Follett Social Studies

Our United States

Program Directors
Phillip Bacon
M. Evelyn Swartz

Authors
Arthur S. Nichols
Stephen S. Birdsall

Follett Publishing Company
Chicago, Illinois

Atlanta, Georgia • Dallas, Texas
Sacramento, California • Warrensburg, Missouri

Teacher Consultants

Joan Sánchez Augerot
Seattle Public Schools
Seattle, Washington

Silvio Guglielmo Benvenuti
Detroit Public Schools
Detroit, Michigan

Margaret L. Boyd
Fairfax County Schools
Vienna, Virginia

Gary L. Caldwell
Omaha Public Schools
Omaha, Nebraska

Elizabeth G. Charette
West Tampa Middle School
Tampa, Florida

Carolyn E. Comey
Washington School #6
Phoenix, Arizona

Patricia DeBardeleben
Treadwell Elementary School
Memphis, Tennessee

Jeanette Hadley
Public School 154, Manhattan
New York, New York

Copyright © 1983 by Follett Publishing Company, a division of Follett Corporation. All rights reserved. No portion of this book may be reproduced in any form without written permission from the publisher. Manufactured in the United States of America.

Lynne K. Hollomon
Portland Public Schools
Portland, Oregon

Dolores K. Horwitz
William Hibbard School
Chicago, Illinois

Sister St. Rita Marotta, I.H.M.
St. Dorothy School
Drexel Hill, Pennsylvania

Edith Naiser
Spring Branch Schools
Houston, Texas

Helen Rogers
Gary School Corporation
Gary, Indiana

Edith B. Rudder
Wake County Schools
Raleigh, North Carolina

Martha Doerr Toppin
Oak Grove Intermediate School
Concord, California

Ronald J. Walker
William H. Ohrenberger School
Boston, Massachusetts

Beautiful Washington, D.C., is a proud symbol of the United States and its heritage. In the cover photograph, the dome of the Capitol rises beyond the Washington Monument, the tallest structure in the city. Museums and government office buildings can also be seen.

Table of Contents

	Page	
	9	The Atlas
	26	A Dictionary of Geographical Terms
	28	The Atlas Tells a Story
Part One	36	**United States History**
Unit 1	38	**America the Beautiful**
	40	A Variety of Landscapes
	44	A Wealth of People
Unit 2	50	**The First Americans**
	52	The First Americans Today
	56	Maps and Pictures Tell A Story of the Settling of the Americas
	60	Indians in the Americas
	65	Indians of the Southwest
	69	Indians of the Great Plains and the Great Basin
	73	Indians of the Eastern Woodlands
	77	Indians of the Northwest Coast
Unit 3	82	**Exploring the New World**
	84	Voyagers of Long Ago
	88	Wanted: A Route to the Indies
	92	Columbus Plans His Voyage
	95	The Voyages of Columbus
	99	Maps and Diagrams Tell a Story of Early Exploration
	103	Spain in the New World
	108	England, France, and the Netherlands Explore the New World
Unit 4	114	**Colonies in North America**
	116	Spanish Settlements in North America
	120	The First English Colonies in North America
	124	Maps and Pictures Tell a Story of Jamestown
	128	French and Dutch Colonies in North America
	132	The Growth of the English Colonies
	137	Life in the English Colonies
	141	The American Indians and the Europeans
Unit 5	146	**Creating a New Nation**
	148	The Struggle for North America
	152	Colonial Cities: Centers of Business and Trade
	156	Breaking Ties with Britain
	161	The Revolutionary War
	166	Forming a New Government
	170	Maps Tell a Story of Distance
	174	The Early Years of the New Government

	Page	
Unit 6	180	**Looking Westward**
	182	The Young Nation
	186	Exploration and a New Territory
	191	Maps and Pictures Tell a Story of the Way West
	195	The United States Expands to the Pacific
	199	Pioneer Life
	204	Progress and Change
	208	Americans Examine Their Country
Unit 7	214	**War and a New Beginning**
	216	Differences in the Growing Nation
	219	The South and Slavery
	224	A Divided Nation
	229	Rebuilding a Nation
	234	Opening the West
	238	Settling the West
	242	Maps, Pictures, and Graphs Tell a Story of Transportation in the West
Unit 8	248	**A Modern Nation**
	250	New Inventions and Industries
	255	A Growing Population
	260	Graphs and Tables Tell a Story of Population Changes
	264	A Need for Change
	269	The United States Becomes a World Power
	274	Good Times and Bad Times
Unit 9	282	**The United States Today**
	284	World War II
	288	The United States, a World Leader
	291	Maps Tell a Story of the United States and the World
	294	Changes in Life in the United States
	298	Changes in the Quality of Life
Part Two	306	**Regions of the United States**
Unit 10	308	**The Northeast**
	311	Where Is the Northeast?
	314	Where Are the People?
	318	What Do the People Do?
Unit 11	326	**The Great Lakes Region**
	329	Where Is the Great Lakes Region?
	332	Where Are the People?
	335	What Do the People Do?

Table of Contents

	Page	
Unit 12	342	**The Midwest Plains**
	345	Where Are the Midwest Plains?
	348	Where Are the People?
	351	What Do the People Do?
Unit 13	358	**The South**
	361	Where Is the South?
	364	Where Are the People?
	368	What Do the People Do?
Unit 14	376	**The Southwest**
	379	Where Is the Southwest?
	381	Where Are the People?
	385	What Do the People Do?
Unit 15	392	**The Interior West**
	395	Where Is the Interior West?
	398	Where Are the People?
	401	What Do the People Do?
Unit 16	408	**The Pacific Coast**
	411	Where Is the Pacific Coast?
	414	Where Are the People?
	417	What Do the People Do?
Unit 17	424	**Alaska and Hawaii**
	427	Where Are Alaska and Hawaii?
	429	Where Are the People?
	431	What Do the People Do?
Unit 18	436	**Canada**
	439	Where Is Canada?
	442	Where Are the People?
	445	What Do the People Do?
Unit 19	452	**Latin America**
	455	Where Is Latin America?
	459	Where Are the People?
	462	What Do the People Do?
Unit 20	470	**The United States in the 21st Century**
	472	The American People in the 21st Century
	476	Technology and the Environment
	482	Appendix
	489	Glossary
	495	Index

Map List

Page		Page	
10–11	World *Political Map*	120	The English Colonies of Jamestown and Plymouth
12–13	World *Physical Map*	124	Lower Chesapeake Bay
14	North America *Political Map*	126	Captain John Smith's Map of Virginia
15	North America *Physical Map*	129	Explorations of the Mississippi River
16	North America Population Map	130	French and English Claims in North America, 1685
17	North America Land Use Map	131	New Netherland
18–19	United States *Political Map*	132	The Thirteen English Colonies
20–21	United States *Physical Map*	145	European Land Claims and Colonies, Early 1700s
22	South America *Political Map*	148	Eastern North America Before 1763
23	South America *Physical Map*	151	Eastern North America After 1763
24	South America Population Map	153	Colonial Trade in 1760
25	South America Land Use Map	163	Major Battles of the Revolutionary War
29	Northern and Southern Hemispheres	170	Washington, D.C.—Map A
29	Eastern and Western Hemispheres	171	Washington, D.C.—Map B
31	Lines of Latitude	172	A Closer Look at Washington, D.C.
32	Low, Middle, and High Latitudes	173	Some Revolutionary War Battles
34	Globe Gores	177	Trouble in the West, 1783–1795
54	Indian Reservations	183	The United States in 1790
56	Routes of the Earliest Americans	184	Routes West: 1800–1850
57	Glaciers over North America	186	The United States in 1803
62	American Indian Tribes in the 1600s	188	The Journey of Lewis and Clark
71	Indian Farm Crops	191	The Narrows—Shaded Relief
81	Indian Tribes in New York State	192	The Narrows—Color Relief
85	Ocean Currents of the North Pacific	192	The Narrows—*Physical Map*
89	Land and Sea Routes to the Indies, 1400s	193	The Narrows—Contour Map
97	The Voyages of Columbus to America	196	Growth of the United States to 1853
99	Norse Routes to North America	217	The United States in 1854
100	Globe of 1492	225	The Confederacy
101	Columbus's First Voyage to the New World	235	Mining Strikes and Mining Towns, 1848–1876
102	Prevailing Winds	236	Cattle Trails, 1860–1880
102	Ocean Currents of the North Atlantic	243	Travel Routes, 1850–1870
104	The Voyage of Magellan, 1519–1522	245	Major Transcontinental Railroads
106	Spanish Exploration in the New World	247	Important Battles of the Civil War
109	Search for a Northwest Passage	251	Growth of Industries and Cities, 1860, 1900, 1920
110	Some French Explorations in the New World	270	United States Possessions in 1900
116	European Claims in North America, Late 1600s		

Map List

Page		Page	
272	World War I	385	Major Petroleum and Natural Gas Deposits
285	World War II	394	The Interior West—*Physical-Political Map*
292	The Caribbean Area		
293	Puerto Rico and the Surrounding Area	395	The Interior West—Locator Map
305	Interstate Highways	397	Annual Precipitation—The Interior West
310	The Northeast—*Physical-Political Map*	397	Growing Seasons—The Interior West
310	Northeast—Locator Map	398	Population Density—The Interior West
312	Regions of the Northeast		
313	Growing Seasons—The Northeast	402	Natural Resources—The Interior West
314	Population Density—The Northeast	407	Government-owned Lands
325	Megalopolis	410	The Pacific Coast—*Physical-Political Map*
328	The Great Lakes Region—*Physical-Political Map*		
328	The Great Lakes Region—Locator Map	410	The Pacific Coast—Locator Map
		413	Growing Seasons—The Pacific Coast
330	Regions of the Great Lakes	414	Population Density—The Pacific Coast
331	Growing Seasons—The Great Lakes Region		
332	Population Density—The Great Lakes Region	423	The Columbia River Basin
		426	Alaska and Hawaii—*Physical-Political Map*
344	The Midwest Plains—*Physical-Political Map*	429	Population Density—Alaska and Hawaii
344	The Midwest Plains—Locator Map	435	Time Zones
347	Growing Seasons—The Midwest Plains	438	Canada—*Physical-Political Map*
348	Population Density—The Midwest Plains	438	Natural Regions of Canada
		438	Canada—Locator Map
351	The Corn Belt	441	Growing Seasons—Canada
351	The Wheat Belt	442	Population Density—Canada
357	Mineral Resources—The Midwest Plains	447	Mineral Resources in Canada
		451	Agricultural Regions—Canada and the United States
360	The South—*Physical-Political Map*		
360	The South—Locator Map	451	Annual Precipitation—Canada and the United States
362	Fall Line Cities		
363	Growing Seasons—The South	454	Latin America—*Physical-Political Map*
364	Population Density—The South		
375	Fun Places to Visit in Florida	454	Latin America—Locator Map
378	The Southwest—*Physical-Political Map*	459	Population Density—Latin America
378	The Southwest—Locator Map	469	Growing Seasons—Latin America
380	Growing Seasons—The Southwest	469	Agricultural Regions—Latin America
381	Population Density—The Southwest	473	U.S. Population, 1970–1980
		484	The Metropolitan Area of Milwaukee

The Atlas

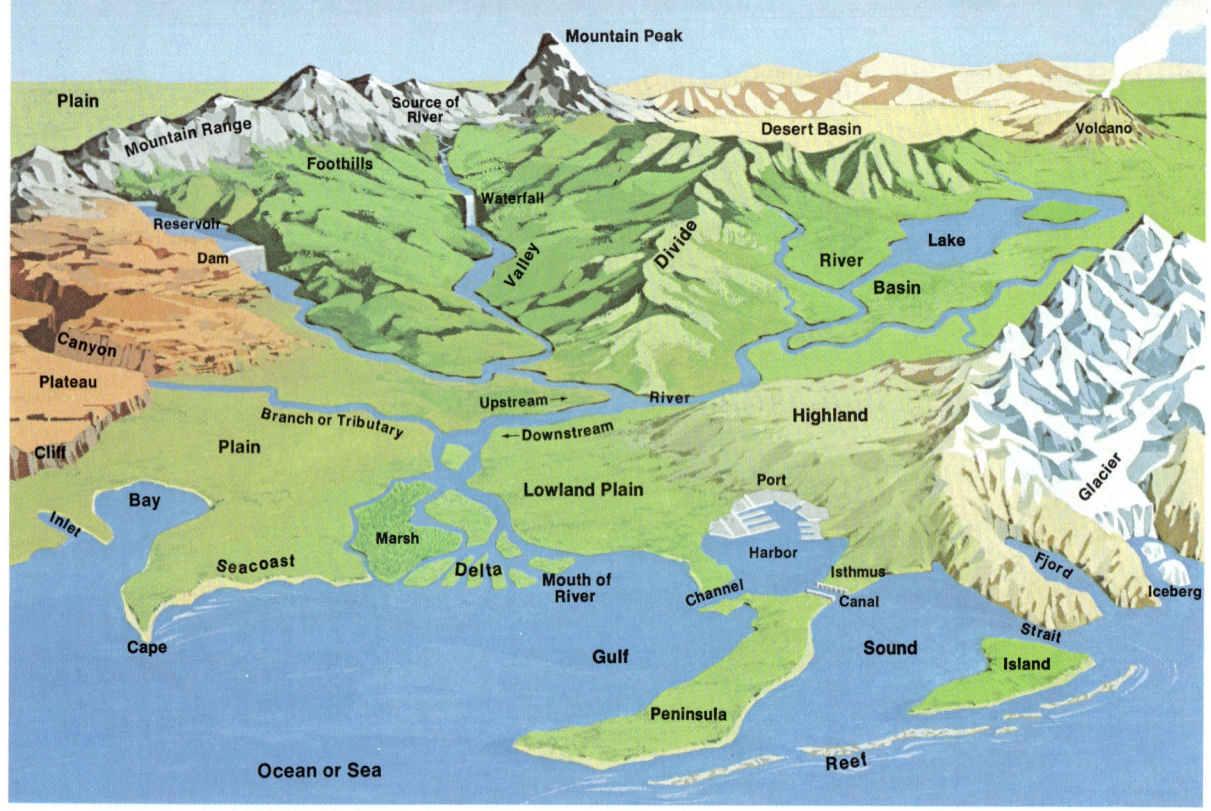

A Dictionary of Geographical Terms

altitude The height above sea level.
basin An area of land largely enclosed by higher land.
bay Part of a body of water that reaches into the land.
bed The bottom of a body of water, as riverbed or ocean bed.
branch A river or stream that flows into a larger river or stream.
canal A channel dug for irrigation or transportation.
canyon A deep, narrow valley with steep sides.
cape A point of land stretching out into a body of water.
channel A narrow body of water connecting two larger bodies of water; the deepest part of a waterway.
cliff A high, steep wall of rock.
coast Land along a sea or ocean.
continent One of the seven largest bodies of land on the earth.
current The flow of a stream of water.
dam A wall built across a river to stop or slow down the flow of water.
delta Land built up by deposits at a river's mouth.
desert A dry, barren area of land where few plants can grow.
dike A wall of earth or stone built by people to hold back flooding.
divide A highest point of land separating river basins.
downstream The direction of a river's flow—toward its mouth.
drainage basin An area of land drained by a river and its tributaries.
elevation The height above sea level.
equator The imaginary line around the earth that is halfway between the North and South poles.
fjord A narrow inlet of the sea between steep banks or cliffs.
foothills Hills at the base of mountains.
glacier A large body of slowly moving ice.
gulf Part of a sea or ocean that reaches into the land.
harbor A sheltered place where ships may anchor safely.
highland An area of hills, mountains, or plateaus.
hill A rounded part of the earth's surface with sloping sides.
iceberg A large floating mass of ice that has broken off from a glacier.
inland Away from the coast.
inlet A small part of a body of water that reaches into a coast.
island Land that is entirely surrounded by water.
isthmus A narrow strip of land that connects two larger land areas.
lake An inland body of water.
latitude The distance in degrees north or south of the equator.
longitude The distance in degrees east or west of the prime meridian.
lowland An area of low and usually level land.
map key An explanation of the meaning of the symbols on a map.
map scale The measuring device found on maps that compares distances on the map with distances on the earth's surface.

marsh An area of low, wet land where tall grasses grow.
mountain High, rocky land, usually with steep sides and a pointed or rounded top, higher than a hill.
mountain peak The pointed top of a mountain.
mountain range A long chain of mountains.
mouth (of a river) The place where a river flows into a larger body of water.
North Pole The point on the earth that is farthest north.
oasis A place in a desert where water is found in a spring or a well, making the growing of crops possible.
ocean One of the four largest bodies of water on the earth.
ocean current A flow of water that moves in a definite direction in the ocean.
pampa A grass-covered plain in South America.
peninsula A body of land nearly surrounded by water.
plain An area of broad, level land.
plateau An area of high, flat land.
port A harbor, town, or city where ships can load and unload their cargoes.

prairie A large plains region with tall grasses.
prime meridian The imaginary line on the earth's surface running through Greenwich, England, from the North Pole to the South Pole. The line is used as the starting point from which degrees of longitude are measured.
rain forest A tropical woodland, with heavy rainfall throughout the year, marked by tall broad-shaped, evergreen trees that form a continuous canopy.
rapids A part of a river, generally shallow, where the current moves swiftly over rocks.
reef A ridge of rock or sand at or near the surface of water.
reservoir A lake where water is stored for future use.
river A large stream of water flowing through the land.
river valley Low land through which a river flows.
savanna A level, tropical grassland with scattered trees.
sea A large body of water, usually salt water, partly or completely enclosed by land.
shore Land next to a lake.
sound A wide channel connecting two bodies of water or an inlet between the mainland and islands.

source (of a river) The place where a river begins.
South Pole The point on the earth that is farthest south.
steppe A vast area of short grass that is often dry and level.
strait A narrow stretch of water that connects two larger bodies of water.
swamp An area of land that is always soaked with water.
tide The regular rising and falling of the water of the ocean and waters connected with the ocean.
timber line A line in mountain regions above which trees do not grow.
tributary A river or stream that flows into a larger river or stream.
tropics The warm region lying on both sides of the equator.
tundra A cold, treeless plain in polar regions.
upstream The direction toward a river's source, opposite to its flow.
valley Low land between hills or mountains.
volcano A mountain formed of rock or ash thrown up from inside the earth.
waterfall Water falling over a steep drop in the land.

Map Symbols

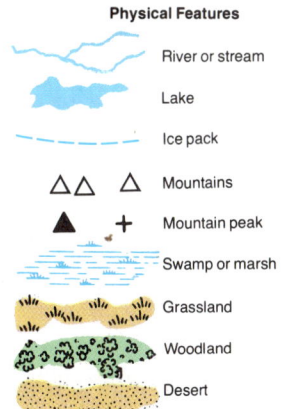

Physical Features
- River or stream
- Lake
- Ice pack
- Mountains
- Mountain peak
- Swamp or marsh
- Grassland
- Woodland
- Desert

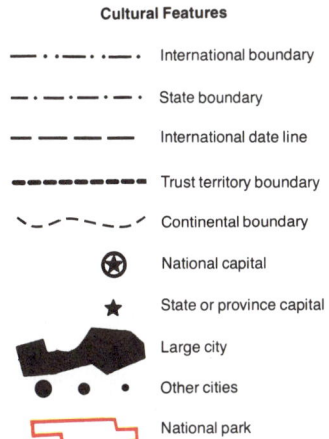

Cultural Features
- International boundary
- State boundary
- International date line
- Trust territory boundary
- Continental boundary
- National capital
- State or province capital
- Large city
- Other cities
- National park

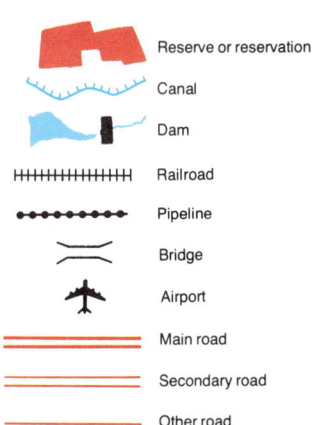

- Reserve or reservation
- Canal
- Dam
- Railroad
- Pipeline
- Bridge
- Airport
- Main road
- Secondary road
- Other road

27

Thinking Skill: Hypothesizing. Have students examine the cover and title of the book and hypothesize about what will be covered. Then have students skim through the book.
Reading Skill: Using textbook features. Before beginning this section, introduce the many features of the textbook. Review the meaning of *atlas* and the many uses of an atlas.

The Atlas Tells a Story

As you read, think about these words.

sphere	sea level	parallel	degree
physical map	political map	latitude	compass rose

A Round Earth

Everyone knows that our earth is round. Yet look around you. Can you really see its roundness?

Proof of roundness. What proof, then, do we have that the earth really is round? Years ago the best proof was watching a tall ship slowly disappear on the horizon. If there really were a sharp edge to the earth, the ship would disappear suddenly. That never happened. Slowly, the ship disappeared as it sailed over the curved surface of our earth.

In recent years you have seen even better proof of the earth's roundness. This proof is seen in the first picture in your Atlas, on page 9. This is a wonderful photograph of our planet, Earth, taken from space. With your finger trace around the edge of Planet Earth on the picture. You can really feel, as well as see, its roundness.

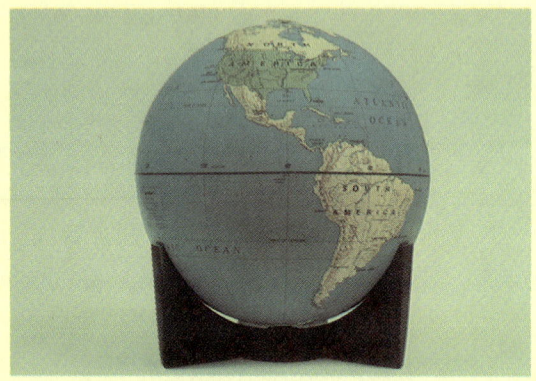

A model of the earth. A globe is a model of our planet. It is a perfect model because everything about it is accurate. The locations, sizes, and shapes of the continents and the oceans are exactly right. Distances and directions are also correct everywhere on a globe. Our views of the earth from space and our globe truly are related to each other. Both help us recognize and remember the round shape of our home, Planet Earth.

As a ship heads away from someone watching it, the ship seems to disappear slowly over the horizon.

Background: Remind the students that people used to think the earth was flat and a ship could fall off the edge. Magellan's voyage (1519–1522) furnished the first positive proof that the world is round.
Reading Skill: Satellite imagery. Ask students how the picture on page 9 was taken.

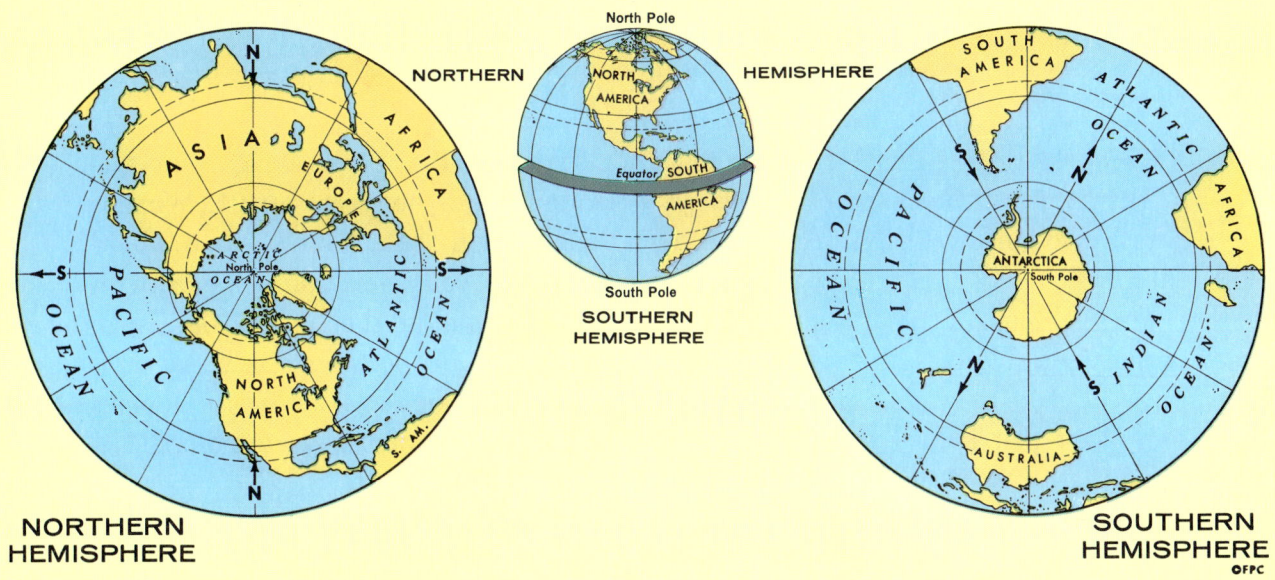

Using Hemispheres

All round objects, no matter what their size, are **spheres**. A ball is a sphere. Planet Earth is a sphere.

When you look at a sphere, you can see only half of it at a time. Try it with your globe. Turn your globe so that you have the Americas facing you. Focus on the equator, halfway between the poles. Why can't you see Asia and Australia?

Four hemispheres. On this page are four different views of the earth. Each is a hemisphere. The equator divides the globe into two of these hemispheres. Places that are north of the equator are in the Northern Hemisphere. Places that are south of the equator are in the Southern Hemisphere.

The hemispheres below are the Eastern and Western Hemispheres. They are formed by dividing the globe from the North Pole to the South Pole. In which two hemispheres is North America? In which two hemispheres is Australia?

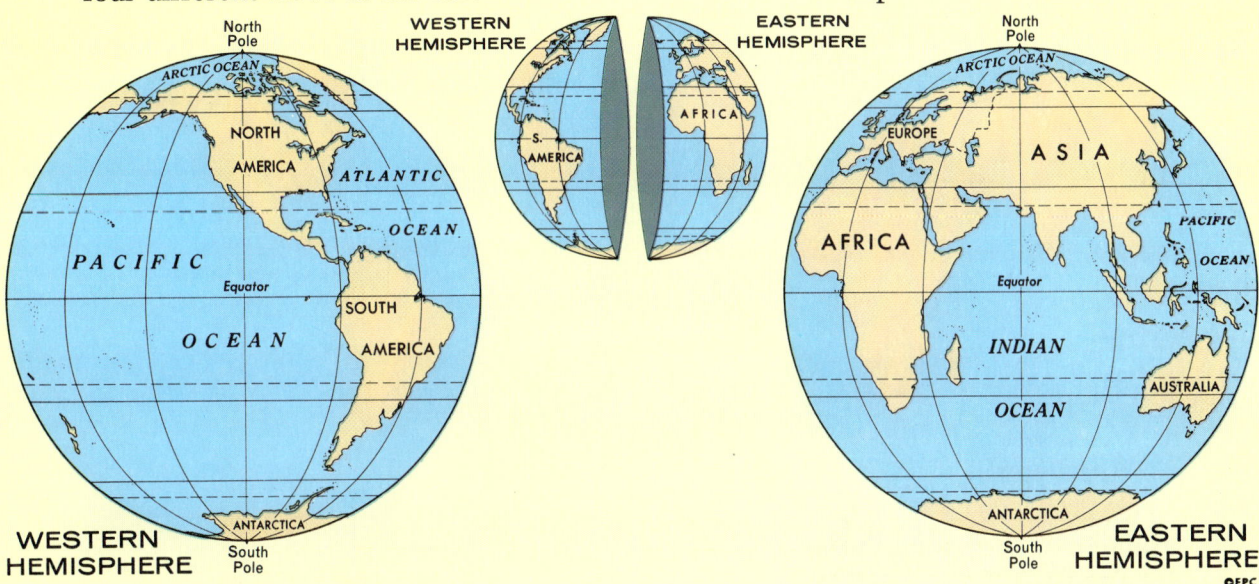

1. Because they are on the opposite side of the globe.
2. North America is in the Northern and Western Hemispheres.

Thinking Skill: Observing. Have students look for examples of spheres in the classroom.

29

Background: The physical map of the U.S. and the political map of the U.S. are drawn to the same scale. They are exactly alike in size. Help students reinforce their knowledge of cardinal directions and in-between directions by planning trips using both maps. This exercise will also provide opportunities for using the scale bar to determine distances to places.

Physical and Political Maps

The Atlas includes many kinds of maps. Two kinds are physical and political maps.

Physical maps. Look at the world map on pages 12–13. It is a **physical map**. A physical map uses shades of black to show land that is hilly or mountainous. Land that is not shaded is nearly flat or completely so.

Physical maps also use colors as map symbols. Check the colors on the world physical map. What does bright green represent? On this map, color shows height, or elevation, above **sea level**. Sea level is the place where the ocean meets the land.

The diagram on this page shows you how to read the key to physical maps. Notice how the shading becomes darker as the land becomes more mountainous. Different colors show different elevations. Shades of blue show the depth of water.

Turn to the physical map of the United States on pages 20–21. What is the elevation of the land where you live? How does your elevation compare with the elevation in the Sangre de Cristo Mountains of northern New Mexico? Which are higher—the Coast Ranges north of San Francisco or the Sierra Nevada just to the east?

Physical maps tell you a great deal about the land and water. They also name many important physical features such as mountains, rivers, and lakes.

Political maps. On pages 18–19 is a **political map** of the United States. Political maps show you how the land is divided into nations and states. Political maps also show you where cities are located and which cities are capitals.

The colors used on political maps are not found on the map key. The only color that stands for anything is blue. What does it show? The other colors just make it easier to see political divisions.

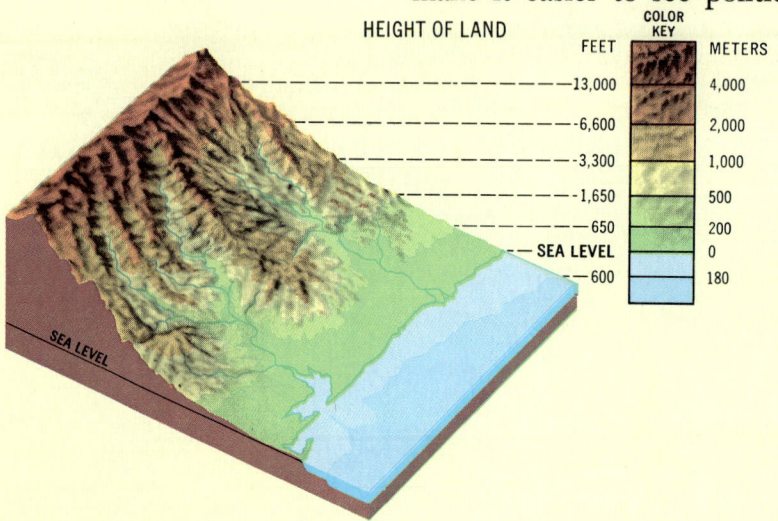

What color shows land lower than 650 feet? What color shows land between 1,650 and 3,300 feet? over 4,000 meters?

1. Land that is below sea level.
2. The Sierra Nevada are higher than the Coast Ranges.
3. Blue areas on political maps show bodies of water.

Sangre de Cristo (sang′grē də kris′tō)

Map Skill: Location. Draw a circle on the board. Put a dot in the middle. It represents the North or South pole, or 90°. The circle is the equator, or 0°. Put an X halfway between the outside and center. Have students discuss how many degrees from the equator or pole it is. Repeat with other X markings. The number for degrees of latitude increases as you move from the equator toward the poles.

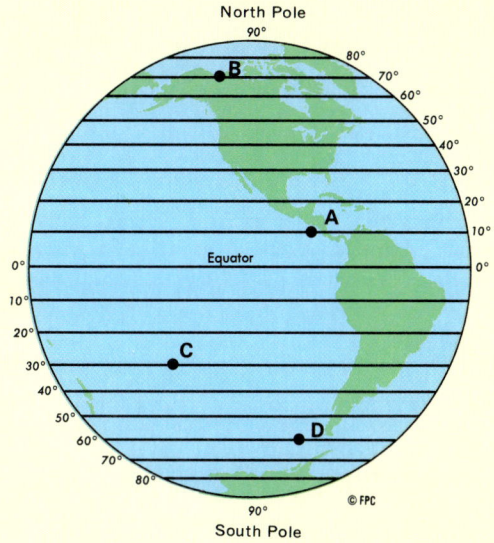

Using Lines of Latitude

Look at the picture of the orange slices on this page. A round orange, a sphere, has been sliced to make it easy to eat. Before eating it, however, we could put the slices back together and re-create the original orange sphere.

Parallel lines. Next to the picture of the orange is a picture of a globe. It, too, appears to have slices through it. Each of these "slices" is a line that runs across the surface of the globe.

These lines are called **parallels**. Parallel lines are like railroad tracks. They always stay the same distance apart. These parallel lines are also called lines of **latitude**. Latitude means distance north or south of the equator. This distance north or south is measured in units called **degrees** rather than in feet, meters, miles, or kilometers. The symbol for *degree* is °.

All measurements of latitude begin at the equator. Since the equator is the beginning place, it is numbered 0°. On the two world maps in your Atlas, pages 10–13, find this 0° line. It is marked Equator and 0°.

Locations north and south. On the map on this page, the lines of latitude are 10° apart. How many degrees is it from the Equator to the North Pole? Find point A. It is on a line marked 10°. This means that A is 10° north of the equator. One degree is equal to about 70 miles (112 km). So A is about 700 miles (1120 km) north of the equator. Find point B. How many degrees north of the equator is point B? How many miles is point B from the equator? 1

Now find point C. It is south of the equator. So we say that point C is located at 30° south latitude. We often shorten this to 30° S. Find point D. What is its location? About how many miles is it from the equator to point D? 2

Look at the political map of the United States in your Atlas, pages 18–19. On this map the lines of latitude are

1. 70° N. 4,900 miles or 7,840 kilometers.
2. 60° S. 4,200 miles or 6,720 kilometers.

Background: In this section reinforce the idea of five special parallels—the equator, Tropic of Cancer, Tropic of Capricorn, Arctic Circle, and Antarctic Circle.

31

1. The lines of latitude are 5 degrees apart.
2. Lisbon, Portugal, and Madrid, Spain.

drawn more often. How many degrees apart are they? At about what latitude do you live? Do you live north or south of the equator? Remember N or S is an important part of your latitude location.

Turn to the world political map on pages 10–11. Find the capital of our country. It is close to 40° N. Follow the 40° parallel eastward across the Atlantic Ocean. When you reach land, you will soon find the capitals of two other countries. What are they?

Tropic lines. The parallels near the equator have low numbers. We call places near the equator the low latitudes. Look again at the map on pages 10–11. If you look carefully just north of the 20° N line, you will find another parallel. It has a dashed (------) line. Look along this dashed line until you find its name. It is the Tropic of Cancer. Now look just south of 20° S. You will find another dashed (------) line. Look along this dashed line until you find its name. What is it? The land and water between these two tropic lines, the low latitudes, are often called the tropics. They have warm weather all year round because the sun is almost always overhead.

Polar lines. Find 60° N on your world map. Now look just to the north of 60° N. Here is another dashed (------) line. It has a special name—the Arctic Circle. South of 60° S you will find yet another dashed (------) line. It, too, has a special name. What is it? These two lines are often called polar lines. They are not far from the North and South poles. The areas between these lines and the poles

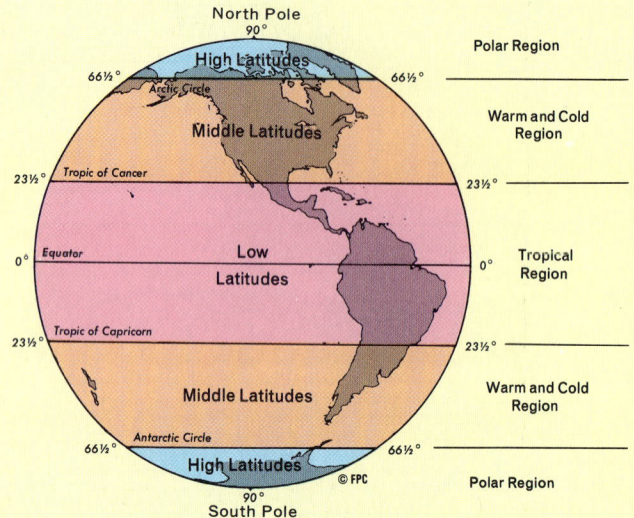

get only slanting rays of sunshine. Sometimes they get no sunshine at all. Most of the time it is very cold in these areas. These are the polar regions. Sometimes they are also called the high latitudes.

Middle latitudes. Between the polar lines and the tropic lines are the middle latitudes. These areas have both hot and cold weather. The diagram on this page shows you the locations of the low, high, and middle latitudes. You can also find these areas on your world map. In what latitude region do you live—low, high, or middle? Is your home area closer to the Tropic of Cancer or to the Arctic Circle? Which, then, is closer to you—the low or the high latitudes?

Finding Directions on Maps

Finding directions is an important map skill. Many maps have a direction finder as part of the map. It may be a simple arrow that points north.

Some maps have a fancy direction finder called a **compass rose**. Look at the

3. Tropic of Capricorn.
4. Antarctic Circle.

São Paulo (sou pou′lō)   Quito (kē′tō)   Belém (bə·lem′)
Map Skill: Location. Have students give directions to items in the classroom by using cardinal and in-between directions.
1. NE, NW, SE, and SW.

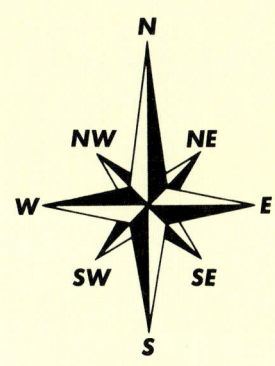

compass rose on this page. It shows not only north, south, east, and west, but it also shows the in-between directions. What are they? How many different directions does this compass rose have?

Where is north? If there is no direction finder on your map, north is almost always toward the top. Remember, however, "up" and "down" are not directions that are used on maps. North means toward the North Pole.

On the maps in your Atlas there is a good clue to direction. Look at the political map of South America on page 22. Find the equator. Take your finger and move toward the top of the page until you come to the next parallel. It says 10°. It is 10 degrees north of the equator. As the number of degrees increases, the farther north or south of the equator you are located.

Locations on maps. Turn to page 22. Use these clues to find this city: It is located almost exactly on the equator. It is the capital of a nation. What is the name of this city? Of what nation is it the capital? How do you know it is a capital?

Now find São Paulo. São Paulo is a large city in Brazil. This city is on a special parallel. What is the name of the parallel? Is this city in the high, low, or middle latitudes?

If you were going to travel from Quito to São Paulo, in what direction would you go? If you were going to travel from São Paulo to Belém, in which direction would you go?

Finding Distance on Maps

By knowing latitude you can measure distances. Remember that one degree of latitude is about 70 miles (112 km).

Turn to the world physical map on pages 12–13. Find the large island of Greenland in the Atlantic Ocean. What line of latitude touches the southern tip of Greenland? What line of latitude runs through the northern portion of Greenland? How many degrees are between these two lines of latitude? How many miles would you have to travel from the southern tip of Greenland to 80° N?

Now find Christmas Island in the Pacific Ocean. It is almost exactly on the

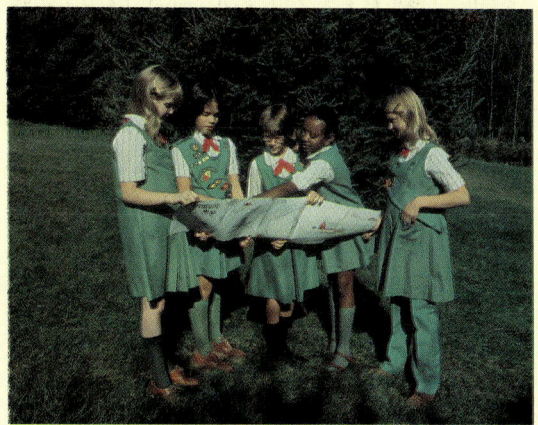

These girls are using maps to locate things that have been hidden for a treasure hunt.

2. Quito. Ecuador. Because it is marked with the symbol for a national capital.
3. Tropic of Capricorn. Low latitudes.
4. Southeast. North.
5. 60° N. 80° N. 20°. 1,400 miles or 2,240 kilometers.

33

Map Skill: Scale. Have students use a string to measure distances on a globe from their community to key places around the world such as London, Tokyo, Buenos Aires, and Cairo.
1. 20° N. 1,400 miles or 2,240 kilometers.
2. It is larger on page 12 than on the globe, and larger still on page 15.

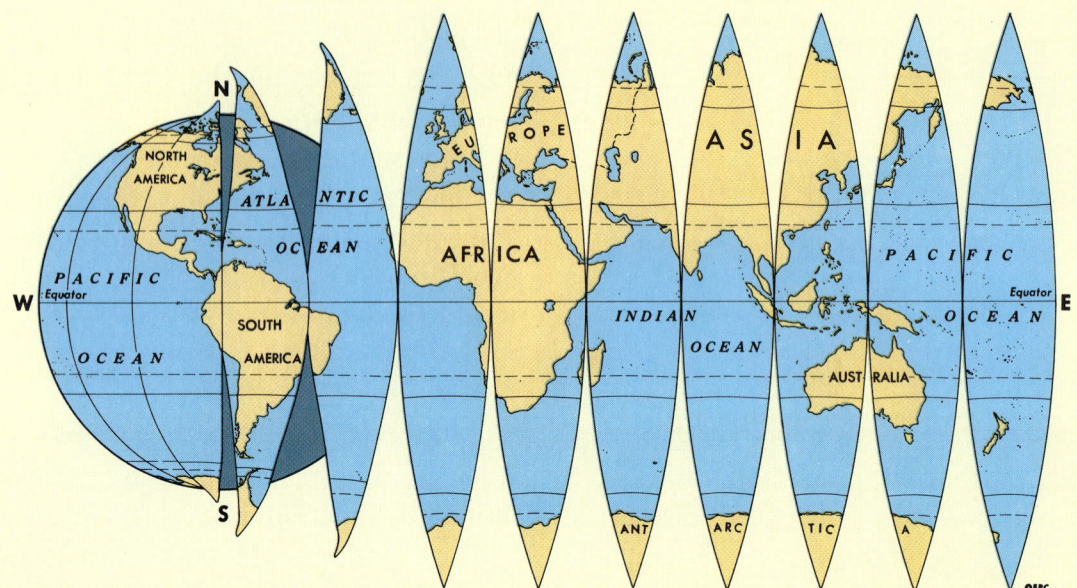

equator. Move your finger north until you find the largest of the Hawaiian Islands. At what latitude is this island? About how many miles is it from Christmas Island to Hawaii?

Problems with distance. You should have found that the distance in degrees and miles between the southern tip of Greenland to 80° N is the same as the distance between Christmas Island and Hawaii. Now use your ruler and your map scale to measure the distance from the southern tip of Greenland to 80° N. Do the same thing from Christmas Island to Hawaii. The distances are not the same according to this measurement.

Distances on a world map simply cannot be accurate everywhere. Too much stretching, tearing, and bending take place when we put the earth's round surface on a flat piece of paper. This distortion is greatest in the high latitudes. Look at the drawing on this page. You can see that the space between the sections of paper increases as you look north and south of the equator.

More than distances become distorted. Look at the shape of Greenland on a globe. Now look at it on page 12. Now look at it on page 15. What happened?

What about area? Look, again, at Greenland on a globe. Look also at Mexico on a globe. They are actually close to the same size. Now compare these two places on the world political map on pages 10–11. Which looks larger? Greenland looks larger on the map because distortion on maps is greatest in the high latitudes. Mexico is in the low latitudes, where distortion is the least on maps.

Many Maps

Each map serves a special purpose. Turn through your Atlas. How many different kinds of maps do you find? In what ways are they different?

Choosing symbols. Many maps use symbols to represent things that are

3. There are political, physical, population, and land-use maps. They are different because they show different areas and have different purposes. Population maps, for example, show how many people live in an area, while land-use maps show how the land is used in an area.

Map Skill: Symbolization. Review symbols used on the United States physical and political maps in the Atlas. Put the sign for degree (°) on the board. Have students list all the things it could represent.

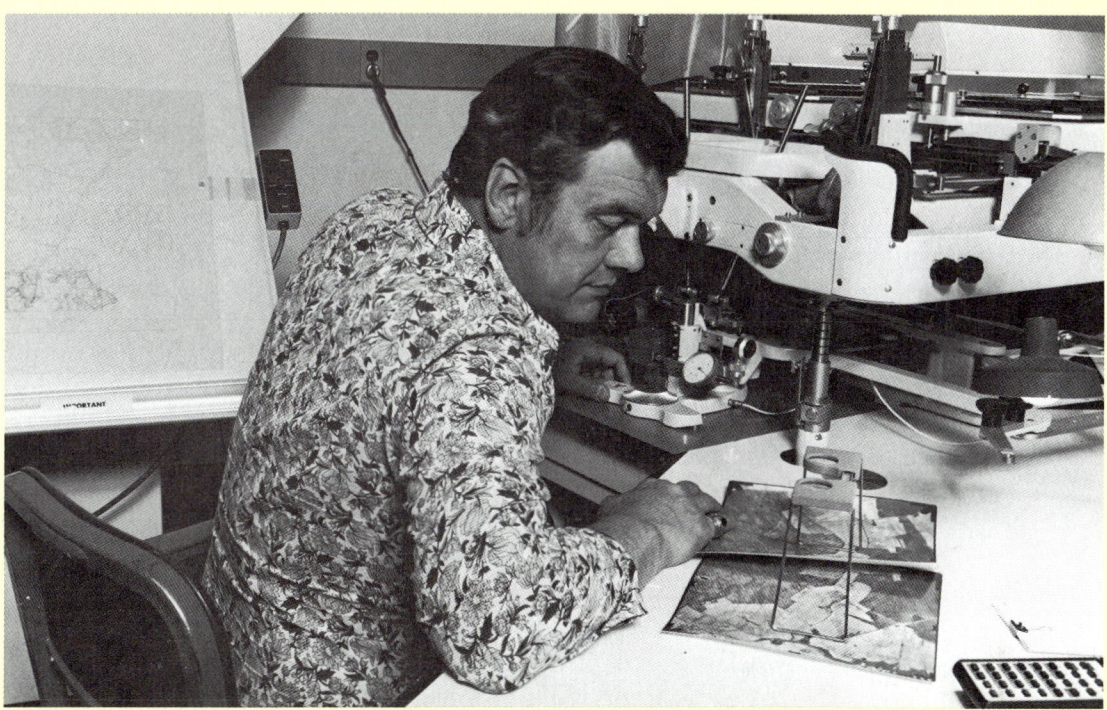

Map makers use special tools to make their maps as accurate as possible. What types of maps did map makers draw for this book?

found on the earth. Sometimes colors are used as symbols. On one map, the color green may represent plains areas. On another, it may represent a forest area. On still another, it may represent farmland. You need to read the map key to know what each symbol means.

Turn to page 27 of the Dictionary of Geographical Terms. Study the list of symbols shown at the top of the page. Some of these symbols may not appear in all map keys. You will need to remember them. Look at the symbols for international boundaries and national boundaries. How are the symbols different? Now turn to the political map of the United States on pages 18–19. Which symbol shows the boundary between Canada and the United States?

Become familiar with the maps in your Atlas. The maps in your Atlas and in other parts of your book will supply you with vast amounts of information. Maps take the place of thousands of words. Reading and using a variety of maps is an important skill.

Checking Up
1. What are two ways that prove the earth is round?
2. In what two hemispheres is our country located?
3. Which is farther from the equator— 30° N or 50° N? How do you know?
4. Approximately how many miles from the equator is 45° S?

Reading Skill: Using textbook features. Have students look at the Dictionary of Geographical Terms on pages 26–27. Ask students to suggest ways in which this textbook feature will be helpful to them in reading the book.

Background: Part One covers the history of the United States. This part begins with an account of the first Americans, the American Indians, and ends with an account of the United States since World War II. Each unit describes in text, pictures, maps, and graphics a period in the development of the American people and our country.

Part One
United States History

United States history is partly the record of how our country grew. Yet it is also the story of how our people became Americans. Although Americans differ in countless ways, a belief in our country unites us. This belief was expressed in 1917 in a statement called the American's Creed.

I believe in the United States of America as a government of the people, by the people, for the people; whose just powers are derived from the consent of the governed; a democracy in a Republic; a sovereign Nation of many sovereign States; a perfect Union, one and inseparable; established upon those principles of freedom, equality, justice, and humanity for which American patriots sacrificed their lives and fortunes.

I therefore believe it is my duty to my country to love it; to support its Constitution; to obey its laws; to respect its flag; and to defend it against all enemies.

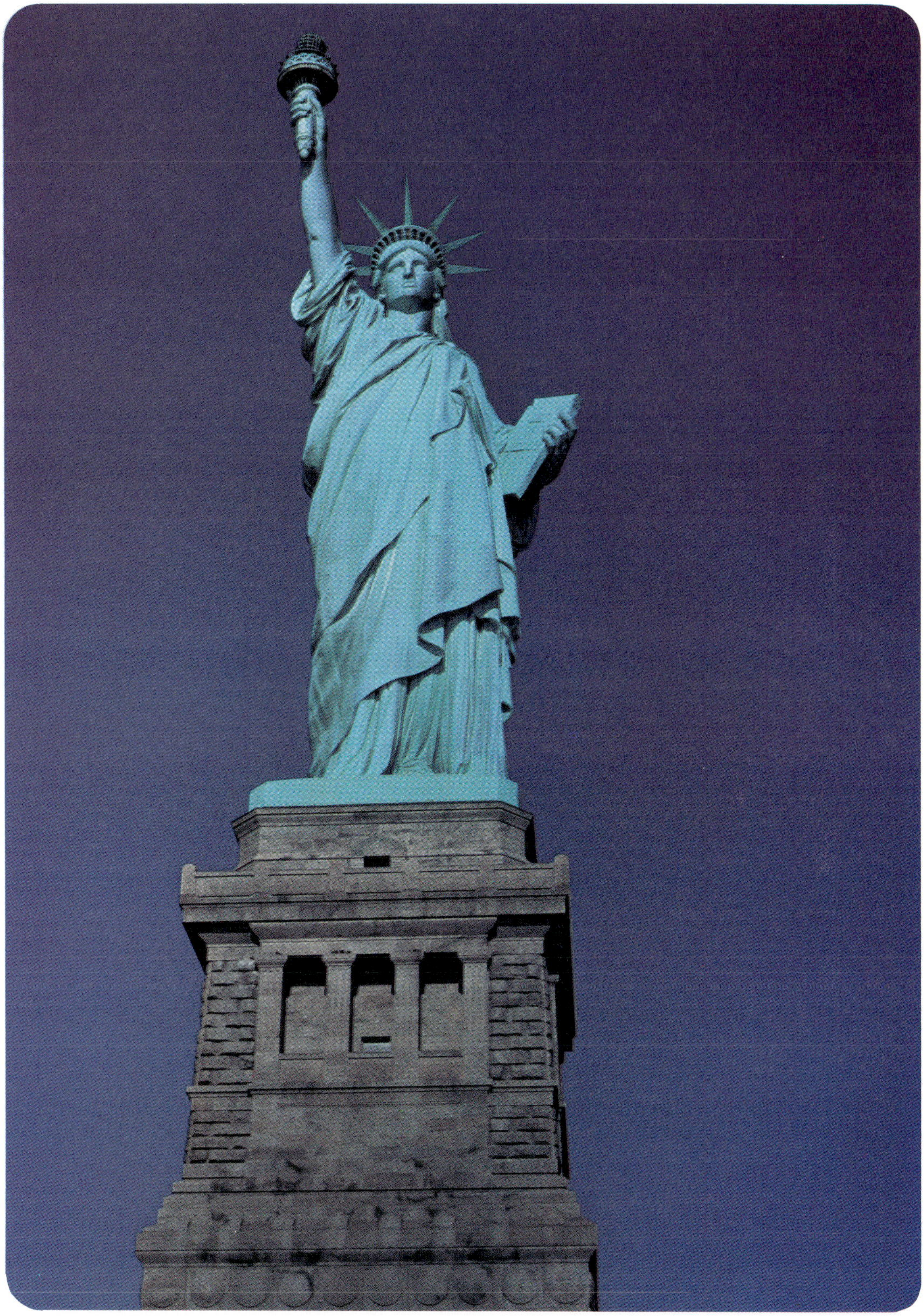

Unit Overview: This unit examines the landscapes and people in the United States.

Unit Objectives
To understand:
- the major landforms in the United States
- the beliefs and spirit of the American people

Suggested Materials
Workbook
Unit Tests

Unit 1

Skills Emphasized
Map Skill: p. 43.
Social Studies Reading Skills: pp. 38, 40, 42, 43, 45, 48, 49.
Thinking Skills: pp. 38, 41, 45, 47, 48, 49.
Communication Skills: pp. 38, 47, 48.
Social Studies Math Skill: p. 44.
Citizenship Skill: p. 38.

Suggested Student Activities
   1. Arrange a bulletin-board mural called "America the Beautiful."
   2. Work in pairs. Make posters illustrating our freedoms.
   3. List ways in which Americans are alike and different.
 * 4. Divide a sheet into four sections. Illustrate the four basic landforms in the United States.
 ** 5. List examples of the kinds of work people do.
*** 6. Illustrate "America the Beautiful."

Skills Emphasized in Suggested Student Activities
Social Studies Reading Skills: Using references, doing research, organizing information.
Thinking Skills: Knowing, comparing, classifying.
Communication Skill: Writing.
Citizenship Skill: Social participation.

America the Beautiful

A river trip through the Grand Canyon would take one almost a mile in the depths of the earth.

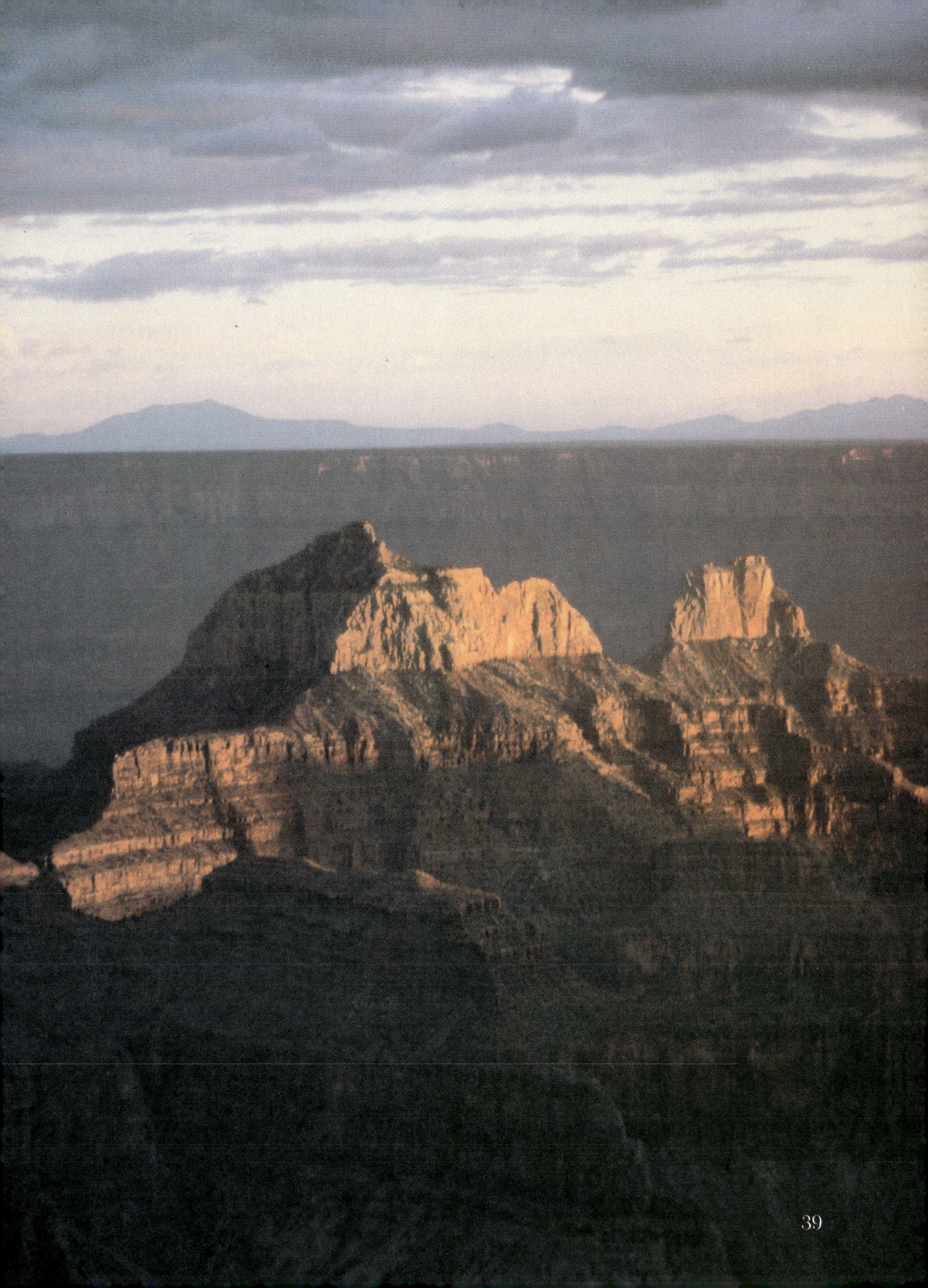

Reading Skill: Using textbook features. Have students locate Unit One in the Table of Contents. Introduce pages 38–39.
Reading Skill: Using textbook features: *As You Read,* 3.

A Variety of Landscapes

As You Read

1. Think about these words.
   landform   heritage
2. Look for answers to this key question.
   What do the photographs in this unit tell you about the United States?
3. Use this reading skill.
   It is important to read the captions of photographs that appear in this text. Captions give information to help you understand photographs. To understand how important captions are, look at every caption in this unit. Write a one-paragraph summary of this unit based on the captions. When you have finished reading the unit, look at your summary. Is your summary a good one? Why or why not?

The United States stretches from the Atlantic Ocean on the east to our Pacific islands on the west. Bordered on the north by Canada and on the south by Mexico, our country is a vast nation on a vast continent.

Our Landscapes

Snowcapped mountains tower over valleys and plains. Deserts, sometimes blooming with flowering cacti, extend for miles in the Southwest. Gently rolling hills curve across the land in many parts of the country. Ships travel on lakes and rivers so wide that you cannot always see from shore to shore. These are only a small part of the variety of landscapes in the United States.

There is much, much more. Volcanoes in Hawaii and Washington spew their hot lava and ash over the land below. Old Faithful, a geyser in Yellowstone National Park, spouts a fountain of water into the air almost every hour.

The first Americans, the Indians, had stories that told of mountains, canyons, and seas. Later Americans have also been inspired by the variety and beauty of the American landscapes. Katharine Lee Bates, awed by the view she saw from Pikes Peak, celebrated our country in "America the Beautiful":

O beautiful for spacious skies,
   For amber waves of grain,
For purple mountain majesties
   Above the fruited plain!
America! America!
   God shed his grace on thee
And crown thy good with brotherhood
   From sea to shining sea!

Reading Skill: Building vocabulary. Have students find the word *cacti* on this page. Ask students what the singular of *cacti* is. Explain that sometimes the plural of a word that ends in *us* is formed by dropping the *us* and adding *i*.

An evening storm will soon drench these Montana wheat fields. Which lines of "America the Beautiful" would describe this scene?

The poet Longfellow once described how the ocean "sends a thrilling pulse through me."

The snowcapped peaks of Utah's Wasatch Range can be seen from many miles away in Salt Lake City.

Thinking Skill: Analyzing. Ask whether any of these pictures could be used to illustrate "America the Beautiful." Have students explain their answers.

41

High-rise buildings line San Francisco Bay. What opportunities might living along a bay offer the people of San Francisco?

Landforms in the United States

The pictures on pages 39 and 41 show the variety of our country's landscapes. Geographers divide these landscapes into four basic **landforms**. A landform is a feature of the earth's surface created by natural forces. All four kinds of landforms are found in the United States.

Level or almost level lands called plains are found in many parts of our country. Coastal plains lie along the Atlantic Ocean from Georgia to Maine.

Reading Skill: Building vocabulary. Have students use a dictionary to look up the meaning of *immense*.

* **Reading Skill:** Using textbook features. Have students use the Atlas and the Dictionary of Geographical Terms on pages 26–27 to review the four landforms identified on pages 42 and 43.

* **Map Skill:** Location. Have students use the map on pages 20–21 to locate the Grand Canyon, the Colorado Plateau, and the Great Plains.

The writer Mark Twain once called the Mississippi "a monstrous big river." Huge tankers now plow its waters.

yon out of the Colorado Plateau. Look at the picture on page 39.

Mountains are another spectacular landform in the United States. There are many mountains in our country, especially in the West and Southwest. The Rockies extend all the way from New Mexico to Alaska. Many people from all over the world like to vacation in these mountain areas.

Hills are another landform. They are rounded and more gently sloping than mountains. Their presence in many parts of our country add to the rich variety of landscapes.

Tucked into these landforms are many natural resources. These valuable resources have helped our country grow. Many waterways crisscross our American landscape. Their names trace our history: Mississippi, Missouri, Delaware, Rio Grande, Platte, Snake, Columbia. Along their routes are another part of our landscape, our great cities. These rivers provide cities with natural highways for trade and transportation.

Other plains cover an immense area in the interior of our country. These are the Great Plains. These grasslands are sometimes called the "breadbasket" of the United States because of the great harvests from the rich farmlands.

High, flat lands, usually found between mountains, are plateaus. Some of our most beautiful scenery is on plateaus. A mighty river carved the Grand Can-

Checking Up
1. What are the four landforms in the United States?
2. What ocean borders the United States on the east? on the west?
3. What country borders the United States on the north? on the south?
4. *What pictures would you choose to illustrate the words in "America the Beautiful"?*

** **Reading Skill:** Using references. Have students look for other pictures of each landform.
Map Skill: Location. Have students use the map on pages 20–21 to locate the rivers mentioned on this page.

Background: In 1863, during the Civil War, President Lincoln gave a speech to set aside part of a battlefield as a cemetery for soldiers who had died at the Battle of Gettysburg. This speech, known as the Gettysburg Address, is still remembered as one of the most inspiring statements about the principles upon which our country was founded.

A Wealth of People

Each year thousands of Americans tour Washington, D.C. Many visit the White House and the Washington Monument.

Four score and seven years ago our fathers brought forth on this continent a new nation, conceived in Liberty, and dedicated to the proposition that all men are created equal.

Abraham Lincoln,
"Gettysburg Address"

The United States is more than beautiful landscapes and rich resources. It is a nation of people whose ideas and beliefs have helped our country become great. These ideas and beliefs are a part of our **heritage,** the customs passed from generation to generation.

The American People

The Indians settled here first. Their languages, customs, and beliefs are a part of our history. Then others came. They came from Europe, Asia, Africa, Latin America, and Canada. Most came because they wanted to come. Some, such as the slaves from Africa, did not. Each group has added to our history and worked to change our country.

Math Skill: Have students figure out how long four score and seven years is (eighty-seven years).

Reading Skill: Building vocabulary. Have students look up the words *heritage* and *precious* in a dictionary and put the definitions in their own words.
Thinking Skill: Analyzing. Have students discuss the privilege and importance of living in a country that has freedom of religion, freedom of speech, and the freedom to vote.

The tradition of a Thanksgiving feast goes back to colonial times. What other holidays celebrate important events in our nation's history and development?

American Beliefs

Although we are different in many ways, Americans have much in common. We share our belief in freedoms that are a part of our heritage.

Freedom of religion. Every American is free to choose any religion. Many of our people came to this country for religious freedom. There are many religions in our country today.

Freedom of speech. In our country we are free to write and speak our ideas and opinions. Freedom of speech is important to us. Many, many people in the world do not have this freedom.

Freedom to vote. Americans are free to choose their own leaders. We can vote for community and national leaders. This is a precious freedom. People in some countries do not have the right to choose their leaders. Many people move to our country to enjoy the freedom to vote.

Williamsburg, Virginia, has been rebuilt to look the way it did in the 1700s.

Thinking Skill: Predicting. Ask how life would be different without these freedoms.

45

Some goods are still made the same way they were long ago.

Our nation's growth depends on jobs done by skilled workers.

More and more jobs, such as welding, are being filled by women.

Our culture places a high value on jobs that help people.

Americans of all backgrounds enjoy the freedom to work and to play.

Americans of all backgrounds enjoy the heritage and culture of Chinese Americans in the Chinatown section of Los Angeles.

Freedom to work. Americans work at many jobs. Some work as doctors or teachers. Others work in factories or on farms. We are free to choose the kind of work we hope to do. In the past, some Americans could not get some jobs because of their race, their sex, or their background. Today we continue to work so that everyone will be free to choose a career.

Today Americans may have different customs, celebrate different holidays, work at different jobs, and vote for different people. Yet we are all alike. We share beliefs in our freedoms. We know that we must continue to work to protect these freedoms. A famous American, Oliver Wendell Holmes, once said,

> One flag, one land, one heart, one hand,
> One Nation, evermore.

Checking Up
1. What does freedom of religion mean?
2. What does freedom of speech mean?
3. Why is the freedom to vote a precious freedom?
4. What answers would you give to the key question at the beginning of this unit?
5. *In what ways do you think Americans are alike?*

Unit 1 Summary
- The United States has a variety of landscapes.
- The people of our country have come from many different places.
- Americans enjoy many freedoms.

Thinking Skill: Analyzing. Ask students what they think Holmes wants us to think about.
Communication Skill: Have each student write a paragraph and find one picture to illustrate each point in the summary.

Unit 1 Review Workshop

What Have You Learned?

1. How far do the Rocky Mountains extend in the United States?
2. Which oceans border the United States?
3. Name the four types of landforms. Describe each type.
4. In which states in this country might you find volcanoes?
5. Name four large rivers that crisscross the United States.
6. Why are the Great Plains called the "breadbasket" of the United States?

Use Your Reading Skills

How would you study the city in which you live? One good way to do so is to read the local newspaper. Get a copy of your local newspaper. Read the newspaper to find out as much as you can about your city and the people who live there. Does the newspaper tell you anything about the landforms or waterways near your city? How do people in your city make a living? What special celebrations do people in your city have? What can people do for entertainment? After you read the newspaper, make a chart like the one here and fill in each of the categories.

Use Your Graphics-Reading Skills

In this unit you have learned that photographs are more than just pretty pictures. They are important tools to help you learn more about a subject. They sometimes give you information that words cannot. Study the photograph on page 49. Then answer the following questions.

1. What landforms do you see in this photograph?
2. What is being grown here?
3. How can you tell that people live here? How do you think some people in this area make a living?
4. Write a short paragraph describing the area shown in this photograph. Be sure your paragraph would help someone learn about this area.

Use Your Research Skills

"America the Beautiful" is only one of many songs that celebrate our country. "The Star-Spangled Banner" is the national anthem, or song, of the United States. "America" is another song that celebrates our country. In your library read the words to all three of these songs. Learn about the history of each song. How does each praise our country?

My City			
Land	Jobs	Celebrations	Entertainment

Thinking Skills: Knowing, analyzing.
Reading Skills: Using references, organizing information, interpreting a visual, doing research.
Communication Skill: Writing.

Learn by Doing

1. One way to learn about the heritage of a country is to learn about its holidays. In the United States, holidays include Memorial Day, the Fourth of July, Labor Day, and others. Make a chart of holidays in the United States and Mexico. Divide your chart into two columns. At the top of one column, write United States. At the top of the other, write Mexico. Then on the left side of your chart, write the name of each month. Put the name of the holiday, the date, and the reason it is celebrated next to the right month.
2. Folk songs are an important part of our heritage. Most of our folk songs originally came from other countries. People who moved to the United States brought these songs with them. Using the library, find one folk song that came from each of these countries: Mexico, England, and Germany. Find one folk song that started in our country.

Read to Learn More

Find the topics listed below in the card catalog of your library. Read all or part of a book listed under one of the topics. Share what you learn with your classmates.

FOLKLORE–UNITED STATES

LAND AND LANDFORMS

NATIONAL PARKS

Reading Skill: Organizing information: *Learn by Doing, 1.*
Thinking Skill: Classifying: *Learn by Doing, 1.*
Reading Skill: Doing research: *Learn by Doing, 1, 2.*
Reading Skill: Using references: *Learn by Doing, 1, 2.*

Unit Overview: This unit examines the first Americans today and long ago, grouping the Indians according to the geographic areas in which they lived.

Unit Objectives
To understand:
- the American Indians, Eskimos, and Aleuts today
- early Indian farmers
- Indians of the Southwest, Great Plains, Great Basin, Eastern Woodlands, and Northwest Coast

Suggested Materials
Workbook
Unit Tests

Unit 2

Skills Emphasized
Map Skills: pp. 50, 53, 54, 58, 65, 80, 81.
Social Studies Reading Skills: pp. 50, 52, 54, 55, 56, 58, 59, 60, 61, 62, 63, 64, 65, 66, 67, 68, 70, 71, 72, 73, 74, 75, 77, 78, 79, 80, 81.
Thinking Skills: pp. 50, 53, 57, 58, 62, 68, 72, 76, 77, 80.
Communication Skills: pp. 50, 64, 74, 79, 81.
Time Skills: pp. 52, 63.
Math Skills: pp. 53, 57.
Citizenship Skills: pp. 50, 56, 68, 75.

Suggested Student Activities
1. Arrange a bulletin-board display entitled "The Homes of the First Americans." Connect student pictures to a map with string to show where the Indians who built each kind of home lived.
2. Work in small groups. Make a movie roll about one Indian group.
3. Make a data chart comparing Indians from various sections of the country.
* 4. Make a display of crops grown by Indian farmers.
** 5. Make a diagram showing all the uses of the buffalo.
*** 6. Invite an Indian to speak to the class.

Skills Emphasized in Suggested Student Activities
Social Studies Reading Skills: Using references, doing research, organizing information.
Communication Skills: Writing, speaking.
Map Skill: Location.
Thinking Skills: Knowing, comparing, classifying.
Citizenship Skill: Social participation.

The First Americans

Indian settlers of the southwestern United States built this home near Canyon de Chelly (də shā), Arizona.

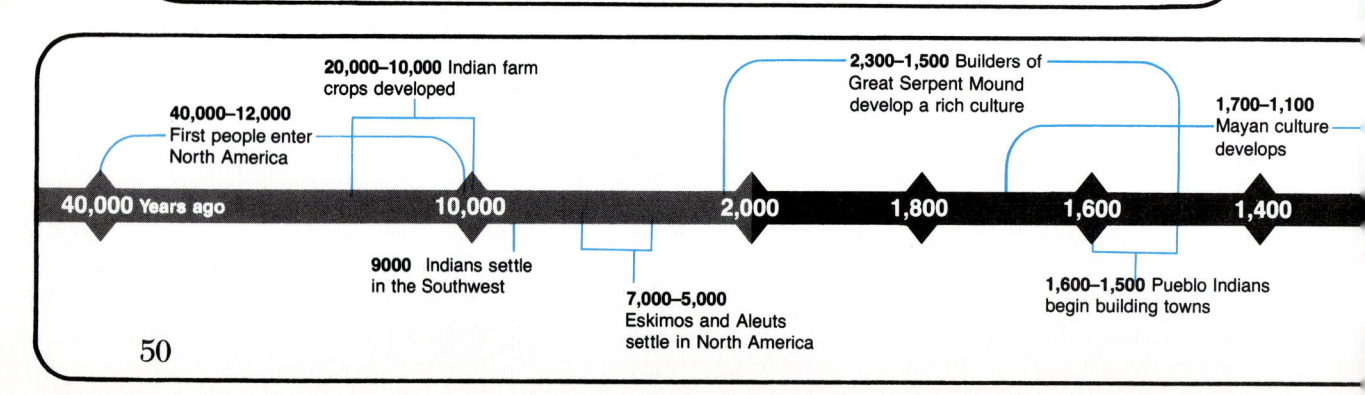

40,000–12,000 First people enter North America

20,000–10,000 Indian farm crops developed

9000 Indians settle in the Southwest

7,000–5,000 Eskimos and Aleuts settle in North America

2,300–1,500 Builders of Great Serpent Mound develop a rich culture

1,600–1,500 Pueblo Indians begin building towns

1,700–1,100 Mayan culture develops

40,000 Years ago — 10,000 — 2,000 — 1,800 — 1,600 — 1,400

1,200	1,000	800	600		400	200 Years ago	

210–200 Many Indians help United States gain independence

700–550 Incan culture develops

160–100 Northwest Coast Indian totem pole period

800–700 Navajos begin moving into the Southwest

700–500 Aztec culture develops

450–390 American Indians begin riding horses

150–90 Most American Indians are moved to reservations

Reading Skill: Recognizing time order: *As You Read, 3.*
Reading Skill: Using textbook features. Have students find Unit 2 in the Table of Contents. Then introduce pages 50–51.

The First Americans Today

As You Read

1. Think about these words.
   ancestor   tribe   reservation
2. Look for answers to these key questions.
   a. How can the influence of American Indians be seen today?
   b. Where do American Indians live today?
   c. Where do Eskimos and Aleuts live?
3. Use this reading skill.
   A time line is a quick and easy way to learn about important events in history. Time lines show the order in which these events occurred. Each of the history units in this text begins with a time line. Before you begin this unit, read the time line on pages 50–51. About how long ago did American Indians reach the Americas? About how many years ago did Indians begin riding horses?

Many Americans today are interested in their **ancestors**. Ancestors are those people from whom you are descended. Your great-grandparents and their parents are some of your ancestors.

The ancestors of most Americans came here from many different countries. People began moving from Europe and Africa to what is now the United States in the early 1600s. There are still many people coming to the United States from all over the world.

Yet there are Americans whose ancestors have been here for thousands of years. These are the American Indians. Sometimes American Indians are called the first Americans or Native Americans. The ancestors of American Indians hunted, fished, and farmed here thousands of years before Europeans and Africans had even heard of the Americas.

Today the influence of the first Americans can be seen almost everywhere. The names of many towns, cities, counties, states, lakes, and rivers are Indian names. Some medicines that American Indians used long ago are used by doctors today. Some of the world's most important crops were first developed and grown by American Indians in North and South America.

In addition to American Indians, two other groups of people lived in North America before the coming of Europeans and Africans. These two groups were the Eskimos (es′kə·mōz′) and the Aleuts (ə·lo͞ots′). They continue to live in parts of Alaska.

Time Skill: Continue to refer to the time line on pages 50–51 throughout the unit.
1. About 12,000–40,000 years ago. About 390–450 years ago.

52

Thinking Skill: Observing. Have students find examples of public places in your community with Indian names (e.g., streets, schools, bodies of water).
Math Skill: Have students compare the size of their community with the number of Indians, Eskimos, and Aleuts living in the United States today.

American Indian Place-Names		
Place-Name	Indian Tribal Language	Meaning
Connecticut	Algonquian	At the long, tidal river
Nebraska	Oto	Flat water
Kentucky	Cherokee	Land of tomorrow or dark and bloody ground
Minnesota	Sioux	Cloudy water
Ashtabula County, Ohio	Algonquian	There are always enough fish moving
Keya Paha County, Nebraska	Sioux	Turtle hills
Chicago, Illinois	Algonquian	Onion place
Opa Locka, Florida	Seminole	Big swamp
Mississippi River	Algonquian	Big river
Klamath River, California and Oregon	Klamath	Tribal name

There are thousands of towns and rivers, as well as many counties and states, with names that come from Indian languages.

Who Is an Indian?

Today over 1,400,000 American Indians, Eskimos, and Aleuts live in the United States. They live in every state and in Washington, D.C. All American Indians have ancestors who belonged to **tribes**, or groups of Indians who shared customs. Most Indians still belong to tribes.

There were hundreds of different tribes of American Indians when the first Europeans came to the Americas. Some of the tribes had no more than fifty people. Others had thousands. Some American Indians lived in towns or villages. Others moved often, carrying their tools and homes with them.

There are now about 250 tribes in the United States. Some still live on the lands of their ancestors. Others live far away from their ancient homelands.

Some Indians still do some things the way their ancestors did. They may speak an Indian language with their families and Indian friends and teach it to their young children. They may continue to practice some of the customs of their ancestors.

Living on Reservations

About half of all American Indians live on lands that belong to a tribe or to several tribes. Most of these lands are called **reservations**. These are lands given to the Indians by the government. The government provides schools, hospitals, and some services to the Indians who live there. Indian tribal councils govern the reservation.

The United States has nearly 300 reservations. They can be found in thirty states. Most, though, are west of the Mis-

Map Skill: Location. Have students locate any reservations in your state on the map on page 54.
Background: Before the coming of Europeans, most Indians did not believe that land could be "owned" by one person alone. Land was for use by the entire tribe.

Navajo (nav′ə·hō′)
*** **Map Skill:** Location. Have students make a map showing any reservations in your state.
*** **Reading Skill:** Doing research. Ask several students to prepare a report on the Navajo.

■ **Indian Reservations**

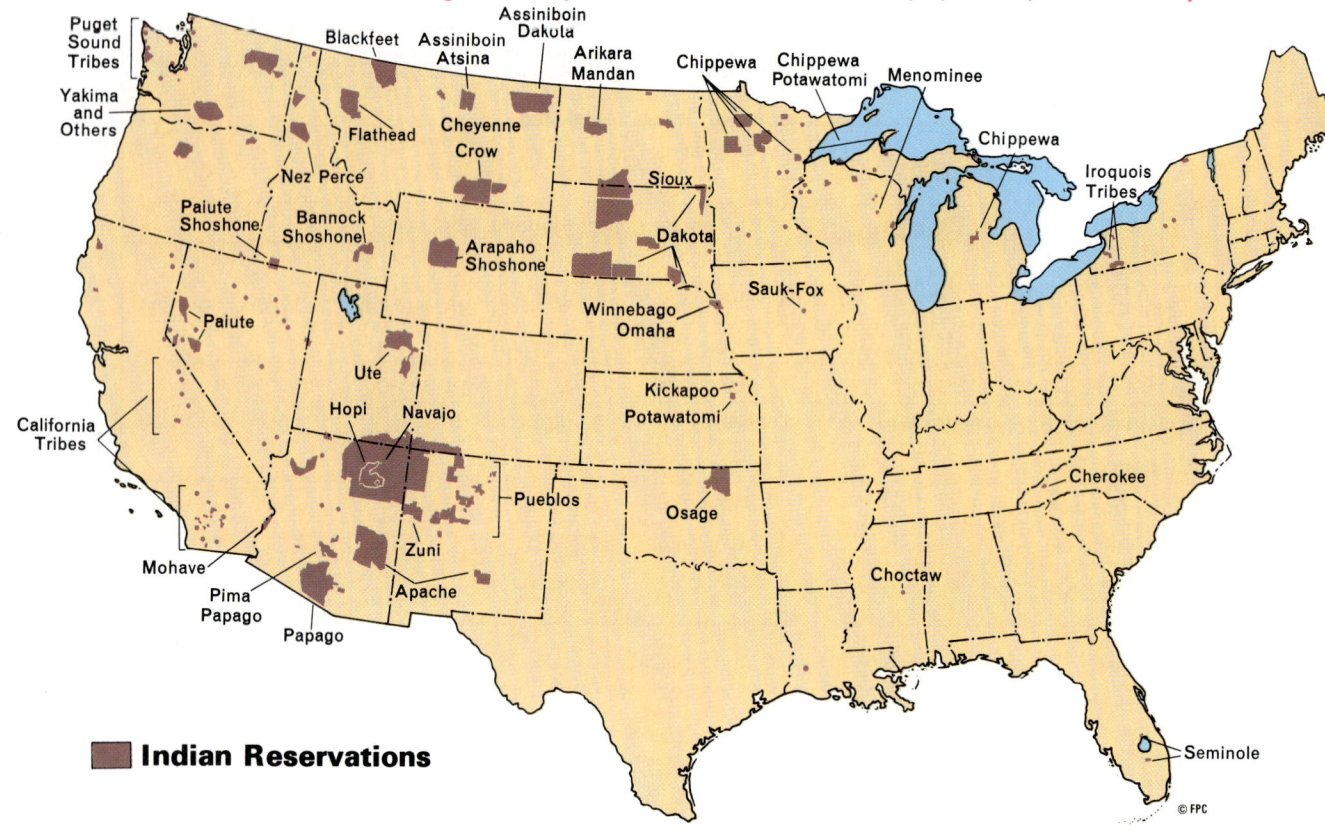

Most Indian tribes had been forced onto reservations by the 1890s. Today some tribes are trying to gain additional reservation land.

sissippi River. Look at the map of reservations on this page. Which states have several reservations? The largest reservation in the country is the Navajo Reservation, which covers parts of Arizona, New Mexico, and Utah. Find this reservation on the map on this page.

On some reservations many of the old ways are kept alive. There children learn some of the old tribal customs. Yet on these same reservations, American Indians may live in modern ways. On most reservations there is a mix of traditional and modern life.

Most American Indians make a living by growing crops and raising livestock. Others work in factories or sawmills owned by the tribes. Some work in the post offices, schools, and stores on the reservations.

Living in Small Towns

Many American Indians leave their reservations, hoping to find better jobs, schools, and places to live. Some find work in small towns near the reservations. They may return to their reservations for holidays, vacations, and family visits. They stay close to their aunts, uncles, cousins, parents, and grandparents.

Living in Cities

Growing numbers of American Indians are moving to large cities such as Los

1. Wash., Idaho, Mont., N.D., S.D., Minn., Nev., Utah, Ariz., and N.M.

Rosebud, South Dakota, is one of many reservation towns in our country.

Many American Indian lawyers work hard to gain rights for Indians.

Angeles, Chicago, Denver, Minneapolis, and Seattle. These Indians work at a variety of jobs. Some become teachers, doctors, or lawyers.

Some of these American Indians live in neighborhoods with other Indians. They go to Indian centers and talk to other Indians. Some also keep the old ways alive in their homes.

Others, though, begin to lose touch with their Indian backgrounds. They move away from the old neighborhoods. They do not return to the reservations.

Eskimos and Aleuts

Eskimos and Aleuts live in the land now called Alaska. They settled there thousands of years ago. Look at the map on page 62. Find the location of the Eskimos during the 1600s.

Now look at the map on pages 20–21. Find the Aleutian Islands off the coast of Alaska. These islands have been the home of the Aleuts for thousands of years.

Today most Eskimos and Aleuts live in small towns and villages. They work in factories, mines, fishing boats, and oil fields. They build modern houses and buy their clothes and food in the towns' stores. Many rely on snowmobiles for winter travel.

A small number of Eskimos and Aleuts still live by hunting and fishing. Throughout the summer and fall, most of these Eskimos and Aleuts hunt caribou, an animal that looks like a large deer. Then as winter draws near, they gather into small groups. They follow many of the ways that their ancestors followed many years ago.

Checking Up
1. Why are American Indians called the first Americans?
2. About how many American Indians, Eskimos, and Aleuts live in the United States?
3. What answers would you give to the key questions at the beginning of this chapter?
4. *Why do you think that life on most reservations has a mix of traditional and modern customs?*

Reading Skill: Interpreting pictures. Ask students how the pictures above help explain the text.
1. Canada and the United States.

Reading Skill: Doing research. Have several students report on the duties of an archaeologist.
Citizenship Skill: Social participation. Invite an archaeologist or a staff member from your area's history museum to speak to the class.

Maps and Pictures Tell a Story of the Settling of the Americas

As you read, think about these words.

| archaeologist | plains | mountain | elevation |
| glacier | plateau | hill | local relief |

Since the 1600s North and South America have been settled by people who moved here from other countries. Most **archaeologists** (är·kē·äl′ə·jəsts), or people who study the way that people lived in the past, believe that American Indians also migrated, or moved, to the Americas. However, archaeologists are not sure exactly when, how, or why the migration was made.

Possible Migration Routes

The early American Indians left no written records. So archaeologists have studied the tools, pottery, and bones that early people left behind. These objects help explain the migration.

Many parts of the story are not known. Archaeologists have different ideas about where American Indians lived before they came to the Americas.

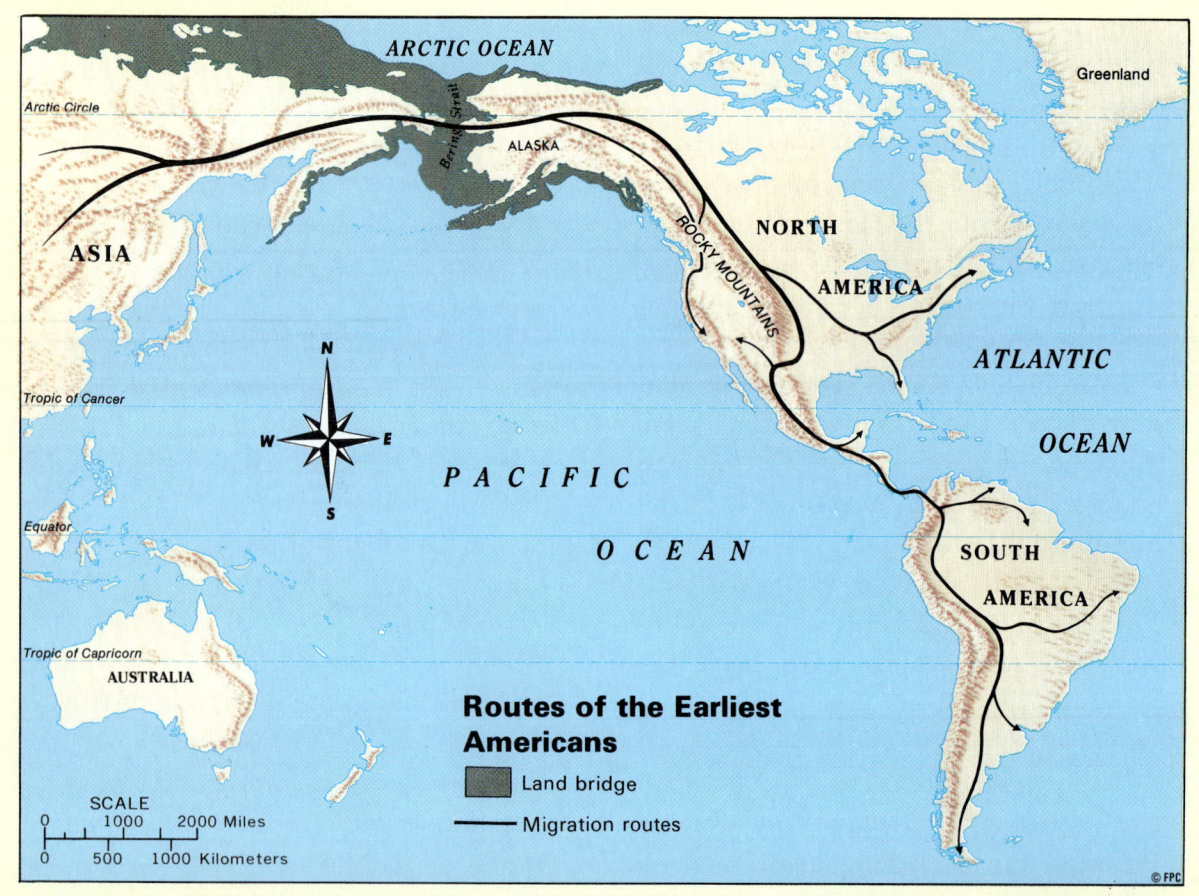

Routes of the Earliest Americans
- Land bridge
- Migration routes

Background: Archaeologists use a method called radiocarbon dating to determine the age of the remains of once living things. Radiocarbon dating is useful in learning about the migration of the earliest Americans.

* **Math Skill:** Talk about how many feet make up 1 mile. (There are 5,280 feet, or 1,609 m, in 1 mile.)
** **Thinking Skill:** Analyzing. Ask students why scientists and historians cannot determine when the first Americans arrived in North America.

Looking toward Asia from Alaska, you can see how close Asia and North America are.

Many archaeologists believe, however, that these early people migrated from Asia thousands of years ago. Look at the map on page 56. What present-day state of the United States is closest to Asia? This area is probably where the first Americans entered North America. What waterway separates North America from Asia? What two large bodies of water does this waterway connect? About how many miles separate Asia from North America at this point?

Some archaeologists believe that these early people may have crossed the Bering Strait by boat. Many others believe that the first Americans migrated over land long ago.

The Ice Age. Thousands of years ago, much of the northern part of North America was covered by thick sheets of ice called **glaciers**. In some places these glaciers were 1 mile (1.6 km) thick. The period of time when glaciers occurred is called the Ice Age.

Look at the map on this page. It shows the location of two large glaciers during the Ice Age. Compare this map with the map of North America on page 14. In which country was most of the eastern glacier? In which country was most of the western glacier?

The land bridge. These glaciers held huge quantities of frozen ocean water.

Glaciers over North America

Extent of ice about 18,000 years ago

1. Alaska.
2. Bering Strait. Arctic and Pacific oceans. About 50 miles.
3. Canada. Canada.

57

Map Skill: Distance. Have students determine roughly how far they might travel if they went 600–1,000 miles away from school. Have them use the map on pages 18–19.

Reading Skill: Using references. Have students look for pictures of animals that crossed the land bridge.

As a result, the level of the oceans dropped. There probably was a bridge of dry land where the Bering Strait is today. This land bridge could have provided the dry land route for the first Americans. Look at the area of the Bering Strait again on the map on page 56. The people probably traveled back and forth between Asia and North America. Some may even have lived on the land bridge. Many people believe that the land bridge could have been 600 to 1,000 miles (966 to 1,609 km) wide.

Why Did Early People Migrate?

It is likely that the migrating people were hunters. The animals that they hunted, such as mammoths, giant sloths, and saber-toothed tigers, used the land bridge too. The first Americans depended on these animals for food, shelter, and clothing. The hunters followed the animals across the land bridge.

Throughout the Americas

The early people who migrated to the Americas did not know that they had discovered a continent. They probably did not think of themselves as explorers. Yet the settlement of the Americas was a great adventure. The journey through the Americas must have been difficult. Yet some people pushed on and on. Some settled in various parts of North America. They were the ancestors of American Indians in what is now the United States. Others migrated farther south. Finally, they reached the southernmost point of South America. Later, their descendants developed the great Indian civilizations of Middle and South America.

Landforms

As these people migrated to all parts of the Americas, they saw many landscapes. These landscapes include the

The ancient mammoth was an important source of food for early Americans. What present-day animal does the mammoth look like?

Thinking Skill: Analyzing. Ask students why most first Americans probably did not think of themselves as explorers.

Reading Skill: Interpreting a picture. Have students look at the picture above and then answer the question in the caption.

Elevation and Relief of Landforms

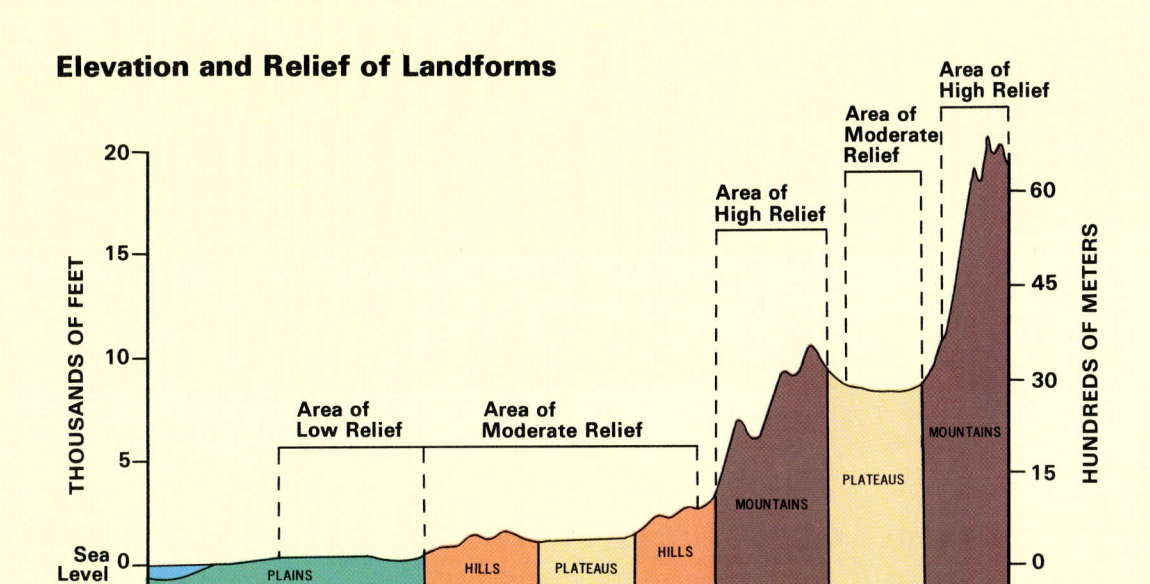

four basic landforms: **plains**, **plateaus**, **mountains**, and **hills**.

These four landforms are classified by **elevation** and **local relief**. Elevation is the height of land above sea level. Local relief describes the differences or changes in elevation from one place to another in the same area.

Plains are almost flat or gently rolling areas. They have low elevation and low local relief. Plateaus, like plains, are generally flat, but they are usually higher in elevation than plains. Local relief of plateaus can be great if rivers have carved deep valleys in a plateau area. Mountains have both high elevation and high local relief. Hills are often worn-down mountains. The local relief of hills is more gently sloping than that of mountains. Hills have lower elevations than mountains. The diagram on this page shows these four landforms.

Compare the map of North America on page 15 with the map of possible migration routes on page 56. As the first Americans began to migrate south from Alaska, which landform was west of their main route? Trace the route across North America to Florida. On which landform did these Indians settle? Now look at Mexico on the map on page 15. On which landform in central Mexico did Indians settle?

Checking Up

1. From where did the first Americans probably come? Where did they enter the Americas?
2. Why did the early people migrate to North America?
3. Which landform lay to the east of the migration route along the Pacific coast of the United States?
4. What are the four basic landforms? How are they different from one another in elevation and local relief?

Reading Skill: Building vocabulary. Have students identify the base word (*migrate*) in *migration*. Talk about building base words with prefixes and suffixes.
1. Mountains. Plains. Plateau.

* **Reading Skill:** Using references. Have students list natural resources found in the United States.
Reading Skill: Using references. Ask students to make a visual list of crops developed and grown by the first Americans.

Indians in the Americas

As You Read

1. Think about these words.
   natural resource   culture
2. Look for answers to these key questions.
   a. Why did American Indians begin to farm?
   b. What crops did Indian farmers grow?
   c. How did the climates and resources of regions influence the way Indian groups lived?

The land on which the first Americans lived had many **natural resources**. Natural resources are those things found in nature that people use. The earliest Americans developed ways of using the many natural resources of the Americas.

Changing Ways of Life

For thousands of years, the first Americans moved south. They followed the animals they hunted. As they moved into new areas, they gradually changed the ways in which they lived.

The end of the Ice Age. There were important changes in the earth at the end of the Ice Age. The climate became warmer. The glaciers melted, leaving lakes and rivers in some places.

Many of the large animals that the first Americans hunted, such as the mammoth, gradually disappeared. Scientists are still not sure why. It may be that the first Americans were such good hunters that they killed most of the large animals. We know, however, that some of the first Americans began to depend more and more on plants and smaller animals for food.

Farming the Land

These early American hunters probably also gathered seeds, nuts, and fruits for food. Yet gathering rarely provided a constant and sure supply of food. After learning many things about plants over a long period of time, the first Americans began to farm. They found that planting seeds provided a more certain supply of food. They carefully chose seeds from the plants that grew well.

It is likely that farming began in Middle or South America. Farming and farm crops gradually spread north to what is now the United States.

Indian crops. Indian farmers developed food crops that now feed millions of people around the world. Corn and white potatoes, two of the world's most important crops, were first grown by Indian farmers. Squash, tomatoes, peppers,

Guatemala (gwät′ə·mäl′ə)
Background: The Indians in the picture below are Menominee. *Menominee* means "wild rice people." The Menominee have always harvested and traded wild rice that grows in nearby lakes. Have students locate the Menominee reservation in Wisconsin on the map on page 54.

Still standing today, these ruins of a Mayan city are in Guatemala.

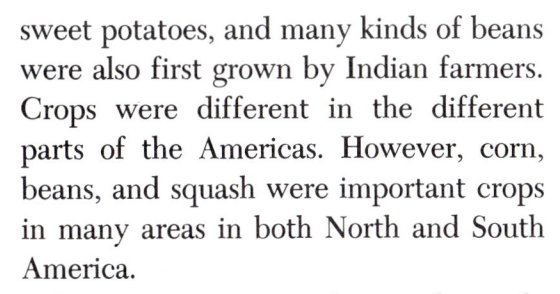

Indians in Wisconsin harvest wild rice, a plant that grows in marshy lakes.

sweet potatoes, and many kinds of beans were also first grown by Indian farmers. Crops were different in the different parts of the Americas. However, corn, beans, and squash were important crops in many areas in both North and South America.

Popcorn was popular with early Americans. Many Indians in the northeast region of North America made maple syrup. American Indians in South America were the first to grow cacao (kə·kou′). The seeds of cacao are still used to make chocolate.

The Growth of Indian Cultures

The arts, customs, and knowledge of a group of people make up their **culture**. All groups of people have cultures.

The development of farming changed many Indian cultures. With food from farming, fewer people were needed to search for food. Those who did not farm could work at other jobs. Some made pottery. Others made clothing and jewelry. In some places people became skilled at designing and building cities.

The Mayas. The Mayas (mī′əz) lived in what is now Mexico and Middle America. They settled there about 2,000 years ago. Look at the map on page 14. Find the Yucatán (yōō′kə·tan′) Peninsula and the country of Guatemala. This was the area in which the Mayas lived. They were excellent farmers. In time, the Mayas became skilled in astronomy, the study of stars and planets. They developed accurate calendars.

Reading Skill: Using references. Ask students to read about maple syrup and then make a chart showing how it is made.
Reading Skill: Doing research. Assign several students to make a display on cacao and its uses.
* **Reading Skill:** Building vocabulary. Talk about the meaning of *culture*.

61

Thinking Skill: Knowing. Ask students which tribes live or once lived in their state. Have students refer to the maps below and on page 54.
*** **Reading Skill:** Doing research. Assign several students to report on the Mayas and the Incas.

American Indian Tribes in the 1600s

·········· Present-day country borders

The Incas. The Incas (ing′kəz) lived in the Andes in what is now Peru in South America. Find this country on the map on page 22. Like the Mayas, the Incas were skilled farmers. They built canals to bring water to dry land. They built terraces that looked like steps going up the sides of mountains. They used the flat land on the terraces for farming. They crafted beautiful gold and silver jewelry. The Incas built long roads and strong bridges through the mountains. Look at the time line on pages 50–51. About how long ago did the Incas prosper? 1

The early people in North America also developed rich cultures. Some of them, too, built towns and made beautiful pottery, jewelry, and other objects.

Reading Skill: Using references. Have students look for pictures of the Mayan and Incan cultures.
* **Reading Skill:** Building vocabulary. Ask students to look up the meaning of *terrace*.
1. About 550–700 years ago.

Background: The Great Serpent Mound, pictured below, takes its name from its snakelike shape. The famous mound is located 60 miles southeast of Cincinnati in Adams County, Ohio. The mound is 1,300 feet long (396 m), 20 feet wide (6 m), and from 2 to 3½ feet high (.6 m to 1 m).
1. Pacific and Arctic oceans.

The Mound Builders

In some areas east of the Mississippi River, there are large earthworks, or hills, called mounds. Look at the picture on this page. Notice that it looks like a hill. It is a special kind of hill. It is a mound. These earthworks were built hundreds of years ago, probably by ancestors of American Indians.

There were many different groups of Mound Builders. They built mounds in many shapes. Some were shaped like animals. Others were pyramids. Some mounds were used for burials. Others were places on which temples were built.

The mound in the photograph above is in Ohio. This mound was designed to look like an animal. It was probably built 1,200 years ago. It may have been used for religious services. No one, however, knows for sure.

The other photograph on this page shows an object found in another mound. From studying objects found in mounds, archaeologists now know that the ancestors of American Indians traded with people in many areas of the country.

Different Regions, Different Ways of Life

There are many different regions in North America. These regions have different climates, landforms, and resources. The American Indian tribes, the Eskimos, and the Aleuts developed different ways of living suitable for each region. They used the natural resources of the region in which they lived for food, clothing, and shelter.

Eskimos and Aleuts

The Eskimos and the Aleuts were in the last group of people to migrate from Asia. They stayed in the Far North. Look at the map on page 62. Find the location of the Eskimos and the Aleuts during the 1600s. Near what bodies of water did these groups live? 1

Theirs was a land of biting cold and strong winds. Summers were short—too

Time Skill: Have students determine roughly the year in which the Great Serpent Mound was built (1,200 years ago). Then have students check the time line on pages 50–51 for other events occurring at that same time.
Reading Skill: Doing research. Ask students to read about the Mound Builders.

Reading Skill: Using references. Have students look for pictures of Aleuts and Eskimos.
Reading Skill: Doing research. Have the class make an illustrated report on the Aleuts and/or Eskimos and their ways of living.

short for farming. Winters were long and cold. During the winter months, deep snow covered the plants and bushes.

The people who settled in this region were mainly hunters. Most lived near the sea in scattered family groups. They harpooned, or speared, and trapped sea animals such as seals, whales, and walruses. The groups that lived farther inland hunted caribou and polar bears with bows and arrows. They also fished in the many clear lakes and rushing streams.

The Eskimos and the Aleuts took everything they needed from the land and the sea around them. Their boats were made of driftwood frames covered with skins. They burned animal fat for heat and light. In the summer they lived in houses made of earth or in stone or log houses covered with soil. When away from home in the winter, they sometimes built shelters from blocks of packed, hardened snow.

The Eskimos and the Aleuts sewed their clothing from the skins of sea and land animals. Men, women, and children all wore hooded coats, pants, stockings, boots, and mittens of fur. In the winter they wore two layers of clothing. The inner layer of fur was turned against the body. The outer layer was turned to the outside.

Southeast Indian Tribes

Much farther south were the southeastern Indians. Look at the map on pages 18–19. The tribes of the Southeast lived in what are now the states of Florida, North and South Carolina, Georgia, Alabama, Mississippi, Tennessee, and Louisiana. Now compare the map on page 62 with the map on pages 18–19. What tribes were in the Southeast?

The Southeast is a land of rich soil and long, hot summers. Most Indians there were farmers. They grew corn, squash, pumpkins, beans, sweet potatoes, and sunflowers in large family gardens.

The most important crop in the Southeast was corn. It was so important that the Creek Indians, a southeastern tribe, even began their new year when the first corn ripened. Every July or August, singing, dancing, feasting, and visiting celebrated the harvest and the new year.

The people also hunted in the forests of the Southeast. They gathered wild fruits and berries. They also used wood from the forests for their homes.

Many tribes lived in large villages. They traded with people of other villages. Sometimes they got together for sports and games. Some of the large tribes formed larger groups that Europeans called nations.

Checking Up
1. What groups settled in the Far North?
2. Who were the Mayas? the Incas?
3. How did the southeastern tribes use natural resources?
4. What answers would you give to the key questions at the beginning of this chapter?
5. *How does farming influence the development of a culture?*

Communication Skill: Listening. Read to the class about the Creek Indians. Have students write three things they learned.

Reading Skill: Using textbook features: *As You Read*, 3.

Indians of the Southwest

As You Read

1. Think about these words.
   adobe   irrigate   hogan
2. Look for answers to these key questions.
   a. Where did the Pueblo and Navajo people live?
   b. Why did the Pueblo Indians irrigate their farms?
   c. In what ways did the Navajo change after they migrated to the Southwest?
3. Use this reading skill.

   Each chapter in this book begins with a list of important social studies words. You will also find these words in bold type as you read the chapters. The Glossary at the back of your book tells you how to pronounce these words and what they mean. Be sure you can pronounce each word and understand its meaning.

The Southwest of the United States is a land of contrasts. Mountains soar above deep canyons. Jagged rocks jut up from the flat desert. Treeless land gives way to dense forests. The land bakes under brilliant blue skies, yet it chills quickly when the sun sets. In the spring, for a few short weeks, wildflowers carpet the desert.

This beautiful land is the ancient home of the Pueblo (pweb′lō) Indians. They settled much of the land where Arizona, New Mexico, Utah, Colorado, and Texas are today. Their descendants still live there. Many other tribes also live in the Southwest today.

Though beautiful, much of the Southwest has a dry climate.

* **Map Skill:** Location. Have students locate the area where the Pueblo settled.
** **Reading Skill:** Organizing information. Have students make individual montages on the Pueblo.

65

This pueblo near Taos (tous), New Mexico, probably looks much the same as it did hundreds of years ago when Europeans first saw it.

The Pueblo

Many tribes in the Southwest developed rich cultures. They became expert farmers who fed many people. They built large homes in towns that you can visit today. Because many of these Indians lived in villages, Spanish explorers called these Indians the Pueblo. *Pueblo* is the Spanish word for "village."

The Pueblo were not just one tribe. They were a group of people who spoke different languages and had different customs. The Hopi (hō′pē) and the Zuñi (zōō′nē) were two Pueblo groups. Find these two tribes on the map on page 62. Now look at the map on pages 18–19. In which states did they live?

The Pueblo people had different ways of living. Yet they were alike in many important ways. All lived in permanent villages. Most of the villages were built on desert land a short distance from water, forests, and mountains. Some villages housed nearly a thousand people.

The houses in the Pueblo villages were built like apartments. Some were four or more stories high. The Pueblo used ladders to get to the higher stories. In times of danger people pulled up the ladders. Most of the houses had underground rooms for special religious meetings and other gatherings. Pictures showing scenes of the life of the people covered the walls.

Some Pueblo built their homes out of stone. Most, though, used **adobe** (ə·dō′bē) bricks. Adobe is a mixture of earth and dried grass. When water was added, the mixture was formed into bricks. The bricks were then dried by the sun. Homes made of adobe were cool during the day and warm at night.

A few early Pueblo groups were cliff dwellers. They built their homes along ledges or in hollow spaces in cliff walls. In time, most of these groups moved to lower land where they could grow crops more easily.

Reading Skill: Interpreting a picture. Ask students what more they can learn about a pueblo from the photograph on page 66.

1. New Mexico and Arizona.

Using the available building materials, the Navajo built this hogan in Arizona. What material do you think was used for this hogan?

Pueblo Farmers

Near the villages were the gardens and fields where the Pueblo grew corn, beans, squash, and sunflowers. They also grew cotton, which they wove into cloth. Farming was difficult in the dry climate of the Southwest. So some Pueblo Indians learned to **irrigate** their fields. They brought water from nearby rivers through a system of ditches or canals.

Some groups of Pueblo grew more food than they needed. They traded this extra food and baskets, pottery, and turquoise jewelry for shells and feathers gathered by Indian tribes along the coast of the Gulf of Mexico.

Hunting and gathering. The Pueblo hunted rabbits and other small desert animals. After the fall harvest, some Pueblo hunters left their villages to hunt buffalo and antelope. Buffalo and antelope skins were made into fur robes and blankets. The people used them during the cold winter months.

Near most Pueblo villages were forested mountain areas. Many kinds of bushes, trees, and plants grew there. The Pueblo people gathered nuts, fruits, and berries in the forests.

The Navajo

The Navajo migrated from the north into the Southwest long after the Pueblo had settled in villages. Find the Navajo on the map on page 62. Now look at the map on pages 18–19. In which states did the Navajo live?

The Navajo were hunters and gatherers, as their ancestors had been. The Southwest, though, did not have many plants and animals. The Navajo had to move several times a year in their search for food.

The Navajo built their homes, called **hogans**, from the materials they found around them. First they cut and stripped three long tree branches. Then they tied these poles together at the top and added

Reading Skill: Following directions. Have the class make a diagram showing how to make a hogan.

67

Navajo sand paintings are often an important part of healing ceremonies.

more poles to this frame. Finally, they covered the frame with mud, bark, and twigs.

Hogans were used mostly in the winter. Often during the summer months, the Navajo did not build hogans. Instead, they made shelters of branches from evergreen trees.

The Navajo and the Pueblo

Navajo groups were scattered over a wide area. However, the groups often joined together to hunt antelope and deer. In time, the Navajo formed close ties with the Pueblo Indians.

The Pueblo taught the Navajo many skills. They taught them to grow beans, corn, and squash. This meant that the Navajo no longer had to depend completely on hunting and gathering food.

The Hopi Pueblo taught the Navajo to weave cloth. The Navajo became expert weavers. They are still famous for their colorful rugs and blankets.

The Navajo learned from the Pueblo, but they did not become like them. They continued to hunt and gather most of their food. They still built hogans in the old way. They still moved two or three times a year, traveling in small groups.

From Hunter to Herder

About 400 years ago, something happened that changed the Navajo way of life. Spanish explorers brought the first sheep and cattle into the Southwest. They also brought the first horses. The Navajo became sheep and cattle herders. Then they moved from place to place, searching for grazing land. With horses they were able to cover great distances. They became an important tribe in the Southwest.

Checking Up
1. How did learning to farm help the Navajo?
2. Why did the Spanish call some Indians in the Southwest the Pueblo?
3. Why were the Pueblo able to trade with other groups?
4. What answers would you give to the key questions at the beginning of this chapter?
5. *Why do you think the Navajo adopted some of the Pueblo Indians' ways of living?*

Indians of the Great Plains and the Great Basin

As You Read

1. Think about these words.
   earth lodge   headwaters   tepee
2. Look for answers to these key questions.
   a. How did the Indians of the Great Plains get their food?
   b. How did the horse change the way the Plains Indians lived?
   c. What kinds of homes were built by the Plains Indians?

From the Mississippi River to the Rocky Mountains and from Canada to Mexico stretches the area known as the Great Plains. On these flat grasslands, summers are hot and dry. Winds often sweep across miles of open land. In the northern part of this area, the winters are cold. Snow often swirls across frozen rivers and lakes, driven by fierce winds. Deep drifts sometimes bury the land.

Dozens of American Indian tribes lived on the Great Plains. The Cheyenne and the Kiowa, the Pawnee and the Comanche lived here. So did the Blackfeet and the Sioux. Find these tribes on the map on page 62.

One of the first tribes to migrate from the east to the Great Plains was the Mandan. They settled along the Missouri River and along the many rivers and streams that flow into the Missouri. Their homes were near where Bismarck, North Dakota, is today. Find this area on the maps on pages 18–21. In which states did the Mandan settle?¹

The Mandan

The Mandan lived in **earth lodges**, or homes made of earth. These were built to last for many years. All the people who were going to live in a lodge helped build it. First they drew a large circle in the earth and dug out the soil inside the circle. They used fire to harden the soil for a floor. Then they built a fire pit in the center of the floor and lined it with stones. Finally, the builders built a frame of wooden poles and covered it with pieces of sod, or grass-covered earth.

Several families lived in each Mandan lodge. The parts were walled off with poles, skins, and grass mats. There was an open area around the fire pit. Here the families gathered for cooking, eating, playing games, and telling stories. Children played in this area in bad weather.

A farming people. The Mandan lived in villages. Each village had several lodges in it. Many Mandan villages were built on high hills, or bluffs, overlooking the Missouri River. On the rich soil of

---

1. North Dakota and parts of South Dakota.
Background: Many of the tribes of the Great Plains, like the Sioux and the Cheyenne, did not move to the Great Plains until the 1600s and 1700s.

Reading Skill: Doing research. Have several students report on the buffalo.
Reading Skill: Using references. Have students look for pictures of Mandan life.

George Catlin was an artist who painted pictures of Mandan homes in the 1800s.

the riverbank below, the Mandan families planted their crops. They grew corn, beans, and squash, just as other Indians in North America did. The Mandan grew more food than they needed. They traded food to other tribes.

A hunting people. During the warm months of the year, the Mandan often left their villages to hunt buffalo on the plains. Groups of Mandan hunters would creep close to the large herds of buffalo. They sometimes wore the skins of wolves or buffalo so the buffalo wouldn't notice them. Buffalo do not see or smell very well. The hunters could get close enough to strike the animals with spears or to shoot them with bows and arrows.

Once in a while, a large hunting party spotted a herd of buffalo on a high cliff near a river. Then they tried to drive the herd over the edge of the cliff. Many of the animals died from the fall.

A trading people. The Mandan lived along the rivers. It was easy for other tribes to travel to Mandan villages. Many Indians came to these villages to trade meat and furs for food. The Mandan villages were trading centers for most of the tribes on the northern half of the Great Plains.

Like Catlin, George Bodmer painted pictures of Mandan earth lodges.

* **Reading Skill:** Organizing information. Have the class build a model lodge.

Reading Skill: Interpreting a map. Discuss the map showing Indian farm crops.
Reading Skill: Doing research. Have several students read more to the class about the Crow.

People Who Made a Difference

Indian Farmers

When Europeans and Africans first came to the Americas, they found crops that were not grown in other parts of the world. Today millions depend on crops that Indian farmers were the first to develop and grow.

Corn now grows in many parts of the world. However, the first crop of corn was probably grown thousands of years ago by Indian farmers in central Mexico. From Mexico, the use of corn spread to other parts of the Americas.

Tomatoes are now a daily food in the United States and other countries. This crop was also first grown by Indian farmers. Some archaeologists believe that tomatoes were first grown in Middle America.

Potatoes, an important food to many people, were first grown by Indian farmers in South America thousands of years ago. Today white potatoes are grown on every continent except Antarctica.

Other important Indian crops were beans and squash. These and the other crops are shown on the map on this page. Which crops were more common in North America? in South America?

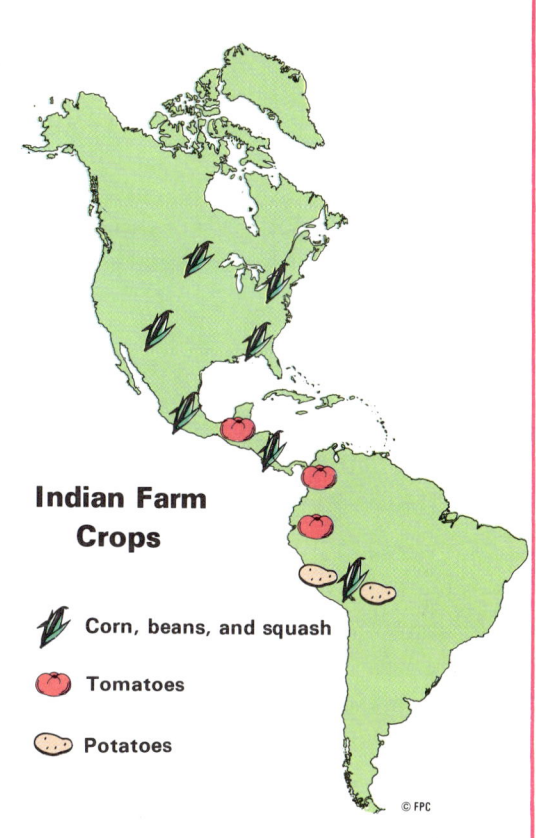

Indian Farm Crops

- Corn, beans, and squash
- Tomatoes
- Potatoes

According to this map, which Indian farm crop was the most common?

The Crow

The Plains tribes got horses from tribes to the south of them. Some tribes, such as the Crow, became hunters who followed the buffalo on horseback. The Crow were part of a tribe called the Hidatsa (hi·dät′sə). Find the Hidatsa on the map on page 62. However, the Crow split off and migrated to the area around the **headwaters**, or beginning, of the Yellowstone River. Find this area on the map on pages 20–21. They rode over this area in search of buffalo.

The **tepee** was the Crow's year-round home. A tepee is like a large tent in the shape of a cone. The Crow tepees, though, were not simple shelters. They were large and beautifully decorated with beads, shells, and feathers. The walls of the Crow tepees were made of buffalo hides that had been carefully sewn together.

Like the Crow, the Blackfeet Indians lived in tepees and hunted buffalo.

Buffalo on the plains. Millions of buffalo, some say as many as 75 million, once roamed the plains. Huge herds stretched as far as the eye could see.

The Crow were great buffalo hunters. They learned to use every part of the animal. They used the hides for winter clothing and for tepees. They made tools from buffalo bones. They dried buffalo meat, pounded it, and then mixed it with fat and berries. This mixture is called pemmican (pem′i·kən). They stored this food for the long winter months.

The Crow made still other uses of buffalo. They brushed their hair with the rough sides of buffalo tongues and stuffed pillows with buffalo hair. They melted buffalo hoofs to make glue. They swatted flies with buffalo tails.

The spread of buffalo hunting. Many other tribes who lived on the Great Plains also learned to hunt buffalo on horseback. Some groups left their farms and permanent villages to become wandering buffalo hunters. Even tribes that lived west of the Rocky Mountains learned to hunt the buffalo. The Shoshone (shə·shō′nē) were one of these tribes.

Thinking Skill: Comparing. Have students compare homes of Indians examined so far. Continue comparing throughout the unit.

The Shoshone

Many of the Shoshone lived in the Great Basin, an area between the Rocky Mountains and the Sierra Nevada. A basin is a wide, shallow, low spot in the earth. The Great Basin is a desert land with few plants and animals. Find this area on the map on pages 20–21.

The Shoshone learned to find food in this dry land. They ate insects and snakes. They gathered seeds in the spring. They dug deep into the earth for roots.

Later, the Shoshone learned from the Crow how to hunt buffalo. This skill changed the Shoshone way of life. They no longer had such a struggle to find food. Each spring they crossed the Rocky Mountains to hunt buffalo. Many months later, they returned to their desert homeland with enough dried buffalo meat for the winter.

When other people began to settle on the plains, many buffalo were killed. The Plains Indians had to change the way they lived.

Checking Up

1. Where did the Mandan live? the Crow? the Shoshone?
2. How did the Crow use the buffalo they killed?
3. What answers would you give to the key questions at the beginning of this chapter?
4. *Why did the Crow Indians develop so many ways to use the buffalo?*

Thinking Skill: Analyzing. Ask students why it was important to use all the buffalo.
Reading Skill: Using references. Have students look for pictures of Shoshone life.

Indians of the Eastern Woodlands

As You Read

1. Think about these words.
   wigwam   longhouse   clan   chief
2. Look for answers to these key questions.
   a. What was the main food crop in the Eastern Woodlands?
   b. What was the Iroquois League?
   c. What role did women play in the Iroquois League?

From the Atlantic Ocean west to the Great Plains, there were once vast forests. These woodlands stretched from the Gulf of Mexico almost to Hudson Bay. Look at the map on page 15. Find this large area on the map. This area, especially the northern part, is sometimes called the Eastern Woodlands. The Eastern Woodlands were once home to many Indian tribes. The Erie, the Chippewa, the Iroquois (ir′ə·kwoi′), and many others lived in the Eastern Woodlands. Find these three tribes on the map on page 62.

Hunting, Gathering, and Growing Food

Food was plentiful throughout most of the Eastern Woodlands. Moose, deer, caribou, rabbits, and other animals lived in the dense forests. Many nuts and berries, and maple trees grew there. Sap from the maple trees could be used for making syrup. Wild rice grew near marshy ponds. Geese and ducks swam in crystal-clear lakes. Fish filled the rivers and streams.

Hunting and fishing. The Indians of the Eastern Woodlands hunted game with bows and arrows. Some groups set fish traps across swift streams. Others speared fish or shot them with bows and arrows. In the winter fishers cut holes in the ice and speared fish through these holes.

Farming. Most of the tribes in this area were farmers. They grew corn, beans, and squash in large family gardens. Corn was the main crop throughout the area.

The Indians found hundreds of uses for corn. They ate corn dumplings, corn soup, and popcorn. They made shoes, masks, and dolls from cornhusks, the leafy coverings of the ears of corn. They also used husks for washing dishes. They even scratched their backs with cornhusks backscratchers.

Using Forest Resources

You have learned that the forests were an important source of food for the Eastern Woodlands tribes. The forests also

* **Reading Skill:** Determining meaning from context. Talk about *crystal-clear*.
Reading Skill: Organizing information. Have students begin a class display on the uses of corn.

73

Indian workers in this scene stretch birch bark over a canoe frame. Many birchbark canoes are still in use today for fishing, hunting, and touring.

provided raw materials for clothing, transportation, and housing. People made shirts, pants, and dresses from deerskin. Many people wove cloth from the plants gathered in the forests. Some sewed hundreds of bird feathers together to make light, beautiful robes.

The two kinds of canoes used throughout the area were built with wood. The dugout canoe was simply a hollowed-out log. The bark canoe had a light frame made of cedar that was covered with birch, spruce, or elm bark.

During the winter, lakes and rivers froze, and deep snow blanketed the woods and fields. The Indians used snowshoes to walk over the snow. They made their showshoes from light wood and strips of hide.

The wigwam. The Eastern Woodlands Indians lived in villages. Some groups built **wigwams** to protect themselves from the cold and snow of winter. The builders began by marking a rectangle or a circle in the earth. They dug holes around the edge and put a long, thin pole in each hole. They brought the poles together at the top and fastened them with roots or thin strips of wood. The poles were covered with branches. Then the builders covered the entire wigwam, except for a smoke hole in the center of the roof, with mats woven from plants called cattails. Finally, the wigwam was covered with sheets of tree bark.

The floor of the wigwam was often carpeted with pine needles. In the center was a fire pit lined with rocks. Around the walls were shelves for sleeping made from poles. These were covered with grass mats and layers of animal furs.

In the spring the families moved the bark and mats to their hunting and fishing grounds. There they set up low shelters with peaked roofs that looked like the tepees used on the Great Plains.

Reading Skill: Using references. Have students look for pictures showing clothing of Eastern Woodland Indians and describe them.
* **Communication Skill:** Speaking. Have students explain how to make a canoe to someone who doesn't know how.

Reading Skill: Using references. Have students look for pictures of Iroquois life.
*** **Citizenship Skill:** Social participation. Invite someone to class to explain lacrosse.

Then and Now

Indian Games

Indians throughout North America played many games. Some were much like those we play today.

Many Eastern Woodlands tribes played a game that was like football and soccer. Two teams played on a flat field with goals something like football goalposts. The field was divided in half. Each team tried to kick a ball through the other team's goal. Sometimes this game lasted for hours, even days. It ended only when one team kicked the ball through the goal a certain number of times.

A game Americans now call lacrosse was first played by Indians in the Eastern Woodlands. The painting above shows a game like lacrosse as it was played by Choctaw (chäk·tô′) Indians.

Men, women, and children all enjoyed a wide variety of games. Look at the painting at right. Name three games you recognize. 1

The Iroquois Indians

The Iroquois, a group of several tribes, lived in what is now the state of New York. These people hunted and fished in the forests and streams near their homes. However, most of their food came from farms around their villages.

Some of the Iroquois villages were made up of fifty or more **longhouses**. These houses had frames of poles covered with bark. They were built in much the same way as wigwams. Longhouses, though, were much larger. Some were more than 100 feet (30 m) long. There were rooms for storing food and for visiting guests. As many as twenty families could live in one longhouse.

Inside each longhouse was a row of fire pits down the center of the building. Two families shared each fire. From the roof poles hung corn and dried apples, pumpkins, and squash. Dried meat and fish were stored in large bowls made of tree bark.

Iroquois clans. Every Iroquois family belonged to a **clan**. A clan was a group of people who had a common ancestor. Each clan had a name such as Bear, Wolf, Turtle, or Beaver. Each clan had a **chief**, or leader.

1. In addition to tobogganing and wrestling, the Indians in this painting are playing kickball and throwing javelins. The women are playing shinny, a form of field hockey.
Reading Skill: Using references. Have students look for other examples of Indian games.

Iroquois longhouses were large enough that people could do many of their daily jobs inside. Why do you think the Iroquois dried their corn inside their longhouses?

An Iroquois woman was a member of the same clan for life. Her husband became part of her clan when she married. Her children were also part of her clan. The women chose the chief of the clan. Sometimes they didn't like the way a chief led the people. Then they chose a new leader.

The Iroquois League. Groups of clans formed tribes. The Mohawk, the Oneida (ō·nīd′ə), the Onondaga (än′ən·dô′gə), the Cayuga (kē·ōō′gə), and the Seneca were all Iroquois tribes. A tribal council made up of clan chiefs led each tribe. About 400 years ago, the five tribes joined together to form a large group called the Iroquois League.

A council of fifty chiefs, chosen by the tribal councils, led the Iroquois League. The chiefs on the league council were peace chiefs. They settled arguments between families, clans, and tribes.

The Iroquois also had war chiefs. They led the warriors in battle against other tribes. A war chief was chosen by the warriors themselves.

Checking Up
1. What was the difference between the Iroquois peace chiefs and the war chiefs? How was each chosen?
2. How did the Eastern Woodlands Indians use the forests?
3. How did the Eastern Woodlands Indians build wigwams?
4. What answers would you give to the key questions at the beginning of this chapter?
5. *How do you think the Iroquois League helped the people?*

Thinking Skill: Analyzing. Have students discuss the role of women.
Background: The Iroquois League usually met every summer to discuss business. Although there were fifty chiefs in the League council, each of the five tribes in the League had only one vote.

Reading Skill: Determining meaning from context: *As You Read, 3.*

Indians of the Northwest Coast

As You Read

1. Think about these words.
   totem pole   fiber   potlatch
2. Look for answers to these key questions.
   a. What natural resources did the Indians of the Northwest Coast use for food?
   b. In what kind of homes did the Indians of the Northwest Coast live? How were these homes built?
   c. In what ways were Indians of the Northwest Coast different from Indians in other areas?
3. Use this reading skill.
   You will sometimes see a word whose meaning you don't know. You do not always have to look up the word in the dictionary. Sometimes you can figure out the meaning of the word by looking at its context. The context of a word may be the sentence in which the word appears. Sometimes the context of a word includes sentences used before or after the word. In this chapter the word *abundant* is used in the third paragraph on this page. Read the two sentences following the word *abundant*. Then read the whole paragraph. How would you define *abundant*? Using the context can help you figure out the meaning of new words.

The Northwest Coast of the United States has many natural resources. The ocean and rivers here are filled with salmon, trout, and shellfish. The moist breezes that often blow from the ocean bring plenty of rainfall, especially during the winters. Temperatures are usually mild. Plants grow everywhere. Forests of cedar and spruce trees soar skyward.

Look at the map on pages 18–19. The Northwest Coast includes the coastline from southeastern Alaska as far south as northern California. It also includes the area as far east as the Cascade Mountains and the Coast Ranges.

In this region many Indian tribes settled and prospered. There was enough food to feed large villages of many families. Homes were built of wood from the abundant forests. Even clothing was made, in part, from wood products. Farming was not common because food and clothing could be easily obtained from the forests.

Thinking Skill: Comparing. Have students compare the Eastern Woodlands and Northwest Coast Indians in terms of their visual arts and crafts.
Reading Skill: Organizing information. Have the class begin a list of the uses of wood in your school.

The Indians' Use of Natural Resources

Many different tribes, speaking different languages, lived in the Northwest. Yet their ways of living were much the same. The areas in which they made their homes had a similar climate and offered similar natural resources. All the Indian groups of the Northwest Coast used the resources there in similar ways.

Food. The Indians got some of their food from the mountains and the forests. They hunted deer, bears, goats, and sheep. During much of the year, people gathered fruits, berries, and nuts in the forests. However, Indians depended on fish for much of their food. Salmon was particularly important. Indians caught salmon in nets and traps as the fish swam up rivers. Some fish were cooked and eaten fresh. Many fish, though, were dried to be eaten later. Shellfish such as clams and oysters also provided many meals for Indian families. Fish caught in the ocean provided food and oil for lamps.

Fishing was so important that many groups became expert in making boats and canoes. Find the Nootka Indians on the map on page 62. The Nootka built oceangoing canoes from hollowed-out logs. These canoes could carry as many as ninety men and women.

Homes. Most of the Northwest Indians lived in villages, especially during the rainy winters. During the summers groups would sometimes move to gather plants and to hunt.

Houses in this area were built of wood. Most houses were large enough

Weaving goat hairs and cedar fibers, Indian workers made beautiful coats.

for several families. Each family had an apartment of its own. In many houses the center of the house was on ground level. The apartments were one level above the center. At the center of the house, people cooked their meals and dried fish.

Totem poles. The Indians of the Northwest made **totem poles**. No other Indian groups made them. Totem poles were tall logs of cedar that had carvings of animals and symbols of ancestors. These Indians made totem poles to tell the story of their ancestors.

Clothing. The climate of the Northwest Coast was mild and rainy. The clothing that Indians wore was often made to protect them more from the rain than from the cold.

Reading Skill: Using references. Have students look for pictures of a potlatch.
** **Communication Skill:** Listening. Read to the class about a potlatch. Have students list three things they learned.

The Indians used **fibers**, or long threadlike strands, from cedar trees to make hats and coats. Sometimes hairs from animals were woven on cedar bark to make clothing. Beautiful designs often decorated the cedar bark clothing.

Trade. The rivers and ocean were more than fishing grounds to the Indian people of this area. The many waterways were also good trading routes. Groups traded with each other and with tribes from other areas. The Northwest Coast tribe known as the Chinook were good traders. They traded dried fish and shells for furs and baskets from Indians in the Great Basin. Find where the Chinook lived on the map on page 62. Now find this same location on the map on pages 20–21. Near what major river did this group live? Why was this a good trading location?¹

Some Important Differences

Farming was not common among the Indians of the Northwest Coast. This alone made Indians here different from many other tribes. Most groups you have learned about had to farm or trade with farming tribes to have enough food.

The potlatch. Another difference between Indians of the Northwest Coast and other Indians was the custom of the **potlatch** (pät′lach′). A potlatch was a feast during which the host gave away presents to everyone at the feast. Often the hosts gave away everything they owned. People who got presents later had potlatches of their own. Then they, too, gave away presents.

Checking Up

1. What was the main food of Indians of the Northwest Coast?
2. What happened during a potlatch?
3. Why were totem poles carved?
4. What answers would you give to the key questions at the beginning of this chapter?
5. *What ways of living of Northwest Coast Indians do you think were influenced by the climate of the area?*

Unit 2 Summary

- American Indians, Aleuts, and Eskimos were the first people to settle in the Americas. They settled here thousands of years ago.
- The ancestors of American Indians migrated from Asia during the last ice age. They probably traveled across a land bridge between Asia and Alaska.
- The first Americans learned to use the resources of the forests, deserts, plains, mountains, and coasts where they lived.
- American Indians grew crops such as corn, beans, and squash. They also hunted and fished.
- The houses that American Indians lived in were made of materials that were plentiful in the area in which each tribe lived.
- Today American Indians live on reservations, in small towns, and in large cities.

1. The Columbia. The Columbia is a large river that many different tribes and groups used for transportation.

Reading Skill: Reading for details. Have students look for one page and paragraph to support each point in the summary.

Unit 2 Review Workshop

What Have You Learned?

1. Who were the first people to live in the Americas? From where do archaeologists think they migrated? Why did the people migrate?
2. What is a reservation? Where are most reservations located?
3. Name two ancient Indian cultures in South America. What were these cultures like?
4. What kind of homes did the Pueblo Indians build? How were their homes different from those of the Mandan Indians?
5. How did the horse change the way of life of the Plains Indians?
6. What were the main foods of Indians in the Eastern Woodlands? on the Northwest Coast?
7. Which groups of American Indians did not farm? Why not?

Use Your Reading Skills

You can improve your vocabulary in many ways. One way is to learn meanings of the parts of words. For example, you read about archaeology in this unit. The word part *-logy* means "the study of." If you remember that meaning, you can figure out the meanings of other words that end with *-logy*. The word part *anthro-* means "human being." What does *anthropology* mean? The word part *geo-* means "earth." What does *geology* mean? Use your dictionary to check your answers.

Use Your Map Skills

The map on the next page shows the major Indian tribes that lived in the state of New York. It also shows some of the waterways and landforms in the state. By studying this map, you can learn more about the Eastern Woodlands Indians. You can also learn about the place-names in and near the state of New York. Study the map and then answer the following questions.

1. Locate the five tribes that were a part of the Iroquois League. Look at page 81 if you need help remembering them. Which of the tribes lived the farthest east? the farthest west?
2. What other tribes lived in or near New York State? Which tribes lived east of the Iroquois? Which tribes lived west of the Iroquois?
3. Which lakes and rivers on this map are named after the five Iroquois tribes?

Use Your Thinking Skills

Read the following descriptions of American Indians. Use the maps, photographs, and text in this unit to identify which tribe or group is being described.

1. This group lives in villages of many longhouses. They grow corn and hunt deer and other animals in the forests.
2. This tribe lived in tepees throughout the year. They followed the great herds of buffalo that once lived on the Great Plains.

Thinking Skills: Knowing, analyzing.
Reading Skills: Building vocabulary, using references, interpreting visuals.
Map Skill: Location.

Indian Tribes in New York State

(Map showing Indian tribes in New York State: Huron, Erie, Seneca, Cayuga, Onondaga, Oneida, Mohawk, Mahican. Includes Lake Ontario, Lake Erie, Lake Champlain, Lake George, St. Lawrence River, Mohawk River, Genesee R., Susquehanna R., Delaware R., Hudson R., Adirondack Mts., Catskill Mts., L. Oneida, L. Onondaga, L. Cayuga, L. Seneca, L. Canandaigua, Otsego Lake. Cities: Oswego, Rome, Buffalo, Avon, Schenectady, Albany, Oneonta, Catskill, Poughkeepsie, New York. Surrounding areas: Canada, Vermont, New Hampshire, Massachusetts, Connecticut, New Jersey, Pennsylvania.)

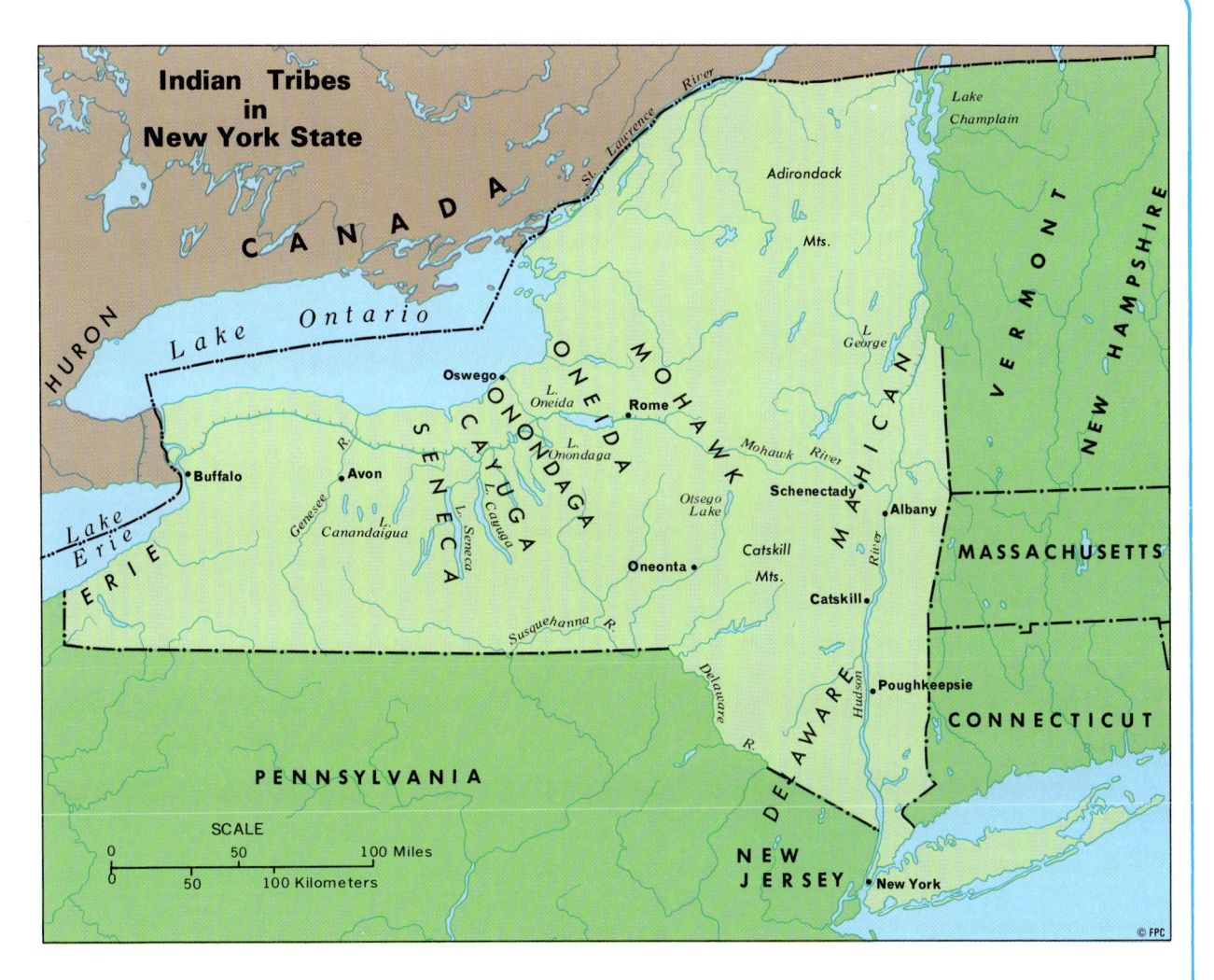

Learn by Doing

Use the map on page 62 and the map of the United States on pages 18–19 to find out which Indian tribes once lived near you. Choose one tribe and find out about the way they lived before other people migrated to this country. What were their houses like? What food did they eat? What was their clothing like? What were their special celebrations? You can find information about and pictures of tribal life in encyclopedias or other books.

Read to Learn More

Find the topics listed below in the card catalog of your library. Read all or part of a book listed under one of the topics. Share what you learn with your classmates.

INDIANS OF NORTH AMERICA
INDIANS OF NORTH AMERICA—ART
MOUND BUILDERS
INDIANS OF NORTH AMERICA—RELIGION

Map Skill: Location: *Learn by Doing, 1.*
Reading Skills: Interpreting visuals: *Learn by Doing, 1;* using references: *Learn by Doing, 1.*
Communication Skill: Speaking: *Learn by Doing, 1.*

Unit Overview: This unit examines early explorers of the New World, focusing on Columbus as well as on early Spanish, English, French, and Dutch explorers.

Unit Objectives
To understand:
- the earliest explorers of the New World
- exploring the West Indies
- Columbus and his voyages
- the extent of Spanish, English, French, and Dutch explorations

Suggested Materials
Workbook
Unit Tests

Unit 3

Skills Emphasized
Map and Globe Skills: pp. 82, 99, 101, 104, 106, 111, 112.
Social Studies Reading Skills: pp. 82, 84, 85, 86, 88, 89, 91, 94, 95, 96, 105, 106, 107, 108, 109, 110, 111, 112, 113.
Thinking Skills: pp. 82, 85, 86, 87, 89, 92, 93, 94, 95, 97, 98, 101, 107, 110, 111, 112, 113.
Communication Skills: pp. 82, 86, 88, 98, 105, 106, 109, 112, 113.
Time Skills: pp. 95, 96, 97, 103, 104, 108.
Social Studies Math Skills: pp. 89, 90, 92, 94, 98, 100, 105, 109.
Citizenship Skill: p. 101.

Suggested Student Activities
1. Arrange a bulletin-board display entitled "Exploring the New World." Focus on a world map. Show each explorer's travels using different-colored string.
2. Make a pictorial time line for use in the classroom.
3. Make a data chart comparing the key explorers named in this unit.
4. Write and illustrate short stories about Christopher Columbus.
** 5. Give individual reports on key explorers mentioned. Include shoe-box dioramas.
*** 6. Look for books on explorers in the library. Arrange a book display.

Skills Emphasized in Suggested Student Activities
Social Studies Reading Skills: Using references, doing research, organizing information.
Communication Skills: Writing, speaking, listening.
Map Skills: Symbolization, location, scale.
Thinking Skills: Knowing, comparing, classifying, analyzing.

Exploring the New World

When Columbus came ashore on San Salvador, he raised the Spanish flag and claimed the land for Spain.

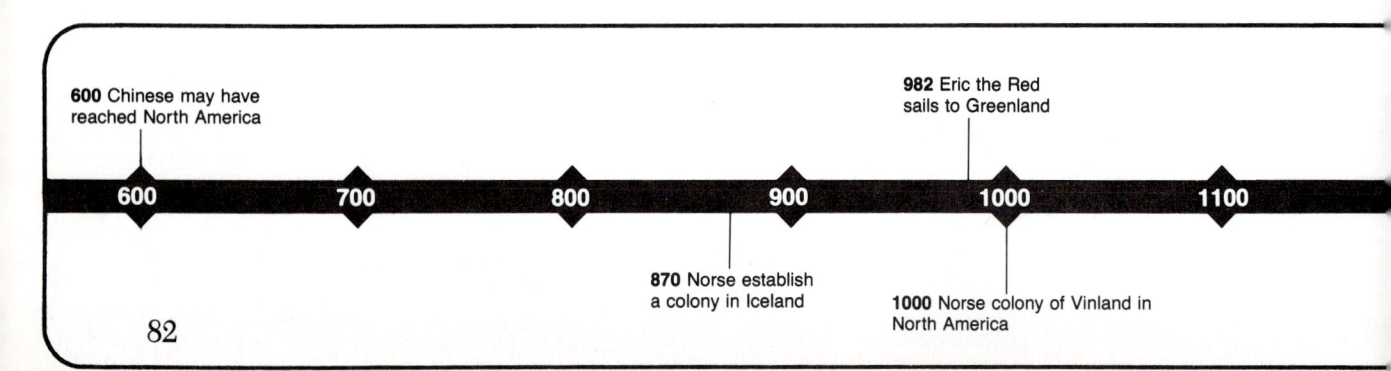

---

600 Chinese may have reached North America

870 Norse establish a colony in Iceland

982 Eric the Red sails to Greenland

1000 Norse colony of Vinland in North America

600 — 700 — 800 — 900 — 1000 — 1100

		1400s Portugal and Spain take the lead in finding a sea route around Africa to reach the Indies	**1534–1536** Cartier explores St. Lawrence River **1500s** Spain builds an empire in the New World	**1540s** Coronado explores American Southwest de Soto explores American Southeast	**1609** Hudson explores Hudson River	
	1271 Marco Polo travels to China					
1200	**1300**	**1400**	**1500**	**1600**		
		1492 Columbus reaches island of San Salvador in the New World	**1521** Cortes conquers the Aztecs		**1610** Hudson explores Hudson Bay	
		1497 John Cabot claims Newfoundland	**1519** Magellan begins his voyage around the world	**1608** Champlain establishes Quebec		

83

Voyagers of Long Ago

As You Read

1. Think about these words.
   ocean current   colony   compass   saga   artifact
2. Look for answers to these key questions.
   a. Why do some historians believe that the Chinese may have reached North America about 1,400 years ago?
   b. Who were the first Europeans to reach North America?
   c. What was Helge Ingstad's discovery?
3. Use this reading skill.
   Every paragraph in a reading selection has a main idea. The sentence that expresses the main idea is called the topic sentence. The other sentences in a paragraph help explain the topic sentence. A good reader must be able to recognize the topic sentence in a paragraph. Find the topic sentence in the first paragraph under the heading "The Chinese." Ask yourself how the other sentences in this paragraph help explain the topic sentence.

For thousands of years, American Indians, Eskimos, and Aleuts were the only people living in North America. During this time voyagers from faraway lands may have reached the shores of North America. We know little about these early voyagers. As far as we know now, only one group left clues behind. From these clues we can guess who they were.

The Chinese

About 1,500 years ago, some people in China believed that a land lay to the east, beyond the great sea. They called this land Fu-Sang. This land may have been Japan. It may also have been North America.

Could the Chinese have crossed the Pacific Ocean? It is possible, say some historians. They point out that a strong **ocean current** flows from west to east across the Pacific. An ocean current is a large river of water moving in the ocean. Look at the map on page 85. Which ocean currents could have carried a ship from China to the west coast of North America?[1]

Historians who think that Chinese explorers did cross the Pacific have studied a Chinese report written about 1,400 years ago. The report describes the trees that grew in Fu-Sang and the food that the people there ate. To some historians, these descriptions sound more like the

1. Kuroshio, North Pacific, and California currents.

84

knarr (när)
*** **Thinking Skill:** Predicting. Ask students where they could look for proof of Chinese journeys to North America.
Reading Skill: Have students look for pictures of Vikings in encyclopedias and other books.

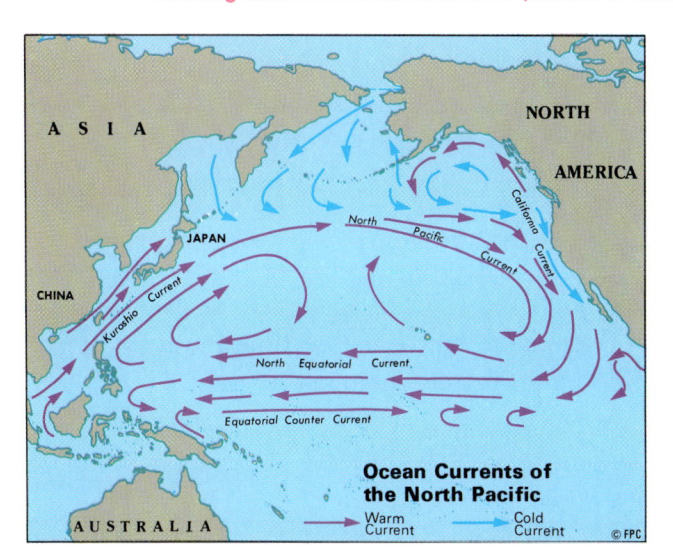

Ocean Currents of the North Pacific

land and people of the Americas than of Japan. They are not certain, though, and they may never be. No one yet has found any proof of Chinese journeys to North America.

The First Europeans in North America

Five hundred years before Christopher Columbus reached North America, the Norse, or Vikings, were in North America. Who were these first Europeans in North America? Where did they come from? How do we know they were in North America?

The Norse built sturdy trading ships called knarrs.

The Norse. A thousand years ago, the Norse were the finest sailors in Europe. The Norse were from Scandinavia (skan′də·nā′vē·ə), today the countries of Norway, Sweden, and Denmark. Look at the world map on pages 10–11 and find these three countries.

In the years between 800 and 1000, Norse traders sailed far from their homeland. During this time the Northern Hemisphere was enjoying the second warmest period since the end of the last ice age, 10,000 years before. Warmer seas encouraged the Norse to explore farther than they had ever explored before. By the middle of the 800s, the Norse had started a **colony** in Iceland in the North Atlantic. A colony is a settlement made by people who leave their own country. Find Iceland on the map on page 10.

Eric the Red. Eric the Red, a tall red-haired Icelander, was a respected Norse sailor in Iceland. However, he had a fiery temper. After one terrible fight Eric had with his neighbors, the leaders of Iceland ordered him to leave the colony for three years. Eric gathered together his family and a few friends and sailed west into the North Atlantic. One week later the group reached a cold, barren shore. Eric claimed the land for Scandinavia and named it Greenland.

Eric and the small group of Icelanders explored Greenland for three years. Then they returned to Iceland. Later, however, Eric returned to Greenland and established a colony there. This colony was closer to North America than any other European settlement.

How Things Work

How the Norse Navigated

At the time the Norse were sailing unknown waters, the **compass** had not been invented. A compass is an instrument with a needle that always points north. Norse sailors had to set their course, or navigate, by the North Star.

The North Star is above the North Pole. By learning to use the Big Dipper as a guide, the sailors could find the North Star and thus north. Once they found north, they could find east, south, and west. They knew that east would be to the right of north, south would be opposite north, and west would be to the left of north. In stormy weather, however, clouds hid the North Star, and high winds blew many ships off course. Ships often sank at sea.

The sagas. For a long time historians believed that the Norse explorers had reached North America. However, they had no proof. They had only the **sagas**. These long stories told of the adventures of Norse heroes.

One of the sagas described the voyage of Bjarni Herjulfsson (byôr′nē här′əlf·sən). According to this saga, in the year 985 Herjulfsson set sail from Iceland. He was on his way to visit his father, who lived in the Greenland colony. A raging storm blew Herjulfsson's ship off course. Finally he spotted land. As the ship drew closer, Herjulfsson became puzzled. Instead of icy mountains, he saw gently rolling hills covered with trees. Deciding that this land did not fit the description of Greenland, he turned northeast and in time reached the Greenland colony.

According to a second saga, Eric the Red's son, Leif, learned of Herjulfsson's discovery of a wooded land far to the west. This saga described how, in the year 1001, Leif Ericson set out in a large ship with a crew of thirty-five. He sailed west to find the wooded land Herjulfsson had described.

From the description in this saga, he came ashore at a place where "the weather was fine. . . . There was no lack of salmon in the river or lake, bigger salmon than they had ever seen." Leif named this new land Vinland.

Leif and his crew spent the winter in Vinland and then returned to Greenland to tell others of this beautiful land to the west. The saga goes on to describe how, during the next fifteen years, the Norse worked hard to establish a colony in Vinland. They built houses, planted crops, and fished in the streams and ocean.

To historians, this gentle land of forests and streams seemed very much like the east coast of North America. However, historians still had no proof that the stories were true.

An important discovery. For many years archaeologists searched the east coast of Canada and the United States

*** **Thinking Skill:** Hypothesizing. Ask students how North America might have been different if the Norse had remained in Greenland and Vinland.

Remains of Norse houses have been found at L'Anse aux Meadows, Newfoundland.

for the remains of a Norse settlement. Among these people was Helge Ingstad (hel′gə ing′städ).

Using the Norse sagas as a guide, Ingstad searched the southeastern shore of Canada. In 1960 in northern Newfoundland, he finally found several half-buried foundations of houses. Find Newfoundland on the map on page 10.

For seven years Ingstad and his team of archaeologists carefully explored the foundations of two large houses and some smaller ones. They found that the houses were built in the same way as the houses in the Norse colony of Greenland. The archaeologists found a bone needle just like the kind used in Norway hundreds of years ago. They also dug up pieces of copper and iron that were made in Norway close to the year 1000.

Ingstad's discoveries proved that the Norse had indeed settled for a time in North America. During the past several years, further discoveries have suggested that the Norse also explored other parts of North America. Thus far, however, the only other **artifact**, or item from the past, that has clearly been identified as Norse is a coin. This coin was found in 1957 along the coast of Maine.

What happened to the Norse colony? According to the sagas, the Indians who lived in North America had welcomed the Norse at first. Later, however, these two groups became enemies. The Indians and colonists fought. Finally, the colonists decided that life in Vinland was just too rugged. They gave up and returned to Greenland.

In time, the Greenland colony also died out. The climate was too cold and the soil too rocky for good farming. The colonists depended on food and supplies sent from Norway. When the leaders in Norway lost interest in Greenland, they stopped sending supplies.

By 1500 the colonies in Vinland and Greenland were forgotten. Europeans did not know what lay west of the great Atlantic Ocean.

Checking Up
1. Who founded the colony of Greenland in the North Atlantic?
2. What proof do we have that the Norse settled for a time in North America?
3. What answers would you give to the key questions at the beginning of this chapter?
4. *How did the sagas help historians discover that the Norse had reached North America?*

Background: The Norse site found by Ingstad and pictured above is in L'Anse aux Meadows (läns ō med′ōz), Newfoundland. Here the sites of eight houses and four boat sheds have been unearthed. Scientists believe that Leif Ericson set up his Vinland colony here, which later Norse expeditions occupied. The site can be found on the map on page 99.

Background: The scarcity of certain spices drew European traders to the Spice Islands (now called the Moluccas). Spices helped season often-tainted European food. The Spice Islands were then the only place in the world where nutmeg and cloves grew. Pepper also grew on nearby islands.
*** **Reading Skill:** Doing research. Have several students report on Constantinople.

Wanted: A Route to the Indies

As You Read

1. Think about these words.
   caravan   mathematics   astronomy   caravel
2. Look for answers to these key questions.
   a. Where are the Indies?
   b. Why did the Europeans want to trade with the Indies?
   c. Why did Europeans begin looking for new routes to the Indies in the late 1400s?

Thousands of miles east of Europe lie China, Japan, India, and the islands off the coast of Southeast Asia. Europeans of the 1400s called these lands in the East the Indies. Find China, Japan, India, and the Spice Islands on the map on page 89.

Marco Polo Travels to the Indies

In the 1200s an Italian merchant named Marco Polo traveled across the rugged mountains, burning deserts, and vast plains between Europe and the Indies. In the East he saw fine silks, gold, and jewels far more beautiful than he had ever seen. He ate food prepared with sharp-tasting spices he had never before tasted.

After spending several years in China, Marco Polo returned to Italy. News about his travels spread through the cities along the Mediterranean Sea. Find the Mediterranean Sea on the map on page 89. Then other traders made their way to the Indies. They brought back small amounts of silks and spices. The Europeans liked these goods from the East. They wanted more.

Trade Routes with the East

In time, long **caravans**, or groups of traders with goods carried by animals, traveled between Europe and the Indies. There were several main routes back from the East. Look at the map on page 89. Trace the land routes from China to Constantinople. In Constantinople the goods were put on ships and brought to European ports along the Mediterranean Sea. Once again they were unloaded and reloaded on animals and carried to cities farther inland.

Sometimes a sea route was used to transport goods most of the way from the Indies to Europe. From the Spice Islands, packages of spices were loaded onto ships. The ships crossed the Indian Ocean and sailed up the Red Sea or the Persian Gulf. Camels carried the spices across the desert to Asian and African ports on the Mediterranean Sea. With

* **Communication Skill:** Listening. Read more about Marco Polo to the class. Have students raise their hands when they hear something new about him.
* **Reading Skill:** Doing research. Ask students to make a list of spices kept in their homes for cooking and then have them report on one spice's origin and cooking uses.

Math Skill: Have students use the map below and the map on pages 10–11 to estimate how far it is from Genoa, Italy, to China, Japan, and the Spice Islands.

Reading Skill: Organizing data. Have students list the problems in sending goods to and from the East.

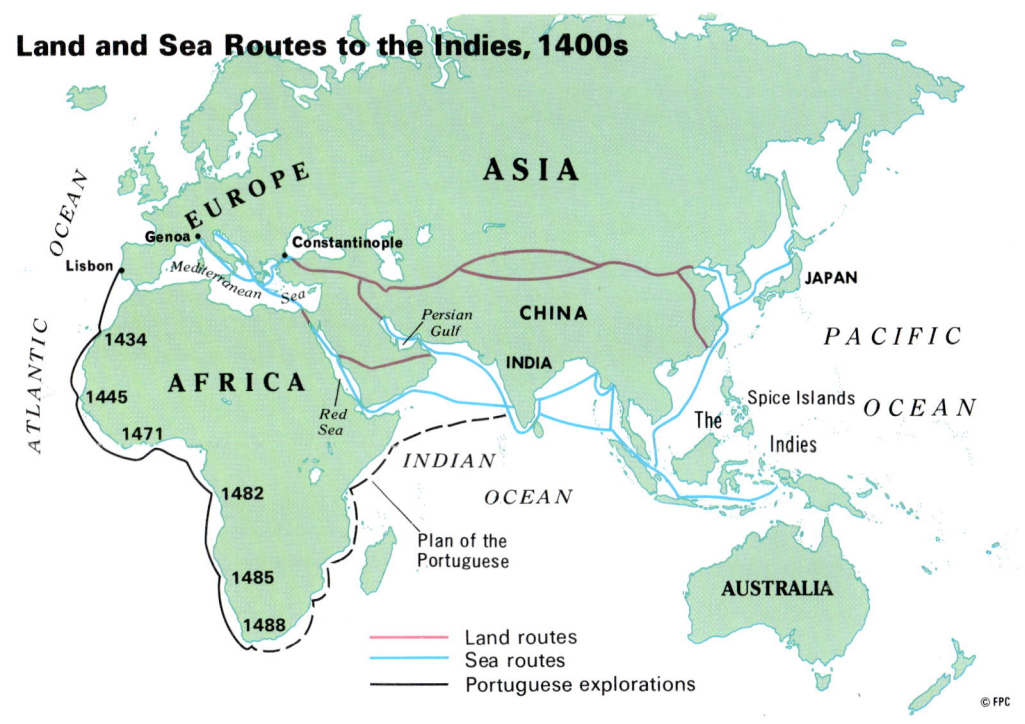

Land and Sea Routes to the Indies, 1400s

How much of the African coast had Portuguese sailors explored by 1445? by 1488?

your finger, trace this route on the map on this page.

The high cost of goods from the East. The trip from the East was long and dangerous. Usually it took months. Sometimes robbers attacked caravans and entire shipments were lost. At every stop traders had to pay the workers who helped with the animals and goods.

The slowness, the danger, and the cost of the long journey made the goods from the Indies very expensive. However, Europeans who had money were willing to pay high prices. Then something happened that slowed trade with the Indies.

New problems for the traders. Late in the 1400s the Turks, warriors from Asia, captured Constantinople. The Turks were enemies of the Europeans. They would not allow goods headed for Europe to pass through Constantinople. Many traders had to find new ways to reach Europe. The new routes were often longer and more difficult than the old one through Constantinople.

European merchants, traders, and sea captains dreamed of a direct sea route to the Indies. "A sea route would be faster and safer," they thought. "The cargoes could be larger and the costs lower." In time, the search for this sea route led Europeans south to Africa and then east to the Indies. This search also led Europeans west to America.

Christopher Columbus

The exhausted sailor lay on the wet sand gasping for breath. In his right

* **Reading Skill:** Building vocabulary. Have students use the Glossary to find the meaning of *merchant*.
Thinking Skill: Analyzing. Ask students why Europeans with money were willing to pay the prices asked for spices.

89

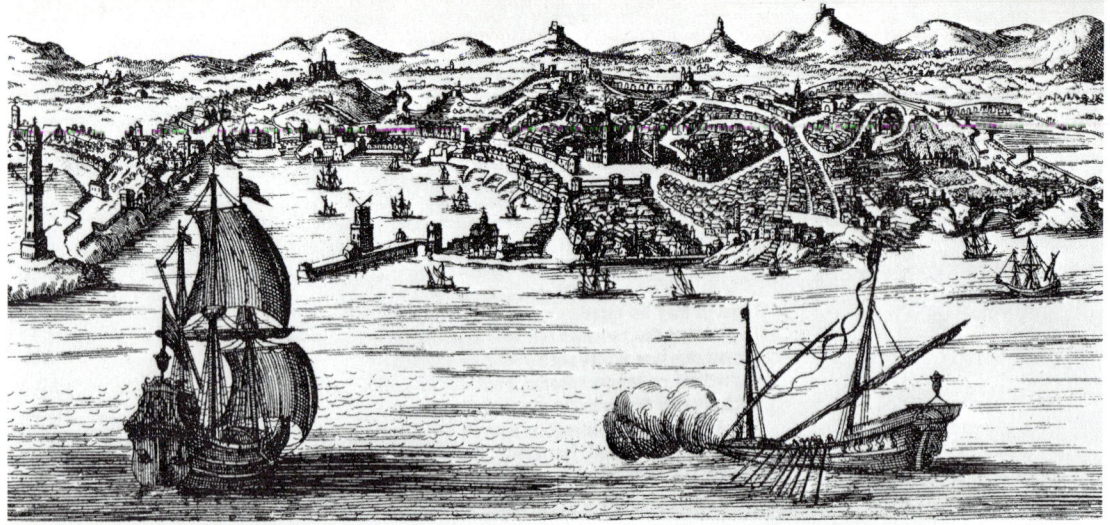

As trade grew between Europe and Asia in the 1400s, ports on the Mediterranean Sea, such as Genoa, became busy trade centers.

hand he clutched a long wooden oar. Two fishers dragged him from the water's edge. "What is your name? Can you hear me?" asked the older of the two, gently touching the sailor's bruised shoulder.

The sailor answered faintly, "Cristoforo. Cristoforo Colombo."

"He is Italian," said the younger fisher. "He must have been on the ship that sank this morning. It's a wonder he is alive!"

The two fishers carried the young sailor to their hut. They cared for him until he began to gain strength. Little by little they learned how the sailor had ended up on a Portuguese (pôr′chə·gēz′) beach far from his homeland.

Boyhood years. Christopher Columbus was born in Genoa, Italy, in 1451. You can find Genoa on the map on page 89. His father and both grandfathers were cloth makers. As a boy he spent long hours among the wool and clacking looms of his father's shop. Yet in his heart he was not a cloth maker. He was a sailor. He dreamed of the day when he could set sail from Genoa. He wanted to sail into the blue waters of the Mediterranean Sea.

In the 1400s Genoa was a lively port. Ships from Asia sailed into its harbor loaded with goods from the East. The sailors and captains told exciting tales of adventure and riches in faraway lands.

Young Christopher grabbed every chance to sail up and down the coast of Italy. He went out on small fishing boats. He rode on the supply ships that traveled to other cities along the Mediterranean coast. In time, the young boy who loved the sea became an expert sailor.

At the age of twenty-five, Columbus signed up with a ship headed for northern Europe. The ship sank in the ocean near Portugal. Columbus swam six miles to shore holding on to an oar. In Portugal a whole new world opened up to him.

Portugal in the 1400s. Portugal was the leading Atlantic sea power in the 1400s. Find Portugal on the map on pages 10–11. Sailors from all over Europe came there to study **mathematics**, the study of numbers, and **astronomy**, the study of the stars. Ships flying the Portuguese flag traveled south along the

Cristoforo Colombo (kris′tō·fôr′ō kə·ləm′bō′)
Genoa (jen′ə·wə)
Math Skill: Ask students to figure out how many kilometers Columbus swam to shore (about 10 km).

* **Reading Skill:** Building vocabulary. Have students use a dictionary to find the meanings of *geography* and *navigation*.

Reading Skill: Using references. Have students look for other pictures of Columbus.

This is one of the many paintings of Christopher Columbus.

west coast of Africa. They were searching for a sea route to the Indies.

When Columbus was well enough to travel, he joined his brother Bartholomew in Lisbon, a busy Portuguese port city. Bartholomew owned a small shop that sold maps, compasses, and other tools sailors needed.

Columbus studied the maps and charts in his brother's shop. He read books on geography and navigation. He visited shipyards and watched shipbuilders work on new ships called **caravels**, the fastest sailing ships of Columbus's day. Everywhere he went, he heard excited talk about finding a sea route to the Indies. Most of the talk was about a route around Africa. Once in a while, though, someone would describe another possible route, across the Atlantic Ocean. An idea began to take shape in Columbus's mind.

Sailing west to reach the East. Most people in Columbus's day thought that the earth was round. They believed that somewhere beyond the Atlantic Ocean lay the Indies. Even the daring Portuguese, though, were not willing to sail far from land into those dangerous unknown waters. For one thing, the sailors had heard tales of boiling seas and great sea monsters. For another, the captains believed the journey would be far too long.

Columbus thought differently. He believed that a route to the Indies across the Atlantic would be shorter and safer than a route around the tip of Africa. He studied maps and figured distances, but he still had one big problem. He did not have the money to buy ships and supplies and to hire sailors. He needed to find someone who had faith in him and who would give him the money to carry out his plan. It took Columbus ten long years to find that person.

Checking Up
1. Who was Marco Polo?
2. What country was a leading Atlantic sea power in the 1400s?
3. What answers would you give to the key questions at the beginning of this chapter?
4. *Why was Columbus's idea about a route to the Indies different from the ideas of most Europeans of the 1400s?*

*** **Reading Skill:** Doing research. Ask several students to read about caravels and then draw models based on their readings.

Math Skill: Have students figure out in miles how far off Columbus's guess was about the distance between the Canary Islands and Asia (about 8,600 miles).
Thinking Skill: Analyzing. Discuss why the experts did not persuade Columbus to change his mind about a voyage west across the Atlantic.

Columbus Plans His Voyage

As You Read

1. Think about these words.
   quadrant   astrolabe
2. Look for answers to these key questions.
   a. Why did Columbus believe that the best route to the Indies was west across the Atlantic Ocean?
   b. Who paid for Columbus's voyage to the Indies in 1492?
   c. What were three things Columbus did to prepare for his voyage?

Columbus's idea was simple. He wanted to sail west to Asia, where he would start a trading colony. Goods could then be taken back to Europe by sea. They could be sold more cheaply than goods brought by the overland route. Columbus was sure that his was the best possible plan and that he was the best possible person to carry it out.

Columbus's Mistakes

Columbus knew much about the earth from his studies of maps and books. Yet he made a serious mistake about what lay between Europe and the Indies. Columbus, along with some other educated people of his time, believed that there was more land than ocean in the world. He thought, for example, that Asia was much larger than it really is. Therefore, he believed Asia would be much closer to the west coast of Europe.

Find the Canary Islands off the west coast of Africa on the map on pages 10–11. Columbus guessed that about 2,400 miles (3,840 k) of open ocean separated the Canary Islands from Asia. Actually, about 11,000 miles (16,960 k) separate them. Also, Columbus did not know that two large continents west of Europe separated Europe from Asia.

Columbus Seeks Help

Columbus first asked the king of Portugal to pay for his voyage. The king asked his advisers to study Columbus's plan. After several months they reported to the king. "Columbus has made a mistake. Asia is more than 10,000 miles west of Africa. The journey would be far too long and expensive and most likely would fail." The king listened to his advisers and would not help Columbus with his plan.

Columbus in Spain. Next Columbus traveled to Spain to ask Queen Isabella and King Ferdinand for help. The queen was interested in Columbus's plan. Her advisers studied his plan. Then they gave the queen the same report that the Por-

Background: Columbus's plan was repeatedly turned down because of his high-priced demands. He demanded three ships fully equipped, the title of Admiral of the Ocean Sea, governorship of all lands he might discover, and 10 percent of all newfound Spanish wealth. Such demands were unheard of then because all new lands and wealth would, of course, belong to the king and queen.

Queen Isabella paid for Columbus's ships, supplies, and crew.

tuguese advisers had given their king: the plan would not succeed.

During the next six years, Columbus asked Queen Isabella for money two more times. His brother Bartholomew tried to get help from the kings of England and France.

In Spain people laughed at Columbus and called him a dreamer. Nevertheless, he refused to give up his idea. Angry and disappointed, he decided to leave Spain. Just then Queen Isabella decided to ignore her advisers and give Columbus what he wanted.

Preparing for the Voyage

Columbus worked for three months to get ready for his voyage. Workers prepared three ships—the *Santa Maria*, the *Niña*, and the *Pinta*—for the trip.

Columbus ordered food and made sure that it was stored safely on board the three ships. He signed up ninety crew members. Most were young Spanish sailors, eager for adventure and riches. Some were gromets, or young boys who had never been to sea or who were learning to be sailors.

On the evening of August 2, 1492, the three ships rested quietly in the small port of Palos on the southwest coast of Spain. The next morning, just before dawn, the three ships moved slowly out of the port toward the sea. Columbus's great adventure had begun at last.

Southwest to the Canary Islands. The three ships sailed southwest with a brisk wind. They stopped at the Canary Islands for repairs and more supplies. Then, on September 6, 1492, the ships again set sail. The course was due west. The goal was the Indies.

How We Know What Happened

The Written Records of Columbus

Historians know very little about how Columbus passed the time while he was waiting to hear if a European king or queen would help him with his voyage. Historians do know, however, that Columbus spent some of this time reading and studying books. Some of these books have been preserved in a museum in Spain. Below are some notes Columbus made in the margins of a book he was studying to help him prepare for his voyage.

> An arm of the sea extends between India [the Indies] and Spain.
>
> Between the end of Spain and the beginning of India [the Indies] is no great width.
>
> The end of Spain and the beginning of India [the Indies] are not far distant but close, and it is evident that this sea is navigable in a few days with a fair wind.

Palos (pä′lōs′)

Thinking Skill: Analyzing. Ask students to read Columbus's notes in the feature above. Then have them look at the world map on pages 10–11 to decide which of Columbus's ideas were wrong.

*** **Math Skill:** Have students figure out how much larger a modern supertanker is than the *Santa Maria.* A supertanker is more than 1,300 feet (396 m) long. (A supertanker is about sixteen times larger.)
*** **Reading Skill:** Organizing information. Have the class make models of Columbus's three ships using a scale of 1 inch = 1 foot.

Columbus's Three Ships

Shown here are models of Columbus's three ships for his first voyage. The *Santa Maria,* at bottom, was probably from 75 to 90 feet (23 to 27 m) long. The *Niña,* at top, and the *Pinta,* middle, were each probably about 70 to 75 feet (21 to 23 m) long.

Life on these ships was far from comfortable. Only the captains of each ship had bunks, so the sailors had to sleep wherever they could find room.

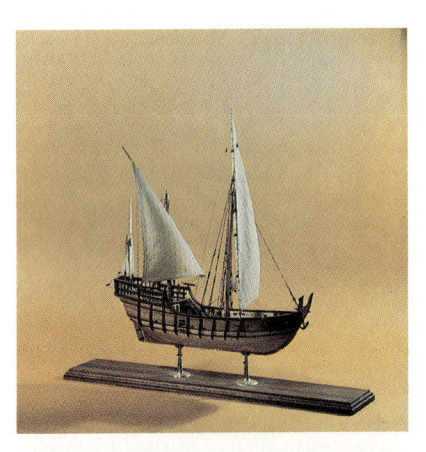

Setting a Course

How did Columbus find his way to the Canary Islands, then west across the Atlantic? For one thing, he had charts showing the coastal waters off Europe and northwestern Africa. These charts had been drawn by Portuguese sea captains as they searched for a route to the Indies.

For the voyage across the Atlantic, Columbus had no charts. No one before had dared to sail so far from the African coast. He had a compass on each ship to help him make sure he was headed due west. He also had on board a **quadrant** (kwäd′rənt) and an **astrolabe** (as′trə·lāb′). These were instruments for measuring how far north of the equator his ships were sailing. In Columbus's time these instruments were not very accurate. They could give Columbus only a rough idea of his position. They could not tell him anything about how far he was from his goal or about whether his course would lead him there.

Checking Up

1. What did Columbus plan to do once he reached the Indies?
2. What answers would you give to the key questions at the beginning of this chapter?
3. *Do you think Columbus would have made his first voyage to the Indies if he had known that Asia was about 11,000 miles west of Europe? Why or why not?*

Thinking Skill: Analyzing. Ask students why the quadrant, astrolabe, and compass were so important to sailors.
** **Reading Skill:** Doing research. Have students look up the words *quadrant* and *astrolabe* in books and encyclopedias.

Reading Skill: Following directions: *As You Read,* 3.
Thinking Skill: Analyzing. Columbus kept two logs of his first voyage, an open one for the crew and a secret one for himself. Ask students why Columbus would keep two different logs.

The Voyages of Columbus

As You Read

1. Think about these words.
   log   New World   colonist
2. Look for answers to these key questions.
   a. Where did Columbus first land in the New World?
   b. How many voyages did Columbus make to the New World?
   c. Why did many people think that Christopher Columbus had found a worthless land?
3. Use this reading skill.
   In some parts of this chapter, you will be asked to follow directions. Sometimes following directions means only that you have to turn to a certain page and look at a map. Make sure you take the time to follow such directions. By doing so, you will gain a better understanding of what you are reading.

Columbus kept a **log**, or written record, of his first voyage across the Atlantic Ocean. Every evening he wrote about what happened during the day at sea. From this log historians know that Columbus had excellent sailing conditions westward across the Atlantic. Even by today's standards, the speed of Columbus's ships was remarkable.

Westward Across the Atlantic

The crew last saw land on the eastern horizon September 9, 1492. By October 10, land had still not been sighted. The crew was restless. Fearing they would never find the Indies, many wanted to return to Spain. Then at two o'clock on the morning of October 12, 1492, the lookout on the *Pinta* saw something like a white cliff shining in the moonlight. He yelled out, *"Tierra! Tierra!"* ("Land! Land!")

The captain of the *Pinta* checked to make sure that indeed land had been spotted. Then, as agreed, a gun was fired to signal that land was just ahead.

The *Santa Maria*, with Columbus on board, approached the *Pinta*. Columbus shouted to the crew on the *Pinta*, "You did find land! Five thousand maravedis [Spanish coins] for you as a bonus!"

At dawn the same morning, Columbus and some of his crew rowed to shore in a small landing boat. On shore, they planted the Spanish flag in the soil and claimed the land for Spain. Columbus named the land he had reached *San Salvador* ("Holy Savior").

tierra (tē·är′ä)   **maravedis** (mär′ə·və·dēz′)
Time Skill: Have students figure out how many days it took Columbus to sail from Palos, Spain, to San Salvador (71 days).

95

Then and Now

The Voyages of Columbus and *Apollo 11*

On October 12, 1492, Columbus set foot in the New World for the first time. More than 477 years later, two of the *Apollo 11* astronauts, Neil Armstrong and Edwin Aldrin, set foot on the moon for the first time.

Columbus and the astronauts were adventurers willing to brave the dangers of a voyage to an unknown place. Their voyages were alike in many ways.

- Columbus and the astronauts were expert navigators. They trained for years for their voyages.
- They learned from the experiences of others. Daring Portuguese sailors had charted the coastal waters off Europe and Africa. Columbus used their charts to plan the first part of his voyage. Unmanned spacecraft had landed on the moon. These spacecraft sent pictures back to earth. Scientists used the pictures to choose a landing spot on the moon.
- Both voyages began with missing information. Columbus did not know exactly how far it was from the Canary Islands to the east coast of Asia. The astronauts did not know whether their spacecraft would land safely on the moon's surface and then lift off again.
- Both voyages were paid for by governments. The Spanish king and queen paid for Columbus's voyage. The United States government paid for the space voyage.
- Columbus and the astronauts faced dangers. In case of trouble, no one was nearby to rescue them.
- Columbus and the astronauts brought back samples from a new land. Columbus brought back people, plants, and animals. The astronauts brought back forty-eight pounds of rocks from the moon.

Astronauts Aldrin and Armstrong raised the United States flag on the moon.

Columbus in the New World

Columbus thought he had landed in Asia or on an island off its coast. In fact, he was nowhere near Asia but on a small island in the Bahamas. Find the Bahamas on the map on page 97. The islands of the Bahamas and other islands nearby are close to the continents of North and South America. All these lands were a **New World** to the Europeans.

As Columbus and his crew explored the island of San Salvador, they met the people already living there. Thinking that he was in the Indies, Columbus called these people Indians.

The Indians showed Columbus their neat gardens of corn, sweet potatoes, and other vegetables that Europeans had never seen before. They offered to guide the Europeans to nearby islands.

Bahamas (bə·häm′əz)

Background: Display and explain to the class Columbus's coat of arms, which King Ferdinand and Queen Isabella granted Columbus after his first voyage. The castle of Castile and the lion of Leon are symbols of Spain. The five anchors represent admiralty. Ask students what the group of islands symbolize and what they might add to Columbus's coat of arms.

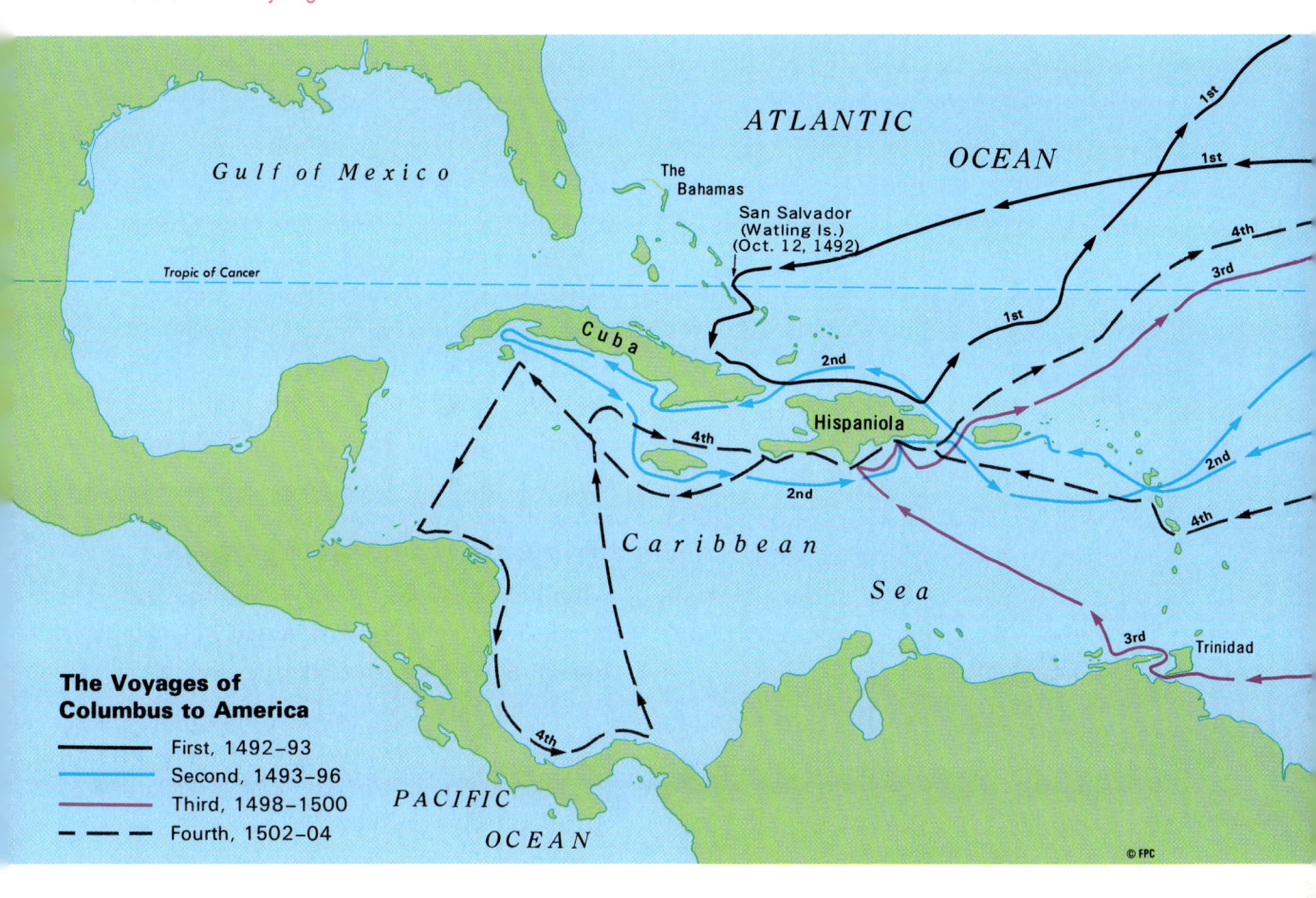

The Voyages of Columbus to America
— First, 1492–93
— Second, 1493–96
— Third, 1498–1500
-- Fourth, 1502–04

Columbus sailed with his crew and Indian guides to Cuba, then to the large island of Hispaniola (his′pən·yō′lə). With your finger, trace Columbus's route on the map above. In Hispaniola Columbus and his crew found a small amount of gold and some plants that smelled like spices. All the while they wondered, "Where are the silks and jewels and rich cities of the East?"

Columbus Returns to Spain

On January 16, 1493, Columbus left the New World for Spain. Two ships, the *Niña* and the *Pinta*, carried parrots, an alligator, a few pieces of gold jewelry, and some interesting-looking plants. Also on board were six American Indians.

The third ship, the *Santa Maria*, had run into large rocks off the coast of Hispaniola. Columbus left the ship and most of its crew behind. He wanted them to build a fort out of wood from the Santa Maria and to keep looking for gold.

The return voyage. The voyage west across the Atlantic had been fairly smooth. The voyage home was far different. The seas were rough, and violent storms threatened to sink the two ships. For weeks at a time, the *Niña* and the *Pinta* were separated. Finally, both ships reached Spain safely on March 15, 1493.

Time Skill: Have students figure out how long the return voyage to Spain lasted (59 days).
Thinking Skill: Analyzing. Ask students why Columbus brought back to Spain the things he did.
Thinking Skill: Predicting. Have students explain why they would or would not have wanted to return to Spain with Columbus, either as a member of his crew or as an American Indian.

> * **Math Skill:** Have students figure about how many colonists were aboard each ship going to Hispaniola (an average of 59 people per ship).
>
> **Communication Skill:** Writing. Ask students to pretend they lived on Hispaniola when Columbus first arrived. Have them write letters to a friend telling about his arrival.

In Spain again. Columbus's arrival caused great excitement in Spain. King Ferdinand and Queen Isabella praised and honored Columbus. They were grateful to Columbus for finding a route to a land of gold and spices.

Columbus could have spent the rest of his life in Spain, but he was still eager for adventure. Soon he began to plan a second voyage across the Atlantic.

The Later Voyages of Columbus

Seventeen ships carrying about 1,000 **colonists**, or people who settle new lands, left Spain in September of 1493. Their goal was to start a Spanish colony in the new land.

Trace the route Columbus took on his second voyage across the Atlantic on the map on page 97. As you can see, Columbus and his crew sailed to Cuba and nearby islands, then to Hispaniola. Here Columbus was saddened to find the fort burned and the Spanish sailors missing. He decided, though, to go ahead with plans to build a permanent settlement in the New World.

Problems with the new colony. Columbus had problems with the new colony from the very beginning. Many of the settlers were not interested in building houses or in planting crops. They wanted to search for gold and riches. Also, hundreds of the settlers became ill and died. The surviving settlers raised cattle and grew cotton and sugarcane. They often traveled into the hills to find gold. They did find some gold but not the great riches promised by Columbus.

The third and fourth voyages. Columbus made two more voyages from Spain to the New World. Trace these last two voyages on the map on page 97. Columbus claimed hundreds of islands and part of South America for Spain. By this time many people in Spain thought that Columbus had found a route to a worthless land. They did not think he had found the rich Indies. Columbus never accepted this idea. He died in 1506 still believing he had reached the Indies.

The Importance of Columbus's Voyages

Looking back, historians know the real importance of Columbus's voyages. He discovered two continents that opened a world that was new to the Europeans of his time. He set up a Spanish colony in the New World. From this colony Spain spread its power into North and South America.

Checking Up
1. Why did Columbus call the people he met on San Salvador Indians?
2. What were two problems Columbus had from the very beginning with his new colony?
3. Name three lands Columbus claimed for Spain.
4. What answers would you give to the key questions at the beginning of this chapter?
5. *Why do you think Columbus continued to believe he had reached the rich Indies?*

> * **Thinking Skill:** Analyzing. Discuss the real importance of Columbus's voyages.

Maps and Diagrams Tell a Story of Early Exploration

As you read, think about these words.
tack   prevailing wind

The Norse Route to North America

The Norse, the first Europeans to come to North America, were expert sailors. They sailed great distances across the rough North Atlantic. First they traveled back and forth between Scandinavia and Iceland. Then they moved on to Greenland. Finally they sailed to North America. Look at the map on this page. With your finger, trace Leif Ericson's route between Greenland and North America. Where did the Norse land in North America? Which direction did they sail to North America? Now trace the same route on your classroom globe.

Find Scandinavia and Iceland on the map pictured on this page. Which looks farther from Greenland—Scandinavia or Newfoundland?

Measuring distances. "The Atlas Tells a Story" section in this book explains why distances on a globe are always accurate. This section also explains why distances on a world map cannot be ac-

This map shows the route that the Norse probably took from Greenland to North America in the early 1000s.

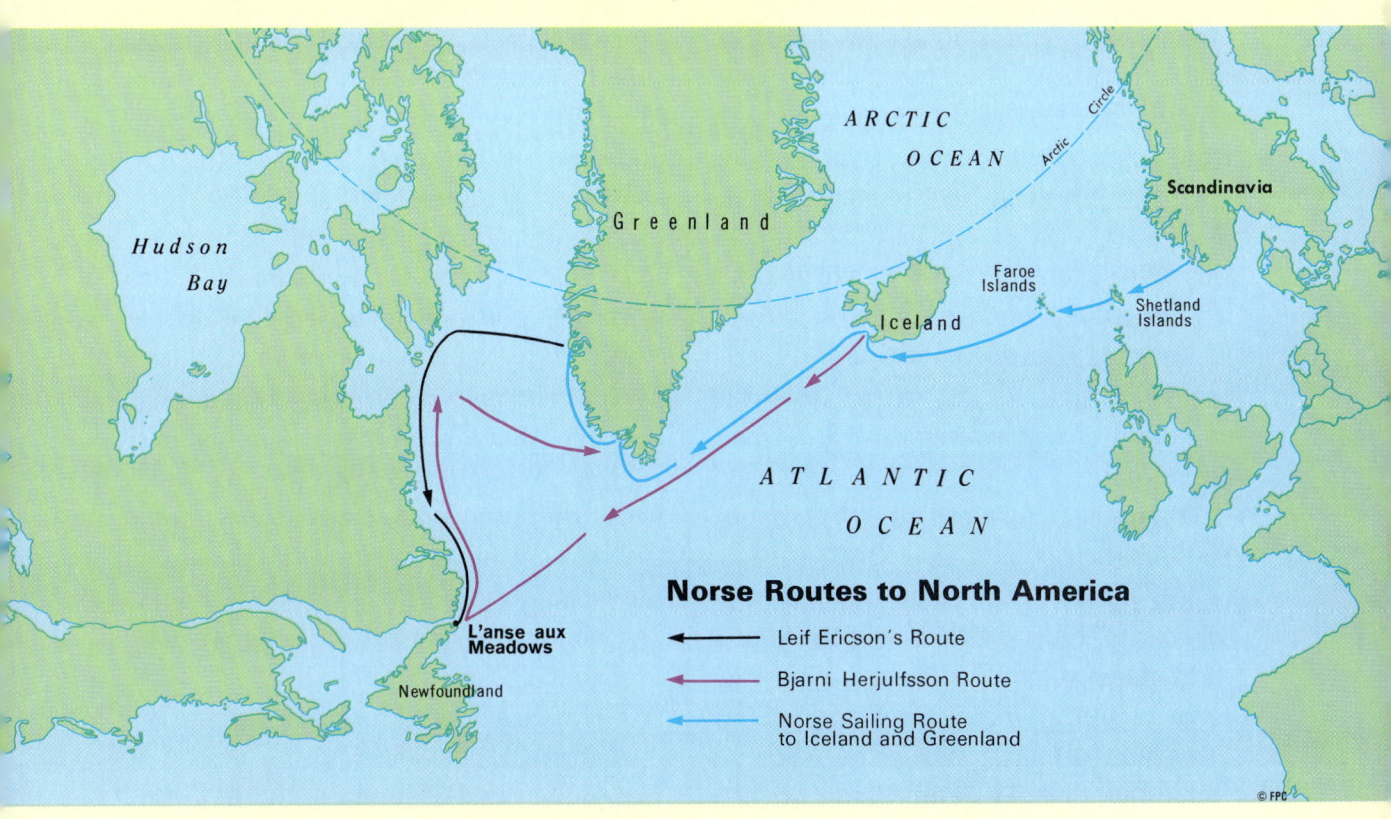

Norse Routes to North America
- Leif Ericson's Route
- Bjarni Herjulfsson Route
- Norse Sailing Route to Iceland and Greenland

1. Newfoundland. West and then south.
2. Scandinavia.

** **Map Skill:** Location. Discuss what part of North America the Norse were exploring. Refer students to the map of North America on page 14.

99

Cipangu (si·pang'gōō)   **Antilla** (an·til'e)
1. No. North and South America. Europeans had not yet discovered these two continents.

curate everywhere. You can measure distances on a globe using a tape measure or a string and a ruler. Just follow these three easy steps.

1. Find the scale on the globe. It tells the number of miles (or kilometers) each inch (or centimeter) on the globe represents.
2. Measure the distance between two places with a tape measure. Or connect the two places with a piece of string and then measure the length of the string with a ruler.
3. Multiply the distance between the two places by the number of miles (or kilometers) represented by each inch (or centimeter) on the globe.

On your classroom globe, find the distance in miles between Scandinavia and Greenland. Then find the distance in miles between Greenland and Newfoundland. How many more miles is it from Greenland to Scandinavia than it is from Greenland to Newfoundland?

Columbus's Route to North America

When Columbus set out across the Atlantic Ocean, no European within memory had dared to sail so far from the coastlines of Europe and Africa. To prepare for his voyage, Columbus studied the maps and writings of astronomers, mathematicians, and navigators.

The picture of a globe on this page shows a globe of 1492. This globe represents much of the knowledge about the earth in 1492. What is interesting about this globe is that it shows the world as Columbus thought of it. Find Cipangu (Japan) on this globe. Notice that an island called Antilia is halfway between Africa and Cipangu. Compare this globe map with the modern map of the world on pages 10–11. Is there an island of Antilia far off the west coast of Africa? What two continents lie between Africa and Asia? Why aren't these continents shown on the globe map of 1492?

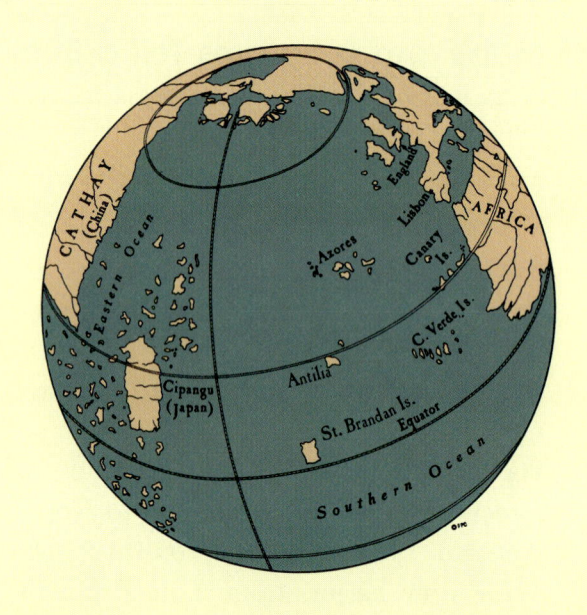

Columbus planned to sail southwest from Spain to the Canary Islands, then west to Cipangu. He hoped to stop at Antilia to rest and take on more supplies. Look at the map on page 101 that shows the route that Columbus took on his first voyage. Which direction did he sail? Trace the same route on your classroom globe. Now measure these distances on the globe.

1. Columbus's route from Spain to the Canary Islands
2. Columbus's route from the Canary Islands to Hispaniola

How long was Columbus's route from

2. Columbus sailed southwest to the Canary Islands and then west across the Atlantic.

Math Skill: Have students practice measuring distances on a globe. Have them measure the distance from their community to several large cities around the world.

100

Map Skill: Location. Have students follow Columbus's journey shown on this map on a globe.
* **Thinking Skill:** Observing. Have students demonstrate tacking by drawing the angles a sailboat would follow if it were tacking.

Columbus's First Voyage to the New World

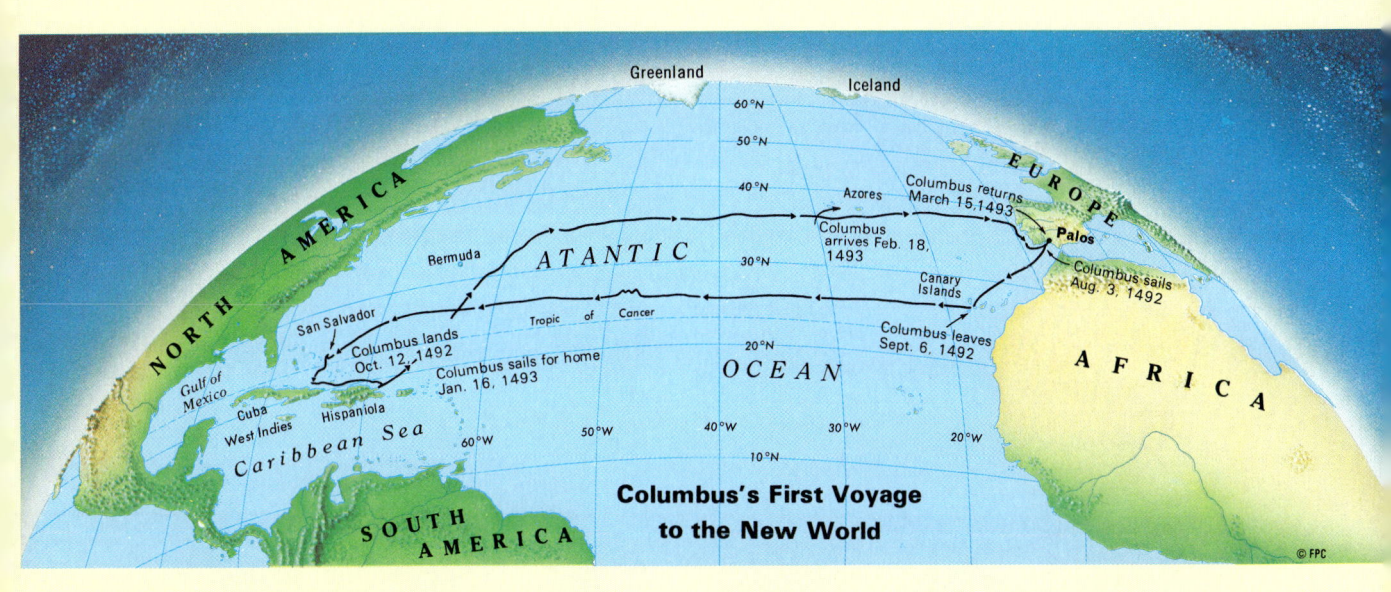

Spain to Hispaniola? Was this longer or shorter than the Norse route from Greenland to Newfoundland?

Movements of Air and Water

The ships used by Columbus were powered by the wind. At times the ships were also carried along by the movement of the ocean currents.

Sailing with and against the wind. A sailboat or a sailing ship is pushed through the water in large part by the wind. The direction that the wind is blowing determines how the boat is sailed. Study diagrams A and B below. Read the caption for each diagram. As you can see, if a sailboat or a sailing ship has to sail into, or against, the wind to reach its destination, it must **tack**, or take a zigzag course. Tacking makes the course longer. However, if the wind is blowing from behind the boat, the boat

By tacking, a sailboat can move in a direction close to that from which the wind is blowing.

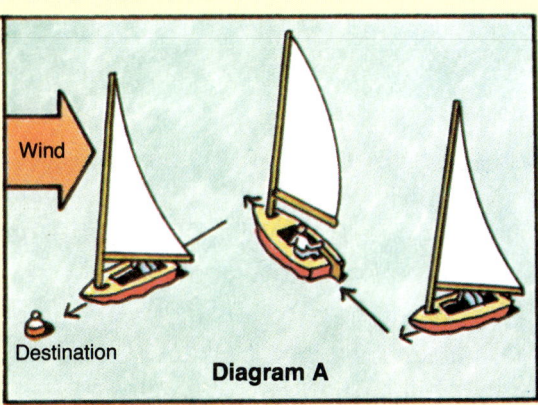

When the wind is blowing from behind the boat, a sailboat can move forward on a straight course.

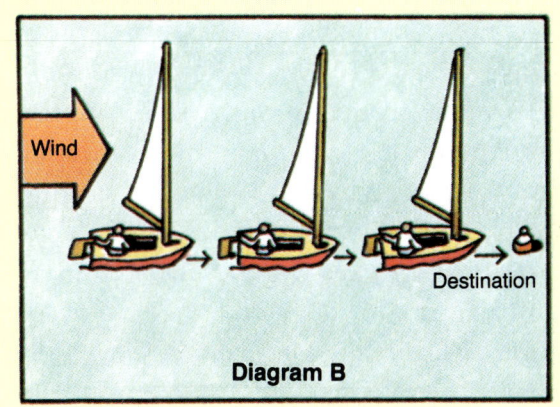

Diagram A

Diagram B

1. Columbus's route was farther than the route the Norse traveled between Greenland and North America.
** **Citizenship Skill:** Social participation. Have someone familiar with sailing talk about special problems with the wind.

101

1. The northeasterly trade winds occur in the low latitudes.
2. Columbus sailed with the prevailing winds.
3. Columbus had to tack because he was sailing against the northeasterly trade winds.
4. From about Bermuda all the way back to Spain.

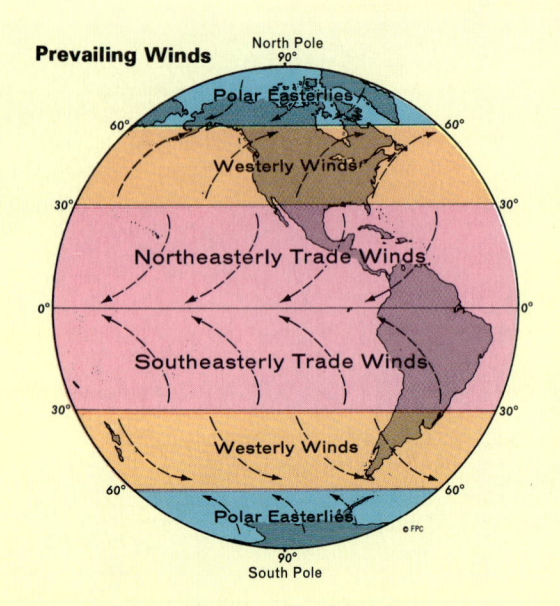

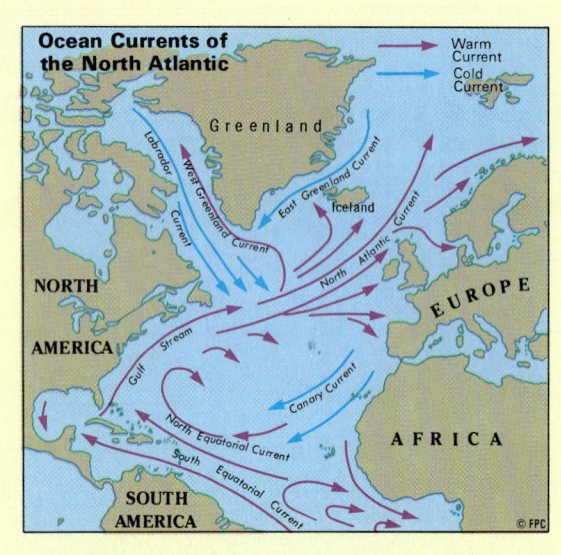

can sail with the wind. The boat can follow a straight course without tacking.

Prevailing winds. Winds that usually blow from the same direction are called **prevailing winds**. They are named for the direction from which they blow. Study the globe map of prevailing winds on this page. Find the Northeasterly Trade Winds. In which latitudes do these winds blow? Now look again at the map on page 101 that shows the route Columbus took to the West Indies. Did Columbus sail with or against the prevailing winds?

Find Columbus's return route on the map on page 101. In which latitudes did he sail on his return route? Compare this map with the globe map of the prevailing winds. Why did Columbus have to tack on the first part of his return route from Hispaniola to Bermuda? During which part of Columbus's return voyage did he have the wind behind him? Why was Columbus's return route a better one than a route sailing straight east from Hispaniola?

Ocean currents. Currents flow like great rivers through the ocean. Traveling with the currents helps ships shorten their traveling time.

Study the map above that shows ocean currents of the North Atlantic. Find the Labrador Current. In which direction does it flow? Does it flow toward the equator or away from the equator? On the way from Greenland to Newfoundland, did the Norse sail with or against the Labrador Current? On the way back to Greenland, did they sail with or against the current? Which trip would have taken less time?

Find the Canary Current. In which direction does it flow? Does it flow toward the equator or away from the equator? On the way from Spain to the Canary Islands, did Columbus sail with or against the current? On the way from the Canary Islands to Hispaniola, was Columbus sailing with the current or against the current?

5. The Labrador Current flows towards the equator. The Norse sailed with this current on their way to Newfoundland and against it on their return to Greenland.
6. The Canary Current flows southwest toward the equator. Columbus sailed with this current across the Atlantic.

102

Spain in the New World

As You Read

1. Think about these words.
   strait   conqueror   empire
2. Look for answers to these key questions.
   a. What was Magellan's plan for reaching Asia?
   b. Who conquered the Aztec empire in Mexico?
   c. Who were two explorers who claimed land in North America for Spain?

News of Columbus's voyages spread quickly through Europe. Soon other daring sailors and explorers crossed the Atlantic to learn about the New World to the west. They mapped much of the eastern coastline of South America and the islands of the Caribbean (kãr′ə·bē′ən) Sea. Find the Caribbean Sea and South America on the map on page 101. In time, they came to know that the New World was a land separate from Asia. Then the search began for a waterway through this new land to the Indies.

Of all the countries in Europe, Spain showed the most interest in the New World. Spain's leaders paid for voyages and colonies. Within forty years after Columbus's first voyage, Spain controlled large areas of land in the New World.

Spanish Ships Circle the Earth

By the end of the 1400s, Portuguese traders were sailing to the Indies by going around the southern tip of Africa. This route often took a year, and the seas around the southern tip of Africa were rough and dangerous.

Ferdinand Magellan, a young Portuguese sailor, made several of these voyages to the Indies. Like most sailors of his day, he had heard about Columbus's discoveries and about other voyages along the coast of South America. He, too, thought that sailing west might be a shorter and safer route to the Indies.

Magellan's plan was to sail across the Atlantic and down the coast of South America. He believed that at some point he would come to a waterway that would lead to the East.

Like Columbus, Magellan needed to find someone who was willing to pay for his voyage. In 1519 the king of Spain finally agreed to help Magellan with his voyage.

Magellan's voyage. On September 20, 1519, five ships and more than 200 men sailed southwest from Spain. Find Magellan's route on the map on page 104.

Magellan (mə·jel′ən)
Time Skill: Ask students how long after Columbus's first voyage Magellan sailed (27 years later).

Time Skill: Ask students about what date Magellan reached Brazil (about December 20).
Background: Remind students of the reversed seasons in the temperate regions of South America.

The Voyage of Magellan 1519-1522

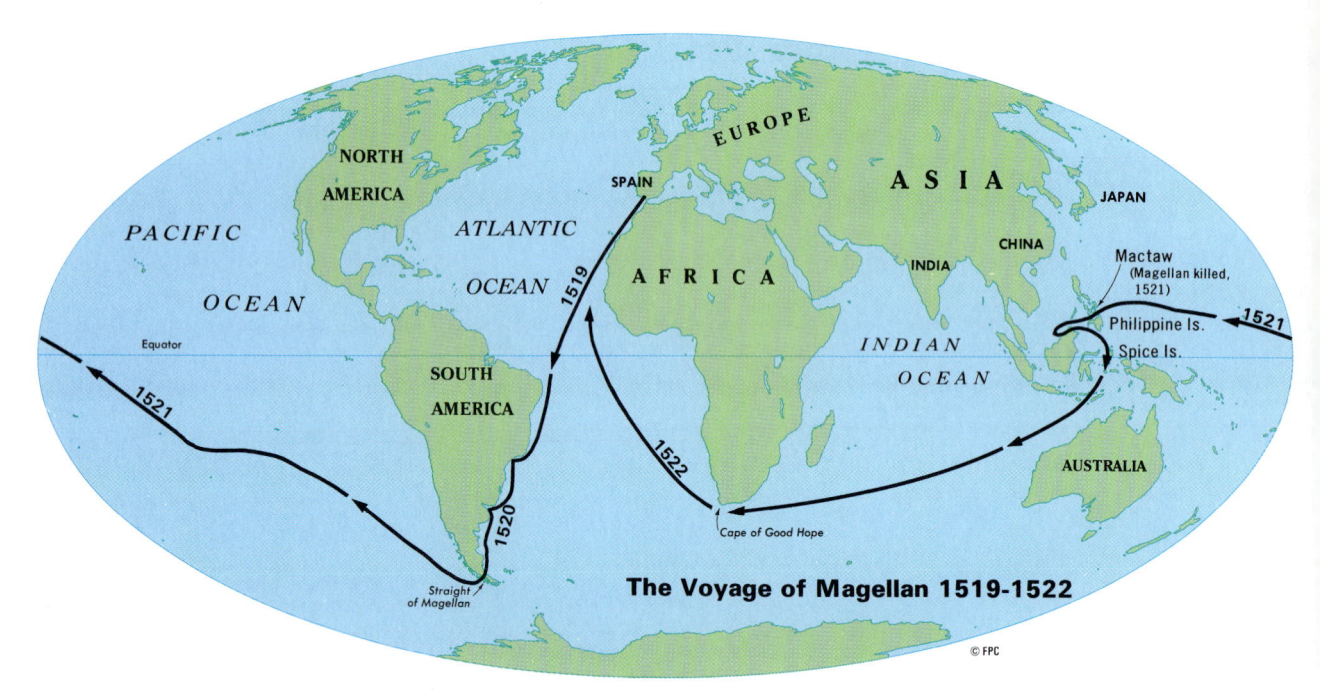

From Magellan's voyage, people learned much more about the distance across the Pacific Ocean and the location of the Americas.

After three months they reached what is now Brazil. Then they headed south. Progress was slow because the ships sailed into every bay and river along the way looking for a waterway through the land. As winter drew near, violent storms struck the coast, and one ship sank in the icy waters. Magellan ordered his captains to drop anchor for the winter months.

In the spring the ships once again made their way south. Within days they reached a waterway that cut far into the land. Magellan carefully guided his ships through this **strait**, or narrow waterway. Find the Strait of Magellan on the map on this page. After thirty-eight days of pitching and rolling, the ships sailed into a calmer sea. Magellan named this sea the *Pacific*, which means "peaceful."

Across the Pacific. Day after day the ships sailed north and west. One month passed. A second month passed. They still had not sighted land. The food ran out and the water spoiled. The desperate sailors swallowed sawdust and chewed on leather straps. Most of the crew became sick, and many died.

Land at last. In early March 1521, after three months of sailing across the Pacific Ocean, Magellan's ships reached the islands that are now called the Philippines. Find the Philippines on the map above. There Magellan was killed in a battle between islanders.

A new leader took charge of the voyage. He decided to abandon one of the ships. The other ships sailed on to the Spice Islands, where they were loaded with spices. The crew then set out across

** **Map Skill:** Distance. Have students trace Magellan's voyage on a globe. Ask how far he traveled.
(About 35,000 miles. Other answers that the students can reasonably support should also be accepted.)
Time Skill: Ask students how long the voyage around the world lasted (about three years).

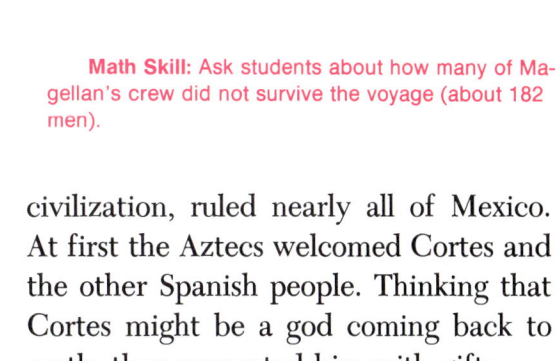

Impressive buildings stood in the Aztec capital of Tenochtitlán.

the Indian Ocean for the long voyage around the tip of Africa.

Only one ship reached Spain. It had been gone for three years. On board were eighteen sick and hungry sailors. They had done something remarkable, something that no one before them had done. They had sailed completely around the world.

Explorers and Conquerors Build an Empire

While Magellan was sailing around the world, other people claimed land in the New World for Spain. Some were **conquerors**, people who took land by force. Hernando Cortes (kôr·tez′) was one of these people. In 1519 Cortes, along with 600 Spanish soldiers, colonists, and priests, set out to establish a trading colony on the east coast of what is today Mexico. Cortes wanted to find gold and to convert the Indians to the Christian religion.

Cortes conquers the Aztecs. In the early 1500s the Aztecs (az′teks), an Indian people who had developed a great civilization, ruled nearly all of Mexico. At first the Aztecs welcomed Cortes and the other Spanish people. Thinking that Cortes might be a god coming back to earth, they presented him with gifts.

Cortes, however, soon imprisoned the Aztec ruler and seized large amounts of Aztec gold. Eventually the Aztecs attacked the Spanish and drove them from the Aztec capital.

Cortes returned. This time he brought thousands of Indians eager to be free from Aztec rule. In 1521 the Spanish and Indians destroyed the Aztec capital. They ruined the temples and made slaves of the proud Aztecs.

People Who Made a Difference

Amerigo Vespucci

In the late 1400s, there lived an Italian navigator named Amerigo Vespucci (ä′mə·rē′gō ve·spōō′chē). Between 1499 and 1504, Vespucci sailed to the New World on both Spanish and Portuguese ships. On one voyage he explored the coast of South America. Vespucci came to believe that this land was not part of Asia but a separate continent. He explained his idea in a book he wrote about his travels.

In 1507 a German map maker printed Vespucci's book and suggested that the land to the west be named after the navigator. Map makers soon began to show the name *Americus* on their maps.

At first *Americus* meant only South America. Later it meant North America as well. Today, almost 500 years after his death, Amerigo Vespucci is remembered as the person for whom the Americas were named.

105

> *** Reading Skill:** Building vocabulary. Have students talk more about the meaning of *empire*. Ask what the strengths and weaknesses of such a system might be.
> ***** Communication Skill:** Writing. Have students write reports on the life of one of these men.

Mexico City was built on the ruins of the Aztec capital. In just a few years, this city became the center of an **empire** in the Americas ruled by Spain. An empire is a large area of land usually ruled by one king or queen. Ships returning to Spain were filled with Aztec jewelry and silver and gold mined from the mountains near the city. Spanish explorers setting out from Mexico City claimed huge areas of land in North and South America. In South America Spanish explorers found a wealth of gold and other precious metals.

The seven cities of gold. In the late 1520s, a Spanish ship was wrecked along what is today the Texas coast. Four men survived the wreck. One was Cabeza de Vaca (kə·vä′thä thā väk′ä), a Spanish explorer. Another was Estevan (es′tā·vän′), an African. The four survivors spent several years imprisoned by the Indians. During this time they heard stories from the Indians about seven great cities that were built of gold.

When Cabeza, Estevan, and the others finally reached Mexico, they told the Spanish ruler the stories they had heard

Spanish Explorations in the New World

- de Leon 1513
- Balboa 1513
- Cortes 1519
- Pizarro 1531-1533
- de Soto 1539-1542
- Coronado 1540-1542

106   **Map Skill:** Location. Have students locate the area between the Texas coast and northern Mexico on the map on page 15. It was in this area that de Vaca traveled.

> *** Reading Skill:** Determining meaning from context. Discuss what made some people search for the Seven Cities of Gold.
>   **Reading Skill:** Building vocabulary. Have students talk about the meaning of *fortune hunters.*

about the seven cities of gold. The Spanish leader, encouraged by the stories, sent a party of explorers led by Fray Marcos (frä′ē mär′kōs) to find the seven cities.

With Estevan as a guide, the expedition explored the lands that are now Arizona and New Mexico. During their explorations Estevan and a few others who were riding ahead came to a Zuñi Indian village. The Zuñis attacked the group of explorers and killed Estevan and many others.

In time Fray Marcos caught up with what was left of Estevan's group. From afar he saw the many-leveled houses of the Zuñis. Their adobe walls gleamed like gold in the bright desert sun.

Fray Marcos reported to the Spanish leader in Mexico that he had found one of the famous cities. He described what he had seen—tall houses with shining golden walls. He also added details from his imagination.

Coronado claims the Southwest. In 1540 Francisco Coronado (kôr′ō·näd′ō) set out to capture the city sighted by Fray Marcos. With him were hundreds of Spanish fortune hunters and soldiers and nearly a thousand Mexican Indians.

The huge army marched north. They captured six Zuñi villages but found no great riches. Look at the map on page 106 and trace Coronado's route. In the area that is now eastern Kansas, Coronado finally gave up his search for great riches.

Coronado's explorations gave Spain large land claims in what is today the southwestern part of the United States. Later, Spanish colonists settled in the areas that Coronado had claimed for Spain.

De Soto claims the Southeast. At the same time that Coronado was searching for the seven cities of gold, Hernando de Soto and 600 Spanish explorers were marching through what is today Florida. They were also looking for the cities of gold. After two years they reached the Mississippi River. They then continued west to what is now Oklahoma. Trace de Soto's route on the map on page 106.

The Spanish empire. Coronado and de Soto claimed vast lands for Spain. However, the heart of the Spanish empire remained in Middle and South America, where riches such as gold were found.

During most of the 1500s, Spain was the only European country to build an empire in the New World. Riches from this empire poured into Spain. The leaders of other European countries began to envy the Spanish king's growing wealth.

Checking Up
1. What lands did Fray Marcos and Estevan explore?
2. What parts of North America did Coronado and de Soto claim for Spain?
3. What answers would you give to the key questions at the beginning of this chapter?
4. *Why do you think the Spanish were eager to build an empire in the New World?*

> **Thinking Skill:** Analyzing. Ask students how horses might have influenced the Indians' way of life.
>   **Background:** It was the Spanish who, during the time of Coronado, first introduced the horse to the Indians of North America. Horses greatly changed the Indian way of life.

Reading Skill: Using textbook features: *As You Read*, 3.

England, France, and the Netherlands Explore the New World

As You Read

1. Think about this term.
   Northwest Passage
2. Look for answers to these key questions.
   a. Why were Europeans looking for a Northwest Passage to the Indies?
   b. Who were two explorers who claimed lands in North America for the French?
   c. What part of North America did Henry Hudson claim for the Netherlands? for England?
3. Use this reading skill.
   In this chapter as well as the other chapters in this book, you will sometimes find a word that is difficult to pronounce. However, its pronunciation is often given in parentheses right after the word. Use the pronunciation key at the beginning of the Glossary to help you read the pronunciation in parentheses. Then pronounce the word. By doing this, you will make sure you pronounce words correctly.

For nearly a hundred years after Columbus's voyages, Spain was the only European country with colonies in the New World. During this time, however, other European countries sent explorers to the new land. From each exploration Europeans learned more about the New World.

John Cabot Sails for the English

John Cabot was an Italian map maker and trader living in England in the late 1400s. For many years Cabot had also thought it might be possible to reach the Indies by sailing west.

Cabot studied his maps closely. He decided that a northern route across the Atlantic would be a more direct route to the Indies than Columbus's route across the middle of the Atlantic. A northern route across the Atlantic and around or through North America was called the **Northwest Passage**.

In 1497 Cabot set out in a small ship with a crew of only eighteen. Trace Cabot's 1497 voyage on the map on page 109. After seven weeks of high waves and strong winds, the crew finally saw land. Look at the map again. Where did Cabot land in North America? 1

1. Newfoundland.
Background: Cabot and his sailors made their landing only a few miles from where the Norse colony had been hundreds of years before.
Time Skill: Ask students how long after Columbus's first voyage Cabot set sail (about five years).

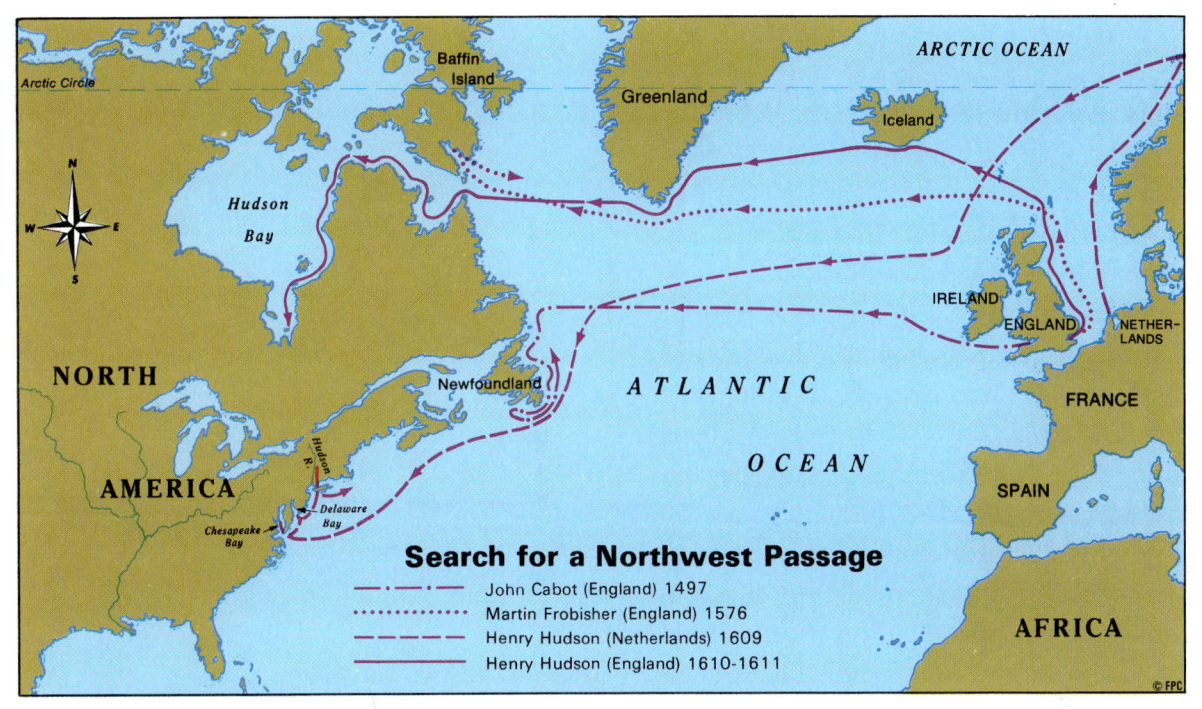

Reading Skill: Doing research. Have students look up the Grand Banks.
*** **Communication Skill:** Speaking. Have several students prepare a report on the Hurons, using the chalkboard as needed for illustrations.

Search for a Northwest Passage
— · — John Cabot (England) 1497
· · · · · Martin Frobisher (England) 1576
— — — Henry Hudson (Netherlands) 1609
——— Henry Hudson (England) 1610-1611

Henry Hudson never returned to England from exploring Hudson Bay. His crew turned against him and set him adrift in a small boat.

Cabot and his men went ashore and claimed this new land for the king of England. He called it Newfoundland. Although Cabot did not find gold or other riches, he did discover one of the world's most important fishing areas off the coast of Newfoundland. This area, called the Grand Banks, still remains one of the richest fishing grounds of the world.

In 1498 Cabot made a second voyage west, this time with five ships. Violent storms forced one of his ships to return to England. Cabot, his crew, and their four ships were never heard from again.

French Explorations in the New World

Between 1534 and 1536, a daring French explorer named Jacques Cartier (zhăk kär·tyā′) made two important voyages to the New World. His goal was to find the Northwest Passage that would lead to the Indies also.

On his first voyage, Cartier sailed into the Gulf of St. Lawrence. Find the Gulf of St. Lawrence on the map on page 110. For five months he explored every bay and inlet, looking for a passage to the Indies.

The next year Cartier made a second voyage. He sailed up the St. Lawrence River as far as the present-day city of Montreal (män′trē·ôl′). Trace Cartier's second voyage on the map on page 110. Near Montreal he found a large Huron Indian village. Cartier made friends with the Hurons and camped near the village during the long winter. In the spring Cartier returned to France.

Math Skill: Have the class use a globe to figure out the approximate distance of Cartier's voyages. (About 5,900 miles on his first voyage; about 6600 miles on his second voyage—total 12,500 miles. Other answers that the students can reasonably support should also be accepted.)

Although Cartier did not find the Northwest Passage, he claimed all the land along the St. Lawrence River for France. He named this land New France.

Growth of the fur trade. For many years the French showed little interest in founding a colony in the New World. During this time, though, the French did fish near the Grand Banks. In time, they formed friendships with the Indians along the coast. The French gave the Indians iron tools. The Indians gave the French furs from animals such as beavers, otters, and bears. These furs became very popular in Europe. As trade between the Indians and the French grew, the French began to think that the New World might be a good place for a colony.

A colony in New France. In the late 1500s, Samuel de Champlain (sham′·plān′), a Frenchman, explored the coast of New France. In 1608 Champlain founded a French colony at Quebec (kwĭ·bĕk′) on the St. Lawrence River. Find Quebec on the map above. From Quebec Champlain pushed inland, searching for the Northwest Passage through America. Along the way he formed friendships with the Indians that made possible the great fur trade that was to grow in later years.

Henry Hudson Sails for the Dutch and the English

During the 1500s the Dutch, or people from the Netherlands, gained a rich empire in the Indies. Dutch ships used the route around Africa to reach this empire. In 1609 the Dutch hired an Englishman, Henry Hudson, to search for a shorter route to the Indies across the Atlantic.

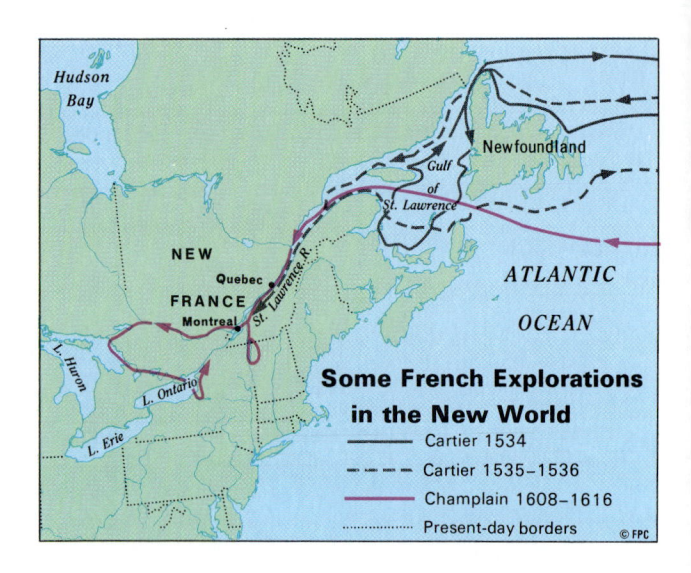

In 1609 Hudson sailed north in his small ship, the *Half Moon*. Freezing winds forced him to change course. He then headed south along the coast of North America. As he explored the coast of North America, he sailed up a river that is today called the Hudson River. Trace Hudson's route on the map on page 109. Hudson claimed the land along the river for the Dutch.

Hudson next sailed to North America for England. This time his search took him far north into what is today Hudson Bay. Find Hudson Bay on the map on page 109. Hudson claimed the land along this bay for England.

By the early 1600s, Europeans had explored and claimed much of North and South America. During the rest of the 1600s, Europeans competed in the race to set up colonies in the New World.

Some French Explorations in the New World
— Cartier 1534
--- Cartier 1535–1536
— Champlain 1608–1616
····· Present-day borders

* **Reading Skill:** Building vocabulary. Discuss the meaning of the title *sir*. Ask students if titles are used in the United States.
    Map Skill: Location. Have students find Roanoke Island on a map of North Carolina.

The Mystery of the Lost Colony

By the late 1500s, the English had become interested in establishing a colony in the New World. During this time they made three unsuccessful attempts to set up a permanent colony in North America. The fate of one of these attempts remains a mystery even today.

In 1583 a group of colonists led by Sir Humphrey Gilbert left England to start a colony in Newfoundland. Although they reached Newfoundland, the colonists did not like Newfoundland's cold climate, so they returned to England.

Two years later a second group of colonists settled in North America on Roanoke Island off the shore of North Carolina. The soil was rich and wood was plentiful. Yet after one year the colonists gave up and went home.

In 1587 a third group came to North America. These colonists also settled on Roanoke Island. Soon after they arrived, the first English child, Virginia Dare, was born in North America.

John White, the governor of the colony, made sure that the colonists built cabins and planted crops. Then he returned to England to buy food and supplies. A war with Spain kept the governor in England for three years. When he returned to Roanoke Island, the colonists were gone. The letters *CRO* were carved on one tree, and the word *Croatoan* (krō′ə·tō′ən) was carved on another.

John White never found the colonists. To this day no one knows for sure what happened to them. Some historians believe they joined the Croatoans, a group of Indians who lived on an island off the coast of North Carolina. These historians point out that some present-day Croatoans have blue eyes and fair hair and that the Croatoan language has some English names and words.

Checking Up

1. Which explorer claimed Newfoundland for England?
2. Where was the first French colony in North America?
3. What answers would you give to the key questions at the beginning of this chapter?
4. *In what ways did the early European explorers face both hardships and disappointments?*

Unit 3 Summary

- Although Columbus is sometimes called the European "discoverer" of the Americas, historians now know that the Norse reached the shores of North America about 500 years before Columbus.
- By the 1400s the Norse colony in North America had been forgotten. People in Europe looked to the Indies as a place to trade their goods for gold, spices, and other riches.
- European sea captains began to search for a sea route to the Indies. Columbus's search in 1492 for a western sea route to the Indies led to his discovery of the New World.
- During the 1500s Spain established colonies in the New World. During this same time England, France, and the Netherlands sent explorers to the New World who claimed large areas of land for these countries.

Reading Skill: Using details to support main ideas. Have students add at least four sentences to each point in the summary to explain it further.
Thinking Skill: Analyzing. Discuss what else might have happened at Roanoke Island.

111

Unit 3 Review Workshop

What Have You Learned?

1. How do historians know that the Norse reached North America about the year 1000?
2. Why did Europeans want a sea route to the Indies?
3. How many voyages did Columbus make to the New World?
4. Who led the first voyage to sail around the world?
5. Which European country was the first to build an empire in the New World?
6. Name three European countries other than Spain that paid for voyages of exploration to the New World in the 1500s.

Use Your Reading Skills

The chart on page 113 lists some of the explorations and discoveries made by Europeans in the hundred years after Columbus's discovery of the New World. Study the chart and then answer the questions below. Answers to these questions will help you understand the order in which Europeans explored and claimed lands in the New World.

1. What important event happened in the New World the same year that Magellan began his voyage?
2. Which country attempted but failed to set up colonies in the New World during the 1500s?
3. At about the same time that Coronado and de Soto were exploring what are today the southeastern and southwestern parts of the United States, what explorer was claiming land along the St. Lawrence River for France?
4. About the same time that Champlain established a colony at Quebec, who was claiming land in the New World for the Dutch?

Use Your Speaking Skills

Magellan's voyage proved many ideas about the world. Below are listed some things that people learned. Study the map on page 104 that shows Magellan's route. Then, using a globe, trace Magellan's voyage with your finger. As you do this, explain how the voyage proved each fact listed below.

1. The earth is round.
2. The land Columbus reached is not part of Asia.
3. The land Columbus reached is not near Asia.

Use Your Map Skills

Compare the map of Spanish explorations on page 106 with the world map on pages 10–11. Then answer the questions below. Answers to these questions will help you see how much of the Americas the Spanish explored in the 1500s.

1. What part of North America did Ponce de León explore?
2. What continent did Pizarro explore?
3. At the time that Ponce de León was

Reading Skills: Interpreting graphics, interpreting facts.
Thinking Skills: Knowing, analyzing, comparing.
Map Skill: Location.
Communication Skill: Speaking.

| European Explorations and Discoveries ||||
Spain	England	France	The Netherlands
1492 Columbus discovers a New World.	1497 John Cabot claims Newfoundland.	1534–1536 Cartier claims land along the St. Lawrence River.	1500s The Dutch gain a rich empire in the Indies.
1519 Cortes reaches Aztec capital. Magellan begins his voyage.	1583–1590 Attempts to establish colonies in the New World fail.	1608 Champlain establishes first French colony at Quebec.	1609 Henry Hudson claims land along the Hudson River for the Netherlands.
1540s Coronado explores the Southwest, and de Soto explores the South.	1610 Henry Hudson explores Hudson Bay.		

exploring North America, what part of the Americas was Balboa setting out to explore?

Learn by Doing

1. Columbus kept a log, or record, of his voyage. The gromets on board his ships, though, could not read or write. However, they probably had much to tell their friends when they got back to Spain. Pretend that you had a chance to talk to one of the gromets on board the *Pinta*. Write a short story in which you describe some of the things the gromet might have told you about his voyage.

2. The Indians in the Southwest told the Spanish explorers from Mexico stories about rich cities of gold to the north. There were villages to the north, but they were far different from those cities described by the Indians. Paint or draw two pictures. In one, show what the explorers expected to find. In the other, show the Zuñi villages as they really were. You may need to turn back to Unit 2 of this book to review the Zuñi Indians.

3. Look in books and encyclopedias to find out about one of the explorers listed below. Then make a report to your class in which you explain what discoveries or explorations were made by this person.

    Juan Ponce de León
    Vasco Núñez de Balboa
    Francisco Pizarro
    Giovanni da Verrazano
    Sir Martin Frobisher

Read to Learn More

Find the topics listed below in the card catalog of your library. Read all or part of a book listed under one of the topics. Share what you learn with your classmates.

THE NORSE   NORTHWEST PASSAGE
MARCO POLO   CHRISTOPHER COLUMBUS

Reading Skills: Organizing information: *Learn by Doing, 1, 2;* using references: *Learn by Doing, 3;* doing research: *Learn by Doing, 3.*
    Thinking Skill: Comparing: *Learn by Doing, 3.*
    Communication Skill: Writing: *Learn by Doing 1, 2.*

Unit Overview: This unit examines the Spanish, English, French, and Dutch colonies in North America with a focus on the growth of the thirteen English colonies.

Unit 4

Unit Objectives
To understand:
- the earliest Spanish, English, French, and Dutch colonies
- the growth of the thirteen English colonies
- interaction between European colonists and the Indians

Suggested Materials
Workbook
Unit Tests

Skills Emphasized
Map Skills: pp. 114, 116, 119, 120, 127, 132, 141, 143, 144.
Social Studies Reading Skills: pp. 114, 116, 117, 118, 121, 122, 123, 124, 125, 127, 128, 129, 130, 131, 132, 133, 134, 136, 137, 139, 140, 143, 144, 145.
Thinking Skills: pp. 114, 118, 119, 120, 121, 123, 128, 130, 133, 136, 137, 139, 141, 144, 145.
Communication Skills: pp. 114, 119, 121, 123, 128, 131, 136, 145.
Time Skills: pp. 125, 136, 141, 142, 143.
Social Studies Math Skills: pp. 122, 140.
Citizenship Skill: p. 134.

Suggested Student Activities
   1. Arrange a bulletin-board display of the thirteen English colonies. Attach information about the origin of each colony to a map of the colonies using different-colored string.
   2. Make individual outline maps of the Spanish, English, French, and Dutch colonies in North America.
   3. Work in groups. Each group should report on one of the thirteen English colonies.
* 4. Make a salt map of the thirteen English colonies.
** 5. Make a display on colonial Jamestown.
*** 6. Give oral reports on famous colonial people.

Skills Emphasized in Suggested Student Activities
Social Studies Reading Skills: Organizing information, doing research, using references.
Communication Skills: Writing, speaking, listening.
Map Skills: Location, scale, distance, symbolization.
Thinking Skills: Knowing, comparing, classifying.

Colonies in North America

English colonists sailed up the James River in 1607.

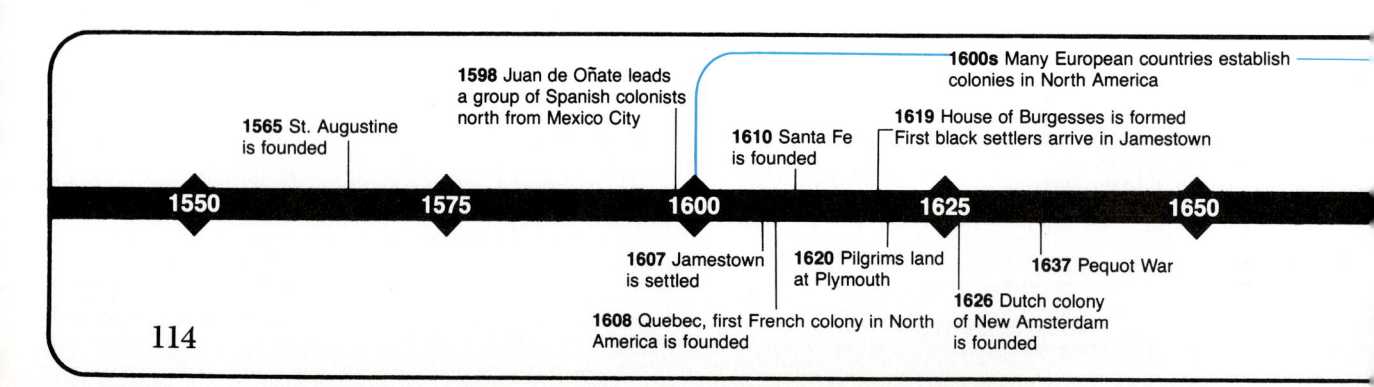

1565 St. Augustine is founded
1598 Juan de Oñate leads a group of Spanish colonists north from Mexico City
1600s Many European countries establish colonies in North America
1607 Jamestown is settled
1608 Quebec, first French colony in North America is founded
1610 Santa Fe is founded
1619 House of Burgesses is formed / First black settlers arrive in Jamestown
1620 Pilgrims land at Plymouth
1626 Dutch colony of New Amsterdam is founded
1637 Pequot War

1550   1575   1600   1625   1650

114

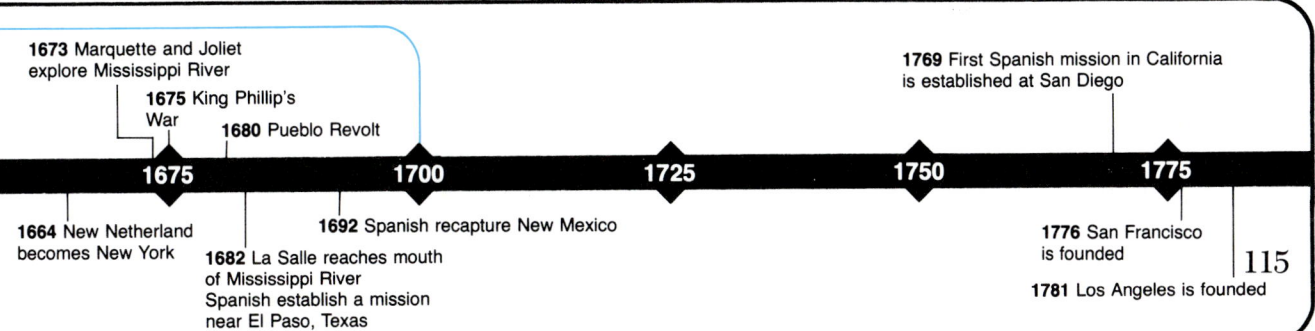

1673 Marquette and Joliet explore Mississippi River

1675 King Phillip's War

1680 Pueblo Revolt

1769 First Spanish mission in California is established at San Diego

1675 — 1700 — 1725 — 1750 — 1775

1664 New Netherland becomes New York

1682 La Salle reaches mouth of Mississippi River
Spanish establish a mission near El Paso, Texas

1692 Spanish recapture New Mexico

1776 San Francisco is founded

1781 Los Angeles is founded

115

Reading Skill: Skimming for information: *As You Read, 3.*
Reading Skill: Using textbook features. Have students find Unit 4 in the Table of Contents and then turn to pages 114–115. Ask students to refer to the time line throughout the unit.

Spanish Settlements in North America

As You Read

1. Think about these words.
   missionary   hacienda   plaza   mission
2. Look for answers to these key questions.
   a. Why did the Spanish want to establish a colony in New Mexico?
   b. What did the Spanish demand of the Pueblo Indians?
   c. In what four present-day states did Spain establish settlements?
3. Use this reading skill.
   Skimming is an important reading skill. To skim a reading selection, look at the pages and read the headings on each page. By skimming you will get a "feel" for the major ideas. Before you begin to read this chapter carefully, skim through the chapter. Then close your book and recall as many of the major ideas in the chapter as you can.

During the 1500s European explorers pushed far inland into North and South America. They discovered that these two continents were much larger than anyone had first believed. In addition, they met the American Indians, whose ways of life were far different from those of Europeans.

As you learned in Unit 3, Spain was the first European country to establish colonies in the new World. In the 1500s Spain's colonies were mainly in Mexico and in South America. However, in the early 1600s Spanish colonists began moving north from Mexico into the vast Southwest claimed by Coronado more than fifty years before.

Which three European nations claimed large areas of land in North America?

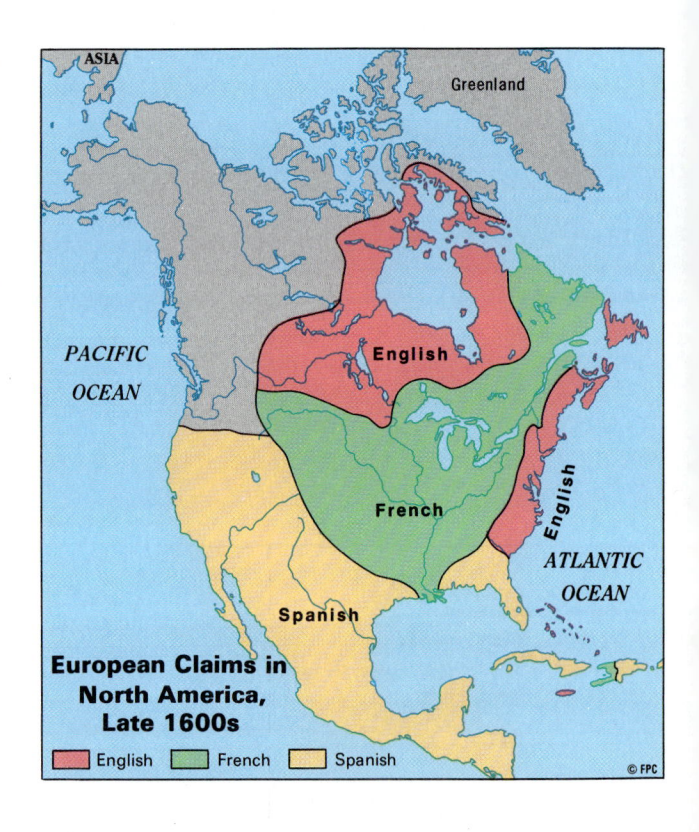

European Claims in North America, Late 1600s

■ English   ■ French   □ Spanish

116   **Map Skill:** Location. Have students use the exploration maps on pages 106, 109, and 110 to show how Spain, England, and France claimed areas of North America based on each country's explorations.

The Palace of the Governors, an adobe and timber structure, was built about 1610 in Santa Fe, New Mexico.

A Spanish Colony in New Mexico

In 1598 a group of Spanish in Mexico led by Don Juan de Oñate (ô·nyä′tä) marched north from Mexico City. They wanted to find new gold and silver mines. They also wanted to bring Spanish rule to the land of the Pueblo and to convert, or change, the Indians to the Christian religion. The Spanish Christian religion was Catholicism.

Oñate's group was made up of several hundred Spanish soldiers, farmers, gold seekers, women, and children. **Missionaries**, people who teach their religion to others, also traveled with the group.

Burned by the blazing desert sun and chilled by the cold night air, the group moved slowly north. Finally they reached the Rio Grande. Find the Rio Grande on the map on pages 18–19.

As Oñate and his group moved north along the Rio Grande, they came to Pueblo Indian villages. At each village Oñate gave the Pueblos a choice: be ruled by Spain or be destroyed.

Most Pueblos were peace-loving farmers. They were eager to please this stranger from the south. Although they probably had no idea what they were promising, the Pueblo agreed to be ruled by Spain.

The new colony. In 1610 the Spanish founded Santa Fe and chose it for the capital of the colony.

Santa Fe is in what is today the state of New Mexico. From Santa Fe, the colonists went in search of gold and silver. The missionaries worked to convert the Indians to the Christian religion. Find Santa Fe on the map on pages 18–19.

The Rio Grande valley was rich in grasses, trees, and wildlife. Yet the colonists soon learned it did not have the riches they wanted. As a result, many colonists chose to brave the long, dangerous trip back to Mexico rather than remain in the new colony.

The missionaries were having more success. They sent reports back to Mexico and Spain about the great numbers of Indians they were converting to the Christian religion. The Spanish leaders decided not to abandon the colony in New Mexico.

Reading Skill: Determining meaning from context. Discuss what Spanish rule meant to a Spanish leader, a Pueblo, and a missionary living in New Mexico in 1610.
Reading Skill: Interpreting a picture. Ask students how the picture helps explain the text.

This painting of a mission near what is now Carmel, California, was drawn in the 1700s.

The Spanish king granted large areas of land to those colonists who were willing to stay in New Mexico. The king also gave the colonists the right to use the Indians as servants or slaves.

Life in New Mexico

Each year the colonists received from Mexico goods such as tools and medicine. Yet they got most of what they needed through their own hard work.

Haciendas. On large farms called **haciendas**, the colonists provided for most of their needs. Parents, children, grandparents, aunts, uncles, and cousins all lived on each hacienda. There were also Indian servants, farm workers, and herders. All these people grew crops, raised cattle and sheep, and cut down trees to build houses and to make furniture. Women and servants of the household did such work as spinning and weaving wool sheared from the sheep on the hacienda.

Towns and villages. Some of the Spanish colonists settled in small towns. Each town was built around a central **plaza**, or public square, with a church in the most important place.

Those who lived on nearby haciendas attended church in town. They also gathered there on market days to trade goods, to exchange news, and to visit the small shops around the plaza.

Missions. In time the Spanish established **missions** in the Southwest. Missions were settlements that centered around a church. Here the Spanish missionaries worked to bring the Indians into missions, where they could learn a new Christian way of life. The missionaries also taught many Indians reading, writing, and new ways of growing crops. In exchange for living in the missions, the Indians gave up their freedom. As a result, the Indians were not allowed to leave the missions.

Other Spanish Colonies in North America

The areas of present-day Florida and Texas were both explored and claimed

Thinking Skill: Analyzing. Ask students why some Spanish colonists did not stay in New Mexico.
Reading Skill: Interpreting a picture. Have students describe the activities in the picture.
*** **Reading Skill:** Using references. Assign written reports on haciendas.

Background: St. Augustine is the oldest city in the United States. The city was founded as a military outpost to repulse British and French attempts to establish colonies along the coast.

for Spain in the 1500s. Later, part of what is today California was also explored and claimed for Spain. Unlike explorers in Middle and South America, Spanish explorers in North America did not find rich treasures such as gold and silver mines. As a result, the Spanish were not as interested in establishing colonies in North America as they were in Middle and South America. In North America Spanish settlements were often missions and military outposts.

Florida. In 1565 Spanish colonists founded St. Augustine in what is today the state of Florida. Find St. Augustine on the map on pages 18–19. Soon missionaries began to build missions. Within fifty years nearly 30,000 Indians were living at missions.

Texas. The Spanish also established missions in what is today Texas. In 1682, for example, the Spanish established a mission near El Paso, Texas. Later, in 1720, another mission was established in San Antonio, Texas. You can find El Paso and San Antonio on the map on pages 18–19. These missions, as well as others in Texas, still stand today. They are a reminder of Spanish rule there.

California. The west coast north of Mexico was the last region to be colonized by Spain. A missionary founded the first Spanish mission in California in 1769 where San Diego is today. Find San Diego on the map on pages 18–19. Later, many other missions were established in California. Many of these missions still exist today and are known for the beauty of their architecture.

Built in St. Augustine, Florida, this fortress was completed in 1696.

Our Heritage from Spain

Spanish rule in North America lasted for several hundred years. Today we are often reminded that the Spanish have been here for many years. Spanish names such as Florida, San Antonio, and San Diego are a part of our language. Many people living in the United States today trace their ancestors back to Spain. Spanish architecture and food are also a part of the culture of the United States today.

Checking Up

1. Who led the group that colonized New Mexico?
2. What answers would you give to the key questions at the beginning of this chapter?
3. *In what ways were Spanish missions similar to haciendas? How were they different?*

** **Communication Skill:** Writing. Have students make pamphlets on St. Augustine past and present.
*** **Map Skill:** Location. Ask students to make maps of California that show the 21 Franciscan missions that once prospered there.
Thinking Skill: Observing. Have students look for examples of Spanish influence in your area.

Thinking Skill: Analyzing. Discuss why the English wanted to establish trading colonies.
Map Skill: Location. Talk about the pros and cons of locating a colony at Jamestown using only the map below.

The First English Colonies in North America

As You Read

1. Think about these words.
   trading company   site
2. Look for answers to these key questions.
   a. Where was the first permanent English colony in North America?
   b. What were two problems faced by the first English colonists in North America?
   c. Why did the Puritans want to start a colony in North America?

Many countries in Europe envied Spain's wealth and power. They, too, sent explorers and later sent colonists to the New World. England was one of these countries.

England in the 1600s

During the early 1600s, some people in England started **trading companies**. Many people put money into these companies. They hoped to make more money from trade.

One of these trading companies was the Virginia Company. The leaders of this company wanted to find a passage through North America to the East Indies. They also wanted to build a trading colony where English goods could be sold. They hoped to find gold and to convert the Indians to Christianity.

The Jamestown Colony

In the winter of 1606, the Virginia Company paid for three ships of colonists to sail to the New World. On board the three ships were 120 people. After several stormy months at sea, the three ships reached Chesapeake Bay in April 1607. They sailed up the James River and dropped anchor near a wooded island in May. They named the place Jamestown in honor of the English king, James I. You can find Jamestown on the map below.

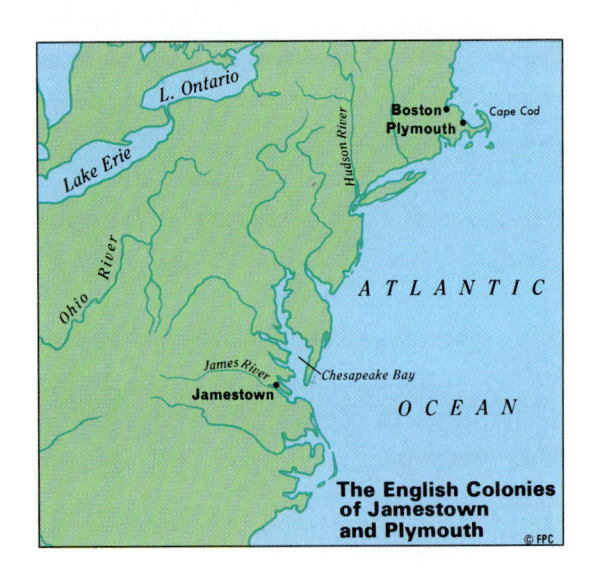

The English Colonies of Jamestown and Plymouth

120

Background: Between 1607 and 1624, more than 6,000 people went to Virginia. In 1625, however, the colony numbered only 1,200 settlers.
Reading Skill: Organizing information. Have students begin a list of the problems the colonists had in Jamestown.

Captain John Smith was a leader of the Jamestown colony.

The Jamestown settlers soon built houses and cleared land for farming.

Starting the colony. The colonists at Jamestown had trouble from the very beginning. The **site**, or location, they had chosen was a poor place for a colony. The land was swampy and was surrounded by a dense forest. The area was also infested with mosquitoes. Food was nearly impossible to grow. At first the colonists would not even try to farm. They lived on the supplies they had brought from England.

In a few months the supplies ran out. Pocahontas (pō′kə·hänt′əs), a Powhatan (pou′ə·tan′) Indian princess, urged the leaders of her tribe to help the colonists. The Powhatan lived farther inland, where the land was fertile and farming was easier. The Powhatan were glad to exchange corn and beans for copper pots and other English goods. However, when the colonists began to steal food, the Powhatan became enemies.

Now the colonists could not even go into the forest to hunt or gather wood. They burned the wood from their houses for heat and fuel. After two years, only fifty-three colonists were alive, and most of them were sick and discouraged. Then Captain John Smith appointed himself the new leader of the colony.

The colony under Smith. Smith was a strong leader who encouraged the colonists to plant corn and to build sturdy houses. Smith also made peace with the Powhatan and traded with them for food. Things improved in Jamestown under Smith's leadership. More colonists arrived until more than 500 English colonists were living in the New World.

In 1609 Smith was hurt by a gunpowder explosion. He returned to England. After he left Jamestown, conditions in the colony reversed. The colonists did not keep peace with the Powhatan, so the Indians no longer helped the colonists. Many colonists died of hunger and disease. For almost ten years, the colonists at Jamestown struggled to survive.

** **Communication Skill:** Writing. Ask students to write short stories or poems about Pocahontas.
Thinking Skill: Analyzing. Discuss the importance of leadership by comparing Jamestown with and without John Smith in charge.

Called *Mayflower II*, this ship is a copy of the one used by the Pilgrims.

The colony becomes successful. In 1613 John Rolfe, a Jamestown colonist, brought the seeds of a mild Caribbean tobacco to Jamestown. On land farther inland, the colonists grew the tobacco. Soon tobacco became an important money-making crop for the colony of the Virginia Company. The colony was finally a success.

The Plymouth Colony

Thirteen years after the founding of the Jamestown colony, another group of English colonists arrived on the coast of what is today Massachusetts. Many of these colonists were seeking religious freedom.

The Puritans. In the 1500s Henry VIII of England had established the Church of England. All people in England had to belong to this church. Some people in England did not want to belong to the Church of England. One of these groups was called the Puritans. One of the leaders of the Virginia Company was a friend of some of the Puritans. He arranged to have the Virginia Company pay for the founding of a Puritan colony in North America.

In the fall of 1620 one ship, the *Mayflower*, left England with 102 passengers and a crew of about 30. Many of the passengers were Puritans. On November 11, 1620, the *Mayflower* reached the coast of what is today Massachusetts. After searching the coast for nearly a month, the Puritan leaders selected

The Indians taught the Pilgrims how to plant corn and squash.

Plymouth as the site for the new colony. You can find Plymouth on the map on page 120.

Unlike Jamestown, Plymouth was a good site for a colony. It had a quiet harbor and freshwater streams. Nearby were fields that had already been cleared by Indians.

Building a colony. The Puritans, who were later called Pilgrims because of their long journey, had reached Plymouth in the midst of winter. At first they lived on board the *Mayflower* and rowed to shore each day. Slowly, they built a large shelter, a storehouse, and then living quarters.

For a while the Indians who lived near Plymouth watched the colonists from afar. Then in early spring, members of the Wampanoag (wäm′pə·nō′ag) tribe came to them in friendship. The chief of the Wampanoag and the leaders of the colony exchanged gifts and promises to live together in peace. Neither side broke this agreement.

The first Thanksgiving. The colonists worked hard through the spring, summer, and early fall. In mid-October after the harvest, they invited many of their Indian friends to a feast of thanksgiving. The colonists wanted to give thanks for their good harvest and for the friendship of the Indians, who had helped make their harvest possible.

The colonists in Jamestown and in Plymouth had to overcome many problems. Yet by the middle of the 1620s, both colonies were firmly established in North America.

American Documents

The Mayflower Compact

The *Mayflower* had set out for the Virginia colony. Plymouth, though, was 200 miles (320 km) north. The Puritans knew that their new colony lay beyond the land and the law of the Virginia colony. Before going ashore at Plymouth, they made an important agreement.

The leaders of the Puritans drew up a document that they called the Mayflower Compact. In all, forty-one of the male colonists on board the *Mayflower* signed the compact. By doing so, they agreed to live under one government. They also promised to follow the laws and rules passed by that government for the good of the colony.

The Mayflower Compact was an agreement to be governed by majority will, or what the majority of people decided. Thus, it stands as one of the important foundations for our present-day government. Nothing quite like the Mayflower Compact was written anywhere else in the world for almost 200 years.

Checking Up

1. What group founded Plymouth colony in 1620?
2. Who was Pocahantas? How did she help the English settlers in the Jamestown colony?
3. What answers would you give to the key questions at the beginning of this chapter?
4. *Why did the colonists in Plymouth get along better with the Indians than the colonists in Jamestown did?*

*** **Reading Skill:** Doing research. Have students look for other maps of Jamestown in atlases and encyclopedias in the library.

Maps and Pictures Tell a Story of Jamestown

As you read, think about these words.
cartographer   symbol

In the spring of 1607, a small group of colonists founded the settlement of Jamestown. This tiny settlement became the first permanent English colony in North America.

Describing the Land

The picture below shows a clearing near the shore of Jamestown Island. Historians think the land in this picture looks much like that first described by the Jamestown colonists. Study the picture. How do you think the colonists might have described this land? Was the land flat or hilly? Was it covered with brush or trees? What had to be done to prepare the land for growing food?

1

This recent picture was taken near the site of the Jamestown colony.

Word descriptions can tell a lot about an area. However, maps were and still are one of the most accurate ways to describe an area. Look at the modern map below. How many things can you learn about Jamestown from this map?

2

John Smith: Explorer and Map Maker

The Virginia Company, which paid for the Jamestown colony, wanted to learn as much as possible about the New World. The colonists were told to begin

Notice that north is at the right on this map. Where is south?

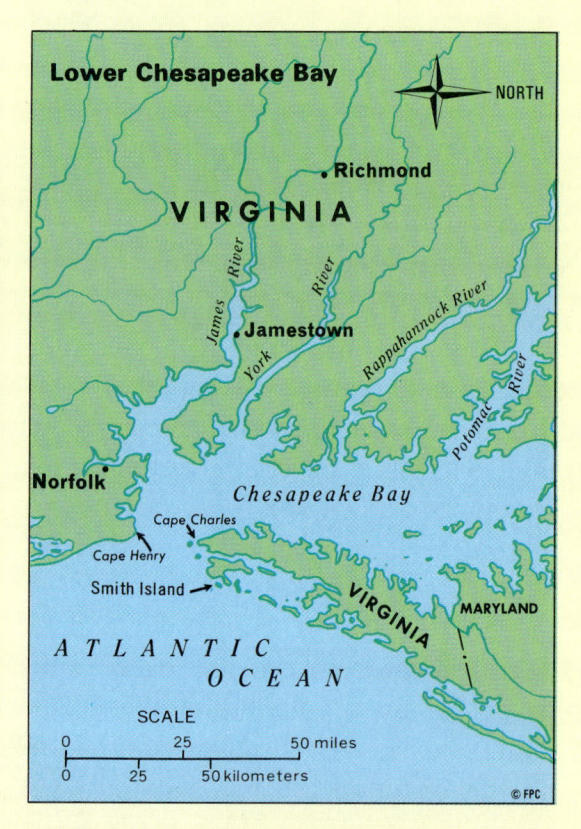

1. A flat, wooded area. Flat. Brush and trees. Trees had to be cut down to clear the land for farming.
2. Jamestown is located on the James River, which feeds into Chesapeake Bay. Jamestown is about halfway between Richmond and the Atlantic Ocean.

Background: The Virginia Company also hoped that expeditions such as Smith's would determine the area's geographic features and natural resources. This information could then be used to attract more settlers to the area and to begin exporting natural resources to England.

exploring the new land as soon as possible. The Virginia Company hoped that the colonists would find both a water passage to Asia and riches such as gold. The discovery of either of these two things would mean great wealth for the Virginia Company and certain success for the Jamestown colony.

Within one week after landing at Jamestown, a small group set out to explore the James River. Captain John Smith was among this small group of explorers. They traveled as far up the James River as the present-day site of the city of Richmond. You can find the James River and Richmond on the map on page 124.

During his first year at Jamestown, Smith made several other journeys up nearby rivers searching for food for the starving colonists. After each of these journeys, Smith wrote down what he had learned about the land near Jamestown in letters and long reports.

About a year after he arrived in Jamestown, Smith and another group set out in a barge to explore Chesapeake Bay and the rivers that empty into the bay. Find Chesapeake Bay on the map on page 124. Their journey took three months and covered 3,000 miles (4,800 km). During this journey Smith began a map of Virginia.

Smith's Map

Smith first drew a sketch of his map. Later, he turned the sketch over to a skilled **cartographer** (kär·täg′rə·fər), or map maker, who made a fine detailed map. This map was printed in England in 1612 and is known as Captain John Smith's Map of Virginia. Part of Smith's map is shown on page 126.

Showing direction. As you may recall, a compass rose is a direction finder. Find the compass rose on Smith's map. Notice the arrowlike design at the right of the compass. This arrow shows that, on Smith's map, north is to the right. Where then is south? east? west? How does Smith's compass rose help you better understand his map? 1

Smith's symbols. On his map Smith wanted to show landforms and what was on the land. He chose **symbols**, or small drawings, to represent trees and hills. Shown here are drawings of some of the symbols Smith used for trees and hills. As you can see in the drawings, Smith's map has several kinds of trees. The map also has hills of different sizes.

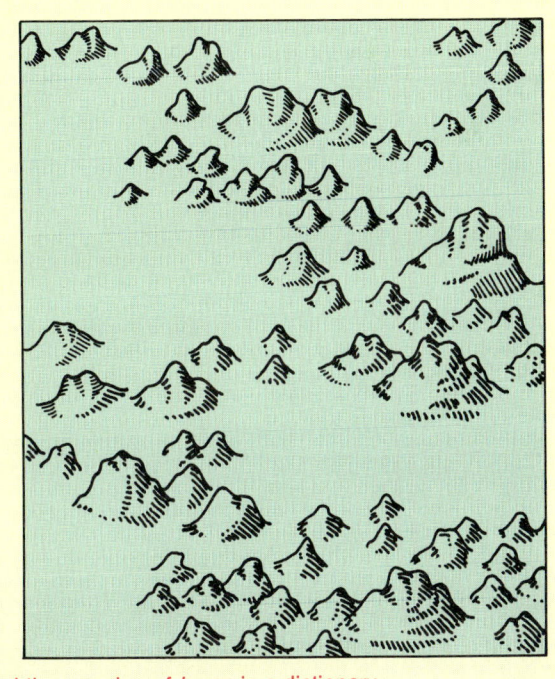

---

* **Reading Skill:** Building vocabulary. Have students find the meaning of *barge* in a dictionary.
* **Time Skill:** Ask students how old Smith's map is.
  1. To the left; to the bottom; to the top. Although many map makers place north at the top of a map, it is helpful to know that north is at the right on Smith's map.

125

1. Mostly plains. Because Smith drew only a few mountain and hill symbols on his map.
2. It is keyed to a darker shade of green.
3. An Indian, small houses, or a sea monster. There were Indians nearby.
4. To describe some of his experiences as a Jamestown settler.

₁ Now study Smith's map below. Was the land shown on Smith's map a hilly area or a plains area? How can you tell? As you learned in Unit 2, cartographers today show landforms by using shades of black and different colors.

₂ As you can see, Smith's map has a lot of trees to show that the area was heavily forested. Look at the key for the land-use map on page 17. How is the forested area shown on this map?

Most people looking at Smith's map would easily understand the symbols for trees and hills. However, Smith's map also has other symbols to give more information about the area. Find two other symbols on Smith's map. How do these symbols tell you something more about the area near the Jamestown colony? ₃

Pictures. In the 1600s most map makers drew pictures that surrounded their maps. Smith's map also had pictures surrounding it. Shown here is one of the pictures from Smith's map. Read the caption for the picture. Why do you think Smith's map includes this picture? ₄

A part of Captain John Smith's Map of Virginia is shown here.

Background: John Smith later explored and mapped the New England coast in 1614. The result of his work was a book, *A Description of New England.* The Pilgrims had read Smith's book and probably named their colony Plimouth in 1620 for the same site so named on a map in Smith's book.
Reading Skill: Interpreting visuals. Ask students how visuals help explain this chapter.

Place-names. Many of the place-names that Smith included on his map are Indian names. They are the names of the American Indians who were living in Virginia when the English colonists first arrived. For this reason Smith's map is an accurate record of the Indian groups who were living in Virginia before the English arrived. Other names Smith used on his map were the names of members of his exploring party or leaders of the Jamestown colony.

Find the place-names listed below on Smith's map and then on the modern map on page 124.

Smith's Map	Modern Map
1. Powhatan River	1. James River
2. Jamestowne	2. Jamestown
3. Patawomeck River	3. Potomac River
4. Cape Henry	4. Cape Henry
5. Smyths Iles	5. Smith Island

Find the Atlantic Ocean on the modern map. What name did Smith give this same body of water? Why do you think Smith chose this name? 1

Think about your comparison of place-names on Smith's map with those on the modern map. Look at the placement of rivers on the two maps. Do you think Smith's map was an accurate one? Why? 2

Smith spent time as a prisoner in the Powhatan chief's lodge.

Checking Up
1. What is a cartographer?
2. How are landforms shown on Smith's map? on modern maps?

** **Map Skill:** Symbolization. Have students draw maps of their neighborhoods similar in format to Smith's map.
1. The Virginian Sea. To honor the Virginia Company, which paid for the Jamestown settlement.
2. Yes. The placement of features, such as rivers, is the same as on modern-day maps.

127

French and Dutch Colonies in North America

As You Read

1. Think about these words.
   port   fort   cargo
2. Look for answers to these key questions.
   a. What was a major French activity in North America in the 1600s?
   b. What lands in North America did France claim in the 1600s?
   c. How did the Dutch lose their colony in North America?
3. Use this reading skill.
   Note taking will help you remember and organize important facts under main ideas. To be a good note taker, you must do several things. First, skim the material in a lesson. Then read the lesson carefully, paying attention to the headings. After you have read a lesson carefully, write down the major headings on notebook paper. Leave plenty of space between each heading. Write down, in your own words, the important ideas under each heading. Follow these steps and take notes as you read this chapter.

The Spanish, English, French, and Dutch all built colonies in the New World during the 1600s. These colonies were quite different from one another. Yet the colonists who settled them shared many of the same experiences.

New France

The lands claimed by France in North America were called New France. As you may remember, the first colony in New France was founded in 1608. This colony was Quebec. During much of the 1600s, however, the French spent most of their efforts exploring North America rather than settling colonies.

French explorations. In the 1670s Louis Joliet (loō′ē zhôl·yā′), a fur trader, and Father Jacques Marquette (zhäk mär·ket′), a Catholic priest, had an amazing journey. They traveled by canoe across Lake Michigan and down the Wisconsin River to the Mississippi River. They traveled the Mississippi as far south as the Arkansas River before turning back. Look at the map on page 129. With your finger trace Joliet and Marquette's route.

In the 1680s Robert de La Salle followed almost the same route. However, he went all the way to the mouth of the Mississippi River. Now follow La Salle's

Explorations of the Mississippi River

→ Marquette and Joliet, 1673
→ La Salle, 1682

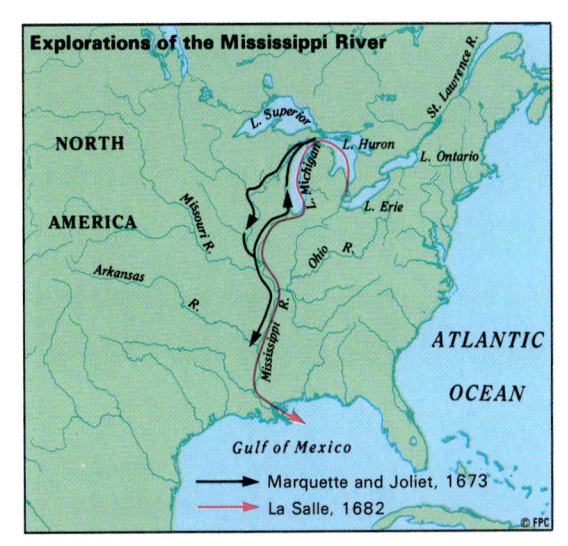

route on the map above. Because of the explorations of Joliet, Marquette, and La Salle, France claimed all the lands along the Mississippi River.

The fur trade. France, like other European countries, was interested mainly in finding treasures in North America. The French found a new treasure in furs. The demand for furs in Europe offered great wealth to fur traders in North America. During the 1600s the fur trade became one of the major activities of the French in North America.

During this time French explorers and traders made fur trading agreements with the American Indians. The Indians often provided furs for the French. The French traded guns and other goods for skins from animals such as beavers and otters.

The French explorers and traders set up inland trade routes that led to **ports**, cities or towns on harbors, along the Atlantic Ocean. From these ports the furs were then shipped to Europe. By the end of the 1600s, a network of fur trading

While exploring the Mississippi River, La Salle met many Indians.

posts and French **forts** linked the Indians of the wilderness of North America with fur dealers based in Atlantic port cities. A fort is a settlement protected by high fences or walls. You can find some of the French forts and trading posts on the map on page 130.

The French and the Indians. French explorers and traders became friends with many of the American Indians. Of-

Explorers such as Joliet and Marquette used Indian canoes to travel on rivers.

129

ten French fur trappers and traders lived among the Indians. Unlike the English and the Spanish, the French did not clear the Indians' land. They were more interested in trapping and trading furs. As a result, the French and the Indians grew to trust each other.

The French also sent missionaries to the New World. French missionaries made friends with the Indians. Many of these missionaries lived and worked with the Indians. They treated the Indians well and tried to teach the Indians the Christian religion.

The Huron and the Algonquin. Sometimes the French sided with one group of Indians against another. The French fur traders worked closely with the Huron and Algonquin (al·gän′kwən) tribes. Look at the map on page 62 and find the locations of these tribes. The Huron and Algonquin were enemies of the Iroquois, whom you read about in Unit 2. They often fought over hunting lands. The French often helped the Huron and Algonquin in wars with the Iroquois.

The growth of New France. In the early 1600s, the French government did not encourage settlers to come to New France. Settlements cost a great deal of money. It was necessary to clear the land and plant crops just to grow food for the settlers. In contrast, the fur trade did not require a large investment of money because land did not have to be cleared and crops did not have to be grown.

However, by the mid-1600s the king of France decided that New France needed more permanent settlers if it were to become the strong colony he wanted. As a result, the king began to send colonists from France to settle and farm the land along the St. Lawrence River in New France. Between 1665 and 1675, many farming villages grew up along the banks of the river. In time small trading posts such as Quebec and Montreal became busy towns. Look at the map above and find the settlements along the St. Lawrence River.

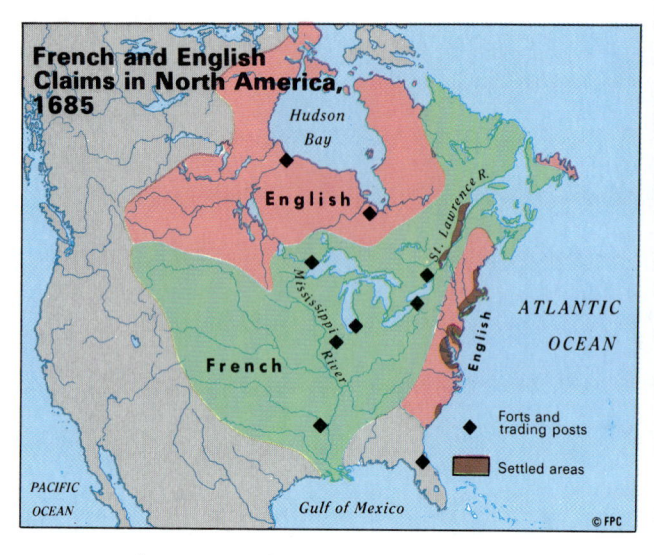

The farm settlements in New France were not very profitable. The settlers grew enough food for themselves. Yet there were no extra crops to ship to Europe. Also, many settlers left the farms to become fur trappers and traders. By the late 1600s, the king of France was no longer sending settlers to New France.

New Netherland

As you read in Unit 3, in the early 1600s Henry Hudson claimed the land along the Hudson River for the Netherlands. Within a few years, Dutch ships were leaving the New World loaded with

*** **Communication Skill:** Writing. Assign short reports on Peter Minuit or Peter Stuyvesant.
  * **Reading Skill:** Determining meaning from context. Ask students what *using the resources of the land* means.

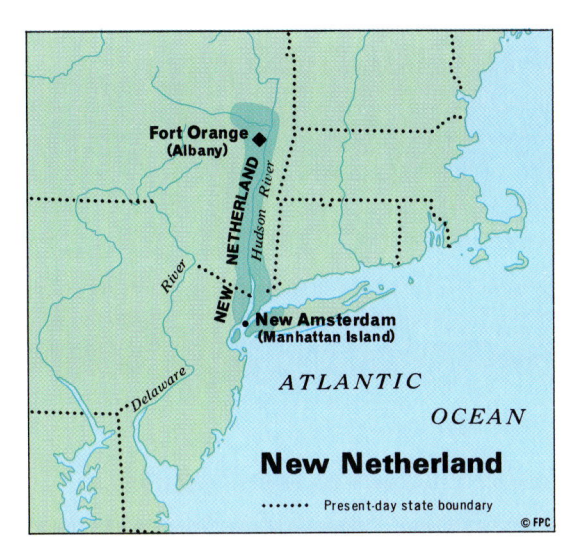

rich **cargoes**, or shipments, of furs. The Dutch soon realized that a colony in North America would be valuable.

In the 1620s a Dutch trading company called the Dutch East Indies Company sent colonists to North America. The company's goal was to set up trading posts along the Hudson River. The Dutch settlements in North America were called New Netherland. Look at the map on this page and find New Netherland.

In 1626 Peter Minuit (min′yə·wət), the newly chosen governor of New Netherland, arrived on what is now Manhattan Island. The Indians there greeted him in friendship and agreed to sell Manhattan to the Dutch. Minuit named the island New Amsterdam, and it became the capital of New Netherland. You can find the town of New Amsterdam on the map on this page.

New Netherland soon attracted many settlers. However, the Dutch began to treat the Indians as enemies. As a result, the two groups often fought.

In addition, the Dutch governors did not always rule the colony wisely. New Amsterdam, for example, had an ocean harbor and was well located for trade with Europe. Yet the governor did little to increase the colony's trade.

New Netherland becomes New York. In 1664 England and the Netherlands were at war. During this time a fleet of English ships anchored off the coast of New Amsterdam. The English captain ordered the Dutch to surrender. The Dutch colonists refused to help their governor, Peter Stuyvesant (stī′və·sənt), fight the English. As a result, New Netherland became the English colony of New York.

At first all the colonists in the New World received help from their homelands. However, in a short period of time they had to provide for their own needs. They learned quickly to use the resources of the land to grow food, to build houses, and to make clothing. They also learned much from the Indians who had lived on the land for thousands of years.

Checking Up
1. Who were three French explorers who claimed lands along the Mississippi River for France?
2. What answers would you give to the key questions at the beginning of this chapter?
3. *Why do you think the French generally had good relations with the American Indians?*

Background: The Indians grew angry as Dutch farmers cleared woods and destroyed the supply of game. In revenge some Indians terrorized the Dutch by burning Dutch homes. In turn, the Dutch often led attacks against the Indians.

Background: In 1691 King William and Queen Mary granted a new charter to the Massachusetts Bay Colony. The charter extended the colony's boundaries to include the Plymouth colony and Maine.
Map Skill: Location. Have students locate the thirteen colonies on the modern-day map on pages 18-19 and then compare the colonial and present-day boundaries.

The Growth of the English Colonies

As You Read

1. Think about these words.
   - subsistence farmer
   - plantation
   - representative government
   - indentured servant
2. Look for answers to these key questions.
   a. What were the thirteen English colonies along the Atlantic coast?
   b. Who were indentured servants?
   c. Why did the number of slaves in the Southern colonies begin to grow in the late 1600s?

Settling the Atlantic coast took over 100 years. At the end of this time, there were thirteen colonies along the eastern seaboard between New France to the north and the Spanish colony of Florida to the south. All thirteen colonies belonged to England. Thus the colonies were under English rule.

The New England Colonies

Tiny Plymouth was the first New England colony. The second was the Masssachusetts Bay Colony. This colony was also founded by the Puritans. Look at the map on this page. What were the New England colonies? How many New England colonies were there? 1

The Massachusetts Bay Colony. The king of England granted the Massachusetts Bay Company a charter to found a colony in North America. In the summer of 1630, seventeen ships set sail from England. On board were nearly 1,000 settlers, many of whom were Puritans.

Upon landing, the settlers founded Boston and other towns. These towns, along with Plymouth, made up the Massachusetts Bay Colony.

The Thirteen English Colonies
- New England Colonies
- Middle Colonies
- Southern Colonies
- Disputed Lands
- ----- Present-Day Borders

132   * **Reading Skill:** Building vocabulary. Have students look up the meaning of *charter* in a dictionary.
1. Conn., R.I., Mass., and N.H. Four.

Reading Skill: Organizing information. Have the class begin a data chart comparing the thirteen colonies.
Thinking Skill: Analyzing. Discuss why this book's authors featured Anne Hutchinson.

People Who Made a Difference

Anne Hutchinson

In 1634 a woman named Anne Hutchinson arrived in the Massachusetts Bay Colony with her husband. In a short time she earned a place among the leaders of the colony.

At first Hutchinson held weekly meetings at which the women of Boston exchanged ideas about sermons and other religious topics. Later, she began to speak out against some of the rules passed by the Puritans of the colony.

Anne Hutchinson's meetings began to attract many people in the colony. Because of her ideas, though, she also had many enemies. Finally, she was brought into court for speaking out against the Puritan leaders. The Puritan court found her guilty, and she had to leave the Massachusetts Bay colony.

Anne Hutchinson and a group of her followers settled on an island, which later became part of Rhode Island. Anne Hutchinson is remembered today as a leader who stood firm in her beliefs and who helped settle Rhode Island, one of the original thirteen English colonies.

In court Anne Hutchinson spoke out for her beliefs.

Rhode Island. The Puritans set up the Massachusetts Bay Colony to seek religious freedom and to practice their own religious beliefs. However, they did not always accept others in the colony who disagreed with their beliefs and rules.

Roger Williams, a Puritan minister, spoke out against many of the rules set by the Puritan leaders of the Massachusetts colony. Puritan leaders made plans to send Williams back to England. Before they could carry out their plans, Williams left Massachusetts. Along with some of his followers, he founded the colony of Rhode Island.

Connecticut. For years farmers from the Massachusetts Bay Colony had been moving into the rich Connecticut River valley. In 1636 Thomas Hooker, a Boston minister, led 100 members of his church south along rough Indian trails into the valley. In time their settlements became Connecticut.

New Hampshire. As the Massachusetts Bay Colony became more crowded, farmers moved north, first to the coast,

---

Thinking Skill: Comparing. Ask students how Hutchinson's and Williams's lives were similar.
Reading Skill: Using references. Have students find pictures of the Connecticut River valley.
* **Reading Skill:** Doing research. Have students list everything a farmer needed to bring to start a farm in the Connecticut River valley.

133

William Penn insisted on fair treatment of the Indians.

then inland to land along the many streams. The towns and farms that grew in this part of New England became known as New Hampshire.

Making a Living in New England

Most of the New England colonists were **subsistence farmers**. They were able to grow only enough for their families. Because of the rocky soil and short summers in New England, they were not able to grow extra crops to sell to other colonists or to send to England.

Farming was the main way of life in New England. Some important industries, though, grew up around the resources of the sea and the vast forests in New England.

Fishing became a major industry for many colonists who lived along the Atlantic coast. Fish were cleaned and dried and then shipped to England. Wood cut from New England's forests was also sent to England. These forests also became the source for a growing shipbuilding industry in New England.

The Middle Colonies

The colonies to the south of New England were the Middle colonies. Look again at the map on page 132. Name the Middle colonies. How many Middle colonies were there? 1

New York. At first New York covered a huge area between New England and Maryland. Because this area was so large, the English king granted parts of New York to other people.

New Jersey. One part of New York became the colony of New Jersey. New Jersey had long been home to farmers from the Netherlands, Sweden, and Finland.

To attract more settlers to their colony, the leaders of New Jersey granted freedom of religion and the right to set up a **representative government**. A representative government is one in which the people elect leaders to govern them.

Pennsylvania. The colony of Pennsylvania was founded by an Englishman named William Penn. As a young man, Penn had converted to the Quaker religion. Quakers refused to support the

*** **Reading Skill:** Doing research. Assign reports on Swedish or Finnish colonial settlements.
Citizenship Skill: Decision making. Ask students if and why they would have settled in colonial New Jersey or Pennsylvania.
1. Penn., Del., N.J., and N.Y. Four.

Background: William Penn made honest treaties with the Indians in Pennsylvania and kept his promises. These actions may not seem unusual today. In the 1600s, though, few English settlers would have done the same.

1. Md., Va., N.C., S.C., and Ga.

Church of England. Also, they would not fight in any war.

William Penn and his Quaker friends wanted to start a North American colony where people from all countries could live in peace. In 1681 the king of England granted Penn a large area of land along the Delaware River. The land had been part of the original colony of New York. Now it became Pennsylvania, whose name means "Penn's Woods."

Delaware. At first this colony was part of William Penn's land grant. In the early 1700s, however, Delaware became a separate colony.

Making a Living in the Middle Colonies

The soil in the Middle colonies was richer and less rocky than that in New England. The growing season was longer. Also, the land was drained by many rivers that could be used to carry farm crops to ports along the coast. Therefore, the Middle colonies became a major farming region.

The Southern Colonies

As you may recall, Jamestown, the first permanent English settlement in North America, became part of the Southern colonies. Look at the map on page 132. Find the Southern colonies. What were the names of the five Southern colonies?

Virginia. The success of the small farms along the rivers near Jamestown soon attracted many wealthy English landowners to Virginia. These landowners bought thousands of acres of land, and Virginia was soon one of the largest colonies along the Atlantic coast.

Maryland. Maryland was founded by Lord Baltimore, an Englishman who was a Catholic. Lord Baltimore wanted his colony to be a safe place for Catholics fleeing unfair treatment in Europe. Both Catholics and people of other Christian religions settled in Maryland. At first this mix caused problems. However, in 1649 the leaders of Maryland passed a law that gave religious freedom to all colonists in Maryland.

The Carolinas. In the mid-1600s, the English king gave eight of his friends permission to start a colony on land between Virginia and the Spanish colony of Florida. The new colony was named Carolina. In time, Carolina was divided into North and South Carolina.

Georgia. Lord John Percival and James Oglethorpe (ō′gəl·thôrp′) founded the colony of Georgia. At first the colony was to be a settlement for people from England who had been jailed for not paying their bills. Later, however, most of those who settled in Georgia were people who wanted to farm like the other settlers in the Southern colonies.

By the late 1600s, New York was a major trade center.

135

*** **Time Skill:** Have students find the dates of English settlement for all thirteen colonies.
Reading Skill: Using references. Assign reports on plantation life.
Communication Skill: Writing. Have students write letters in which they try to persuade a friend in England to come to Virginia and work as an indentured servant.

Making a Living in the Southern Colonies

As in New England and the Middle colonies, most people in the Southern colonies earned a living by farming. Most farming in the South, though, was different from farming in the other two regions. Landowners in the South grew great amounts of one crop, such as tobacco, rice, or cotton. Their huge farms were called **plantations**. They shipped most of the crop to England, where it was sold or exchanged for English-made goods.

Indentured servants. Many of the early colonists in North America were **indentured servants**. Indentured servants were men and women who were too poor to pay for the trip to the New World. They wanted to come, so they promised to serve an owner for five or more years. In exchange, the owner paid for their trip and gave them a place to live and work. At the end of their service, they were free to buy their own land or practice a trade. Many workers were needed to plant and harvest crops on large plantations in the South. As a result, many of the first indentured servants settled in the Southern colonies.

Slaves. Within twenty-five years after the founding of Jamestown, slave dealers began to sell captured Africans as slaves to the English colonists. Children born to these Africans also were slaves. Slaves had no say in where they lived or worked.

For many years the number of slaves in the colonies was small. However, as large plantations spread throughout the South, more and more workers were needed. By the late 1600s, a steady stream of slaves was being brought into the colonies. Although most slaves lived in the Southern colonies, some also lived in the other colonies.

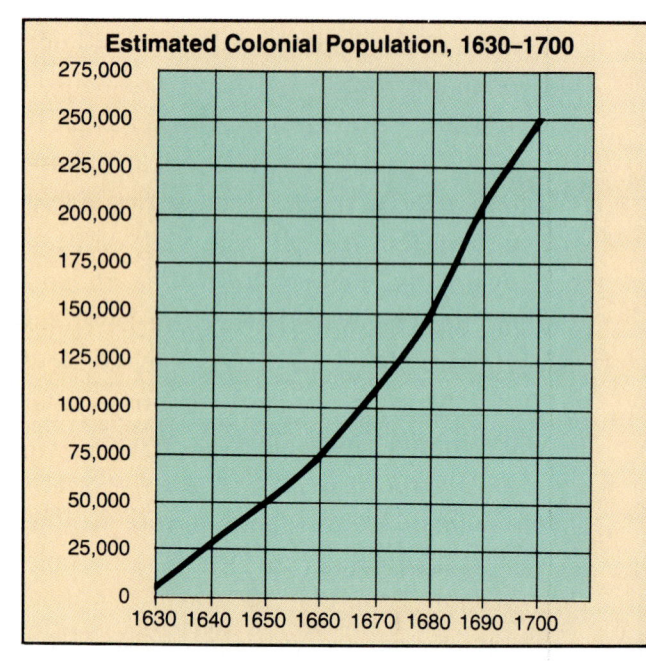

Look at the graph on this page. About how many people were living in the English colonies in 1630? How many were living in the colonies by 1700? 1

Estimated Colonial Population, 1630–1700

Checking Up

1. Who was Roger Williams?
2. Why were most farmers in New England subsistence farmers?
3. What answers would you give to the key questions at the beginning of this chapter?
4. *How were ways of making a living in the various English colonies similar? How were they different?*

Thinking Skill: Evaluating. Discuss the pros and cons of having indentured servants from both a servant's and an owner's viewpoint.
1. About 5,000 people. About 250,000 people.

Reading Skill: Using textbook features: *As You Read, 3.*
Thinking Skill: Comparing. Have the class begin a chart comparing colonial life with life today. The chapter's major topic headings can serve as categories.

Life in the English Colonies

As You Read

1. Think about these words.
   legislature   apprentice   frontier
2. Look for answers to these key questions.
   a. In what ways were the English colonial governments similar?
   b. What were three activities carried out on colonial farms?
   c. Why were most colonial farms and towns located near rivers or the seacoast?
3. Use this reading skill.
   This chapter describes what life was like for the early colonists. As you read this chapter, try to think how early colonial life compares with life in the United States today. For example, when you come to a major topic heading in the chapter, such as "Colonial Government," try to think of one way in which colonial governments were like our government today. Then try to think of one way in which they were different. By taking time to think about what you are reading, you will gain a greater understanding of our heritage from colonial times.

More than half of the people living in the English colonies came from England. Others came from different countries in Europe. With these colonists came a variety of ways of making clothing, building houses, and growing and preparing food. In time these ways changed. By the early 1700s, life in the English colonies was far different from life in England or in any other European country.

Colonial Governments

Although the king of England ruled all the colonies, each colony had some form of representative government. The first lawmaking body in the colonies began with the House of Burgesses in Virginia in 1619. Representatives to the House of Burgesses were chosen by free white men over seventeen years old. The House of Burgesses met once a year to make laws about such things as prices, boundary disputes, and trade with other countries.

New England and the Middle colonies also had **legislatures**, or governing bodies, that passed laws. However, as in the South, not all people could vote. In general only white adult men who owned land in the colonies were allowed to vote.

*** **Reading Skill:** Doing research. Have several students report on the House of Burgesses.

137

Early New England towns were built around a village green, or common. The church, school, and inn often stood closest to the village green. Colonists made community decisions at town meetings.

Colonial Farms

As you have learned, most of the people in the English colonies were farmers. Except for the large plantations in the South, farms were small, usually between 50 to 100 acres (20 to 40 ha). Each farm produced almost all of what a farm family needed.

Farm families, for example, made bread from the grains harvested from their fields. They ate the meat of their chickens, hogs, and cattle. Each year farmers sheared their sheep. Then the women of the household spun thread and wove cloth from the wool. Farmers used the wood from the trees on their farms to build and heat their houses.

Colonial Towns and Cities

Towns and cities were busy places. They were centers for the industries, such as iron making and shipbuilding, that grew up in the colonies in the late 1600s and early 1700s.

Business in the colonies. Most goods in the English colonies, however, were not made in large factories or mills. Instead they were made at home or in small shops in colonial towns.

Colonial shops were usually owned by people who were skilled in a trade such as clockmaking or glassblowing. These people were masters of a craft.

In early colonial days, a child learned a trade by working under the watchful eye of a master. The child, called an **apprentice**, went to live and work with the master at about the age of twelve. The master taught the apprentice a trade. At about the age of twenty-one, the apprenticeship was over, and the young person was free to open a shop.

Pilgrim dress and crafts are part of a restored colonial village in Plymouth.

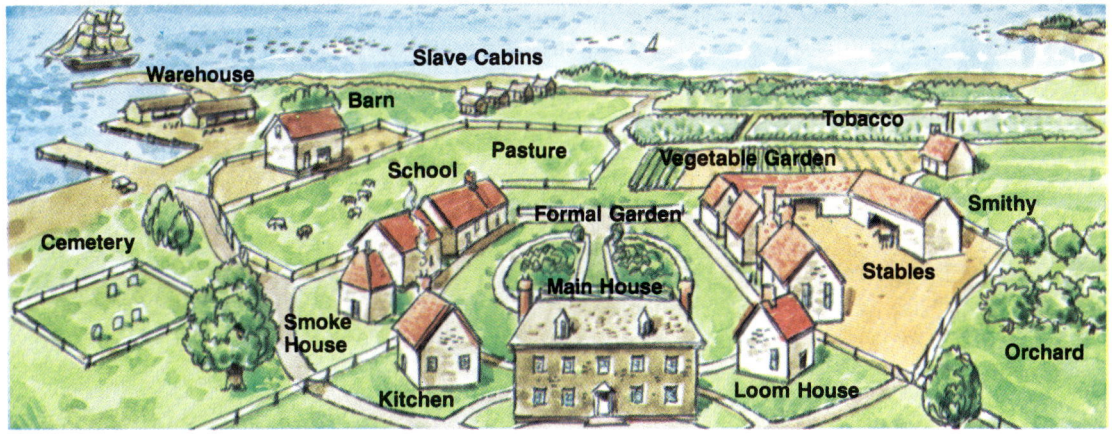

What similarities can you find between this picture of a plantation and the picture of a New England village on page 138?

Citizenship

A Contribution to Education

Good citizenship often means giving time or money to improve your community. In early colonial days, there were many colonists who helped make the colonies a better place in which to live. One such person was John Harvard.

John Harvard was a Puritan minister in the Massachusetts Bay Colony in the early 1600s. When Harvard died, he left his library of 400 books and also a large sum of money to a college in the Massachusetts town of Cambridge.

This college had been founded in 1636. At first the college had few books and little money. Its founders were not certain that the school could remain open. Then they received word of John Harvard's gift. The grateful founders changed the name of the college from Cambridge College to Harvard College. Today, this college is Harvard University. It is the oldest university in the United States. It is also one of the best-known universities in the world.

Transportation

Roads and waterways linked cities and farms and villages. Outside the towns, roads were rough paths. Stumps, mudholes, and many small rocks made travel slow and difficult.

Because the roads were so poor, colonists often traveled by boat rather than by carriage and wagon. It is not surprising that most cities, villages, and farms were on or near a waterway.

Colonial Houses

Almost all houses in the colonies were built of wood. On the **frontier**, or western edge of the colonies near the wilderness, famers lived in small log cabins. Most colonists had more comfortable homes, however, than the farmers on the frontier. The few wealthy merchants and landowners lived in fine houses filled with furniture made in Europe.

Even the finest colonial houses were not like our homes today. The houses were heated only by fireplaces. Most light came from a few whale oil lamps. Only in the houses of the rich did dozens of costly candles burn each evening. None of the houses had running water or indoor bathrooms.

Background: New England town meetings were a direct democracy in that the town's citizens voted on all decisions about their towns.
*** **Reading Skill:** Doing research. Assign reports on Harvard University as it is today.
Thinking Skill: Analyzing. Discuss apprentice programs, such as carpentry, that exist today.

Background: In the early days most furniture was imported, but in time more and more furniture was made by colonial craftworkers. Some carved and painted the furniture with original designs.
Math Skill: Discuss what *built to scale* means.

Then and Now

Colonial Furniture

In 1942 Mrs. James Ward Thorne presented the Art Institute of Chicago with a wonderful gift. It was a collection of miniature rooms. They traced the history of American houses and furniture from the 1600s to the present day.

The Thorne rooms were built to scale. Each room and piece of furniture is one-twelfth of its actual size. Great care was

What item was used to spin wool?

How many different pieces of furniture can you find in the picture above?

taken so that even the tiniest chair and candle would look exactly like the real pieces.

Shown at the top is one of Mrs. Thorne's American rooms. It is a model of the living room and kitchen of a house built in Massachusetts in the 1600s. Compare this model with the picture at the left of the present-day room furnished with colonial furniture. What items are similar in the two pictures? Why do you think some people today enjoy furnishing their homes with items similar to those used by the early colonists in North America?

Education

Colonial boys and girls either did not attend school at all or went for only a few years. Many were taught to read and write by their parents. Sometimes women held classes in their homes to teach reading and writing to neighborhood children.

Those who did attend colonial schools studied mostly reading, writing, and arithmetic. The sons of rich colonists were tutored at home and then were sent to school in England.

Checking Up

1. What was the first law-making body in the colonies?
2. What was an apprentice?
3. What answers would you give to the key questions at the beginning of this chapter?
4. *Why do you think early colonial life might have been more difficult than life today? In what ways might it have been easier?*

Reading Skill: Using references. Have students find pictures of colonial homes and furniture.
* **Reading Skill:** Building vocabulary. Have students find the meaning of *tutor* in a dictionary.

* **Map Skill:** Location. Have students locate the Indian tribes that once lived in the thirteen English colonies on the map on page 62.
** **Thinking Skill:** Knowing. Discuss whether people in the United States and in the world still get and die from smallpox, measles, or whooping cough.

The American Indians and the Europeans

As You Read

1. Think about these words.
   population   alliance
2. Look for answers to these key questions.
   a. What were two wars fought in New England between the colonists and the Indians?
   b. How did border struggles in the Southeast between the French, Spanish, and English affect the Indians there?
   c. What was the result of the Pueblo Revolt of 1680?

The Europeans who came to colonize North America did not arrive on the shores of an empty wilderness. As you learned in Unit 2, North America was home to people who had lived on the land before history was written. These people were the American Indians.

A Changing Way of Life

As the **population**, or number of people, in the European colonies in North America grew, the Indians' way of life began to change. The Europeans pushed farther and farther inland and settled new lands. As the Europeans moved farther inland, many Indians were pushed away from their homelands. Also, thousands of Indians died of European diseases such as smallpox, measles, and whooping cough.

Each group of American Indians has its own special history of dealings with the European settlers. Only a few of these histories are described in this chapter. They will give you some idea of what happened when colonists from Europe moved into the land of the Indian.

At first, most Europeans and Indians made friendly trade agreements.

*** **Time Skill:** Have students make time lines of important Indian events that occurred during the European colonization of the United States from 1500 to 1776. Students should use the time lines on pages 50–51, 82–83, and 114–115.

Metacomet was called King Philip because of his proud manner.

Indians were introduced to owners of the Georgia colony in England.

Eastern Woodland Tribes of New England

You read about some of the Eastern Woodland Indians in Unit 2. Look back at the map on page 62 and find the Pequot (pē′kwät′) Indians.

The Pequot War. In 1637 the English, angered over the murder of a colonist, burned a Pequot village. Pequot warriors attacked, and a war began.

The Pequot War was short but bloody. The colonists were determined to drive the Pequot out of the Connecticut River valley. Within one month most of the Pequot Indians had been killed. The rest were sold as slaves.

King Philip's War. Forty years passed before a second war was fought between the New England colonists and an Eastern Woodland tribe. This war was called King Philip's War. It was led by Metacomet, the son of the Wampanoag chief who had helped the Pilgrims when they first landed at Plymouth. The colonists called him King Philip.

Metacomet believed that his people could not live in peace with the white colonists. For nearly two years, Metacomet led the Wampanoag in war against the colonists. Hundreds of colonists and Indians were killed.

Tribes of the Southeast

The Creek and the Choctaw (chäk′tô′) lived in what is today the southeastern part of the United States. Find these two tribes on the map on page 62.

The French, Spanish, and English fought on and off for control of the southeast. For many years the Indians did not take sides in these fights. Finally, the tribes formed **alliances**, or friendly agreements. The Choctaw, for example, took the side of the French. The Creek joined the English, which meant that they became enemies of the Choctaw. Thousands of Indians from many different tribes eventually died in the European border struggles in this part of North America.

Background: Many of the early Europeans in the Southeast were fur traders. They bartered woven cloth, metal tools, and firearms for furs and deerskins that the Southeast Indians trapped.

Time Skill: Have students use the time line on pages 114–115 to figure out how many years the Wampanoag and the Pilgrims lived in peace before King Philip's War (55 years).

*** **Reading Skill:** Determining meaning from context. Discuss what is meant by the sentence "The Indian culture did not die."

The Pueblo Revolt

As you remember, the Spanish took over Pueblo lands in the Southwest in the early 1600s. In 1680, however, the Pueblo rose up against the Spanish. They killed hundreds of Spanish men, women, and children and destroyed every church. Within ten days the revolt was over. The last of the Spanish colonists had given up and had fled south.

The Pueblo victory did not last long, however. Twelve years later, Don Diego de Vargas (vär′gäs) recaptured New Mexico for Spain.

The coming of the Europeans changed the way many Indians lived. Still, the Indians kept alive many of their ceremonies and religious practices. The changes in the Indian ways of life were far reaching, but the Indian culture did not die.

Checking Up

1. Who recaptured New Mexico for Spain after the Pueblo Revolt?
2. What answers would you give to the key questions at the beginning of this chapter?
3. *In what different ways did population growth in the European colonies affect the lives of the Indians?*

Unit 4 Summary

- By the early 1600s Spain, France, the Netherlands, and England all had colonies in North America.

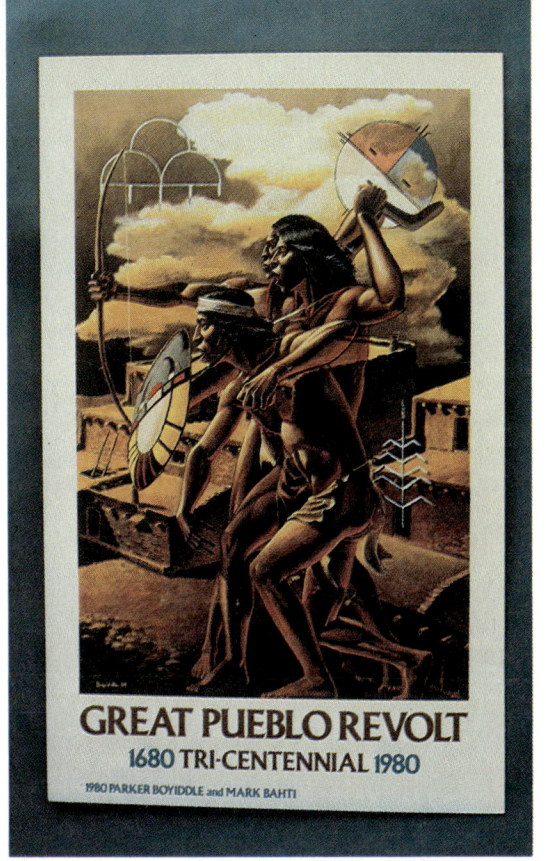

The Pueblo Revolt of 1680 is remembered in this recent poster.

- Spain's colonies were in the southern and southwestern part of what is today the United States.
- The colony of New France centered around the St. Lawrence River, the Great Lakes, and the entire Mississippi River valley.
- The Dutch and the English colonies were along the Atlantic coast.
- The English led the colonization of the Atlantic coast. Beginning with the tiny colonies of Jamestown and Plymouth, English leaders started thirteen colonies.
- All the European colonies were carved from lands that were the homeland of the American Indians. Gradually the Indians were pushed farther west.

** **Time Skill:** Ask students why the Pueblo revolt was commemorated in 1980. (It was 300 years after the event.)
Map Skill: Location. Have students find a map that supports each point in the unit summary.
Reading Skill: Interpreting visuals. Discuss how the chapter's visuals help explain the text.

Unit 4 Review Workshop

What Have You Learned?

1. What Spanish leader founded the colony of New Mexico?
2. Why were the Spanish not as interested in establishing colonies in North America as they were in Middle and South America?
3. Where did the English found their first permanent colony?
4. What were two major activites of the French in North America during the 1600s?
5. Which of the thirteen English colonies was first a Dutch colony?
6. How did most English colonists make a living?
7. What were two wars fought between the European colonists and the American Indians?

Use Your Reading Skills

It is often easier to understand information that has been organized into chart form. Divide a sheet of notebook paper into three columns. Head the first column "New England Colonies," the second column "Middle Colonies," and the third column "Southern Colonies." Study the following list of words. Then make a chart by writing each word or phrase in the correct column.

Jamestown
Plymouth
Anne Hutchinson
plantations
William Penn
Powhatan
New Amsterdam
Quakers
Mayflower Compact
House of Burgesses
New York
shipbuilding
New Jersey
Boston

Use Your Map Skills

The map on the next page shows the parts of North America claimed by England, France, and Spain by the early 1700s. Study the map closely. Then answer these questions.

1. Where was most of the land claimed by Spain?
2. Where were the thirteen English colonies in North America?
3. What colony in the Southeast was not an English colony?
4. French land claims were along which waterways?
5. Find the area that is now the United States. Which country claimed the largest part of this area?

Use Your Math Skills

Sometimes in order to understand the information on a graph, you need to use your math skills. Study the graph on page 136. Then answer the questions that follow. Answers to these questions will give you a greater appreciation of how fast the population increased in the English colonies during the 1600s.

1. How many years of population growth does this graph show?
2. About how many more people were living in the English colonies in 1650 than in 1630?

Reading Skill: Organizing information.
Thinking Skills: Knowing, analyzing.
Map Skill: Location.

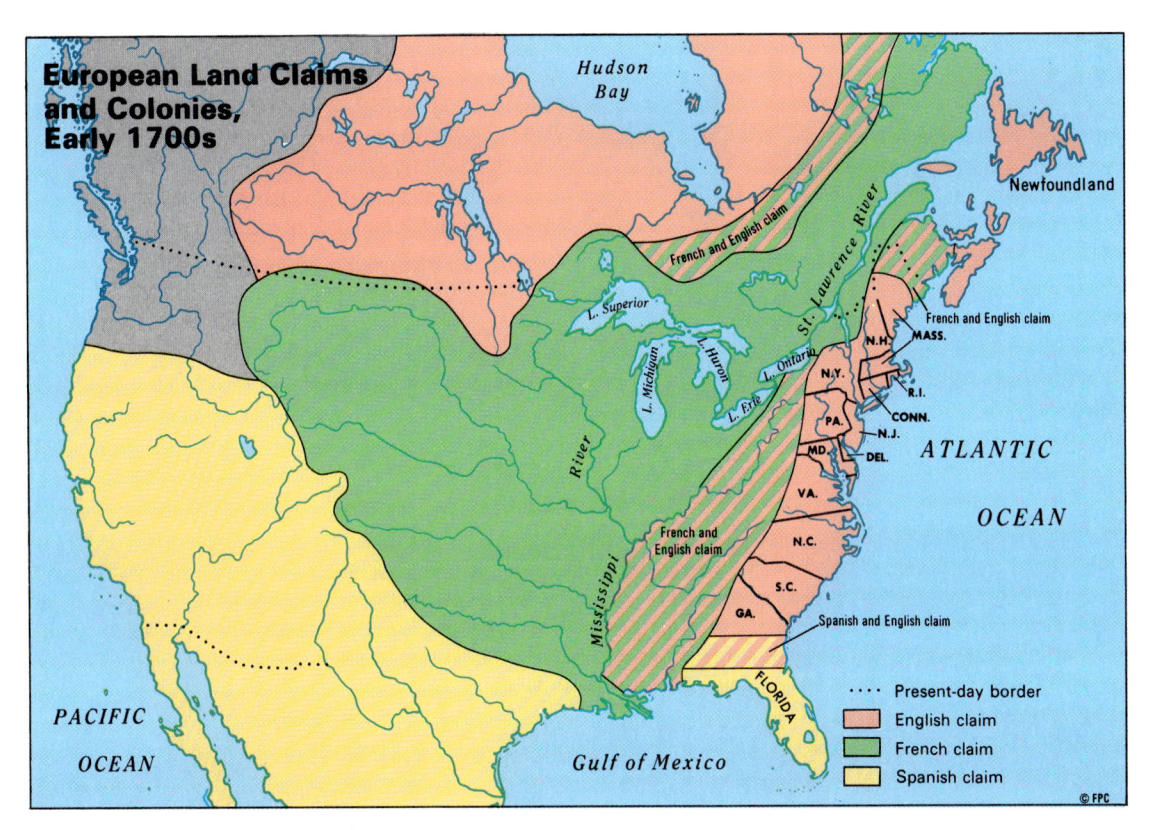

European Land Claims and Colonies, Early 1700s

3. During which ten-year period did the population of the colonies increase the most?
4. How many more people were living in the colonies in 1700 than in 1630?

Learn by Doing

1. Choose one of the thirteen English colonies, or the colony of New France or New Mexico. Imagine that you are a leader of the colony. You want to convince people in your homeland to settle in your colony. Make a poster or pamphlet that shows all the good things about your colony.
2. Below are the names of some of the leaders in colonial North America. Each wanted freedom for a certain group of people. Look in books and encyclopedias to find out more about one of these people. Write a short report in which you name the group of people this person led and what the leader did to gain their freedom.

James Oglethorpe	Thomas Hooker
Roger Williams	El Popé
George Calvert	Metacomet

Read to Learn More

Find the topics listed below in the card catalog of your library. Read all or part of a book listed under one of the topics. Share what you learn with your classmates.

INDENTURED SERVANT	PLYMOUTH
FUR TRADE, FRENCH	PLANTATION

Reading Skills: Organizing information: *Learn by Doing, 1*; using references: *Learn by Doing, 2*; doing research: *Learn by Doing, 2*.
Thinking Skill: Analyzing: *Learn by Doing, 1*.
Communication Skill: Writing: *Learn by Doing, 2*.

Unit Overview: This unit examines the years of transition from the thirteen British colonies to the new United States of America.

Unit Objectives
To understand:
- the French and Indian War
- colonial cities
- causes of the Revolutionary War
- the Revolutionary War
- the Constitutional Convention
- George Washington's term as President

Suggested Materials
Workbook
Unit Tests

Unit 5

Skills Emphasized
Map Skills: pp. 146, 151, 154, 155, 157, 170, 172, 178.
Social Studies Reading Skills: pp. 146, 148, 149, 150, 151, 152, 154, 155, 156, 157, 158, 159, 162, 164, 167, 168, 169, 172, 174, 175, 176, 177, 178, 179.
Thinking Skills: pp. 146, 148, 149, 153, 154, 155, 156, 157, 158, 160, 161, 163, 164, 167, 168, 170, 171, 174, 175, 176, 177, 178, 179.
Communication Skills: pp. 146, 150, 158, 159, 160, 161, 162, 163, 166, 170, 175.
Time Skills: pp. 146, 148, 149, 151, 157, 161, 163, 165, 169, 172, 174.
Social Studies Math Skills: pp. 153, 159, 160, 169, 170, 171, 173.
Citizenship Skills: pp. 163, 179.

Suggested Student Activities
   1. Arrange a bulletin-board display entitled "The Constitution."
   2. Make a movie roll on the key events in George Washington's life.
   3. Make a large map of events during the Revolutionary War.
* 4. Arrange a display on the Declaration of Independence.
*** 5. Organize a mural about women during the Revolutionary War.
** 6. Make a chart of the Bill of Rights.

Skills Emphasized in Suggested Student Activities
Map Skills: Distance, scale, symbolization.
Social Studies Reading Skills: Using references, doing research, organizing information.
Thinking Skills: Knowing, comparing, classifying.
Communication Skill: Writing.
Time Skill.

Creating a New Nation

People visit Independence Hall in Philadelphia to see where the Declaration of Independence was signed.

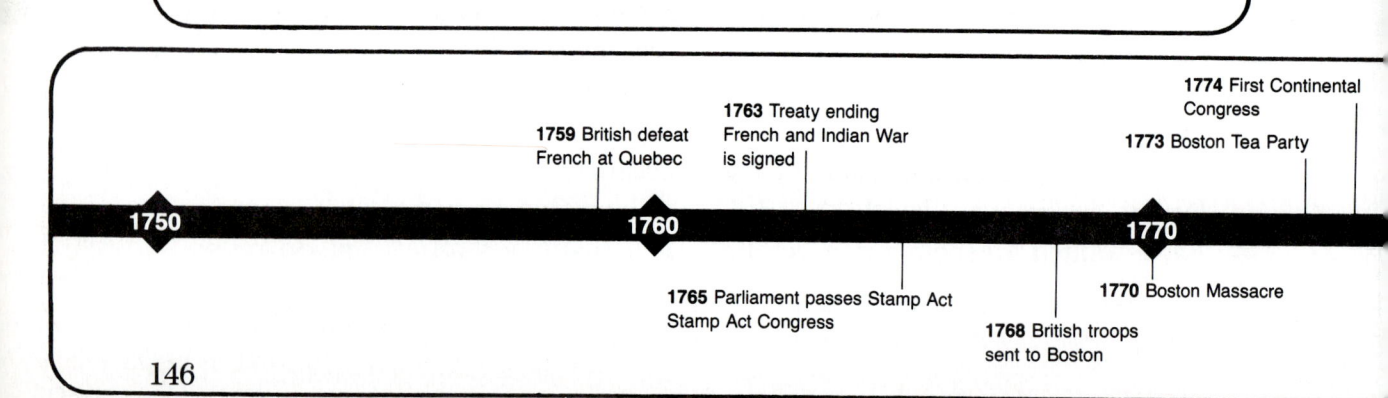

1750 — **1759** British defeat French at Quebec — **1760** — **1763** Treaty ending French and Indian War is signed — **1765** Parliament passes Stamp Act Stamp Act Congress — **1768** British troops sent to Boston — **1770** Boston Massacre — **1770** — **1773** Boston Tea Party — **1774** First Continental Congress

1777 Americans win the Battle of Saratoga	1787 Constitutional Convention	
1781 Americans win the Battle of Yorktown	1791 Bill of Rights is adopted	
1783 Treaty of Paris ending the Revolutionary War is signed		

1780 — **1790** — **1800**

- **1776** Declaration of Independence is signed
- **1775** Revolutionary War starts with the battles of Lexington and Concord Second Continental Congress
- **1789** George Washington becomes first President
- **1797** John Adams becomes President

147

The Struggle for North America

> **As You Read**
>
> 1. Think about these words.
>   ally   militia   treaty
> 2. Look for answers to these key questions.
>   a. What two things did the French do to claim lands west of the Appalachians?
>   b. Why did the British colonists want the French out of lands west of the Appalachians?
>   c. Why was the British victory at Quebec important?

As you learned in Unit 4, the French had carved out settlements along the St. Lawrence River and the Great Lakes in the early 1600s. At the same time, the English were settling much of the land along the Atlantic coast.

In the early 1700s, the English Kingdom, which included Wales, became a more powerful country. It joined with Scotland to become Great Britain.

The British and French were both proud of their growing colonies in North America. Yet France and Great Britain both dreamed of controlling even more lands in North America and in Europe.

The Struggle for More Land

France and Great Britain fought four wars during the 1600s and the 1700s. They fought each other in Europe and in North America. In North America the wars were fought to answer one important question: Who would control the eastern part of North America?

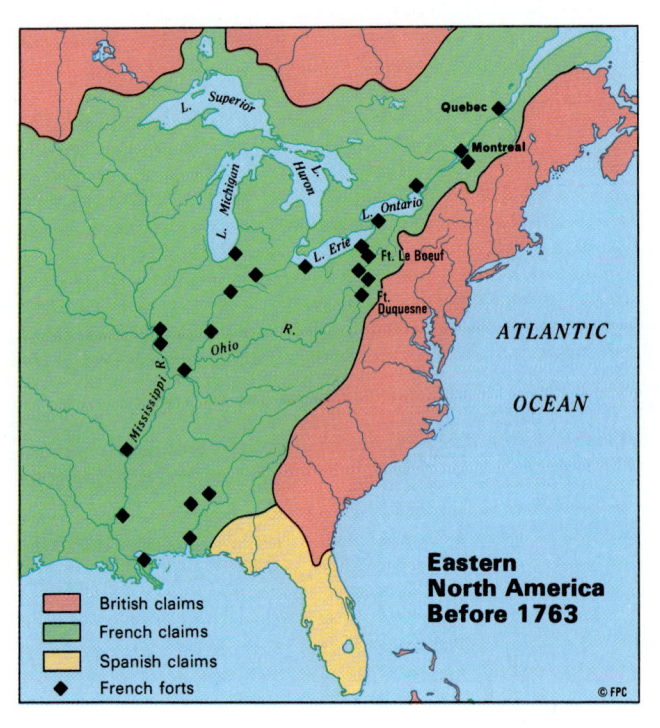

Eastern North America Before 1763

- British claims
- French claims
- Spanish claims
- ◆ French forts

The French claim. France claimed the eastern part of North America between the Mississippi River and the Appalachian Mountains. Find this area on the map on this page. French fur traders had set up trading routes and built trading

148

Background: George Washington had trained to be a surveyor. At age 17 he was appointed surveyor of Culpeper County, Virginia, and was kept busy surveying land grants.

Thinking Skill: Classifying. Have students make charts of the war using words, dates, places, and people for categories.

posts throughout the entire Mississippi River valley.

The British claim. Yet the British claimed these same lands west of the Appalachians. Over the years many British colonists who lived along the Atlantic coast had decided to move west. They settled the western edges of Pennsylvania, Virginia, and North Carolina near the Appalachians.

Some even wanted to move west of the Appalachians. These British settlers wanted more farmland and a greater share of the fur trade. They also wanted safety for their frontier settlements.

The French and Indian War

By the mid-1700s, the French had become worried about their lands west of the Appalachians. The British had set up companies to develop fur trading and farming north of the Ohio River in the Ohio River valley. Find this area on the map on page 148. Already one Virginia planter had hired a young man named George Washington to survey future plantation sites in the Ohio River valley.

Strengthening French claims. The leaders of New France decided to remind everyone in the British colonies that land west of the mountains was French. In 1749 these leaders sent a group of Frenchmen and Indians south of Lake Erie along the Allegheny River to the Ohio River. As they traveled along the rivers, they stopped to post metal markers on shore. These markers were to remind the Indians and the British that this land was French.

In 1753 the governor of New France ordered log forts built along these same rivers. These forts were for the soldiers who would protect the French claim to the Ohio River valley. Look at the map on page 148. How many French forts were built before 1763? 1

Word of these new forts reached the governor of Virginia. Virginia, along with some other colonies, claimed some of these lands as their own. The governor was alarmed and angered. "How dare the French move into British territory!"

Washington in the wilderness. The governor of Virginia sent George Washington to warn the French to leave British land. Washington delivered the governor's message to the French commander at Fort Le Boeuf (lə bəf). Find this fort on the map on page 148. The commander was polite, but he refused to withdraw his troops. Washington returned to Virginia.

The first shots. The next year the Virginia governor sent Washington back to the Ohio River valley with 150 Virginia soldiers. They were to capture Fort Duquesne (doō·kān′). However, the colonists failed to take the fort. A few days later, they did capture a group of French soldiers. During the fight shots were exchanged between French and British colonists. These shots marked the beginning of the French and Indian War.

Who fought the war? The French soldiers came from France and from the colony of New France. Fighting with the French were their Huron and Algonquin **allies**, or friends. You learned in Unit 3

---

* **Reading Skill:** Building vocabulary. Discuss the meaning of *survey* and how it relates to George Washington.

Time Skill: Have students begin a pictorial time line of George Washington's life.

1. Twenty-four French forts.

Background: Charles Willson Peale painted this portrait of Washington in 1772. At that time Peale was the leading portrait painter in the colonies. He was a Patriot and fought in the Revolutionary War. Peale is best known for painting portraits of the leading civil and military leaders during the war and for opening the first natural history museum in this country.

George Washington first served as a colonel in the Virginia militia.

Washington had warned the British about an ambush in the forest.

that the French had helped the Huron and Algonquin fight the Iroquois.

British troops arrived to defend the colonies. They were helped by colonial **militia** (mə·lish′ə). The militia of each colony was a group of farmers and shop owners who served as soldiers in times of emergency. The Iroquois, enemies of the Huron and Algonquin, also fought with the British.

British losses. British troops marched first against Fort Duquesne. They were joined by colonial militia led by George Washington. Their total force numbered about 1,500.

As the troops neared Fort Duquesne, shots rang out. They seemed to come from everywhere. The soldiers were surrounded, trapped by the enemy hidden in the forest! Some 850 Frenchmen and Indians had waited silently for the British to appear.

Washington was nearly killed by bullets that ripped through his coat. Twice the horses he rode were shot out from under him. Only about 500 of the 1,500 British and colonial troops lived through that bloody battle in July 1755.

The British defeat at Fort Duquesne was the first of many British losses. It began to look as if the French and Indians would win the war. Then the best British troops and the finest young generals were sent to America.

The British start winning. One by one, key French forts fell into British hands. Finally, the British were ready to attack the French stronghold of Quebec. After a long and fierce battle, the colonists of New France surrendered their capital city on September 18, 1759.

The French did not admit they had lost the war until their defeat at Mon-

*** **Communication Skill:** Speaking. Ask students to role-play interviewing a French soldier, an Indian ally of the French, and a militiaman about the battle near Fort Duquesne.
Reading Skill: Interpreting a visual. Discuss how the top right picture illustrates the text.

** **Map Skill:** Location. Have students make individual maps of eastern North America before and after 1763.
*** **Reading Skill:** Interpreting graphics. Have students use the information on the maps on pages 148 and 151 to make two separate pie graphs comparing the Spanish, French, and British land claims.

treal a year later. However, the British victory at Quebec proved that the British had won the right to control eastern North America.

Results of the War

The French and Indian War ended with the signing of a peace **treaty** in 1763. This agreement signed by both sides was called the Peace of Paris. France gave New France and the land between the Appalachians and the Mississippi River to Great Britain. Spain, which had been a French ally, gave Florida to Great Britain. To make up for this loss, France gave Spain the port of New Orleans and all the French lands west of the Mississippi River.

Compare the map on page 148 with the map on this page. Who now controlled the Mississippi River? Why did the British now say that they controlled half of North America? What lands were still claimed by France?

France was no longer powerful in North America. French trading posts and forts were abandoned. British colonists could now travel west of the Appalachians to settle rich new farmlands in the Ohio River valley.

Eastern North America After 1763

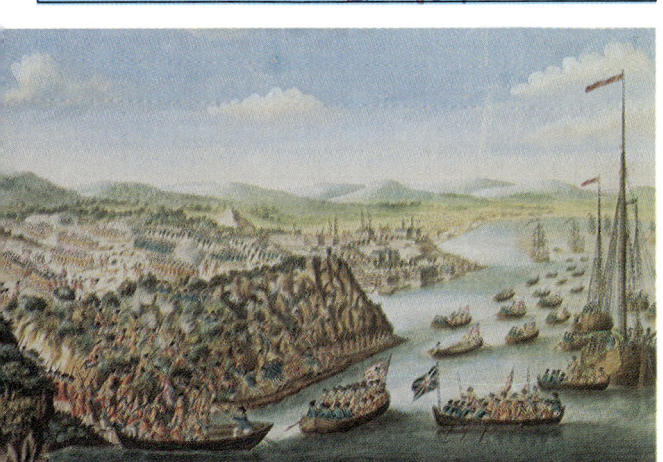

- British Claims
- Spanish Claims

The British landed more troops to fight the French for control of Quebec.

Checking Up

1. Why did the French worry about their lands west of the Appalachians?
2. What lands did France give Great Britain and Spain after the French and Indian War?
3. Which Indian tribes fought on the side of the French? of the British?
4. What answers would you give to the key questions at the beginning of this chapter?
5. *Why do you think Great Britain wanted to control the eastern part of North America?*

** **Reading Skill:** Doing research. Assign additional reading about the French and Indian War.
  Time Skill: Ask students how many years the French and Indian War lasted (nine years).
  1. The British. Because the British controlled all the lands east of the Mississippi River. None in North America.

Background: People of all nationalities were willing to come to the thirteen colonies and become British citizens because only Britain let foreigners settle in its colonies.
Reading Skill: Using references: *As You Read, 3.*

Colonial Cities: Centers of Business and Trade

As You Read

1. Think about these words.
   cash crop   merchant
2. Look for answers to these key questions.
   a. What did Philadelphia, New York, Boston, Charleston, and Newport have in common?
   b. What goods did the colonies ship to Great Britain?
   c. What goods did the colonies buy from Great Britain?
3. Use this reading skill.
   As you read this chapter, you may find words that you do not know. If the word is not listed in the Glossary, you should use a dictionary instead. A dictionary tells you the meaning of words. It also tells you how to pronounce words. Remember to use a dictionary when you read words that you do not understand.

The population of the thirteen British colonies grew rapidly from 1700 to 1770. In each colony new settlements were started, and older towns increased in size. More food and goods were needed for the growing population. As a result, trade between the colonies and Britain increased.

The Growth of the Colonies

Look at the chart on page 153. Notice that the population kept growing between 1700 and 1770. Some of the growth came about because colonists often had large families. In addition, more and more people from Britain, Ireland, France, and Germany came to the colonies to live.

The Growth of Colonial Cities

The population of the cities also increased as people arrived from nearby farms and from overseas. Philadelphia, New York, Boston, Charleston, and Newport were the five largest cities. Find these cities on the map on page 153.

Now look at the population chart on page 154. Which city had the largest population in 1743? in 1760? In which city did the population decrease between 1743 and 1760?

Colonial cities changed as more people moved to these urban areas. Many older cities began as farming communities. For example, in the early days farmers and their families lived in Boston and worked in the fields outside the city. As Boston

Reading Skill: Organizing information. Have students list reasons for the colonies' growth.
1. Boston; Philadelphia. Boston.

152

* **Thinking Skill:** Analyzing. Discuss why the largest cities were located near water.
* **Math Skill:** Have students use the graph below to figure out which decades had the most growth and the least growth (1760–1769; 1710–1719).

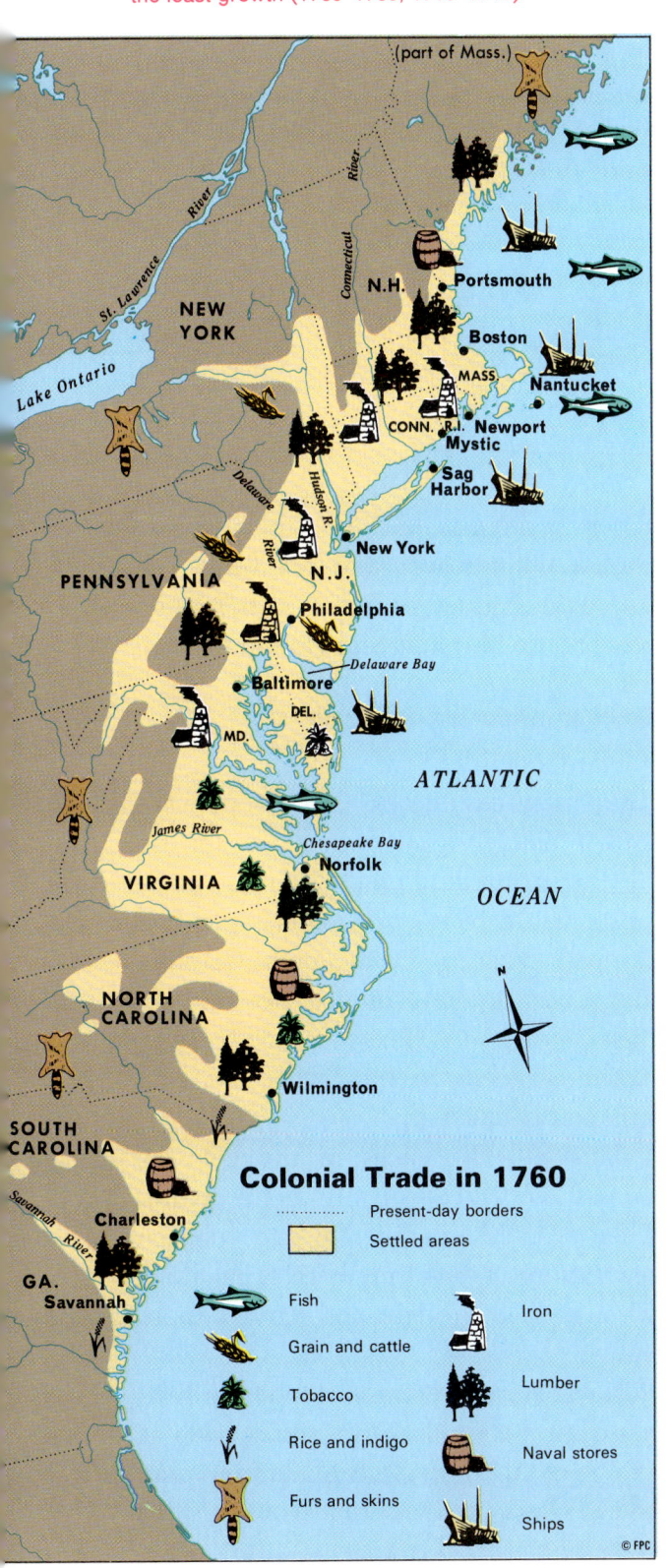

Which colonies on the trading map grew farm products?

grew, however, farmers moved away. There was not enough farmland left near the city. Boston was no longer a farming community. People had moved and begun new communities.

The largest cities were the centers of colonial trade. Look again at the map on this page. Where was each city located? All were seaports on bays or rivers leading into the ocean. All had harbors where trading ships could dock. If the city was on a river, other boats carried goods from farms and settlements farther west to the city. Which river flows into Philadelphia? into the city of New York? 1

Changing Patterns of Trade

In the early days, almost all colonial trade was with Britain. The colonies shipped raw materials such as lumber, tobacco, and furs to Britain. In return they

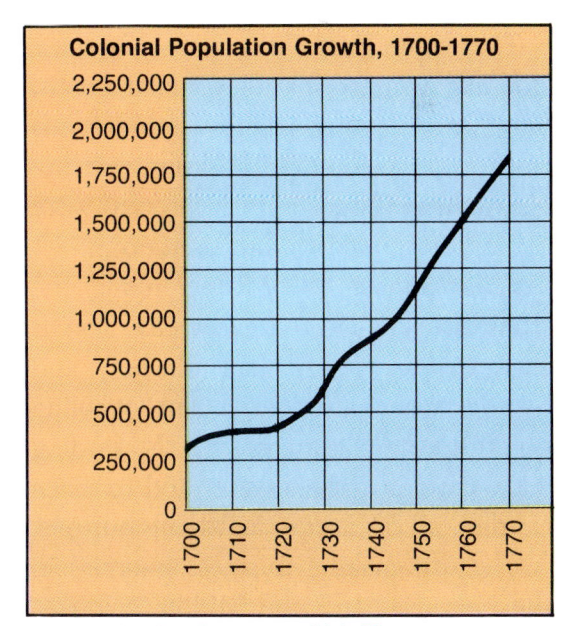

Colonial Trade in 1760

- Fish
- Grain and cattle
- Tobacco
- Rice and indigo
- Furs and skins
- Iron
- Lumber
- Naval stores
- Ships

Present-day borders
Settled areas

Colonial Population Growth, 1700-1770

Math Skill: Have students compare the graphs on pages 136 and 153 to figure out which 70-year period had steadier growth and more overall growth (the graph on page 136; the graph on page 153).
Thinking Skill: Knowing. Review why almost all colonial trade was with Britain.
1. Delaware River; Hudson River.

Growth of Five Colonial Cities, 1743–1760		
	1743	1760
Philadelphia	13,000	23,750
New York City	11,000	18,000
Boston	16,382	15,631
Charleston	6,800	8,000
Newport	6,200	7,500

received manufactured goods such as nails, farm tools, glass, and cloth. British ships, made from colonial lumber, carried the goods back and forth.

In time both manufacturing and farming became big business. Colonial industries such as shipbuilding and flour milling began producing finished goods. Other countries in Europe and their colonies in Africa and the West Indies began to trade with the thirteen colonies. A lively trade started among the colonies themselves.

New England Colonies and Trade

The New England colonies became shipping centers for all colonial goods. Ships from New England carried goods from every colony. In addition to shipping, other important industries were fishing, iron making, and lumbering.

From almost every town along the coast, fishers went out every day. Towns such as Nantucket, Sag Harbor, and Mystic were also important whaling ports. Locate these cities on the trading map. Parts of whales were used to make candles, oil for lamps, and bone buttons.

The iron-making business boomed in the New England and Middle colonies. Iron mills produced bars of iron that would later be shaped into nails or tools. For a long time, most of the iron bars went to Britain.

Middle Colonies and Trade

The Middle colonies shipped grain, meat, and furs. Farmers shipped barrels of wheat, corn, and salted meat down rivers to ports along Delaware Bay. Locate Delaware Bay on the trading map.

Fur traders traveled along the Hudson River to the city of New York in boats loaded with beaver and fox furs. The furs were shipped to Britain, where they were made into hats and clothing.

Southern Colonies and Trade

Planters in the Southern colonies grew three main **cash crops**. Cash crops were grown mostly for sale rather than for use by the planters. From Virginia, Maryland, and North Carolina, planters shipped tobacco. From South Carolina and Georgia, they shipped rice and indigo (in′di·gō′), a blue dye used to color cloth. Colonists in the South also sold furs and deerskins.

The 500,000 slaves in the colonies around 1770 lived mainly in the South. They worked on the rice and tobacco plantations. Great numbers of workers were needed to plant and harvest these crops.

Naval stores were also shipped to Britain from the South. Naval stores, such as tar, were liquid products made from pine trees. These products kept wooden ships watertight.

Slaves loaded and unloaded British ships that docked at plantations and towns in the Southern colonies.

Trading with the World

Trading ships built in New England sailed around the world. Ships returned from the West Indies with sugar and molasses. Molasses, a sugar product, was used to make rum in the colonies. Trappers sometimes traded their furs for rum.

Some New England **merchants**, or traders who bought and sold goods, made great fortunes in the slave trade. Their slave ships brought captured Africans to sugar plantations in the West Indies. Later, ships brought Africans to the thirteen colonies.

Close Ties with Britain

The colonists depended on Britain for goods they did not produce. They also depended on Britain for their cultural heritage, or way of living. The colonists did not want to forget that they were part of Britain.

Early colonial settlements looked like British towns. British plays were often performed in the Middle and Southern colonies. Wealthy merchants and planters visited Britain every few years.

The ties binding the thirteen colonies to Britain seemed strong. However, signs of trouble were beginning to be seen. Much of the trouble centered on trade. Since the colonies could trade with other parts of the world, maybe they did not need to depend on Britain as much as they had in the past.

Checking Up

1. Name two other places besides Britain that traded with the colonies.
2. What were three important goods produced in the New England colonies? in the Middle colonies? in the Southern colonies?
3. What answers would you give to the key questions at the beginning of this chapter?
4. *Why were seaports the colonial centers of trade?*

*** **Map Skill:** Location. Have students draw maps that show what was traded among the colonies, Britain, Africa, and the West Indies. Have them label the products at their place of origin.
   Thinking Skill: Analyzing. Discuss why the colonies had close ties with Britain.
 * **Reading Skill:** Determining meaning from context. Talk about the meaning of *signs of trouble*.

Reading Skill: Distinguishing fact from opinion: *As You Read,* 3.
Reading Skill: Doing research. Assign additional reading about the duties of Parliament.
Thinking Skill: Analyzing. Discuss why it was important that the colonists became used to governing themselves.

Breaking Ties with Britain

As You Read
1. Think about these words.
   tax   boycott   congress   repeal   Patriot
2. Look for answers to these key questions.
   a. Why did the British king forbid the colonists to settle lands west of the Appalachian Mountains?
   b. How was the Stamp Act different from other taxes passed by Parliament?
   c. Why was the First Continental Congress important?
3. Use this reading skill.
   It is important to read all the facts about an event before you form an opinion, or idea, about the event. For example, in this chapter you will read that some British soldiers killed four colonists in Boston. The colonists called this event the Boston Massacre. The British called it a terrible accident. After you read this chapter, think about these two opinions. Why did the colonial and British opinions differ? Be sure you can support your answer from facts you have read.

During the late 1700s, some colonists decided it was time to cut their close ties with Britain. These colonists felt that Britain had not paid much attention to its colonies during the French and Indian War. However, after the war King George III and Parliament, the British lawmaking body, became more interested in the thirteen colonies.

Government in the Colonies

The British king or queen had always chosen the governor and council of each colony. However, the British government was too busy fighting wars to give them much advice. Instead, the colonial assemblies decided many important matters in each colony. They got people to join the militia. They also collected money to run the colonial governments. The colonists became used to governing themselves.

King George III ruled Great Britain from 1760 to 1820.

The king says no. The colonists, however, did not always have the final word on colonial matters. For example, in the 1763 treaty ending the French and Indian War, the French gave the British control of lands west of the Appalachians. The colonists wanted to settle these lands.

In 1763 the king declared all lands west of the Appalachians to be Indian land. Many colonists were angry. They had fought the French to win these lands. Many settled there anyway.

Taxes in the Colonies

The British government needed more money after the war. The war had been costly, and troops were still needed in the colonies to protect frontier settlements. Parliament passed new laws to make people in Britain and in the colonies pay more **taxes**. Taxes were money collected to run the government.

The Acts of Trade. Before the war Parliament had passed a group of laws called the Acts of Trade. Some of these laws helped the colonies. Others did not.

Merchants and shippers were supposed to pay taxes on goods they shipped into or out of their colonies. Many did not. However, after the war those who did not pay were fined or arrested. So, many merchants stopped trading with other countries.

The Sugar Act. Parliament next passed the Sugar Act in 1764. The act taxed molasses. The tax increased the price of rum, which was made from molasses. This tax angered many colonists.

A stamp attached to a paper showed that the Stamp Act tax had been paid.

A New Kind of Tax

For a long time, only goods shipped to and from the colonies had been taxed by Parliament. The colonial assemblies approved all other taxes. Later, Parliament tried raising money a new way. In 1765 Parliament passed the Stamp Act. This act put a small tax on every important colonial paper, such as legal papers and newspapers. The colonies were to use this tax money to pay for the British troops stationed in the colonies.

The leaders in Parliament thought that the Stamp Act was quite fair. The colonists, however, were angry. They believed that only the colonial assemblies should have the right to tax the colonies. Some people burned the stamps. Others broke into the homes of stamp sellers. Most colonists, however, did not take part in these actions. Yet they refused to use the stamps. They also **boycotted**, or did not buy, many British goods. The effect of the boycott was felt in both Britain and the colonies.

Some Patriots, called the Sons of Liberty, burned the hated stamps.

The Stamp Act Congress. Massachusetts now called a meeting, or **congress**, of all the colonies. This was the first time that a meeting of all the colonies was held. Representatives from nine colonies met in New York in October 1765 to discuss their common problems.

The representatives pointed out that the colonists were not represented in Parliament. They could not vote on laws passed by Parliament. They agreed that only their assemblies should pass laws making colonists pay taxes to Britain. "No taxation without representation" became the famous cry.

Meanwhile, the king and Parliament saw that the Stamp Act was causing too much trouble. So Parliament passed a law that took back, or **repealed**, the tax. The leaders in Parliament, however, said they still had the right to tax the colonies and would do so.

Reading Skill: Interpreting a visual. Discuss how the picture explains many colonists' opinion of the Stamp Act.

New Taxes on Trade

Parliament next passed the Townshend Acts. These acts taxed glass, paper, and tea shipped from Britain. They also let British troops search the homes of some colonists.

To the shocked colonists, the new laws were not fair. Stories against Britain appeared in colonial newspapers. Many colonists again agreed to boycott British goods. A small group of colonists even dared to talk about freeing the colonies from British rule. They called themselves **Patriots**. They wanted the colonies to become a separate country.

Trouble in Boston

Then in 1768 more British troops were sent to Boston to keep order. Many people thought of the troops as enemies. An uneasy quiet settled on Boston for two years. Then something happened that proved more trouble was to come.

The Boston Massacre. On a quiet evening in March 1770, a group of young Bostonians spotted a British guard outside the Customs House. They tossed snowballs and then sticks at him. Other soldiers came to help the guard. The crowd started pushing and shouting insults. By then, the captain of the soldiers was shouting to his men, "Hold your fire!" Yet some soldiers fired. Four colonists fell dead in the winter snow.

Although the British called the shooting an accident, Patriots called it the Boston Massacre. They said the shooting was one more reason the colonies should separate from Britain.

Thinking Skill: Analyzing. Discuss the meaning of *No taxation without representation*.
Reading Skill: Interpreting data. Have students illustrate the story of the Boston Massacre.
Communication Skill: Listening. Read a colonist's and a British officer's account of the Boston Massacre. Ask students which description is more credible.

Background: Tea was also shipped to other colonies. However, Patriots in Philadelphia and New York refused to let the ships land. Ships docked in Charleston, but the tea was put into warehouses, where it rotted.
*** **Communication Skill:** Writing. Have small groups prepare features on the Boston Tea Party.

Repeal of the Townshend Acts. The same day as the Boston Massacre, Parliament repealed all the new taxes except one. They kept the tax on tea as a sign of Parliament's right to tax the colonies. Many colonists continued to boycott tea.

The Boston Tea Party

For the next three years, there was little trouble. Then a British trading company sent ships loaded with tea to the colonies. The people in Boston did not intend to buy the taxed tea. Some Boston Patriots did plan a "tea party," however.

A daring raid. On the night of December 16, 1773, three ships loaded with tea were resting in Boston Harbor. A group of fifty citizens, made up to look like Mohawk Indians, boarded the ships. They broke open nearly 350 chests of tea worth $75,000 and dumped the tea into the harbor.

The king punishes Boston. When word of the tea party reached King George, he ordered the port of Boston closed. No ships could leave or enter the harbor until the colonists paid for the destroyed tea. No town meetings could be held in Massachusetts unless the governor, who was appointed by the king, agreed. More troops arrived in Boston, and the colonists were ordered to feed and house them.

With the port closed, trading and shipping stopped. Yet help was on the way. Colonial assemblies as far away as Charleston voted to send food and money to Boston.

Many colonists cheered when they saw the British tea being dumped into Boston Harbor. The crowd watching numbered about 5000.

Reading Skill: Interpreting a visual. Ask students how the picture above adds to the text.
* **Math Skill:** Have students figure out how much one chest of the Boston tea cost (about $215).
*** **Reading Skill:** Doing research. Have students report on one of these famous Patriots: Samuel Adams, John Hancock, Patrick Henry, James Otis.

Background: Printer William Bradford made his newspaper below look like a tombstone to protest the Stamp Act. He announced that his paper was "expiring" because of the new tax on newspapers.
Thinking Skill: Observing. Point out that *s*'s were once printed as *f*'s, as the paper below shows.
Math Skill: Have students compare the number of newspapers printed then and now.

Then and Now

Newspapers

The earliest newspaper printed in the colonies was the *Boston News-Letter*. It first appeared in 1704. By early 1765 there were almost twenty-five colonial papers. Every colony except Delaware and New Jersey had at least one paper.

All were four-page papers that came out once a week. Each paper usually printed 1,500 copies. People read the papers and then passed them on to others to read.

Most of the news was about events in Britain and in the rest of Europe. The stories were often copies from London newspapers that shippers and colonists brought back from London. The papers also printed some local news. Reports about the colonial assemblies appeared. Advertisements for British and colonial goods were also part of the newspapers.

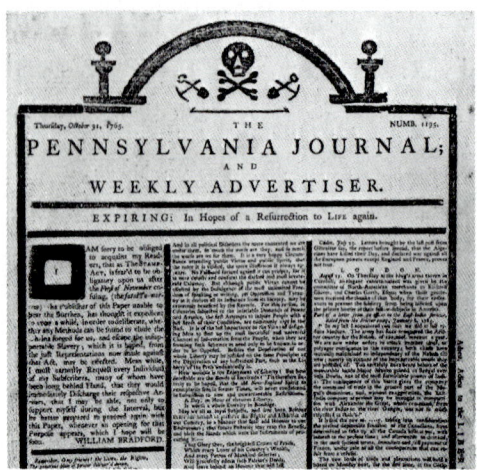

The Pennsylvania Journal and other colonial papers protested the Stamp Act.

Today over 1,700 newspapers are printed each day in cities across the United States. They carry up-to-date news from around the world.

The First Continental Congress

Alarmed colonial leaders decided to meet in Philadelphia in September 1774. Representatives, or delegates, from almost every colony attended this First Continental Congress.

After a month of discussion, the delegates took a strong stand. A message was sent to the king and to all the colonists. It said that the colonists would still be loyal to the king, but the king must allow them self-government.

The delegates agreed that the colonies would stop trading with Britain. The delegates also decided that the colonies would take over the mail service. Colonial leaders would use the mail service to keep in close touch.

The king and leaders in Parliament refused to let the colonies govern themselves. Once again some Patriots called for a break with British rule. The colonial ties with Britain were being stretched now to the breaking point.

Checking Up

1. What goods did the colonists boycott?
2. Name two events that angered colonists in Boston.
3. What answers would you give to the key questions at the beginning of this chapter?
4. *Give the meaning of this saying: "No taxation without representation."*

** **Thinking Skill:** Knowing. Have students find out how many copies of their local paper are printed each day or each week.
Communication Skill: Writing. Have the class make a newspaper of events in this chapter.
* **Communication Skill:** Listening. Read additional information about the First Continental Congress.

Background: General Thomas Gage was the British governor of Massachusetts. In 1774 he had been appointed governor and commander of the British troops in Massachusetts. He and George Washington once served together during the French and Indian War.

Time Skill: Have the class begin a time line of events during the Revolutionary War.

The Revolutionary War

As You Read

1. Think about these words.
   minuteman   independent
2. Look for answers to these key questions.
   a. What happened on July 4, 1776?
   b. Which were the two most important battles fought during the Revolutionary War?
   c. Which nations helped the Americans win the Revolutionary War?

The mists cleared slowly as dawn broke on Lexington Green. In the faint light, two groups of soldiers faced each other across the green. On one side, well-armed British soldiers stood in orderly rows. On the other side, colonial farmers, shop owners, doctors, and lawyers lined up. Then a shot was fired, and another and another.

Eight Patriots died on Lexington Green. They were the first to die in the war later called the Revolutionary War. The date was April 19, 1775.

The Fighting Begins

From Lexington the British soldiers marched to neighboring Concord. There they exchanged fire with farmers and other citizens of that tiny town.

The first shot. No one knows who fired the first shot at Lexington. A British soldier might have fired first. The soldiers had marched all night from Boston. By morning they were weary and expecting trouble. Or it could have been one of the Patriots. They had drilled for months. Their promise "to fight on a minute's notice" gave them the nickname **minutemen**.

The British governor of Massachusetts had learned that Patriots were storing gunpowder and other war supplies in Concord. He ordered the troops to march to Concord and destroy the forbidden supplies. Lexington was on the way to Concord.

Lexington militia defended their town in the first battle of the war.

* **Thinking Skill:** Analyzing. Discuss why no one knows who fired the first shot at Lexington.
Communication Skill: Writing. Have students write stories about what happened at Lexington.

161

The warning. The minutemen in Lexington and Concord knew that the British were coming. They did not, however, know when or by which route. Then on the evening of April 18, 1775, Patriots Paul Revere and William Dawes learned that British troops in Boston were gathering near the Charles River.

Revere told the news to two Patriots, who then slipped into Old North Church. There they hung two lanterns. The minutemen spotted the signal. They knew then that the British were coming by water. At the same time, Revere and Dawes rode horseback through the countryside spreading the word, "The British are coming!"

The Second Continental Congress

News of the fighting at Lexington and Concord spread throughout the colonies. Colonial militias began drilling. Colonial leaders planned to meet and discuss their problems at the Second Continental Congress in Philadelphia.

Although members of the Congress wanted peace with Britain, they prepared for war. They started the Continental Army, made up of militia from each colony. They elected George Washington of Virginia to be commander in chief of the new army.

The fighting goes on. The delegates to the Congress talked and argued through the long, hot summer. Meanwhile, fighting went on between colonial and British troops. They fought battles at Bunker Hill and at British Fort Ticonderoga. Locate both places on the map on page 163.

The Declaration of Independence told what Americans were fighting for.

Declaring independence. Finally, after months of discussion, a delegate from Virginia suggested that the Congress declare the thirteen colonies **independent**, or free, from Britain. A five-member committee went to work on the declaration. Thomas Jefferson wrote the final document.

On July 4, 1776, the delegates accepted the Declaration of Independence. One by one, the representatives from each colony signed the Declaration. The Declaration of Independence signaled the birth of a new country—the United States of America. The colonists were proud to call themselves Americans.

Ideas in the Declaration of Independence. The Declaration listed the colonists' complaints against King George III. It also said that all people are created equal. This meant that all citizens share the same rights. These rights include the rights to life, liberty, and the search for happiness.

> **Communication Skill:** Writing. Have each student report on a signer of the Declaration.
> **Thinking Skill:** Knowing. Discuss some nations that have recently declared their independence.
> **Time Skill:** Have students compare the length of time that the thirteen British colonies existed with the time that the United States has been a nation.

The Declaration said that a government is formed to serve the people. If a government fails to protect the rights of the people, the people have the right to change the government.

Choosing loyalty. Some colonists would not fight Britain. They were called Loyalists. Some Loyalists joined the British army. Others fled to Canada or to Britain. Most, though, remained in the colonies and quietly hoped for peace.

Fighting for Independence

Washington's army was made up of volunteers. They usually signed up for one year. Soldiers of the Continental Army received little pay. When their terms ended, most returned to their farms or shops. Some later rejoined the army. Soldiers joined and left so often that Washington seldom knew how many troops he had.

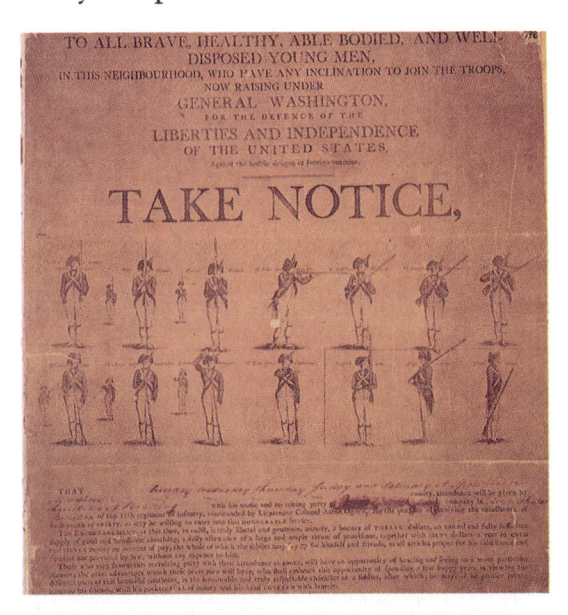

Major Battles of the Revolutionary War
- ★ U.S. Victory
- ★ British Victory
- → U.S. Troops
- → British Troops
- ···· Present-Day Borders

Men from every state left their families and jobs to join the Continental Army.

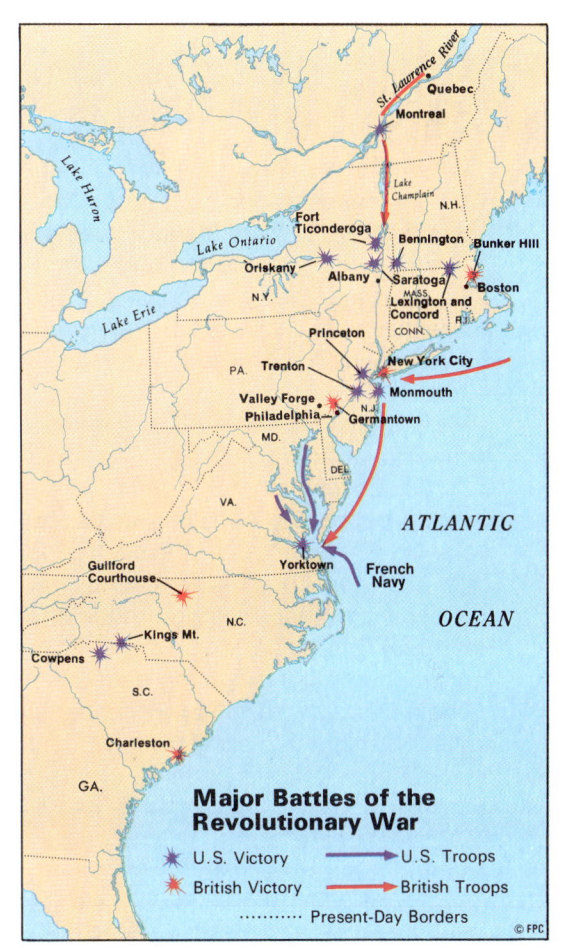

The course of the war. Most of the early battles took place in the North. The Patriots regained Boston. However, British soldiers took over New York and Philadelphia. British ships carrying more troops docked at these ports.

Fighting also took place in the South and near the Great Lakes. There was fighting along the St. Lawrence River as well as along the Mississippi and Ohio rivers on the western frontier. In western New York, U.S. troops fought Iroquois tribes who had sided with the British. At sea the U.S. navy captured ships loaded with British war supplies.

> **Citizenship Skill:** Decision making. Ask students if and why they would have fought as a Patriot or as a Loyalist.
> **Thinking Skill:** Classifying. Have the class make a chart of the war using key names, dates, places, and words.

Background: King George III hired nearly 30,000 Germans to reinforce British troops. These Germans fought in most of the major battles. After the war nearly 5,000 remained here to begin a new life.
Monmouth (män′məth)
* **Reading Skill:** Organizing information. Have students list the roles of women during the war.

People Who Made a Difference

Women in the War

When the men went off to fight the war, life changed for everyone. Most women stayed home to manage the family farms or shops. Some wives, however, went with their husbands to camp. There they cooked, washed, and nursed the wounded. Some women even fought in the war.

Mary Ludwig Hays earned her name Molly Pitcher at the Battle of Monmouth in 1778. Locate the battle site on the map on page 163. All day she carried water in a pitcher to the tired troops. Later that day her husband, who fired one of the cannons, was wounded. Mary Hays took his place loading and firing the cannon until the fighting ended.

Lydia Darragh (dăr′ō) of Philadelphia saved Washington's army from a British attack. British officers had been housed with her and her family. One day in 1777, she heard some of the officers planning a surprise attack on Washington's camp outside the town. Darragh slipped out of town and walked more than 13 miles to warn the U.S. army of the plan. When the British marched to the camp, the Patriots were ready.

Mary Ludwig Hays loaded and fired a cannon at the Battle of Monmouth.

People remember Deborah Sampson as our country's first woman soldier. Dressed as a boy, she asked to serve in a Massachusetts fighting group in 1782. She fought in several battles and was wounded twice.

Women found ways to help fight the war. Whether they sewed shirts for the soldiers or nursed the wounded, they helped win the Revolutionary War.

Winning the War

For a long time, no one could tell who would win the war. Two battles were the keys to a United States victory. These two important battles were fought at Saratoga and Yorktown. Locate these battle sites on the map on page 163.

The Battle of Saratoga. In 1777 British troops planned to march south from Quebec to Albany, New York. Their plan was to separate New England from the rest of the colonies. Follow the route from Quebec to Albany on the map on page 163.

The British never made it to Albany. When the British got to Saratoga, they found that U.S. troops outnumbered them two to one. Without help, the British could not hold off the enemy. Help never came. On October 17, 1777, more than 5,000 British troops surrendered at Saratoga.

Aid from abroad. News of the great victory at Saratoga reached Europe. France decided to help the United States defeat their common enemy, Great Britain. The French sent badly needed clothing, firearms, and money. They also sent

*** **Reading Skill:** Doing research. Assign reports on these famous women: Mary K. Goddard, Nancy Hart, Sybil Ludington, Martha Washington.
Thinking Skill: Analyzing. Discuss why the Battle of Saratoga was so important.
Reading Skill: Using references. Assign additional reading about the Marquis de Lafayette.

Generals Lafayette and Washington visited their troops at Valley Forge during the cold winter of 1777–1778.

part of their army and navy, including the famous General Lafayette (läf′ē·et′). Soon Spain and the Netherlands also helped. They loaned the United States money to help pay for the war.

The Battle of Yorktown. The other important battle was fought in October 1781 at Yorktown. The British army waited at Yorktown for more troops. British ships sailing from Britain and New York were expected soon.

Meanwhile, thirty French ships carried U.S. troops to Virginia. Washington marched south to Virginia with more troops. As the troops neared Yorktown, they cut off the British escape by land.

French ships later met the British navy on its way to help the British troops. For two hours the cannons fired. The French navy won. The British navy sailed back to New York. The British at Yorktown could no longer count on a quick escape by sea.

The British troops at Yorktown were trapped. Less than three weeks later, the British army surrendered. The date was October 17, 1781, exactly four years after the British surrender at Saratoga.

With the defeat at Yorktown, the British had had enough of war. The king and Parliament were willing to make peace with the United States.

The Treaty of Paris. In 1783 representatives from Britain and the United States signed a peace treaty. Britain gave the United States the land east of the Mississippi River and south of Canada, except for Florida. Britain returned Florida to Spain. Even more important, the British agreed that the thirteen colonies were indeed independent.

Checking Up

1. Who were the minutemen? Where did they fight the British?
2. Who wrote the final Declaration of Independence? Who approved it? Where did this take place?
3. What answers would you give to the key questions at the beginning of this chapter?
4. *Why was it important for the Americans to have allies during the Revolutionary War?*

Background: Another result of the war was the end of the Iroquois League described on page 76. Two Iroquois tribes had sided with the Patriots; the other tribes had joined the Loyalists.
Time Skill: Have students use the time line on pages 146–147 to figure out how long the war lasted (eight years).

Background: After the war most states ignored the pleas of Congress for money. Money was needed to run the government and to repay French and Dutch war loans.
** Communication Skill: Listening. Read a story about Daniel Boone.

Forming a New Government

As You Read

1. Think about these words.
   convention   democratic republic
   constitution   amendment
2. Look for answers to these key questions.
   a. Why did fifty-five Americans meet in Philadelphia in 1787?
   b. What are the three branches of our country's government?
   c. What is the Bill of Rights?

With the signing of the Declaration of Independence, the thirteen colonies became the first thirteen states of the United States of America. During the war all the states had worked together to defeat the British and to become a new country. After the war the country's leaders had to find other ways to unite the states and solve their problems.

Problems in the West

As you learned earlier, King George had closed the lands west of the Appalachians to settlers in 1763. Now settlers poured into the forests and farmlands of what later became the states of Kentucky and Tennessee. Who would govern this new frontier? What should be done about the Indians in the West?

Other problems needed solutions. British troops still held seven forts just south of the Canadian border on United States land. Spain also had forts on U.S. land near the important port of New Orleans. In the Southeast, Creek, Choctaw, and Chickasaw tribes raided frontier villages. In return settlers destroyed Indian fields and villages.

Other Problems

In the port cities along the Atlantic coast, shipping had slowed. Before the war, colonists sold almost all their goods to Britain and its other colonies. Now Britain would not allow any U.S. ships to dock at its colonies in the West Indies. Remember that the West Indies were an

Daniel Boone led groups of pioneers to the Kentucky wilderness.

George Washington watched with pride as the delegates to the Constitutional Convention signed the Constitution.

important part of colonial trade. So U.S. merchants had to set up new trade routes with other countries.

In addition, some states acted like separate nations. They argued over borders and taxed trade with other states. Some even issued their own money.

The Constitutional Convention

Some kind of plan was needed to unite the states. The country's leaders called a special meeting, or **convention**. In the spring of 1787, delegates from the states met in Philadelphia. Their purpose was to write a **constitution**, or plan of government, for the United States. Among the fifty-five delegates elected to the Constitutional Convention were shippers, planters, teachers, and lawyers. The people at this convention were later called the founders of our country.

The delegates chose George Washington as president of the convention. Then they began working. The delegates took four months to write the United States Constitution. By the fall of 1787, they were ready to present the new Constitution to the rest of the country.

The Constitution

The Constitution called for three branches of government: the executive branch, the legislative branch, and the judicial branch. The Constitution stated the duties of each branch. No branch was given more important duties than the other two. The writers of the Constitution did not want any one branch to be stronger than the other two. Our government still follows this plan.

Form of government. The writers of the Constitution remembered the famous saying "No taxation without representation." They remembered that the colonists had to pay British taxes. Yet no colonists could be in Parliament.

Thinking Skill: Analyzing. Talk about others in this country—shopkeepers, plantation owners, craftworkers—who were affected by the loss of British markets after the war.

* **Reading Skill:** Determining meaning from context. Review the meaning of the phrase *No taxation without representation.*

Background: Most of the delegates to the Constitutional Convention had attended the two Continental Congresses and helped write their new state constitutions.
Thinking Skill: Analyzing. Discuss why the delegates are called the founders of this country.
Reading Skill: Organizing information. Have the class make a chart of the delegates.

The writers of the Constitution made sure that the former colonists would have some say in their new government. The writers chose to make the United States a **democratic republic**. The people would govern. They would decide what plan of government they wanted. Making such decisions makes our government democratic. However, the people decided to elect representatives to run the government and make the laws. Choosing representatives makes our government a republic. So in a democratic republic, the people govern through their representatives.

The executive branch. The President is the head of the executive branch. The President is elected for a four-year term by the people. The Vice-President helps the President.

United States Documents

Using the Constitution

The United States has changed in many ways since the late 1700s. Yet the Constitution, written in 1787, describes the plan of government that our country still uses today.

The Constitution divides our government into three branches. The first chart below lists important powers of these branches. The second chart below lists limits on each branch.

Powers of the Three Branches of Government		
Legislative Branch *Congress* • Makes laws • Approves appointments made by the President • Declares war	**Executive Branch** *President* • Suggests laws • Approves or disapproves laws • Sees that laws are carried out	**Judicial Branch** *U.S. Supreme Court* • Decides if a law disagrees with the U.S. Constitution • Decides cases between states • Judges whether or not people's rights have been taken away

Limits on the Three Branches of Government		
Congressional Limits • President can refuse to approve laws passed by Congress • Supreme Court can do away with a law if the law does not follow the Constitution	**Presidential Limits** • Congress must approve Presidential appointments • Congress can pass some laws without the President's approval • Congress can remove the President	**Judicial Limits** • President appoints Supreme Court and other judges • Congress can remove a judge

---

** **Thinking Skill:** Observing. Explain the three parts of the Constitution—the preamble, articles, and amendments.
*** **Thinking Skill:** Analyzing. Ask students to use the chart above to give examples of the checks-and-balances system of government.

Math Skill: Have students tell how many senators and representatives represent their state.
*** **Reading Skill:** Using references. Ask students to name the nine current Supreme Court justices.
* **Math Skill:** Ask students how many constitutional amendments are in effect (twenty-six).

The legislative branch. This branch is called the Congress. It is made up of two groups of elected representatives. One group is the Senate. Each state now elects two people to serve as senators for a six-year term. The second group is the House of Representatives. The number of representatives from each state depends on its population. The greater the population, the more representatives a state has. Representatives to the House are elected every two years.

The judicial branch. This branch is made up of certain courts throughout the country. The highest court is the Supreme Court in Washington, D.C. Today nine justices, or judges, serve on the Supreme Court. Each is chosen by the President and approved by the Senate. They serve on this court for life.

Accepting the Constitution

For the Constitution to become law, at least nine of the thirteen states had to approve it. In each state people were elected to study the Constitution and decide if it should become law.

In many states the supporters of the Constitution had a hard time getting others to believe that this was a good plan of government. However, each state finally voted to accept the Constitution. Some people, though, were still troubled. They thought the Constitution should say more about the rights of each citizen.

The Bill of Rights

Wisely, the writers of the Constitution had planned a way to make changes in the Constitution. These changes are called **amendments**. Amendments either add to or take out parts of the Constitution. After the Constitution became law, ten amendments were added in 1791. These amendments are known as the Bill of Rights.

The Bill of Rights states that the government can never take away the rights and freedoms of United States citizens. It then lists these rights and freedoms. The First Amendment, for example, says every citizen in this country has the right to worship freely, speak freely, and print all the news.

The founders included in the Constitution everything they thought would be needed for our government to run well. The founders even put in the Constitution the oath, or promise of trust, that every President would repeat before accepting this important job.

Checking Up
1. Name two problems in the lands west of the Appalachians after the Revolutionary War.
2. What are three duties of Congress? of the President?
3. What answers would you give to the key questions at the beginning of this chapter?
4. *Look again at the chart on page 168. Name one duty that involves at least two branches of government. Why is it important that both branches have some say in this matter?*

*** **Time Skill:** Ask students to list the first thirteen states in the order they accepted the Constitution (Del., Pa., N.J., Ga., Conn., Mass., Md., S.C., N.H., Va., N.Y., N.C., and R.I.).
** **Reading Skill:** Paraphrasing. Read the Bill of Rights. Then have the class paraphrase each amendment to the Bill of Rights.

Thinking Skill: Knowing. Ask students where their state capital is located and what state functions take place there.
Map Skill: Scale. Have the class make a display of maps with different scales.
Communication Skill: Writing. Ask students to make travel brochures of Washington, D.C.

Maps Tell a Story of Distance

As you read, think about these words.
capital   map scale   Capitol

Imagine that you are going to visit Washington, D.C., the **capital** of the United States. The President, Congress, and the Supreme Court all have offices there. Many other government offices are also in this city.

To plan a trip there, you would need to know how far your town is from Washington, D.C. You would need a map to measure the distance between the two places. Then you would need to know how to measure distances accurately on a map.

Describing Map Scale

Somewhere on most maps is a **map scale** of miles and/or kilometers. The scale tells the relationship between distance on the map and distance on the earth. In other words, the scale shows that so much distance on the map is equal to so much distance on the earth's surface.

Reading a map scale. Look at the map of Washington, D.C., on this page. The map shows the capital and the area surrounding it. Find the map scale in the lower left-hand corner.

Read the line under the scale that begins, "One inch . . ." Map makers use this scale to tell you how much smaller the area on the map is than the real area. So one inch on this map stands for about four miles of the real area in Washington, D.C.

Locate Arlington Cemetery and the **Capitol** on this map. Congress works in the building known as the Capitol. If you measure the distance between these places, it is about one inch. The real distance is about four miles.

Map scale is usually written in miles and kilometers. The numbers above the line show the scale for miles. What do the numbers below the line show? Those rows of numbers above and below the line begin with zero. What is the highest number above the line? below the line? What do both numbers mean?   1   2

Washington, D.C.—Map A

1 Capitol
2 Washington Monument
3 Lincoln Memorial
4 White House
5 Jefferson Memorial
6 Arlington Cemetery

SCALE
ONE INCH — ABOUT 4 MILES

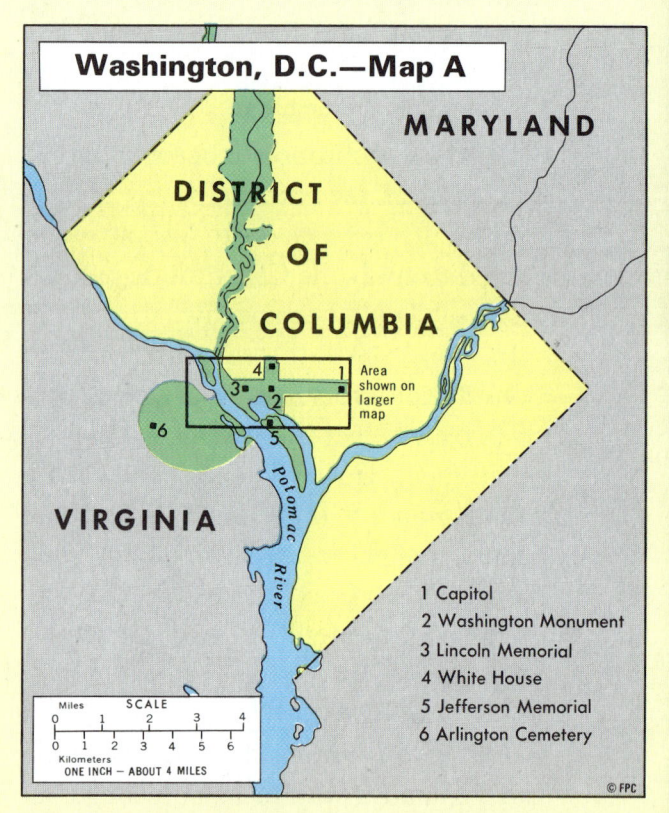

Math Skill: Have students figure out how far 4 miles is from their school. Then have them tell what to include on a map in a square inch surrounding their school if the map scale is 1 inch = 4 miles.
1. The scale for kilometers.
2. 4; 6. One inch on the map equals about 4 miles, or about 6½ kilometers.

Thinking Skill: Comparing. Discuss how the maps on pages 170 and 171 are the same and different.
Math Skill: Have students figure out how far four-tenths of a mile is from their school. Then have them tell what to include on a map in a square inch surrounding their school if the map scale is 1 inch = .4 mile.

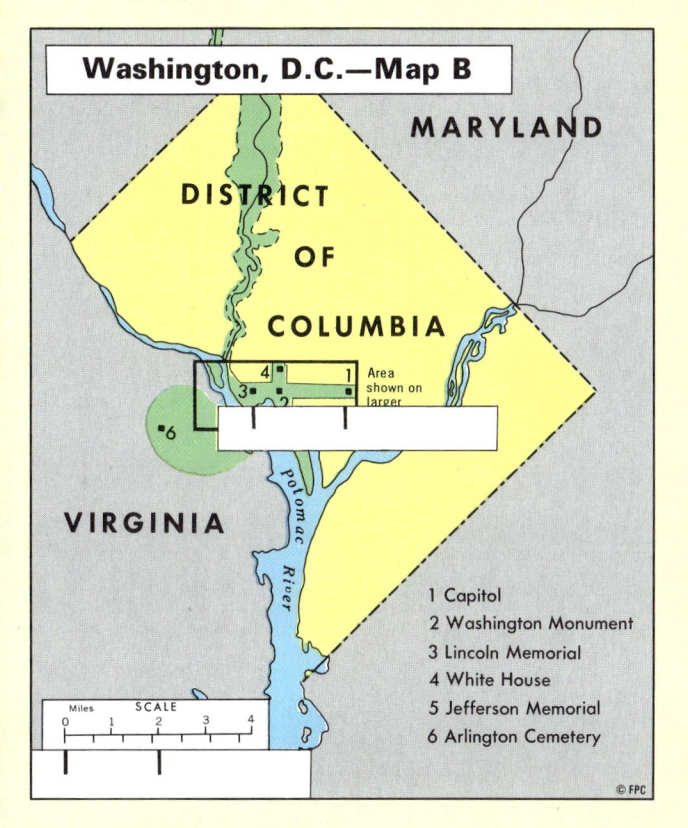

Washington, D.C.—Map B

MARYLAND
DISTRICT OF COLUMBIA
VIRGINIA
Potomac River

1 Capitol
2 Washington Monument
3 Lincoln Memorial
4 White House
5 Jefferson Memorial
6 Arlington Cemetery

Area shown on larger

SCALE Miles 0 1 2 3 4

Measuring Scale

Let's say you want to learn the distance in miles between the Lincoln Memorial and the Capitol. All you need is a strip of paper and a pencil. Place the edge of the paper on the map above so that it touches the two tiny squares that stand for these two places. Mark the paper at each point.

Next, place the paper under the map scale with one mark on zero. Where the second mark falls on the map scale is the number of miles between the two buildings. How many miles is the Lincoln Memorial from the Capitol?

Use the map on page 170, paper, and pencil to find roughly these distances:
1. the miles between the Capitol and the White House
2. the kilometers between the Capitol and the White House
3. the miles between the Lincoln Memorial and the Jefferson Memorial
4. the kilometers between the Lincoln Memorial and the Jefferson Memorial

Changing scale. The map of Washington, D.C., on page 172, shows a smaller area of the city than the map on page 170. It is the same area as the area boxed on the map on page 170.

Read the line above the map scale on page 172 that begins, "One inch . . ." In other words, one inch on the map stands for four-tenths of a mile of the real area of Washington, D.C. Four-tenths of a mile is about three city blocks.

Different maps have different map scales. On the map on page 170, one inch stands for about four miles. On the map on page 172, one inch stands for only four-tenths of a mile. Being able to compare map scale helps you understand how much area a map shows.

Look again at the scale on the map on page 172. The length of the line is equal to how many miles? kilometers?

Using Scale

On the map on page 172, measure the distance between the Capitol and the White House in miles and in kilometers. Then find the number of miles and kilometers between the Lincoln Memorial and the Jefferson Memorial. Check these distances with the distances you found on the map on page 170. Distances measured on the map on page 172 should be very close to the distances measured on

1. About 2 miles. 2. About 1½ miles.
3. About 2½ kilometers. About 1 mile. About 1½ kilometers.
4. 1 mile; about 1⅝ kilometers.

171

Reading Skill: Building vocabulary. Have students find the meaning of *tidal basin* in a dictionary.
Time Skill: Ask students to figure out how long their walk around Washington, D.C., would take if they walked a mile in 15 minutes (about 55 minutes).
***Map Skill:* Scale. Have students examine other maps of Washington, D.C., and determine their scale.

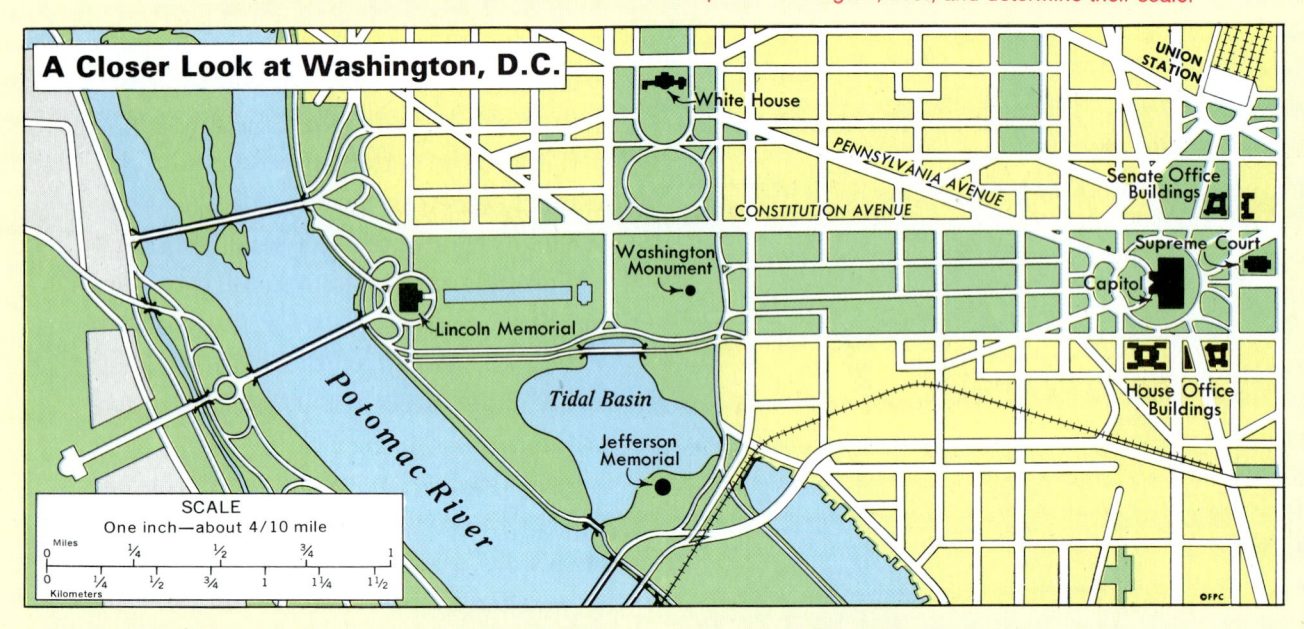

A Closer Look at Washington, D.C.

SCALE
One inch—about 4/10 mile

the map on page 170. This is because you are measuring the same distances on both maps.

To plan a trip. Use the map on this page to plan a walk around Washington, D.C. Begin at the White House. Now find the distance between the White House and the Washington Monument. Then go to the Lincoln Memorial, to the Jefferson Memorial, and back to the White House. How many miles would you walk altogether? ¹

On the map you used a straight line to measure between two places. Yet you cannot always travel in straight lines from one place to another. Look again at the map. You would have a difficult time trying to walk in a straight line from the Lincoln Memorial to the Jefferson Memorial. There is a tidal basin full of water in the way! You would have to follow the roads instead. However, people usually use straight lines when measuring map distance. Most of the time, people want to know only *about* how many miles it is from place to place.

Knowing how to use a map scale helped you find the distances between the places on your walking tour. Now you are ready to plan an even bigger trip. How far is it from your town to Washington, D.C.? Use the map on pages 18–19 to find out.

Before you start measuring, study the scale on page 19. Read the line above the map scale. About how many miles are represented by one inch on the scale? About how many kilometers are represented by one inch on the scale? ²

Remember the map on page 170 has a scale of one inch for every four miles. The map on this page has a scale of one inch for every four-tenths of a mile. The difference between these map scales means that the second map shows a smaller area than the first map. Now the map of the United States has a scale of one inch for every 210 miles. Of the

Map Skill: Distance. If the students' town is not on the map on pages 18–19, have them measure the distance between their state capital and Washington, D.C.
Reading Skill: Doing research. Have students read more about the history of Washington, D.C.
1. About 3½ miles. 2. About 210 miles. About 350 kilometers.

Background: In June the British army left Fort St. Johns on the Richelieu River and then rowed up Lake Champlain. The march then slowed down as the soldiers cleared a road through thick forests for the supply wagons and cannons. The army reached Saratoga in early October.

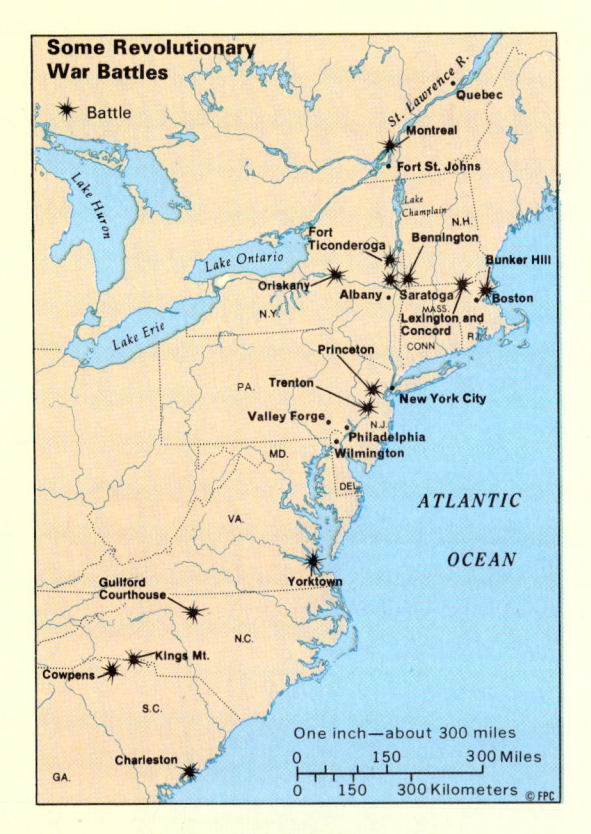

Some Revolutionary War Battles

three maps, which shows the greatest area? How do you know?

To reread history. You have measured distances on several different maps. You planned two trips using map scale. Knowing how to find distances between places on a map can also make history more real for you.

The Battle of Saratoga. As you learned earlier, the British planned a grand march from Quebec, Canada, to Albany, New York. The British army never reached Albany. Instead, the British army surrendered to the United States army at Saratoga, New York. Find all three places on the map above.

You can now use the map scale to find out about how many miles the British marched to their surrender. First measure from Quebec to Fort St. Johns, where the British prepared to march into the United States. Then measure from Fort St. Johns to Saratoga. What was the total distance of the march?

It seems hard to believe that it took the British almost five months to travel about 350 miles. Yet remember that you measured the march using straight lines. Straight lines measure the shortest distance between two places. The British, though, could not travel in a straight line. They had to travel, for example, across Lake Champlain and then over the rugged Adirondack Mountains.

The Battle of Yorktown. You can also measure the famous march of Washington's army to meet the British at Yorktown. Washington left his camp near New York City in late August 1781. He then traveled to Philadelphia, Wilmington, and finally Yorktown. Measure the distance from city to city starting with New York City. About how far did Washington march altogether?

One month later Washington was setting up camp in sight of Yorktown. Washington's army had traveled about 350 miles in one month! Washington had known that only a quick surprise would trap the British army.

You can make history come alive for you if you can locate historical places on maps and use map scales. You have learned how one army met its defeat and how another army won the Revolutionary War. You can measure distances to places all around the world if you know how to make map scales work for you.

* **Math Skill:** Have students figure out about how many miles Washington's army traveled each day (about 12 miles a day).
   1. The U.S. map. Of the three map scales, the U.S. map shows the largest area equaling an inch.
   2. About 350 miles.   3. About 350 miles.

173

Reading Skill: Using details to support main ideas: *As You Read, 3.*
Time Skill: Ask students how long ago Washington first became President.
Thinking Skill: Comparing. Have students tell on which day the President now takes office.

The Early Years of the New Government

As You Read
1. Think about these words.
   political party   pioneer
2. Look for answers to these key questions.
   a. Why did George Washington go to New York in 1789?
   b. Why was the Treasury Department so important?
   c. What two events made the West safe for settlers?
3. Use this reading skill.
   A careful reader looks for details to support the main ideas in a reading selection. In this chapter you will read that George Washington was a skilled planner and leader. As you read, look for two details to support the idea that Washington was a skilled planner and leader.

The crowd cheered wildly as a tall, white-haired man stepped out onto the balcony of Federal Hall in New York City. Thousands jammed Wall Street, hoping to get a look at this most famous of all Americans. They listened in silence as George Washington repeated the oath, or promise, that all Presidents since him have made:

> I do solemnly swear that I will faithfully execute the office of President of the United States and will, to the best of my ability, preserve, protect, and defend the Constitution of the United States.

The date was April 30, 1789. General George Washington had just become President George Washington, the first President of the United States.

The crowd gave three big cheers when Washington became our first President.

Washington enjoyed life at his plantation, Mount Vernon.

The Quiet Years

At the end of the Revolutionary War, Washington had said a tearful good-by to his officers. He had returned home to Mount Vernon. There he lived a quiet life for the next seven years. A stream of visitors and letters, however, kept Washington up-to-date on all the latest news.

In April 1789 Washington received word that he had been elected President. Two days later he set out for New York City, then the country's capital. Once again Washington put duty to his country before his desire to stay on the land that he loved.

Washington as President

When Washington took office, no one was collecting taxes to run the government. The United States still owed money to people at home and in Europe. The money had been borrowed to fight the Revolutionary War. There were no courts. The country had an army of only a few hundred troops and no navy at all.

Washington was a skilled planner and leader. He talked with representatives in Congress about the needs of their states. He asked them for names of people who might be willing to serve in the government. Most of the representatives were old friends who were glad to work with Washington.

After careful thought Washington made his key appointments. He chose Thomas Jefferson as secretary of state and Alexander Hamilton as secretary of the treasury. Others became secretary of war and attorney general. After Congress set up the court system in 1789, Washington appointed John Jay the first chief justice, head of the U.S. Supreme Court.

The Treasury Department. Without money, the government could not work. So the Treasury Department, which took care of the money, soon became the most important department. Treasury workers began collecting taxes on goods shipped to and from the United States.

These taxes kept the government running and paid its bills. When war loans were repaid, some European countries were willing to loan our government more money. They also began buying more U.S. goods.

Two Different Views

Alexander Hamilton had strong ideas about running the government. He believed that the country's leaders should be educated and own property. He also believed that the United States should focus on trade. Not everyone, including Thomas Jefferson, agreed with Hamilton. Jefferson believed that all citizens should have some say in running the gov-

Thomas Jefferson dealt with the governments of other countries.

Alexander Hamilton took charge of the country's money.

ernment. He also thought that the United States should focus on farming.

Hamilton and Jefferson never did agree about running the government. Some representatives in Congress and other citizens agreed with Hamilton. They formed a group called the Federalist party. Those who shared Jefferson's ideas started a group called the Republican party. These were the first groups in the country that had their own ideas about running the government. Today we call such groups **political parties**.

Problems for the President

Once again the United States was being drawn into a war. This time the French asked their ally the United States to help them fight the British. For a while Americans could not decide what to do. Then the British began to stir up trouble in the western lands of the United States. It seemed as if war with Britain could not be avoided.

Trouble in the West. As you may remember, the British still had forts on U.S. land after the Revolutionary War. They did not intend to give up these forts. Washington sent Chief Justice Jay to Britain in 1794 to settle this problem.

British soldiers at the forts brought together many of the Indian tribes that lived in the western lands. The soldiers gave them firearms to fight the Americans. However, U.S. troops defeated the Indians. At the peace talks that followed in 1795, the Indians signed a treaty. They gave up all their land east of the Mississippi River and between the Great Lakes and the Ohio River.

In Britain Chief Justice Jay had also signed an important treaty. In the treaty,

176

Background: In 1794 the British built one more fort, Fort Miami, about 100 miles south of Detroit. The British then held eight forts on U.S. land. Some of the forts were located in the Northwest Territory, which was then considered the West. Even though Congress had opened this area to settlement, Indian tribes still lived there as shown on the map below.

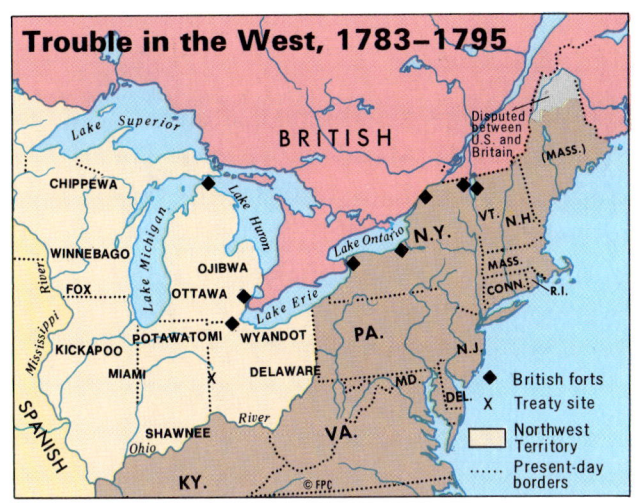

Trouble in the West, 1783–1795

British troops and Indians fought to keep western lands for themselves.

the British agreed to remove their troops from the United States. At last, Americans could safely settle the rich land north of the Ohio River. People who ventured into unsettled lands were some of our first **pioneers**.

Washington's Farewell

President Washington had kept the country out of war, even when many citizens wanted war. Now with his second four-year term as President ending, he looked forward to returning to the peace and quiet of Mount Vernon.

In March 1797 Washington turned over his office to John Adams of Massachusetts. Adams had been elected President in late 1796. Washington went home to Mount Vernon. There he died on December 14, 1799.

The whole country was saddened by the loss of one of its first heroes. A Virginia leader described the place held by his good friend Washington with these words: "First in war, first in peace, and first in the hearts of his countrymen."

Checking Up

1. Name two things that John Jay did for his country.
2. Why did some Americans want to go to war against Britain?
3. What answers would you give to the key questions at the beginning of this chapter?
4. *How did the treaty signed by the Indians in 1795 affect settlers?*

Unit 5 Summary

- The British defeated the French in the French and Indian War. The French gave the British all their lands in eastern North America.
- New British laws and taxes hurt colonial trade. The colonists refused to pay many of these taxes.
- Actions of the British king and Parliament angered the colonists. They signed a Declaration of Independence and declared war on Britain.
- The colonies won the Revolutionary War and became the United States of America.
- The country's leaders wrote a new plan of government called the Constitution and later added the Bill of Rights.
- George Washington served as our first President.

Thinking Skill: Evaluating. Talk about why Washington's friend had described him well.
Reading Skill: Organizing information. Have students write ten true-false statements based on each point in the unit summary. Have them exchange papers.

Unit 5 Review Workshop

What Have You Learned?

1. What lands in North America did Britain, Spain, and France control after the French and Indian War?
2. What two types of goods did the colonies ship to Britain? Name two examples of each type.
3. Why did the colonists think the Stamp Act was unfair?
4. Why did Thomas Jefferson write the Declaration of Independence?
5. What are the three branches of government? Name two duties of each branch.
6. How does an amendment change the Constitution? What do we call the first ten amendments added to the Constitution?
7. Beginning with the French and Indian War, name three different jobs that George Washington performed for his country.

Use Your Reading Skills

Many events led up to the Revolutionary War. What happened is fact. What the colonists thought about what happened is opinion. Read the following sentences. Tell which sentences state facts and which sentences state opinions. Give reasons for your answers.

1. Only the colonies should have taxed the colonists.
2. The Sugar Act taxed molasses.
3. The Stamp Act was unfair.
4. All colonists were lawbreakers.
5. British troops killed innocent citizens in the Boston Massacre.
6. Parliament had a right to tax the thirteen colonies.
7. The king punished Boston for the Boston Tea Party.

Use Your Map Skills

Maps show two different kinds of borders: natural borders and political borders. Natural borders are features of the earth that separate areas. These borders can be mountains or bodies of water such as lakes and rivers. Political borders are such things as borders between countries and borders between states. People decide where to put political borders.

Study the physical map of the United States on pages 20–21. Use the map to answer these questions.

1. What two bodies of water form the eastern border of Delaware?
2. What river forms the border between Pennsylvania and New Jersey?
3. Is the border that separates Virginia and North Carolina a natural or a political border?
4. Which mountains form the western boundary of most of the original thirteen colonies?
5. Which colonies had the ocean for a border?

Use Your Thinking Skills

The picture on page 179 shows three carpenters at work in Colonial Williams-

Reading Skills: Distinguishing fact from opinion, interpreting graphics.
Thinking Skills: Knowing, analyzing.
Map Skill: Location.

burg, Virginia. Colonial Williamsburg is a restored, or rebuilt, colonial village. Visitors can see how people lived and worked in the 1700s. By studying this picture, you can learn about a colonial trade. Gathering information from a picture is an important skill. Study the picture and then answer the questions below.

1. What are the carpenters making?
2. How many different kinds of tools can you find?
3. Which tools are similar to tools we use today?
4. Why would some of the items being made take less time to make today?

Learn by Doing

1. In the library find a book or an encyclopedia about Washington, D.C. Read about these famous places there: the White House, the Capitol, the Supreme Court building, and the Washington Monument. Then choose the three places you would most like to visit. Be ready to explain why you would visit those places.
2. Ask a classmate to read the Bill of Rights with you. Then together make a poster giving examples of what each amendment means.
3. Keep a record for one week of what the President does every day. Write down also where you found your information. Then match as many of the items you find with the President's duties listed on the chart on page 168.

Read to Learn More

Find the topics listed below in the card catalog of your library. Read all or part of a book listed under one of the topics. Share what you learn with your classmates.

PRESIDENTS (U.S.)   SHIPBUILDING
WHALING (HISTORY)
U.S. HISTORY (COLONIAL PERIOD)

Reading Skills: Using references: *Learn by Doing, 1, 3*; organizing information: *Learn by Doing, 2.*
Thinking Skill: Classifying: *Learn by Doing, 3.*
Citizenship Skill: Decision making: *Learn by Doing, 1.*

Unit Overview: This unit examines the new nation focusing on settlement of the West and the industrial revolution.

Unit Objectives
To understand:
- settlement in the West
- the industrial revolution
- rights in early America

Suggested Materials
Workbook
Unit Tests

Unit 6

Skills Emphasized
Map Skills: pp. 186, 191, 192, 194, 213.
Social Studies Reading Skills: pp. 180, 182, 183, 184, 185, 187, 188, 189, 190, 192, 195, 196, 197, 198, 199, 200, 201, 202, 203, 204, 206, 207, 209, 210, 211, 212, 213.
Thinking Skills: pp. 180, 185, 187, 188, 189, 193, 194, 195, 197, 198, 201, 202, 205, 206, 207, 210, 211, 212, 213.
Communication Skills: pp. 180, 184, 186, 190, 196, 201, 203, 205, 208, 210, 213.
Time Skills: pp. 184, 190.
Math Skills: pp. 183, 184, 189, 200, 202.
Citizenship Skills: pp. 191, 207.

Suggested Student Activities
1. Make brown-bag puppets and write biographies of famous people during this period. Arrange them on a bulletin board.
2. Make posters advertising the new lands.
3. Begin a "Famous Inventors" class booklet.
* 4. Make a montage of things we have as a result of the industrial revolution.
** 5. Make a movie roll and script on pioneer life.
*** 6. Arrange a display of books on this period of U.S. history.

Skills Emphasized in Suggested Student Activities
Social Studies Reading Skills: Organizing information, doing research, using references.
Communication Skill: Writing.
Thinking Skills: Knowing, comparing, classifying.

Looking Westward

In the early 1800s, horse-drawn barges moved people and goods from Buffalo to Albany on the Erie Canal.

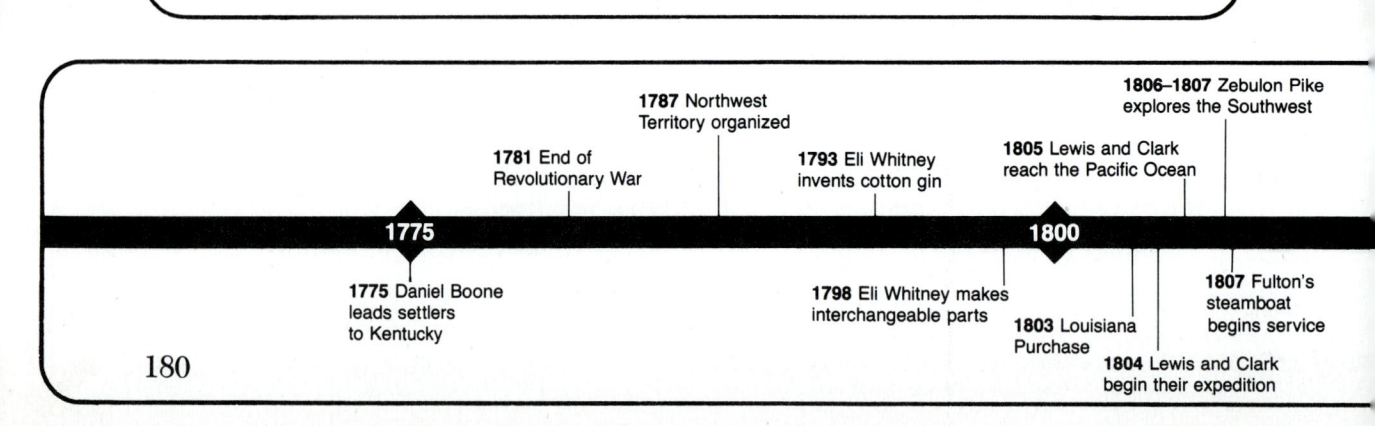

1775 Daniel Boone leads settlers to Kentucky
1781 End of Revolutionary War
1787 Northwest Territory organized
1793 Eli Whitney invents cotton gin
1798 Eli Whitney makes interchangeable parts
1803 Louisiana Purchase
1804 Lewis and Clark begin their expedition
1805 Lewis and Clark reach the Pacific Ocean
1806–1807 Zebulon Pike explores the Southwest
1807 Fulton's steamboat begins service

1819 The United States buys Florida

1825 Erie Canal opens between Albany and Buffalo

1830–1838 Removal of Indians from Southeast

1834 McCormick reaper first used

1846–1848 Mexican War

1853 Gadsden Purchase

1825

1850

1812–1814 War of 1812

1811 Work on National Road begins

1832 Samuel Morse invents telegraph

1836 Texas revolts from Mexico

1849 California gold rush

181

Reading Skill: Discovering cause and effect: *As You Read*, 3.

The Young Nation

As You Read

1. Think about these words.
   territory   toll   canal   steamboat
2. Look for answers to these key questions.
   a. What was the pattern of settlement in the West?
   b. What developments in transportation helped the settlement of the United States?
   c. Why was water transportation important to early settlers?
3. Use this reading skill.
   It is important to understand the relationship between cause and effect. When something happens, it is called an effect. The reasons for the event are its causes. In this chapter you will learn that many people settled in the Northwest Territory. Several things are probable causes of this settlement. After reading the chapter, explain how each of the following were causes of settlement: the Erie Canal, the National Road, the *Clermont*.

Even during the Revolutionary War, Americans moved west. Hunters and trappers moved west because the lands were full of deer, beaver, and bear. Farmers traveled west because the soil was rich and deep. When the Revolutionary War ended in 1781, thousands of people went west.

New Land, New States

Look at the map on page 183. Find the area known as the Northwest Territory. Find the area known as the Southwest Territory. These **territories** were lands that belonged to the United States but were not yet states. Which river formed most of the western border of both the Northwest and the Southwest territories? Which mountains formed most of the eastern border of both territories? Now find the Ohio River. This river was also part of the border between the two territories.

When Americans began moving west after the Revolutionary War, these territories were known as the West. For years hunters and trappers had used this land. As families began settling there, the hunters and trappers moved farther west. Farmers and families following hunters and trappers became a pattern of settlement in our country.

The Northwest Territory. The government decided that when 60,000 people

1. Appalachian Mountains.

Reading Skill: Using textbook features. Introduce the unit by discussing pages 180–181. Refer to the time line throughout the unit.

Reading Skill: Using references. Have students look for pictures of these main routes west.
Math Skill: Have students talk about the width of the road and compare it with the width of a modern road.

The U.S. in 1790
- 13 original colonies
- (1791) Date state was admitted
- Present-day borders

had settled in a particular area of this territory, they could ask to become a state. New states carved out of the Northwest Territory would have the same rights and duties as the original states. In time, the Northwest Territory became the states of Ohio, Indiana, Illinois, Wisconsin, and Michigan.

The Southwest Territory. Even during the Revolutionary War, people settled in what are now Kentucky and Tennessee. Tennessee and parts of Georgia, Alabama, and Mississippi were in the Southwest Territory.

The Ways West

It was not easy for the settlers to travel west. Indians, hunters, and trappers had made trails the settlers could use, but these were not much more than narrow dirt paths for walkers.

The roads west. From 1800 to 1815, there were three main routes west. They were the Mohawk Turnpike, the Pennsylvania Road, and the Great Valley Road. The Great Valley Road connected the Wilderness and Nashville roads. Find these roads on the map on page 184.

In 1811 the government began building the National Road. The National Road was built on the old Cumberland Road. Find the Cumberland Road on the map. The National Road was a much better road. It was 30 feet (9 m) wide and had a foundation made of sand, crushed rock, and earth. Settlers using this road could reach the Ohio River at Wheeling. Then they could travel down the Ohio River to the territories.

Private companies also began building new roads or improving old ones. These companies charged **tolls**, or payments, for use of the roads.

Thousands of people used the roads on their way west. Some walked with their belongings on their backs. Others rode in covered wagons. Some even pushed their possessions west in wheelbarrows!

The Erie Canal. Although roads had improved by the early 1800s, it was still difficult to travel across land. It was even harder to send goods the settlers needed or farm products they wanted to sell. Transportation by water was easier and less expensive. Rivers were important in the settling of our country. In fact, many early settlements were along rivers.

Background: Settlers traveling on the Ohio River used keelboats, long, narrow boats that were pulled or rowed.
** **Reading Skill:** Doing research. Have several students make a visual report on the Erie Canal.

***Communication Skill:** Writing. Have students write features on the Erie Canal.
Math Skill: Have students compare the width of the Erie Canal with the width of the National Road (the Erie Canal was wider). Ask them why the canal was wider.

Routes West: 1800–1850

- Canals
- Roads 1800–1815
- Roads 1815–1850

However, water routes and rivers did not always link all the parts of the territories. So in the 1820s Americans began building **canals**. Canals are waterways built by people. The canals linked rivers and lakes. Boats that were pulled by horses carried people and freight up and down the canals.

The Erie Canal was one of the first and most important canals. It connected Lake Erie and the Hudson River. Find the Erie Canal on the map on page 184. It was 363 miles (581 km) long and 50 feet (15 m) wide. When it was completed in 1825, there was an all-water route between Buffalo and New York City.

Time Skill: Ask students how many years old the Erie Canal is.
* **Reading Skill:** Using references. Have students look for pictures of the Erie Canal.

* **Reading Skill:** Building vocabulary. Discuss the meaning of "The Star-Spangled Banner."

Our National Anthem

In 1814 a captured American named Francis Scott Key watched British ships fire on Fort McHenry, Maryland. When he saw that the United States flag was still flying, he wrote down his thoughts. His words became our national anthem, "The Star-Spangled Banner."

Oh! say, can you see, by the dawn's early light,/What so proudly we hailed at the twilight's last gleaming?/Whose broad stripes and bright stars, thro' the perilous fight,/O'er the ramparts we watched were so gallantly streaming?/And the rockets' red glare, the bombs bursting in air,/Gave proof thro' the night that our flag was still there./Oh! say, does that star-spangled banner yet wave/O'er the land of the free and the home of the brave?

Throughout the night Key watched as the British failed to take Fort McHenry.

Steamboats. The **steamboat**, a boat driven by the power of steam, improved water transportation. In 1807 Robert Fulton's steamboat, the *Clermont*, made its first trip up the Hudson River. Soon steamboats became an important means of transportation on rivers, lakes, and oceans.

The United States and Great Britain

While Americans were busy settling the country, the United States had some problems with other countries. One of these was Great Britain.

The War of 1812. Although the United States owned the Northwest Territory, the British still had forts nearby. The Americans wanted the forts removed. Some Americans wanted to settle on Canadian land. Americans also wanted the British navy to stop interfering with their ships and trade.

In June 1812, Congress declared war on Great Britain. Battles were fought on land and sea, even on Lake Erie.

No boundaries changed because of the War of 1812. Nevertheless, U.S. ships could at last travel the oceans safely. The United States and Great Britain were again at peace.

Checking Up

1. Which areas were considered the west in 1790?
2. What states were once part of the Northwest Territory? of the Southwest Territory?
3. What answers would you give to the key questions at the beginning of this chapter?
4. *How do you think the Erie Canal helped the growth of New York City?*

* **Thinking Skill:** Knowing. Have students learn "The Star-Spangled Banner."
*** **Reading Skill:** Using references. Have students look for pictures and data on Fulton.

Exploration and New Territory

As You Read

1. Think about these words.
   expedition   journal
2. Look for answers to these key questions.
   a. Why was the Louisiana Purchase important to the United States?
   b. What route did Lewis and Clark take to the Pacific Ocean? What route did they take on their trip back to St. Louis?
   c. What lands in addition to the Louisiana Purchase were opened to settlement in the early 1800s?

The boundaries of the United States changed greatly in the early 1800s. In 1803 the United States purchased an area called Louisiana from France. In 1819 the United States bought an area called Florida from Spain. You can see these areas on the map on this page. Both purchases added important new land to our rapidly growing country.

The Louisiana Purchase

Look again at the map on this page. The Mississippi River was the western boundary of the United States in 1803.

Map Skill: Location. Have students compare this map and the one on page 183. Ask them how the United States had changed.

Communication Skill: Listening. Read additional data on the Louisiana Purchase to the class. Have students write down five facts about the Louisiana Purchase.

Reading Skill: Organizing data. Have the class list reasons the Louisiana Purchase was a "bargain."
Thinking Skill: Analyzing. Discuss the importance of Lewis's and Clark's having "special skills."

Much of the land that lay just west of the river was called Louisiana. At that time, this area was much larger than the present state of Louisiana.

For many years Louisiana belonged to Spain. In 1800 the French bought the land from Spain. Thomas Jefferson offered to buy Louisiana from the French. The French agreed to sell Louisiana for $15 million.

That was a lot of money. Yet the purchase was a bargain. Look at the map on page 186. Compare the size of Louisiana with what was the rest of the United States. The Louisiana Purchase doubled the size of the United States!

Jefferson believed that the Louisiana Purchase was important to the United States. The port at New Orleans handled goods shipped down both the Ohio and the Mississippi rivers. The United States now controlled both sides of the Mississippi. The river was like a great highway through the middle of the country.

The Louisiana Purchase was important for another reason. For a long time people had looked for a water route across America to Asia. Jefferson believed that such a route might be in this area. Perhaps the Missouri River was part of this route. No one knew for sure because most of the Louisiana Purchase was unexplored. Only the American Indians and some trappers who lived in the area knew what the land was like.

Jefferson decided to send an **expedition** through the Louisiana Purchase. An expedition is a journey made for a special purpose. The special reason for this expedition was to find out what we had bought. Did a water route to Asia run through the area? What else was there?

Lewis (left) and Clark (right) traveled nearly 8,000 miles.

The Lewis and Clark Expedition

Jefferson chose Meriwether Lewis to lead the expedition. Lewis then chose an old friend of his, William Clark, to help him. Both men knew how to survive in the wilderness.

Lewis and Clark picked forty-five men to go on their expedition. Some were soldiers. Some were hunters and trappers. Each one had a special skill. Lewis and Clark and their group prepared for the long expedition.

Lewis and Clark set off on a journey that was something like Columbus's voyage. Both groups wanted to find a water route that would lead to Asia. Both groups knew part of their routes. Yet neither group knew exactly where its journey would end. Lewis and Clark did not know exactly where the Missouri River would lead them. Nor did they know

Background: Meriwether Lewis had been Jefferson's personal secretary. Both Lewis's and Clarks's families had been neighbors of Jefferson in Virginia.

The Journey of Lewis and Clark

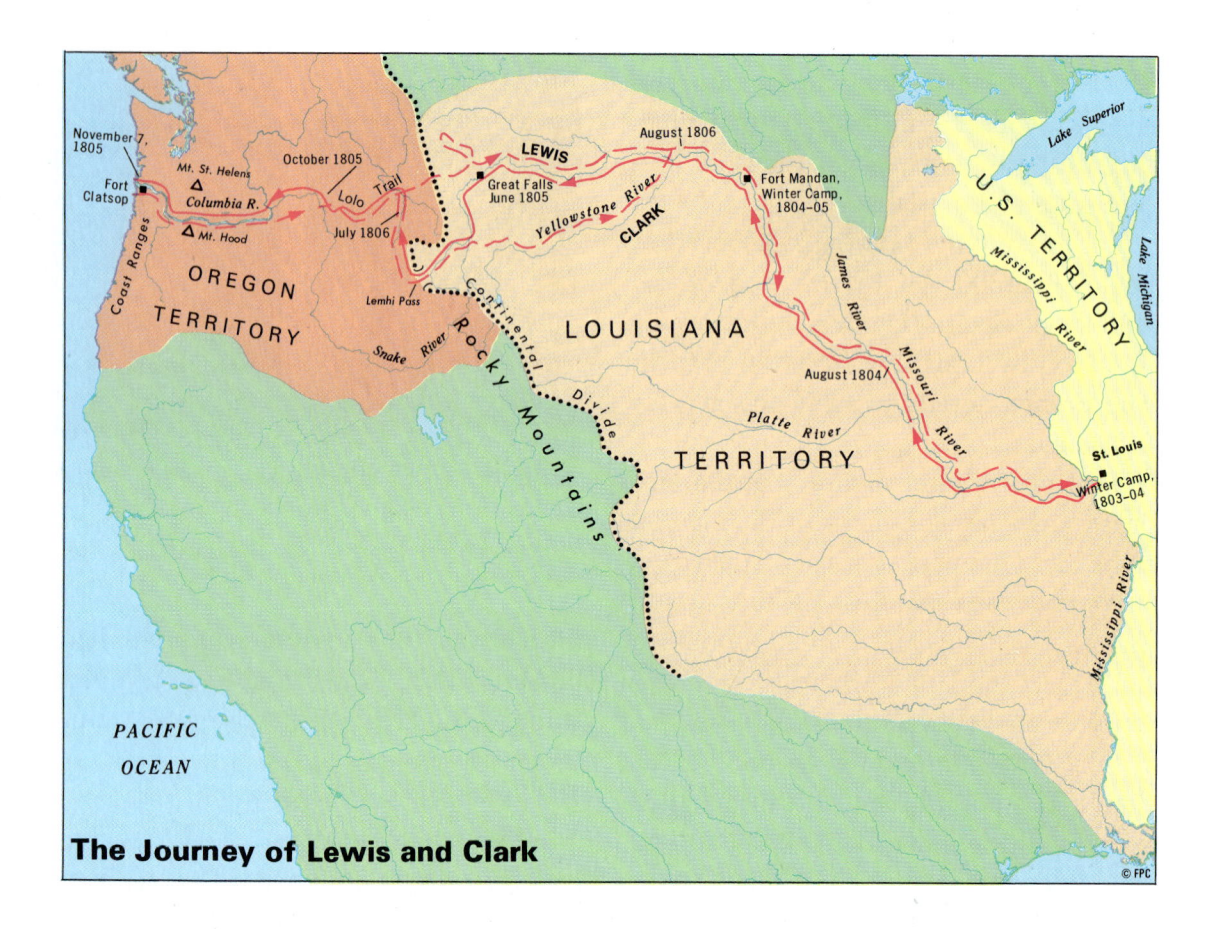

much about crossing the Rocky Mountains. So like Columbus, they started a trip to unknown land.

The journey up the Missouri. Jefferson wanted the group to travel up the Missouri River, so the expedition left from St. Louis in May of 1804. Three boats carried the explorers and their supplies up the Missouri River. Sometimes thunderstorms soaked the men and their supplies. They were bitten by mosquitoes, ticks, and sometimes even snakes. Look at the map on this page. It shows the route of the expedition.

Finally, in late October, Lewis and Clark reached the villages of the Mandan Indians. You read about the Mandan in Unit 2. Lewis and Clark decided to spend the winter near these Indians. During the long winter, they drew maps of the land they had seen in their **journals**, or notebooks. They even drew pictures of plants and animals living in the new land.

To the Pacific—1805. In the Mandan villages, Lewis and Clark met a French trader, Charbonneau (shär′bə·nō′), and his Shoshone Indian wife, Sacagawea (sak′ə·jə·wē′ə). Lewis wanted Sacagawea to go with the group. He knew that she could speak the language of the Shoshone Indians, who lived to the west of the Mandans. Sacagawea, her husband, and their baby joined the expedition

William Clark made this full-page drawing of a salmon trout in his diary.

when it left the Mandan villages in early April 1805.

By June of 1805, a little more than a year after beginning their trip, Lewis and Clark had reached a series of waterfalls on the Missouri River. Find the Great Falls of the Missouri on the map on page 188. From this point on, the journey became even more difficult. The expedition was now in the Rocky Mountains. The land was steep, rough, and rocky. Often the men had to drag the canoes they were now using overland. The rocky soil cut up shoes and boots. Lewis and Clark found that there was no easy way through the mountains.

Finally, in August of 1805, the expedition reached the Shoshone. Sacagawea's brother was a chief of the tribe. The Shoshone guided Lewis and Clark through the mountains along the Bitterroot River and the Lolo Trail. Find this route on the map on page 188.

Lewis and Clark then canoed down rivers until they reached the Columbia River. After traveling down the Columbia for about three weeks, they at last saw the Pacific Ocean! They had reached their destination. Look at the map again. In what month did they finally reach the Pacific? How long had they been gone?

The return to St. Louis. Lewis and Clark spent the winter of 1805–1806 near the Pacific. In April of 1806, they began the trip back to St. Louis, where they arrived on September 23, 1806. Follow this route on the map on page 188.

Lewis and Clark crossed plains and mountains to reach the West.

Lewis and Clark had found unknown animals and plants. They had proved that it was possible to travel across the country. However, the old dream of a direct water route to the Pacific died with their return.

Zebulon Pike Explores the West

Zebulon (zeb′ū·lon) Pike was another explorer who learned about the land west of the Mississippi River. In 1806 Pike led a group of soldiers on an expedition through the southern part of the Louisiana Purchase. Pike and his party passed through what is now Missouri, Arkansas, Oklahoma, and Colorado. In the Rocky Mountains of Colorado, Pike turned south and entered Spanish territory. Although Pike and his men were captured by the Spanish, they were released, and they returned to the United States.

Pike published a book about his travels in 1810. This book, along with the accounts of Lewis and Clark, excited Americans. Although the new land held danger, it also held new promise for settlers. Now settlers pushed west of the Mississippi River. Farms and towns began to spring up along the Mississippi and Missouri rivers. Soon, more and more people would follow and add to the growth of the western settlements.

The Removal of the Indians

Meanwhile, American Indians continued to hold on to some land east of the Mississippi River. Many tribes in Georgia, Alabama, and Mississippi had large farms and villages. Settlers, though, wanted this land too.

In 1830 the United States government began to move Indian tribes to lands west of the Mississippi River. The Indians had to leave their homes, farms, and towns. One of the tribes forced from their land was the Cherokee. Almost one-third of them died on the trip west. The Cherokee called this forced journey "the Trail of Tears." Most of the Indians had to live on reservations in what is now the state of Oklahoma.

The United States had expanded greatly in the twenty years between 1800 and 1820. Although there was still eastern land for settlement, Americans continued moving west and south. They settled on the lands of the Louisiana Purchase and Florida.

Checking Up

1. What two purchases in the early 1800s greatly increased the size of the United States?
2. In what ways was the Lewis and Clark expedition like the voyage of Columbus?
3. What was the most difficult part of the Lewis and Clark expedition? Why was this part of the journey difficult?
4. What answers would you give to the key questions at the beginning of this chapter?
5. *Why were the explorations of Lewis and Clark and of Pike important to settlers?*

Maps and Pictures Tell a Story of the Way West

As you read, think about these words.
pass   contour line   contour map

Explorers like John Smith, Lewis and Clark, and Zebulon Pike did more than travel through unexplored lands. They drew maps of the lands they explored. The maps they drew helped settlers travel to and through new territories.

How Maps Show Landforms

You can show many different things on a map. John Smith and Lewis and Clark tried to show landforms on the maps they drew. They tried to show what the land they explored was like.

Settlers needed to know about the landforms in the areas through which they were going to travel. They needed to know where they would find hills and mountains and **passes**, or gaps in the hills and mountains.

You may remember that early map makers like John Smith simply drew pictures of mountains on their maps. Look at the drawing (left, below). This drawing shows the Narrows and the hills around it. The Narrows was an important pass through the Appalachian Mountains on the Cumberland Road. The drawing is like those John Smith used on his map of Virginia. Both show the location of hills. However, neither one shows how high the hills are. They do not show elevation or local relief.

The drawing (right, below) shows more detail about the landforms and landscape of the Narrows. As you learned in the Atlas section, shades of black tell you that land is hilly or mountainous. This drawing shows that the land around the Narrows is hilly.

Color on maps. Cartographers, or mapmakers, often use colors to show elevation of an area. The maps of the Narrows on page 192 for example, use colors to show the elevations of the hills in this

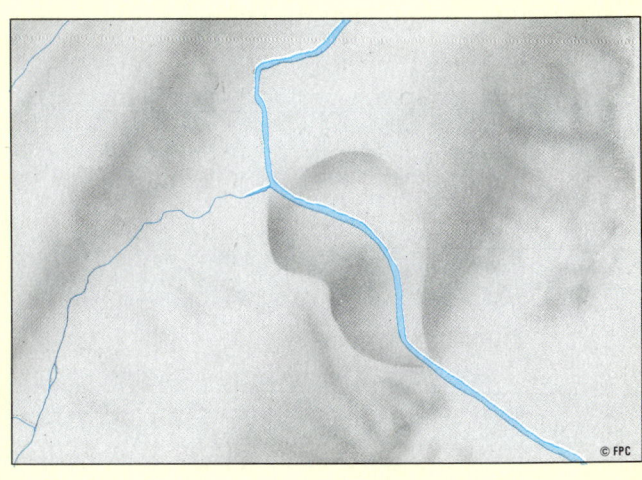

---

* **Map Skill:** Location. Have students make drawings and relief maps of their neighborhoods.
** **Citizenship Skill:** Social participation. Invite a cartographer to speak to the class.

*** Map Skill:** Symbolization. Have students make color-shaded maps of their neighborhoods.

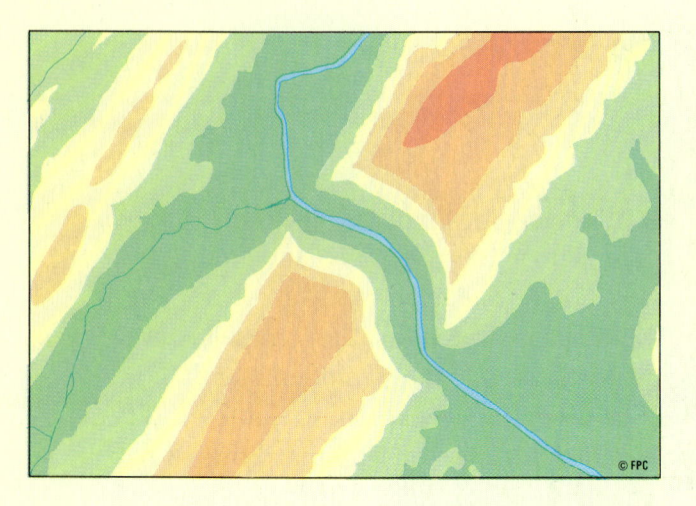

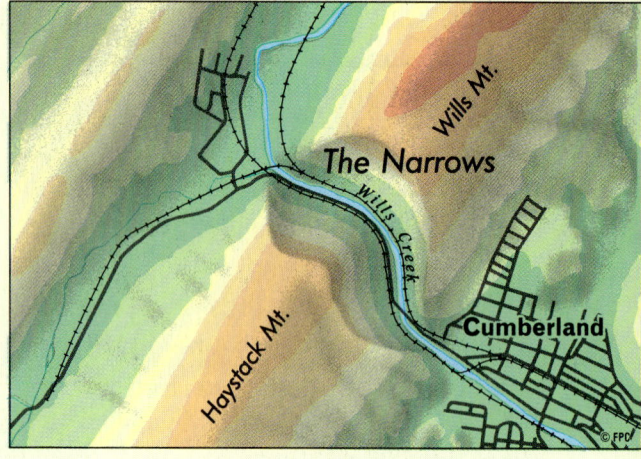

area. How many different colors are used to show different elevations on the map at left? Which color is used to show the highest elevation above sea level? Which color is used to show the lowest elevation above sea level? You may recall that maps that use both color and gray shading to show elevation and local relief are called physical maps. At right is a physical map of the Narrows. Which color on the physical map shows the highest elevation above sea level? Which color is used to show the lowest elevation above sea level? Many of the maps in this book are physical maps. They help give you a good idea of what the land in an area looks like.

Contour Maps

Physical maps provide important information about a particular area in a way that is easy to read. Yet there are still other ways to draw maps to tell you about an area.

Look at the diagrams of the mountains shown on page 193. These diagrams show two mountains sliced at five different elevations. On a physical map, the elevations of these mountains would be represented by different colors. One color would represent all the land between two particular elevations. However, in the diagram at the top of page 193, there is a **contour line** for each of the five different slices, or elevations of the two mountains. For example, one line in the diagram joins all points that are 650 feet above sea level. Find this line. Such a line is a contour line. Find the contour line that joins all points that are 1,650 feet above sea level. Now find the contour line that joins together all points that are 3,300 feet above sea level. On a **contour map**, the differences in elevation are shown by different contour lines instead of by different colors.

Using contour maps. Look at the contour map of the Narrows on page 193. Compare this map of the Narrows with the two other maps. You can use the contour map of the Narrows to find the same information that the other two have. You can find even more information. Using the contour map, find the

192

1. Brown. Green. Brown; green—with the gray shading of relief underneath the colors.
*** Reading Skill:** Using references. Have students look for other examples of contour maps.

View from Above

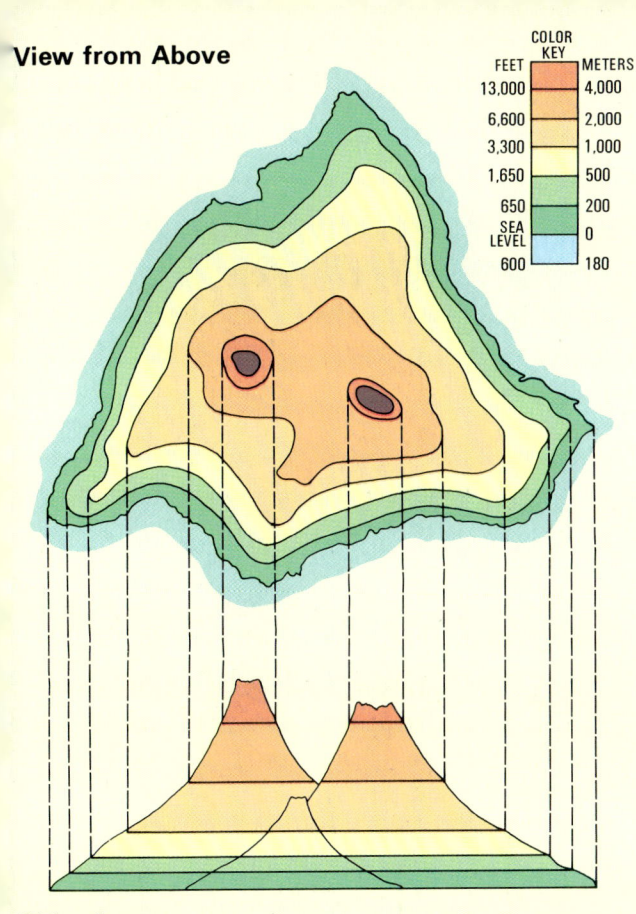

Side view

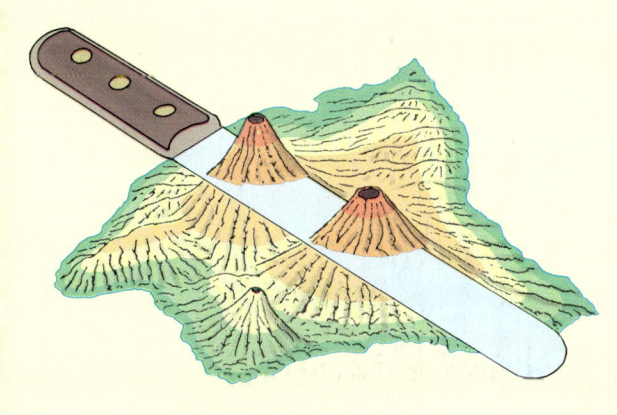

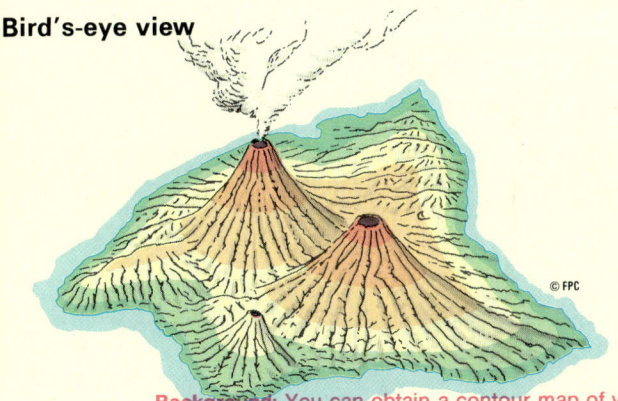

Bird's-eye view

COLOR KEY

FEET	METERS
13,000	4,000
6,600	2,000
3,300	1,000
1,650	500
650	200
SEA LEVEL	0
600	180

1. About 800 feet (244 m).

Thinking Skill: Analyzing. Discuss how the contour lines depict the "slices" made in the hills.

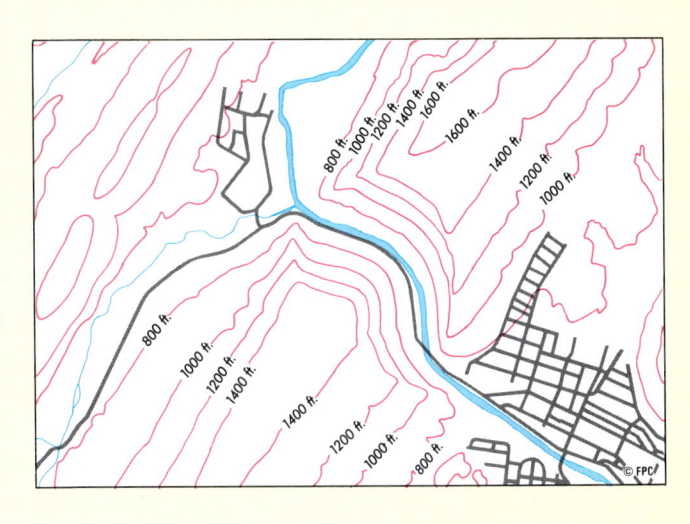

highest elevation of the land surrounding the Narrows. What is the elevation of the pass called the Narrows? How many different contour lines do you see on this map? Remember that each contour line shows a different elevation.

Contour maps and landforms. You can find out about the landforms of an area using a contour map. Remember that landforms are described by both elevation and local relief. To find the elevation of an area on a contour map, you read the numbers on the contour lines. To find the local relief of an area, look at the changes in the numbers on the contour lines. On contour maps of plains and plateaus, the contour lines are far apart. Plains and plateaus are flat or gently rolling. There are no great changes in elevation on plains or plateaus, so there are few contour lines to show changes in elevation.

There are more lines on a contour map of hills and mountains. Hills and mountains have great local relief, or many changes in elevation. So a map maker must use many contour lines to show

Background: You can obtain a contour map of your area by writing to Eastern Distribution Branch, U.S. Geological Survey, 1200 S. Eads St., Arlington, VA 22202 (for the United States east of the Mississippi River and Minnesota) or to Western Distribution Branch, U.S. Geological Survey, Box 25286, Federal Center, Denver, CO 80225 (for the western United States and Louisiana).

* **Map Skill:** Symbolization. Have students take photographs of their neighborhoods.
* **Thinking Skill:** Comparing. Have students compare the maps they've drawn of their neighborhoods with the photographs of their neighborhoods. Ask them which gives a more accurate portrait of their neighborhoods.

1 these changes on a contour map. Look again at the contour map of the Narrows. What landform do you think surrounds the Narrows?

In addition, you can see how steep a hill or mountain is by looking to see how close together the contour lines are. If the contour lines are close together, you can tell there is a sharp increase in elevation. If the contour lines are far apart, you can tell the slope is gentle. Where is the steepest slope of the Narrows?

A contour map has certain advantages over a physical map. Usually contour maps have many more contour lines than physical maps have colors. Most physical maps have about six different colors with which to indicate elevation. Contour maps can have as many contour lines as necessary. As a result, it is easier to find the elevations of specific points on contour maps than it is on physical maps.

Each type of map gives important information about the land in a particular area. Photographs can also give important information about the land. The photograph above shows the Narrows as it looks today. Compare the photograph with each of the maps of the Narrows. What advantages or disadvantages do you think the photograph has compared with the maps in supplying information about the land around the Narrows?

Checking Up
1. What is a physical map? What does this kind of map show?
2. What is a contour map? In what ways does a contour map differ from a physical map?
3. Using a contour map, how can you determine the steepness of a hill or a mountain?
4. How can you identify the four landforms using a contour map?

194

1. Hills.

Reading Skill: Seeing relationships: *As You Read, 3.*

The United States Expands to the Pacific

As You Read

1. Think about these words.
   volunteer   annex   wagon train
2. Look for answers to these key questions.
   a. Why did many settlers in Texas want the area to become part of the United States?
   b. What lands did the United States gain in the 1840s?
   c. What trails were important to settlers?
3. Use this reading skill.
   This chapter focuses on how the United States got new territory. One area, Texas, became part of the United States in 1845. Another area, Oregon, became part of the United States in 1846. Settlement in both areas had some things in common. As you read this chapter, look for ways in which the settlement of both areas was the same. When you look for similarities, you are making comparisons. Making comparisons is an important reading skill.

The pioneers did not stop westward movement at the Mississippi River. In the 1800s settlers heard about rich, new land in places called Texas, Oregon, and California. So they continued their move westward into new areas that soon became part of our country.

Texas Becomes Part of the United States

In the 1820s traders from the United States traveled on the Santa Fe Trail to the old Spanish town of Santa Fe. Find the Santa Fe Trail on the map on page 196. The traders rode over plains and brightly colored plateaus in the Southwest. They traded manufactured goods to Mexicans and Pueblo Indians for gold and silver. Settlers soon followed traders to the Southwest.

In 1823 Stephen Austin led 300 families into a part of Mexico called Texas. The people settled in a region of rich soil near the Sabine River. By 1834 there were about 22,000 settlers from the United States in Texas. Find Texas on the map on page 196.

These settlers were used to the customs and laws of the United States. Many of them were eager to have Texas become a state of the United States. Others wanted Texas to become an independent country. Whichever they wanted,

Sabine (sə·bēn′)
Thinking Skill: Evaluating. Ask students what advantages there were in becoming a state rather than becoming an independent country.

195

***Communication Skill:** Speaking. Have several students prepare a mock radio interview with Santa Anna and Sam Houston.
Reading Skill: Determining meaning from context. Discuss the meaning of *Remember the Alamo*.

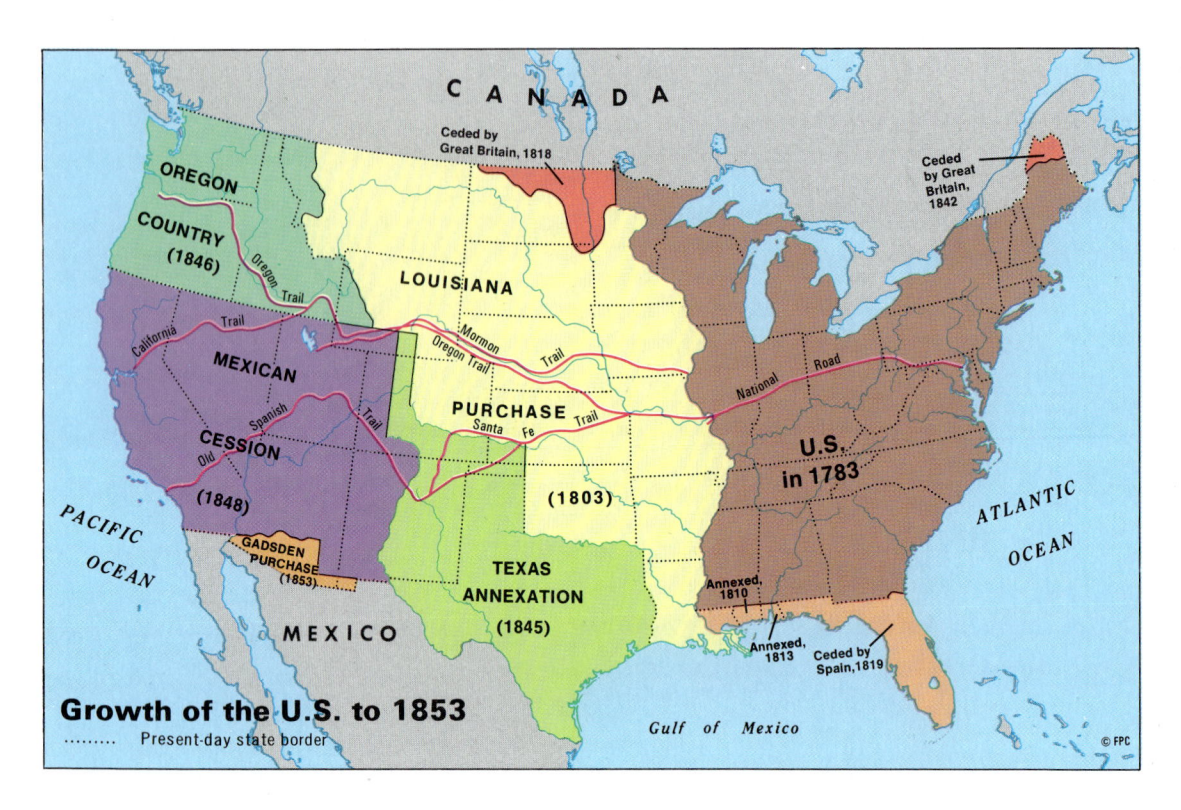

most of the settlers wanted Texas to be separated from Mexico. In 1835 the president of Mexico, Santa Anna, refused to allow any more settlers into Texas.

Because of Santa Anna's action, settlers from the United States revolted. They set up their own government. They drove out Mexican army troops. So Santa Anna brought 3,000 soldiers across the Rio Grande to put down the revolt.

"Remember the Alamo!" In early 1836 Santa Anna led his 3,000 soldiers in an attack on a fort called the Alamo (al′ə·mō). Only 200 settlers were defending the fort. The settlers held the fort for ten days. However, Santa Anna's troops finally took the fort.

Another Texan, Sam Houston, was determined to keep on fighting after the defeat at the Alamo. He gathered a group of **volunteers**, people who decided on their own to become soldiers. Houston led this group in a surprise attack on Santa Anna on April 21, 1836. The soldiers cried, "Remember the Alamo!" as they attacked. The surprise was complete. Houston's army took Santa Anna prisoner. Texas won its independence.

Visitors still tour the Alamo, where Texas fought to be free.

196

Background: The difficulties encountered on the Oregon Trail included scorching deserts, contaminated water, and warfare against Indian tribes. More than 30,000 people died on the Oregon Trail during the 1840s and 1850s.

Texans honored Sam Houston (above) by naming a new city Houston in 1836.

The Texans now wanted to be **annexed**, or added, to the United States. In late 1845 Texas was admitted as a state.

A War—and New Territory

Texas still had many disagreements with Mexico about its borders. The United States considered the Rio Grande to be Texas's southern border. Mexico thought the border should be farther north. In 1846 the two countries went to war about where the border was to be.

The United States attacked Mexico in several different places. One army fought in Mexico. Another entered what is now New Mexico and captured Santa Fe. This same army marched into California. There other settlers joined with the army to take over California. By 1848 Mexico signed a peace treaty.

In the treaty Mexico agreed that the Rio Grande was the border of Texas. It also sold California, most of what is now New Mexico, Nevada, and Arizona, and parts of Colorado and Utah to the United States. This area is sometimes called the Mexican Cession. In 1853 Mexico sold another piece of land to the United States. This area was called the Gadsden Purchase. Find these two areas on the map on page 196.

The Oregon Territory

Find the Oregon Territory on the map on page 196. This territory was claimed by both the United States and Great Britain. In the early 1800s, the Oregon Territory was home to Indians and a few British and U.S. traders and trappers. The trappers marked trails through the woods and mountains of the territory. These trails connected with trails that trappers had made in the Rocky Mountains. The trails of the trappers made the Oregon Trail. Find the Oregon Trail on the map on page 196.

The Oregon Territory was a land of tall forests, tumbling rivers, mild winters, and rich soil. By the 1840s settlers began moving to the territory. **Wagon trains**, or long lines of covered wagons, crossed plains and mountains to reach Oregon.

The British considered Oregon to be a trading post, not a colony. By 1846 there were so many Americans in Oregon that Great Britain and the United States had to decide who owned the territory. In 1846 Great Britain and the United States agreed on the border between the state of Washington and Canada.

The journey west. It was a hard trip. The settlers had to take food and sometimes water. They carried tools, furni-

Thinking Skill: Analyzing. Ask students why the Mexican Cession and Gadsden Purchase were so important.
  * **Reading Skill:** Organizing information. Have students build or draw a wagon train.

The search for gold in California often involved the whole family.

ture, and seeds. Their Conestoga (kän'ə·stō'gə) wagons carried everything they thought they would need.

Usually an experienced trader or trapper led the wagon train. Many of the trips started at towns on the Missouri River. An entire wagon train often had to cross wide, swift rivers. Sometimes the fast river currents swept wagons away. After a wagon train crossed the Rocky Mountains, it faced the worst part of the trip. It had to cross hundreds of miles of desert. Often horses and cattle died of thirst. Sometimes people died too. In spite of the hardships, however, thousands made the trip and reached Oregon.

The settlers used many different trails to travel to the West. Settlers of the Southwest used the Santa Fe and Old Spanish trails. The first settlers of Utah used the Mormon Trail. Find each of these trails on the map on page 196.

California and Gold

The rich soil and mild climate lured settlers to Oregon. In California, however, it was gold.

The gold rush. In 1848 a workman discovered flakes of gold on John Sutter's property in California. Sutter's ranch was in northern California, near the location of Sacramento today. Sutter tried to keep the discovery a secret. The news of the discovery spread anyway. People began to stream into California.

The Gold Rush was on! Farmers, sailors, preachers, and shopkeepers gave up everything to go to California. Some followed the Oregon Trail part of the way. Then the gold hunters took the California Trail to the gold fields. Find the California Trail on the map on page 196. Many others sailed there, crossing the Isthmus of Panama to get from the Caribbean Sea to the Pacific Ocean. Find Panama on the map on pages 10–11.

About 80,000 people reached California between 1848 and 1849. In 1850 California became a state. By 1852 the population of California was nearly 250,000. In 1859 Oregon also became a state. The United States had reached the Pacific Ocean!

Checking Up
1. Who was Stephen Austin?
2. How did the United States get Texas and California?
3. Why did the population of California increase between 1848 and 1849?
4. What answers would you give to the key questions at the beginning of this chapter?
5. *How were traders and trappers important to the settling of the West in the early 1800s?*

Pioneer Life

As You Read

1. Think about these words.
   corduroy road   plank road   springhouse   mill
2. Look for answers to these key questions.
   a. Who were the early pioneers?
   b. Why did pioneers move west?
   c. What was early pioneer life like?

Some settlers gave up on the westward journey and went back home. Others died along the way. Yet thousands were successful and completed the trip to the new land in the West.

They cleared forests for farms. They started towns and built roads. They were the pioneers—settlers of the Northwest and Southwest territories, Texas, Oregon, and California.

In the early 1800s, Americans built a government while they settled a country. Here people in Philadelphia gather to vote.

Reading Skill: Determining the author's purpose. Ask students why this picture was added to a chapter on pioneer life.
*** **Reading Skill:** Organizing information. Have students make shoe-box dioramas of pioneer life.

199

How Things Work

Conestoga Wagons

Conestoga wagons helped Americans move west. These wagons carried people and their tools, seeds, furniture, and food to the new land.

The Conestoga wagons were first built in southeastern Pennsylvania. Look at the Conestoga wagon in the photograph below. The large wheels helped the wagon move through mud. Its length—17 feet (5 m)—provided space for the people and goods. The ends of the wagon were high to keep things from falling out.

The boat-shaped body also helped center the load inside the wagon. As a result, a family's belongings were less likely to be damaged by being jostled on rough roads. The boat shape of the Conestoga wagon was so well known that many people called them "prairie schooners" after the ships called schooners.

Who Were the Pioneers?

The pioneers came from many places. Some came from the states along the Atlantic coast. Some came from earlier settlements in the Northwest and Southwest. Still others came from Norway, Sweden, Germany, Great Britain, and Ireland.

Often people from the same place settled together. In 1805 about 200 people left East Granville, Massachusetts. They made the long trip to Ohio. There they started their new town. They named it Granville after their Massachusetts home. People from Sweden often settled in the north central part of the Northwest Territory. There the land was somewhat like the land they left. There were other Swedish people, too, who spoke their language and kept their customs.

Some early pioneers settled in one place for just a few years. When the land began to fill with farms and towns, they started their westward journey again. Sometimes they went by themselves. Sometimes people like Daniel Boone helped them find new areas to settle. Boone and other pioneers like him looked for land where there were no settlements. It has been said that some pioneers moved as soon as they could see the smoke from another family's cabin.

A Country of Farms and Farmers

Most pioneers went west with dreams of owning their own farms. There was so much land, and the land was so rich, that they knew they could have a farm big enough to support their families better than they had before.

Families could buy land from the government. After buying the land they traveled to their new home. Most pioneers timed their journeys so they would arrive on their new land in early spring or summer. One of the first things they did when they arrived was build a shelter. These shelters were made of logs and leafy branches.

Homes. One of the very first jobs for the pioneers was clearing the forest and building a home. This was hard work. Often families helped one another.

Almost all the early pioneers in the West lived in log cabins. The log cabins were simple. There was usually one room where the family ate, did their chores, and slept. Rough logs, held together with mud, formed the walls of the cabin. Sometimes a floor was made of wooden planks. Often the floor was just packed dirt. There were few glass windows. Usually the pioneers used animal skins or greased paper for window coverings. These coverings helped keep out rain, snow, and insects.

The pioneers in the West learned how to use the forests where they settled. How did this family use the forest's products?

***Reading Skill:** Determining meaning from context. Have students describe a corduroy road to someone who hasn't seen one.
Thinking Skill: Observing. Ask students what kinds of roads are in their area.

One of the most important parts of the cabin was the stone fireplace. It provided warmth and heat for cooking. In winter the family tried to keep close to the fireplace. Even there they could feel the cold wind that seeped through the cracks between the logs.

Life on pioneer farms. The people in a pioneer family had to provide almost everything that they needed. Everyone worked hard, even the children. They chopped trees to burn in the fireplace. They made their own clothing and furniture. They grew their own food. They repaired whatever needed fixing.

In the forests they hunted deer, bears, ducks, geese, and wild turkeys. Pioneers collected wild fruits and nuts in the same forests. The streams and rivers in most places were filled with fish. The pioneers used the resources of the land in much the same way as the Indians had.

Then and Now

Roads

The pioneers of the early 1800s wanted well-built roads. Most of the time, these settlers traveled over roads that were just wide paths. During rainy weather wagons could sink several feet into mud. Sometimes pioneers packed logs and brush in low, wet places in the roads. This helped some. The photograph below shows the Natchez Trace. This was one of the first roads in the United States. Even today, you can still see the deep ruts of the wagon wheels.

The drawing at right shows some of the ways that early pioneers improved roads. **Corduroy roads** were easier to travel on than dirt roads. A corduroy road was built of logs. Some of the logs

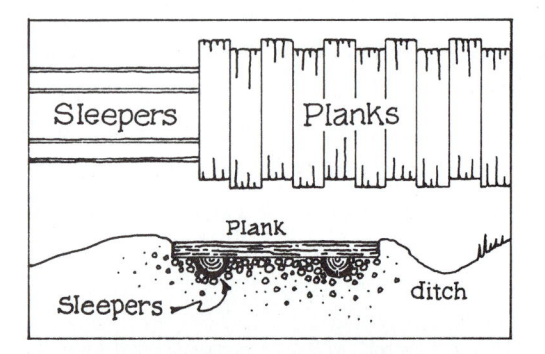

Crushed gravel was placed under cut logs to help support plank roads.

were placed in such a way as to support the other logs. **Plank roads**, roads built of heavy, thick boards, were easier to travel on than corduroy roads. Look at the drawing of plank roads at right. Why do you think plank roads were better than corduroy roads? 1

Today there are about 3 million miles (6.3 million km) of roads in the United States. That means that our roads are long enough to circle the world more than 150 times! Most roads now are paved with hard, strong materials like concrete. Most roads today are smooth and comfortable to ride on. Good roads are still important to this country.

---

1. Plank roads had more support for the weight of vehicles and were therefore less likely to be adversely affected by rain and mud.
Math Skill: Ask students how far it is around the world (24,902 miles, or 40,075 k).

Because pioneer families supplied most of their own food, they did not have the variety of foods we enjoy today. Like many Indian tribes, pioneer families depended on corn for much of their food. Corn bread and corn cakes were common foods for pioneer families. Farmers raised some livestock for food.

Although animals were important for food, pioneer farmers had other uses for them. Horses and oxen pulled the wagons and carts that pioneers used for transportation. Farmers also used horses, donkeys, and oxen to pull plows to prepare fields for seeding.

Unlike Americans today, the pioneers did not have refrigerators or freezers. They did, however, have ways of preserving, or keeping, food. They knew how to preserve meat by salting it. They stored vegetables, milk, butter, and eggs in **springhouses**. A springhouse was a deep pit dug in a cool area.

Most early pioneers made most of their own clothing. The materials they used were cotton, wool, and flax. The thin fibers of the flax plant could be spun into linen thread. Pioneers used dyes made from plants to color their clothes.

The development of towns. Small towns started in the new territories too. Stores, banks, and churches were important places in these areas. Most towns had a general store that sold things settlers needed. Knives, axes, iron nails, farm tools, and calico for dresses and shirts could be bought in the general store. The stores also sold sugar, salt, dishes, needles, and thread. A trip to town to shop was a special event.

A quilting bee was a frontier party at which people made beautiful quilts.

Often towns grew up around **mills**, or places where grains were ground into flour. Because farmers took their corn and wheat to the mills, stores and banks located there too. They knew they would have customers. Some of these early towns became large cities. This was especially true of those towns on rivers.

Checking Up

1. Name two ways pioneer life was like that of the Indians.
2. Describe log cabins. Why were fireplaces in log cabins important?
3. What answers would you give to the key questions at the beginning of this chapter?
4. *Why do you think people from the same place often wanted to settle together?*

Reading Skill: Organizing information: *As You Read, 3.*

Progress and Change

As You Read

1. Think about these words.

   industrial revolution   textile   steam engine   factory   cotton gin   reaper   telegraph

2. Look for answers to these key questions.
   a. What was the first industry started in the United States?
   b. How did the industrial revolution change farming in the United States?
   c. How did great American inventors help to start an industrial revolution in the United States?

3. Use this reading skill.
   Note taking will help you remember the main ideas about what you read. To be a good note taker, you must do several things. First skim the lesson, noticing the headings and illustrations. Then read the lesson carefully. Write down each heading. Under each one write the main ideas of the section. Use these notes to write a summary of this chapter.

In the late 1700s, the **industrial revolution** began in Great Britain. The industrial revolution was the time when machines began doing the work people had done by hand. These new machines could do the work of many people.

In the late 1700s and early 1800s, the industrial revolution spread to the United States. The industrial revolution did not occur in all parts of the United States at the same time. The first **factories**, or places where machines produced goods, were in Massachusetts, Rhode Island, Connecticut, and New York. These states had rivers and waterfalls for power to run the machines.

Early Industry in the United States

The first industries made **textiles**, or cloth. These textile industries used cotton grown in Georgia, South Carolina, and Louisiana.

Cotton factories. In 1793 Samuel Slater opened the first factory in the United States that made cotton thread and cloth. Slater had been to England and made copies of machines that spun thread. These machines did work that had been done by hand. Slater's machines were powered by the river flowing beside his factory.

By 1840 there were about 1,200 cotton factories in the United States. Most

* **Reading Skill:** Building vocabulary. Discuss the meaning of *industrial revolution.*

Textile machines like these made cotton thread and cloth far more cheaply than people could by hand.

of them were in the Northeast. Most used waterpower to run the machines.

The success of these factories brought about many changes. Thousands of people came to the factory towns to find jobs working with the new machines. The growth of the factories caused some towns to grow into cities.

The success of the cotton factories made changes in other places too. The demand for cotton increased. An American inventor helped farmers in another part of the United States meet this growing demand.

The Cotton Gin and the South

In 1792 Eli Whitney was visiting a friend in Georgia. He noticed that the cotton grown on his friend's farm was full of seeds. The seeds were difficult to pick out by hand. So Eli Whitney worked to invent a machine called the **cotton gin**. It separated the seeds from the cotton fibers. The first cotton gin, operated by hand, did the work of ten people. When the cotton gin was powered by water, it did the work of fifty.

The invention of the cotton gin changed the United States in many ways. Farmers in Georgia, Alabama, Mississippi, and Louisiana began planting more and more cotton. Factories in both the northeastern United States and Great Britain bought all the cotton farmers could grow. Cotton became such an

Whitney's gin used teeth of small saws to pull cotton fibers from the seeds.

* **Communication Skill:** Writing. Choose a student or a group of students to write a feature on Eli Whitney. Have them illustrate their feature.
    Thinking Skill: Observing. Have students describe a cotton gin to someone who has never seen one.

important crop that it became known as "King Cotton."

Eli Whitney's other invention. Eli Whitney made another invention that helped United States industry. In 1798 Whitney accepted an order from the United States government to make 10,000 rifles. At that time rifles were made by hand, one by one. Whitney thought that it would be easier and faster to make rifle parts by machine. Machines could make all the parts that could be used in any of the 10,000 rifles. When all the parts were made, the rifles could be put together quickly. Whitney had developed the idea of interchangeable parts. Soon many businesses and factories were using interchangeable parts.

The Rise of Railroads

The growth of businesses and factories created a need for good transportation. Factories needed raw materials. Factory owners needed to send finished goods to places where people could buy them.

The canals built in this country helped solve part of this problem. However, the shortest route between farm and factory was not always by canal. Moreover, in the North, where the factories were, canals and waterways often froze in the winters.

Fortunately, in the 1830s a new form of transportation developed. It was the railroad. Like the machines in Slater's factory, the railroad was a British invention. However, by 1831 a train called "the Best Friend of Charleston" was making regular runs carrying passengers within Charleston, South Carolina.

Many of the first trains used horses to pull cars on a track. Yet it was the **steam engine** that made railroads fast and efficient. Steam engines used the powerful force of boiling water to drive the train.

People take a ride on the first train of an early New York railroad. What other means of transportation did trains borrow from?

Two workers using a reaper could cut five or six acres of grain a day.

The Industrial Revolution Comes to the Farm

Farmers, like most people in the early 1800s, did much of their work by hand. One of their hardest jobs was harvesting grain by hand.

In 1834 Cyrus McCormick invented the **reaper**, a machine that harvested grain. A horse or team of horses pulled the reaper. McCormick's reaper made harvesting much easier and faster. Farmers in Ohio, Indiana, Illinois, and other places increased the amount of land they planted in grain. They started to grow more grain to sell. They sent the grain by railroad to cities like New York City and Philadelphia. There it was shipped to Great Britain and many other countries in Europe. United States grain became as important as United States cotton to eastern cities and Great Britain. The states in the old Northwest Territory became the breadbasket, the center of grain growing, for part of the world.

Changes in Communication

How did a person in the early 1800s send a letter to someone in a distant city? It could be sent by stagecoach, boat, or railroad. All these ways took time. Yet once again a United States inventor changed that.

Samuel Morse was a painter. However, in 1844 after twelve years of hard work, Morse set up the first telegraph lines. The **telegraph** is a way of sending messages on electrical wires. The electrical wires were connected to poles. The first telegraph lines were between Baltimore and Washington, D.C. Messages went back and forth between these two cities in a few seconds. By the 1850s telegraph lines linked cities and towns just as the railroads did.

The United States had expanded to the Pacific Ocean in the 1840s. Yet the inventions of its own people had truly linked the country.

Checking Up

1. Where did the industrial revolution begin?
2. What effect did textile factories have on the South?
3. What invention changed farming in Ohio, Indiana, and Illinois?
4. What answers would you give to the key questions at the beginning of this chapter?
5. *How did the inventions you read about bring the country closer together?*

Americans Examine Their Country

As You Read

1. Think about these words.
   slavery   abolish   suffrage
2. Look for answers to these key questions.
   a. Why were slaves important especially in the South?
   b. What was the main goal of the abolitionists?
   c. What was meant by woman suffrage?

You have read about many important inventors in the United States during the late 1700s and early 1800s. These inventors, like many other Americans, were curious people. They wanted to know how and why things worked. Americans in the 1840s and 1850s also began looking carefully at how they lived. Many thought there should be important changes in life in the United States.

Slavery

Many Americans wanted to stop **slavery**. Slavery is the ownership of people by other people. In the 1700s slavery existed in most of the colonies. By the 1840s slavery was against the law in most northern states. It then existed mainly in the southern states. Within the southern states, slavery was most common within cotton-growing areas.

Eli Whitney's cotton gin made cotton easier to clean and prepare for the textile factories. In the last chapter you read that the demand for cotton increased. The slaves who planted, harvested, and cleaned the cotton became more and more valuable to their owners. To cotton growers, slavery was a business.

Cotton is a plant that quickly uses up the food in the soil. It was almost impossible to grow cotton in the same fields year after year. So cotton growers often moved to new areas. By the 1840s cotton growing, and the slaves who worked in the cotton fields, seemed to be more widespread in the United States than ever before. The number of slaves had increased from about 700,000 in 1790 to more than 3 million in 1850.

The Abolitionist Movement

Abolitionists (ab'ə·lish'ə·nists) were people who believed that slavery was wrong. They wanted to **abolish**, or get rid of, slavery. They believed it was wrong for one person to own another person.

The abolitionists wanted slavery to be against the law. Some abolitionists wanted the government to stop the spread of slavery into the new territories.

Background: In some areas of the United States, such as the Northwest Territory, slavery had always been illegal.
*** Communication Skill: Speaking. Have several students prepare speeches for and against slavery.

Abolitionists protested against slave auctions. Slaves were bought and sold like any other good.

They wanted to abolish slavery over a long period of time. Other abolitionists wanted slavery abolished all over the United States immediately.

In the 1830s and 1840s, the abolitionists began making speeches about their beliefs. They published newspapers about slavery and abolition. One famous abolitionist newspaper was *The Liberator*. It was published in Boston by William Lloyd Garrison.

Beginning in 1831, Garrison used his newspaper to convince others that slavery was wrong. He wrote that slaves should be freed immediately. At first Garrison's ideas were very unpopular. In 1835 he was attacked by a mob who hated his ideas. Yet Garrison still spoke

Garrison denounced the evils of slavery in his paper, *The Liberator*. He published the paper until slavery was abolished in 1865.

Reading Skill: Doing research. Have students research Garrison's life and write three additional paragraphs to add to the section about him.

Reading Skill: Building vocabulary. Have students look up the meanings of *masthead* and *auction*.

209

*** **Communication Skill:** Writing. Have several students write a feature on Harriet Tubman.
Thinking Skill: Analyzing. Ask students how Frederick Douglass made a difference.

Harriet Tubman made nineteen trips to the South to help slaves escape.

out against slavery. In the first issue of *The Liberator*, he had told his readers his feelings about slavery: "I will not excuse. I will not retreat an inch. And I will be heard."

Some abolitionists were former slaves. One of these people was Harriet Tubman. She helped slaves escape from the plantations on which they worked. In ten years she helped more than 300 slaves escape to northern states.

By 1850 there were thousands of abolitionists. They were writing and speaking in most parts of the country, even in the southern states. The questions about slavery that abolitionists had brought up troubled the entire country.

The Move for Greater Rights

Some of the abolitionists were also concerned about the rights of women. For most of the 1800s, women in the United States could not vote. They could not be elected President, senator, or representative. In the early 1800s, women could not even go to college.

People Who Made a Difference

Frederick Douglass

Like Harriet Tubman, Frederick Douglass was a former slave who became an abolitionist. Douglass was one of the most effective speakers of all the abolitionists. He made many speeches in the 1840s in Massachusetts. Douglass was able to tell listeners about the wrongs of slavery. He had experienced those wrongs himself.

Douglass was also a writer whose books reached a wide audience. He had learned to read and write while still a slave. His first book, *Narrative of the Life of Frederick Douglass*, was one of the first books to tell what slavery did to people.

---

* **Reading Skill:** Doing research. Have students research the life of Frederick Douglass and add two paragraphs to this feature.

Thinking Skill: Analyzing. Ask students if they would have wanted to go to this convention.
Reading Skill: Doing research. Have students look for additional information about Lucretia Mott and Elizabeth Cady Stanton.

Many people began working to improve the rights of women in the United States. These people said that women should be allowed to vote and go to college. Changes began to be made. In 1835 Oberlin College in Ohio became the first college to admit women. In 1837 Mount Holyoke (hōl′ē·ōk) College became the first women's college in the United States.

Those who worked for women's rights thought that woman **suffrage** was the most important right. Suffrage is the right to vote. In 1848 two women, Elizabeth Cady Stanton and Lucretia (lū·krē′shə) Mott, organized a convention, or a meeting for a specific purpose, in Seneca Falls, New York. More than 1,000 people from eleven states went to the convention. This was the beginning of the organized effort to get women the right to vote.

The struggle to improve the rights of women was hard. Yet people continued to work for these rights. They also continued to work for abolition.

Oberlin College has been a center for civil rights since its beginning.

Checking Up
1. Why did abolitionists want to stop slavery?
2. What was the Seneca Falls Convention of 1848?
3. What answers would you give to the key questions at the beginning of this chapter?
4. *Why do you think some people who were slaves became abolitionists?*

Unit 6 Summary
- In the move westward, traders and trappers were usually the first people in a new territory. They were followed by settlers and their families. The development of roads, canals, steamboats, and railroads helped pioneers move west.
- The Louisiana Purchase more than doubled the size of the United States. Lewis and Clark explored this new territory.
- The United States gained Texas, the Mexican Cession, and Oregon in the 1840s.
- Pioneers supplied most of their needs themselves.
- The industrial revolution changed the way most Americans lived. Machines began to do the work people had.
- In the 1840s and 1850s, Americans began to work to abolish slavery. Some tried to get voting rights for women.

Unit 6 Review Workshop

What Have You Learned?

1. How were the Erie Canal, the National Road, and the steamboat important to the settling of the West?
2. Who wrote the words of our national anthem? When was the national anthem written?
3. What were Lewis and Clark looking for on their expedition?
4. What new lands did Zebulon Pike explore?
5. How did the United States get the land that is now Arizona and New Mexico?
6. Describe the homes in which most early pioneer families lived.
7. How were Conestoga wagons built to withstand the rugged trip west?
8. What were Eli Whitney's two important inventions?
9. Who were the abolitionists?
10. Why were many people in favor of woman suffrage?

Use Your Reading Skills

You can improve your vocabulary in many ways. One way is to learn meanings of parts of words. For example, you read about an expedition in this unit. The word expedition uses the word part *ped*. The word part *ped* means "foot" or "moving on foot." If you remember that meaning, you can figure out the meanings of other words that contain *ped*. How do you *pedal* a bicycle? How does a *pedestrian* move from place to place? Use your dictionary to find out the meanings of the following words: *centipede*, *pedestal*, *pedometer*, and *pedigree*. Explain what the word part *ped* has to do with the meaning of each word.

Use Your Time Skills

The table on page 213 shows the populations of five states from 1790 to 1830. These five states were some of the first places that pioneers settled after the Revolutionary War. Study the table. Then answer the questions below.

1. Which state had the largest population in 1790? in 1830?
2. Why do you think there are no population figures for Ohio, Indiana, and Illinois in 1790?
3. During which ten-year period did the population of Ohio grow the most?
4. During which ten-year period did the population in a state of the Southwest Territory grow the most?

Use Your Thinking Skills

Using the map on page 184, write a sentence that tells whether each of the following statements is true or false. Include reasons that show why the statement is true or false.

1. All the roads built by 1815 went in a western direction.
2. All the roads built by 1815 were in states that had been the original thirteen colonies.

Reading Skills: Building vocabulary, using references, interpreting visuals.
Thinking Skills: Knowing, analyzing.

Population of Selected States						
	1790	1800	1810	1820	1830
Kentucky	74,000	221,000	407,000	564,000	688,000
Tennessee	36,000	106,000	262,000	423,000	682,000
Ohio	N/A	45,000	231,000	581,000	938,000
Indiana	N/A	6,000	25,000	147,000	343,000
Illinois	N/A	N/A	12,000	55,000	157,000

N/A: Not available

3. By 1815 there were many canals built that were connected to the Missouri River.
4. All canals built between 1815 and 1850 connected rivers with lakes.
5. By 1850 there were more roads and canals in the Northwest Territory than in any other part of the United States.

Learn by Doing

1. Imagine that you are with the Lewis and Clark expedition. Write a journal about your trip. Write about what you would see and hear as you leave the Mandan villages on the way to the Great Falls of the Missouri River. What is the weather like? What landforms do you see? What rivers? What animals? Use the map of Indian tribes on page 62. What tribes are nearby? You may even want to include some drawings. Share your journal with your classmates.
2. Read more about the forms of transportation that the early settlers used: Conestoga wagons, keelboats, stagecoaches, and steamboats. Use books and encyclopedias to help you with your research. Then write about the advantages and disadvantages of each form of transportation. Be sure to include information about the speed with which each form of transportation moved.
3. Prepare a report on the tools used by pioneers for farming and for building homes. One good source of information is in the books of the writer Eric Sloane. In which ways were early American tools different from tools used today? How are they like tools used today? In your report, include drawings of some of the early American tools.

Read to Learn More

Find the topics listed below in the card catalog of your library. Read all or part of a book listed under one of the topics. Share what you learn with your classmates.

ERIE CANAL   CALIFORNIA GOLD RUSH
OREGON TRAIL   FRONTIER LIFE

Communication Skill: Writing: *Learn by Doing, 1.*
Map Skill: Location: *Learn by Doing, 1.*
Reading Skills: Interpreting visuals, using references: *Learn by Doing, 1, 2.*
Thinking Skill: Analyzing: *Learn by Doing, 1, 2.*

Unit Overview: This unit examines the Civil War period—before, during, and after the war.

Unit Objectives
To understand:
- the causes of the Civil War
- the Civil War
- the effects of the war
- the settlement of the West after the war

Suggested Materials
Workbook
Unit Tests

Unit 7

Skills Emphasized
Map Skills: pp. 214, 216, 217, 219, 236, 237, 246.
Social Studies Reading Skills: pp. 214, 216, 217, 218, 219, 220, 221, 222, 223, 225, 226, 227, 228, 229, 230, 231, 232, 233, 234, 235, 236, 237, 238, 239, 240, 241, 243, 245, 246, 247.
Thinking Skills: pp. 214, 217, 218, 220, 221, 222, 223, 225, 226, 229, 231, 237, 239, 240, 241, 246.
Communication Skills: pp. 214, 222, 224, 225, 227, 228, 235, 236, 237, 240, 246, 247.
Time Skills: pp. 214, 224, 226, 234, 236, 238, 240, 241.
Social Studies Math Skills: pp. 223, 233, 236.
Citizenship Skill: p. 227.

Suggested Student Activities
   1. Arrange a bulletin-board display on each section of the United States—the North, South, and West—before the Civil War.
   2. Make a map of Civil War battles. Plot all the battles on the map on page 247.
   3. Draw a large map of the United States in 1853. Then draw in each new state created after 1853 to the present day.
 * 4. Make a model of a plantation.
 ** 5. Make a pictorial graph of travel during this period.
*** 6. Make a pictorial time line using each event in the unit time line on pages 214–215.

Skills Emphasized in Suggested Student Activities
Map Skills: Location, scale, distance, symbolization.
Social Studies Reading Skills: Using references, doing research, organizing information.
Thinking Skills: Knowing, comparing, analyzing.
Communication Skill: Writing.
Time Skill.

War and a New Beginning

One of the famous battles of the Civil War was fought at this site in Gettysburg.

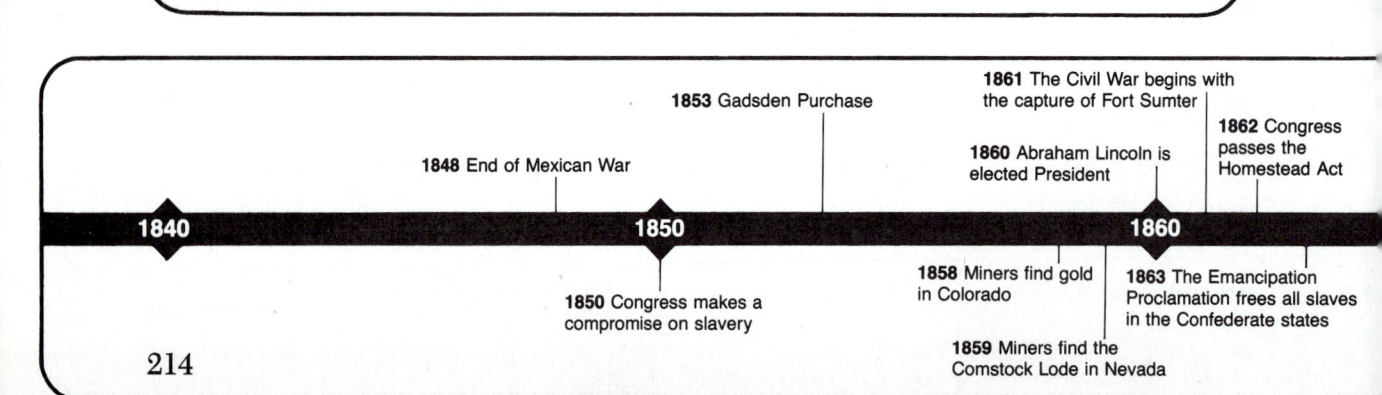

1848 End of Mexican War
1850 Congress makes a compromise on slavery
1853 Gadsden Purchase
1858 Miners find gold in Colorado
1859 Miners find the Comstock Lode in Nevada
1860 Abraham Lincoln is elected President
1861 The Civil War begins with the capture of Fort Sumter
1862 Congress passes the Homestead Act
1863 The Emancipation Proclamation frees all slaves in the Confederate states

1840   1850   1860

214

1868 The Fourteenth Amendment to the Constitution becomes law

1867 The Chisholm Trail opens

1869 The first transcontinental railroad is completed

1870 The Fifteenth Amendment to the Constitution becomes law

1877 Union troops leave the South

1870 — **1880** — **1890**

1865 The Civil War ends with the Confederate surrender at Appomattox Court House

President Lincoln is killed

The Thirteenth Amendment to the Constitution becomes law

1876 Centennial celebration

1873 Joseph Glidden invents barbed wire

1890 All Plains Indians are living on reservations

Differences in the Growing Nation

As You Read

1. Think about these words.
   tariff   compromise
2. Look for answers to these key questions.
   a. What were the three main sections of the United States by the mid-1800s? How did they differ?
   b. What problems caused disagreements between the North and the South?
   c. Why did the South want slavery to continue?
3. Use this reading skill.
   A good reader skims a chapter several times to find its main ideas. Before you begin reading this chapter, skim it more than once. The first time, look at the headings and words in bold type. The second time, look carefully at the illustrations. Then close your book and write one sentence that tells what this chapter is about.

By 1850 the United States was a nation of thirty-one states and several territories. The nation stretched from the Atlantic to the Pacific. As you read in Unit 6, by 1853 its borders with Canada and Mexico had become the same as they are today. By 1850 the United States had more than 23 million people. Over the next ten years, its population grew to well over 31 million.

Growing Differences

While the United States was growing in population, the country was also growing apart. Different parts of the country were not developing in the same ways.

The map on page 217 shows the United States in 1854. By studying this map, you can see how the country had developed into three sections. In general, those states east of the Missouri River where slavery was not allowed made up the North. States where slavery was allowed made up the South. The other states and territories made up the West.

Problems developed between the North and the South. Because the West had so few people, and because its economic life was different, it was not deeply involved in the disagreements between the North and the South.

Population and politics. The North had more than half of the nation's population by 1850. Thus, the North had more members than the South in the House of Representatives. In the Senate the North and South were even. Yet people in the South feared that the North

Map Skill: Location. Have students compare the number of U.S. states and territories shown on the map below with the map on pages 18–19. Have them list which states developed from which territories on the map below.

*** Reading Skill:** Building vocabulary. Discuss the meaning of *tariff*.

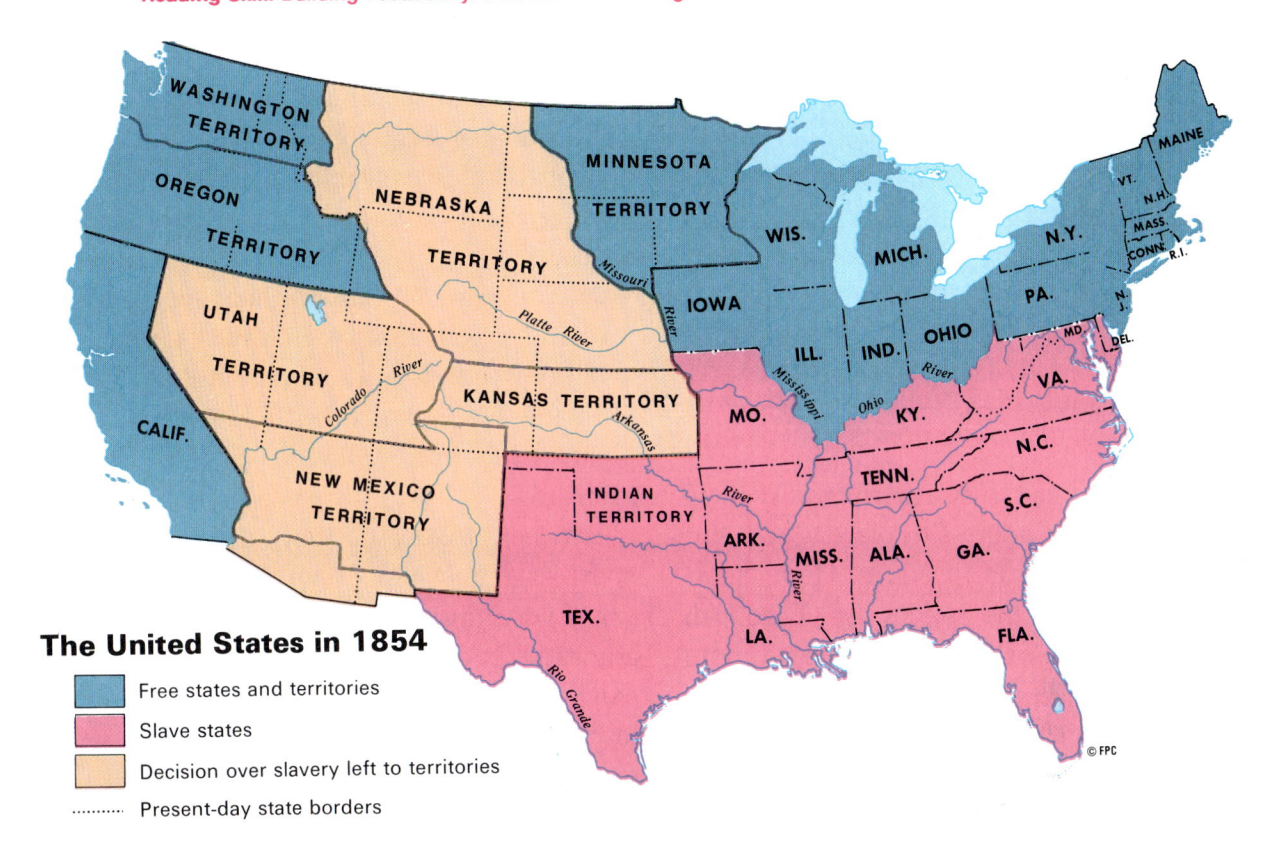

The United States in 1854

- Free states and territories
- Slave states
- Decision over slavery left to territories
- .... Present-day state borders

would continue to make gains in Congress. They were afraid that the laws made by Congress would favor the interests of the North.

Transportation. One of the disagreements was about transportation. Most of the nation's factories were in the North. Business owners wanted more roads, canals, and railroads so they could ship their products to other parts of the country for sale. The North wanted the government to spend more money on improving transportation.

The South was not against improving transportation. However, it did not need new roads or railroads as much as the North did. Most people in the South made a living by farming. Farm products could be shipped from the South by water. The South had plenty of riverways and good seaports. Southerners complained that too much government money was being spent on improving transportation in the North.

Taxes. The government got most of its money by taxing goods that were shipped into the United States from overseas. Such taxes are called **tariffs**. There were sharp differences between the North and the South about tariffs.

Factory owners in the North wanted protection against cheaper products brought from Europe. If European clothing or furniture, for example, sold for less money than similar products made in the United States, people would buy the

Thinking Skill: Classifying. Ask students to list the problems that developed between the North and South that led to the Civil War.

217

Thinking Skill: Analyzing. Discuss why some people were for tariffs and others against them.

Northern factories produced most of the nation's finished goods.

cheaper products. Northern factory owners wanted Congress to place a high tariff on goods from overseas. High tariffs would raise the prices of European goods. People would then buy more United States products.

Southerners, who had few factories, were against the tariffs. They wanted to be able to buy products at the lowest possible price.

Slavery. The most bitter disagreements between North and South were about slavery. By the mid-1800s, all the northern states had done away with slavery. The South continued to support it. The owners of large southern plantations depended on slave labor to grow their large crops of cotton, sugarcane, and tobacco.

As you read in Unit 6, many people wanted to end slavery entirely. A few abolitionists were in the South, but most of them were in the North. The southern planters felt that ending slavery would ruin them.

Between 1820 and 1860, there were many arguments in Congress over slavery. Every time a territory asked to be admitted as a new state, the argument came up again. Would the new state allow or forbid slavery? Several times Congress worked out **compromises**. That is, they made deals that would partly satisfy both the North and the South. When Missouri was admitted as a slave state, for example, Maine was admitted as a free state. Such compromises kept the balance between free and slave states.

None of the compromises really satisfied anyone for long. They did not put an end to the conflict over slavery.

By 1850 most slaves on farms and plantations worked in cotton fields.

Checking Up
1. Why did the North and South differ on transportation? on tariffs?
2. What answers would you give to the key questions at the beginning of this chapter?
3. *How did compromises satisfy the North and the South for awhile?*

Background: In the Missouri Compromise of 1820, Congress forbade slavery north of the 36°30' N parallel except for Missouri and allowed slavery south of the line. In the Compromise of 1850, Congress let the settlers of the New Mexico and Utah territories decide whether they wanted slavery.

* **Reading Skill:** Developing vocabulary. Review the meaning of *abolitionist*.

Reading Skill: Interpreting visuals: *As You Read, 3.*
Reading Skill: Organizing information. Have students begin lists of words and phrases that describe plantations.

The South and Slavery

As You Read

1. Think about these words.
   underground railroad   rebellion
2. Look for answers to these key questions.
   a. What was life in the South like for plantation owners? for small farmers? for slaves?
   b. What kinds of work did slaves do?
   c. How did slaves try to fight against slavery?
3. Use this reading skill.
   Pictures can tell you a great deal about life in earlier times. Study the pictures in this chapter carefully. Read the captions to learn more about the pictures. Then write a short paragraph describing the South and slavery from what you learned from the pictures.

During the first half of the 1800s, the North became more industrialized. The South had some industry, but it remained mostly agricultural. These differences helped the country grow apart.

Plantations and Farms

The South was mainly a land of large plantations and small farms. Its richest people were the owners of the large plantations. These were the people who had the most power in the South. They were the strongest supporters of slavery because they depended on slaves to work their plantations.

King Cotton. Some planters, especially those in Virginia, North Carolina, and Tennessee, grew tobacco. Rice and sugar were the important crops in Louisiana. Rice was also important in Georgia and South Carolina. The most important crop in nearly all the South, however, was cotton.

The industrial revolution had increased the demand for cotton. Factories in the North and in Britain were making huge amounts of cotton cloth. As better machines speeded up the work, the need for cotton increased. Because the demand for cotton was high, the price of cotton also increased.

Planters could make great profits by selling cotton to these factories. The South's long growing season, with its plentiful rainfall, was well suited to the growing of cotton. Cotton became so important to the South that people called it "King Cotton."

Plantations. A large cotton plantation included many hundreds of acres of

Map Skill: Location. Ask students to make farm product maps of the pre–Civil War South.
** Reading Skill: Using references. Have the class look for other pictures of plantations.

Thinking Skill: Comparing. Discuss how the acreage and products of a plantation compare with those of a modern-day farm.

Reading Skill: Determining meaning from context. Talk about why many plantations were compared with small towns.

Cotton bales were sent by steamboat to ports like New Orleans.

land. About half of the acres were planted in cotton. The other half were used to grow food crops to feed the family of the plantation owner and the slaves.

Plantations and farms were spread far apart. It was a long trip from one to the next. The nearest town or city might be a day's journey away. Planters could not depend on town workers for any of their needs. So every plantation was really like a small town. The owner ran it, but the slaves did all the work. A large plantation might have more than a hundred slaves.

There were many buildings on a plantation. The slaves lived in small cabins away from the big house. A plantation also included stables and barns for the farm animals and a warehouse to store the crops until they were ready to be shipped. Other buildings included workshops of various kinds. Blacksmiths and brickmakers had their own shops. Sometimes one building was for the slaves to weave cloth for their own clothes.

Other farmers. Not all the southern farmers had large plantations. Most, in fact, had smaller farms. Instead of big houses, farm families lived in small wooden houses or log cabins. Many had only one or two rooms.

On a small farm, much of the work was done by the family itself. Most farm families did not have slaves. If they did, it was usually one or two, seldom more than ten. These farmers worked alongside their slaves.

The farmers raised farm animals and grew food crops for their own use. If they could manage it, they tried to plant a few acres in cotton or some other crop to sell for extra money.

Most planter families lived in big houses filled with fine furniture.

220

Background: Many plantation homes, such as Rosalie in Natchez, Mississippi, pictured above, have been restored and are open to the public. Tourism maps of the South locate these mansions.

* **Reading Skill:** Developing vocabulary. Review the purposes of a blacksmith's shop.

Thinking Skill: Observing. Ask students to describe the slave quarters in the top picture and then compare their structure and surrounding grounds with the photograph of the planter's home on page 220.
** **Reading Skill:** Organizing information. Have students make pictorial summaries of a slave's life.

Many slaves lived in small cabins in the slave quarters. There they ate their meals and visited one another.

The poorest farmers lived on the least desirable land. Their farms were small, and the soil was so poor that they could just barely manage to make a living. The poor farmers owned no slaves, but even they supported slavery. Many of them hoped that they might somehow manage to become slave owners.

A Slave's Life

A slave's life was one of hard work. From the time slave children were old enough to get around on their own, they were put to work. They continued to work until they were too old or until they died. They were bought and sold as though they were no more than pieces of property. In fact, most slave owners thought of them as property.

Farming. Most of the slaves on a farm or plantation worked in the fields. They

Often house slaves did not have as many hardships as field slaves.

* **Reading Skill:** Using references. Have the class look for other pictures of slaves working in the pre–Civil War South.

221

planted the crops, cared for them, and harvested them. Other slaves took care of the farm animals. Those with special skills worked as blacksmiths, carpenters, or brickmakers, or at other special jobs. Skilled slaves were especially prized by the slave owners.

Work began early in the morning, often before the sun rose. It continued until darkness fell. At the busiest times of the year, such as harvesttime, slaves might be kept working well into the night. Sundays and a few holidays were their only days of rest.

Slaves also worked as servants in the big house. They cooked and served meals, cleaned, and did the washing.

Slaves had little time to themselves. Many planters, however, let their slaves have small gardens of their own near the slave cabins. Some slaves were able to make a little money selling vegetables they grew themselves. A few were able to buy their freedom with this money.

City workers. Not all the slaves worked on farms and plantations. Many were servants for people living in towns and cities. Slaves also worked in factories, stores, and other businesses. Some plantation owners "rented" their slaves to a factory owner when they were not needed on the plantation.

Flight to Freedom

Slave owners often claimed that their slaves were happy. The slaves certainly would not have agreed. They were told when to work, where to work, and how to work. They were punished if they did not obey their masters or if they did not work hard enough. Slave families were often torn apart when members were sold separately. What the slaves wanted more than anything else was freedom.

Runaway slaves reach another underground railroad stop.

Thousands managed to escape from their owners. They tried to make their way to the North, where they would be free. The route to freedom was called the **underground railroad**. Runaway slaves traveled at night to escape being caught. They moved from one place of safety to the next until they reached freedom. People who were against slavery—both black and white, in both the North and the South—helped the escaping slaves. They hid them during the day and told them which way to travel to keep from getting caught. They provided food and money for the runaways.

> **Background:** In 1850 Congress passed the Fugitive Slave Act. The law made it a serious crime to help slaves escape and gave law officers the right to capture escaped slaves in any state and return them to their owners.
>
> **Thinking Skill:** Hypothesizing. Ask students whether they would have helped slaves escape.

RUNAWAYS.

TWENTY-FIVE DOLLARS REWARD. — Runaway from my place, in Chesterfield county, Va., my Negro Man BEN JOHNSON, of black color, about 5 feet 10 inches high, weighs about 175 lbs., apparently 45 or 50 years old, and is a good cook, and is probably hiring himself to cook in Richmond or Petersburg. The above reward will be paid for his safe delivery to me at PULLIAM & Co.'s office, or safe lodgment in some jail. He came from Petersburg. Left home 1st March last.
ap 17-tf   ALBERT C. PULLIAM.

Many southern newspapers regularly carried notices about runaway slaves.

Slaves who were caught trying to escape were punished. Sometimes they were beaten or whipped. Many owners, however, did not want to hurt their slaves so badly that they would be unable to work. They punished runaways by giving them extra work, locking them up, or putting them in chains.

Slave uprisings. Slaves also tried to escape by fighting their way to freedom. There were a number of slave **rebellions**, or uprisings, in the South. Slaves would gather together to march north. On their way north, they fought against anyone who tried to stop them.

Most of these rebellions failed. The slaves seldom had many weapons. They could not defeat the well-armed whites who tried to stop them. Many people, both black and white, were killed in rebellions.

Free Blacks

There were more than 4 million black people in the United States by 1860. Most of them were slaves, but almost half a million were free. Some had bought their freedom. Others had escaped from slavery. Many had always been free.

Most of the free blacks lived in the North. Some remained in the South, especially in larger cities, where they had less trouble. Free blacks in the South had to carry papers with them at all times to prove that they were not runaway slaves.

Free blacks, especially in the North, worked at nearly every kind of job there was. Many farmed or worked in factories. Some were teachers, doctors, preachers, lawyers, or writers. A few became wealthy business owners.

Although they were free, they still had problems. In the South laws kept free blacks from getting some jobs. Yet they could also be arrested for not having a job. They could even be sold back into slavery. Even in the North, black people often faced problems. In some states they could not vote. Some senators even tried to pass a law to keep blacks out of the army and navy. The law failed, and blacks continued to serve in both. The time was not far off when their help would be needed.

Checking Up

1. What was the underground railroad?
2. Where did most free blacks live?
3. What problems did free blacks have in the South? in the North?
4. What answers would you give to the key questions at the beginning of this chapter?
5. *What arguments would you use to convince a slave owner that slavery was wrong?*

> *** **Math Skill:** Have students use encyclopedias or other books to figure out the total U.S. population by 1860 and compare it with the total black population then, which is mentioned on this page.
> *** **Reading Skill:** Organizing information. Have small groups of students describe frames they would include in a filmstrip on slavery.

Communication Skill: Writing. Organize a class biography of Abraham Lincoln.
1. The Utah, New Mexico, Nebraska, and Kansas territories.

A Divided Nation

As You Read

1. Think about these words.
   secede   Union   civil war   blockade   civilian
2. Look for answers to these key questions.
   a. What events led to a war between the North and the South?
   b. What advantages did the North have in the war? the South?
   c. How did the North defeat the South?

Feelings between the North and the South grew more and more bitter. Abolitionists continued to demand an end to slavery. Most southerners believed they should have the right to decide what was best for them. People in the South thought the federal government should stay out of such matters as slavery.

Drifting Toward War

As you know, Congress made several compromises on the issue of slavery in the mid-1800s. Some of these compromises said that states formed from territories could be slave or free, depending on what the people in the new states decided. Look at the map of the United States in 1854 on page 217. What were four territories in which the decision about slavery would be left to the people in these areas?¹ As new states were formed in the mid-1800s, arguments over slavery increased.

The Republican Party. A new political party was formed in the 1850s. It was called the Republican Party. The Republican Party was against the spread of slavery. Most Republicans lived in the North. The Democrats remained strong in the South.

Abraham Lincoln. In the late 1850s, the Republicans found a new leader. He

Lincoln was one of four men in the race for President in 1860.

Time Skill: Have students make a time line for this chapter. Have them write down each date and event mentioned in this chapter in the correct time order.

224

Reading Skill: Determining meaning from context. Discuss the meaning of *A house divided against itself cannot stand.*

* **Reading Skill:** Building vocabulary. Have students find the meaning of *confederate* in a dictionary.

1. Tex., Ark., La., Tenn., Miss., Ala., Ga., Fla., S.C., N.C., and Va./Mo., Ky., W.Va., Md., and Del.

was a young lawyer from Illinois. His name was Abraham Lincoln. Lincoln ran for the United States Senate in 1858. Although Lincoln lost the election, his campaign speeches had impressed many people. He believed the nation could not continue to be half-slave and half-free. Lincoln said, "A house divided against itself cannot stand."

The Union breaks up. Lincoln became the Republicans' choice to run for President of the United States in 1860. Lincoln easily won the election.

Most southerners did not like Lincoln. Lincoln's stand against slavery worried most people in the South. Even before Lincoln took office as President, seven southern states decided to **secede**, or withdraw, from the **Union**. In other words, they declared themselves no longer part of the United States of America. Four more southern states soon joined them. They formed a new government called the Confederate States of America.

Look at the map below. Which states made up the Confederacy? Which southern states that allowed slavery remained in the Union?

The government of the United States refused to accept the Confederacy as a separate nation. Lincoln and people in the North believed that secession was not legal. The Constitution, they said, did not allow states to leave the Union. Both sides were willing to fight for their beliefs.

The Civil War

After withdrawing from the Union, the Confederates started to seize United States army forts and weapons in the South. On April 12, 1861, Confederate soldiers attacked Fort Sumter in South Carolina. The next afternoon the commanding officer surrendered the fort to the Confederates. The war had begun. The North would fight to save the Union. The South would fight to become an independent country.

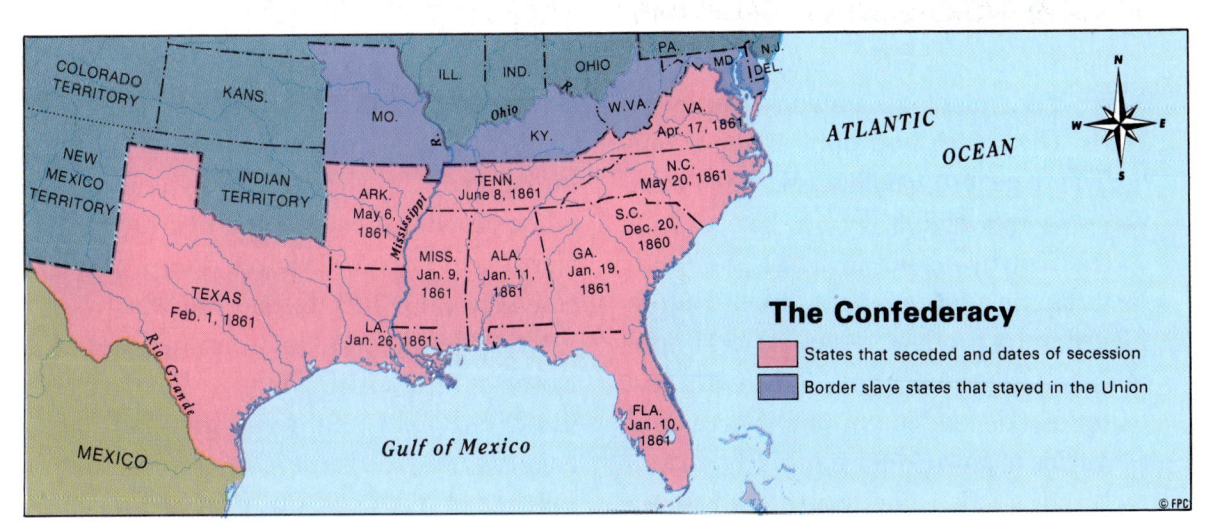

The Confederacy

- States that seceded and dates of secession
- Border slave states that stayed in the Union

*** **Thinking Skill:** Hypothesizing. Ask students to speculate what would have happened if Maryland had seceded. Washington, D.C., lies between Maryland and Virginia.

Communication Skill: Speaking. Ask students to role-play two sons living on a Kentucky farm who have decided to enlist—one as a Union soldier and the other as a Confederate soldier.

People watched the attack on Fort Sumter from their rooftops.

Northerners called those who seceded rebels. They called the war a rebellion. Southerners called it the War Between the States. Today most people refer to it as the Civil War. A **civil war** is a war in which people of the same country fight against each other.

North and South compared. The North had about 20 million people by 1861. The South had only about 9 million, and nearly 4 million of these were slaves or free blacks.

The North was far ahead of the South in industrial development. It had more factories to produce weapons and supplies for its army. The South, with few factories, depended on the North and countries in Europe for most of its manufactured goods. The North had more roads and railroads to move troops and equipment. At the start of the war, for example, the North had 22,000 miles (35,200 km) of railroad tracks. The South had only 9,000 miles (14,400 km).

Still, the South had some important advantages. The South needed only to protect its territory from northern armies. The North needed to invade the South and force it to surrender in order to save the Union. It usually takes larger armies and more equipment to invade and conquer an area than to defend it. Thus, the North needed larger armies and more equipment to defeat the South. In addition, the South had the military advantage of fighting on familiar, southern territory.

The fighting. Civil War battles took place in two major areas in the South—in Virginia and along the Mississippi River. The earliest important battles took place in Virginia. The North's early attempts to take Richmond, the Confederate capital, failed. Both sides soon realized that the war would not be over in a few months.

For two years General Robert E. Lee's Confederate forces defended Virginia against Union forces. Then in 1863, threatened by shortages of food and other supplies, Lee decided to attack the North. He hoped a victory there would convince the North to end the war.

Confederate and Union armies met at Gettysburg, a small town in Pennsylvania. Find Gettysburg on the map on page 247. After three days of fighting, Lee had to pull back. His plan had failed.

** **Communication Skill:** Listening. Read the Emancipation Proclamation to the class.
* **Reading Skill:** Building vocabulary. Discuss the purpose of a naval blockade.
Reading Skill: Doing research. Assign features on these Civil War women: Clara Barton, Belle Boyd, Charlotte Grimké, Mary Livermore, and Elizabeth Van Lew.

American Documents

The Emancipation Proclamation

President Lincoln put out a presidential order on January 1, 1863. This order is called the Emancipation Proclamation. The order freed all slaves in the Confederate states.

Although Lincoln could not immediately enforce the Emancipation Proclamation, it was an important document. It clearly showed that if the Union won the Civil War, slavery would be abolished.

It was not until Union forces were victorious in the South that they were able to set slaves free on the basis of the Emancipation Proclamation. In 1865 the Thirteenth Amendment to the Constitution made slavery illegal.

In the other major area of fighting, along the Mississippi River, the North was victorious. The North had gradually gained control of the entire Mississippi. This split the Confederacy in half, separating Arkansas, Louisiana, and Texas from the rest of the Confederacy.

In the battles to gain control of the Mississippi River, the North finally found a general who could lead troops to victory. Ulysses S. Grant led the army that defeated the South's forces at Vicksburg, Mississippi. Lincoln put Grant in command of all Union forces the following year.

Another success of the North was its naval **blockade** of the South. Union ships blockaded, or prevented other ships from entering and leaving, southern ports. This meant the South could no longer get money by shipping and selling its cotton and tobacco to England. It could no longer receive supplies from overseas. Before long, the South faced shortages of almost everything.

Soldiers and civilians. As the war continued, so did the suffering, especially in the South. The death rate was high on both sides. Thousands of soldiers were killed in battle. Many died of sickness or from wounds that could not be treated properly. In all, about 700,000 soldiers from both the North and the South died.

Civilians, or people who were not in the armed forces, suffered too. Southern towns and cities were destroyed. Armies marched over and fought on farmlands, destroying crops and killing farm animals. Food shortages became serious in much of the South.

Women on both sides helped in the war effort. Many took care of farms while the men were away fighting. Some cared for wounded soldiers.

Women nursed the wounded, made uniforms, and rolled bandages.

** **Citizenship Skill:** Social participation. Invite someone to speak to the class about the Civil War.
Communication Skill: Writing. Have students write reports on General Ulysses S. Grant, General Robert E. Lee, or other Civil War generals.

Background: Other key battles were Bull Run, Shiloh, Seven Days', Antietam, Perryville, Fredericksburg, Chancellorsville, Chickamauga, Chattanooga, the Wilderness, Franklin, and Nashville. The sites of some of these battles are on the map on page 247.

Reading Skill: Using references. Assign additional reading about the Civil War.

Generals Robert E. Lee (seated left) and Ulysses S. Grant (seated center) met to discuss the terms of surrender.

Some black people also took an active part in the war. More than 185,000 blacks served in the Union army.

The end. After the Union victories at Gettysburg and Vicksburg, it was clear that the South could not win. Yet it continued to fight on.

To bring the war to an end, the North planned a number of harsh attacks on the South. Union troops led by General William T. Sherman swept across the state of Georgia, destroying all that stood in their way. After reaching Savannah, Sherman moved his troops northward across the Carolinas. Meanwhile, General Grant launched an attack on Richmond.

Lee, in command of the Confederate soldiers, was forced to pull his troops out of the Confederate capital. Finally, on April 9, 1865, Lee surrendered to Grant at Appomattox (ap'ə·mat'əks) Court House, Virginia. The war was over. The Union had been saved.

Checking Up

1. Why did most southerners dislike Abraham Lincoln?
2. Why were the battles at Gettysburg and Vicksburg important?
3. What answers would you give to the key questions at the beginning of this chapter?
4. *Why do you think Lincoln wanted to save the Union even if it meant fighting a war?*

Communication Skill: Listening. Read diary accounts of the war written by soldiers. Sources include *The Life of Billy Yank* and *The Life of Johnny Rebel*, both by Bell Wiley, and *The Blue and the Gray* by Henry S. Commager.

Thinking Skill: Predicting. Have students speculate about what types of problems southerners, particularly freed slaves, faced in rebuilding the South.
** Reading Skill: Using references. Ask students to find other pictures of war damage in the North or the South.

Rebuilding the Nation

As You Read

1. Think about these words.
   Reconstruction   sharecropping   segregation
2. Look for answers to these key questions.
   a. What was Reconstruction?
   b. What problems did black people face after the Civil War?
   c. How did the Freedmen's Bureau help freed slaves?

Both the North and the South suffered because of the Civil War. The North, however, was able to recover more quickly. Little of the fighting had taken place in northern states.

However, in the South, many towns and cities lay in ruins. Roads, railways, and bridges had been destroyed. Farmland had been torn up by battles and marching soldiers.

Reuniting the Nation

After the war all the states had to be united again as one country. In addition, the southern states needed help rebuilding their homes, cities, and farms. The

Richmond, Virginia, the capital of the Confederacy, was one of the hardest-hit cities during the war.

229

* **Reading Skill:** Building vocabulary. Discuss why the period after the Civil War was called Reconstruction.

** **Reading Skill:** Organizing information. Ask students to list the key points and dates for the Thirteenth, Fourteenth, and Fifteenth amendments. Information is also given on page 227.

slaves who were now free people needed help too. After the war a period of **Reconstruction**, or rebuilding and reuniting the nation, began.

The job of reuniting the country led to arguments in the government. The problem again concerned secession. How could states that had seceded become a part of the United States again?

Lincoln's plan. President Lincoln wanted to bring the country together again as quickly and as painlessly as possible. Even before the war ended, he announced his plan for Reconstruction. As President he had the power to pardon, or forgive, people. Lincoln planned to pardon anyone from a state that had seceded. He would ask only that the person sign a promise to remain loyal to the United States. Once 10 percent of the people of a southern state had done so, that state could be readmitted.

Congress opposed Lincoln's plan. The leaders of Congress said that Congress, not the President, had the right to decide how to allow the southern states back into the Union. Most members of Congress wanted to punish the South for the war. They wanted to keep the former leaders of the Confederacy from taking power again.

Five days after the war ended, Lincoln was shot and killed by John Wilkes Booth. Vice-President Andrew Johnson became President. Johnson tried to follow Lincoln's plans, but Congress opposed him.

Congress takes charge. Congress began a plan for the reconstruction of the South. The former Confederacy was divided into five military zones, with Union soldiers stationed in each zone. An army general ruled each zone and directed the setting up of new state governments. Former Confederate leaders were not allowed to serve in government offices.

Congress also took the lead in making changes in the Constitution of the United States. The Thirteenth Amendment ended slavery. The Fourteenth Amendment was approved in 1868. It stated that all people in the United States had the same rights. Black people could not be treated differently by laws than white people. Southern states were not allowed back into the Union until they had approved this amendment. The Fifteenth Amendment, approved in 1870, gave freed slaves the right to vote. One by one the southern states were readmitted to the Union.

Problems for Blacks After the War

After the Civil War, there were problems ahead for the freed slaves. They owned no property. They had little or no money to start farms or businesses. Some were skilled workers. Finding a job, however, was difficult because so many factories, businesses, and farms had been destroyed in the South.

Farm workers. Some blacks left the South and moved west, where there was more land available. Most blacks, however, stayed in the South, where the land still belonged to white owners. Without slave labor, though, the big landholders

Background: When Johnson tried to follow Lincoln's plan for Reconstruction, the House of Representatives voted to impeach Johnson. Impeachment is the first step in removing a President from office. However, after a trial in the Senate, Johnson remained in office. His removal had failed by only one vote.

Living conditions for sharecroppers were poor. Long, hard hours made life difficult for the sharecropping family.

could not operate their plantations as they had before the war. Few plantation owners had enough money to pay wages to farm workers. The only way they could hope to get crops planted and make a living was by renting land or by a system called **sharecropping**. By this system, poor people, both blacks and whites, farmed pieces of land that belonged to the plantation owners. For the use of this land, the sharecroppers paid the plantation owners with a share of the crops they grew.

The sharecroppers had to follow the owner's orders. The owner of the land told the sharecroppers what to plant. When a crop was harvested, a large part of it went to the owner of the land.

More and more landowners began to use the sharecropper system. Because few blacks had money to pay rent, most earned a living by sharecropping. Few sharecroppers ever managed to save any money from year to year. They were unable to buy their own land and escape from sharecropping.

Blacks in the cities. Soon after the war, many blacks went to large towns or cities in the South to try to find work. Before long, some southern cities had more black than white people. This situation began to bother some white southerners.

Many southern towns and cities passed laws called black codes. These codes limited the freedom of black people. Curfews, for example, forced blacks to stay off the streets after a certain time at night. Also, blacks without jobs could be arrested.

Life During Reconstruction

Even before the war ended, plans to help the freed slaves were made. After the war, several improvements helped blacks.

The Freedmen's Bureau. In 1865 Congress set up an agency called the Freedmen's Bureau. This agency helped the former slaves. The bureau provided food for the hungry and medical care for the sick.

Thinking Skill: Comparing. Have students compare their predictions of freed slaves' needs with their actual needs described on pages 231–232.
** **Reading Skill:** Doing research. Have several students report on the Freedmen's Bureau.

Background: In 1870 Hiram R. Revels of Mississippi became the first black to serve in the U.S. Senate. Revels served one year. In 1874 Blanche K. Bruce, also of Mississippi, became the first black to be elected to a full six-year Senate term. Not until 1966 would another black, Edward Brooke of Massachusetts, be elected to a full six-year term in the Senate.

People Who Made a Difference

Blacks in Government

During the time of Reconstruction, many black leaders in the South entered politics and were elected to office. Two blacks served in the United States Senate. Fourteen blacks were elected to the House of Representatives. They were the first black people to serve in the nation's Congress. Blacks also helped write new state constitutions in the South, and they were elected to many state offices.

Most of the blacks in government were hardworking and fair-minded people. They did not try to make laws that would favor blacks over whites. They tried to serve their local communities, their states, and their nation well.

These blacks served in the Louisiana state legislature during Reconstruction.

The Freedmen's Bureau ran schools day and night for freed slaves.

Most blacks had little or no education. Before the war it was against the law in most of the South to teach slaves how to read and write. The Freedmen's Bureau set up thousands of new schools for black people. The Freedmen's Bureau also set up colleges for blacks. At colleges such as Howard University in Washington, D.C., and Fisk University in Tennessee, blacks received an education for such professions as teaching, law, and medicine.

Gains during Reconstruction. With the help of the Freedmen's Bureau and the protection of northern soldiers, black people began to use their new rights. They turned out to vote in large numbers. Many blacks were elected to political offices in the South.

Resentment over Reconstruction. Reconstruction helped many people, especially blacks. Many whites in the South,

*** **Reading Skill:** Doing research. Have students look up Howard University and Fisk University in encyclopedias and other books.

The Fifteenth Amendment gave blacks the right to vote.

however, did not like what happened after the war. Many did not want blacks to vote and hold government offices. Some claimed that the newly freed slaves were not ready for full citizenship. Others feared that blacks would have more political power than whites would.

Many white southerners resented northerners who moved to the South after the war and were elected to office. White southerners also resented some of their own people who took part in Reconstruction governments. Although Reconstruction helped many in the South, especially the freed slaves, Reconstruction governments sometimes misused money. Many white southerners resented this misuse of money.

The End of Reconstruction

Slowly the South began to recover. The new state governments raised taxes to help the war-torn region. Roads, railways, and bridges were rebuilt. Businesses were given help so they could start up again.

Reconstruction came to an end in 1877 when the last of the federal troops were removed from the South. Once the soldiers were gone, white southerners gained control of most of the state governments.

The new southern governments worked to undo the rights that blacks had gained during Reconstruction. Laws favoring **segregation**, or separating black people from white, were passed. On trains, for example, blacks were not allowed to sit in the same area as whites. Some southerners used violence and terror to keep blacks from voting. Some southern legislatures passed laws that made it almost impossible for blacks to vote. In a few years, blacks lost most of the rights they had gained during Reconstruction. It would be many years before black people would enjoy the full rights of citizenship again.

Checking Up
1. What was the sharecropping system?
2. What changes were made by new amendments to the Constitution?
3. What answers would you give to the key questions at the beginning of this chapter?
4. *What do you think was the biggest problem facing the nation after the Civil War? Explain your answer.*

Math Skill: Have students use the time line on pages 214–215 to figure out how many years passed from the beginning of the war until Reconstruction ended (16 years).
Reading Skill: Developing vocabulary. Ask students to write one-paragraph summaries of this chapter that use the chapter's vocabulary words listed on page 229.

Reading Skill: Using textbook features: *As You Read*, 3.
* Reading Skill: Building vocabulary. Discuss the meaning of *opening the West*.

Opening the West

As You Read

1. Think about these words.
   prospector   lode
2. Look for answers to these key questions.
   a. How did prospectors and miners help settle the West?
   b. How did new railroads influence the cattle business?
   c. What was a cowhand's life like?
3. Use this reading skill.
   Finding information in the Appendix is an important reading skill. Use page 482 in the Appendix to find out what states were admitted to the Union between 1865 and 1890.

Before the Civil War, many people traveled to the Far West, to California or the Oregon Territory. Most of the West, however, was still occupied by Indians and was largely unsettled by others.

For many years there was little to attract settlers to the vast land between the Missouri River and the West Coast settlements. Travelers west had to pass over hundreds of miles of grassland that made up the Great Plains. Because the Great Plains were believed to be too dry for good farming, farmers were not attracted to the area.

West of the Great Plains were the steep, rugged mountains of the Rockies. Between the Rockies and the mountains on the West Coast was the Great Basin, a vast dry area. The Mormons, a religious group, settled in the Great Basin at Salt Lake City, Utah, in the 1840s. The Mormons dug canals and ditches to irrigate the land for farming. With the exception of the Mormons, though, few settlers were attracted to the area.

Prospectors and Miners

The discovery of gold in California in 1848 started the "gold fever" that lasted for the next thirty years. Gold seekers who were unlucky in California began to search for gold in other areas.

Gold fever. In 1858 a group of **prospectors**, people looking for gold or other minerals, became lucky. They found small amounts of gold near Denver, Colorado. Newspapers spread the story of the new gold find. Thousands of people from all over the nation set out for Colorado. Look at the map on page 235 and find the areas where gold was discovered in Colorado.

The amount of gold found in Colorado was less than people had hoped. Many

Time Skill: Review the early settlement of the West Coast discussed on pages 195–198.
*** **Reading Skill:** Organizing information. Have students make pictorial charts of various ways of mining in the 1800s.

Background: Prospectors in the West were gradually replaced by mining companies as more minerals were discovered in rock and not near the surface. The companies had the money to buy expensive machines to mine the ore and to hire miners.

1. Calif.; Wash., Ariz., N.Mex., Wyo., Idaho, Mont., and Dakota territories.

Mining Strikes and Mining Towns 1848–1876

disappointed people packed up and returned home. Others, however, continued to search for gold and other minerals elsewhere in the West.

A large deposit of silver was discovered in Nevada in 1859. This deposit became known as the Comstock Lode. A **lode** is a rich deposit of metal. Again, the news of the discovery brought many more people into the area. The Comstock Lode turned out to be the richest deposit of silver in the United States. Find the Comstock Lode on the map on this page.

Mining towns. Prospectors continued to search for other sources of gold and silver. Discoveries were made in many areas in the Rocky Mountains. Look again at the map on this page. What were three states or territories, in addition to Colorado and Nevada, where gold or silver was found? 1

As prospectors and miners rushed into a new area, towns sprang up quickly. Some of the mining towns became deserted after the gold or silver ran out. There was nothing to keep people there anymore. Yet other towns continued to grow. Some miners settled down in places like Denver. Families began to build farms or ranches in the area. Businesses grew. In this way, gold fever helped settle a large part of the West.

Cattle Ranchers

Cattle raising had begun in Texas long before it became part of the United States. By 1865 there were about 5 million head of cattle in Texas.

Once the Civil War was over, Texans were able to sell their cattle in the North,

Helena, Montana, began as the mining town Last Chance Gulch in 1864.

Reading Skill: Interpreting graphics. Discuss how the photograph above explains the text.
*** **Communication Skill:** Writing. Assign reports on the history and development of mining towns listed on the map above.

235

where there was a greater demand for beef. All the ranchers had to do was get their cattle from Texas to the railroad—a distance of about 1,500 miles (2,400 km)!

Cattle drives. The first long cattle drive to the Kansas Pacific Railroad took place in 1866. Ranchers rounded up herds of cattle and drove them from southern Texas to the railroad at Sedalia, Missouri. Find the Sedalia Trail on the map on this page.

By the following year, the railroad crossed part of Kansas. An Illinois meat dealer, Joseph McCoy, sent out word that he would buy cattle at Abilene, Kansas. The cattle herders followed a new trail to Abilene—the Chisholm Trail. Abilene quickly grew into the first of the important "cow towns." Between 1868 and 1871, nearly 1½ million cattle passed through it. Follow the route of the Chisholm Trail on the map of cattle trails on this page.

As the railroad workers continued building tracks farther west, other cattle trails came into use. By the time the first railroad across the country was completed in 1869, ranchers had a choice of several trails to follow. Other cow towns in Kansas, Nebraska, Wyoming, and Montana became important.

Cowhands. The ranchers hired cowhands to take care of the cattle. Movies and television shows have made the life of cowhands look exciting and full of adventure. The truth is that cowhands spent most of their time doing hard, dull jobs. On the long drives, cowhands spent the whole day on horseback on a dusty trail. They had to keep the cattle moving and chase after strays. A cattle drive from Texas to Kansas lasted about three months.

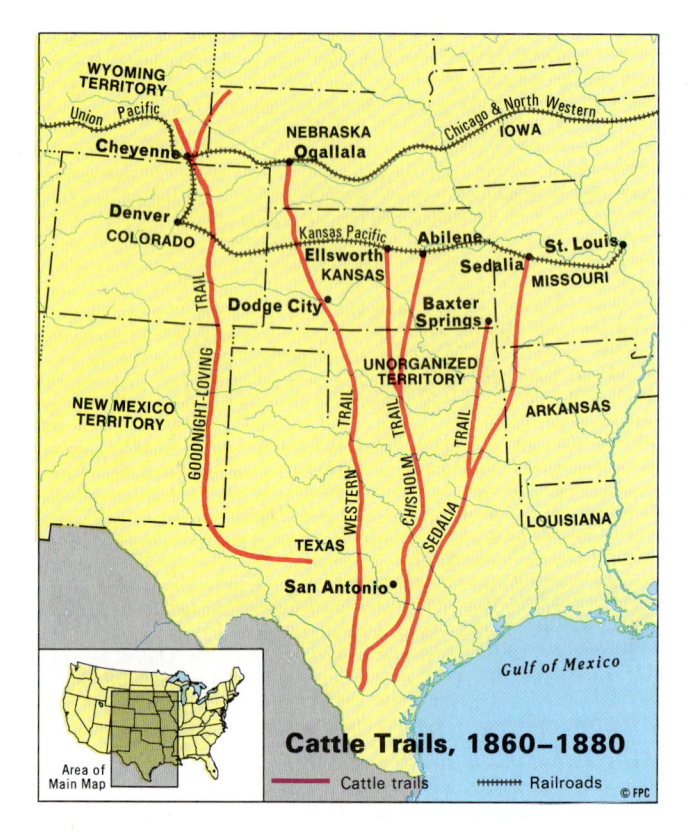

The rest of the year, cowhands rode up and down the open range, or unfenced land, as the cattle grazed on the grassland. Their main job was to see that the cattle from their ranch did not get mixed up with the cattle herds of other ranchers.

Ranching changes. During the 1860s and 1870s, cattle ranching began to spread beyond Texas. It moved into the northern plains states and even into Canada. As more and more railroad lines were built, the need for long drives faded. By the 1880s there were railway lines running through much of the cattle

Cattle Trails, 1860–1880

Thinking Skill: Comparing. Have half the class write reports about cowhands on television and the other half about cowhands in encyclopedias or other books. Have the class compare reports.
* **Communication Skill:** Writing. Ask students to compose poems or songs about cowhand life.
* **Reading Skill:** Building vocabulary. Review the meaning of *open range.*

Cowhands spent weeks out on the range driving cattle to market. At night they gathered around the chuck wagon for dinner.

country. Not many ranchers had to drive their cattle more than a few hundred miles to a railroad.

Ranching also changed when the ranchers began to build fences around their ranches. This happened after a time of trouble in the 1880s.

In the late 1800s, the Great Plains had two of the worst winters people could remember. Between them was an especially dry summer. The drought dried up much of the grass cattle fed on. The winter cold froze thousands of cattle to death. Many more starved because they could not find grass to eat under the snow. Some ranchers lost as many as nine out of every ten animals they owned.

Ranchers began to build fences to keep their cattle from straying. They started to grow hay to feed their herds through the winter. At the same time, more and more farmers were beginning to settle on the plains. They, too, built fences around their property. The days of the open range were over.

Checking Up
1. How did geography influence the settlement of the West?
2. How did cattle ranching change in the 1880s?
3. What answers would you give to the key questions at the beginning of this chapter?
4. *In what ways do you think television and movies show the life of a cowhand as one full of adventure?*

Map Skill: Distance. Ask students to figure out which trail on the map on page 236 passed through the most states and territories and which passed through the fewest (Goodnight-Loving Trail; Chisholm Trail).
Thinking Skill: Analyzing. Discuss the importance of ranchers' building fences.

Reading Skill: Organizing information. Have students list problems the Plains Indians faced.
*** Time Skill: Have students research the number of buffalo that exist today in this country.

Settling the West

As You Read

1. Think about these words.
   sod   barbed wire
2. Look for answers to these key questions.
   a. Why were Indian tribes in the West driven from their homelands?
   b. What had happened to most Indians by 1890?
   c. What were some of the problems faced by the early settlers on the Great Plains? How did the settlers solve these problems?

As you may remember from Unit 2, many Indian tribes had lived in the West for longer than anyone could remember. Others, like those who traveled the Trail of Tears you read about in Unit 6, had been forced to the West years before the Civil War.

Indians on the Plains

The Indians in the West were mainly left in peace until after the Civil War. Then more and more new settlers arrived. They began to push the Indians off their homelands.

The miners were the first people to move into Indian lands in the West. They rushed into areas where gold or silver was found. They built towns. Ranchers and farmers soon followed the miners.

The new settlers paid no attention to the rights of the Indians. The United States government had made many treaties with Indian tribes. The treaties had promised that the Indians would not be bothered on their lands. Again and again, the treaties were broken as new settlers forced Indian tribes from their territory.

Mass killing of the buffalo helped crush the Plains Indians. Large herds of buffalo often wandered across the tracks and stopped trains. So the railroads paid people to kill the buffalo. Other people hunted them for their skins, which were used to make leather. Buffalo were killed by the millions. By 1889 there were fewer than 500 buffalo left. The Indians, who had lived by hunting buffalo for thousands of years, could no longer follow their old way of life.

As more and more farmers and ranchers settled the plains, they asked the United States Army to protect them from the Indians. Wars broke out between Indian tribes and army soldiers. Many people on both sides were killed.

The Indians fought well, but they could not hold out long against the army. One by one, the Indian tribes were de-

238   **Background:** One tribe that fought back was the Nez Percé who lived in Oregon and Idaho. The tribe did not want to go to a reservation. Chief Joseph tried to lead his people to Canada. After a 1,500-mile march and several battles, the tribe gave up and went to a reservation.

Thinking Skill: Evaluating. Discuss the decision of the U.S. government to move the Plains Indians onto reservations.

Reading Skill: Organizing information. Have students make charts about farming on the plains, listing problems and solutions.

feated. The Indians were forced to leave their villages and their hunting grounds. They were herded onto reservations, where they had to live according to the rules of the United States government. By 1890 nearly all the Indians of the West were living on reservations established by the government.

Farming the Plains

The government encouraged people to settle new lands in the West. In 1862 Congress passed the Homestead Act. This law offered government land to any family that would settle on it, build a house, and farm the land. Much of the available farmland was on the Great Plains.

Farming problems. Farming on the plains was not easy. Farmers needed to solve many problems before they could make a living on the dry grasslands.

Buffalo blocked trains causing problems for the railroads.

Finding enough water was one problem. Farmers who did not have a nearby river or stream dug deep wells. They built windmills to pump the water up from the wells. People who could not afford wells and windmills collected rainwater in barrels. This water had to last them from one rainfall to the next.

A lone Indian listens to the strange hum of the telegraph wires. The technology of white settlers had invaded the Indians' homeland.

Background: Some farmers bought their lands from railroad companies that had built railroads on the plains. The railroads were glad to sell land to farmers. Farmers would use the railroads to travel and to get their crops to market. The money would also help build more railroads.

Reading Skill: Interpreting visuals. Discuss how the bottom picture explains the text.

How We Know What Happened

The Diary of Laura Ingalls Wilder

One good way of learning about the past is by reading diaries. You may have heard of Laura Ingalls Wilder. She wrote about her childhood on a pioneer farm in *Little House on the Prairie* and many other books. In 1894 she and her husband, Manly, made a trip across the Great Plains. Her diary of that trip gives a good picture of the hardships of travel in that area. In the following selection, the Wilders are waiting to cross the Missouri River by ferry.

It was leaving just as we drove down to the landing at 6 o'clock and while we were waiting for it to come back a bad-looking storm came up. It was not rain, only wind and dust.

We had to face the river to keep the wagon's back to the wind so that it would not be blown over. The wind lifted the hind wheels twice before Manly could get them roped down.

At fifteen Laura Ingalls taught in a one-room schoolhouse in South Dakota.

Plains farmers tried new methods of farming. Rather than planting so crops grew closely together, farmers spaced crops to prevent one plant from robbing another of precious water. After a rain the farmers turned the soil over quickly. They buried the wet soil under a layer of dry soil. This method kept the soil from drying out too fast.

New farming machinery also helped the plains farmers. Better plows made it easier to turn the soil over quickly. New reapers helped harvest the wheat that most farmers grew. Wheat, actually a grass, was one crop that grew well in the grasslands of the Great Plains.

Homes and fences. Another problem faced by farmers was the lack of wood. There were not enough trees on the dry plains to supply wood for homes, buildings, and fences.

The farmers solved their housing problem by using **sod**, the tightly-packed mixture of soil and tangled grass roots found on the grasslands. The sod was cut into squares, which were then piled up to build houses.

In 1873 Joseph F. Glidden, an Illinois farmer, helped solve the fence problem. He invented **barbed wire**, a wire with twisted points, or barbs, spaced along it. The sharp barbs kept animals from

Sod houses were usually cool in summer and fairly warm in winter.

breaking through the wire fence. At last farmers could fence in their property and enclose the cattle.

A hard life. One by one, the farmers solved their problems. Still, they did not have an easy life. The lack of rain was always a problem. In some years so little rain fell that farmers lost their crops. The winters were hard too. Temperatures fell far below freezing. Snowstorms often buried farmhouses under many feet of drifting snow.

In some years great swarms of grasshoppers swept over the plains by the millions. They darkened the sky like a great living cloud. The grasshoppers could eat a farmer's entire crop within minutes.

Some people could not take the hard life of farming on the plains. They gave up and returned east. Most farmers, however, remained, and many more continued to settle there. By 1890 the last unoccupied part of the nation had been settled.

Checking Up
1. How did buffalo hunters influence the life of the Indians?
2. Why did farmers on the Great Plains often build sod houses?
3. What answers would you give to the key questions at the beginning of this chapter?
4. *Why do you think farmers settled the Great Plains even though farming there was difficult?*

Unit 7 Summary
- The North and the South began to differ on such things as transportation, tariffs, and especially slavery.
- Differences between the North and the South led to the Civil War.
- After the Civil War, Congress began Reconstruction to reunify the nation and to rebuild the South. Changes in the Constitution freed the slaves and gave black people the right to vote.
- In the years after Reconstruction, a number of segregation laws were made by southern states. These laws limited the rights of blacks and kept blacks separate from whites.
- Miners, cattle ranchers, and farmers settled the West between the end of the Civil War and 1890.
- As more and more settlers moved west, Indians lost their lands.
- By 1890 most Indians had been forced to live on reservations.

1. About 98 miles a week; about 420 miles a month.
2. The stagecoach. Thick straps held the stagecoach body to make the ride smooth. The stagecoach. The stagecoach would probably go faster; it appears to be lighter in weight and to have less wind resistance because it does not have the billowy cloth top found on the Conestoga wagon.

Maps, Pictures, and Graphs Tell a Story of Transportation in the West

As you read, think about these words.
overland   transcontinental

People used different means of transportation to reach the West. Between 1850 and 1900, transportation in the West improved greatly. Studying the kinds of transportation and how transportation improved will help you better understand the settlement of the West.

Early Transportation in the West

As you learned in Unit 6, Conestoga wagons carried settlers from the East to California and Oregon. A Conestoga wagon averaged about 14 miles (22.4 km) a day. A trip from Missouri to California took about five months. How many miles could a Conestoga wagon travel in a week? in a thirty-day month?

Stagecoaches. Thousands of people settled Oregon and California in the 1840s and 1850s. These people needed a faster, more convenient method of transportation than the Conestoga wagon. This need was met by the stagecoach.

Study the picture of the stagecoach on this page. Compare this picture with the picture of the Conestoga wagon on page 200. Which vehicle looks more comfortable? Why? Which vehicle looks like it could travel faster? Why?

Stagecoaches had been used since colonial days in the East. As the frontier of the country moved west, stagecoach service was provided farther and farther west. Look at the map on page 243. Trace three stagecoach routes to California. Through which states and territories did these routes pass?

The average stagecoach speed was about 5 miles per hour. How many miles would a stagecoach travel in an eight-hour day? How many more miles a day could a stagecoach travel than a Conestoga wagon?

Although the stagecoach was an improvement over the Conestoga wagon, stagecoach travel had its share of problems. Coaches often got stuck in mud or holes. There was also the constant threat of attacks by Indians or robbers.

Two straps held the stagecoach body to make the ride smoother.

3. Central Overland Route: Mo., Kan., Neb., Wyo. Terr., Utah Terr., Nev., and Calif.; Butterfield Overland Route: Mo. or Tenn., Ark., Unorg. Terr., Tex., N.Mex. Terr., Ariz. Terr., and Calif. Students can also trace the paths of the unnamed stagecoach routes on the map.
4. 40 miles. About 26 miles more during an eight-hour day.

Background: The Concord coaches were made in Concord, New Hampshire, and then shipped west.
*** **Reading Skill:** Doing research. Have several students report on stagecoach travel.
1. Mo. or Tenn. (starting points), Ark., Unorg. Terr., Tex., N.Mex. Terr., Ariz. Terr., and Calif. To avoid having to cross the Rocky Mountains.

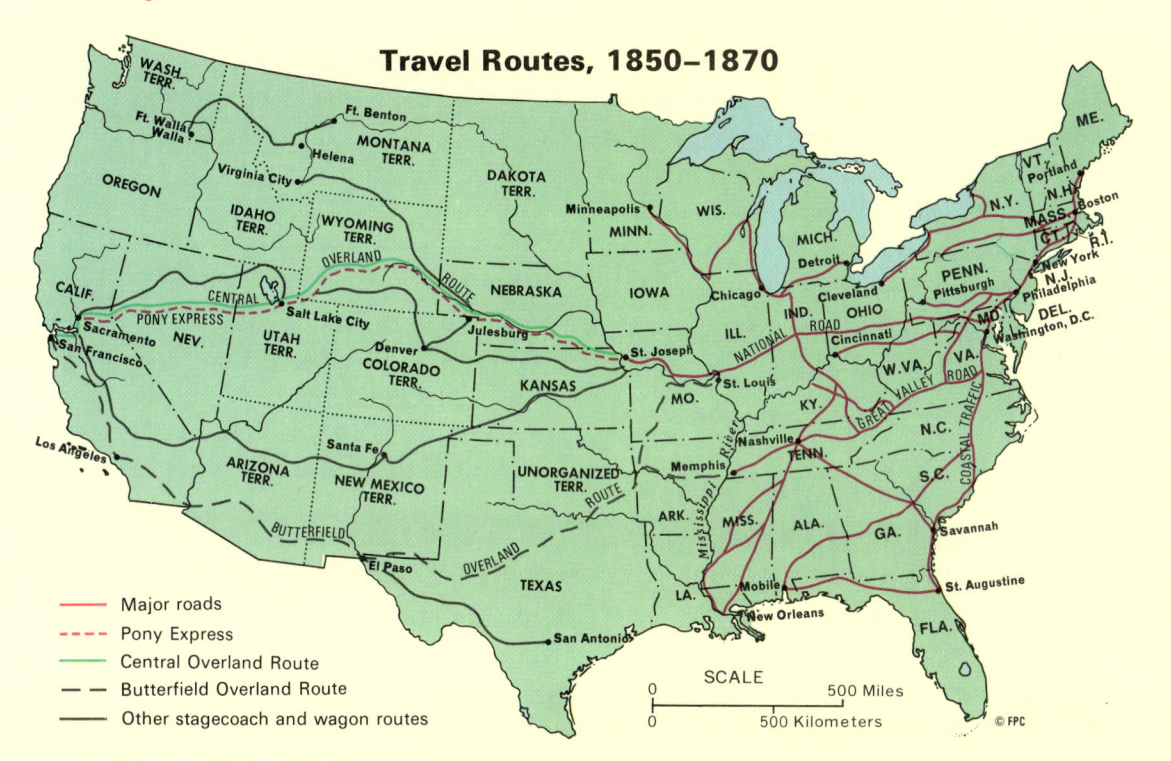

Travel Routes, 1850–1870

- —— Major roads
- ---- Pony Express
- —— Central Overland Route
- — — Butterfield Overland Route
- —— Other stagecoach and wagon routes

Stagecoaches carry the mail. The stagecoach improved mail service to the West. Early settlers in Oregon and California had had to wait 2½ months to receive mail from the East. Mail traveled from the East Coast by ship to Panama in Middle America. The mail was then transported across the narrow strip of land at Panama. From Panama the mail was carried by ship to California. Trace this route on the map on pages 10–11.

As more people settled the West, demand grew for faster mail service. In 1857 Congress passed a bill that called for stagecoaches to carry both passengers and mail **overland**, or across the land, to the West.

Congress gave the first mail route to the Butterfield Overland Mail Company. Find this mail route on the map on this page. Through which states and territories did this route pass? Look at the physical map on page 15. Why do you think this company chose such an indirect route?   1

The first overland mail coach left St. Louis in September 1858. Twenty-four days later the mail reached San Francisco. About how much faster was overland mail service than the earlier ship service?   2

The Butterfield Overland Mail Company ran its route until March 1861. It stopped as the Civil War began. Why would the war put an end to service on this route? The mail route was then   3 given to the Central Overland Company. It ran its route in thirty-five days. Locate the Central Overland route on the map on this page. Now look at the physical

2. About seven weeks faster.
3. Because much of its route ran through states and territories that either joined or sympathized with the Confederacy. Congress, who authorized the company to deliver the mail, believed the mail might be delayed or stopped in Confederate areas.

243

Background: Pony Express riders stopped and changed horses every 10 miles at one of the 190 stations that had been built along the 1,966-mile route. Riders switched every 70 miles.
1. Because the route crossed much more mountainous and hilly terrain.
2. The Central Overland Route. 3. About 184,000 miles. 4. About three weeks' time.

map on page 15. Why did the Central Overland route take eleven days longer?

The Pony Express. Even though mail reached California in about a month, some people wanted the time reduced even more. The stagecoach company of Russell, Majors, and Waddell believed it could deliver the mail from Missouri to California in about ten days. It planned to use a number of riders on horseback to carry the mail.

On April 3, 1860, the Pony Express began. Locate its route on the map on page 243. Which stagecoach route did the Pony Express follow?

Pony Express riders traveled through rain and snow. They braved Indian attacks and robbers. Yet the route worked! The first scheduled Pony Express delivery reached California in 10½ days.

The Pony Express stopped running on October 24, 1861. It stopped when the first telegraph line connected California and New York. There was now no need to wait for messages to come by Pony Express.

The Railroads Take Over

In the fifty years after the Civil War, the growth of a **transcontinental**, or across the continent, railroad system brought vast changes to the country. Transportation of people and goods became faster and cheaper. In the West cities grew, and the population of the region increased greatly.

Study the graph on this page. How many more miles of railroad track were there in 1900 than in 1850?

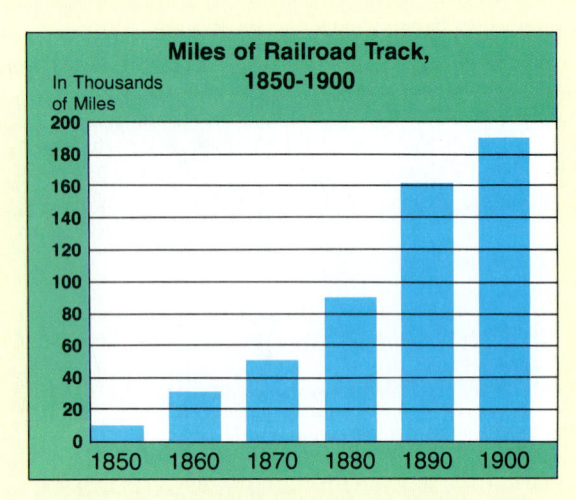

Miles of Railroad Track, 1850–1900

(Bar graph showing miles of railroad track in thousands from 1850 to 1900.)

The first transcontinental railroad was completed in 1869. The Central Pacific and the Union Pacific connected in Utah. Now passengers could go from Nebraska to California in just one week. A stagecoach could travel this distance in about one month. About how much time was saved by train travel?

In addition to greater speed, trains were more comfortable than stagecoaches. Compare the picture on page

The Pullman sleeping car improved train travel.

244

Reading Skill: Doing research. Have students find out the name of the railroad that runs nearest their homes, what it carries, and how often it runs by their homes.

1. On trains there were comfortable chairs and beds for people, room for people to walk around, more windows to see the view, and conductors to help passengers.

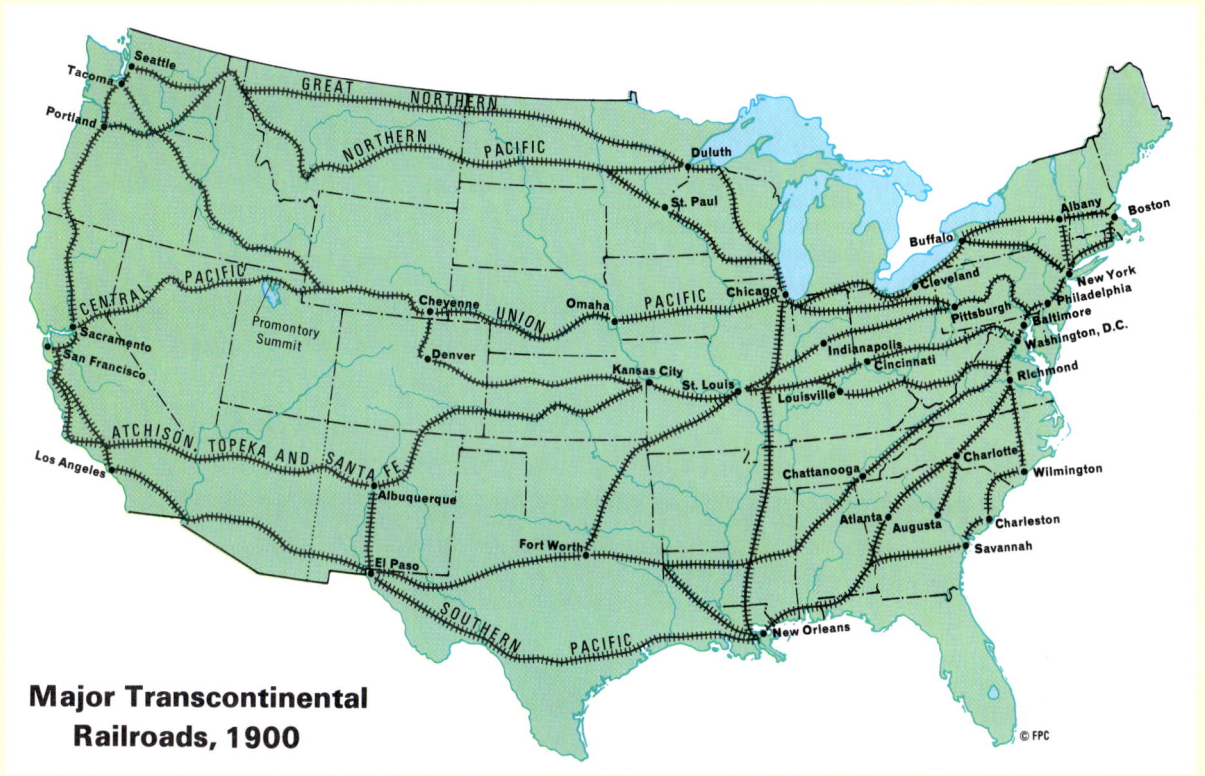

Major Transcontinental Railroads, 1900

Thousands of Asian and European immigrants came to the United States in the 1800s to help build the transcontinental railroads.

242 with the picture on page 244. In what ways were trains more comfortable than stagecoaches?

By 1883 four transcontinental railroads had been built. By the 1890s a fifth transcontinental railroad was completed. Look at the map above. Name the five transcontinental railroads.

The first western railroads followed the old trails of the West. Look at the map in Unit 6 on page 196 and then look at the map of railroads above. Which trails did the Union Pacific and Central Pacific follow? Which did the Atchison, Topeka, and Santa Fe follow?

Now look at the map on page 243. Which stagecoach route did the Union Pacific and Central Pacific follow? Today Interstate 80 follows a similar route. Why do you think a modern highway would follow a route that is more than a hundred years old?

Look again at the map of railroads. What differences do you see between the patterns of railroads in the West and in the East? What reasons might explain the different patterns?

Checking Up

1. What were two means of early transportation to the West?
2. Why did the Pony Express end?

2. The Great Northern; Northern Pacific; Central Pacific and Union Pacific; Atchison, Topeka, and Santa Fe; and Southern Pacific railroads.
3. Mormon Trail or Oregon Trail and California Trail. Santa Fe Trail and Old Spanish Trail.
4. Central Overland. Because people already live along the route who need transportation.

245

Unit 7 Review Workshop

What Have You Learned?

1. What were three problems that caused disagreements between the North and the South in the mid-1800s?
2. What kind of work did most plantation slaves do?
3. How did some slaves escape to the North?
4. When did the Civil War begin? How long did it last?
5. What were two improvements made for blacks during the time of Reconstruction?
6. What problems did blacks face after the end of Reconstruction?
7. What were three groups of people who helped settle the West?
8. What changes did the growth of railroads bring to the West?
9. What happened to the Indian tribes as more and more people moved into and settled the West?

Use Your Reading Skills

Learning to use new words is an important reading skill. Write one sentence for each of the vocabulary words listed below. By using these words in sentences, you will better understand the meaning of the vocabulary words introduced in this unit.

tariff	civilian
compromise	segregation
secede	prospector
civil war	lode

Use Your Group Skills

The last question in the "Checking Up" section of each chapter is a thought question. Different students may have different answers to these questions. Choose one of the thought questions from this unit and write a paragraph giving your answer to it. Be sure to give reasons for your answer. Share your answer with others in the class.

Use Your Map Skills

It is important to understand the part geography played in the Civil War. The map at right shows some of the important battles in the war. Study the map carefully. Think about the landforms and location of battle sites. Then answer the following questions.

1. In which state were the greatest number of battles? Name three battles that took place in this state.
2. Compare this map with the map of the United States on pages 20–21. Were most battles fought on plains or in mountainous areas? Why?
3. You learned in this unit that the Union navy blockaded the Confederacy. At which places on the Atlantic Ocean and the Gulf of Mexico were there naval battles?
4. Along what rivers in the South were important Civil War battles fought? Why do you think there were so many Civil War battles fought on or near waterways?

Reading Skills: Building vocabulary, interpreting graphics.
Thinking Skills: Knowing, analyzing.
Communication Skill: Writing.
Map Skill: Location.

Important Battles of the Civil War

★ Battles

- Union states
- Border states
- Confederate states

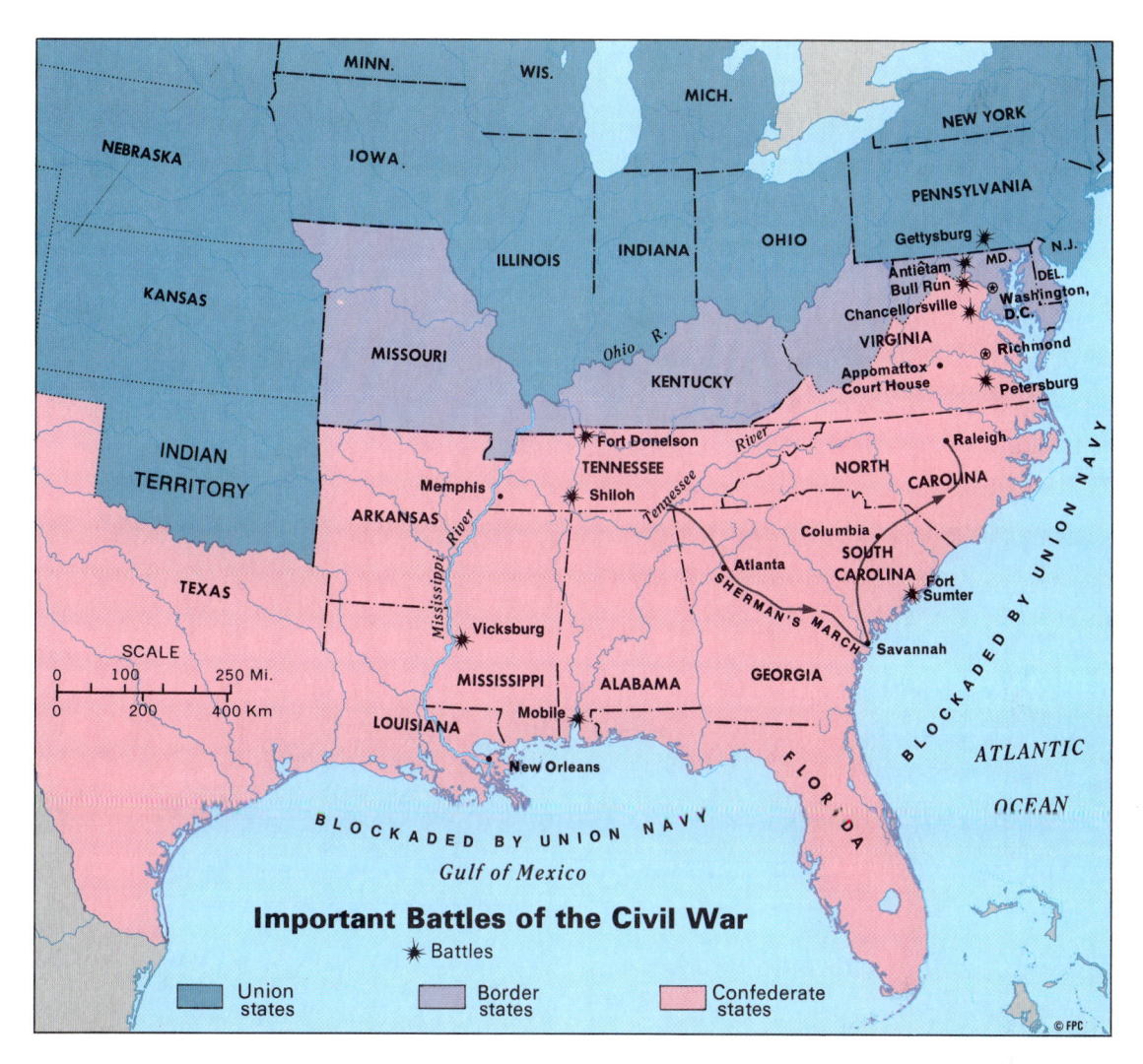

Learn by Doing

1. Using the information in this unit and books about the settlement of the West, work with others to draw a mural of how the West was settled. Be sure to include drawings of the Plains Indians, mining camps, cattle ranchers, cowhands, and farmers. Display your mural for others to see.

2. Look in books and encyclopedias to find out more about the building of the first transcontinental railroad, the Central Pacific and the Union Pacific. Make a report to the class about the construction of this railroad.

Read to Learn More

Find the topics listed below in the card catalog of your library. Read all or part of a book listed under one of the topics. Share what you learn with your classmates.

MINES AND MINING   SLAVERY
RECONSTRUCTION   COWHANDS

Reading Skills: Organizing information: *Learn by Doing, 1, 2*; doing research: *Learn by Doing, 1, 2*; using references: *Learn by Doing, 1, 2*.
Communication Skill: Speaking: *Learn by Doing, 2*.

247

Unit Overview: This unit examines the growth of the nation from the late 1800s to the 1930s.

Unit Objectives
To understand:
- the country's industrial growth
- new inventions
- the growing United States population
- the rise of the United States to become a world power

Suggested Materials
Workbook
Unit Tests

Unit 8

Skills Emphasized
Map Skills: pp. 253, 270, 273.
Social Studies Reading Skills: pp. 248, 250, 251, 252, 253, 254, 255, 256, 257, 258, 259, 261, 263, 264, 265, 266, 267, 268, 269, 270, 271, 272, 273, 274, 276, 277, 278, 279, 280, 281.
Thinking Skills: pp. 248, 251, 255, 258, 260, 261, 264, 265, 266, 267, 269, 270, 272, 274, 276, 278, 279, 280, 281.
Communication Skills: pp. 248, 251, 253, 265, 267, 268, 271, 273, 280, 281.
Time Skills: pp. 248, 250, 253, 262, 266, 268, 269, 272, 273, 276, 279, 280, 281.
Social Studies Math Skills: pp. 251, 259, 260, 261, 269, 271, 277.
Citizenship Skills: pp. 252, 254, 256, 257, 258, 262, 267, 268, 277, 278.

Suggested Student Activities
    1. Arrange a bulletin-board display of important inventions.
    2. Make a movie roll on the key inventions of Thomas Edison.
    3. Make a pictorial time line of the airplane's development.
  * 4. Arrange a display on the life and works of Mark Twain.
  ** 5. Make mobiles of new technological advances discussed in the unit.
*** 6. Make a model of the Panama Canal.

Skills Emphasized in Suggested Student Activities
Reading Skills: Organizing information, using references, doing research.
Thinking Skills: Knowing, comparing, classifying.
Communication Skill: Writing.
Time Skill.

A Modern Nation

Steel production has helped make the United States one of the world's great industrial nations.

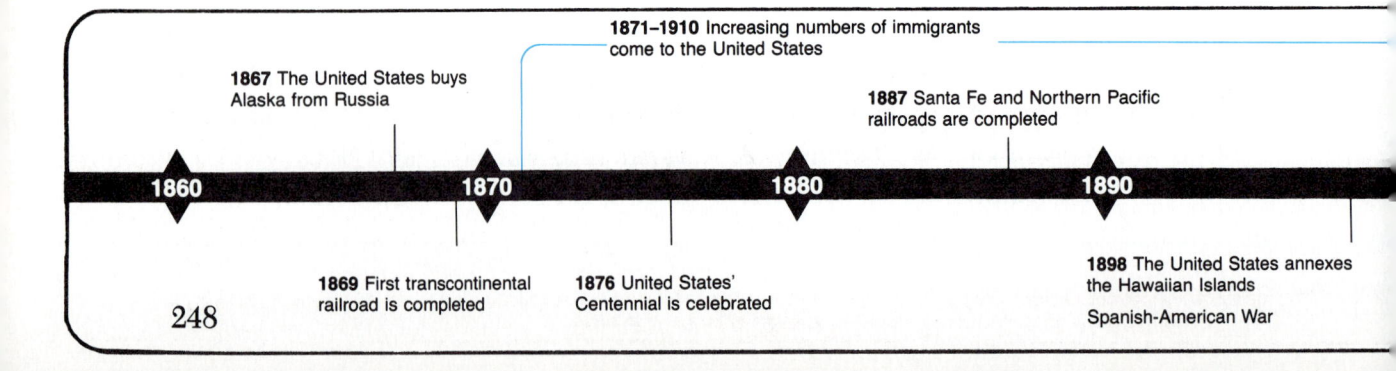

1867 The United States buys Alaska from Russia

1871–1910 Increasing numbers of immigrants come to the United States

1887 Santa Fe and Northern Pacific railroads are completed

1860 — 1870 — 1880 — 1890

1869 First transcontinental railroad is completed

1876 United States' Centennial is celebrated

1898 The United States annexes the Hawaiian Islands

Spanish-American War

248

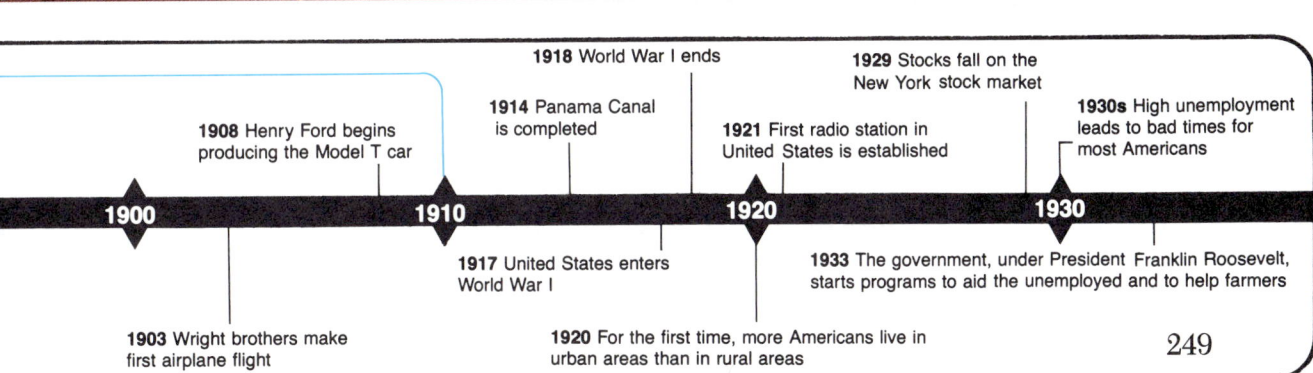

1903 Wright brothers make first airplane flight

1908 Henry Ford begins producing the Model T car

1914 Panama Canal is completed

1917 United States enters World War I

1918 World War I ends

1920 For the first time, more Americans live in urban areas than in rural areas

1921 First radio station in United States is established

1929 Stocks fall on the New York stock market

1930s High unemployment leads to bad times for most Americans

1933 The government, under President Franklin Roosevelt, starts programs to aid the unemployed and to help farmers

1900 — 1910 — 1920 — 1930

New Inventions and Industries

As You Read

1. Think about these words.
   patent   technology   assembly line   refining   union
2. Look for answers to these key questions.
   a. What were two major reasons for industrial growth during the 1800s?
   b. What were three important inventions made during the late 1800s?
   c. Why were labor unions formed during the late 1800s?

By 1880 the United States looked quite different from the way it had in earlier times. Businesses and industries had grown immensely. More than 90,000 miles of railroad tracks connected many parts of the country. New inventions were changing the way people lived and worked.

People Who Made a Difference

Thomas Edison

People can thank Thomas Alva Edison for the electric light that fills our homes and streets at night. Edison was not the first person to make an electric lamp. In 1879, however, he became the first to make a small electric light that would shine for a long time. His invention made it possible for millions to enjoy bright light in their homes. Edison's light bulb was also much safer and cheaper than the candles and gaslights used before.

The practical light bulb was just one of more than 1,000 inventions that Edison made during his lifetime. Some of the other inventions made by Edison were the phonograph and one of the first successful motion picture cameras.

Edison shows how to use the first office dictating machine.

Edison was a genius who worked long hours. Sometimes he worked days at a time without sleeping. Today Thomas Edison is remembered as an inventor who greatly changed the way people live all over the world.

Math Skill: Ask students to figure out how many more patents were granted from 1860 to 1890 than from 1790 to 1860 (404,000 more patents).
*** **Reading Skill:** Using references. Have students find out how a person applies for a patent.
** **Communication Skill:** Speaking. Have students plan skits about U.S. inventors and their inventions.

Growth of Industries and Cities

granted 36,000 **patents** to U.S. inventors with new ideas. A patent is the right to make, use, or sell an invention. However, in just thirty years, from 1860 to 1890, the government granted 440,000 patents. An age of **technology** (tek·näl′ə·jē) was developing in the United States. Technology refers to scientific advances in such things as tools, machines, and transportation.

With new technology, factories in the United States turned out more and more goods. By 1900 the United States had become the world's greatest industrial power. Study the three maps on this page. How many more states had major industrial areas in 1900 than in 1860? How many more states had major industrial areas in 1920 than in 1900?

United States inventors. United States inventors, finding new ways of doing things, helped make the growth in industry possible during the late 1800s. The English scientist Michael Faraday began working with electricity as early as the 1830s. The United States inventors Thomas Edison and William Stanley put electricity to practical use. Light bulbs, streetcars, and subways, run by electricity, were soon used in many places.

Nikolaus Otto invented the gasoline engine in Germany in 1878. Henry Ford, a United States inventor and businessman, developed a gasoline engine to run an automobile. In 1908 Ford began selling an automobile that even working people could afford. To make his Model T car, Ford developed an **assembly line**. On an assembly line, the main body of

Population of Cities
- 100,000–500,000
- 500,000–1,000,000
- Greater than 1,000,000

■ Major industrial area
■ State
■ Territory

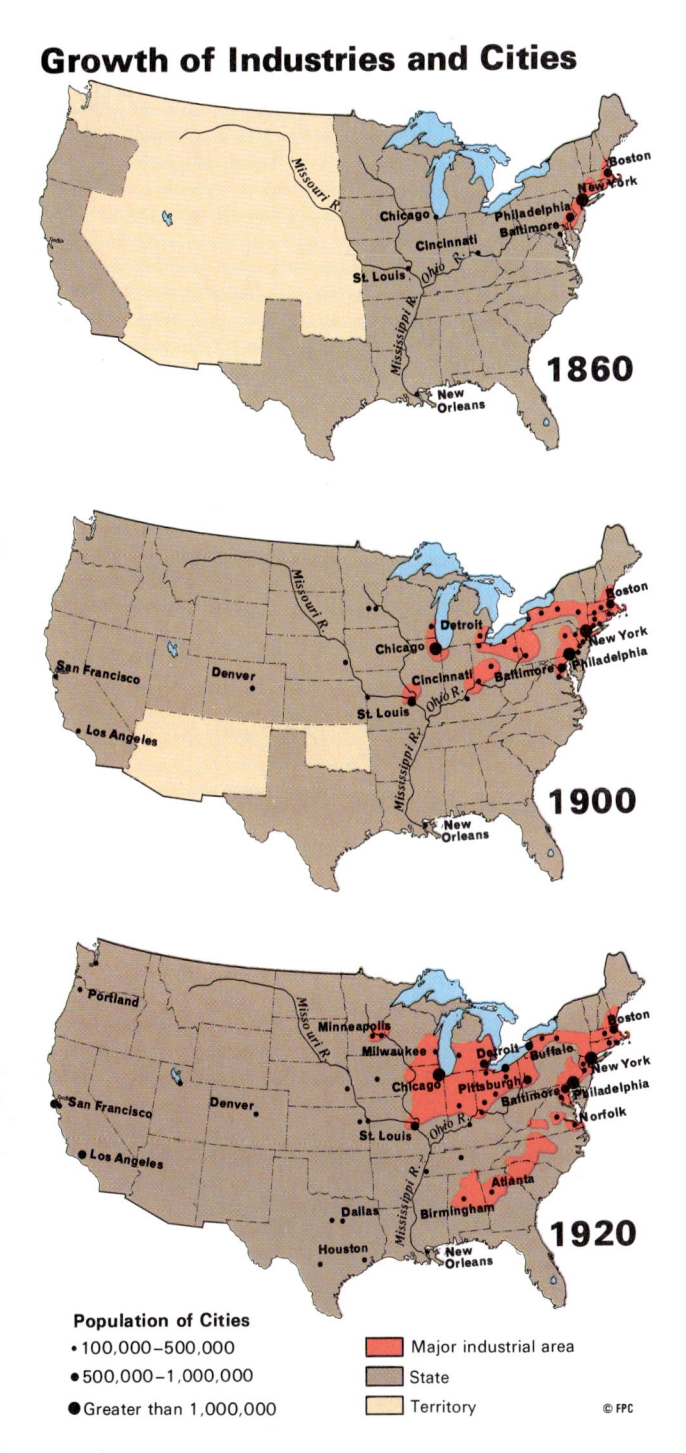

Inventions and the Growth of Industry

In the seventy years from 1790 to 1860, the United States government

Thinking Skill: Hypothesizing. Ask students what they would invent to solve one of the nation's problems today. Have them describe their inventions.

1. Eight more states (Md., Ohio, Mich., Ind., Ky., Ill., Wis., and Mo.). Seven more states (Maine, Minn., Iowa, Ala., Ga., S.C., and N.C.).

Citizenship Skill: Social participation. Ask students to role-play working on an automobile assembly line.

This Model T car owner knew the reasons for building hard-paved roads.

the car moved on a belt past workers. Each worker put a different part of the car into place. Cars could be made faster and cheaper this way.

The gasoline engine also helped people make an old dream come true—the dream of flying. In 1903 two brothers, Orville and Wilbur Wright, made the first real airplane flight at Kitty Hawk, North Carolina. It lasted only twelve seconds. Six years later, however, Orville Wright flew an airplane over Washington, D.C., for more than an hour. A new industry, based on the building of airplanes, developed.

Another United States inventor sparked a great change in communication. In 1876 the United States held a world's fair in Philadelphia, Pennsylvania. It was called the Centennial Exposition in honor of the 100th birthday of the United States. During the fair the visiting emperor of Brazil walked up to a stand run by Alexander Graham Bell. The emperor picked up a strange instrument shaped like a cone. He put it to his ear and cried out, "It speaks! It speaks!"

After that, visitors to the Centennial Exposition rushed to see and hear something called the "telephone." By the mid-1920s, there were 16 million telephones in the United States.

Study the chart of inventions on this page. What were three other important inventions made during the late 1800s? 1

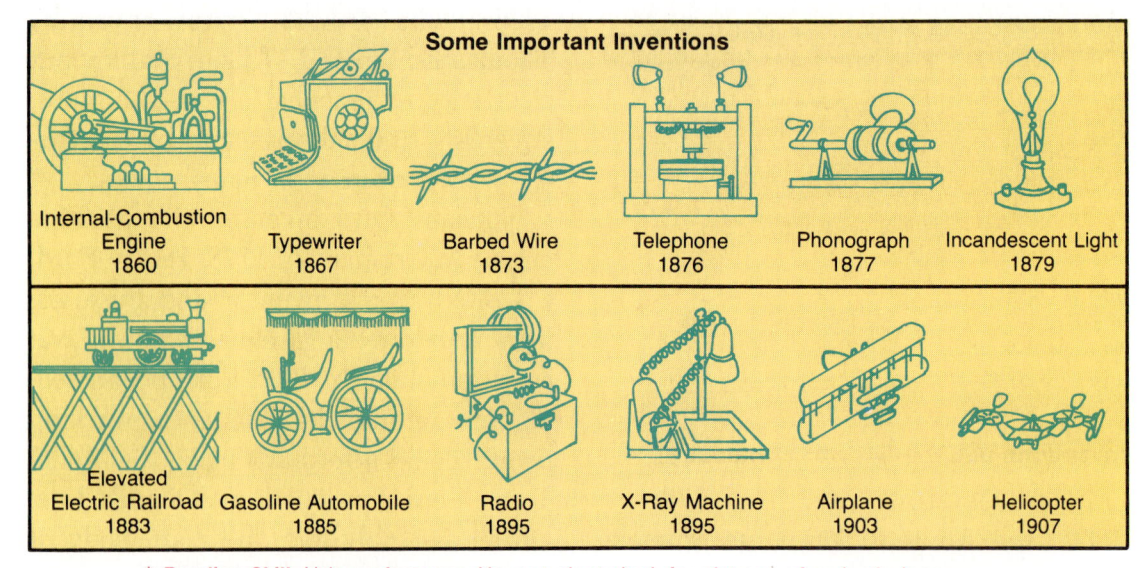

Some Important Inventions

| Internal-Combustion Engine 1860 | Typewriter 1867 | Barbed Wire 1873 | Telephone 1876 | Phonograph 1877 | Incandescent Light 1879 |

| Elevated Electric Railroad 1883 | Gasoline Automobile 1885 | Radio 1895 | X-Ray Machine 1895 | Airplane 1903 | Helicopter 1907 |

* **Reading Skill:** Using references. Have students look for pictures of early airplanes.
Reading Skill: Organizing information. Have students research the history and function of the inventions listed on the chart above.
1. Typewriter, barbed wire, phonograph, elevated electric railroad, radio, and X-ray machine.

> **Time Skill:** Discuss why the world's fair in 1876 was called the Centennial Exposition and why the nation's 200th birthday celebration in 1976 was called the Bicentennial.
> **Reading Skill:** Organizing information. Have students list this country's natural resources.
> **Reading Skill:** Building vocabulary. Review the meaning of *food processing*.

The Wonders of the Centennial Exposition

The Centennial Exposition of 1876 was the first world's fair hosted by the United States. The fair, which was held in Philadelphia, was a showcase for the latest inventions and scientific discoveries of the time.

New machines, such as the Corliss steam engine, which ran all the machinery in one large building, were displayed. A person who visited the fair could also see such wonders as an ice-cream soda fountain, a glass-enclosed elevator that rose 185 feet, and a 15-foot-high church made of sugar.

A writer for a popular United States magazine of the time described the wonders of the fair this way:

> One thinks only of the glorious triumphs of skill and invention. . . . All that Great Britain and Germany have sent is insignificant in amount when compared with our own contributions; the superior elegance, aptness, and ingenuity [skill] of our machinery is observable at a glance.

Many of the 10 million fairgoers saw the largest steam engine of its day.

The Growth of Big Business

Besides new inventions, other changes helped spark a boom in industry and business after the Civil War. One was the vast system of railroads that connected many cities. Railroads made it possible to send goods rapidly and inexpensively to most parts of the country.

The rich natural resources of our country also helped businesses and industries. Huge forests provided the raw materials for a growing lumber and paper industry. Rich farmlands produced abundant crops. These crops were the source of an expanding food-processing industry.

As people settled the country in the 1800s, they discovered even more natural resources. The discovery of iron ore and oil sparked the growth of two of our country's largest industries.

The steel industry. In England in the mid-1800s, Henry Bessemer developed an inexpensive way to take the impurities out of iron ore. This was an important discovery because iron ore is used to make steel. Also in the mid-1800s, huge amounts of iron ore were found in Michigan and Minnesota, near Lake Superior. Soon Americans were making steel to build railroads, bridges, and automobiles. By 1900 the United States led the world in steel production.

The oil industry. Oil was becoming big business too. In 1859 Edwin Drake

> **Map Skill:** Location. Have students trace possible routes of iron ore being shipped from Minnesota to Pennsylvania steel mills on the railroads' map on page 245.
> **Communication Skill:** Writing. Assign reports on Henry Bessemer and Edwin Drake.

Pennsylvania was the leading oil-producing state in the late 1800s.

drilled a hole seventy feet deep in Titusville, Pennsylvania, and found oil. Other people began drilling oil wells all over northwestern Pennsylvania. More oil was soon discovered in other parts of the country. New products from oil, such as gasoline, were also developed. By 1900 the United States was an important oil-producing country.

Problems bring changes. The industries that developed were often controlled by a few people. By 1900, for example, Andrew Carnegie owned or controlled each step in the steelmaking process. He made millions of dollars. Like Andrew Carnegie in steel, John D. Rockefeller became the most powerful person in the United States oil industry. By 1900 Rockefeller's oil company controlled the drilling and the **refining** of oil. Refining is the process by which the impurities of a mineral are removed.

Powerful business leaders who controlled all parts of a business could raise prices whenever they wanted. They could also lower prices to force smaller companies out of business. Soon many Americans began to say that laws should be made to limit the power of such powerful business people. In the late 1800s and early 1900s, the federal government made laws to break up the power of big companies.

The Rise of Labor Unions

As industries grew in the United States, more and more people went to work in factories. In addition to men, women and children worked in the factories. Factory workers often worked twelve to fourteen hours a day for low pay. Women and children were usually paid even less than men.

In the late 1800s, many workers began to organize labor **unions**. A union is a group of people who join together to work for things they believe they should have. By working as a group, labor union members believed they would be better able to bargain with business owners for better wages and working conditions.

Reading Skill: Doing research. Have students make charts showing how oil is mined and processed into gasoline and other oil products.

Checking Up
1. What was the Centennial Exposition?
2. Name two major industries in the United States in 1900.
3. What answers would you give to the key questions at the beginning of this chapter?
4. *How do you think inventions such as the electric light bulb, the telephone, and the automobile changed the way people lived and worked?*

Background: Both Andrew Carnegie and John D. Rockefeller gave away millions of dollars to charities. Carnegie gave money for education, libraries, and the cause of world peace. Rockefeller gave to foundations and organizations such as the Rockefeller Foundation and the University of Chicago.

** **Citizenship Skill:** Social participation. Invite a union member to speak to the class.

Reading Skill: Interpreting graphics: *As You Read, 3.*
Reading Skill: Determining meaning from context. Discuss why the United States was called a nation of immigrants.

A Growing Population

As You Read

1. Think about these words.
   immigrant   ethnic group
2. Look for answers to these key questions.
   a. What were two reasons for the great population increase in the United States after the Civil War?
   b. How did immigration to this country change in the late 1800s?
   c. Why did the population of cities increase in the late 1800s and early 1900s?
3. Use this reading skill.
   A table is a good way to find information. There are two tables in this chapter. Before you read this chapter, study the tables on page 256 and page 259. Then write one sentence for each table that summarizes the kind of information shown in the table.

After the Civil War, the population of the United States increased greatly. One reason for this population increase was that families were larger than they are now. Families with ten or more children were not unusual. This helped the population grow. Yet another reason for this population growth was that more **immigrants** came to the United States during this time than ever before. An immigrant is a person who comes to a country to make a permanent home.

A Nation of Immigrants

Our country has been called "a nation of immigrants." Since early colonial times, people from other parts of the world came to settle here. After the Civil War, boats crowded with people arrived daily in the United States. The millions of immigrants who came to the United States were seeking a better life.

Why the immigrants came. Some people came to the United States for religious freedom. As you may remember from Unit 5, the Bill of Rights guarantees people in the United States the right to worship in their own way. By the late 1800s, the United States had become a country of many different religions.

Many left their homelands to escape hunger and poverty. Some parts of Europe suffered from poor crops in the middle and late 1800s. Many Irish people, for example, left Ireland as a result of a potato crop failure in the 1840s.

Whatever the reason, some immigrants believed they could improve their

Thinking Skill: Hypothesizing. Ask students whether they would have immigrated to the United States in the late 1800s if they had lived in Europe and, if so, why.
Reading Skill: Organizing information. Have students list reasons immigrants came to the United States.

255

Many Asian immigrants worked during the day and went to school at night.

lives by working in the growing industries of the United States. Others wanted to start farms on the millions of acres of farmland still available in the United States. For the immigrants the United States was a land of opportunity. Even the words at the base of the Statue of Liberty in New York Harbor welcomed the immigrants to the United States:

Give me your tired, your poor,
Your huddled masses yearning to breathe free.

Immigrants from many lands. Most of the first immigrants to the United States came from Britain and other countries in northern and western Europe. After the Civil War, just as before, the largest group of immigrants came from northern and western European countries such as Britain, Ireland, Germany, Norway, and Sweden. Look at the world map on pages 10–11 and find these countries. As you may recall from Unit 7, large numbers of Asians from China and Japan also came to the United States after the Civil War.

Immigrants from northern and western Europe often moved west and became farmers. For example, many people from Norway, Sweden, and Germany settled in farming states such as Minnesota, Illinois, and Iowa. Many immigrant farmers settled near people with similar cultures. Soon settlements that were mostly Norwegian, Swedish, or German grew in these areas.

By the 1880s immigrants from countries in southern and eastern Europe began to arrive in greater numbers. These immigrants came from countries such as Italy, Hungary, and Poland. You can find these countries on the world map on pages 10–11.

Look at the table on this page. During which years did Germany and England have the largest numbers of immigrants arriving in the United States? During which years did Russia and Italy have the largest numbers?

Immigrants Arriving in the United States				
Year	England	Germany	Russia	Italy
1866	95,000	116,000	300	1,000
1876	29,000	32,000	5,000	3,000
1886	63,000	84,000	18,000	21,000
1896	25,000	32,000	51,000	68,000
1906	67,000	38,000	216,000	273,000

Background: More than 70 percent of all immigrants arrived in New York City. There they passed through immigration centers where officials recorded immigrants' names, countries of origin, ages, occupations, and religions. The city's first immigration center, Castle Garden, began in 1855. It was replaced by the center on Ellis Island in 1892 and remained in operation until 1954.

How We Know What Happened

The Story of a Young Immigrant Girl

In 1894 Mary Antin moved with her family from Russia to the United States. She was only thirteen years old when she arrived in the United States. She later wrote a book about her experiences as an immigrant. The selections below are from Mary's book, *The Promised Land*. As you read the selections, think what it would have been like to be an immigrant in the late 1800s.

Mary's first impressions about life in the United States:

> So in the evening of the first day my father conducted us to the public baths. As we moved along in a little procession, I was delighted with the illumination [brightness] of the streets. So many lamps, and they burned until morning, my father said, and so people did not need to carry lanterns. In America, then, everything was free, as we had heard in Russia.

New York's tenement-lined streets in the late 1800s were often dirty and crowded.

This family waits on Ellis Island in New York Harbor.

Mary's first impression of her new home:

> What would the . . . sight-seer say about Union Place, . . . where my new home waited for me? He would say that it is no place at all, but a short box of an alley. . . .
>
> But I saw a very different picture. . . . I saw two . . . rows of brick buildings, loftier than any dwelling I had ever lived in. Brick was even on the ground for me to tread on, instead of common earth or boards.

The languages and customs of people from southern and eastern Europe were quite different from those of most Americans. As a result, immigrants from southern and eastern Europe usually settled in cities. They lived in the cities to be close to others from their homeland. Soon **ethnic groups**, or groups that share the same ancestry, customs, and language, formed neighborhoods in cities. People from Europe and Asia soon were joined by people from Latin America.

Reading Skill: Interpreting visuals. Discuss how the picture to the right above explains the text.
Citizenship Skill: Social participation. Ask students to role-play some first days' experiences of immigrants in this country in the late 1800s.
* **Reading Skill:** Building vocabulary. Review the meaning of *custom*.

257

These immigrant children of the early 1900s are learning to say the Pledge of Allegiance in a New York City public school.

Problems faced by immigrants. Life was often difficult for the immigrants arriving in the United States. Many immigrants were poor. Many did not speak English. Some were not educated and had few skills. So they had to take unskilled jobs in factories or as farm hands. Those immigrants who worked in the cities often had to live in crowded, poor sections. Many children had to work just as their parents did.

Citizenship for immigrants. Many immigrants went to night schools for adults to learn to speak English and to learn a skilled trade such as bricklaying or dressmaking.

United States citizenship was granted to immigrants who could pass certain tests. Immigrants had to take a test, for example, that proved they could speak, read, and write basic English. They also had to take a United States history test. No person could become a citizen who was not twenty-one years old or older and who had not lived in the United States for at least five years. Today immigrants have to take the same kinds of tests to become United States citizens.

Population Growth in the Cities

At the same time that the population of the United States was increasing

Math Skill: Ask students to figure out how many more people live in the cities listed in the table below in 1980 than in 1880. Refer students to the population chart of cities on page 483 (New York: 5,159,332 more; Chicago: 2,501,887 more; Philadelphia: 841,040 more; Detroit: 1,086,999 more; Cleveland: 413,676 more).

greatly, so, too, was the population of its cities. New cities developed as well. Many of these cities grew up along transportation routes just as the older ones had. Now, however, the important transportation routes were the railroads.

Study the table on this page. Which cities had a population increase of more than one million people for all the years shown? Look at the three maps on page 251. How many more cities of 100,000 were there west of the Mississippi River in 1900 than in 1860?

Population Growth of Selected Cities, 1880–1940				
City	1880	1900	1920	1940
New York, NY	1,911,698	3,437,202	5,620,048	7,454,995
Chicago, IL	503,185	1,698,575	2,701,705	3,396,808
Philadelphia, PA	847,170	1,293,697	1,823,779	1,931,334
Detroit, MI	116,340	285,704	993,678	1,623,452
Cleveland, OH	160,146	381,768	796,841	878,336

The increasing numbers of immigrants who arrived in the United States in the late 1800s and early 1900s help explain the population growth of cities. In 1900, for example, two out of every three immigrants lived in cities.

Farm workers also began to move to the cities. As you may remember from Units 6 and 7, many advances were made in farm methods and machines during the mid-1800s. New machines took over many of the tasks that had been done by hand in the past. Many farm workers, therefore, moved to the cities to find jobs in the new factories and businesses that developed in the late 1800s and early 1900s.

By the late 1800s, signs of the modern age could be seen in many large cities.

Checking Up
1. What were three reasons that immigrants came to the United States?
2. Name two problems immigrants had.
3. What answers would you give to the key questions at the beginning of this chapter?
4. *What problems might you and your family have as immigrants to a different country today?*

Reading Skill: Interpreting visuals. Discuss how the picture above explains the text.
1. New York, Chicago, Philadelphia, and Detroit. Seven more cities.

Math Skill: Have students use the line graph below to figure out which twenty-year period had the most population growth and which had the least (1900–1920; 1800–1820).

Graphs and Tables Tell a Story of Population Changes

As you read, think about these words.
migration   rural   urban

As you learned in the last chapter, during the late 1800s and early 1900s the population of the United States increased faster than it ever had before. Look at the line graph on this page that shows population growth in the United States between 1800 and 1940. About how many people lived in the United States in 1800? in 1880? How many more people were there in 1920 than in 1880? How much greater was the population increase between 1880 and 1940 than between 1800 and 1880?

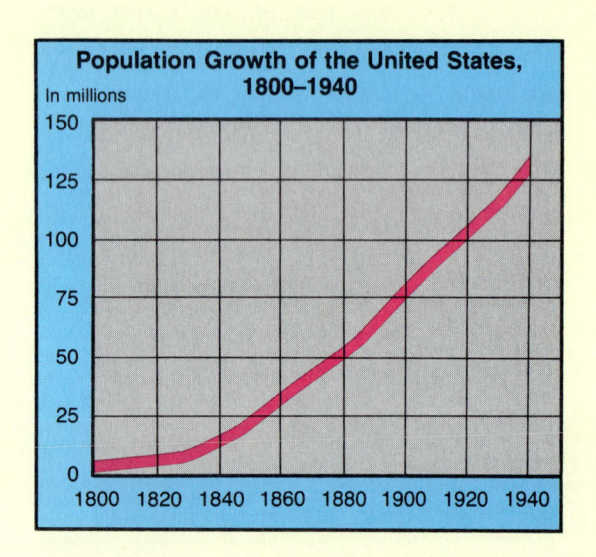

Population Growth of the United States, 1800–1940

Immigration to the United States

In 1820 the United States government started to keep a record of the number of immigrants coming into the country. Between 1820 and 1880, about 10 million immigrants came to the United States. As you may remember from the last chapter, even greater numbers of immi-

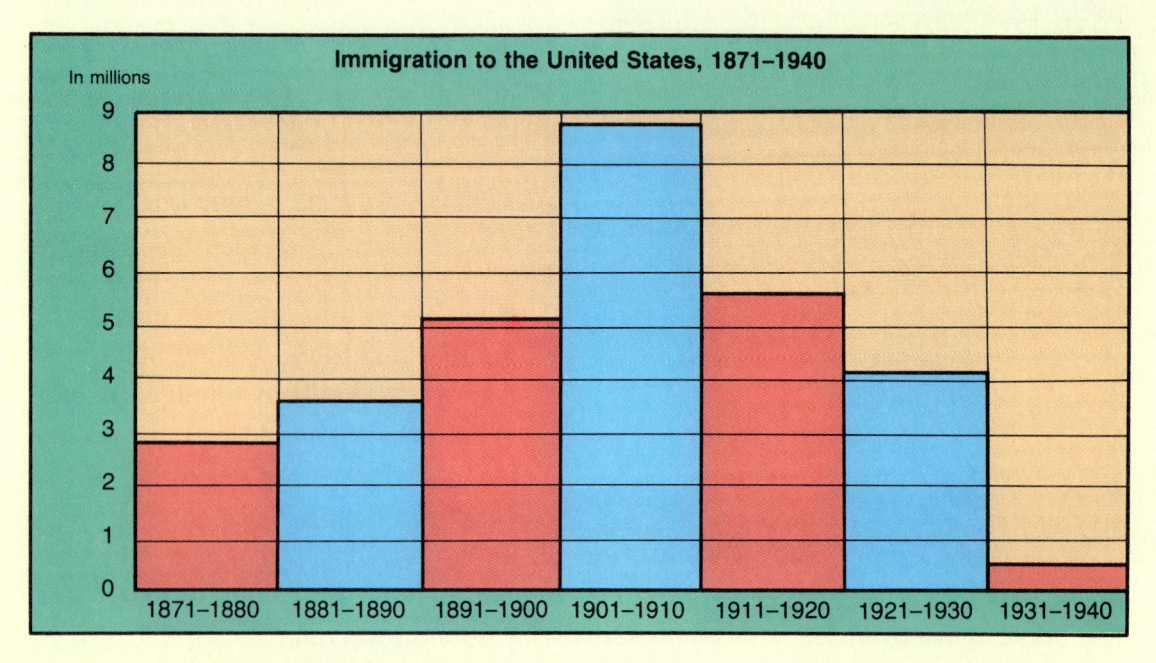

Immigration to the United States, 1871–1940

Thinking Skill: Analyzing. Talk about why it was important that the government began recording the number of immigrants coming to this country.

1. About 5 million people; about 50 million people. About 55 million more people. About 75 million more people.

*** **Math Skill:** Ask students to figure out about how many immigrants came to the U.S. from 1871–1940 using the bar graph on page 260 (about 30,600,000 people).
  Thinking Skill: Analyzing. Discuss why Congress put limits on immigration.

grants came to the United States in the late 1800s and early 1900s.

The bar graph on page 260 shows the number of immigrants to the United States between 1871 and 1940. By studying the bar graph, you can see a great increase in immigration between 1871 and 1910. During these years the United States needed workers to build its railroads and to work in its growing factories. Immigrants came to fill the many jobs that were available in the United States.

Study the bar graph again. About how many immigrants came to the United States between 1871 and 1880? between 1881 and 1890? During which ten-year period did the greatest number of immigrants come to the United States?

Congress eventually passed laws in 1917 and in 1924 to limit the flow of immigrants into the country. In 1917, for example, the government passed a law that no one could be admitted to the United States who could not read or write. Then in 1924, Congress set a limit on the number of immigrants that could be admitted to the country in any given year. The government had set limits on immigration from Asia in the late 1800s. However, the laws passed in 1917 and in 1924 set limits on all immigrants.

Look at the bar graph again. How many more immigrants came to the United States between 1901 and 1910 than between 1921 and 1930?

Where did the immigrants come from? Look at the key to the graphs on this page. This key lists the origins, or

Origins of United States Immigrants, 1820–1930

Key:
- Asia
- Latin America
- Southern and Eastern Europe
- Canada
- Northern and Western Europe
- Other

1820–1860: 95% Northern and Western Europe, 3% Canada, 2% Other

1861–1900: 68% Northern and Western Europe, 22% Southern and Eastern Europe, 7% Canada, 2% Asia, 1% Other

1901–1930: 58% Southern and Eastern Europe, 23% Northern and Western Europe, 11% Canada, 5% Latin America, 3% Asia

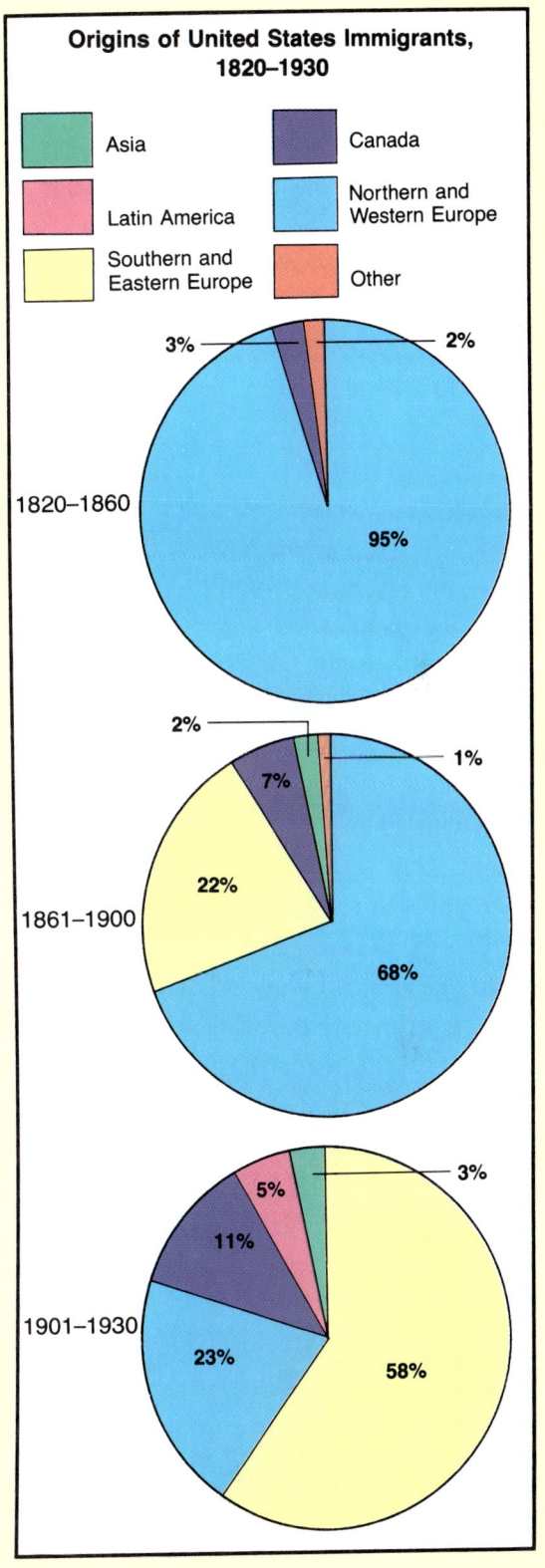

Reading Skill: Interpreting graphics. Discuss how the bar graph on page 260 verifies the immigration limits set in 1917 and 1924. Refer students to the figures for 1911–1920 and 1921–1930.
  1. About 2,800,000 people; about 3,500,000 people. From 1901–1910.
  2. About 4,600,000 more people.

261

Background: The average trip by steamship for European immigrants lasted 14 days in 1867 and only 5½ days in 1897. Passengers were given their own berths and three meals a day.
Citizenship Skill: Social participation. Have students ask their families if any of their relatives immigrated to this country between 1820 and 1930, their countries of origin, and where they settled.

homelands, of the immigrants who came to the United States between 1820 and 1930. Notice that Europe is divided into two areas. As you may recall, northern and western Europe includes such countries as Britain, Germany, Ireland, Belgium, Denmark, Norway, and Sweden. Southern and eastern Europe includes such countries as Italy, Poland, Greece, Hungary, and Spain.

Now study the three pie graphs. From which part of the world did most of the immigrants come between 1820 and 1860? Which area showed the greatest increase in number of immigrants in the years between 1861 and 1900?

During which period of time did Asia have large numbers of immigrants coming to the United States? Many Asians came to the United States in the mid-1800s to help build the railroads in the West. By the end of the 1870s, there were almost 150,000 Chinese living in California. The Chinese worked for long hours at wages below what most Americans would accept.

Many Americans feared that the Chinese would drive down working wages for all Americans. In part, this is why feelings against the Chinese developed in the United States in the 1870s. As a result of these feelings, Congress passed a law in 1882 that cut off Chinese immigration.

How does the third pie graph show government limits on immigration from Asia? During which period of time did Latin America have large numbers of immigrants coming to the United States?

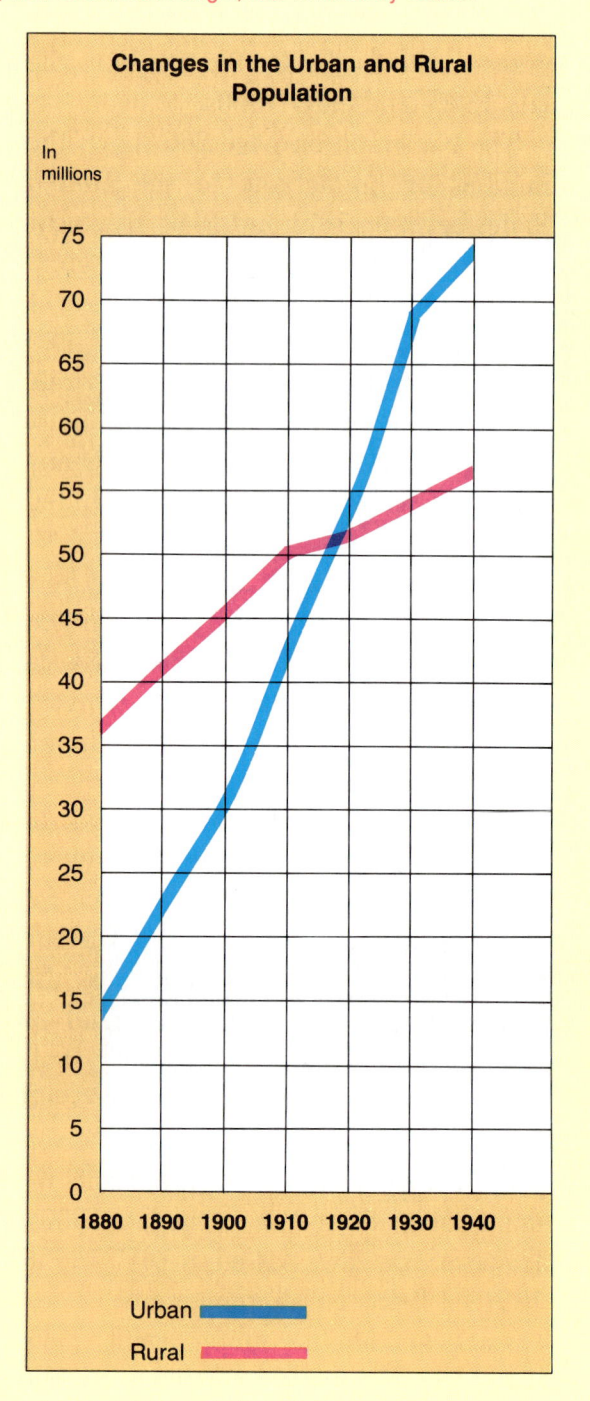

Changes in the Urban and Rural Population

Migration

At the same time that the population of the United States was greatly increasing, another change began to occur in

---

262   **Time Skill:** Ask students how long their families have lived in this country.
1. Northern and western Europe. Southern and eastern Europe.   2. From 1861–1930.
3. From 1901–1930.

* **Reading Skill:** Using references. Have students make montages of urban and rural areas.
1. Red. Blue. About 36 million people. About 14 million people.
2. About 1918.

Growth of Black Population in Selected Cities, 1870–1930				
City	1870	1890	1910	1930
Baltimore, MD	39,558	67,104	84,749	142,106
Cincinnati, OH	5,900	11,655	19,639	47,818
New York, NY	13,072	36,620	91,709	327,706
Philadelphia, PA	22,147	39,371	84,459	219,599
Washington, D.C.	35,455	75,572	94,446	132,068

the population. This change had to do with population **migration**, or the movement of the population. As you learned in the last chapter, many Americans began to migrate, or move, from **rural** areas to **urban** areas in the late 1800s and early 1900s. A rural area is one that is away from cities. An urban area is a city and its surrounding towns.

Rural to urban migration. The opportunity for jobs in the cities attracted many rural Americans to the cities. Better farm methods and machinery that were developed in the late 1800s had left many farm workers without jobs.

Look at the line graph on page 262. Notice that there are two colored lines on the graph. Which color shows the rural population? Which color shows the urban population? About how many people lived in rural areas in 1880? How many people lived in urban areas during this same year?

By what year did the United States have more people living in urban areas than in rural areas? About how many more people were living in urban areas than in rural areas by 1930? by 1940?

Migration of blacks. After the Civil War, many black Americans, like other Americans, began moving to cities. Black Americans, many of whom had been farm workers, were also seeking better job opportunities in the cities. Although the greatest numbers of black people moved to northern cities, many also moved to cities in the South.

Study the table on this page. Which city had the largest black population in 1870? in 1910? in 1930? Which city's black population increased the most between 1870 and 1910? between 1910 and 1930?

Checking Up
1. What is the difference between an urban area and a rural area?
2. What were two major changes in the population of the United States during the late 1800s and early 1900s?

3. About 15 million more people in 1930; about 17 million more people in 1940.
4. Baltimore; Washington, D.C.; New York. New York; New York.

Reading Skill: Using references: *As You Read*, 3.
Thinking Skill: Analyzing. Discuss why so many immigrants settled in the nation's largest cities along the Atlantic seaboard.

A Need for Change

As You Read
1. Think about these words.
   poverty   tenement   conservation
2. Look for answers to these key questions.
   a. What were two problems faced by cities in the late 1800s and early 1900s?
   b. What were three advances in education during the late 1800s?
   c. How did President Theodore Roosevelt help conserve the country's natural resources?
3. Use this reading skill.
   Words that are sometimes difficult to understand are defined in the text and in the Glossary as well. However, you may occasionally come across a word whose meaning you do not know. When this happens, use your classroom dictionary to look up the meaning of the word. Two words that are used, but not defined, in this chapter are *slum* and *ratified*. Before you read this chapter, check the meanings of these words in a dictionary. Making sure you know the meanings of these words will help you read with better understanding.

Although the United States was a land of opportunity with many freedoms, there were problems in the country. There were problems, for example, with housing and education. Other problems arose because not everyone enjoyed the same freedoms and rights. During the late 1800s and early 1900s, Americans tried to find ways to correct many of these problems.

The Need to Improve Cities

Many of the people who moved to the cities lacked the skills necessary to find jobs that paid high wages. Many lived in **poverty**, or as poor people. As more and more people moved to cities, overcrowded slums became a problem.

The streets of New York were alive with activity in the 1890s.

Background: In 1901 the New York State legislature forbade the building of dumbbell-shaped tenements—long, narrow buildings with six or seven rooms at each end.
Thinking Skill: Analyzing. Talk about why laws were passed setting building standards.

Citizenship

Jane Addams

Jane Addams was born in 1860 in a small town in Illinois. Although her family was wealthy, Jane Addams spent her life working to make life better for poor people and children.

As a young woman, she had seen the terrible living conditions of the poor in Chicago. In an attempt to make a better life for these people, she established Hull House in 1889 in Chicago. At Hull House she organized activities such as a day nursery and a handicraft workshop. Immigrants could go to Hull House to learn to speak English. They could also take classes to become United States citizens. Gradually other houses similar to Hull House were established in Chicago and in other cities.

Jane Addams also worked to get laws passed to end child labor and to set up a court system for children who had committed crimes. Presidents and lawmakers listened to Jane Addams. During her life many of the changes she worked for were put into practice.

Jane Addams chose an immigrant neighborhood in which to start Hull House.

In the slums poorly built **tenements**, or run-down apartment buildings, crowded against one another. Little sunlight or air got into the tiny apartments. Usually there was no running water. Many families had to get water from the same faucet, usually located outside the tenement building.

In 1890 a European immigrant named Jacob Riis wrote a book called *How the Other Half Lives*. In this book Riis described the horrible living conditions in tenements in New York City. His book helped Americans see the need to improve living conditions in the cities.

By the early 1900s, some improvements were made. Laws were passed setting standards for buildings. Some playgrounds were built for children. Settlement houses were also started to help the poor. Settlement houses were community centers where people could go to take classes to learn a skill. Classes were also offered to teach immigrants to speak English and to become United States citizens.

Advances in Education

From earliest times Americans had considered education important to the growth of the country. Schools were not the first building a community built, but once built, the schoolhouse was often the most valued building in the community.

Thinking Skill: Observing. Discuss why Presidents and lawmakers listened to Jane Addams.
Communication Skill: Writing. Have students add to the feature about Jane Addams.
Reading Skill: Organizing information. Have students list the country's social problems and solutions discussed in this chapter.

Thinking Skill: Comparing. Have students compare school subjects taught in the late 1800s with those taught now.
** **Time Skill.** Have students find out when the first school was built in their community.
Reading Skill: Interpreting visuals. Ask students to describe the photograph below.

Until the late 1800s, farm children usually attended a one-room school. There one teacher taught all the grades, one through eight. In cities there were schools with classrooms for each grade. Most children did not go to high school. They left school at the end of the eighth grade or even earlier.

Teachers taught mainly reading, writing, and arithmetic. Geography, history, and spelling were also taught. There were few books. Textbooks were often old and had been used by students years earlier.

During the late 1800s and early 1900s, there were many changes in education. More schools were built. Before 1870 there were only 200 public high schools in the country. In 1880 there were 800 public high schools. By 1918 all states had laws requiring children to attend school. The number of children who attended schools increased greatly in the early 1900s.

The first public kindergarten was started in 1873. In the years that followed, more and more public schools established kindergartens.

As roads and transportation improved, the one-room schoolhouse in the country began to disappear. Children could now travel to larger schools in nearby towns. These schools had teachers who could teach more subjects, such as science, foreign languages, and physical education.

Education also improved for women and blacks. During the early 1800s, most colleges did not admit women. By 1900, though, women were admitted at many colleges. Blacks had not been admitted at most colleges either. After the Civil War colleges for black students opened, and more black people were able to earn a college education.

In 1897 the teacher and students of Nelson, Wisconsin, posed for their class picture. Only one teacher taught every student at this schoolhouse. Then, as now, communities were proud of their local schools.

** **Communication Skill:** Listening. Read excerpts from some of Mark Twain's books to the class.
*** **Reading Skill:** Using references. Have students look up the meaning of *Mark Twain* and the author's true name in encyclopedias and other books.

Then and Now

The Stories of Mark Twain

A great book is one that people continue to enjoy over the years. In the late 1800s, as education improved in our country, books and the authors who wrote them became popular. No writer in this period was more popular than Mark Twain. Today people still enjoy the stories written by Mark Twain.

Twain's stories are popular because they are filled with true and often funny descriptions of life. Many of Twain's stories are about his early life along the Mississippi River.

Twain got the idea for one of his earliest stories while living in a mining camp in the West. There he heard a tall tale about a jumping frog. He decided to set the story down in writing. In the late 1860s, the whole country was laughing at *The Celebrated Jumping Frog of Calaveras County*. However, Twain's best-known and best-loved stories described life along the Mississippi River.

Mark Twain returned to his boyhood home of Hannibal, Missouri, in 1902.

Books such as *The Adventures of Tom Sawyer* and *The Adventures of Huckleberry Finn* quickly became favorites, and remain favorites, of young and old alike.

Protecting Our Natural Resources

At the beginning of the 1900s, some Americans began to see the need for **conservation**. Conservation is the protection of natural resources. As early as the 1870s, scientists had warned that Americans were destroying their forests and wasting or spoiling other resources as well. Lumber companies, for example, did not replant trees after cutting down a forest.

At the end of the 1800s, the federal government took some steps to protect the country's natural resources. In 1891 Congress passed a law that gave the President the right to set aside some forestland in the United States.

Ten years later President Theodore Roosevelt set aside almost 150 million acres of timberland in the western United States as a national forest preserve. Roosevelt also set up programs to make better use of the country's water supply. He got money from Congress to start irrigation projects.

Later Presidents followed President Roosevelt's lead. By 1916 the National Park Service was established to supervise the sixteen national parks that had come into existence.

* **Thinking Skill:** Classifying. Have students list ways to conserve natural resources.
Citizenship Skill: Social participation. Invite a conservation officer, a park ranger, or a member of a conservation organization to speak to the class.
*** **Reading Skill:** Doing research. Have students identify the first sixteen national parks.

*** **Reading Skill:** Doing research. Assign additional reading on the Meat Inspection Act and the Pure Food and Drug Act.
** **Citizenship Skill:** Social participation. Invite someone from a meat market or grocery to speak about the Meat Inspection Act and the Pure Food and Drug Act.

The Roosevelt Dam near Phoenix has supplied irrigation water since 1911.

The Need to Improve Life for All Americans

During the early 1900s, other improvements were made that resulted in a better life for many Americans. In 1906, for example, the federal government passed the Meat Inspection Act and the Pure Food and Drug Act. These laws helped protect Americans from the unclean handling of meat and the unsafe making of food and medicine.

Better living conditions did not mean, however, that all Americans shared equal rights. In particular, black people and women did not have equal rights.

Segregation. Remember that a number of segregation laws were made in the South after the Civil War. These laws worked to keep blacks separate from whites. Although there were no segregation laws in the North, blacks fared little better there. In the North blacks were often unable to buy houses in white neighborhoods. Blacks were usually as segregated from whites in the North as they were in the South.

Women's rights. In the 1800s such leaders as Elizabeth Cady Stanton, Carrie Chapman Catt, and Susan B. Anthony worked to win the right to vote for women. In 1869 women in the Wyoming Territory did gain the right to vote. Women's groups continued to work for voting rights throughout the country. Over the years they succeeded in a number of states. However, it was not until 1920, after the Nineteenth Amendment was ratified by the states, that women everywhere in the United States won the right to vote.

Checking Up
1. What were two improvements many cities made in the early 1900s?
2. What is conservation?
3. What was the Nineteenth Amendment? When was it passed?
4. What answers would you give to the key questions at the beginning of this chapter?
5. *How do you think advances in education helped the United States?*

Time Skill: Review the woman suffrage movement discussed on pages 210–211.
*** **Communication Skill:** Speaking. Assign oral reports on Elizabeth Cady Stanton, Carrie Chapman Catt, and Susan B. Anthony.
Time Skill: Have students figure out how long all women in this nation have had voting rights.

Reading Skill: Using textbook features: *As You Read, 3.*
Thinking Skill: Analyzing. Discuss why Alaska was called "Seward's Icebox."

The United States Becomes a World Power

As You Read

1. Think about these words.
   isthmus   neutral
2. Look for answers to these key questions.
   a. What were two ways the United States gained overseas territories in the late 1800s?
   b. Why did the United States government decide to build the Panama Canal?
   c. Why did the United States enter World War I?
3. Use this reading skill.
   The Appendix in the back of your book contains additional information that you will find helpful in learning about the United States. One of the items you will find in the Appendix is a list of United States Presidents and the years they served as President. Before you read this chapter, look at the list of Presidents on pages 486–488. Then name the Presidents who served between 1877 and 1945.

Buying and selling goods and raw materials involved the United States in worldwide trade. Industries needed markets for their goods. Some also needed raw materials from other countries. By the late 1800s, United States businesses and industries were trading with countries all around the world. The United States was fast becoming a world power. Many Americans believed the time had come when our country might expand its borders.

The United States Buys Alaska

In 1867 President Andrew Johnson's secretary of state, William H. Seward, persuaded Congress to buy Alaska from Russia. You can find Alaska on the map on page 14. Russia sold Alaska to the United States for $7,200,000. To Secretary Seward, this seemed like a bargain price. Yet many Americans thought the government was wasting money foolishly. They called the purchase "Seward's Icebox."

The purchase of Alaska proved to be a wise one, however. The fish, gold, oil, lumber, and other products of Alaska were worth much more than the cost of the land. In just one year, the value of Alaska's salmon catch alone is eight times the price paid for Alaska in 1867.

*** **Time Skill:** Have students make time lines showing important dates and events in Alaska's history.
   Math Skill: Discuss the fee paid for Alaska.

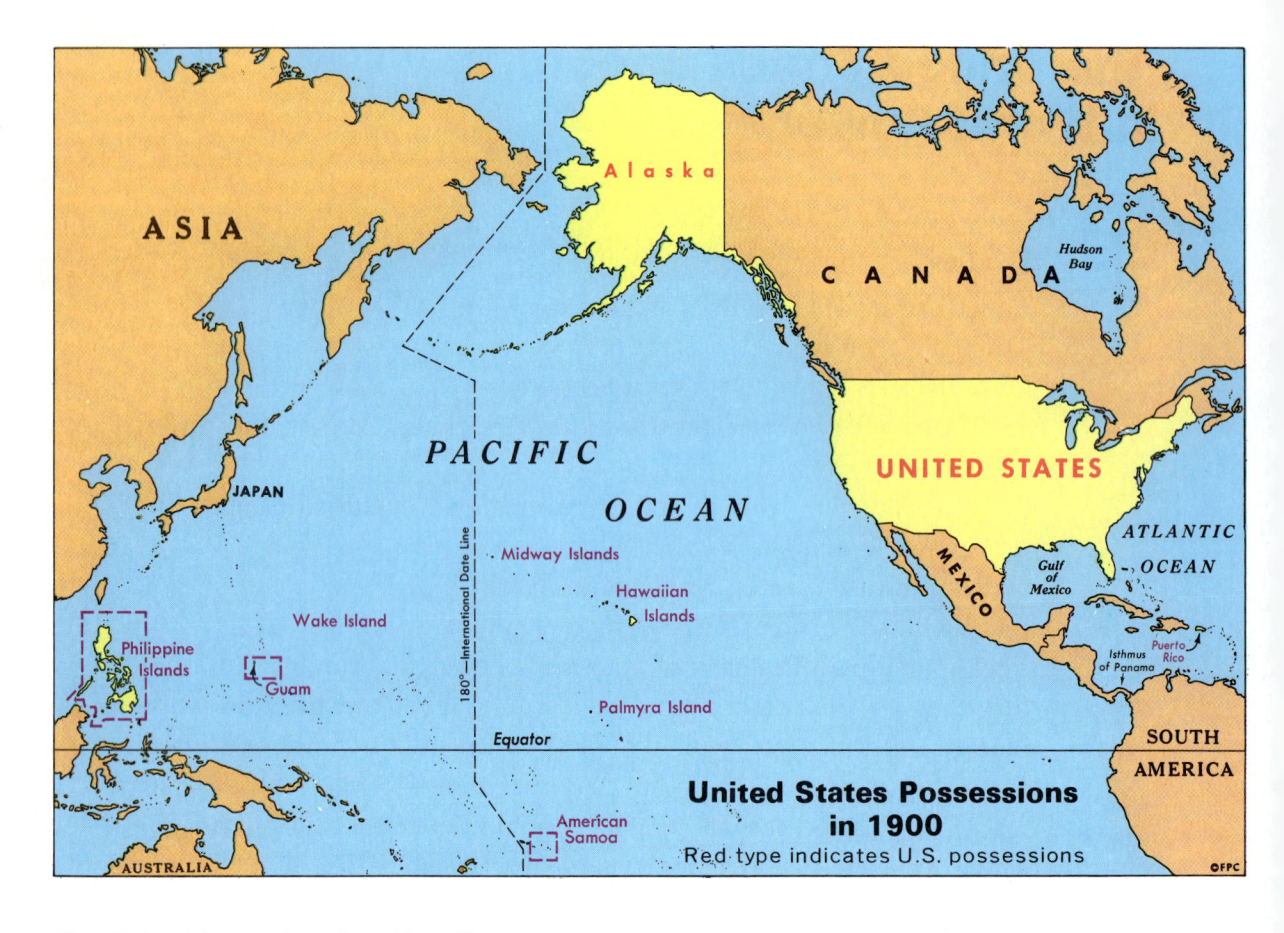

Background: Queen Liliuokalani (li·lē′ə·wō·kə·län′ē) became Hawaii's last royal ruler when some Americans removed her from office in 1893 and established the Republic of Hawaii.

United States Possessions in 1900
Red type indicates U.S. possessions

The United States Acquires Hawaii

In the late 1700s, ships from the United States sailing the Pacific Ocean stopped at the Hawaiian Islands for fresh water and supplies. You can find the Hawaiian Islands on the map above.

Then in the early 1800s, missionaries from the United States went to the islands. They brought the Christian religion to the Polynesian (päl′ə·nē′zhən) people who had lived on the islands for hundreds of years. They also built schools and taught the Polynesians to read and write.

As the years passed, many Americans visited the islands. They saw that the islands were an ideal place to grow pineapples and sugarcane, crops that did not grow well in most parts of the United States. Some of these people bought large areas of land and started plantations. The islands soon prospered.

For many years the Americans and the Polynesian kings and queens got along quite well. As time went on, however, some Polynesians began to worry that the Americans were gaining too much power on the islands.

In 1891 a new queen came to the throne. She tried to work against United States influence. In 1893 Americans living on the islands overthrew the queen and set up a government under their control. Then in 1898 Congress voted to

---

** **Map Skill:** Location. Have students compare U.S. possessions in 1900 with U.S. possessions today using the map above and the map on pages 10–11.
* **Thinking Skill:** Observing. Have students bring in pineapple and sugarcane to taste.
*** **Reading Skill:** Doing research. Assign additional reading on Hawaii's history.

annex, or add, the Hawaiian Islands to United States territory. Like Alaska, Hawaii also became a valuable territory, and later a state, of the United States.

War with Spain

During the closing years of the 1800s, a dispute over Cuba led to a war between the United States and Spain. Cuba is an island in the West Indies. You can find Cuba on the map on pages 10–11.

Cuba had belonged to Spain since Columbus first discovered it. In the 1890s the Cubans started a rebellion against Spain.

Many Americans thought the United States should help the Cubans win their independence from Spain. By the late 1800s, many Americans owned large sugar plantations and other businesses in Cuba. These people, too, were concerned with the outcome of the Cuban rebellion against Spain.

To protect Americans' lives and property, the United States sent its battleship *Maine* to Havana harbor in Cuba. In February 1898 the *Maine* exploded and sank, and 260 U.S. sailors died. No one knew exactly what had caused the explosion. At the time, however, many Americans were convinced the Spanish had blown up the ship. The United States went to war with Spain in 1898.

The United States army and navy defeated the Spanish forces in a few months. Cuba eventually became independent. The United States took over the Spanish islands of Puerto Rico in the West Indies and Guam and the Philippines in the Pacific. Find these islands on the map on page 270.

Winning the Spanish-American War gave the United States important new territory. Guam, for example, became an important military base for the United States.

More than 13,000 ships pass through the Panama Canal locks each year.

The United States Builds a Canal

Find the Isthmus of Panama on the map on page 270. As you can see, an **isthmus** is a narrow strip of land that connects two larger land areas. The Isthmus of Panama connects North and South America.

For many years people had wanted to shorten the water route from the Atlantic Ocean to the Pacific Ocean by building a canal through the isthmus. Ships from the eastern coast had to travel around the southern tip of South America to reach the Pacific Ocean. A canal through the Isthmus of Panama would shorten the long, costly trip by 7,000 miles (11,200 km).

After gaining overseas territories in the late 1800s, the United States government became especially interested in

Reading Skill: Organizing information. Have students make fact charts about the Panama Canal.
Time Skill: Ask students to make time lines about events occurring during Theodore Roosevelt's years as President. Refer students to Roosevelt's listing in the Presidents' chart on page 487.

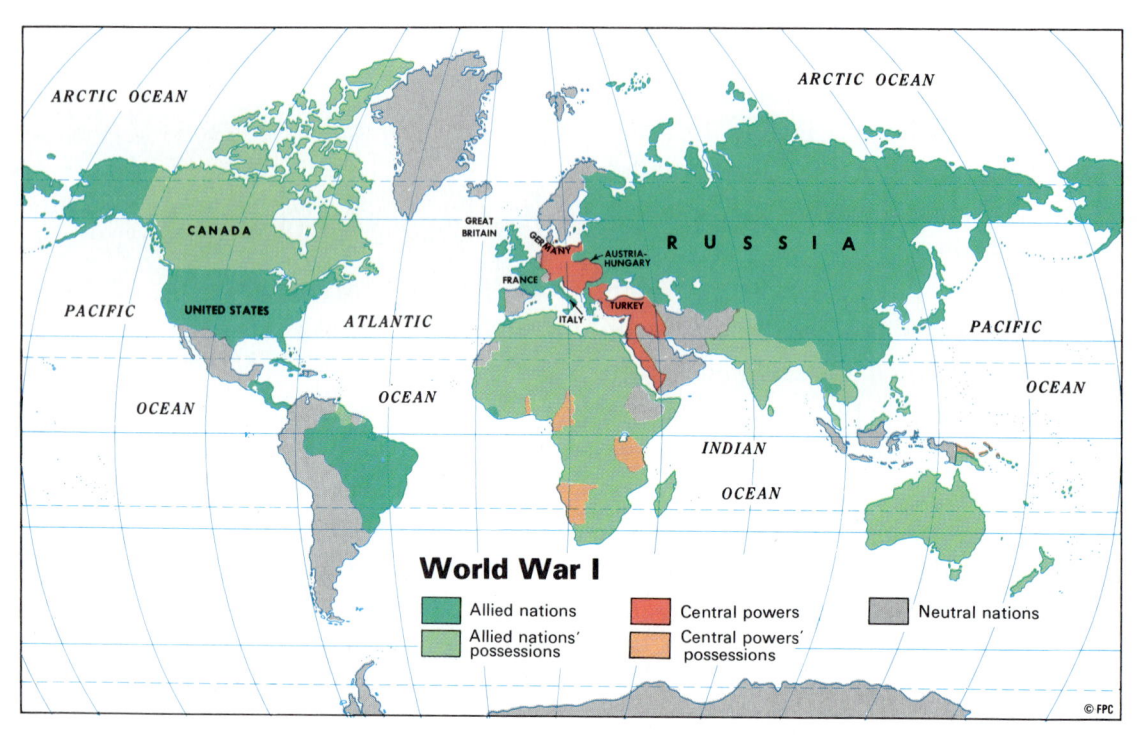

World War I

- Allied nations
- Allied nations' possessions
- Central powers
- Central powers' possessions
- Neutral nations

Which continents had neutral countries? Which continents had countries involved in World War I? How do you think the war affected the Central Powers' possessions?

finding a shorter route to its new lands in the Pacific. President Theodore Roosevelt decided that the United States should build a canal.

At this time the Isthmus of Panama was part of the South American country of Colombia. Colombia refused to give the United States the right to build the canal. So President Roosevelt helped the people in the Isthmus of Panama become an independent country. The new country of Panama quickly made an agreement that allowed the United States to build the canal.

The building of the canal took ten years. Finally, in 1914, the canal was finished. The canal was one of the great engineering accomplishments of the 20th century. The canal enabled ships to travel more quickly from the Atlantic to the Pacific.

World War I

As a world leader, the United States became involved in world affairs. In part, this is why the United States got drawn into World War I.

In the early 1900s, the countries of Europe began to divide into two enemy groups. Each group built up its armies and navies. Germany, Austria-Hungary, and Turkey were in one group called the Central Powers. Britain, France, and Russia were in the other group called the Allies. Find these two groups of countries on the map above.

Thinking Skill: Analyzing. Discuss the responsibilities a world power had in world affairs in the early 1900s and those it has in today's world.
Reading Skill: Doing research. Have several groups report on key aspects of World War I.

Map Skill: Location. Ask students whether the Allied nations or the Central Powers held more possessions during World War I (the Allied nations). Have them use the map on page 272.
* **Reading Skill:** Building vocabulary. Review the meaning of *neutral*.
*** **Communication Skill:** Writing. Assign features on Woodrow Wilson.

Distrust and bad feelings between the two groups finally led to the outbreak of war in 1914. Because so many countries were involved in the war, it has come to be called World War I.

The United States tries not to take sides. At the beginning of the war, the President of the United States, Woodrow Wilson, announced that the country would stay **neutral**, or not take sides. As the war went on, however, it became increasingly difficult for the United States to stay neutral.

German submarines began to attack neutral ships carrying supplies to Britain and France. The Germans also attacked and sank neutral passenger ships carrying Americans.

The United States enters the war. President Wilson warned the Germans to stop the attacks on neutral ships. In 1917, however, after the Germans sank five United States cargo ships in a period of a few weeks, Congress declared war on Germany.

By June 1917, only two months after Congress declared war, the first United States troops arrived in Europe. In the United States, people everywhere helped support the war effort. Women went to work in the factories to replace the men who had left to fight the war in Europe. Factories stopped making other goods and made weapons instead. People conserved food so that more food could be shipped to the soldiers in Europe.

With the help of the Americans, the war soon turned in favor of the Allies. On November 11, 1918, Germany surrendered to the Allies, and World War I ended.

These American soldiers are on their way home after the Allies' victory.

Checking Up
1. How did the United States acquire Alaska? Hawaii?
2. What were the results of the Spanish-American War?
3. When did World War I end?
4. What answers would you give to the key questions at the beginning of this chapter?
5. *How do you think the Panama Canal helped increase worldwide trade?*

Reading Skill: Organizing information. Have students list causes for World War I.
Time Skill: Have students figure out how many years the United States was actually involved in the war (less than two years).

Thinking Skill: Classifying. Have students list text examples of prosperity in the 1920s and examples of hardships in the 1930s.
Reading Skill: Organizing information. Ask students to make charts showing jobs related to the automobile industry.

Good Times and Bad Times

As You Read

1. Think about these words.
   consumer goods   suburb   stock
2. Look for answers to these key questions.
   a. How did the automobile industry lead to the growth of other industries?
   b. What were three major changes in the way people lived during the 1920s and the 1930s?
   c. Why were the 1930s a time of hardship for most Americans?

In the years after World War I, the United States experienced both good times and bad times. During most of the 1920s, business and industry prospered. Americans during this time were able to buy and enjoy more goods than ever before. Yet there were problems. These problems led to severe hardships for most Americans during the 1930s.

Businesses and Industries Prosper

After World War I, factories stopped making weapons and started again to produce **consumer goods**, or goods used by people, such as cars and refrigerators. During this time new businesses were started as well.

More goods and more jobs. At the end of World War I, there were about 9 million automobiles in the United States. Ten years later there were 26 million automobiles. During this time thousands of workers found jobs in the growing automobile industry.

The automobile industry led to the growth of other businesses and industries. Industries that made products used in the manufacture of automobiles, such as steel, glass, and rubber, grew during this time. With more cars in use, more gasoline and oil were needed to run cars. As a result, the oil industry grew as well. New roads were built to accommodate increased car traffic. Many workers found jobs in road construction. New businesses, such as gas stations, opened to provide service to the increasing number of car owners.

New products for the home were also developed. Toasters, irons, and vacuum cleaners were popular consumer goods in the 1920s. Making and selling these new goods meant that there were more jobs for people.

Still, not all parts of the country were enjoying prosperity during the 1920s. During this time gas and electricity were used more and more as sources of power.

Compare this picture of New York with the painting on page 259. How had city life changed by the 1920s?

So less coal was used, and many coal miners lost their jobs during the 1920s.

Problems for farmers. Farmers also experienced bad times. During World War I, farmers in the United States did very well. Soldiers and the people in the war-torn countries of Europe needed food. Farmers in the United States produced large crops to provide troops with food during the war.

For Sale signs like this one were common in the 1930s.

After the war, however, as the European countries recovered, the demand for farm crops from the United States was not as great. Farmers were unable to sell all their crops. Because demand was lower, prices for the crops fell. Many farmers could not make the payments on their farms. Many farmers lost their farms.

Cities Continue to Grow

The number of people working on farms dropped by one million during the 1920s. Because of the poor conditions for farmers, people continued to move from farming areas to the cities. They went to the cities to seek jobs in the many factories and businesses just as people did at the beginning of the 1900s.

In 1920 the government reported that, for the first time, more Americans lived in urban areas than in rural areas. It was mainly in the cities that Americans in the 1920s tried out new ways of living and working.

Reading Skill: Interpreting data. Have students illustrate changes for women during the 1920s.
Thinking Skill: Analyzing. Discuss how the automobile changed the way people lived.
*** Time Skill: Display books written during the 1920s.

Living During the Twenties

During the 1920s there were many changes in the way people in the United States lived. Changes were especially great for women.

Changes for women. During the 1920s modern machines such as the vacuum cleaner and the washing machine made housework much easier. Women were also able to buy baked goods such as bread and cakes in stores for the first time. They no longer had to spend hours preparing food and doing housework. Women had more free time to do other things.

Many women decided to take jobs outside the home. Some women took office jobs such as secretarial work. A few trained for professions such as medicine and law.

Changes brought by the automobile. The automobile also brought changes in the way people lived. It made it possible for people to travel farther and faster than they had before. Families with automobiles could now take vacations in faraway states.

Automobile and bus transportation led to the growth of **suburbs**, or small towns surrounding cities. By car, by bus, or by train, people could easily and quickly get to work in the businesses and factories of the city. Yet they were able to live in the less crowded suburbs.

Airplanes bring changes. During the 1920s new and improved airplanes were built. Airports were also built. More and more people, as well as mail, traveled by airplanes.

The airplane also gave the 1920s some of its greatest heroes. In May 1927 Charles A. Lindbergh took off from Roosevelt Field in New York City in his small plane, the *Spirit of St. Louis*. The flight took 33½ hours. Lindbergh became the first person to cross the Atlantic alone by plane. After he landed in Paris, France, "Lucky Lindy" was the hero of millions around the world. One year later Amelia Earhart became the first woman passenger on a flight across the Atlantic. In 1932 Earhart became the first woman to fly alone across the Atlantic Ocean.

Radio. Radio had been invented before World War I. At first, most Americans looked on it as little more than a toy. During the 1920s, however, radio filled homes with entertainment and news about the world. By the end of the 1920s, 10 million radio sets were in use in the United States. No longer a toy, radio had become for Americans an important source of knowledge, culture, and fun.

These youngsters needed earphones to listen to the early radio sets.

276

* **Reading Skill:** Using references. Have students look for other photographs taken during the 1920s.
*** **Math Skill:** Have students figure out how much faster a plane today travels than a DC-3. Boeing 747 jets now fly at 561 miles per hour (391 more miles per hour).

The Golden Age of Airplanes

During the 1920s and the 1930s, many advances were made in the design of airplanes. These advances led to the development of bigger planes that could fly faster, higher, and longer distances than ever before.

The planes used during World War I were made mostly of wood and had little navigation equipment. These planes were stronger than those made before the war, but they were still dangerous.

During the 1920s engineers designed safer and more powerful planes. The first all-metal plane was built in 1924. By 1926 Henry Ford had designed a three-engine, all-metal plane that could carry ten passengers at 100 m.p.h. (160 kph).

During the 1930s engineers designed pressurized, or airtight, cabins. Because there is less oxygen at higher altitudes, the pressurized cabin made airplane travel safer and more comfortable.

During the 1930s advances were also made in navigation equipment for airplanes. Pilots, for example, were able to receive radio messages from the ground. The automatic pilot was also developed. This device made it possible for pilots to fly without actually seeing the ground. As a result, pilots could fly in bad weather and at night.

The most advanced airplane built during the 1930s was the DC-3 pictured at the right. This plane could carry up to twenty-one passengers and fly at a speed of 170 m.p.h. (274 kph). The DC-3 became the most widely used airplane in history.

Fighter planes such as this one were first used in combat in World War I.

Lindbergh flew more than 3,600 miles in the *Spirit of St. Louis* to reach Paris.

DC-3 planes first carried passengers in 1936. Some still make local flights.

Motion pictures. Along with radio, motion pictures also grew into a popular form of entertainment during the 1920s. Movies during the early 1900s had no sound. These movies were called silent films. The words of the actors were flashed on the screen, so people had to read what the actors were saying.

277

Reading Skill: Building vocabulary. Review the meanings of *pressurized* and *automatic pilot*.
Citizenship Skill: Social participation. Invite a pilot to speak to the class.

Background: Thousands of people, as well as many banks and businesses, lost money in the stock market crash of October 1929. Stockholders suddenly found that their stocks' values had dropped far below what they had paid for them, and no one wanted to buy stocks at earlier selling prices.
Thinking Skill: Observing. Show a silent movie to the class.

During the 1930s these youngsters could see two movies and take home door prizes for only twenty cents at their local theater.

In 1927, however, movies began to have sound. It was not long before silent films were a thing of the past. Soon after, color was added to films.

Soup lines were set up to feed workers who had lost their jobs.

All these improvements made movies great entertainment. Americans flocked to see them. By 1930 almost every town had at least one movie theater.

A Time of Hardship

During the 1920s many people bought **stocks,** or shares of ownership, in companies. When business was good, the price of stocks went up. When business was bad, the price of stocks went down. During the late 1920s, business was not always good. Factories in the United States were producing more goods than they could sell. Some factories and businesses had to close. Many people lost their jobs. Then in October 1929, the price of all stocks fell. More factories and businesses failed, and millions of people lost their jobs.

278
Reading Skill: Building vocabulary. Discuss the meaning of *depression*.
Citizenship Skill: Social participation. Invite someone who lived through the Great Depression to speak to the class.

President Franklin Roosevelt, who took office in 1933, promised to lead the country back to prosperity. To put people back to work, the government started programs for building huge dams, highways, and schools.

Government money was used to help farmers get a fair price for their crops. Laws were passed to set fair wages for workers and to help unemployed people. A law was also passed to provide old-age insurance so people too old to work would have some income. Business in the country recovered slowly, however. During most of the 1930s, millions of people remained out of work.

In the 1930s dust storms swept across the Great Plains and ruined farms.

Checking Up

1. What were three industries that grew during the 1920s?
2. Why did farmers have bad times in the 1920s?
3. What answers would you give to the key questions at the beginning of this chapter?
4. *Why do you think products such as the radio and new home appliances changed the way people lived?*

Unit 8 Summary

- During the late 1800s, more inventions were made than ever before. These inventions helped speed the growth of new industries.
- By the end of the 1800s, the United States had become the world's greatest industrial power.
- Cities grew fast after the Civil War. Millions of immigrants settled in cities. Also, many people from rural areas moved to the cities.
- During the late 1800s and early 1900s, people worked to solve some of the problems caused by the rapid growth of industries and cities.
- During the late 1800s, the United States gained overseas territories.
- After World War I, goods were produced that changed the way people lived.
- In the late 1920s, prosperity ended. The 1930s were a time of hardship.

Unit 8 Review Workshop

What Have You Learned?

1. What were two inventions that led to the growth of new industries and businesses in the late 1800s and early 1900s?
2. Why did people organize labor unions in the late 1800s?
3. Why did the population of United States cities increase greatly after the Civil War?
4. What were three improvements made in the late 1800s and early 1900s that led to a better life for most American citizens?
5. What overseas lands did the United States acquire in the late 1800s?
6. Why were the 1920s good times and the 1930s bad times for most people in the United States?

Use Your Reading Skills

Study the table on page 259 and then answer the questions below. Answers to these questions will help you better understand city population growth between 1880 and 1940.

1. What was the population of Detroit in 1880? in 1920?
2. Which city had the second largest population in 1880? in 1920?
3. Which city had the most people in 1880? in 1940?
4. How many more people lived in Chicago in 1940 than in 1880?
5. Which city had the greatest population increase for all the years shown?

Use Your Thinking Skills

Being able to gather information from a painting is an important skill. Study the painting of the one-room school. Then answer the questions below. Answers to these questions will help you see how much schools have changed over the years.

1. While students of one age group read for the teacher, what are the other students doing?
2. What things can you find in the picture that would probably not be found in a classroom today?
3. Describe the differences in clothing between today's students and those in the painting. How do teachers dress differently today?
4. What are three things you have in your classroom that the students in the painting probably didn't have?

Use Your Research Skills

In this unit you have read about many of the inventions made during the late 1800s and early 1900s. Use the chart of inventions on page 252 and select one invention to research. Read about this invention in your school encyclopedia. Then write a short report in which you tell who made the invention and why the invention was important.

Learn by Doing

1. Work with other students to paint a mural that shows how the United

Reading Skills: Interpreting visuals, using references.
Thinking Skills: Knowing, comparing, analyzing.
Communication Skill: Writing.
Time Skill.

States changed in the late 1800s and early 1900s. In your mural include drawings of important inventions and industries during this time. Show also the changes in clothing styles and the different forms of entertainment people began to enjoy, such as radio and motion pictures.

2. Write a short story in which you describe the experiences of an immigrant who came to the United States in the late 1800s. To get ideas for your story, you might try to learn when members of your own family first came to the United States, why they came, and where they settled. Be sure to include in your story some of the difficulties immigrants faced when they first settled in the United States.

3. Work with others to put together a class newspaper about the 1920s. Write articles for your newspaper about problems farmers faced in the 1920s. Include articles about heroes of the time, such as Charles Lindbergh and Amelia Earhart. Include advertisements for new products of the 1920s in your newspaper. Share your newspaper with others in your class.

Read to Learn More

Find the topics listed below in the card catalog of your library. Read all or part of a book listed under one of the topics. Share what you learn with your classmates.

CENTENNIAL	CONSERVATION
IMMIGRATION	AUTOMOBILE

Reading Skills: Organizing information, using references: *Learn by Doing*, 1, 2, 3.
Thinking Skill: Analyzing: *Learn by Doing*, 2, 3.
Communication Skill: Writing: *Learn by Doing*, 2, 3.
Time Skill: *Learn by Doing*, 1, 2, 3.

Unit Overview: This unit examines the United States from World War II to the present.

Unit Objectives
To understand:
- World War II
- the United States as a world leader
- recent changes in life in the United States

Suggested Materials
Workbook
Unit Tests

Unit 9

Skills Emphasized
Map Skills: pp. 285, 286, 290, 291, 293, 304.
Social Studies Reading Skills: pp. 282, 284, 285, 286, 287, 288, 289, 292, 294, 296, 297, 298, 301, 304, 305.
Thinking Skills: pp. 282, 284, 287, 289, 295, 299, 304.
Communication Skills: pp. 282, 285, 287, 288, 296, 305.
Time Skills: pp. 287, 289, 290, 304, 305.
Math Skills: pp. 295, 296, 300.
Citizenship Skills: pp. 286, 290, 300.

Suggested Student Activities
1. Arrange a bulletin-board display entitled "The United States Today."
2. Make a class time line of the years beginning with World War II. Include the 100 most important events.
3. Make a class booklet on the 1980s.
* 4. Make a time capsule for this year.
** 5. Arrange a stamp display using only U.S. stamps.
*** 6. Have students dress in the costume of their favorite person in U.S. history.

Skills Emphasized in Suggested Student Activities
Social Studies Reading Skills: Organizing information, using references, doing research.
Communication Skills: Writing, speaking.
Thinking Skills: Knowing, synthesizing, evaluating.

The United States Today

Millions watched the lift-off of the space shuttle *Columbia* on its first voyage into space.

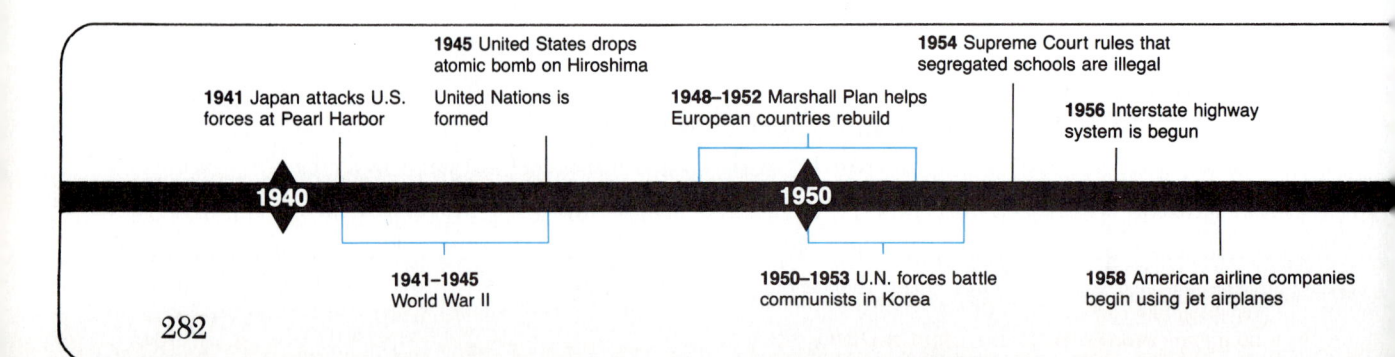

1941 Japan attacks U.S. forces at Pearl Harbor
1941–1945 World War II
1945 United States drops atomic bomb on Hiroshima
United Nations is formed
1948–1952 Marshall Plan helps European countries rebuild
1950–1953 U.N. forces battle communists in Korea
1954 Supreme Court rules that segregated schools are illegal
1956 Interstate highway system is begun
1958 American airline companies begin using jet airplanes

1940 — 1950

1965–1973 U.S. forces fight communists in Vietnam

1960 First communications satellite is launched

1981 The space shuttle *Columbia* makes first flight into space

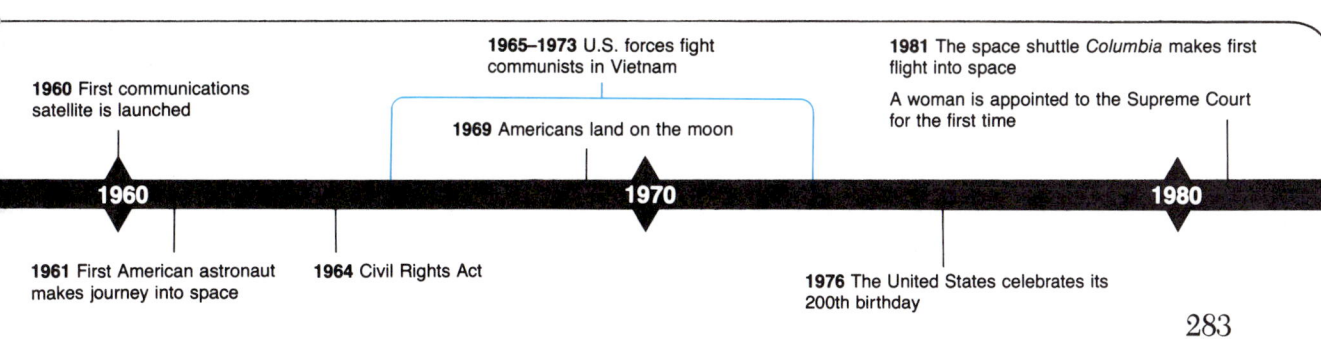

A woman is appointed to the Supreme Court for the first time

1969 Americans land on the moon

1960 — 1970 — 1980

1961 First American astronaut makes journey into space

1964 Civil Rights Act

1976 The United States celebrates its 200th birthday

283

> **Reading Skill:** Using textbook features. Introduce the unit using pages 282–283. Ask students to refer to the time line throughout the unit.
> **Thinking Skill:** Analyzing. Discuss why Germans and Italians allowed Adolf Hitler and Benito Mussolini to become dictators.

World War II

As You Read

1. Think about these words.
   dictator   armed forces   rationing
2. Look for answers to these key questions.
   a. What countries made up the Axis? the Allies?
   b. What is a dictatorship? Who was the dictator of Italy? Who was the dictator of Germany?
   c. Why did the United States become involved in World War II on the side of the Allies?

For President Franklin Roosevelt and most other Americans, the 1930s were a time when problems within the country seemed more important than any problems outside the country. Yet by the late 1930s, the problems of the world began to demand the attention of Americans.

Between the Wars

The United States was not the only country to have problems in the 1920s and 1930s. Other countries around the world had problems too. In Europe, for example, many people did not have jobs. In some places food was scarce and food prices were high.

Many people in European countries looked for strong leaders who would help them solve their problems. In Italy and Germany, two new leaders gained power. They were **dictators**, people who have total control over their own governments. In Japan and the Soviet Union, new leaders also came to power. These leaders, like the leaders in Germany and Italy, had little concern for the rights of individuals.

Dictators in Italy and Germany. In 1925 Benito Mussolini became the dictator of Italy. He promised to make Italy strong again by building up the **armed forces**. Armed forces are the army, navy, and air force of a country.

A few years later, in the 1930s, Adolf Hitler became the dictator of Germany. Hitler gained power because he promised the people that he would make jobs for everyone. He said that he would make Germany a strong country again.

Unfortunately, the German people lost a great deal with Hitler as their leader. They lost freedoms such as the freedom of speech and the right to vote for people of their choice. People who did not agree with Hitler were jailed or killed.

Hitler blamed many of Germany's problems on one group of people—the Jews. The hatred that Hitler felt for the countries that had defeated Germany in World War I and his hatred of democ-

---

** **Reading Skill:** Have students look for pictures of Adolf Hitler and Benito Mussolini.
Thinking Skill: Hypothesizing. Talk about whether a person could ever become dictator of the United States.

*** **Communication Skill:** Speaking. Assign oral reports on the Holocaust.
Reading Skill: Organizing information. Have students list causes for World War II.

racy became a total, unreasoning hatred of Jews. Hitler began a policy of killing all the Jews in Germany and in areas controlled by Germany. Years later, by the end of World War II, his soldiers and police had killed over 6 million Jews—men, women, and children. This mass murder of the Jews is called the Holocaust (häl′ə·kôst′).

Like Mussolini, Hitler built up Germany's armed forces. In 1936 the two dictators joined their forces in a partnership called the Axis (ak′səs).

Military power in Japan. In the 1930s some military officers became the leaders in Japan. They, too, prepared their people for war. In 1940 Japan joined Germany and Italy as part of the Axis.

The Soviet Union. In 1929 a strong leader, Joseph Stalin, came to power in the Soviet Union. The Soviet Union had a communist system of government. A communist government is one that owns all property and controls the economy. Like Hitler, Stalin killed many millions of people who opposed his policies.

The War Begins

Several events happened that caused the beginning of the Second World War. In the 1930s Japan invaded China, and Italy attacked Ethiopia, a country in eastern Africa. Germany was able to take over many countries in Europe without going to war. However, when Germany invaded Poland in 1939, Great Britain

By 1942 Axis forces occupied most of Europe, including parts of the Soviet Union. Which other continents were occupied by the Axis?

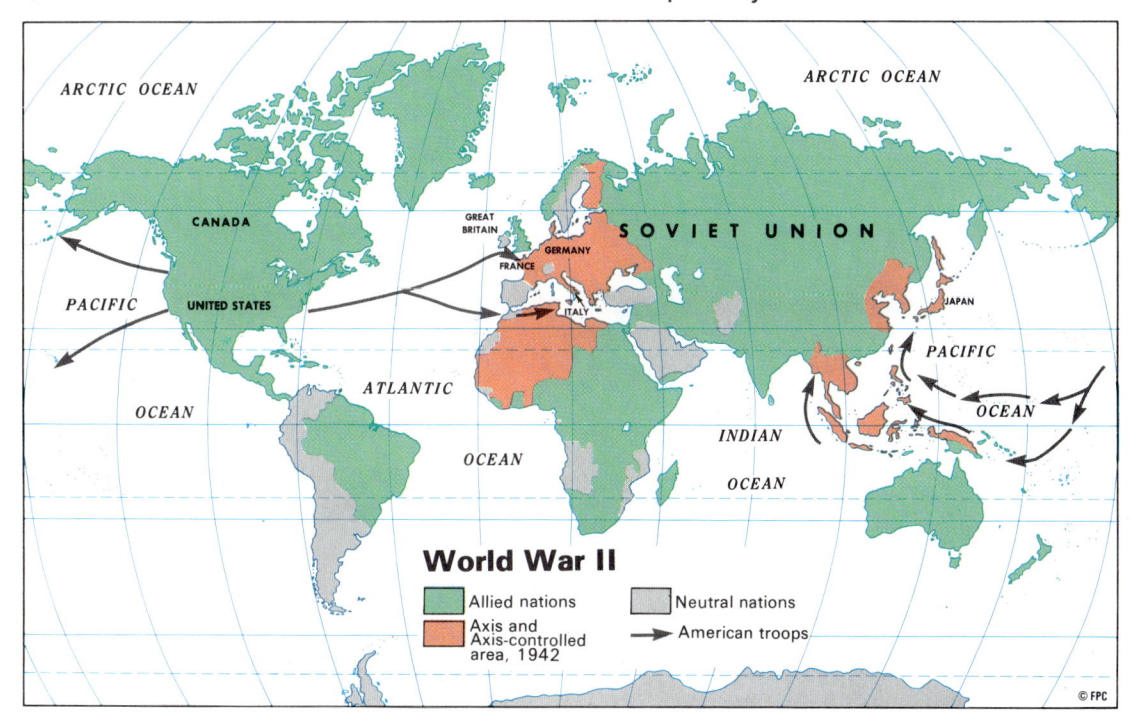

Background: The map above shows the balance of world power in October 1942 when the extent of Axis-controlled areas was at its peak.
Map Skill: Location. Ask students which continents had neutral nations during the war, using the map above (South America, Africa, Europe, and Asia).

and France declared war on Germany and Italy. World War II had begun.

Germany quickly conquered France and other European countries. Italy took over countries in southeastern Europe. Thousands of miles from Europe, Japan conquered much of China and other lands in Southeast Asia as well as islands in the Pacific. In June 1941 Germany invaded the Soviet Union. The war now involved more people and more countries than any other war in the history of the world. The map on page 285 shows how many countries were involved in the conflict.

The United States and World War II

At first, many Americans wanted the United States to remain neutral, just as it had been before World War I. Yet most Americans did not want the Axis powers to win. So the United States government gave help to the Allies, the countries fighting the Axis countries. The United States sent food, ships, tanks, guns, and other goods to help the Allies win.

The United States enters the war. The United States finally found it impossible to stay out of the war. On December 7, 1941, Japanese planes attacked the U.S. naval base at Pearl Harbor, Hawaii. Many Americans were killed. Many ships were damaged or destroyed. The next day the United States declared war on Japan. Three days later the United States also declared war on Germany and Italy. The United States had joined the Allies.

Millions of Americans served in the armed forces. Soldiers, sailors, and fliers fought all over the world. The map on page 285 shows the areas in which Americans served. Thousands of Americans were killed and wounded in land, sea, and air battles.

The war effort at home. While the armed forces were fighting around the world, millions of Americans helped at home. Workers in industries made goods needed to win the war. Many of these workers were women. They took over jobs men had done before they went to war. Women became an important part of the wartime labor force.

Because the armed forces needed so many goods, people at home had **rationing**. Rationing means that the government decides how much of some goods people are to receive. During World War II sugar, meat, coffee, gasoline, and shoes were rationed.

People in Axis-occupied Europe welcomed the U.S. troops.

Children in New York City collected newspapers to help the war effort.

People at home helped in other ways too. There was a national speed limit of 35 miles per hour. This reduced speed helped save gasoline. Some people grew their own vegetables in gardens called victory gardens.

Unfortunately, some people at home were treated unfairly. Some Americans feared that Japanese Americans who lived on the West Coast would try to help Japan. So the government ordered Japanese Americans to be sent to special camps. These Americans lost their businesses and homes. Yet not one case ever proved that a Japanese American was giving help to Japan. In fact, many Japanese Americans fought bravely against Axis forces in Europe.

The War Ends

At the beginning of the war, the Axis won many battles. As the war went on, however, the Allies began to hold back the Axis forces. In 1944 Allied forces, under the leadership of General Dwight D. Eisenhower, invaded France. They pushed the Germans back toward Germany. The Soviet Union, fighting in eastern Europe, also forced the Germans back toward Germany. Caught between two powerful forces, the German and Italian forces could not win. First Italy gave up. Then in May 1945, Germany surrendered. The war in Europe was finally over.

Japan, however, fought on. Then the United States used a new weapon, the atomic bomb. One atomic bomb was dropped on the Japanese city of Hiroshima (hir′ə·shē′mə). Much of the city was destroyed, and thousands of people died. Three days later another atomic bomb was dropped on Nagasaki. Overpowered by this new weapon, Japan surrendered in August 1945. World War II ended.

Checking Up

1. How did Americans at home help fight the war?
2. On what continents did United States armed forces fight?
3. Who was General Dwight D. Eisenhower?
4. What answers would you give to the key questions at the beginning of this chapter?
5. *Why do you think people sometimes call World War II a global war?*

Reading Skill: Using references. Have students find other pictures of war damage in Europe or Asia.
*** Communication Skill: Speaking. Assign oral reports on the Marshall Plan.

The United States, a World Leader

As You Read

1. Think about these words.
   agency   developing nation
2. Look for answers to these key questions.
   a. In what ways did the United States try to help keep the peace in the world?
   b. How did the United States help other countries after the end of World War II?
   c. Why have there been problems between the United States and communist countries?

After World War II, factories that had produced goods for the war began to produce consumer goods. United States businesses and industries produced goods for people in this country and in other countries. The United States became the strongest industrial nation in the world.

The United States also became a world leader of nations. As a world leader, the United States made plans to keep the peace.

The United States Helps Rebuild Countries

Millions of people, both civilians and soldiers, died during World War II. In Europe, Asia, and Africa, many towns, cities, and farms had been damaged or destroyed. People needed food, homes, and jobs. They needed to rebuild their countries. Many people in the United States believed they should help people who had suffered during the war.

Help for Europe and Japan. Many countries needed help to rebuild after the war. One American, General George Marshall, had a plan for such help. He thought the United States should provide money and goods to help countries re-

The Marshall Plan provided money, food, and machinery to rebuild Europe.

288

cover. He thought we should even help countries that had fought against us.

One American who agreed with Marshall was President Harry Truman. He asked Congress to provide money for the Marshall Plan. Congress agreed. Because of help from the United States, Germany and other countries in Europe rebuilt factories, railroads, and homes that had been destroyed during the war. Soon these countries began to recover from the effects of the war.

The United States helped Japan too. With United States leadership and guidance, Japan developed a democratic government. In addition, the United States provided millions of dollars for the Japanese to rebuild industries and businesses. Today Japan is one of the most important industrial nations in the world.

A new organization. During World War II, the Allies worked closely together to defeat the Axis. In 1945 many of the Allied nations formed the United Nations, a new organization to help keep peace among nations.

The United States led the world in trying to make this new organization work. It gave money and provided land for the United Nations headquarters in New York City. Here representatives of countries could meet to try to settle problems.

Some **agencies**, or groups, under the United Nations have tried to help countries in other ways. These agencies have sent people to countries to help farmers produce more food. Doctors have worked with people to prevent illnesses and diseases.

The UN agency UNICEF distributes food to millions of hungry children.

The United States and Developing Nations

After World War II, many European colonies in Africa and Asia became independent nations. They formed their own governments. Yet they also had problems.

Many of the people in these new nations lived in poverty. Many could not read or write. Often farmers grew only enough food for their own families. In many of the new nations, there was not enough food for all the people. Because of their lack of technology and industry, these new nations are often called **developing nations**.

The United States has tried to help the developing nations. Our country has sent food and medicine to these countries. Even more important, people have been sent to help. One special group of people is the Peace Corps. Started by President John F. Kennedy in 1961, members of the Peace Corps live and work with the

Background: More than 75,000 Peace Corps workers have served in Latin America, Africa, Asia, and the Pacific islands. Volunteers serve for two-year periods in nations that request Peace Corps workers. Workers study the host country's language and culture before they serve.
** **Citizenship Skill:** Social participation. Ask a former Peace Corps worker to speak to the class.

A Peace Corps worker helps an African build a school in Sierra Leone.

people in developing nations. They have helped build schools, roads, and other things people need.

The United States and Communist Countries

During World War II, the United States and the Soviet Union were allies. After the war, conflicts between the two countries began.

The communist government of the Soviet Union is unlike our own. The Soviet government owns most of the land, businesses, and industries. People are not free to choose their own leaders. People do not have the freedom of speech or most of the freedoms we enjoy. The Soviet Union's system of government and our system represent two totally different views of government.

The Soviet Union has tried to force other countries to become communist. It has placed communist leaders in control of other countries. Many countries in eastern Europe, as well as China and Cuba, have become communist.

At the same time, the United States has tried to keep other countries from becoming communist. Our government has supplied food, money, and other help to countries fighting communists. It even fought wars against communism in Korea and Vietnam.

Although there are deep disagreements between the United States and the Soviet Union, both are trying to develop understanding. The two countries have cooperated on a space mission. There is trade between the two nations. The United States has tried hard to keep peace.

Checking Up
1. Why was the United Nations founded?
2. Describe the communist system of government in the Soviet Union.
3. Why are some nations called developing nations?
4. What answers would you give to the key questions at the beginning of this chapter?
5. *Why do you think the United States helped rebuild countries after World War II?*

*** **Map Skill:** Location. Have students use the map on pages 10–11 to name some communist nations.
Time Skill: Ask students to use the time line on pages 282–283 to figure out how long U.S. troops fought in the Korean and Vietnam conflicts (four years; nine years).

Maps Tell a Story of the United States and the World

As you read, think about these words.

latitude   degree   prime meridian
parallel   longitude meridian

In the years since the beginning of World War II, people in the United States have become more and more aware of the world. It is important for you to be able to find specific locations in the world on a map or globe.

Lines of Latitude and Longitude

One of the easiest ways to find places on a map or globe is by using lines of latitude and lines of longitude. This system of lines can help you locate any place on earth.

Latitude. In the Atlas skills section on pages 31–32 of this book, you learned about lines of **latitude**. These lines, called **parallels**, are used to locate places north and south. The starting point of the parallels is the equator.

The unit of measure that people use to number the parallels is called a **degree**. The symbol for *degree* is written this way: °. In addition to numbering parallels, people also mark them with one of two letters, *N* or *S*. If the parallel is marked with an *N*, it is north of the equator. If the parallel is marked with an *S*, it is south of the equator.

Longitude. Just as people use parallels to locate places north and south, they also use lines of **longitude** to locate places east and west. The starting point for the lines of longitude is called the **prime meridian** (mə·rid′ē·ən). The prime meridian is an imaginary line that runs from the North Pole to the South Pole through Greenwich (gren′ich), England. Look at the Atlas map on pages 12–13. Trace the prime meridian from the North Pole to the South Pole. Through what continents does it run?

Like lines of latitude, lines of longitude are measured by degrees. The prime meridian is marked as 0° because it is the starting point for lines of longitude. Because lines of longitude, or **meridians**, are used to find locations east and west, they are marked with either a *W* or an *E*. The *W* means that the meridian is west of the prime meridian. The *E* means that the meridian is east of the prime meridian.

Finding Locations

Let's practice using lines of latitude and longitude to locate places in one part of the world. You may recall that every line of latitude and longitude does not appear on maps and globes. Look at the map of the Caribbean area on page 292. You can see parallels and meridians. Find the parallel marked 10°N. Which parallel is the next one to the north? Find the meridian marked 65°W. Which meridian is the next one to the west?

Every location in the world has a specific latitude and longitude. To find a location, you locate the proper line of

1. Europe, Africa, and Antarctica.
2. 15° N.
3. 70° W.

1. 25° N and 80° W.
2. Nassau. 75° W and 80° W.
3. Jamaica.
4. Between 17° N and 20° N. Between 65° W and 70° W.

latitude and the proper line of longitude and follow the two lines to the point where they intersect. Look again at the map on this page. Find Miami, Florida. What are the lines of latitude and longitude that intersect close to Miami?

Sometimes you have to estimate a location's latitude or longitude. Look again at the map of the Caribbean. Find the 25°N parallel. The capital of the Bahamas lies along this latitude. What is the capital? Between what two lines of longitude is it located?

As you can see from this map, most countries are too large to have just one latitude and longitude. So geographers will often use the latitude and longitude of the center of the country to tell people where that country is located. For instance, a geographer might say that Cuba is located at 22°N and 80°W. Find Cuba on the map on this page. Which country in the Caribbean is located about 18°N and 78°W?

Look at the map of a smaller area of the Caribbean on page 293. Between what parallels is the area shown on this map? Between what meridians is this area? How many degrees are there between marked parallels? between marked meridians? Compare this map with the map of the entire Caribbean on this page. Locate the area shown on page 293 on the map of the entire Caribbean.

A map like the one on page 293 can help you pinpoint some locations more easily. Which island has its center about 18°N and 67°W? Which city on this is-

292

* **Reading Skill:** Building vocabulary. Review the meaning of *estimate*.
5. Puerto Rico.

1. San Juan. Mayagüez is located about 18° N and 67° W.
2. The Dominican Republic.
3. The ships are probably not directly threatened by the hurricane.

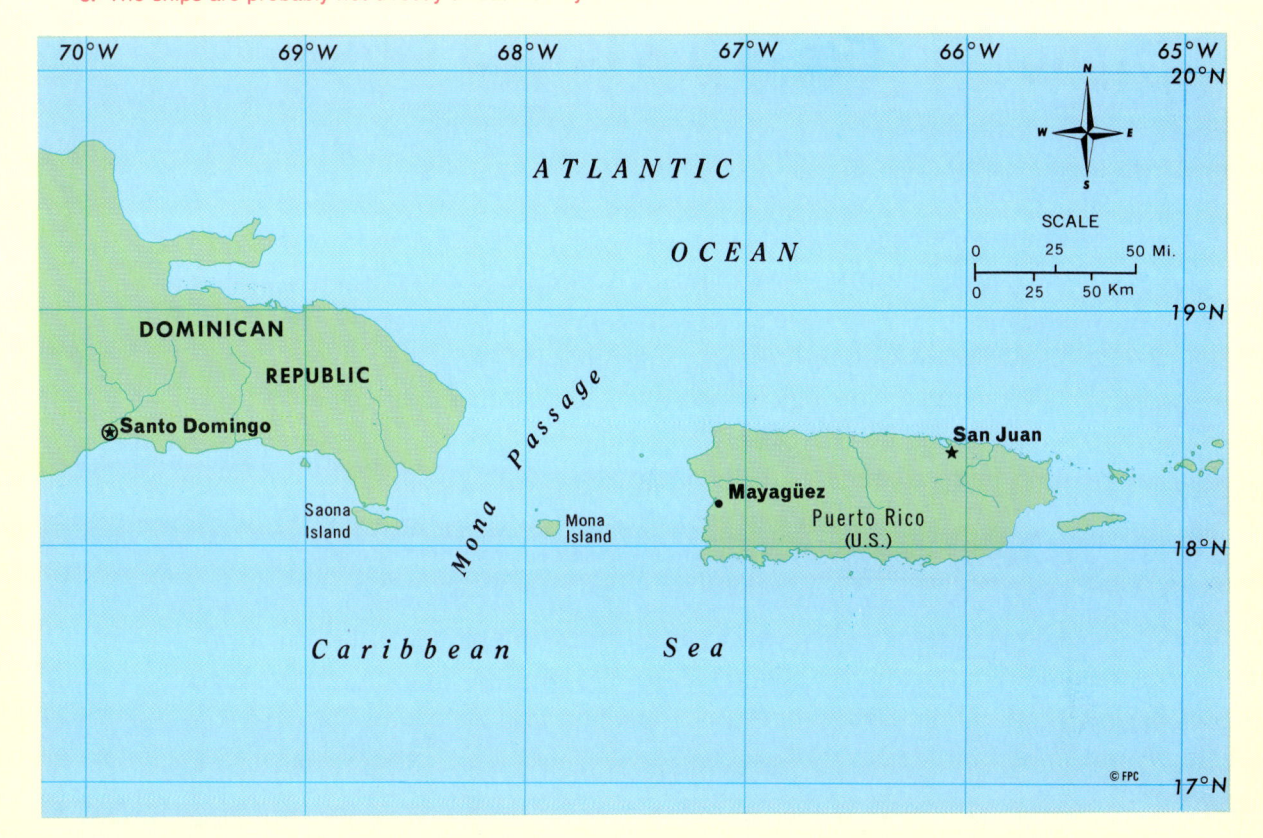

land is located about 18°N and 66°W? Where would you say the Puerto Rican city of Mayagüez (mī′ə·gwez′) is located? Puerto Rico is not a state but a commonwealth of the United States.

Imagine that you hear on television about a hurricane in the Caribbean area. The report says that the hurricane's center is located about 17°N and 68°W. The storm is said to be moving in a northwesterly direction. Which country is threatened by the hurricane? The same report mentions that a fleet of ships are in the Mona Passage. About where is the Mona Passage? Are these ships threatened by the hurricane?

An ability to use latitude and longitude will help you find places all over the world. Since the United States is now concerned with every part of the world, it is important to know how to locate countries, cities, and waterways.

Checking Up

1. What is a parallel? How are parallels numbered?
2. What is a meridian? How are meridians numbered?
3. How do parallels and meridians help you locate specific places?
4. How do geographers give the location of countries that are too large to be located at just one latitude and one longitude?

Map Skill: Location. Have students use longitude and latitude to locate their community on the map on pages 18–19.

Reading Skill: Previewing a reading selection: *As You Read, 3.*

Changes in Life in the United States

As You Read

1. Think about these words.
   interstate highway   computer   astronaut
   satellite   expressway
2. Look for answers to these key questions.
   a. How has technology helped the connection among places and people in the United States?
   b. How have satellites helped improve communication?
   c. What do we learn from our explorations of space?
3. Use this reading skill.
   Before you begin to read this chapter, preview the lesson. To preview a lesson means to look ahead at it. Study the photographs, the heads, and the chart in this chapter. Read the captions of each of the photographs. Previewing a reading selection will help you focus on the important ideas.

Once there were millions of acres of land to settle in the United States. For many years, settlers crossed the country to start new homes. Technology has helped Americans settle the land and change their ways of living. You read about some of this technology in Unit 8. Technology continues to change the ways Americans live.

Transportation Links the Land

The first roads and railroads helped people settle new areas. They connected the farms, towns, and cities. When the automobile was invented, faster transportation became possible.

After World War II, more and more people bought automobiles. Today there

This home's solar panels will trap the sun's rays to provide energy for heat.

Reading Skill: Interpreting visuals. Ask students how the picture on this page helps explain recent changes in life in the United States.

294

** **Thinking Skill:** Observing. Ask students to find out the size of the largest plane used at the airport closest to their school.

Travel Times from Kansas City, Missouri, to Portland, Oregon	
Type of Transportation	Estimated Travel Time
1840s Conestoga Wagon	3,120 hours
1940s Automobile	36 hours
1980s Jet Airplane	4 hours

are more than 110 million cars in the United States. That means there is one car for every two people in our country.

As more cars were made and sold, more and better highways were needed. The **interstate highways** that were started in 1956 truly connected the land. An interstate highway connects two or more states. These four-lane highways crisscross the country north and south, east and west. Automobile travel became even faster.

Improved airplanes also made faster travel possible. In 1958 airlines began carrying passengers on jet airplanes. Passenger jets can now travel at speeds of 550 miles per hour. Now hundreds of thousands of people travel by jet airplanes. There are more than 4,000 airports within the United States. Trips that took the pioneers many weeks can now be made in just a few hours. Look at the chart on this page. How long did it take to go from Kansas City, Missouri, to Portland, Oregon, in the 1840s? How long did it take by automobile in the 1940s? How long did it take by jet airplane in the 1980s?

Communication Links the Land

Improved communication also connected people in the United States. Technology improved the telephone and made it possible for people to talk with other people not only in the United States but around the entire world as well. By the 1980s about 160 million telephones connected homes, businesses, and industries.

Television also improved communication. Although television was invented in the 1920s, it was not common in U.S. homes until the 1950s. Then the number of televisions increased rapidly. Television has become an important way of providing information and entertainment for millions of people.

Both telephones and televisions have been improved by the use of **satellites**. A satellite is an electronic object that circles the earth. Signals are relayed from a satellite to earth so that instant communication between distant places is possible. Through the use of satellites, people can make long-distance calls to almost any place in the world. People can also see world events on television as they are happening. Communication not only connects people all around the United States. It also connects people all around the world.

Computers have also improved communication. Computers store and print information. Americans now use computers to run machinery and to conduct business. Banks and schools use computers to store records. Some people even use computers in their homes.

*** **Math Skill:** Have students find out and compare costs of calls to other countries.
1. About 3,120 hours. About 36 hours. About 4 hours.

** **Reading Skill:** Doing research. Have the class make a space traveler book with biographies of other astronauts.

* **Communication Skill:** Writing. Have students write summaries of the recent events in the U.S. space program.

People Who Made a Difference

Alan Shepard

Explorers have played an important part in our history. Some explorers, like Columbus or Lewis and Clark, opened up new lands. Others, like Eli Whitney, were explorers in that they opened up new possibilities, new ways of doing things.

In the 1960s the U.S. astronauts were a new type of explorer. Astronauts both explored new areas and opened up new ways of communication and travel.

The first U.S. astronaut to make a voyage into outer space was Alan Shepard. On May 5, 1961, he climbed into a space capsule and was launched. Shepard was in space only fifteen minutes. However, this successful flight convinced people that space travel was an adventure worth pursuing.

Shepard trained for months before his Project Mercury flight into space.

From City to Suburb

The first migrations of settlers in the United States were from east to west. You may recall from Unit 8 that people began moving from the cities to suburbs in the 1920s.

Beginning in the 1950s, more and more people moved out of the cities to live in the suburbs. Better transportation and more **expressways**, highways that link the suburbs with the cities, made this shift of population possible. Each day thousands of people drove or traveled by train to their jobs in the cities.

Some suburbs had been small towns. Others were brand-new. They were built to give city workers places to live outside the city. By the 1980s more people lived in suburbs than in central cities.

The United States Goes to School

Education has been a part of the history of the United States for many years. You learned in Unit 8 that there were 800 high schools in 1880. Now, about 100 years later, there are about 24,500 public high schools. About 13 million students attend these schools.

Just as more students started attending high school, so did more of these students go on to college. In 1980 about 30 out of every 100 students who graduated from high school attended college.

Space, a New Frontier

In 1957 the Soviet Union launched the first orbiting spacecraft around the earth. This event sparked a new effort. Soon after, the United States began a

* **Math Skill:** Explain that 30 out of 100 can also be written as 30%. Review the definition of *percent*. Remind students that the word *percent* means "hundredths," or "out of 100." For example, 50% is $50/100$, or 50 out of 100. Explain that percentages of less than 50% are less than half and percentages of more than 50% are more than half.

The success of the space shuttle *Columbia* may make frequent flights into space a reality.

space exploration program. Its **astronauts**, or pilots and technicians who work in spacecraft, began to explore space.

In 1969 Neil Armstrong, Edwin Aldrin, and Michael Collins were in a spacecraft that went to the moon. Neil Armstrong, the first person to walk on the moon, said, "That's one small step for a man, one giant leap for mankind."

Millions of people watched Armstrong's moon walk. Television communication took this important event right into people's homes as it happened. Later, scientists studied samples of dust and rock brought back from the moon. Although astronauts have not yet traveled to the other planets, photographs teach us about them. Just as the astronauts explore space, so scientists explore the information from space.

The first astronauts were all men. Now women are astronauts too. They also prepare to explore the vast distances of the new frontier in space.

Our country is enormous. Millions of people of many backgrounds have settled here. We depend in many ways on technology to link us together.

Checking Up

1. What developments in transportation helped the growth of suburbs?
2. What important event in U.S. history took place in 1969?
3. What answers would you give to the key questions at the beginning of this chapter?
4. *Why do you think Americans want to explore space and other planets?*

Background: The United States developed spacecraft able to reach the moon in 1962. Thus, the U.S. space program perfected a system for sending people to the moon within seven years.

Reading Skill: Determining meaning from context. Discuss Armstrong's statement when he stepped onto the moon.

Reading Skill: Using textbook features: *As You Read*, 3.

Changes in the Quality of Life

As You Read
1. Think about these words.
   equality   integrated   discriminate
2. Look for answers to these key questions.
   a. What important victories have blacks won in their efforts to win equality?
   b. What other groups of Americans have worked to gain equality?
   c. How are Americans today like Americans of the past?
3. Use this reading skill.
   As you know, there is a unit summary at the end of each unit. After you finish reading this unit summary, review your entire reading of United States history. Reread the unit summaries for Units 2–8. Think about the important points of each unit.

The history of the United States has been one of change. The land has been changed as people moved and settled. Technology has helped change the way people live. Many jobs that took hours or days are now done much more quickly by machines and computers. Improved transportation has brought our country closer together. There have been good times and bad times. There have been many years of peace and some years of war.

Throughout our history, one thing has been clear. There has been a continuing search for improvement in the quality of life. Having automobiles, riding in airplanes, and being able to produce plenty of food are important. Yet there are many other things that contribute to our quality of life.

The Rights of All Americans

In this book you have read about the struggle of some Americans to win **equality**. Equality means that each person has the same rights. In the 1950s and 1960s, many groups began to win important victories in their efforts to achieve equality.

Equal rights. Before 1954 many places in the United States, such as schools, restaurants, and movie theaters, were segregated. However, many people were working hard to change the laws allowing this old practice.

Then in 1954, the United States Supreme Court said that segregated schools broke the laws of our country. The Supreme Court ruled that schools had to be **integrated**. Integrated means made available to all people regardless of race or

298   **Reading Skill:** Organizing information. Have students list things that contribute to our quality of life.
      Reading Skill: Building vocabulary. Discuss the meaning of *equal rights*.

Henry Cisneros, a Hispanic American, became mayor of San Antonio in 1981.

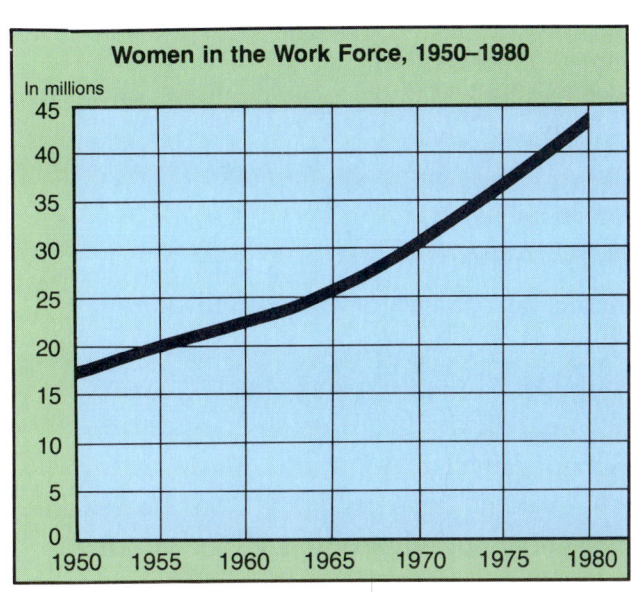

In 1963 Martin Luther King, Jr., led a civil rights march in Washington, D.C.

background. After that ruling more blacks and whites attended school together.

Black leaders such as Martin Luther King, Jr., continued to work hard for equality. In 1964 the Congress of the United States passed a civil rights act. This law made it illegal to **discriminate** against anyone because of race, religion, the place he or she came from, or sex. To discriminate means to show a preference in the treatment of a particular group of people. This law and others help people in their efforts to end discrimination.

Today Hispanic Americans, American Indians, Asian Americans, and women also work for equality. Hispanic Americans, those Americans who speak Spanish as a first language, are working hard to elect some of their leaders to political office. American Indians work to see that treaties made years ago with the United States are honored.

Women have begun to enter professions that were once closed to them. The number of women in the labor force has increased. Look at the graph on this page. About how many women were working in 1955? About how many women were working in 1980?

There have been improvements in opportunities for handicapped Americans. Changes in streets, curbs, and transportation make it possible for handicapped people to get around more easily. There are greater job opportunities for them today too.

Women in the Work Force, 1950–1980

Thinking Skill: Observing. Ask students what aids and programs for handicapped Americans their community provides.
Cisneros (sis·năr′ōs)
1. About 20 million. About 43 million.

299

Citizenship Skill: Social participation. Have students interview people who are able to vote and find out how many voted in the last presidential election.
Background: As recently as 1918–1919, influenza, or flu, killed 20 million people.

Then and Now

United States Voters

The right to vote has always been an important freedom to Americans. In your study of United States history, you learned that many groups have worked hard to get that right. In Unit 8 you learned that women worked hard to get the right to vote. In this unit you read about the 1964 Civil Rights Act. This act helped blacks get full voting rights.

Even though the right to vote is often called our most important right, many Americans do not use this right. The table at right shows the number of voters in some recent presidential elections. The table also shows the percentages of the total voting population that did vote. In which election listed did the highest percentage of people vote? What percent of the total voting population voted in that election?

Voters in Presidential Elections		
Election Year	Number of Voters	Percent of Total Voting Population
1944	47,977,000	56.0%
1956	62,027,000	59.3%
1960	68,838,000	62.8%
1972	77,719,000	55.0%
1980	84,263,000	52.5%

As you can see, in most presidential elections only about half the people who can vote actually do vote. When you reach voting age, your responsibility to your community and your country will be to use your right to vote intelligently.

Improvements in Health Care

In years past many people including many children died from diseases such as influenza, diphtheria, and measles. For many years doctors and scientists in the United States and other countries worked to wipe out such diseases. They developed many shots and inoculations (in·äk′yə·lā′shənz). An inoculation is a shot that helps people develop a resistance to a certain disease. One way Americans fought diseases is by building better sanitation and water systems. In Unit 8 you read about poor people who lived in crowded tenements. Many people in those buildings became sick and even died from the bad water and unclean conditions.

What has been the result of all this work? Many people in the United States live longer than ever before. In 1900 the average American lived about forty-seven years. Today the average American can look forward to living about seventy-three years.

American Ideals

The 1900s have been a time of remarkable change for the United States. Technology has changed the way Americans live. Groups of people who for years did not enjoy full equality have, since the 1950s, gained many rights. Many parts of American life—our homes, our transportation, our education, and our health care—have changed so greatly that

Math Skill: Ask students how much longer the average American will live in the 1980s than in 1900.
1. 1960. 62.8%.

Daniel Inouye, a Japanese American, has served in the Senate since 1962.

Sandra O'Connor became the first woman on the Supreme Court in 1981.

many people think our country has changed completely.

Yet the most important parts of our country remain much as they have for many years. The American people still have a belief in the freedoms that are a part of our heritage. The freedom of religion, the freedom of speech, and the freedom to vote are as important to Americans today as they were to Americans 200 years ago. These freedoms still attract people from all over the world. Americans still work to make this country strong. Our belief in our heritage is a strong link to the American past.

Checking Up

1. How did the Supreme Court help blacks in their struggle to win equality?
2. What is one result of the improvements in health care in the United States?
3. What answers would you give to the key questions at the beginning of this chapter?
4. *How do you think a belief in Americans' ideals links us to our past?*

Unit 9 Summary

- The United States hoped to stay out of World War II but was drawn into the conflict. Our victory in the war made us the most powerful country in the world.
- The United States helped countries rebuild after World War II. More than ever before, the United States was involved with the rest of the world.
- Many great advances in technology changed the way Americans lived and worked.
- Many groups of Americans worked hard in the 1950s and 1960s to win equal rights.

Reading Skill: Organizing information. Have students write four-paragraph summaries of this unit. One paragraph should explain each point in the unit summary.

Stamps—The Story of United States History

You have just finished reading about the history of the United States. Many people and events are part of our story. Some people and events have been commemorated, or honored, on our postage stamps. There are many stamps that celebrate great moments in our history. They tell of exploration and discovery. They praise the first Americans, the American Indians. Some commemorate the development of our special form of government. Still others show the settlement of this vast continent. Other stamps praise developments in transportation and communication. There are also stamps that show places and people who represent the ideals and beliefs of Americans. There are also stamps showing American flowers and animals.

Each of the stamps you see on these two pages will remind you of an important part of our history. Look carefully at each stamp. What does each stamp tell you about our history? Which stamps tell you about the ideals and beliefs of the United States and its people? Use these stamps to help review your study of our country and its history.

Background: These are but a few of the hundreds of U.S. stamps depicting our country and its people. The hobby of stamp collecting is called philately (fə·lat′əl·ē).

1620 THE LANDING OF THE PILGRIMS
U.S. POSTAGE 6 CENTS
5c
FRIENDSHIP – THE KEY TO WORLD PEACE
CHILDREN'S STAMP
1956
3¢ UNITED STATES POSTAGE 3¢
EXPO'74 · US10¢
PRESERVE THE ENVIRONMENT
UNITED STATES POSTAGE
3¢
IWO JIMA
UNITED STATES POSTAGE
15 CENTS 15

Unit 9 Review Workshop

What Have You Learned?

1. Why did the United States enter World War II?
2. What was the Marshall Plan? How did it help countries help themselves?
3. What special kinds of problems do developing nations have? How have the United States and the United Nations helped these countries?
4. When did televisions become common in United States homes?
5. What developments in transportation helped the growth of suburbs?
6. In what year did Americans first land on the moon?
7. What did the Civil Rights Act of 1964 change?
8. How have doctors and scientists improved the health of Americans?

Use Your Reading Skills

Two important social studies vocabulary words are *decade* and *century*. Both words refer to units of time. A decade is a period of ten years. For example, the decade we are in now is sometimes called the 1980s. A century is a period of 100 years. The current century is sometimes called the 1900s. Read the following references to periods of time. Decide whether the references are to decades or to centuries.

1. 1801–1900
2. 1901–1910
3. the 1800s
4. 1922–1931
5. 1845–1944
6. 1901–2000
7. 2011–2020

Use Your Math Skills

In this unit you learned about the development of the interstate highway system and the development of jet travel. Both changed the ways Americans lived. If you can average 50 miles per hour on the interstate highway system and about 500 miles per hour on a jet, about how long would each of the following trips take by car? by jet?

1. a trip of 50 miles; a trip of 500 miles
2. a trip of 100 miles; a trip of 1,000 miles
3. a trip of 250 miles; a trip of 2,500 miles
4. a trip of 400 miles; a trip of 1,600 miles

Use Your Map Skills

The map at right shows the interstate highway system in the mainland of the United States. Study the map carefully. Then answer the following questions about traveling on this highway system.

1. Find Interstate 80 outside San Francisco, California. Follow its path east across the country. With what large eastern city does it connect?
2. What interstates would you use traveling from Chicago, Illinois, to New Orleans, Louisiana?
3. One interstate highway goes all the way from Miami, Florida, to northern Maine. Which one is it?
4. Imagine that you are driving from Philadelphia, Pennsylvania, to Phoe-

Reading Skill: Building vocabulary.
Thinking Skill: Knowing.
Map Skill: Location.
Time Skill.

Interstate Highways

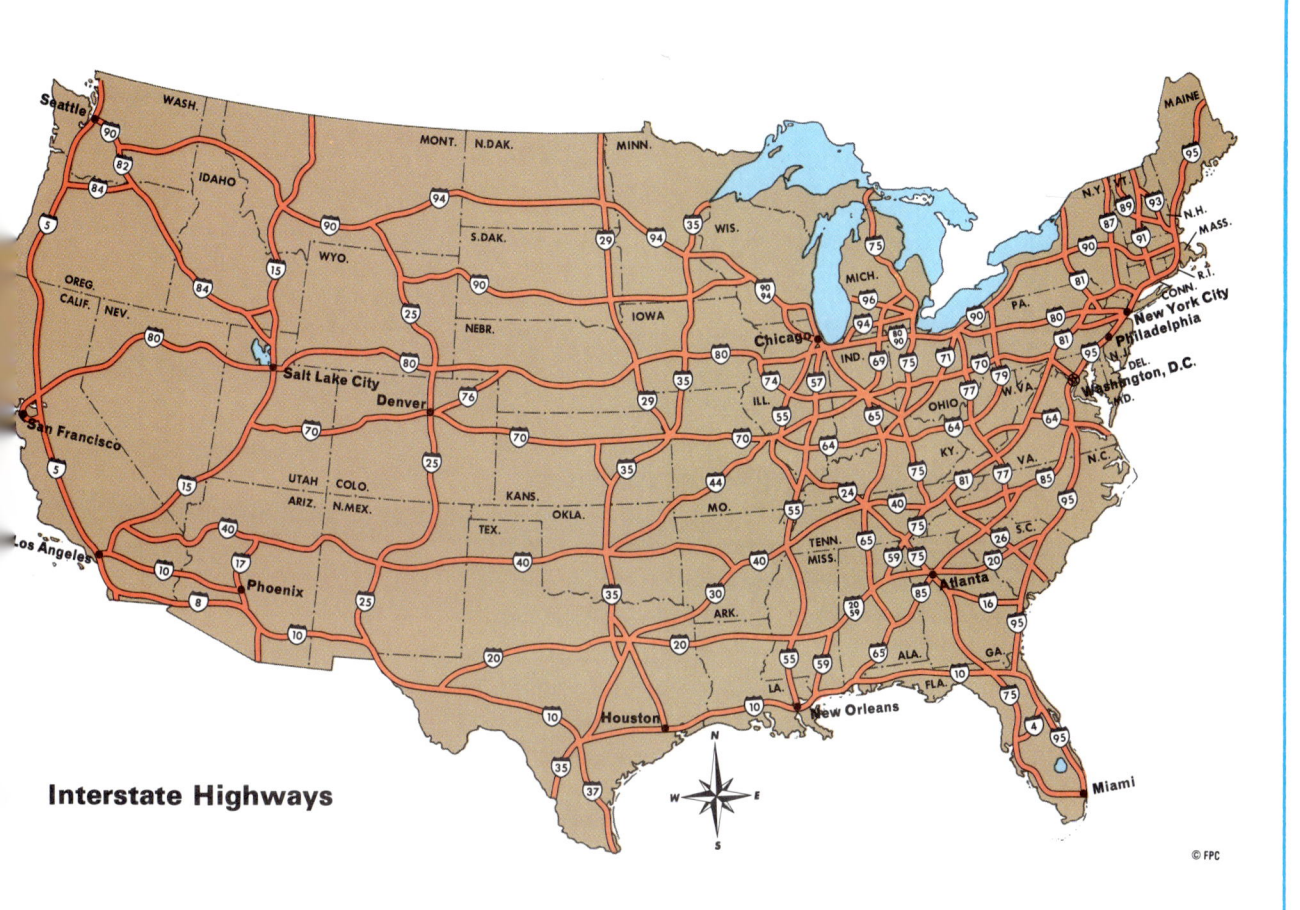

nix, Arizona. You hear that there are heavy snows in both Ohio and western Pennsylvania, so you want to avoid traveling through those areas. What interstates might you use?

Learn by Doing

1. In this unit you learned that most Americans participated in the effort to win World War II. Find out how children your own age in school helped the war effort. Write a report about the ways children helped.
2. You have now read about life in the United States over a period of many years. Review U.S. history by preparing a mural of life in the United States. On your mural show how Americans lived in the 1750s, the 1850s, and the 1950s, as well as how they live now. You might want to show what kinds of homes and what kinds of transportation people used.

Read to Learn More

Find the topics listed below in the card catalog of your library. Read all or part of a book listed under one of the topics. Share what you learn with your classmates.

WORLD WAR II	TELEVISION
COMPUTERS	SPACEFLIGHT

Reading Skills: Using references, organizing information: *Learn by Doing, 1, 2.*
Communication Skill: Writing: *Learn by Doing, 1.*
Time Skill: *Learn by Doing, 2.*

Background: The units that describe the regions of the United States and Canada and Latin America make liberal use of "data banks," or collections of maps, graphs, tables, and charts that help students ascertain the unique characteristics of each region. Since the data banks use many of the same kinds of graphics from unit to unit, students can easily compare the different regions.

Part Two
Regions of the United States

Part One of this book tells some of the story of United States history. Yet there is more to learn. An important part of our story is about the regions of our country.

This section of the book divides our country into eight regions. Each has its own characteristics. The landforms, resources, and climate of each region tell us about that part of the country. The people who settled each area were influenced by these features. Even today, the regions differ from one another in population patterns and in jobs people have.

The map at right shows these eight regions. Find the state in which you live. In which region is your state? Differences among regions have helped build our strength. As you read each unit, you will study graphs, tables, charts, and maps that will help you understand each region and compare one with the others. You will learn how these regions contribute to our country. You will also learn about Canada and Latin America, our neighbors to the north and south. Studying Part Two will help you understand more about our United States.

Alaska

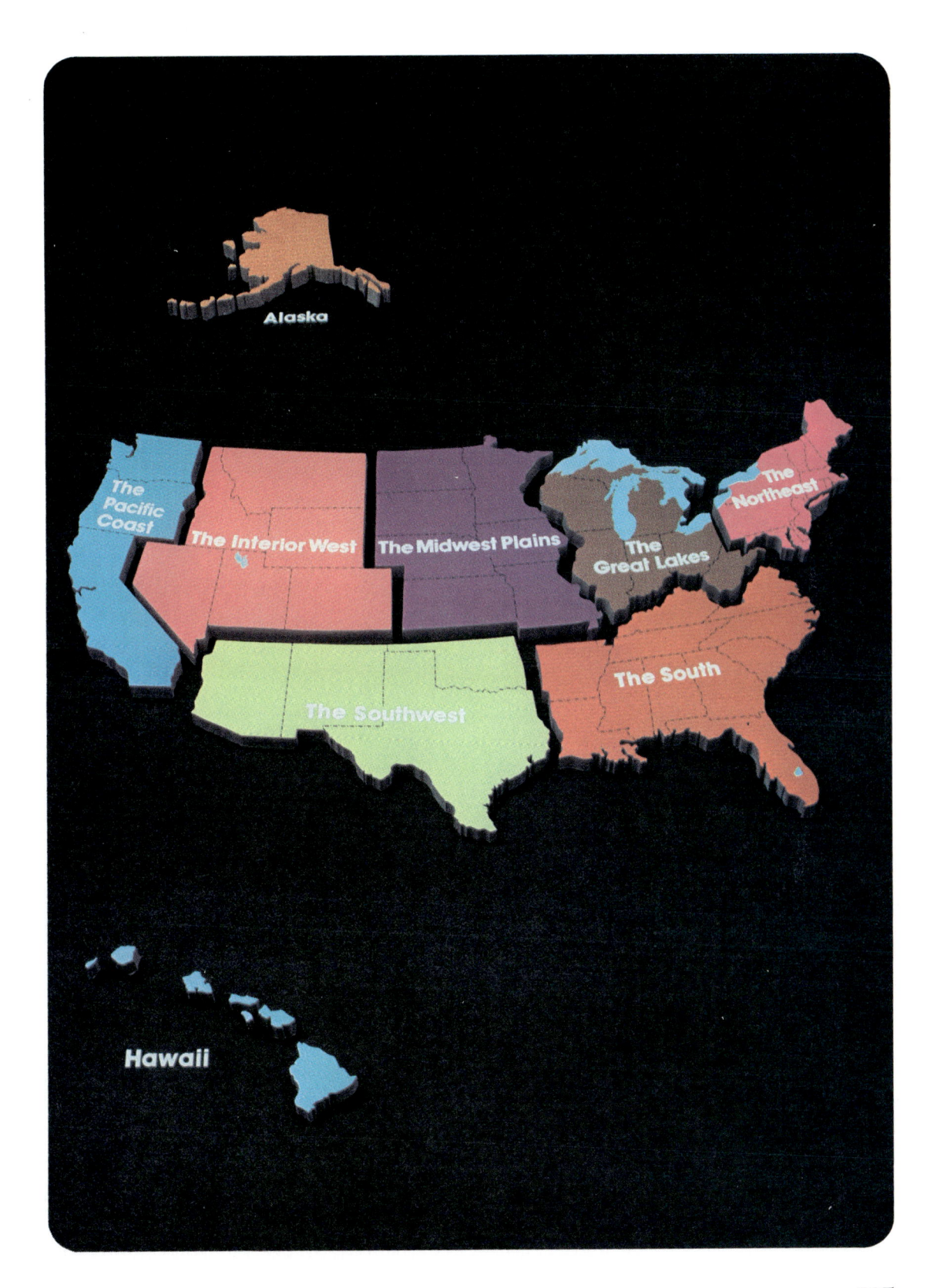

The Pacific Coast
The Interior West
The Midwest Plains
The Great Lakes
The Northeast
The Southwest
The South

Hawaii

Unit Overview: This unit examines the Northeast region, its population density, and its main types of employment.

Unit Objectives
To understand:
- the eleven states in this region
- where the people live in this region
- the main ways people make a living in this region
- graphics, including pie graphs, line graphs, bar graphs, and special-purpose maps

Skills Emphasized
Map Skills: pp. 308, 324.
Social Studies Reading Skills: pp. 308, 311, 313, 314, 315, 316, 318, 319, 320, 321, 323, 324, 325.
Thinking Skills: pp. 308, 313, 314, 317, 318, 324, 325.
Communication Skills: pp. 308, 320, 325.
Time Skills: pp. 315, 325.
Social Studies Math Skills: pp. 315, 318.
Citizenship Skill: p. 308.

Suggested Materials
Workbook
Unit Tests

Unit 10

Suggested Student Activities
1. Work in groups. Each group should prepare a display about one of the eleven states in this region.
2. Post magazine and newspaper articles about this region on a bulletin board.
3. Begin a class data-retrieval chart on this region. Information will be added later about other regions.
* 4. Make shoe-box dioramas of occupations in this region.
*** 5. Work in pairs. Write reports on the topics listed on page 320.

Skills Emphasized in Suggested Student Activities
Map Skill: Location.
Social Studies Reading Skills: Doing research, using magazines and newspapers.
Thinking Skills: Observing, comparing.
Communication Skills: Listening, speaking, writing.
Citizenship Skill: Social participation.

The Northeast

During rush hours many people travel on the George Washington Bridge and the other major bridges and highways in New York City.

309

Region of the Northeast
Physical-Political Map

☆ National Capital
★ State Capital
• Other Cities

SCALE
One inch—about 110 miles

Miles: 0, 50, 100, 150
Kilometers: 0, 50, 100, 150, 200

HEIGHT OF LAND
- 3,300 TO 6,600
- 1,650 TO 3,300
- 650 TO 1,650
- 0 TO 650 FEET

DEPTH OF WATER
- 0 TO 600 FEET
- BELOW 600 FEET

S.C. 310

© FPC

Profile
Feet: 2,000 / 1,000 / Sea level / -1,000

Pittsburgh — Johnstown — Susquehanna River — Philadelphia — Atlantic Ocean

LOCATION MAP

Reading Skill: Interpreting maps: *As You Read, 3.* Also use page 309 as you introduce this unit.
1. Me. (Augusta), N.H. (Concord), Vt. (Montpelier), Mass. (Boston), R.I. (Providence), Conn. (Hartford), N.Y. (Albany), N.J. (Trenton), Pa. (Harrisburg), Del. (Dover), Md. (Annapolis).

Where Is the Northeast?

As You Read This Unit

1. Think about these words.
   population density   megalopolis
2. Look for answers to these key questions.
   a. Which eleven states make up the Northeast?
   b. Which part of the Northeast has the largest population? Which part has the smallest population?
   c. What are the three main ways that people make a living in the Northeast?
3. Use this reading skill.
   This unit, as well as the following units about the regions in the United States, begins with a physical-political map. You will also find an inset map on the same page. What does the inset map on page 310 show? Use the scale on the map on page 310 to find out how many miles the Northeast stretches in an east-west direction. How many miles does the Northeast stretch in a north-south direction?

Can you imagine a region of our country that has all these things: a rocky coast, rich farmlands, lakes, and forests? There are also beaches and harbors for summer fun and excellent mountains and snow for skiing. In this same region you can see places famous in American history. Here, too, are some large and important cities.

The Region

1 The Northeast is made up of eleven states. Look at the map on page 310. Name the eleven states that make up this region. Find the capital of each state. Notice that the District of Columbia is also a part of the Northeast.

The Northeast stretches from the Atlantic Ocean to as far west as Lake Ontario and Lake Erie. Which two states border on these lakes? Which of the states border on the Atlantic Ocean? Which states border on Canada? What symbol shows this boundary? 2

The Land

Look at the profile beneath the map on page 310. This profile shows a cross section of the Northeast from the western boundary of Pennsylvania to the Atlantic Ocean. Find Johnstown and Philadelphia on the profile. Compare their elevations. These two places show the range in elevation in this region. Us-

2. N.Y. and Pa./Me., N.H., Mass., R.I., Conn., N.Y., N.J., Del., and Md./Me., N.H., Vt., and N.Y./Two dots and a dash.

311

Large tankers carry goods into and out of Boston's fine harbor.

1. Plains; plateaus.
2. Northeastern Seaboard, Western Pa. and Western N.Y., and Rugged Interior. Rugged Interior. Western Pa. and Western N.Y.

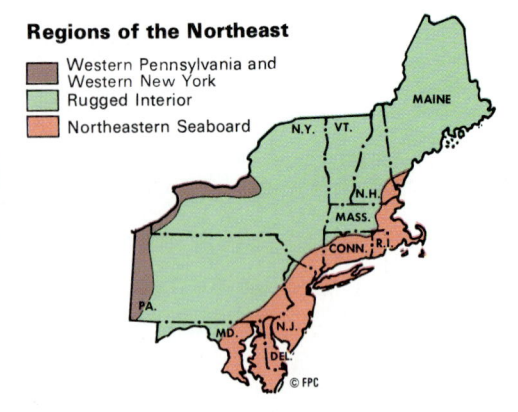

Regions of the Northeast

- Western Pennsylvania and Western New York
- Rugged Interior
- Northeastern Seaboard

ing the profile and the map, describe the landforms in this region. Look at the pie graph on page 313. Which is the most common landform in the Northeast? the least common?

Based on the location of these landforms, the Northeast can be divided into three smaller parts. Look at the map on this page. What is the name of each part? Which part is the largest? Which part is the smallest?

Name the states that are almost totally made up of plains. Which of these states are in the Northeastern Seaboard? What kind of landform is found in western Pennsylvania and in western New York along Lake Ontario and Lake Erie?

The Rugged Interior, which is more than three-fourths of the Northeast, is made up of highlands. These highlands include plateaus, hills, and mountains. Name the states that are almost totally made up of highlands. Using the map on page 310, locate five mountain ranges in the Northeast. These small mountain ranges belong to a larger range called the Appalachian Mountains.

In addition to mountain ranges, the Rugged Interior is marked by plateaus

Look carefully at this map. Which states or parts of states are within each subregion of the Northeast?

cut by streams. A plateau is usually a large, generally level area of high land. The Allegheny Plateau in Pennsylvania, however, is not level at all. Over thousands of years, streams have carved it into steep slopes and narrow valleys. Find the Allegheny Plateau on the map on page 310.

The maps and the graph on these pages show how the land in the Northeast ranges from coastal lowlands to mountains. How do these different landforms help explain why the Northeast is divided into three smaller regions?

The Climate

Yearly patterns of temperature and precipitation help determine the climate of an area.

Temperature. The climate is not the same in all parts of the Northeast. For example, temperatures along the Northeastern Seaboard differ from those in the Rugged Interior. Look at the climatographs on page 313. They show the aver-

3. Md., Del., N.J., R.I., and Conn./ All of them/Plains.
4. Penn., N.Y., Vt., N.H., Me., and Mass./Allegheny, Catskill, Adirondack, Green, and White mountains.

312

Reading Skill: Doing research. Have students find current weather information in newspapers or on radio or television. Chart the results for one week.
Thinking Skill: Comparing. Make comparisons with your area's climate when appropriate.

age monthly temperatures for Mount Washington and Washington, D.C. Find each place on the map on page 310.

1   Which place has a higher average temperature for July? Which place has a lower average temperature for January? Which place has more months of average temperature above 70 °F (21 °C)? Elevation above sea level is the chief reason for these differences. Highlands are cooler than lowlands. Temperature drops about 3.6 °F (2 °C) for each 1,000 feet (300 m) of elevation.

Precipitation. Study the graphs again on this page. Compare the average monthly precipitation of Mount Washington with that of Washington, D.C.
2   Which location has more precipitation?

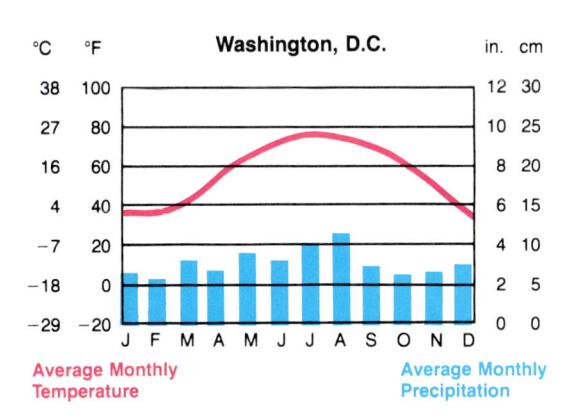

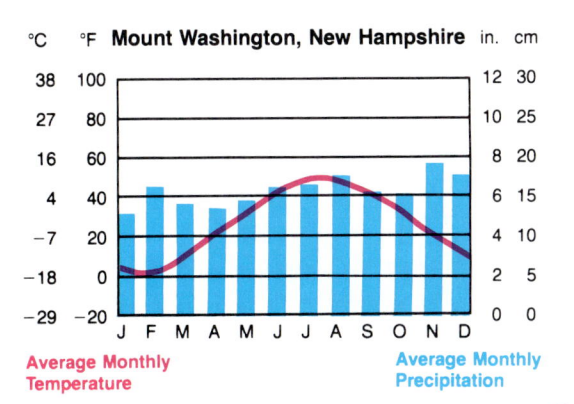

Landforms of the Northeast

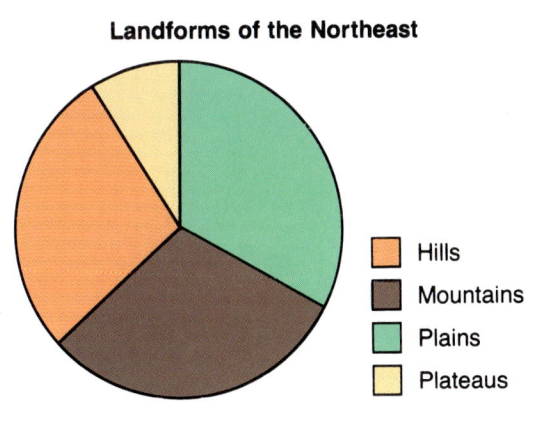

- Hills
- Mountains
- Plains
- Plateaus

The growing season. Temperature and precipitation help determine the length of the growing season. Look at the map on this page. How many months is the growing season along the Northeastern Seaboard? in western Pennsylvania and western New York? How long is the growing season in the Rugged Interior?

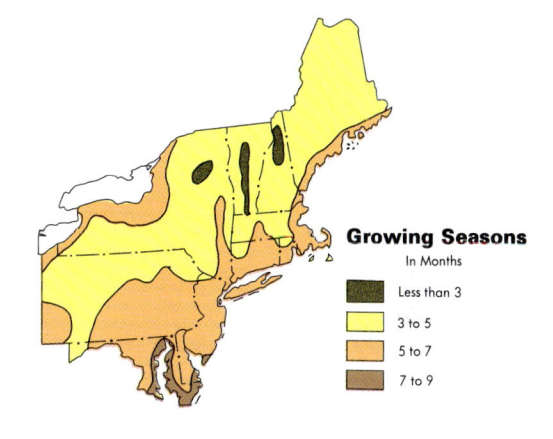

Washington, D.C.

Average Monthly Temperature
Average Monthly Precipitation

Mount Washington, New Hampshire

Average Monthly Temperature
Average Monthly Precipitation

1. Washington, D.C./Mount Washington/Washington, D.C.
2. Mount Washington.

Growing Seasons
In Months
- Less than 3
- 3 to 5
- 5 to 7
- 7 to 9

Checking Up

1. What are the names of the three parts of the Northeast?
2. Which of these parts has mainly hills and mountains? plains?
3. *Why do you think the Rugged Interior has a shorter growing season than the other two parts of the Northeast?*

Background: Ethnic groups make up a large part of the people living in Northeastern Seaboard cities. Explain how the people of an ethnic group share the same customs and language.
Thinking Skill: Classifying. Have students work in pairs to find three pictures of urban areas and three of rural areas in the Northeast. Share these with the class.

Where Are the People?

The Northeast is the most densely populated area of our country. In fact, when people think of the Northeast, they often think of crowded cities bustling with activity. However, this picture is true for only part of the Northeast.

Where the People Live

Turn to the population map on page 16. Compare it with the map of the three parts of the Northeast on page 312. Which of the three parts has the most people? the fewest people? What is the major landform in each of these areas?

Now look at the map on page 310. Where are most of the cities in the Northeast? What is the major landform in this area? What connection can you find between landform and population?

An area both rural and urban. The Northeast is an area where people live in both urban and rural settings. Look at the pie graph on this page. Where do most of the people in the Northeast live?

The key to the population map on this page shows the **population density,** or the average number of people living within a square mile or square kilometer. What is the population density for most of the Northeastern Seaboard? for most of the Rugged Interior? for western Pennsylvania and western New York?

Urban Growth in the Northeastern Seaboard

The Northeastern Seaboard has always been the most densely populated area of our country. Migration is one of the reasons why this area has so many people.

As Unit 8 explains, in the years from 1820 to 1920, millions of people came to the United States from Europe. They settled along the Northeastern Seaboard to work in the cities and in the factories. The factories in the cities were growing rapidly, and they needed workers.

Immigration from Europe slowed in the 1920s. About this same time, however, many people in our country were

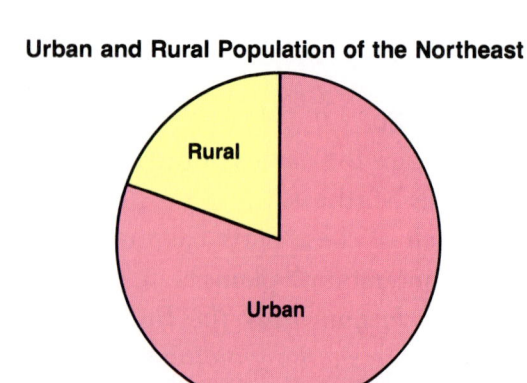

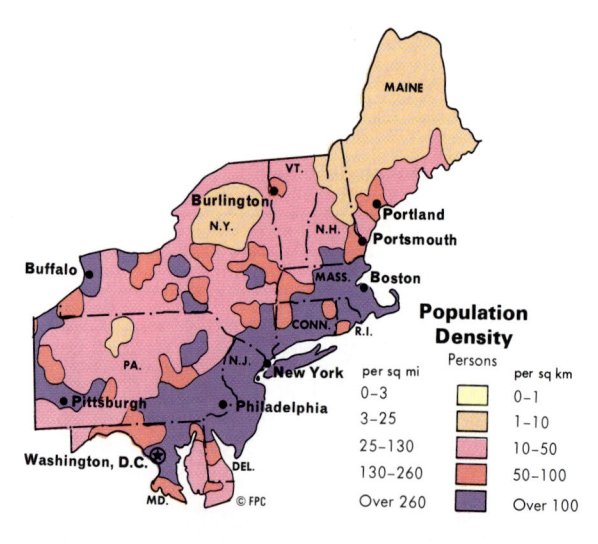

Urban and Rural Population of the Northeast

Population Density

Persons per sq mi	per sq km
0–3	0–1
3–25	1–10
25–130	10–50
130–260	50–100
Over 260	Over 100

* **Reading Skill:** Interpreting graphics. Review how to interpret the map above and the climatographs on page 313.
 1. Northeastern Seaboard. Plains. More people settle a plains area than a hilly or mountainous area.
 2. Urban areas.

Crowds and heavy traffic are common sights in New York City, one of the most densely populated areas of our country.

moving from rural areas to urban areas. One reason was that new farm machinery replaced many farm workers. For example, in the 1920s and the 1930s many black people from the South moved to work in the cities in the Northeastern Seaboard. Also during the 1930s, people from the island of Puerto Rico began to move to cities on the Northeastern Seaboard. They, too, were looking for better job opportunities.

Population growth. Study the line graph of population growth in the Northeast on this page. During which period

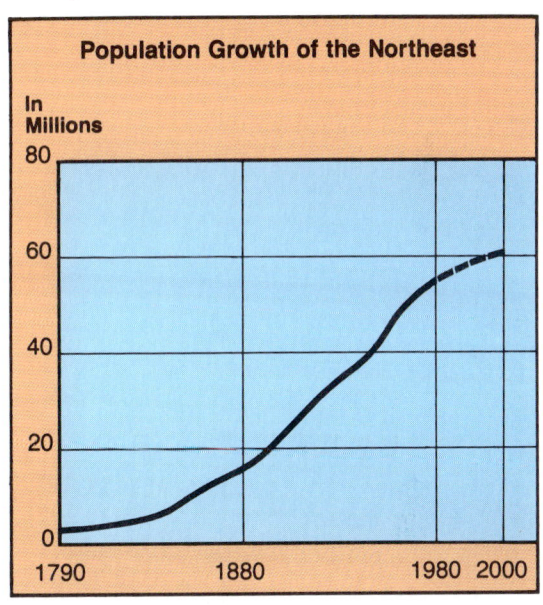

Population Growth of the Northeast

Population Growth of Selected Cities in the Northeast			
City	1790 Population	1880 Population	1980 Population
Baltimore, MD	13,503	332,313	786,775
Boston, MA	18,320	362,839	562,994
New York, NY	49,401	1,911,698	7,071,030
Philadelphia, PA	28,522	847,170	1,688,210
Pittsburgh, PA	Not Available	156,389	423,938
Washington, DC	Not Available	147,293	637,651

Time Skill: Have students use current statistics to support predictions of population growth.
* **Math Skill:** Have students work in pairs to interpret these graphics.
** **Reading Skill:** Recognizing the author's purpose. How do these graphics help support the text?

***Reading Skill:** Building vocabulary. Have students use other sources to define *megalopolis* and figure out why the megalopolis in the Northeast is sometimes called Bonnywash.
1. Between 1880 and 1980.
2. New York; New York. New York. 5,159,332 people.

of time did the population of the Northeast grow the most? Now look at the table on page 315 that shows population growth in some of the cities of the Northeast. Which city grew the most between 1790 and 1880? between 1880 and 1980? Which was the largest city in 1980? How much did its population grow between 1880 and 1980?

The growth of megalopolis. During the 1950s, cities and suburbs of the Northeastern Seaboard grew at a tremendous rate. As they grew, they began to merge. By the 1960s, the entire area between Boston and Washington, D.C., was almost completely urban. Such a large urban area is a **megalopolis.** Look at the map on page 325. Locate the area that this megalopolis includes.

The Less Crowded Areas of the Northeast

In contrast to the crowded, urban area of the Northeastern Seaboard, the Rugged Interior is mostly rural. The cities in

Resort areas in the Rugged Interior, like Big Bromley Ski Area in Vermont, attract many vacationers each year.

316

1. People mainly settled the mountain valleys, not the mountainous or hilly areas of this region.
2. Plains. Availability of good farmland and good water transportation.
3. All of them; all of them.
4. To move to warmer climates, to less congested rural areas, or to areas with a lower cost of living.

Recent Populations of Selected Cities in the Northeast				
City	1950 Population	1960 Population	1970 Population	1980 Population
Baltimore, MD	949,708	939,024	905,759	786,775
Boston, MA	801,444	697,197	641,071	562,994
New York, NY	7,891,957	7,781,984	7,894,862	7,071,030
Philadelphia, PA	2,071,605	2,002,512	1,948,609	1,688,210
Pittsburgh, PA	676,806	604,332	520,117	423,938
Washington, DC	802,178	763,956	756,510	637,651

the Rugged Interior tend to be smaller and farther apart than those along the Northeastern Seaboard. Look at the map on page 310. How can the landforms of the Rugged Interior help explain the size and location of its urban areas?

1

Again look at the map on page 310. What is the major landform in western Pennsylvania and in western New York? Look at the population map. Why might there be more people here than in the Rugged Interior?

2

Changes in Population

In recent years, some of the cities of the Northeast have decreased in population. Look at the table on this page. Which cities have decreased in population since 1970? Which cities have decreased in population since 1960?

3

There are several reasons for this decrease. Some people have moved from cities to suburbs. Improved means of transportation make it easier to ship goods all over the country. Thus, some factories have moved to the Rugged Interior and other less urban regions in the United States. People have moved to these areas to work in the factories. What other reasons can you think of to explain why people might leave cities? Although people continue to come to cities in the Northeast, their numbers do not equal those who have left.

4

In contrast, parts of the Rugged Interior are gaining more people. Relocated industries provide more jobs. The lakes and mountains attract more tourists each year. More tourists mean more jobs in resort areas.

Look again at the graph of population growth for the Northeast on page 315. How many people are expected to be living in the Northeast by the year 2000? How many more people will this be than in 1980?

5

Checking Up

1. Where do most of the people in the Northeast live?
2. Why have some cities decreased in population in recent years?
3. *Why is the Northeastern Seaboard so densely populated?*

5. About 62 million people. About 10 million people.
** **Thinking Skill:** Predicting. Talk about how students could use population data for the year 2000.

Reading Skill: Skimming. Have students skim this section to identify the region's main occupations.
Thinking Skill: Analyzing. Help students focus a discussion on reasons for the main occupations of this region's workers.

What Do the People Do?

Many people live and work in the fast-paced urban areas of the Northeastern Seaboard and in western Pennsylvania and western New York. Others in the Northeast live and work in the quieter, more rural areas of the Rugged Interior.

Making a Living in the Northeastern Seaboard

From early in our history to today, the Northeastern Seaboard has been a trade and transportation center. Many people in this region still work in trade and transportation.

A trade and transportation center. Most of the earliest cities along the Atlantic seaboard grew because of their ties with Europe. European trade was important to these cities. Thus, people remained close to the ocean and its good harbors.

Find Boston on the map on page 310. Located on a bay, Boston has a good harbor sheltered from the Atlantic Ocean. Find New York City, Philadelphia, and Baltimore on the map. They also have good harbors.

Our country depends on many goods from other countries. We also need to sell our own goods in other countries. A large number of goods enter our country through the harbors and airports of the port cities in the Northeastern Seaboard. In these cities, goods are transferred from ships and planes onto trucks and trains to travel inland. Goods brought to

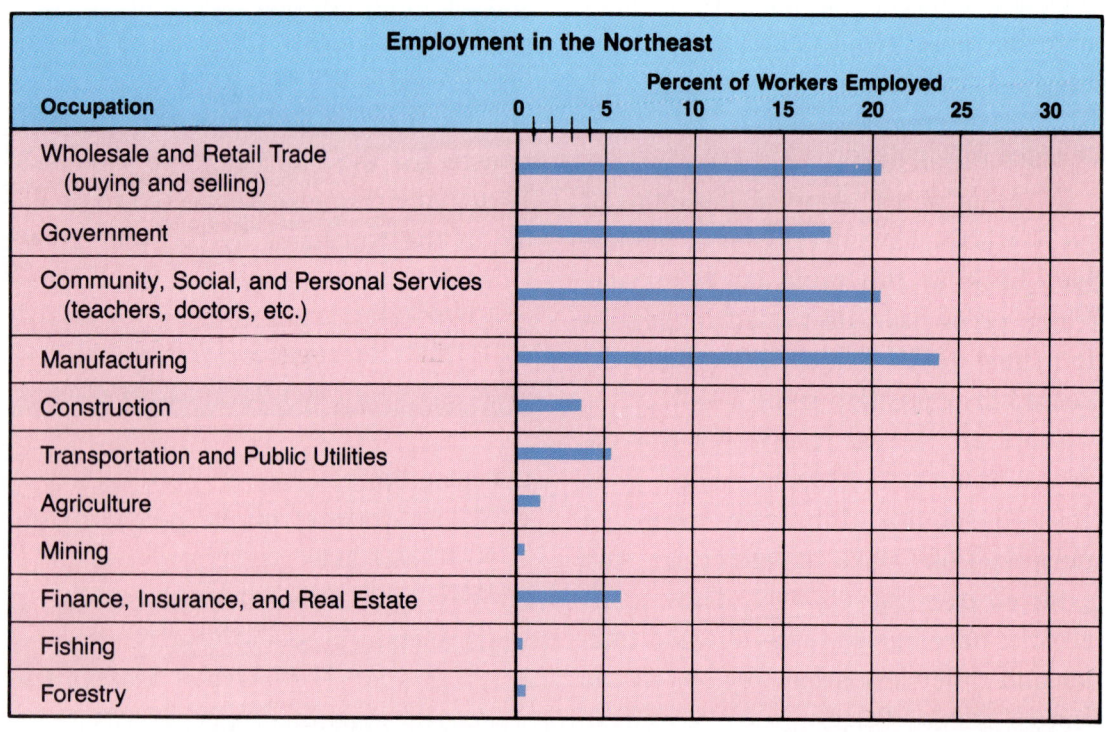

Employment in the Northeast

Occupation	Percent of Workers Employed
Wholesale and Retail Trade (buying and selling)	~20
Government	~17
Community, Social, and Personal Services (teachers, doctors, etc.)	~20
Manufacturing	~22
Construction	~5
Transportation and Public Utilities	~6
Agriculture	~2
Mining	<1
Finance, Insurance, and Real Estate	~6
Fishing	<1
Forestry	<1

* **Math Skill:** Review the definition of percent. Remind students that the word percent means hundredths, or the number out of 100. For example, 50% means $50/100$ or 50 out of 100. Explain that percentages of less than 50% are less than half, and percentages of more than 50% are more than half. Use examples from the graphs on pages 318 and 319 to explain further how to read percentages.

* **Reading Skill:** Seeing relationships. Some students may need help seeing the relationships among graph figures on pages 318–319.
  1. About 6%; about 21%.
  2. About 23%.

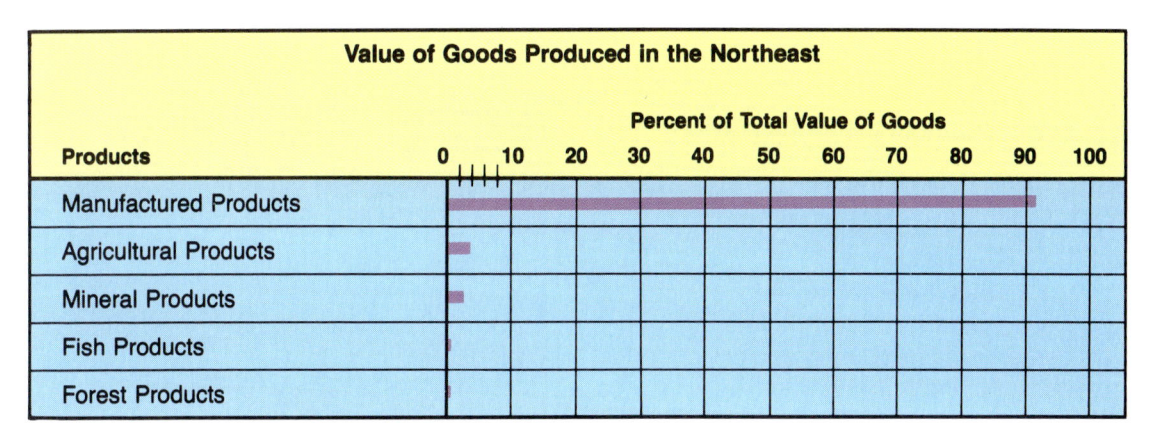

Value of Goods Produced in the Northeast											
Products	\multicolumn{11}{l	}{Percent of Total Value of Goods}
	0	10	20	30	40	50	60	70	80	90	100
Manufactured Products											
Agricultural Products											
Mineral Products											
Fish Products											
Forest Products											

the port cities by trucks and trains are sent to other countries on ships and planes.

Look at the bar graph of employment on page 318. What percent of the workers in the Northeast work in the transportation industry? in wholesale and retail trade?

A manufacturing center. When colonial settlers began to do their own manufacturing, they did so in the port cities along the Northeastern Seaboard. Today the Northeastern Seaboard is one of the major manufacturing regions in our country. Look at the bar graph of employment on page 318. What percent of the people in the Northeast are employed in manufacturing?

Now look at the bar graph on this page. This graph shows the total value of goods in the Northeast. What is the percent of value for manufactured goods? What connection can you make between the number of people employed in manufacturing and the value of manufactured goods in the Northeast?

Other major occupations. The Northeastern Seaboard is also our country's banking and financial center. For example, in New York City many people work in banks that serve our country and other countries. Look again at the employment graph on page 318. What percent of people in the Northeast work in banking and finance?

Washington, D.C., our country's capital, is along the Northeastern Seaboard. Thousands of people who live in or near Washington, D.C., work for the many government agencies in this area. What percent of people in the Northeast work in government?

Making a Living in the Rugged Interior

There are some small but excellent farming areas in the valleys of the highlands in the Rugged Interior. Some of these areas are the Great Valley in Pennsylvania, the Connecticut River Valley, and the Aroostook Valley in Maine. Find these valleys on the map on page 310. Now look at the growing seasons map on page 313. What is the growing season in these areas?

Almost all the food needs of the megalopolis are produced in other parts of the

Aroostook (ə·roos′tək)
3. About 92%.
4. About 6%.
5. About 17%.

319

Careers

Where Some of the People Work

Pictured here is Seventh Avenue in New York City. Seventh Avenue is the center of our country's clothing business. Buyers from retail stores, or stores that sell directly to customers, come from all parts of the country to buy clothes from Seventh Avenue wholesale merchants. These wholesale merchants sell goods in large quantities to retail stores.

The picture above shows the floor of the New York Stock Exchange in New York City. The New York Stock Exchange is a vital part of our country's business. The people shown in the picture are called brokers. Brokers buy and sell stocks, or shares of a company.

The inside of the United States Treasury Building in Washington, D.C., is shown above. The people who work in this building work for our government's Department of the Treasury. Some of the people who work for the Department of the Treasury print our money.

Reading Skill: Using details. Have students identify a page and paragraph to support each point in the unit summary.
1. Allegheny and Monongahela rivers.
2. Manufactured goods; fish or forest products.

country. These foods can be economically shipped great distances. However, milk cannot. Therefore, dairy farms in the Rugged Interior produce milk for much of the megalopolis.

Besides farming, some people make a living in the Rugged Interior by quarrying stone. There are deposits of granite and marble in Vermont, for example. Some people also make a living in the lumber industry. The forests of Maine, Vermont, and New Hampshire produce lumber and wood pulp.

Making a Living in Western Pennsylvania and Western New York

Western Pennsylvania is rich in coal deposits. Thus, many people mine coal in this area.

Pittsburgh is the major city in western Pennsylvania. Find Pittsburgh on the map on page 310. What two rivers join to form the Ohio River in Pittsburgh? Because of Pittsburgh's good location for shipping, and because it is close to the coal, Pittsburgh is a center of the iron and steel industry. This industry depends on the coal mined in the area.

Western New York has two major areas of industry. The Buffalo area is a shipping and food-processing center. Find Buffalo on the map on page 310. Buffalo is at the eastern end of shipping routes from the Great Lakes. Buffalo is a good place to process goods that have been shipped by lake.

The Niagara Falls area of western New York is a center of the energy industry. The falls provide waterpower to generate electricity. This electricity provides power for homes and factories in the Northeast.

Look at the bar graph on page 319 that shows the value of goods. Which goods are most important economically? least important economically?

Look again at the employment graph on page 318. What are the three main occupations in the Northeast? Do most of the people in each group live in the Northeastern Seaboard, in the Rugged Interior, or in western Pennsylvania and western New York?

Checking Up
1. Name two ways that people make a living in the Rugged Interior.
2. What answers would you give to the key questions at the beginning of this unit?
3. *Why are the cities of the Northeastern Seaboard major trade centers?*

Unit 10 Summary
- The Northeast can be divided into three smaller parts based on landforms.
- The Northeastern Seaboard is a business and manufacturing center.
- The Rugged Interior is primarily a rural and agricultural area.
- The area of western Pennsylvania and western New York is a center of industry and trade.

3. Manufacturing; community, social, and personal services; and wholesale and retail trade. The Northeastern Seaboard.

FACTS ABOUT THE NORTHEAST						
	Nickname	Capital* and Largest Cities	State Bird	Farm Products and Natural Resources	Manufactured Products	Did You Know This?
Connecticut	The Constitution State	Hartford* Bridgeport New Haven Waterbury Stamford	American Robin	Dairy and poultry products, tobacco, cattle Stone, gravel, sand	Chemicals, printed and published material, instruments, transportation equipment	The first atomic-powered submarine was launched in Connecticut.
Delaware	The First State	Dover* Wilmington Newark Elsmere Milford	Blue Hen Chicken	Soybeans, corn, dairy products, hogs Sand, gravel	Processed foods, rubber, metals, machinery	Delaware was the first state to ratify the Constitution.
Maine	The Pine Tree State	Augusta* Portland Lewiston Bangor Auburn	Chickadee	Poultry and dairy products, potatoes Seafood, timber, sand, gravel, zinc	Paper, leather, processed foods, lumber	Mount Katahdin, in Maine, is the first point in the United States to be touched by morning sunlight.
Maryland	The Old Line State	Annapolis* Baltimore Rockville Hagerstown Bowie	Baltimore Oriole	Dairy products, corn, soybeans, cattle Sand, gravel, coal	Processed foods, metals, electrical equipment, machinery	Fort McHenry, in Maryland, is where Francis Scott Key saw the flag that inspired our national anthem.
Massachusetts	The Bay State	Boston* Worcester Springfield Cambridge New Bedford	Chickadee	Dairy and poultry products Seafood, stone, sand, gravel	Machinery, electronic equipment	The first shot of the Revolutionary War was fired in Massachusetts.
New Hampshire	The Granite State	Concord* Manchester Nashua Portsmouth Dover	Purple Finch	Dairy and poultry products, hay, cattle Sand, gravel, stone	Electronic equipment, machinery, paper	The first presidential primaries are held in New Hampshire.

Reading Skill: Interpreting facts. Students could work in small groups and use the Facts chart to write ten true-false questions about the region. Have groups exchange questions and answer them.

	Nickname	Capital* and Largest Cities	State Bird	Farm Products and Natural Resources	Manufactured Products	Did You Know This?
New Jersey	The Garden State	Trenton* Newark Jersey City Paterson Elizabeth	Eastern Goldfinch	Dairy products, hay, vegetables Stone, sand, gravel, zinc, seafood	Chemicals, processed foods, electrical equipment, machinery	Princeton and Trenton in New Jersey each served as the nation's capital from 1783 to 1784.
New York	The Empire State	Albany* New York City Buffalo Rochester Yonkers	Bluebird	Dairy products, hay, cattle, corn, poultry products Stone, zinc, salt	Printed and published material, instruments, machinery	New York City is the largest city in the United States.
Pennsylvania	The Keystone State	Harrisburg* Philadelphia Pittsburgh Erie Allentown	Ruffed Grouse	Dairy products, hay, corn, cattle, poultry products Coal, stone, lime	Metals, machinery, processed foods, instruments, chemicals	Pennsylvania was the first state to build a modern four-lane turnpike.
Rhode Island	The Ocean State	Providence* Warwick Cranston Pawtucket East Providence	Rhode Island Red Chicken	Dairy products, potatoes, poultry products, hogs Sand, gravel, stone, seafood	Metals, textiles, processed foods, machinery	The oldest existing synagogue in the nation is in Newport, Rhode Island.
Vermont	The Green Mountain State	Montpelier* Burlington Rutland South Burlington Barre	Hermit Thrush	Dairy products, hay, cattle, poultry products Asbestos, stone, timber, gravel	Machinery, metals, paper, instruments	Vermont was an independent country for fourteen years, from 1777 to 1791.

Unit 10 Review Workshop

What Have You Learned?

1. What is the major landform of the Northeastern Seaboard? of the Rugged Interior? of western Pennsylvania and western New York?
2. Why did people migrate to the cities of the Northeastern Seaboard from the 1820s to the 1930s?
3. Why have some cities decreased in population in the last twenty to thirty years?
4. What is a megalopolis?
5. What are three ways that people make a living in the Rugged Interior? in the Northeastern Seaboard?
6. What are the major centers of industry in western Pennsylvania and western New York?

Use Your Reading Skills

It is important to be able to read tables. Some information is best understood in table form. Study the table on page 317. Then answer the questions which follow.

1. Which city had the greatest decrease in population during a 10-year period? which 10-year period?
2. During which 10-year period did Philadelphia's population go below 2,000,000?
3. During which 10-year period did a city's population grow? Which city had this population increase?
4. What happened to the population of all six cities between 1970 and 1980?

Use Your Thinking Skills

A. In reading this unit, you have learned how landform and climate influence where people live. Landform and climate influence how people make a living. Tell how the items below also influence where people live and how they make a living.
   1. Good *harbors* on the Northeastern Seaboard
   2. *Coal* in western Pennsylvania
   3. The *location* of Buffalo at the eastern end of the Great Lakes
B. What reasons would you give for each of the following?
   1. Population loss in cities of the Northeastern Seaboard
   2. Growing population of areas in the Rugged Interior

Use Your Map Skills

The map here shows the area of the megalopolis along the Northeastern Seaboard. Study the map and answer the following:

1. What states or parts of states does this megalopolis include?
2. Name three cities in this megalopolis that are located on harbors.
3. How many miles is it from New York City to Boston? from Baltimore to New York City?
4. What city in this megalopolis is the farthest inland from the Atlantic Ocean? About how many miles inland is this city?

Reading Skill: Interpreting a table.
Thinking Skills: Knowing, analyzing.
Map Skills: Location, symbolization, distance, scale.

Megalopolis

5. Use the map scale to estimate in miles, then in kilometers, the distance this megalopolis stretches from Manchester, New Hampshire, to Washington, D.C.

Learn by Doing

1. Imagine you have had a month's vacation in Vermont or New Hampshire. Write a letter telling a friend what things you did and what you saw in this state.
2. Read more about one group of immigrants who settled in the cities of the Northeastern Seaboard in the 1800s or early 1900s. You may want to choose a group that a member of your family belonged to. Write a report about this group of immigrants. In your report, tell why they came to the cities of the Northeastern Seaboard, what they did when they came, and what their lives in their new homes were like.
3. Look for jobs advertised in the classified section of your local newspaper. Make a list of ten jobs. Try to classify each job according to the categories used in the employment graph on page 318.
4. Fishing is an important way of making a living in both Maine and the Chesapeake Bay area of Maryland. Read about people who fish. Draw five pictures that show the steps they go through. Write a caption for each picture.

Read to Learn More

Find the topics listed below in the card catalog of your library. Read all or part of a book listed under one of the topics. Share what you learn with your classmates.

TRADE	WASHINGTON, D.C.
TRANSPORTATION	NEW YORK CITY

Reading Skills: Using references, reading widely: *Learn by Doing, 2,3,4* and *Read to Learn More.*
Thinking Skills: Classifying: *Learn by Doing, 3;* synthesizing: *Learn by Doing, 3,4.*
Communication Skills: Writing: *Learn by Doing, 1,2,4;* speaking: *Read to Learn More.*
Time Skill: *Learn by Doing, 1.*

Unit Overview: This unit examines the Great Lakes Region, its population density, and its main types of employment.

Unit 11

Unit Objectives
To understand:
- the six states in this region
- how population density varies within this region
- the main ways people make a living in this region
- graphics

Suggested Materials
Workbook
Unit Tests

Skills Emphasized
Map Skills: pp. 326, 340.
Social Studies Reading Skills: pp. 326, 329, 331, 332, 334, 335, 337, 338, 340, 341.
Thinking Skills: pp. 326, 331, 334, 335, 336, 338, 340.
Communication Skills: pp. 326, 336, 341.
Time Skills: pp. 333, 337.
Social Studies Math Skill: p. 334.
Citizenship Skills: pp. 326, 336, 338.

Suggested Student Activities
1. Work in groups. Each group should prepare a report about one of the six states in this region.
2. Post magazine and newspaper articles about this region on a bulletin board.
3. Add to the class data-retrieval chart begun in Unit 10.
4. Work in small groups. Make product report charts on this region.
* 5. Review outlining skills by using unit headings and subheadings. Write unit summaries.
** 6. Work in pairs. Write reports on the career topics listed on page 336.

Skills Emphasized in Suggested Student Activities
Map Skill: Location.
Social Studies Reading Skills: Doing research, using magazines and newspapers, outlining.
Thinking Skills: Observing, comparing.
Communication Skills: Listening, speaking, writing.
Citizenship Skill: Social participation.

The Great Lakes Region

Diversey Harbor on Lake Michigan and Lincoln Park are highlighted in the foreground of this picture of Chicago's skyline.

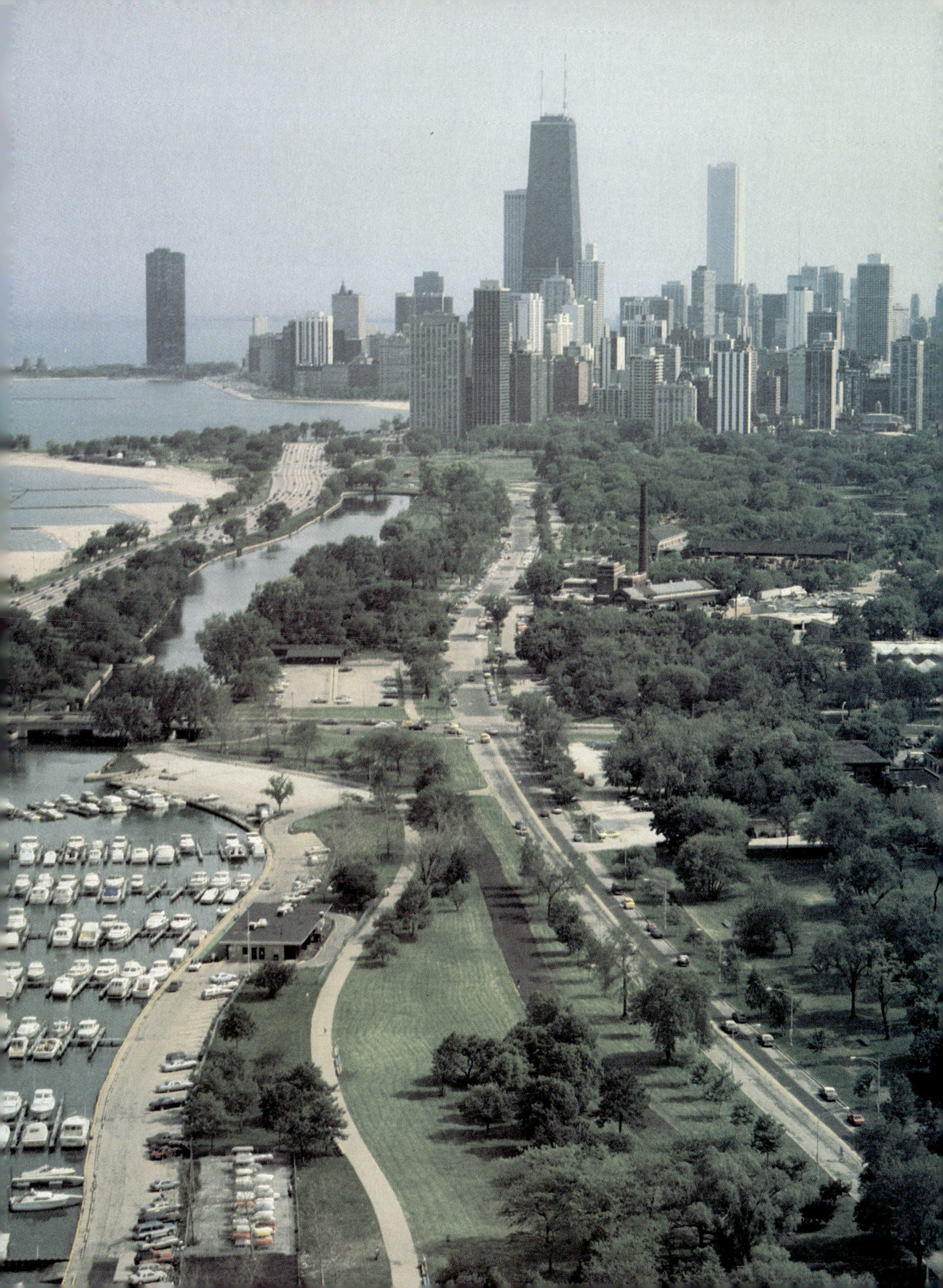

Region of the Great Lakes
Physical-Political Map

Reading Skill: Summarizing. *As You Read, 3.*
1. Wis. (Madison), Mich. (Lansing), Ill. (Springfield), Ind. (Indianapolis), Ohio (Columbus), W.Va. (Charleston).

Where Is the Great Lakes Region?

As You Read This Unit
1. Think about these words.
   economy   heavy industry   corn belt
2. Look for answers to these key questions.
   a. Which six states make up the Great Lakes Region?
   b. How does population density in the four parts of the Great Lakes Region differ?
   c. What are three major ways that people make a living in the Great Lakes Region?
3. Use this reading skill.
   At the close of every unit in this book, there is a Unit Summary. Making summaries is an important reading skill that you can use often. After you have studied each chapter in this unit, make a list of the subheadings in the chapter. Close your book. Say to yourself the important points that you remember from each subheading. Then open your book and check to see how complete your summary of the chapter was.

Three important waterways nearly surround the Great Lakes Region of the United States. In fact, the region is named for one of the waterways, the Great Lakes. The Great Lakes, the Mississippi River, and the Ohio River are three of the most important waterways in the United States. These waterways have helped the Great Lakes Region become both a great industrial center and an important farming center.

The Region

The Great Lakes Region is made up of six states. Look at the map on page 328. Name the six states. What is the capital of each state? Use the map scale to find out about how many miles the Great Lakes Region stretches in an east-west direction, and in a north-south direction.

Find the Mississippi River on the same map. Which states in this region border the Mississippi River? Find the Ohio River. Which states in this region border the Ohio River?

The Great Lakes are the largest group of freshwater lakes in the world. Look at the map of the United States on pages 18 and 19. How many Great Lakes are there? Using the map on page 328, name the four Great Lakes that border this region. Which states in this region border

1
2. Ill. and Wis./Ill., Ind., Ohio, and W.Va.
3. Five. Lakes Superior, Michigan, Huron, and Erie.

2

3

329

1. Wis., Mich., Ohio, Ind., and Ill./Canada.
2. Plains; plateaus/W.Va., Ill., and Ind.; Wis., Mich., and Ohio/W.Va.
3. Farmlands, Northlands, Southern Great Lakes Region and Ohio River Valley. Southern Great Lakes Region.

1 the Great Lakes? What other country borders the Great Lakes? Find the boundary between these two countries.

The Land

The Great Lakes Region does not have as wide a variety of landforms as the Northeast. Look at the profile on page 328. Compare the elevation of Rock Island, Illinois, with the elevation of Cleveland, Ohio. How much difference in elevation is there between these two cities?

Yet not all the Great Lakes Region is the same. Look at the pie graph on this page. Which is the most common landform? the least common? Study the map on page 328 to find these landforms. Which states in the region have the greatest variety? the least? In which state are the Appalachian Mountains?

Although the Great Lakes Region cannot be divided based on landforms, there are four distinct areas. These areas are different because of the ways the people in these areas make a living.

Look at the map on this page. What are the names of the four areas of the Great Lakes Region? In which area are

Landforms of the Great Lakes Region

- Hills
- Mountains
- Plains
- Plateaus

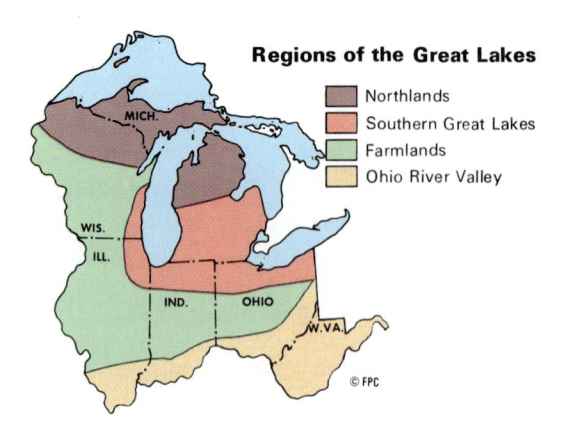

Regions of the Great Lakes
- Northlands
- Southern Great Lakes
- Farmlands
- Ohio River Valley

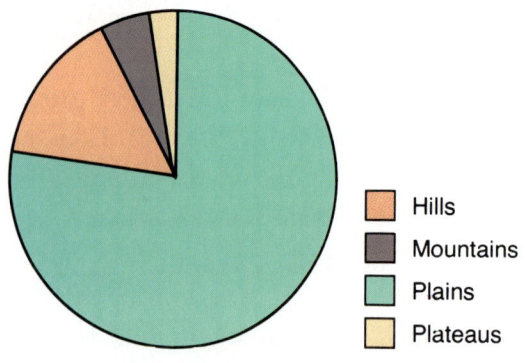

Study this map of the subregions of the Great Lakes Region. Which state does not border one of the Great Lakes?

Chicago, Detroit, Milwaukee, and Cleveland? The **economy,** or the way people manage their resources, of this area is based on industry and business.

Which area of the Great Lakes Region is named after a river? Use the map on page 328 and name the states or parts of states included in this area of the Great Lakes Region. The economy here depends upon good river transportation and large coal deposits. West Virginia, for example, ships many goods on the Ohio River.

The Northlands area of the Great Lakes Region has long, hard winters and short, cool summers. Farming and tourism are the principal ways people make a living in this area. Which states or parts of states are included in the Northlands area of the Great Lakes Region?

Which states or parts of states are included in the Farmlands area of the Great Lakes Region? The farms of this area provide foods for all regions of the country.

4. Ohio River Valley; Ill., Ind., Ohio, and W.Va.
5. Wis. and Mich.
6. Wis., Ill., Ind., and Ohio.

330

Thinking Skill: Comparing. Have students compare this region's climate with that of other regions and their own area.
** **Reading Skill:** Doing research. Have students look for data on this region in an almanac.

The maps and graphs in this section help describe the Great Lakes Region. Which area is the largest? the smallest?

The Climate

Temperature and precipitation help determine the climate of an area.

Temperatures. As you might expect, temperatures differ from area to area in the Great Lakes Region. Look at the graphs that show average monthly temperatures for Sault Sainte Marie (sü′sānt mə·rē′), Michigan, and Cincinnati, Ohio, on this page. Find these places on the map on page 328. Which place has a higher average temperature in July? Which place has a lower average temperature in January?

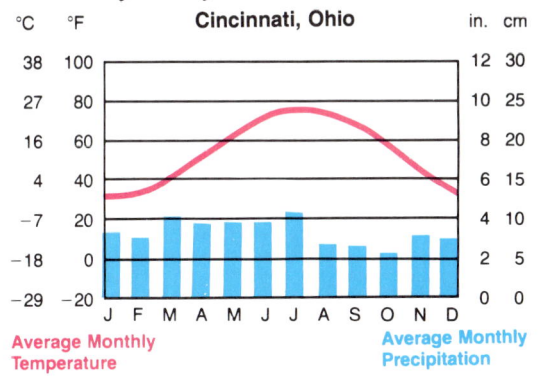

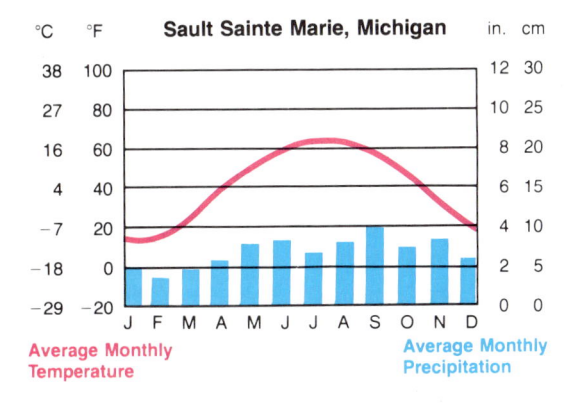

Precipitation. Study again the graphs for Sault Sainte Marie and Cincinnati on this page. Which place has more precipitation each year? How much more? Use both temperature and precipitation information to predict in what months Sault Sainte Marie would be likely to receive snow.

Growing Seasons. The frost-free period of time during which crops can grow is very important to farmers. Look at the map on this page. How many months is the growing season in each area of the Great Lakes Region? Which area has the shortest growing season? Why? Which area has the longest growing season? What is the economy of this area based on?

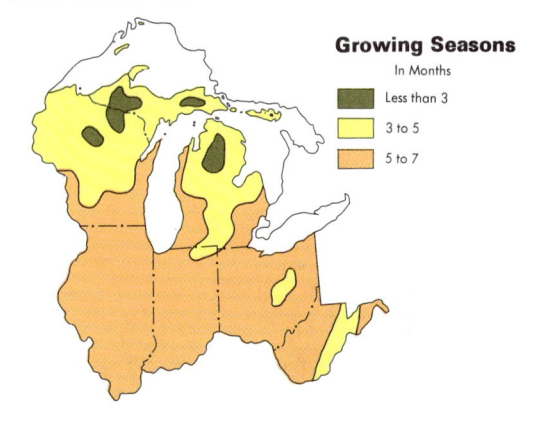

Checking Up

1. Name the three most important waterways in the Great Lakes Region.
2. What are the four areas of the Great Lakes Region?
3. *In what ways do the temperatures and precipitation within this region differ?*

1. Cincinnati. Sault Sainte Marie.
2. Cincinnati. 7–10 inches. Jan., Feb., March, April, Nov., and Dec.

331

Where Are the People?

A large expanse of the Great Lakes Region is made up of people living in rural areas dotted with small cities. But the Great Lakes Region also has some of our country's largest and busiest cities.

Where the People Live

Compare the population map on page 16 with the map of the four parts of the Great Lakes Region on page 330. Which of the four parts of the Great Lakes Region has the most people? Which part has the fewest people?

Now look at the map on page 328. Where are most of the large cities? What connection do you see between population density and cities? What is similar about the location of these cities?

The urban and rural population. Look at the pie graph on this page. Do most people in the Great Lakes Region live in rural or in urban areas?

Look at the population map on this page. Study the key. What is the population density for most of the Northlands? for most of the Southern Great Lakes Region? for the Farmlands? for the Ohio River Valley?

The Southern Great Lakes Region

By the late 1800s large industries, such as the iron and steel industry, had

Urban and Rural Population of the Great Lakes Region

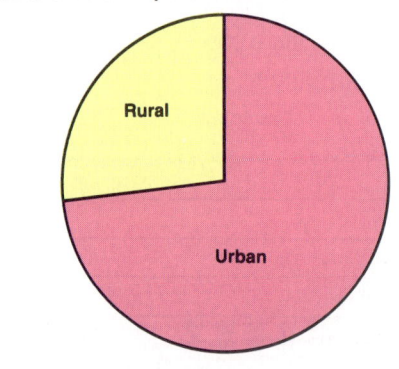

Many people live or work in high-rise buildings in Chicago.

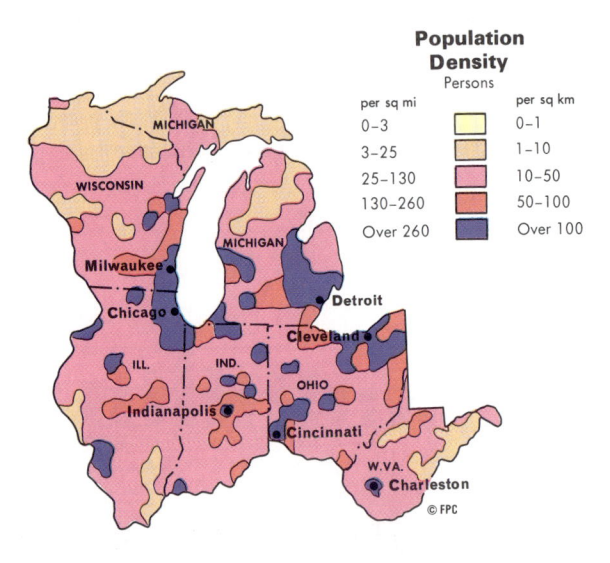

1. Along the southern shores of Lakes Michigan and Erie. Population density is greatest in areas where there are large cities. They are located along waterways.
2. Urban areas.

1. The many hills and mountains make farming nearly impossible and transportation costly. So people have been slow in settling these areas except in the mountain valleys.

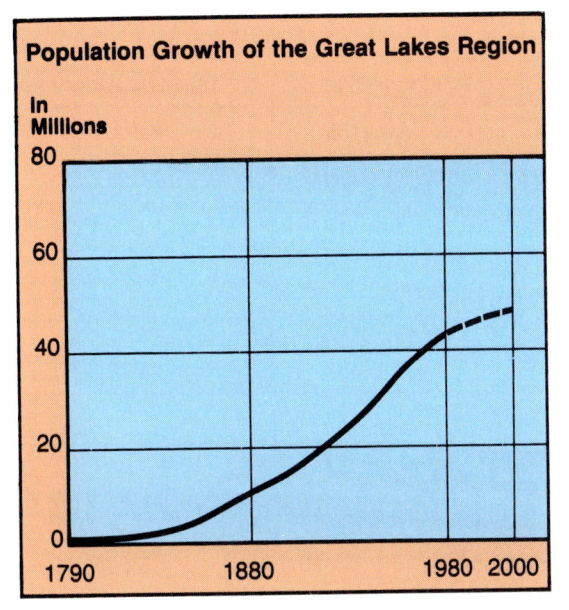

Population Growth of the Great Lakes Region

(Line graph showing population in millions from 1790 to 2000, rising from near 0 in 1790 to about 45 million by 1980, with a dashed extension to 2000.)

Compare this town in the Farmlands with Chicago, pictured on page 332.

developed along the southern shores of Lake Michigan and Lake Erie. The growth of these industries attracted many people, including immigrants, to the cities in this area.

Later, in the 1920s and the 1930s, people from rural areas moved to these cities. Advances in farm methods and machinery had left many farm workers without jobs. During this time a large number of rural black people moved from the South to cities such as Chicago, Cleveland, and Detroit. In more recent years people from other countries, especially countries in Latin America, have also moved to cities along the lakes.

Population in the Other Parts of the Region

The other three parts of the Great Lakes Region are not nearly as densely populated as the Southern Great Lakes Region. In fact, much of the Great Lakes Region is made up of rural populations. However, by looking at the population map on page 332, you can see that there are smaller urban areas outside the Southern Great Lakes Region. Use the map on page 332 to find the names of two of these cities.

The Northlands and West Virginia are the most rural areas in the Great Lakes Region. Study the map on page 328. How might the location or the landforms of these areas explain why they are sparsely populated?

The Population Growth of the Region

Look at the line graph of population growth in the Great Lakes Region on this page. During which years did the population of the Great Lakes Region grow the most? Now look at the table on page 334. What was the largest city in 1880? How many people lived there then? Which city grew the most between 1880 and 1980?

Changes in Population

Like the Northeast, some of the cities in the Great Lakes Region have had a population decrease in recent years.

2. Between 1880 and 1980. Chicago. 503,185 people. Chicago.
Time Skill: Have students list ways that this region has changed over time. Discuss reasons for each change.

Math Skill: Use the tables below to make further comparisons.
Thinking Skill: Hypothesizing. Review the meaning of *hypothesizing*. Discuss what this region may be like in the year 2000.
1. All of them.

Population Growth of Selected Cities in the Great Lakes Region			
City	1790 Population	1880 Population	1980 Population
Chicago, IL	Not Available	503,185	3,005,073
Cincinnati, OH	Not Available	255,139	385,457
Cleveland, OH	Not Available	160,146	573,822
Detroit, MI	Not Available	116,340	1,203,339
Indianapolis, IN	Not Available	75,056	700,807
Milwaukee, WI	Not Available	115,587	636,212

Recent Populations of Selected Cities in the Great Lakes Region				
City	1950 Population	1960 Population	1970 Population	1980 Population
Chicago, IL	3,620,962	3,550,404	3,366,957	3,005,072
Cincinnati, OH	503,998	502,550	452,524	385,457
Cleveland, OH	914,808	876,050	750,903	573,822
Detroit, MI	1,849,568	1,670,144	1,511,482	1,203,339
Indianapolis, IN	427,173	476,258	744,624	700,807
Milwaukee, WI	637,392	741,324	717,099	636,212

1 Look at the table just above. Which cities have had a population decrease since 1970?

In part, this population loss has happened because some factories and businesses have moved out of the cities to suburbs or more rural areas. These areas are less crowded, and the land is often less expensive. Better transportation allows people and businesses to locate farther from urban areas.

Some parts of the Great Lakes Region are gaining population. Some smaller cities are growing as industry and businesses relocate in these areas. Also, the quiet beauty of the Northlands has attracted people who want to live away from busy urban areas.

Look at the graph of population growth for the Great Lakes Region on page 333. About how many people are expected to live in the region by the year 2000? How many more people will this be than the 1980 population? 2

Checking Up
1. Name three large cities in the Great Lakes Region.
2. Which parts of the Great Lakes Region have been gaining population in recent years?
3. *Why did urban growth occur along the southern shores of Lake Michigan and Lake Erie?*

2. About 49 million people. About 5 million more people.
Reading Skill: Skimming. Have students locate cities in other regions that have about the same population as the cities named above.

> **Background:** Thousands of ships containing iron ore and other goods pass through the Soo Canals each year. The Soo Canals connect Lakes Superior and Huron near Sault Sainte Marie, Mich. Have students locate the canals on the map on page 328.
> **Reading Skill:** Seeing relationships. Discuss how the picture below supports the text.

What Do the People Do?

Steel plants, like this one in Gary, Indiana, provide work for many people.

Huge factories, rich farmlands, and important raw materials all play major roles in the economy of the Great Lakes Region. Some people make a living in the industrial centers of the region. Others make a living from the land.

Making a Living in the Southern Great Lakes Region

Cities grew along the southern shores of the Great Lakes. These cities have easy access to important sources of raw materials. The lakes and rivers near these cities provide an easy way to move raw materials from their sources to the factories in the cities. In turn, finished goods can be shipped by water to markets in other parts of the country.

A region of manufacturing. Most of the cities in the Southern Great Lakes Region have industries that are known as **heavy industries**. These factories produce steel parts for heavy equipment.

Coal and iron ore are needed to make steel. Iron ore, mined near the shores of Lake Superior, is shipped by lake to steel mills on the southern shores of Lake Erie and Lake Michigan. Coal is also mined in the Great Lakes Region. River barges and railroads carry this coal to steel mills.

In addition to the steel industry, the automobile and the rubber industries are also centered in the Southern Great Lakes Region. Find Detroit, Michigan, and Akron, Ohio, on the map on page 328. The automobile industry is centered in Detroit, and the rubber industry is in Akron. How do you think Detroit's location helped the growth of its industries? 1

Large food-processing plants are also located in many of the cities in the Southern Great Lakes Region. Crops grown in the Farmlands can be transported easily by truck, railroad, or river barge to these food-processing plants.

Other occupations. Look at the bar graph of employment on page 337. What percent of the workers in the Great Lakes Region work in manufacturing? in wholesale and retail trade? in transportation? In what areas of the Great Lakes Region do most of the people who work in these occupations probably live? 2

Look at the graph on page 337. What is the percent of value for manufactured products? What connection can you make between the number of people employed in manufacturing and the value of manufactured products?

> **Thinking Skill:** Analyzing. Discuss why manufacturing is important to the region and the nation.
> 1. Access to many waterways made it easy to ship raw materials and finished goods in and out.
> 2. About 29%; about 20%; about 5%. Southern Great Lakes Region and Ohio River Valley.
> 3. About 84%.

335

Communication Skill: Speaking. Students who prepared reports on these careers could give them.
Thinking Skill: Comparing. The Merchandise Mart in Chicago has twenty-four stories. Compare it with the tallest building in your area.

Careers

Where Some of the People Work

The huge office building pictured on this page is the Merchandise Mart in Chicago. This building is one of the largest buildings in the world. It is a major center of wholesale buying. Almost 20,000 people work here each day.

Coal is one of the United States' most important resources. The miners in this West Virginia mine work hard hundreds of feet underground. Because the price of oil will continue to rise, the importance of the coal in the Great Lakes Region will continue to grow.

This picture shows an assembly line at an automobile plant in Michigan. The assembly line involves a group of workers who put together one particular product. Great numbers of motors or car bodies can be made in one day this way. There are many automobile plants in the Great Lakes Region.

Citizenship Skill: Social participation. Have students role-play assembly-line production. Decide on a simple product to produce.

336

Reading Skill: Summarizing. Students could work in pairs to summarize the graphs below. Share summaries with the entire class.
Time Skill: Have a small group report on changes in farm equipment over time.
1. Soybeans, wheat, oats, hay, tomatoes, beans, and fruit.

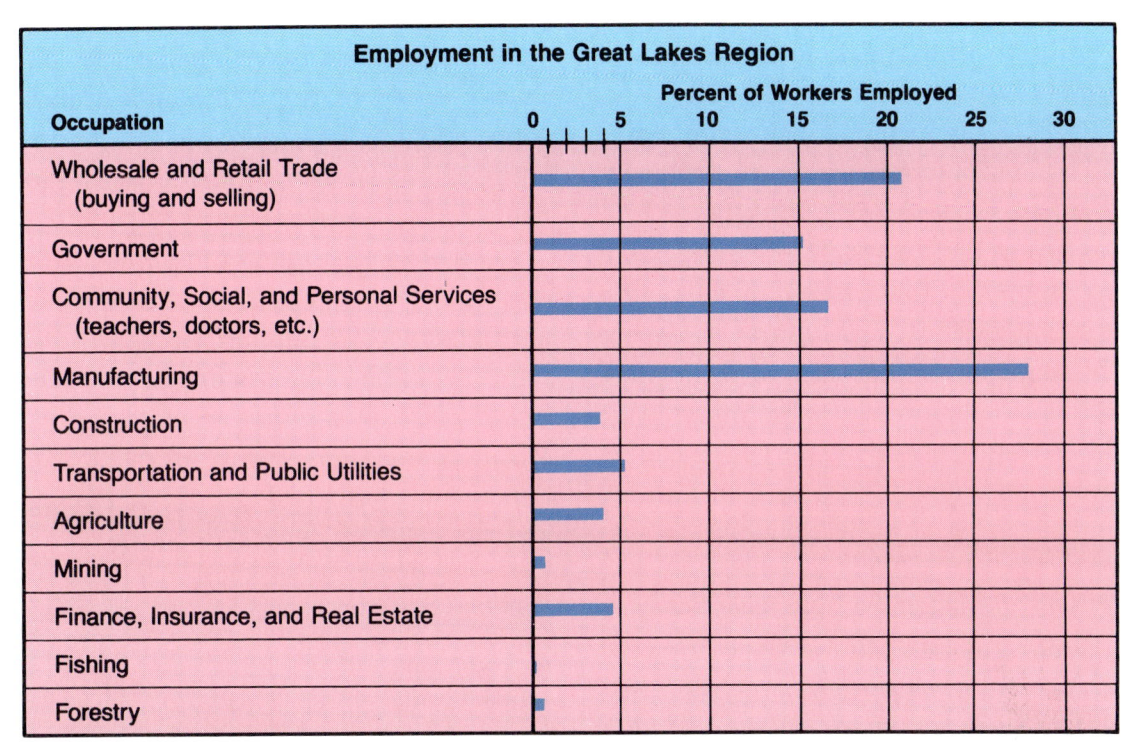

Employment in the Great Lakes Region

Occupation	Percent of Workers Employed
Wholesale and Retail Trade (buying and selling)	~21
Government	~15
Community, Social, and Personal Services (teachers, doctors, etc.)	~17
Manufacturing	~29
Construction	~4
Transportation and Public Utilities	~5
Agriculture	~4
Mining	<1
Finance, Insurance, and Real Estate	~4
Fishing	<1
Forestry	<1

Making a Living in the Farmlands

Corn is the major crop of the Farmlands today. This area is often called a part of the **corn belt**. The corn belt is a large corn-growing region that extends into the Midwest Plains. Billions of bushels of corn are grown each year in the Farmlands Region. Some of the corn is fed to cattle and hogs to fatten them for market.

Milk products are also important in the Farmlands. Dairy farms in Wisconsin are among the most important in our country. Look at the chart on page 339. What other crops are grown in the Great Lakes Region?

Recent changes. Once farmers did almost everything by hand. Today many large farms have machinery to help with the work.

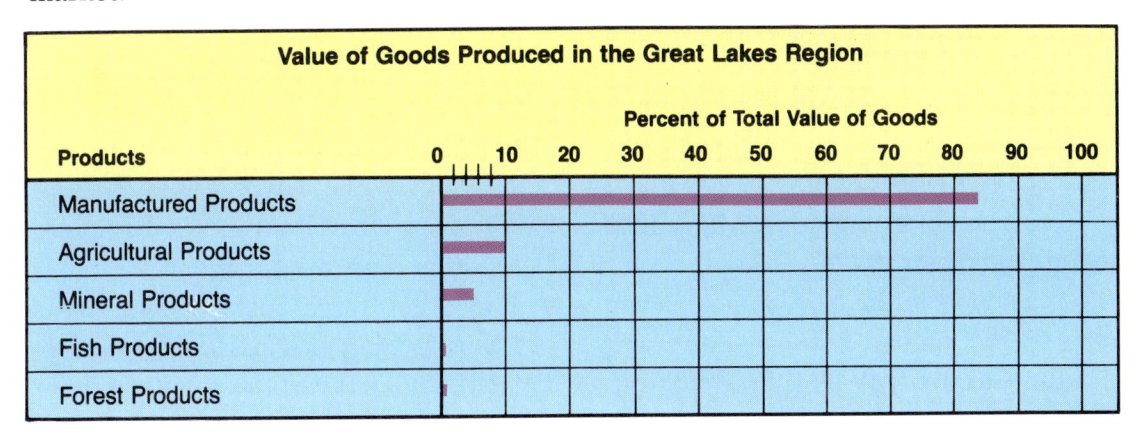

Value of Goods Produced in the Great Lakes Region

Products	Percent of Total Value of Goods
Manufactured Products	~85
Agricultural Products	~10
Mineral Products	~5
Fish Products	<1
Forest Products	<1

337

Reading Skill: Interpreting graphics. Have students find one graphic in this unit that supports each point of the unit summary.
1. About 4%. A small number of farmers grow a large amount of farm products in this region.
2. Less than 1%. A small number of workers mine and process a large amount of mineral deposits.

Also, many farmers no longer grow a variety of crops. Instead, they often specialize, or produce one main crop. Some of the major crops are corn, soybeans, and hay.

Look at the bar graph for employment on page 337. What percent of the people are employed in agriculture? Compare this figure with the value of farm products in the graph at the bottom of page 337. What connection can you make between the number of people in farming and the value of farm products?

Making a Living in the Ohio River Valley

Rich coal deposits in West Virginia, along with transportation on the Ohio River, have led to an important coal-based industry in the Ohio River Valley. Many people in West Virginia mine coal. Some people in the cities in the Ohio River Valley work in factories that make chemicals from coal.

Rich coal deposits are also found in Indiana and Illinois. Cities such as Terre Haute, Indiana, have become industrial centers that use coal as a raw material for many of their factories.

Making a Living in the Northlands

Although not many deposits of high-grade iron ore are left in the Northlands, there are still large deposits of low-grade iron ore near Lake Superior. Many people mine and process this iron ore.

Some people in the Northlands make a living in the lumber industry. For example, the Fox River Valley in Wisconsin has large papermaking factories.

The tourist industry provides jobs for many people in the Northlands today. More and more people visit the Northlands each year to fish in the lakes and camp in the forests.

Look at the bar graph for employment on page 337. What percent of the people are employed in mining? Compare this figure with the value of mineral products in the graph at the bottom of page 337. What connections can you make between the number of people in mining and the value of mineral deposits?

Checking Up
1. What is the major crop of the Great Lakes Region?
2. What answers would you give to the key questions at the beginning of this unit?
3. *What geographic advantages aided the growth of manufacturing in the Southern Great Lakes Region?*

Unit 11 Summary
- Three of our country's most important waterways have been important to the growth of manufacturing and farming in the Great Lakes Region.
- The Southern Great Lakes Region is an urban industrial center.
- The other three parts of the Great Lakes Region are less densely populated, and many of the people in these areas mine or farm.

Thinking Skill: Comparing. Have students compare the chart on page 339 with *Facts* charts of other regions.

FACTS ABOUT THE GREAT LAKES REGION

	Nickname	Capital* and Largest Cities	State Bird	Farm Products and Natural Resources	Manufactured Products	Did You Know This?
Illinois	The Prairie State	Springfield* Chicago Rockford Peoria Decatur	Cardinal	Hogs, cattle, soybeans, corn, dairy products, poultry Coal, petroleum, zinc, natural gas	Iron and steel, machinery, processed foods, printed and published materials	Illinois produces more corn than any other state in the country.
Indiana	The Hoosier State	Indianapolis* Fort Wayne Gary Evansville South Bend	Cardinal	Corn, hogs, soybeans, wheat, tomatoes, poultry Coal, petroleum, limestone	Iron and steel, soap, refined oil, aviation and railroad equipment, farm equipment, auto parts	The world's largest manufacturer of diesel engines is in Columbus, Indiana.
Michigan	The Wolverine State	Lansing* Detroit Grand Rapids Flint Warren	Robin	Dairy products, corn, livestock, cherries, beans, apples Iron ore, petroleum, copper, salt, limestone	Automobiles and automobile parts, furniture, breakfast foods, chemicals	Michigan, which borders on four of the five Great Lakes, has the longest shoreline of any inland state. Its shoreline is 3,288 miles (5,292 km).
Ohio	The Buckeye State	Columbus* Cleveland Cincinnati Toledo Akron	Cardinal	Soybeans, corn, oats, grapes, dairy products, hogs Lime, coal, clay, petroleum, natural gas	Steel, rubber, jet engines, machine tools, auto parts, glass	Ohio produces more rubber than any other state.
West Virginia	The Mountain State	Charleston* Huntington Wheeling Parkersburg Morgantown	Cardinal	Cattle, corn, dairy products, hay, fruits, tobacco Coal, natural gas, petroleum	Chemicals, iron and steel, glass, aluminum	More coal is mined in West Virginia than in any other state.
Wisconsin	The Badger State	Madison* Milwaukee Racine Green Bay Kenosha	Robin	Dairy products, corn, hay, poultry, soybeans, livestock, grapes Timber, stone, zinc, sand, gravel	Processed foods, metals, machinery, pulp, paper products, transportation equipment	The first kindergarten in the United States was started in Wisconsin in 1856.

Citizenship Skill: Social participation. Students could review this unit by using this chart's data in a Twenty Questions format.

Unit 11 Review Workshop

What Have You Learned?

1. What are the three major waterways of the Great Lakes Region?
2. How are the land and climate of the Northlands different from those in the Farmlands?
3. Why is the Southern Great Lakes Region so densely populated?
4. What geographic advantages aided the growth of industries in cities such as Chicago and Detroit?
5. Describe how farm methods have changed in recent years.
6. Why is coal important to the people of the Ohio River Valley?

Use Your Reading Skills

The chart on page 339 includes some facts about the states in the Great Lakes Region. Use the chart to answer the following questions.

1. What are the largest cities in Indiana? in Illinois?
2. Which states have minerals as natural resources?
3. Which states manufacture iron and steel?
4. Which states grow both corn and fruit?

Use Your Thinking Skills

Being able to use information to make a reasonable judgment is an important skill. Study the picture on page 341 and then answer the questions below.

1. What buildings are shown in the picture? How do you think each building is used?
2. What animals does this farmer raise?
3. What crop does this farmer grow?
4. Judging from the picture, tell whether or not the farmer specializes. Give reasons for your answer.

Use Your Map Skills

By studying the map on page 328, see if you can answer the following questions. Answers to these questions will help you see how the waterways in the Great Lakes Region have been so important to the growth of farming and manufacturing in the area.

1. Which of the Great Lakes would a ship loaded with iron ore that started in Superior, Wisconsin, travel to reach steel factories in Cleveland, Ohio? in Gary, Indiana?
2. What river would a barge filled with lumber starting in Wausau, Wisconsin, travel to reach the Mississippi River?
3. Which rivers would a barge loaded with farm products starting near Terre Haute, Indiana, have to travel to reach the Mississippi River?

Use Your Writing Skills

In this unit, you learned that the populations of both large and smaller cities have changed in recent years. Turn to page 334 and review the text and charts on population changes.

340

Reading Skills: Interpreting graphics, summarizing.
Thinking Skills: Knowing, analyzing.
Map Skill: Location.

Now write three paragraphs, using your own words to describe city population changes in the Great Lakes Region. In your first paragraph, tell what changes have taken place. In your second paragraph, give some reasons for these changes. In the last paragraph, give examples of cities that have changed in population since 1970.

Learn by Doing

1. Soybeans, raised in the Great Lakes Region, are important to us. Use an encyclopedia to discover what things are made from soybeans. Make a chart of drawings or pictures to show soybean products. Explain the use of these products to your class.
2. Find out how steel is made. Use encyclopedias or other books. Then draw a diagram that shows the steps.
3. Many people in the Great Lakes Region have made important contributions to our society. Find out about one of the people listed below. Then write a report about this person.

   Bill Mauldin   Frank Lloyd Wright
   Carl Sandburg   John Harold Johnson
   George Szell   Coleman Young

Read to Learn More

Find the topics listed below in the card catalog of your library. Read all or part of a book listed under one of the topics. Share what you learn with your classmates.

SOO CANALS   DAIRY FARMING
GREAT LAKES   IRON AND STEEL

Reading Skill: Using references: *Learn by Doing, 1,2,3* and *Read to Learn More.*
Communication Skills: Speaking: *Learn by Doing, 1* and *Read to Learn More;* writing: *Learn by Doing, 1,2,3.*

Unit Overview: This unit examines the Midwest Plains Region, its population density, and the major crops grown there.

Unit Objectives
To understand:
- the seven states in this region
- how population density varies within this region
- the major crops grown in this region
- graphics

Suggested Materials
Workbook
Unit Tests

Unit 12

Skills Emphasized
Map Skills: pp. 342, 349, 356.
Social Studies Reading Skills: pp. 342, 345, 346, 348, 349, 350, 351, 353, 354, 356, 357.
Thinking Skills: pp. 342, 349, 351, 352, 356, 357.
Communication Skills: pp. 342, 347, 349, 353, 354, 357.
Time Skill: p. 357.
Social Studies Math Skills: pp. 347, 350, 352.
Citizenship Skill: p. 342.

Suggested Student Activities
   1. Work in groups. Each group should prepare a booklet about one of the seven states in this region.
   2. Post magazine and newspaper articles about this region on a bulletin board.
   3. Add to the class data-retrieval chart begun in Unit 10.
   4. Make salt model maps of the Mississippi River. Label key points.
 * 5. Work in small groups. Make model farms or report on farm products.
*** 6. Work in pairs. Write reports on topics listed on page 353.

Skills Emphasized in Suggested Student Activities
Social Studies Reading Skills: Doing research, using magazines and newspapers.
Communication Skills: Writing, speaking, listening.
Citizenship Skill: Social participation.
Map Skills: Location, distance, scale.
Thinking Skills: Observing, comparing.

The Midwest Plains

Fields of golden, ripe wheat, such as this one in Kansas, dominate the landscape in many of the states on the Midwest Plains.

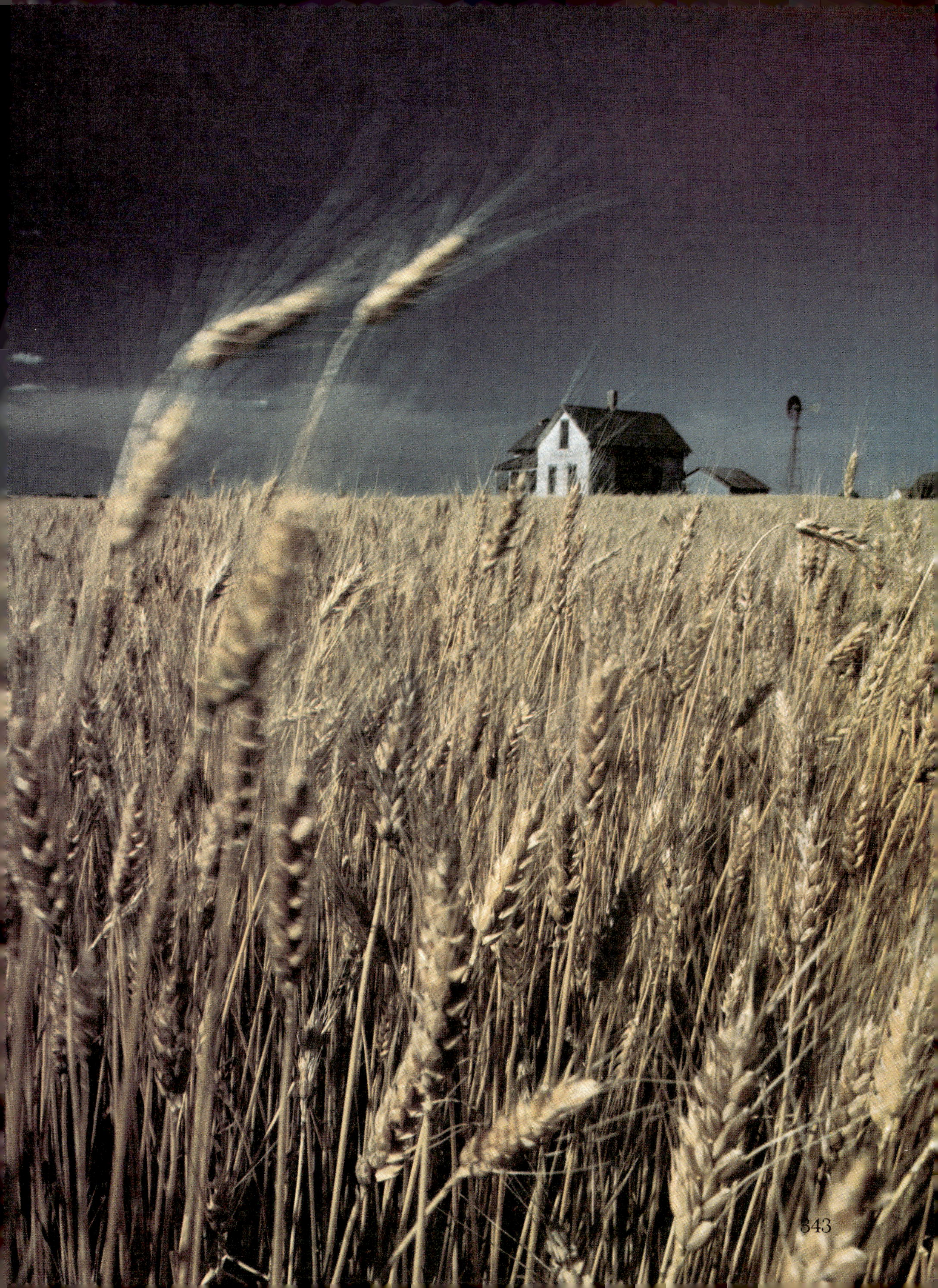

Region of the Midwest Plains
Physical-Political Map

★ State Capitals ● Other Cities

SCALE One inch—about 120 miles

Miles: 0, 50, 100, 150, 200, 250
Kilometers: 0, 50, 100, 150, 200, 250, 300, 350

HEIGHT OF LAND
- 6,600 TO 13,000
- 3,300 TO 6,600
- 1,650 TO 3,300
- 650 TO 1,650
- 0 TO 650 FEET

DEPTH OF WATER
- 0 TO 600 FEET
- BELOW 600 FEET

LOCATION MAP

Profile
FEET — Scotts Bluff, Sand Hills, Missouri River, Cedar Rapids, Mississippi River
4,000 / 3,000 / 2,000 / 1,000 / Sea level

344

Reading Skill: Interpreting graphics: *As You Read, 3.*

Where Are the Midwest Plains?

As You Read This Unit

1. Think about these words.
   erosion   continental   wheat belt
2. Look for answers to these key questions.
   a. Which seven states make up the Midwest Plains?
   b. How does the population density within the Midwest Plains vary?
   c. What are the major crops grown in the Midwest Plains?
3. Use these reading skills.
   In each of the regional units there are many graphics: charts, graphs, diagrams, illustrations, and maps. You must study the graphics in this unit very carefully in order to understand the Midwest Plains. As you come to each graphic in this unit, read the title and any labels. Ask yourself these questions: Is something being measured? Are several things being compared? Is something being described or explained? Finally, how does this graphic help me understand the Midwest Plains?

The Midwest Plains Region of our country has many rich farms. The rich soils and the flat plains make farming easier in this region than in many other parts of the United States. The plains in this region seem to stretch forever. Of course, there are hills and even mountains in the Midwest Plains. Large cities, located on the great rivers of the Midwest Plains, are trade and transportation centers for the entire country. For the most part, though, this is a region of farms that cover the plains.

The Area

The Midwest Plains are made up of seven states. What are they? Name the capital of each state. Use the map scale to find out about how many miles the Midwest Plains stretch in an east-west direction, then in a north-south direction. What two states in this region are the farthest north? What country borders these two states? Find the Mississippi River. Which states in the Midwest Plains border the Mississippi River? Which states border the Midwest Plains on the south? on the west?

The Land

Look at the profile at the bottom of page 344. Find Scottsbluff, Nebraska, and Cedar Rapids, Iowa. Compare the elevations of these two places. Now look

1. Mo. (Jefferson City), Kans. (Topeka), Iowa (Des Moines), Nebr. (Lincoln), Minn. (St. Paul), S.Dak. (Pierre), N.Dak. (Bismarck).
2. Minn., N.Dak./Canada.
3. Mo., Iowa, Minn./Okla., Ark., Tenn./Colo., Wyo., Mont.

345

1. Western part.
2. Mountains.
3. The Ozark Plateau is in Missouri.
4. South Dakota, Wyoming.

at the physical-political map and compare the general elevations of the western and of the eastern parts of this region. Which part has higher elevations? Where is the point of highest elevation in this region?

The landforms. The name of this region tells you which landform is most common. Look at the pie graph on this page. Which is the least common landform in the region?

Landforms of the Midwest Plains

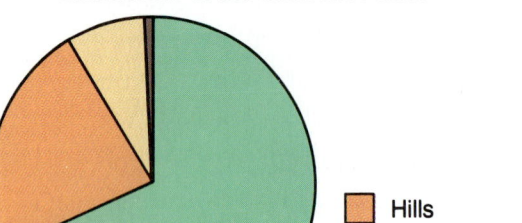

- Hills
- Mountains
- Plains
- Plateaus

The Midwest Plains Region also has plateaus, hills, and mountains. These other landforms are scattered across the region. On the map on page 344, find the Ozark Plateau. In which state is it located? Find the Black Hills. In which states are the Black Hills?

Parts of the Midwest Plains are like nothing else in the entire country. Look at the photo on this page. These areas are called Badlands. Early European settlers called them Badlands because they could grow almost nothing and because traveling was so difficult in these areas. **Erosion,** or the wearing away of the earth by wind and water, created the Badlands. Look at the map on page 344. In which state are the Badlands?

Few plants can grow in the Badlands.

Rivers of the Midwest Plains

The Mississippi River forms most of the eastern boundary of the Midwest Plains. This river is an important shipping route for both the Midwest Plains and the Great Lakes Region. Use the map on page 344 and follow the course of the Mississippi River from Minneapolis to Saint Louis. Find the Missouri River on the map on page 344. What cities are located on this river? The Missouri has always been an important transportation route into the interior of the Midwest Plains. There are also other important rivers in the Midwest Plains. Use the same map to find the Red River between Minnesota and North Dakota. Find the Platte River in Nebraska.

The Climate

The climate of the Midwest Plains is called **continental.** In a continental climate, summers are hot and winters are cold. There are no large bodies of water in the Midwest Plains to make the winter and summer temperatures milder.

Temperatures. Temperatures within the Midwest Plains vary from season to season and from place to place. Look at the graphs on page 347. Compare the average monthly temperatures of Williston, North Dakota, and Springfield, Missouri.

5. South Dakota.
6. Kansas City, Omaha, Pierre, Bismarck.
*** **Reading Skill:** Doing research. Have groups of students report on the key rivers of the region.

1. Springfield. Williston.
2. Differences in temperature: Dec., about 21°; Jan., about 25°; Feb., about 23°. Northern location.
3. Williston: May, June, July. Springfield: April, May, June. Springfield.

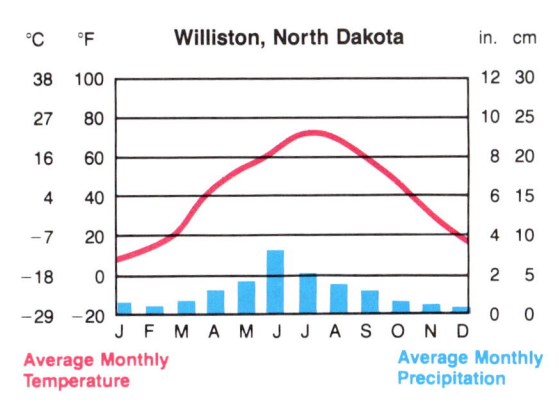

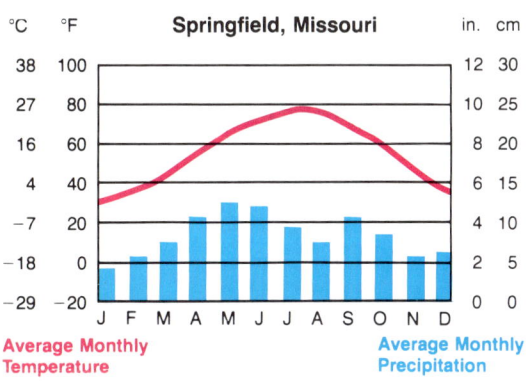

Williston, North Dakota

Average Monthly Temperature
Average Monthly Precipitation

Springfield, Missouri

Average Monthly Temperature
Average Monthly Precipitation

1 Which place has a higher average July temperature? Which place has a lower average January temperature?

2 What are the differences in temperature for the months of December, January, and February between the two places? Why is it so much colder in Williston than in Springfield during these months? Temperatures in the northern part of the Midwest Plains are generally lower than in the southern part.

Precipitation. Look again at the graphs on this page. Compare the average monthly precipitation of Williston with that of Springfield. During which three months does each place receive the most precipitation? Which place receives more precipitation during an average year? Most places in the western part of the Midwest Plains receive less precipitation than do places in the eastern part. This difference in precipitation is particularly important to farmers. What crops they grow depends partly on the amount of precipitation in that area.

3

The growing seasons. Look at the map on this page. How many different growing seasons are there in the Midwest Plains? How long is each one? Where is the longest growing season in this region? Why? Where is the shortest growing season in this region? Why?

You can see that the climate within the Midwest Plains varies from place to place. The amount of precipitation decreases from east to west. The length of growing seasons increases from north to south.

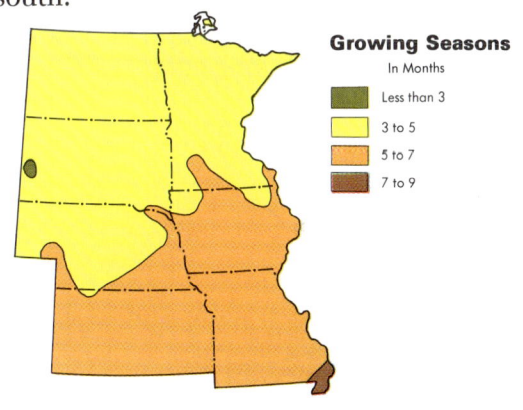

Growing Seasons
In Months
- Less than 3
- 3 to 5
- 5 to 7
- 7 to 9

Checking Up

1. What is the difference in elevation between the western and eastern parts of the Midwest Plains?
2. Why do the temperatures differ within this region?
3. *How does the climate within this region vary?*

Communication Skill: Listening. Have students listen for current weather reports on this region.
Math Skill: Review the meaning of *average.* Have students find out the average rainfall and temperature for your community at this time of year.

1. Eastern part. Western part. Decreases from east to west. More people in the area of greater precipitation.
2. Less densely populated.

Where Are the People?

A definite population pattern appears across the Midwest Plains. People are clustered in cities. Many of the cities have grown at key trading locations. Most of these locations are along rivers. Some of these cities were at first trading posts for Indians and settlers. They eventually grew into cities. More people live in the cities than in the towns and on the farms. Most of the land between cities is farmland.

Where the People Live

Look at the population density map on this page. Compare this density map with the map of the Midwest Plains on page 344. Where are the most densely populated areas of the Midwest Plains? Where are the least populated parts? How does the pattern of population density change from east to west? What connection do you see between population density and the climate patterns of the Midwest Plains?

Look back at the population map on page 16. Are the Midwest Plains more densely or less densely populated than

Urban and Rural Population of the Midwest Plains

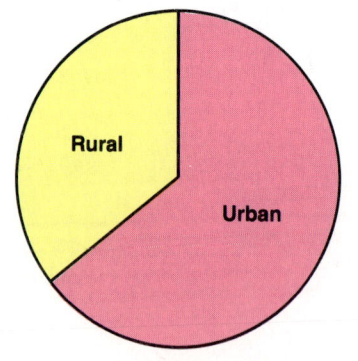

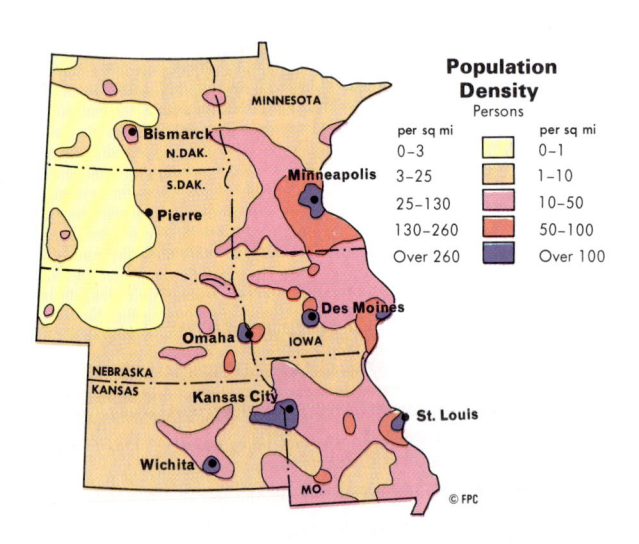

Recent Populations of Selected Cities on the Midwest Plains				
City	1950 Population	1960 Population	1970 Population	1980 Population
Kansas City, MO	456,622	475,539	507,087	448,159
Minneapolis, MN	521,718	482,872	434,400	370,951
Omaha, NE	251,117	301,598	347,328	311,681
St. Louis, MO	856,796	750,026	622,236	453,085
St. Paul, MN	311,349	313,411	309,980	270,230
Wichita, KS	168,279	254,698	276,554	279,272

1. Urban areas.
2. East Saint Louis. Council Bluffs, Iowa.
Reading Skill: Skimming. What cities in other regions are about the same size as these cities?
Map Skill: Location. Have students locate each of the cities listed on the table.

the Great Lakes Region? than the Northeast region?

Cities in the Midwest Plains. Many people in this region live in cities. Look at the pie graph on page 348. Where do most of the people live?

The location on rivers of many cities in the Midwest Plains has created an interesting feature. Today there are many "twin" cities. For example, Minneapolis, Minnesota, is across the Mississippi River from Saint Paul. Find these two cities on the map on page 344. What city is across the Mississippi River from Saint Louis, Missouri? What city is across the Missouri River from Omaha, Nebraska?

Interesting Places To Visit

Mitchell, South Dakota, has its own kind of festival each year. People here use different colors of corn to create the Corn Palace during Corn Palace Week.

The Boundary Waters Canoe Area in northern Minnesota covers about a million acres (404,700 hectares) of wilderness. There are 1,000 lakes here where people can fish and canoe.

Reading Skill: Interpreting pictures. Have students look for pictures of urban and rural areas.
Thinking Skill: Analyzing. Talk about why these places would be important to the region.
** **Communication Skill:** Writing. Interested students could design posters advertising these places.

349

1. Saint Louis. Omaha. Wichita. Kansas City, Minneapolis, Saint Louis, Saint Paul.
2. Decreased. Decreased. Rural.
3. Between 1880 and 1980.
4. Northeast. Midwest Plains. Northeast. Midwest Plains.

Look at the table on page 348. What is the largest city in the Midwest Plains? Which cities have gained people since 1950? Which cities have lost people since 1950? As you have read about the Midwest Plains, you have seen some differences between the eastern and the western parts. In which of these parts are the cities that have gained people?

The population patterns. You saw on the pie graph on page 348 that a large percentage of people in the Midwest Plains live in urban areas. Now look at the pie graphs below. What happened to the rural population between 1920 and 1950? between 1950 and the present? In 1920, did more people live in rural or urban areas?

Urban and Rural Population of the Midwest Plains, 1920 and 1950

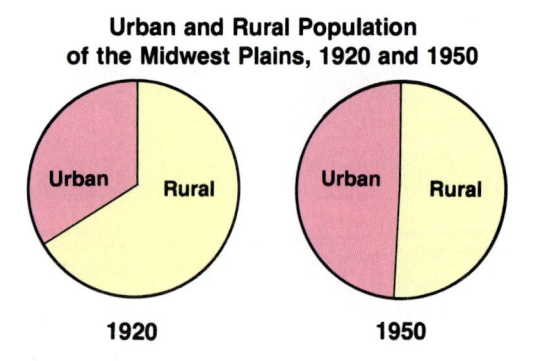

1920 | 1950

The rural population has been declining for a long time. However, the urban population has declined in some places too. Look at the line graph of population growth for the entire Midwest Plains on this page. When did the greatest growth in population occur? What is the prediction for the population growth between 1980 and 2000? Compare this prediction with the prediction for the Northeast on page 315, then with the prediction for the Great Lakes Region on page 333. Which region is expected to have the greatest population growth? the least? Which of these three regions had the largest population in 1980? the smallest population in 1980?

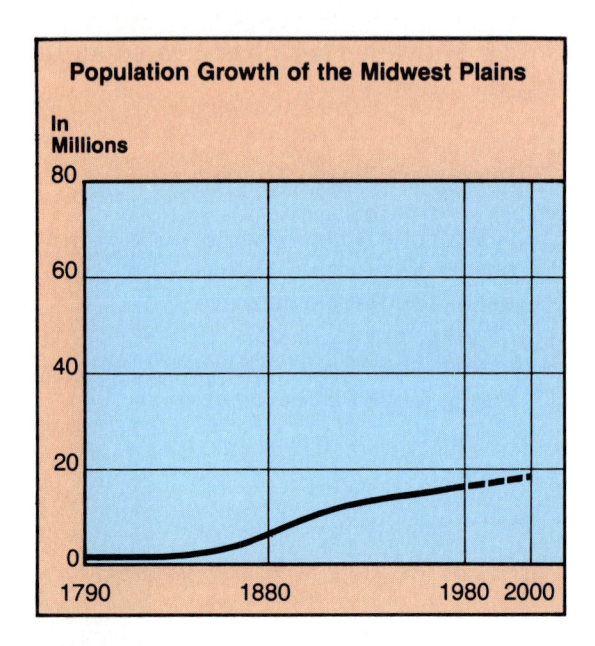

Population Growth of the Midwest Plains
In Millions

Although the population of the Midwest Plains is not as large as some other regions, the region is a most important part of the United States. Other regions depend on the farms in the Midwest Plains.

Checking Up
1. Do more people in the Midwest Plains live in rural or in urban areas?
2. What are the three largest cities in the Midwest Plains?
3. *Why are most major cities in the Midwest Plains located on rivers?*

Reading Skill: Recognizing main ideas. Talk about the importance of population patterns.
Math Skill: Ask how the prediction for the population of this area in the future compares with other regions students have read about.

350

1. Iowa, Nebr., S.Dak., Minn., Mo., Ill., Ind., and Ohio./Iowa.
2. Kans., Nebr., S.Dak., and N.Dak.

What Do the People Do?

You have learned that, in the past, most people in the Midwest Plains lived in rural areas. Today the population is largely urban. People earn their living in a variety of ways.

A Region of Farms

Farming within the Midwest Plains is widespread and important. The farms vary in size and in what they produce. The size and kind of farm depend on its location.

The corn belt. In Unit 11, you learned about the part of the Great Lakes Region where corn is the major crop. This corn belt extends into the Midwest Plains. Look at the map below. Which states are part of the corn belt? Which state in the Midwest Plains is almost totally within the corn belt?

All farms in the corn belt do not grow only corn. In addition to corn, farmers grow soybeans. Soybeans provide food for livestock and people. Farmers in the corn belt of the Midwest Plains also raise millions of beef cattle and hogs.

The wheat belt. Look at the map below. This map shows what is called the **wheat belt** of the United States. More wheat grows here than in any other region of the United States. Which states in the Midwest Plains are within the wheat belt? Farms in the wheat belt also produce rye, barley, hay, flaxseed, and potatoes.

Farmers in the wheat belt grow two kinds of wheat. Find North and South Dakota on the map on page 347. Here in the northern part of the Midwest Plains, the growing season is short. How long is the growing season in most of the Dakotas? Farmers in the northern part of the Midwest Plains grow spring wheat. Spring wheat is planted in May. It grows quickly in the short spring and during the hot summer days. Farmers harvest the ripe grain in the fall.

Look again at the growing seasons map on page 347. How long is the growing season in Kansas and southern Nebraska? In this southern part of the Midwest Plains, farmers grow winter

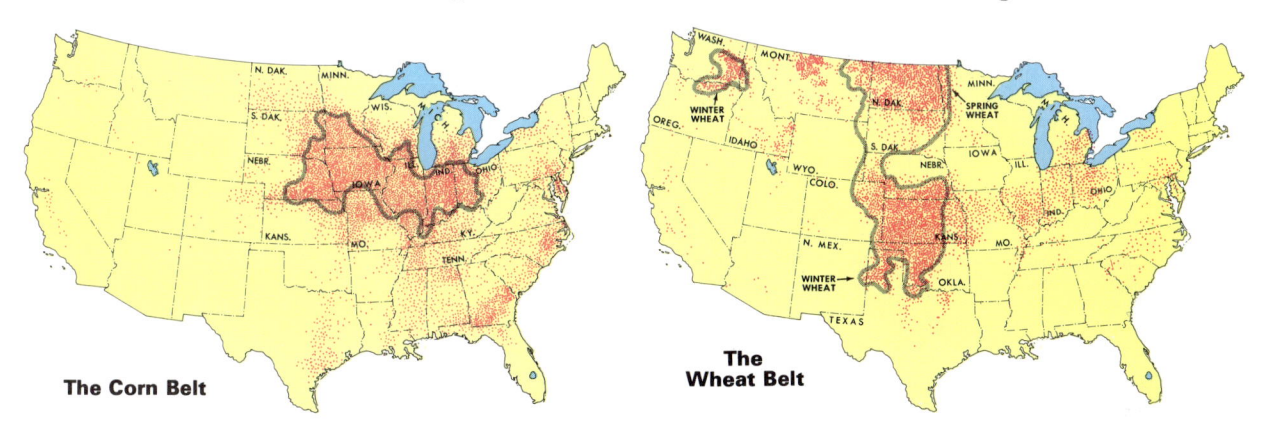

The Corn Belt

The Wheat Belt

Reading Skill: Previewing. Before reading ask students to identify the main occupations.
Thinking Skill: Comparing. Have students make a chart comparing the corn belt and wheat belt.

wheat. Winter wheat is planted in fall and grows quickly in warm fall weather. During the winter, the wheat stops growing but does not die. In spring, the wheat begins growing again. Farmers then harvest the wheat in June or July. Winter wheat gives a better yield than spring wheat. In addition, winter wheat usually brings the farmer a higher price.

Farms in the wheat belt are different from farms in the corn belt. Usually wheat farms are larger than farms in the eastern part of the Midwest Plains. The wheat farms of the western Midwest Plains are often 1,000 acres (405 hectares) and sometimes as large as 2,000 acres (809 hectares). An acre is about the same size as a football field. At one time farms in the corn belt were as small as 160 acres (65 hectares). Today corn belt farms are often larger. Because the eastern part of the Midwest Plains receives more precipitation than the western part, farms in the corn belt get good yields and this is enough to pay for the farmers' work even with small acreage.

Nonfarming lands. Not all areas in the Midwest Plains are good for farming. Northern Minnesota's climate is too cool and the soil too poor for most farming. However, this area is the leading iron ore–mining region in the United States. About half the iron ore mined in this country comes from northern Minnesota.

The Ozark Plateau is generally too hilly to be farmed. The Sand Hills of Nebraska and the Badlands areas have soil that is too poor for farming. However, each of these areas has beautiful scenery that attracts tourists.

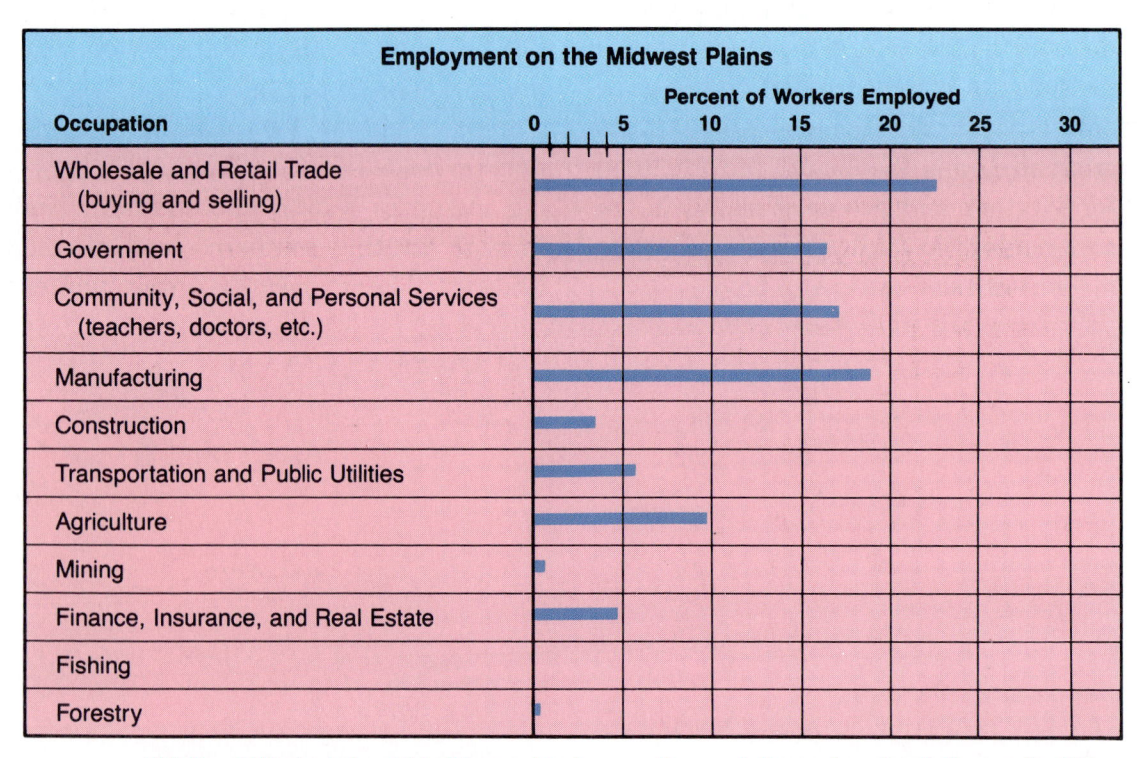

Employment on the Midwest Plains

Occupation	Percent of Workers Employed
Wholesale and Retail Trade (buying and selling)	~22
Government	~15
Community, Social, and Personal Services (teachers, doctors, etc.)	~15
Manufacturing	~19
Construction	~4
Transportation and Public Utilities	~6
Agriculture	~8
Mining	~1
Finance, Insurance, and Real Estate	~4
Fishing	—
Forestry	~1

1. About 10%. About 19%.
2. Wholesale and retail trade and manufacturing.

*** **Reading Skill:** Doing research. Have a small group of students prepare a chart showing the iron ore mining process.

Careers

Where Some of the People Work

The picture at the right shows the Mayo Clinic in Rochester, Minnesota. Founded in 1889 by William Mayo and his two sons, this medical center is world famous for its medical research. The Mayo Clinic is one of the largest medical centers in the world. The staff numbers about 500, and almost 225,000 patients a year receive treatment here.

The picture at the left shows an Iowa farmer. Some Iowa farmers own and farm more than 400 acres (162 hectares) of rich Iowa farmland. These farmers grow mainly corn and some soybeans. They also raise hogs. They use some of the corn and soybeans to feed their hogs. They sell the rest. When the hogs reach market size, they are also sold.

At the right is a picture of an open-pit iron ore mine in Minnesota. Open-pit miners remove a thin layer of earth so they can then mine the iron ore underneath. Find the Mesabi Range on the map on page 344. The iron ore mined in the Mesabi Range and elsewhere in northern Minnesota is usually shipped from the port at Duluth to factories in the Great Lakes Region.

Cities and the Jobs They Create

Although many people depend on the farms of the Midwest Plains, farming is by no means the only way, or even the most common way, that people make a living. Look at the bar graph of employment on page 352. What percent of the workers are in agriculture? What percent work in manufacturing? Of all the occupations listed in the bar graph, which two occupations employ the most workers? These people live in the cities.

Communication Skill: Listening. Establish a purpose for listening.
Communication Skill: Speaking. Students who prepared reports on these careers could give them.

353

1. About 6%. **2.** About 39%; about 55%.
Reading Skill: Determining meaning from context. Talk about the food-processing industry.
Communication Skill: Writing. Students could work in pairs. Have them use the data on page 355 to write state riddles. Share them with the class.

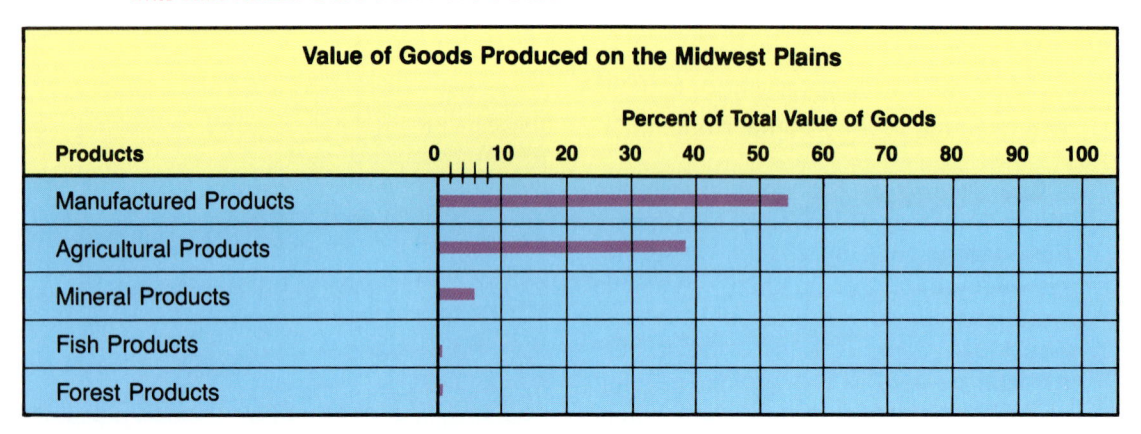

Value of Goods Produced on the Midwest Plains

Products	Percent of Total Value of Goods
Manufactured Products	~55%
Agricultural Products	~39%
Mineral Products	~6%
Fish Products	<1%
Forest Products	<1%

Most people in the Midwest Plains live in urban areas. Cities serve as centers of trade and as centers for processing the farm products from the surrounding countryside. The food-processing industry employs thousands of people in Minneapolis, Omaha, Saint Louis, and Kansas City. Food processing prepares farm products for human or animal use.

Because the Midwest Plains are in the middle of the country and because so much of the country needs these farm products, cities here are centers of transportation. Saint Louis, Omaha, and Kansas City, Missouri, are particularly important rail and trucking centers. Look at the bar graph on page 352. What percent of the people work in transportation and public utilities?

1

Look at the bar graph of the value of goods in the Midwest Plains on this page. What percent of the total value of goods is farm products? manufactured goods? Look again at the bar graph on page 352. Find the percent of people working in agriculture. What connections can you make about the number of people in agriculture and the value of the goods they

2

produce? Find the percent of people working in manufacturing. What connections can you make about the number of people in manufacturing and the value of the goods they produce?

3

Checking Up
1. Which cities in the Midwest Plains are centers of transportation?
2. What answers would you give to the key questions at the beginning of this unit?
3. *Why do you think food-processing companies are located in this region?*

Unit 12 Summary
- Plains are the most common landform in this region.
- Although the Midwest Plains are an important farming area, more people live in urban than in rural areas.
- Many industries in the Midwest Plains process or ship farm products from the region.

3. There is a small number of farmers producing a great deal of wealth.
Reading Skill: Reading for details. Have students decide which of the three main selections in this unit contains each point in the summary.

FACTS ABOUT THE MIDWEST PLAINS

	Nickname	Capital* and Largest Cities	State Bird	Farm Products and Natural Resources	Manufactured Products	Did You Know This?
Iowa	The Hawkeye State	Des Moines* Cedar Rapids Davenport Sioux City Waterloo	Eastern Goldfinch	Corn, hogs, soybeans, cattle, dairy products Stone, sand, gravel	Machinery, processed foods, chemicals, electrical equipment	Iowa has the largest farm population of any state in the nation.
Kansas	The Sunflower State	Topeka* Wichita Kansas City Overland Park Lawrence	Western Meadowlark	Cattle, wheat, corn, hogs, hay Petroleum, natural gas, stone, salt	Processed foods, machinery, chemicals	The first newspaper in Kansas was printed in the Shawnee Indian language.
Missouri	The Show Me State	Jefferson City* St. Louis Kansas City Springfield Independence	Bluebird	Soybeans, cattle, hogs, corn, dairy products Lead, clay, limestone	Transportation equipment, processed foods, chemicals, machinery	Mark Twain's childhood home in Hannibal is open for public tours.
Minnesota	The Gopher State	St. Paul* Minneapolis Duluth Bloomington Rochester	Common Loon	Corn, dairy products, soybeans, hogs, beef cattle Lead, clay, iron ore	Machinery, processed foods, metals, electrical equipment	The source of the Mississippi River is Lake Itasca in Minnesota.
Nebraska	The Cornhusker State	Lincoln* Omaha Grand Island Fremont Bellevue	Western Meadowlark	Corn, cattle, hogs, soybeans, hay Petroleum, natural gas	Processed foods, machinery, electrical equipment, chemicals	Nebraska is the only state in the nation that has a one-house legislature.
North Dakota	The Flickertail State	Bismarck* Fargo Grand Forks Minot Jamestown	Western Meadowlark	Wheat, beef cattle, hay, dairy products, potatoes Natural gas, petroleum, coal	Machinery, processed foods, printed and published materials	Lewis and Clark met their guide, Sacagawea, in North Dakota.
South Dakota	The Sunshine State	Pierre* Sioux Falls Rapid City Aberdeen Watertown	Ring-necked Pheasant	Beef cattle, corn, hogs, hay, wheat, dairy products Gold, sand, gravel	Processed foods, machinery, lumber	The Homestate Mine at Lead, South Dakota, is the largest gold mine in the United States.

Communication Skill: Writing. Students could work in pairs. Have them use this data to write state riddles. Share them with class.

Unit 12 Review Workshop

What Have You Learned?

1. What are the Badlands? How were these landscapes created?
2. How do precipitation patterns differ within the Midwest Plains? How do temperature patterns differ within the Midwest Plains?
3. Why is the eastern part of the Midwest Plains more densely populated than the western part?
4. What are "twin" cities?
5. What are the differences between spring and winter wheat?
6. Why are some cities in the Midwest Plains centers of transportation?
7. How has the rural population of the Midwest Plains changed since 1920?

Use Your Reading Skills

You learned in this unit that the farms in the western part of the Midwest Plains are generally larger than the farms in the eastern part. Make an outline listing advantages large farms would have in the western part. Make another outline listing advantages a smaller farm might have in the eastern part. You should look carefully at the tables, charts, and graphs in this unit for clues. Use resources from your classroom or school library as well. What effect might high land prices have on the advantages in your outlines? What effect might climate have on the advantages in your outlines? What about the high prices of tractors and other machinery, fuel, and fertilizers?

Use Your Research Skills

One of the most important uses of a dictionary is to find out where particular words first came from. The origin of a word is called its etymology. Dictionaries often give etymologies after the pronunciation of a word.

The name of each state in the Midwest Plains has an interesting etymology, or origin. Find the etymology of each state name. You may have to use more than one dictionary. Different dictionaries may not give exactly the same information or details. What do all the names have in common? Why do you think there are so many Indian names in this region and not in the Northeast?

Use Your Map Skills

Look at the map on page 357 and answer the following questions. Answers to these questions will help you understand more about the mineral resources in the Midwest Plains.

1. Which states produce petroleum? natural gas? Which state produces both petroleum and natural gas?
2. In what part of the Midwest Plains does gold mining take place? Use the map on page 344 and name the landform in which this mining takes place.
3. This map shows that there is mining in Missouri. Look at the product key and name the kinds of mineral products in Missouri. In which part of the state is most of the mining?

Reading Skills: Using references, interpreting graphics, outlining.
Thinking Skills: Knowing, comparing.
Map Skills: Location, symbolization.

Mineral Resources

- Coal
- C — Copper
- Gold
- I — Iron Ore
- L — Lead
- Natural Gas
- Oil
- Sa — Salt
- S — Silver
- Z — Zinc

4. Again, turn to the map on page 344. What city in Kansas is close to the Kansas oil and natural gas fields? What city is near the deposits of iron ore in Minnesota? What effects on a city do you think these minerals have?

5. Coal is one of our country's most important sources of energy. In which states in the Midwest Plains is there coal mining?

Learn by Doing

1. Turn back to the map of American Indian reservations on page 54. Compare this map with the map of the Midwest Plains on page 344. In which states of the Midwest Plains are there Indian reservations? As you can see, there are many large reservations in this region. Prepare an oral report on one of these reservations. In your report, tell about which tribe lives on the reservation, their history, and their life on the reservation today. Use books and encyclopedias to help you prepare your report.

2. In this unit you have read about two different kinds of wheat. There are also many other kinds of wheat. Use encyclopedias or other books to find out about some of these other kinds of wheat. Prepare a report for your class. Describe the different kinds of wheat, where and how these kinds of wheat were developed, and how each kind of wheat is used.

3. Some of you may wish to compare modern farming with the farming of 100 years ago. One way to make the comparison is to learn about modern farm machines (such as combines). What do they do? Then find out how these same jobs were done in the past. Make a chart comparing the two different methods of farming.

4. Prepare a report on the history and growth of one pair of "twin" cities. How is each city like its twin? How is it different? Which is larger? When were the cities founded? What do the people do now?

Read to Learn More

Find the topics below in the card catalog of your library. Read all or part of a book listed under one of the topics. Share what you learn with your classmates.

MISSOURI RIVER   FOOD
BLACK HILLS   FORT LEAVENWORTH

Reading Skill: Doing research: *Learn by Doing, 1,2* and *Read to Learn More.*
Communication Skill: Speaking: *Learn by Doing, 1,3* and *Read to Learn More.*
Time Skill: *Learn by Doing, 2.*
Thinking Skill: Comparing: *Learn by Doing, 1,2,3.*

Unit Overview: This unit examines the South, why its population is growing, and the major ways its people make a living.

Unit Objectives
To understand:
- the eleven states in this region
- why the population is growing in this region
- the major occupations in this region
- graphics

Skills Emphasized
Map Skills: pp. 374, 375.
Social Studies Reading Skills: pp. 358, 361, 362, 364, 365, 366, 368, 369, 370, 371, 374, 375.
Thinking Skills: pp. 358, 363, 367, 371, 374, 375.
Communication Skills: pp. 358, 370, 375.
Time Skill: p. 368.
Social Studies Math Skill: p. 374.
Citizenship Skills: pp. 358, 365, 366.

Suggested Materials
Workbook
Unit Tests

Unit 13

Suggested Student Activities
1. Work in groups. Each group should prepare a picture chart about one of the eleven states in this region.
2. Post magazine and newspaper articles about this region on a bulletin board.
3. Add to the class data-retrieval chart begun in Unit 10.
4. Have each state group write for information on their state. This could include travel information.
** 5. Make mobiles of tourist attractions in each state.
*** 6. Work in pairs. Write reports on the career topics listed on page 370.

Skills Emphasized in Suggested Student Activities
Social Studies Reading Skills: Doing research, using magazines and newspapers.
Thinking Skill: Comparing.
Communication Skills: Speaking, writing, listening.
Citizenship Skill: Social participation.

The South

Forests of pine trees cover much of the landscape in the South.

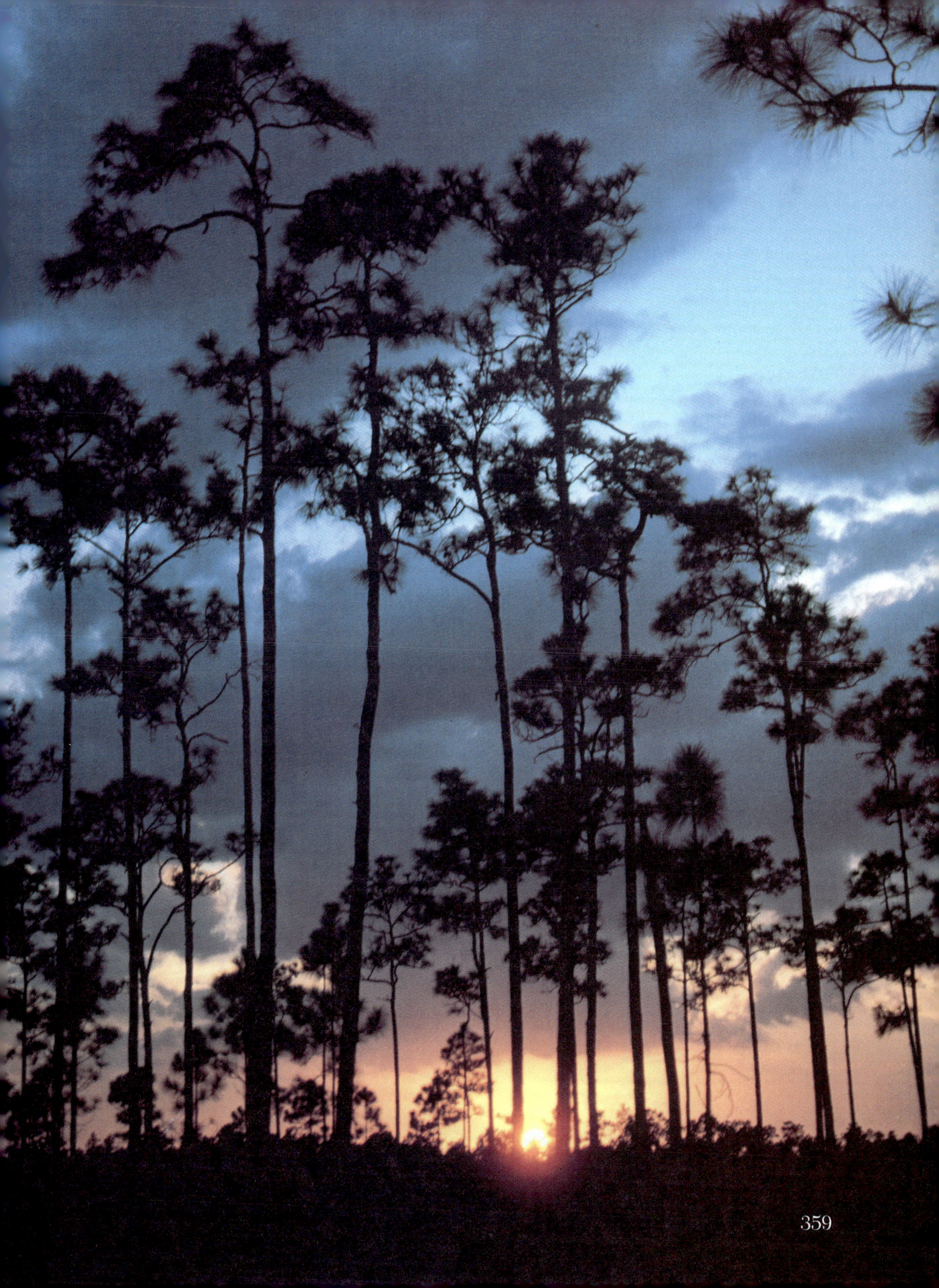

Region of the South
Physical-Political Map

⊛ National Capitals
★ State Capitals
• Other Cities

SCALE
One inch—about 165 miles

Miles: 0, 50, 100, 150, 200
Kilometers: 0, 50, 100, 200, 300

HEIGHT OF LAND
- 6,600 TO 13,000
- 3,300 TO 6,600
- 1,650 TO 3,300
- 650 TO 1,650
- 0 TO 650 FEET

DEPTH OF WATER
- 0 TO 600 FEET
- BELOW 600 FEET

Profile
Feet 4,000 / 2,000 / Sea level
Mississippi River — Memphis — Chattanooga — Blue Ridge Mountains — Charlotte — Atlantic Coastal Plain

360

Reading Skill: Interpreting pictures: *As You Read, 3.*
1. Walt Disney World, New Orleans, and Peachtree Center. Forests, coal, iron ore, oil, natural gas. Wood processing and textile.

Where Is the South?

As You Read This Unit

1. Think about these words.
   Piedmont   sunbelt   textile   petrochemical
2. Look for answers to these key questions.
   a. Which eleven states make up the South?
   b. What are two reasons why the population of the South is growing?
   c. What are three major ways people make a living in the South?
3. Use this reading skill.
   To get the most from each unit, remember that you must "read" and study photographs just as carefully as the words of the text. Before you begin reading this unit, look through the unit and study each photograph. Use the photographs to answer these questions about the South. Where are three major tourist areas in the South? What natural resources can be found in the South? What are two major industries of the region?

Today the South is one of the fastest growing parts of our country. New businesses and industries are growing and moving there. One of the newest and busiest airports in our country is in Atlanta, Georgia. Recreation areas such as Walt Disney World in Florida and the Superdome in New Orleans attract many visitors.

The South is also a region rich in history. St. Augustine, Florida, began as a Spanish city over 300 years ago. In Williamsburg, Virginia, homes built by some of the first English settlers in America have been restored. In some of the states of the South, you can see where battles were fought during the Civil War.

The Region

The South is made up of eleven states. Look at the map on page 360. Name the eleven states that make up the South. What is the capital of each state? Use the map scale on page 360 to find out about how many miles the South stretches in an east-west direction, then in a north-south direction.

All the states in the South border important waterways. Which states border the Mississippi River? the Ohio River? Which states border the Atlantic Ocean?

The Land

The South is a region with a variety of scenery. Some states have seaside

2. Ark. (Little Rock), La. (Baton Rouge), Miss. (Jackson), Ala. (Montgomery), Ga. (Atlanta), Fla. (Tallahassee), S.C. (Columbia), N.C. (Raleigh), Va. (Richmond), Ky. (Frankfort), Tenn. (Nashville).
3. La., Ark., Miss., Tenn., and Ky.; Ky./Fla., Ga., S.C., N.C., and Va.

361

* **Reading Skill:** Building vocabulary. Have students who need help with the pronunciation and meaning of *Piedmont* use the Glossary and a dictionary.
1. Plains.
2. N.C., S.C., and Ga.

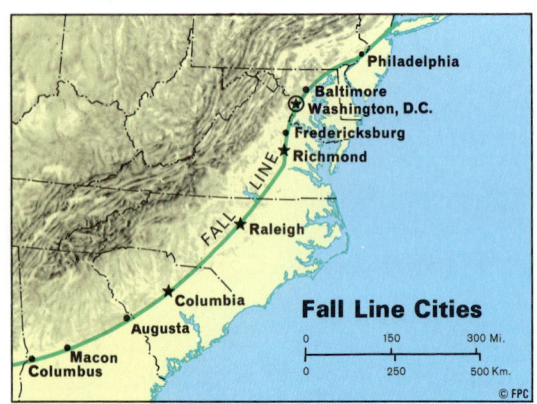

Fall Line Cities

Where rivers flow from the Piedmont to the plains, waterfalls form.

beaches lined with palm trees. Some parts of the South have lush pine forests. Still other areas of the South have beautiful mountains and green valleys.

The landforms. The varied scenery in the South can be explained in part by the different landforms. Look at the profile at the bottom of page 360. Find the elevation for Memphis and Chattanooga. Why would you expect Memphis to have a lower elevation than Chattanooga?

Study the pie graph on this page. Which landform is the most common in the South?

1

The plains. Find the Gulf Coastal Plain on the map on page 360. This area includes the western half of Florida and most of the states of Alabama, Mississippi, and Louisiana.

Now find the Atlantic Coastal Plain on the same map. What states are included in this lowland area?

2

A highland area. Using the map on page 360, follow the Atlantic Coastal Plain west to the **Piedmont.** The word *piedmont* means "at the foot of the mountains." The Piedmont is a hilly area at the foot of the Appalachian Mountains. Many rivers flow from the Piedmont to the Atlantic coast. Name three of these rivers.

3

The mountains. West of the Piedmont is an area of mountains. Look at the map on page 360 and find the Great Smoky Mountains and the Blue Ridge Mountains. These mountains are part of the Appalachian Mountains, which stretch from Alabama northward into Canada. Mount Mitchell is the highest peak in the Appalachian Mountains. Find Mount Mitchell on the map on page 360. What is its elevation? In what state is Mount Mitchell located?

4

There is another area of mountains in the South. This area is in northwestern Arkansas. Look at the map on page 360 and find the Boston Mountains in this area. Compare this mountain area with the Appalachian area.

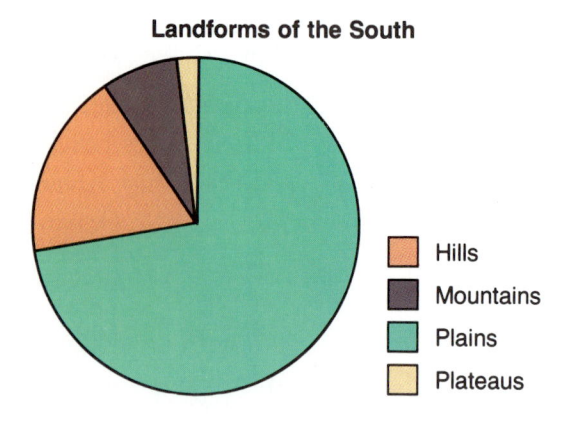

The Climate

Many people think of the South as a part of the **sunbelt.** The sunbelt includes the southern row of states that stretches from the Atlantic Ocean to the Pacific

Landforms of the South

- Hills
- Mountains
- Plains
- Plateaus

3. Altamaha, Savannah, and Santee rivers.
4. 6,684 ft./N.C.

362

Thinking Skill: Comparing. Have students find the average precipitation and temperature in your community for this month. Then compare it with Miami's figures on the climatograph.
1. 5. No. Higher elevation and farther distance from the equator.
2. Miami. Miami. About 20 inches more.

Ocean. Although the South is included in the sunbelt, the climate within the region varies. For example, only Florida has warm, summerlike temperatures all year long.

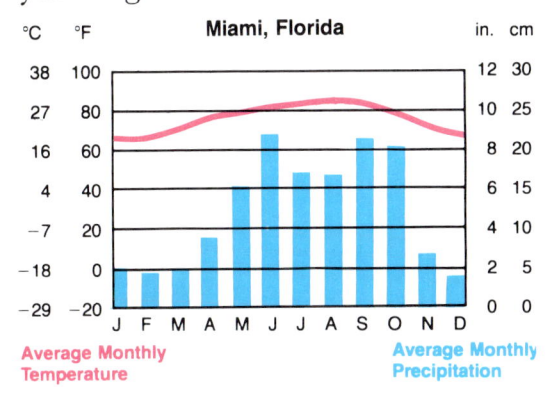

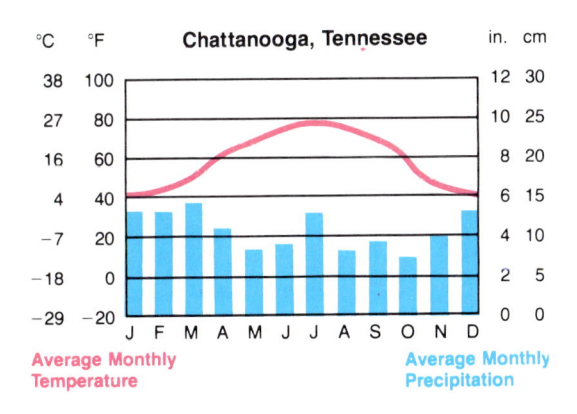

Compare the average monthly precipitation of Chattanooga and Miami. Which place gets more precipitation? Now look at the graph on page 331. Does Miami or Cincinnati get more precipitation? How much more?

The growing seasons. The South has one of the longest growing seasons in our country. However, some parts of the South have more frost-free months than other parts. Look at the growing-seasons map on this page. Which state has the longest growing season? How many frost-free months do most areas in this state have? How long is the growing season in the mountainous parts of Tennessee? What are two reasons for the difference in the length of growing season in Florida and in the mountainous parts of Tennessee?

Temperature. Look at the two graphs on this page. For how many months does Chattanooga have temperatures below 50 °F (10 °C)? Does Miami have any months with average temperatures below 50 °F (10 °C)? Find Chattanooga and Miami on the map on page 360. Why do you think Chattanooga is cooler than Miami?

Precipitation. The South gets more precipitation than many other parts of our country. However, the amount of precipitation within the South varies.

Growing Seasons
In Months
- 3 to 5
- 5 to 7
- 7 to 9
- 9 to 12
- All year long

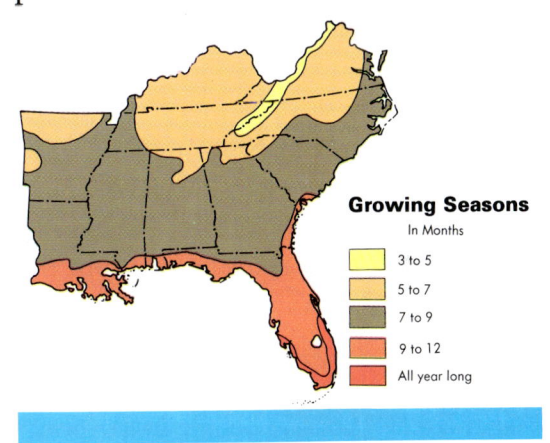

Checking Up
1. What are the important waterways that border most of the South?
2. Name the two major plains in the South.
3. *How does the climate within the South vary?*

*Reading Skill: Determining meaning from context. Have students check a dictionary for the meaning of *boom*. Which graphic illustrates its meaning?
1. Urban areas.

Where Are the People?

A population boom is sweeping the South. During the 1970s, for example, more than six million people moved to the South. New industries attract many of these people. Some people move to the South, however, simply to enjoy a warmer climate.

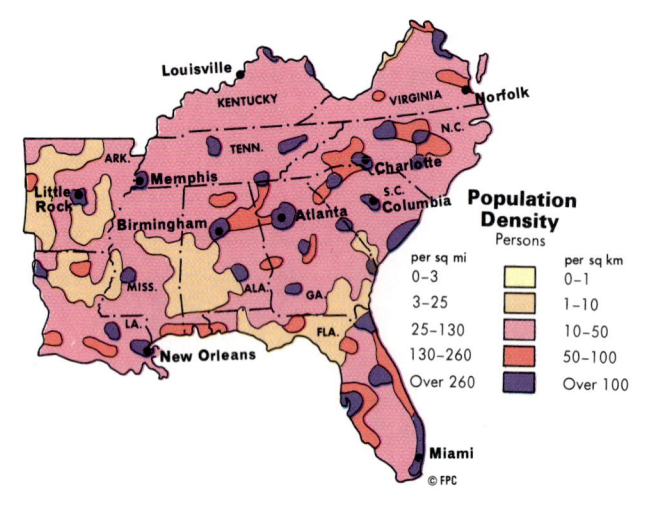

Urban and Rural Population of the South

Population Density (Persons)

per sq mi	per sq km
0–3	0–1
3–25	1–10
25–130	10–50
130–260	50–100
Over 260	Over 100

Using this map, name three densely populated areas of the South.

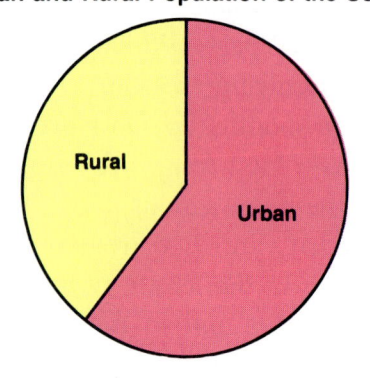

Where the People Live

Look at the map on page 16. How is the population distribution in the South different from the population distribution in the Northeast? How might landforms account for this difference?

The urban and rural population. For much of its history, the South has been mainly a rural region. Today the South is different. Look at the pie graph on this page. Do most of the people in the South today live in urban or rural areas?

1

Now look at the population map on this page. What is the population density for most of the South? Which states in the South have areas where there are over 260 people per square mile? As you can see from the map there are a number of densely populated areas in the South.

Population Growth in the South

Look at the line graph on page 365. What was the population of the South in 1790? in 1880? Now look at the table on page 366 that shows population growth in selected cities. What was the population of Richmond in 1790? in 1880? Which city listed in the table had the greatest population increase between 1790 and 1880?

2

3

Today's population boom. The population boom in the South today is partly due to businesses from northern areas of our country that are relocating in the South. Many people are moving to the South to fill the jobs created by these new businesses.

There are several reasons for businesses and industries to relocate in the South. The South has good transportation. Atlanta, Georgia, is the business center of the South. Find Atlanta on the

2. About 1.5 million people; about 13 million people.
3. 3,761 people; 63,600 people. New Orleans.

Reading Skill: Using details to support main ideas. Have students make a list of reasons for the population boom mentioned on page 364.
Citizenship Skill: Role-play various situations in which one person tries to persuade another to move to this region.

Population Growth of the South

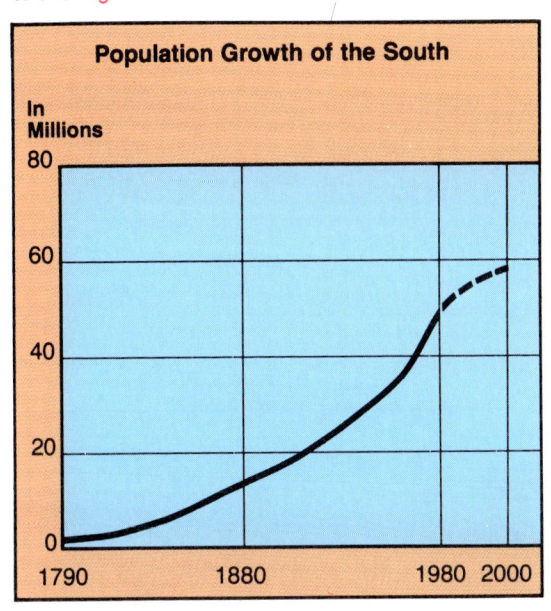

map on page 360. Railroad lines, highways, and airlines connect all parts of the South with Atlanta. It is easy for businesses to move people and goods throughout the South.

Many industries and businesses move to the South to get away from cold northern winters. During the winter it is expensive to heat factories in the North. Winter weather conditions in the North, such as ice and snow, can make transportation hard. In addition to the weather, land is cheaper, and taxes are lower in the South.

New coastal developments, such as this one in Sarasota, Florida, are often made by filling in swampland.

Reading Skill: Interpreting pictures. Have students look for pictures of urban and rural areas in the South.

Reading Skill: Skimming. What other cities in earlier units compare in population with Atlanta and Miami?

Reading Skill: Doing research. Divide the class into small groups. Have each group give a visual report on one key city in the South.

Population Growth of Selected Cities in the South			
City	1790 Population	1880 Population	1980 Population
Atlanta, GA	Not Available	37,409	425,022
Charlotte, NC	Not Available	Not Available	314,447
Memphis, TN	Not Available	33,592	646,356
Miami, FL	Not Available	Not Available	346,931
New Orleans, LA	Not Available	216,090	557,482
Richmond, VA	3,761	63,600	219,214

The sunshine and generally warm weather of the South also attract many people. Retired people, especially, move to Florida. In addition to the weather, these people like the year-round recreational activities such as golf, boating, and fishing. These same attractions bring an increasing number of tourists to the South each year. As a result, many people have moved to the South to work in the hotels and resorts of the region.

Look at the line graph on page 365. How many more people were in the South in 1980 than in 1880? Now look at the table on this page. Which city was the largest in 1790? in 1880? Which city

1

Cultural Influences

French Cultural Influence in New Orleans

New Orleans was founded by the French in 1718. Many of the original French buildings have been saved. You can see them in an area called the French Quarter. These buildings often are built around courtyards. Many of the buildings, such as the one at the right, have fancy grillwork. Strict laws keep the buildings just the way French architects designed them.

French food is plentiful in the many fine restaurants and open-air cafés in the French Quarter. People work to keep the French culture very much alive in this southern city.

Citizenship Skill: Social participation. Invite someone to class to demonstrate French cooking, to explain a menu written in French, or to show slides of New Orleans.

1. About 37 million. Richmond; New Orleans.

Thinking Skill: Predicting. Discuss what the South might be like in the year 2000 if the population predictions are correct.
*** **Thinking Skill:** Synthesizing. Have students look again at the picture on page 365 and design a development for the year 2000.

Recent Populations of Selected Cities in the South				
City	1950 Population	1960 Population	1970 Population	1980 Population
Atlanta, Ga	331,314	487,455	496,973	425,022
Charlotte, NC	134,042	201,564	241,178	314,447
Memphis, TN	396,000	497,524	623,530	646,356
Miami, FL	249,276	291,688	334,859	346,931
New Orleans, LA	570,445	627,525	593,471	557,482
Richmond, VA	230,310	219,958	249,621	219,214

had the greatest increase in population between 1790 and 1880? between 1880 and 1980?

Use the tables on this page and 317 to compare the 1980 population of cities in the South with cities in the Northeast. Which region has more cities with a population over 500,000?

Recent Population Patterns

Study the table on this page that shows recent populations in selected cities. Which cities have had a population increase for each of the years listed? Which cities have had a population decrease? Compare this table with the table of recent populations in selected cities in the Northeast on page 317. Which region has more cities that have continued to grow?

A changing population. After World War I, many black people left the South. They went to northern cities looking for better jobs. During this same time, many of the blacks who stayed in the South moved from the rural areas to the cities. They, too, were seeking better job opportunities in the cities.

With more and more industries relocating in the South, many blacks are now moving to the South. In fact, some cities, such as Atlanta, Georgia, have more black people than white people.

In recent years many people from Cuba have also moved to the South. Most have settled in Florida. These people left their homeland to get away from the dictatorship of Fidel Castro. In 1980 more than 100,000 Cubans arrived in Florida.

Look again at the line graph that shows population growth in the South. How many people are expected to be living in the South by the year 2000? About how many more people will this be than in 1980?

Checking Up
1. When did the population of the South first start to increase greatly?
2. Name two groups who have added to the population of the South.
3. *Why is the South experiencing population growth today?*

1. New Orleans. Memphis.
2. The Northeast.
3. Charlotte, Memphis, and Miami. Atlanta, New Orleans, and Richmond. The South.
4. About 60 million people. About 10 million people.

367

Background: Pine forests are the source of a raw material used to make turpentine. Farmers drain the sap from their pine trees to sell to factories that make turpentine.
Reading Skill: Organizing Information. Have students make a bulletin-board display about the uses of trees.

What Do the People Do?

The economy of the South is changing. The South used to be a region where most of the people farmed, and cotton was "king." Agriculture is still important in the South. However, today business and industry are also important.

The Agricultural South

Fewer farm workers are needed today because of the use of modern farm machinery. Even with fewer people farming, the South is still a major producer of farm products.

North Carolina, Virginia, and Kentucky are the top tobacco-growing states in our country. Rice and soybeans are also important crops. Cotton is still grown in parts of the South. Today, however, much of the cotton grown in the United States is produced outside the South. Texas, for example, is a large cotton-growing state.

In Florida, citrus groves produce many of the country's oranges, grapefruit, lemons, and limes. Look at the chart on pages 372 and 373. Name four other crops that are grown in the South. 1

Some people raise cattle, especially in the inland parts of Florida. The most important animal for the southern farmer, however, is the chicken. Three out of four broiler chickens in the United States come from the South.

Southern forests are an important source of income. Some farmers lease their forest land to paper companies.

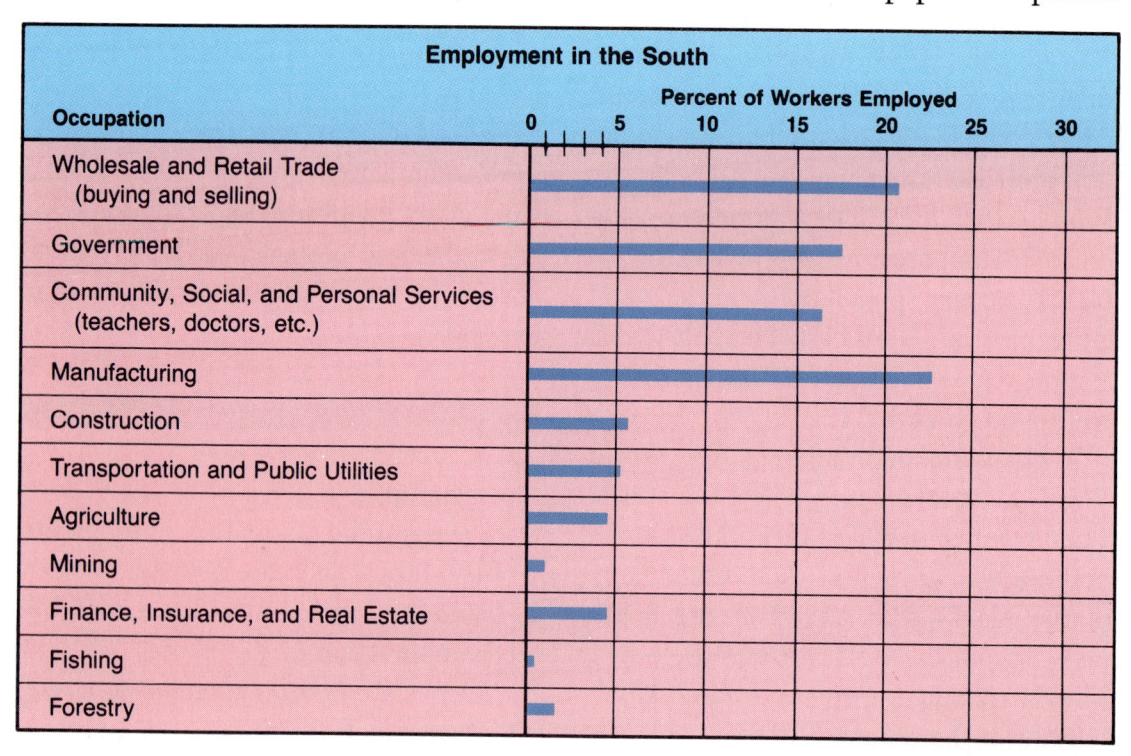

Employment in the South

Occupation	Percent of Workers Employed
Wholesale and Retail Trade (buying and selling)	~20
Government	~17
Community, Social, and Personal Services (teachers, doctors, etc.)	~16
Manufacturing	~22
Construction	~6
Transportation and Public Utilities	~6
Agriculture	~4
Mining	~1
Finance, Insurance, and Real Estate	~5
Fishing	<1
Forestry	<1

Time Skill: Have students make charts showing the steps involved, from planting to finished product, in producing some key farm products such as cotton.

1. Corn, peanuts, sugarcane, tomatoes, peaches, pecans, hay, or apples.

***Reading Skill:** Doing research. Several students could report on papermaking.
   1. About 5%; about 2%.
   2. About 15%; about 1%. Agriculture and forestry are not the largest employers or producers of goods in the South.

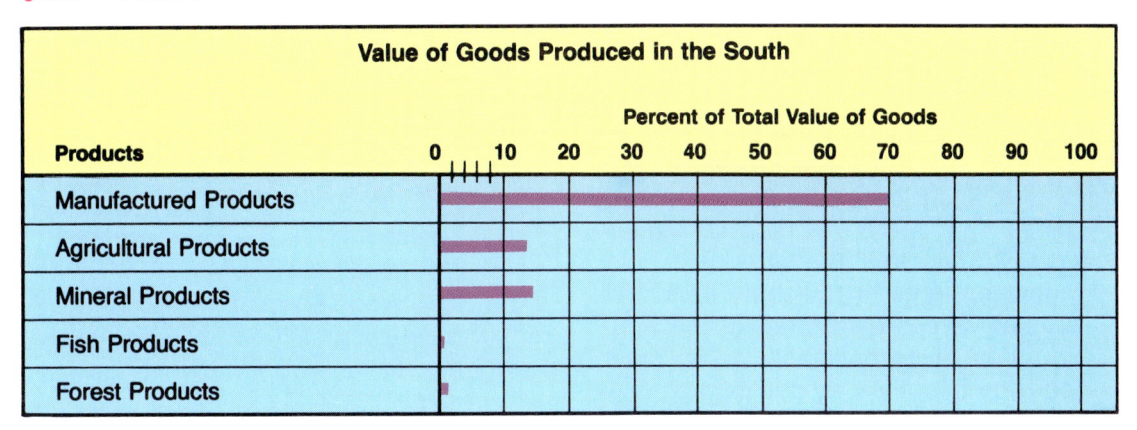

Value of Goods Produced in the South		
Products	Percent of Total Value of Goods 0 10 20 30 40 50 60 70 80 90 100	
Manufactured Products	~70%	
Agricultural Products	~15%	
Mineral Products	~15%	
Fish Products	<1%	
Forest Products	~1%	

The companies manage the land, cut the wood for pulp, and replant the trees.

1 Look at the bar graph of employment on page 368. What percent of the workers in the South are employed in agriculture? in forestry? Compare these figures to the graph of the value of goods on this page. What is the value of agricultural
2 products? of forest products? What connections can you make about the number of people in agriculture and in forestry and the value of agricultural and forest products?

The Industrial South

The South started to become more industrialized after the Civil War. The first factories were built along the fall line in the Piedmont. These were **textile,** or cloth-making, factories. The machines in the factories needed the power from the rivers that flowed over the rapids.

In the years after 1900, the South discovered its forests were a great source of wealth. Papermaking plants developed near the coastal areas where many pine trees grew. Furniture factories were built in the Appalachians and in the Piedmont. These areas grew the hardwood trees needed for making fine furniture.

The South also began to mine minerals. Coal was discovered in Kentucky, Virginia, and Alabama. In fact, Birmingham, Alabama, became a leading steel-producing city because large amounts of iron ore and coal are nearby.

Many people work in textile mills in the South. These workers are inspecting cloth in a textile mill in South Carolina.

369

Reading Skill: Listing. Have students make a list of occupations needed at Walt Disney World and the surrounding Orlando community.

Reading Skill: Recognizing propaganda. Have students look for ads about Walt Disney World and try to find examples of propaganda.

Careers

Where Some of the People Work

At the spot where Atlanta began, there was a single peach tree in a forest of pines. That peach tree became famous. Today Peachtree Street is a popular shopping area in Atlanta. Peachtree Center Complex, pictured at the right, includes office buildings, a big hotel, and the country's second largest merchandise mart.

Many people work at Walt Disney World in Orlando, Florida. In fact, Walt Disney World employs more of Orlando's people than any other employer. Many other jobs have been created by the hotels and restaurants that were built to serve visitors to Walt Disney World.

The Pentagon Building in Arlington, Virginia, is the headquarters of our country's Department of Defense. This building is the largest office building in the world. More than 26,000 people work here.

Communication Skill: Speaking. Students who prepared reports on these careers could give them.
Communication Skill: Listening. Establish a purpose for listening.

* **Reading Skill:** Determining meaning from context. Discuss the meanings of *distribution* and *financial centers.*
    1. The Mississippi River.
    2. Manufacturing. Wholesale and retail trade.

Present-day industries. Wood processing and furniture making are still major industries in the South. Much of the furniture made in the United States today comes from the rural areas of the South.

The textile industry of our country is centered in the South. There are many textile mills in small to medium-sized cities between southern Virginia and northern Georgia.

Recent oil and natural gas discoveries in Louisiana and off Louisiana's shore have led to a growing **petrochemical** industry. Petrochemical industries use oil and gas as chemical building blocks to make goods such as plastics, paints, and fertilizers.

Transportation centers. Industries often locate in cities near water because water transportation is inexpensive. These industries get raw materials and send off finished products by boat. Find Memphis, Baton Rouge, and New Orleans on the map on page 360. On what river are these cities located? These cities are transportation centers. The factories in the cities depend on inexpensive water transportation.

Some cities are located on ocean harbors. Find Mobile, Tampa, and Norfolk–Newport News on the map on page 360. These cities are also transportation centers and depend on oceangoing ships to transport goods to and from their factories and mills.

The business center of the South. Atlanta, Georgia, is the business center of the South today. Its good location for air and highway travel has helped Atlanta become the distribution center for the South. As a distribution center, Atlanta has factories and warehouses from which goods can be shipped throughout the South.

Businesses from all over the world have offices in Atlanta. Atlanta is also the financial center of the South. Large banks serve the needs of the many national and international companies in this region.

Look at the bar graph of employment on page 368. Which occupation employs the most people in the South? Which occupation has the second greatest number of people?

Checking Up
1. Why is the petrochemical industry growing in the South today?
2. What answers would you give to the key questions at the beginning of this unit?
3. *Why might the South continue to experience industrial growth?*

Unit 13 Summary
- The South today is a region that is growing and changing. Its population is increasing, and its economy is becoming more industrialized.
- The South still remains an important agricultural region. It produces crops that are not grown in many other parts of our country.

Thinking Skill: Analyzing. Discuss the importance of transportation centers.
Reading Skill: Interpreting visuals. Have students find three pictures to support each point in the unit summary.

FACTS ABOUT THE SOUTH

	Nickname	Capital* and Largest Cities	State Bird	Farm Products and Natural Resources	Manufactured Products	Did You Know This?
Alabama	The Yellowhammer State	Montgomery* Birmingham Mobile Huntsville Tuscaloosa	Yellowhammer	Cotton, corn, soybeans, peanuts, fruit, cattle, hogs, poultry, dairy products Coal, iron ore, timber, natural gas	Iron and steel, cement, fertilizer, chemicals, rubber, aluminum, lumber, textiles	Alabama Space and Rocket Center in Huntsville has the world's largest collection of missiles and space equipment.
Arkansas	Land of Opportunity	Little Rock* Fort Smith North Little Rock Pine Bluff Hot Springs	Mockingbird	Cotton, rice, soybeans, poultry, cattle Timber, petroleum, natural gas, coal, bauxite ore	Processed foods, lumber, paper products, chemicals, rubber, plastic products, clothing	Arkansas produces 97 percent of the country's supply of bauxite ore, the source of aluminum.
Florida	The Sunshine State	Tallahassee* Jacksonville Miami Tampa St. Petersburg	Mockingbird	Citrus fruits, sugarcane, tomatoes, soybeans, cattle, dairy products Limestone, phosphate rock, timber, seafood	Processed foods, chemicals, electronic equipment, lumber, paper products	*Apollo 11*, the first spacecraft to land men on the moon, was launched from Cape Canaveral, Florida, in 1969.
Georgia	Empire State of the South	Atlanta* Columbus Macon Savannah Albany	Brown Thrasher	Poultry, cattle, cotton, corn, soybeans, tobacco, peanuts, peaches, pecans Timber, marble, clays, granite	Textiles, processed foods, transportation equipment, pulp, paper products	Atlanta, Georgia, was the birthplace of Martin Luther King, Jr.
Kentucky	The Bluegrass State	Frankfort* Louisville Lexington Owensboro Covington	Kentucky Cardinal	Tobacco, horses, corn, dairy products, hogs, cattle, soybeans Coal, natural gas, petroleum	Tobacco products, machinery, iron and steel, processed foods, chemicals	The storehouse of our nation's gold, Fort Knox, is located in Kentucky.
Louisiana	The Pelican State	Baton Rouge* New Orleans Shreveport Lake Charles Lafayette	Pelican	Cattle, poultry, dairy products, cotton, rice, sugarcane, soybeans Petroleum, natural gas, salt, sulfur, timber, furs	Chemicals, petroleum, coal products, processed foods, pulp, paper products	In 1956 Louisiana opened the world's longest bridge, the Lake Pontchartrain Causeway.

	Nickname	Capital* and Largest Cities	State Bird	Farm Products and Natural Resources	Manufactured Products	Did You Know This?
Mississippi	The Magnolia State	Jackson* Biloxi Meridian Gulfport Greenville	Mockingbird	Cotton, soybeans, corn, rice, hay, cattle, dairy products Timber, shrimp, petroleum, natural gas	Lumber, furniture, paper, clothing, chemicals, processed foods, transportation equipment	A petrified forest near Flora, Mississippi, has giant stone trees that date back 30 million years.
North Carolina	The Tar Heel State	Raleigh* Charlotte Greensboro Winston-Salem Durham	Cardinal	Tobacco, corn, cotton, soybeans, cattle, hogs, vegetables, dairy products Timber, seafood, stone, clay	Textiles, pulp, paper products, clothing, steel, chemicals, machinery	North Carolina is our country's largest furniture producer.
South Carolina	The Palmetto State	Columbia* Charleston Greenville Spartanburg Rock Hill	Carolina Wren	Peaches, tobacco, cotton, peanuts, corn, soybeans, poultry, dairy products Timber, seafood, stone, clay	Textiles, pulp, paper products, clothing, steel, chemicals, machinery	In 1831 Charleston, South Carolina, became the first city in the nation to have a steam locomotive in service.
Tennessee	The Volunteer State	Nashville* Memphis Knoxville Chattanooga Clarksville	Mockingbird	Tobacco, cotton, soybeans, corn, cattle, dairy products Coal, marble, limestone, phosphate rock, zinc, timber	Chemicals, textiles, electrical machinery, processed foods, lumber	Nashville, Tennessee, has the world's only reproduction of the Parthenon, the ancient temple in Athens, Greece.
Virginia	The Old Dominion State	Richmond* Norfolk Arlington Virginia Beach Newport News	Cardinal	Tobacco, corn, hay, peanuts, soybeans, hogs, apples, dairy and poultry products Coal, lime, zinc, stone, seafood	Textiles, tobacco products, chemicals, lumber, paper products, furniture	Williamsburg, Virginia, a popular tourist attraction, has restored more than eighty of the city's original buildings to their appearance in the 1700s.

Communication Skill: Writing. Have students use this chart to write ten fact questions about states in the South. Have students exchange papers and answer the questions.

Unit 13 Review Workshop

What Have You Learned?

1. What is the most common landform in the South?
2. How do the growing seasons within the South vary?
3. What are two reasons for the population boom in the South?
4. What are three important agricultural crops of the South?
5. What are three important industries in the South today?
6. In what ways is Atlanta the business capital of the South?

Use Your Reading Skills

It is easier to understand ideas if you have details or facts to explain these ideas. Find details in this unit to explain or support the following major ideas.
1. The South is changing.
2. The South is a naturally rich area.

Use Your Map Skills

As you have learned, there are many different kinds of maps. Some maps, for example, use symbols to show such things as the farm crops of a region. The map at the right uses symbols to show places to visit in Florida. This map also shows some of the major highways and cities in Florida. Study the map key and then answer these questions:
1. What two cities have historical places to visit?
2. Walt Disney World and Sea World are near what city?
3. What interesting place could you visit in Sarasota? in Tampa?
4. What highways could you take to get from Orlando to Sarasota?
5. How many miles would you drive to get from Tampa to Orlando? from Tampa to Fort Myers? If you traveled at fifty miles per hour, how many hours would it take you to get from Tampa to Fort Myers?

Use Your Math Skills

As you remember from reading Unit 10, highlands are cooler than lowlands. Temperature drops about 3.6 °F (2 °C) for each 1,000 feet (300 m) of elevation.

Try to solve this problem. Assume the elevation at the foot of Mount Mitchell is 4,684 feet (1,405 m). Mount Mitchell is 6,684 feet (2,005 m) high. Now assume it is 80 °F (27 °C) at the foot of Mount Mitchell. What is the temperature at the top of Mount Mitchell?

Learn by Doing

1. Choose a state in the South other than Florida. Look in books and encyclopedias to find out about historical and interesting places to visit. You may also want to use a road atlas so you can include some of the major highways on your state map. Then draw a map using symbols to show these places.
2. Look up the word *petrochemical* in an encyclopedia. Find the products that

Reading Skill: Using details to support main ideas.
Thinking Skill: Knowing.
Map Skills: Location, symbolization, distance.
Math Skill.

Fun Places to Visit in Florida

- ■ Historical
  1. St. Augustine
  2. Thomas Edison Winter Home
- ▲ Scenic-Interesting
  3. Kennedy Space Center
  4. Disney World
  5. Sea World
  6. Cypress Gardens
  7. Busch Gardens
  8. Circus Hall of Fame
  9. Lion Country Safari
  10. Everglades National Park
  11. Florida Keys

are made from petrochemicals. Make a bulletin-board display by drawing pictures of these products.

3. Rayon and nylon are two important textiles produced in the South. Look in books and encyclopedias to find out how they are made. Draw diagrams to explain these processes. Use the diagrams to report to your class what you have learned.

4. Look through current magazines and newspapers to find out more about the South today. Take notes from what you have read. Organize your notes into topics such as people in the news, population changes in the South, industries of the South, and tourist attractions in the South. Use your notes to write a paragraph or two about each topic. Make a folder of your information to share with your class.

Read to Learn More

Find the topics listed below in the card catalog of your library. Read all or part of a book listed under one of the topics. Share what you learn with your classmates.

TEXTILES	EVERGLADES
SHENANDOAH VALLEY	NEW ORLEANS

Reading Skill: Using references: *Learn by Doing, 1,2,3,4* and *Read to Learn More.*
Thinking Skill: Classifying: *Learn by Doing, 4.*
Map Skill: Symbolization: *Learn by Doing, 1.*
Communication Skill: Writing: *Learn by Doing, 4.*

Unit Overview: This unit examines the Southwest region, its population density, and the major ways its people make a living.

Unit Objectives
To understand:
- the four states in this region
- how population density varies within this region
- the main ways people make a living in this region
- graphics

Skills Emphasized
Map Skills: pp. 376, 380, 385, 386.
Social Studies Reading Skills: pp. 376, 379, 381, 383, 384, 385, 388, 389, 390, 391.
Thinking Skills: pp. 376, 382, 385, 387, 388, 390.
Communication Skills: pp. 376, 384, 386, 387, 391.
Time Skill: p. 391.
Social Studies Math Skill: p. 390.
Citizenship Skills: pp. 376, 383, 388.

Suggested Materials
Workbook
Unit Tests

Unit 14

Suggested Student Activities
   1. Work in groups. Each group should make a movie roll on one of the four states in this region.
   2. Display newspaper and magazine articles about this region on a bulletin board.
   3. Add to the class data-retrieval chart.
 * 4. Work in small groups. Make product or resource displays on this region.
*** 5. Write reports on career topics listed on page 386.
 ** 6. Invite someone who has visited or lived in this region to speak to the class.

Skills Emphasized in Suggested Student Activities
Map Skill: Location.
Social Studies Reading Skills: Using references, organizing information, doing research.
Thinking Skills: Classifying, knowing, comparing.
Communication Skills: Writing, speaking, listening.
Citizenship Skill: Social participation.

The Southwest

This oil rig is off the Texas coast in the Gulf of Mexico. Workers live on some offshore oil rigs.

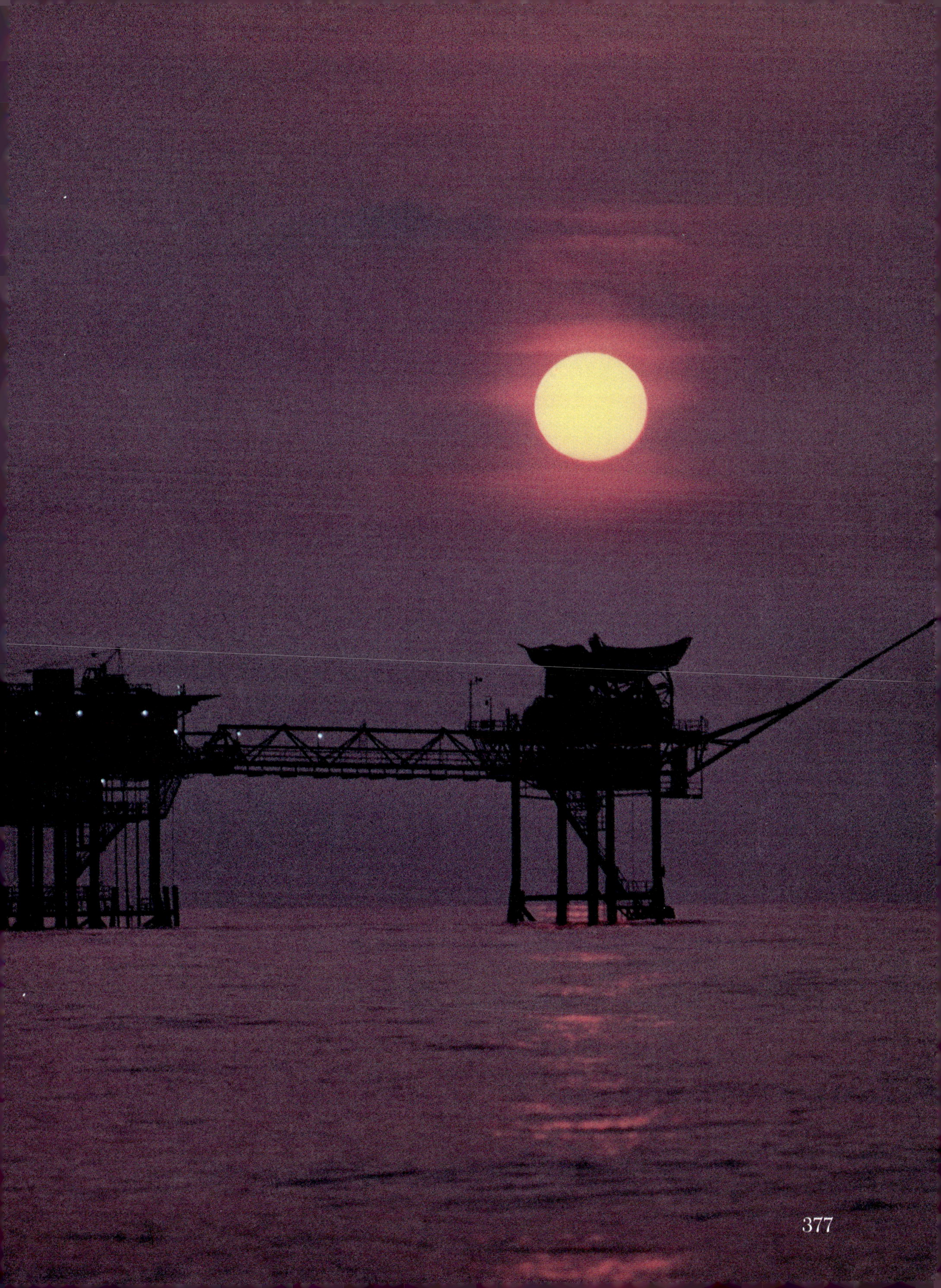

Region of the Southwest
Physical-Political Map

★ State Capitals   • Other Cities

SCALE
One inch—about 135 miles

Miles 0 50 100 150 200 250 300
Kilometers 0 50 100 200 300 400

HEIGHT OF LAND
- OVER 13,000 FEET
- 6,600 TO 13,000
- 3,300 TO 6,600
- 1,650 TO 3,300
- 650 TO 1,650
- 0 TO 650 FEET

DEPTH OF WATER
- 0 TO 600 FEET
- BELOW 600 FEET

Profile

Feet
12,000
10,000
8,000
6,000
4,000
2,000
Sea level

Texarkana — Lubbock — Rio Grande — Phoenix — Colorado River

Life on the Navajo Reservation in the Southwest has a mixture of the old and the modern.

history of the Southwest, Mexican immigrants have come to live in Texas, Arizona, and New Mexico. Most have come to this region with hopes of finding jobs and a better life.

The Mexican mark on the Southwest is unmistakable. You can find it everywhere, especially in the architecture, the food, and the language. In fact, Spanish is a commonly used language in the Southwest.

The Indian heritage of the Southwest. The influence of American Indians is also strong in the Southwest. Indian artists of several tribes in the Southwest craft beautiful jewelry, pottery, baskets, and weavings. People all over the United States treasure these examples of Indian culture. Many people attend festivals held on Indian reservations. You learned in an earlier unit that Oklahoma was a territory with many reservations for Indian tribes that had been removed from their homes in the East. Today Oklahoma has the largest Indian population of any state. The Navajo Indian Reservation in Arizona, New Mexico, and Utah is the country's largest reservation.

The influence of these two cultures, Mexican and Indian, helps to make the Southwest different from any other region in the United States.

Checking Up
1. Where are the areas of greatest population density in the Southwest?
2. What happened to the population of the Southwest's cities between 1950 and 1980?
3. *Why are many parts of the Southwest not as densely populated as the Gulf Coast of the Southwest?*

---

* **Reading Skill:** Using references. Have students look for pictures of Spanish architecture.
*** **Communication Skill:** Writing. Have students prepare reports on the Navajo, including posters showing Navajo pottery, jewelry, and other goods.

** **Reading Skill:** Listing. Have students name as many sources of water as they can.
*** **Reading Skill:** Organizing information. Have students make a montage of uses of water in the Southwest.

cook, and bathe, but farms and factories need water also. On the map on page 378, you can see that there are many rivers in the Southwest. These rivers, however, cannot meet people's needs for water. As a result, farms and many towns and cities drill wells to provide more water.

Look at the illustration of a well on this page. Find the **water table** in the illustration. The top of the underground area in which water has collected is called the water table. You can see that the well must be drilled below the water table to reach the water underground.

Unfortunately, the supply of water underground is limited. Many parts of the Southwest are using large amounts of this water. Growing cities like Phoenix and Albuquerque need more and more water for homes and businesses. As a result, more wells are drilled. As more wells are drilled and more water is pumped to the surface, the water table is lowered. As the water table drops, drilling becomes more expensive and water becomes less plentiful.

Even cities near the Gulf of Mexico don't always have enough fresh, or salt-free, water. They, too, must drill wells for fresh water. So even the area of the Southwest near the gulf faces the problem of a water shortage.

Farms and factories seem to need more and more water. Good supplies of clean, inexpensive water are a problem in many parts of the world. It is a problem that the Southwest is facing now.

A Region of Many Cultures

The Southwest is a region where many different kinds of people and cultures exist side by side. The different cultures give the Southwest a special atmosphere.

The Mexican heritage of the Southwest. You already know that most of the Southwest was part of Mexico until 1848. Many Americans in the Southwest have ancestors who lived in Texas, Arizona, and New Mexico when these states were a part of Mexico. Throughout the

What signs of the Mexican heritage do you see in this Texas city?

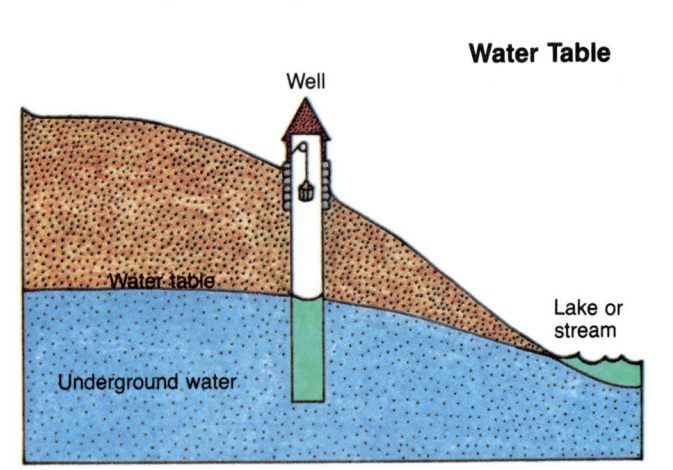

Water Table

Well
Water table
Lake or stream
Underground water

Reading Skill: Paraphrasing. Have students paraphrase the text that explains the diagram above.
Citizenship Skill: Social participation. Invite a Spanish speaker to teach the class some Spanish, such as signs, numbers, or greetings.

Thinking Skill: Analyzing. Talk about why this region is growing and list reasons in order of importance.

Thinking Skill: Comparing. Have students compare this region's predicted growth rate with your own region's.

Recent Populations of Selected Cities in the Southwest				
City	1950 Population	1960 Population	1970 Population	1980 Population
Dallas, TX	434,462	679,684	844,401	904,078
El Paso, TX	278,778	356,268	393,476	425,259
Fort Worth, TX	130,485	276,687	322,261	385,141
Houston, TX	596,163	938,219	1,232,802	1,594,086
Phoenix, AZ	108,818	439,170	581,562	764,911
San Antonio, TX	408,442	587,718	654,153	785,410

1. Look at the table on this page. Which cities had a population increase between 1950 and 1980? Which cities had a population decrease between 1950 and 1980? Which city's population went over 1,000,000 between 1960 and 1970?

2. The tremendous growth in population of the cities in this region is even more evident when compared with the population changes of cities in other regions. For example, the table on page 317 shows that most cities in the Northeast were losing people between 1950 and 1980. How many people left Baltimore between 1950 and 1980? How many people moved into San Antonio between 1950 and 1980?

3. Look at the pie graph on this page. Do more people live in urban or rural areas? The Southwest is largely a region of growing cities, but it also has many farms, ranches, and small towns.

4. The line graph on this page shows the population growth, both real and predicted, of the entire region from 1790 to 2000. When did the greatest growth in population occur? What is the predicted population growth between the years of 1980 and 2000?

Urban and Rural Population of the Southwest

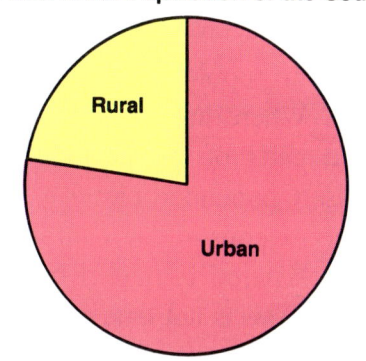

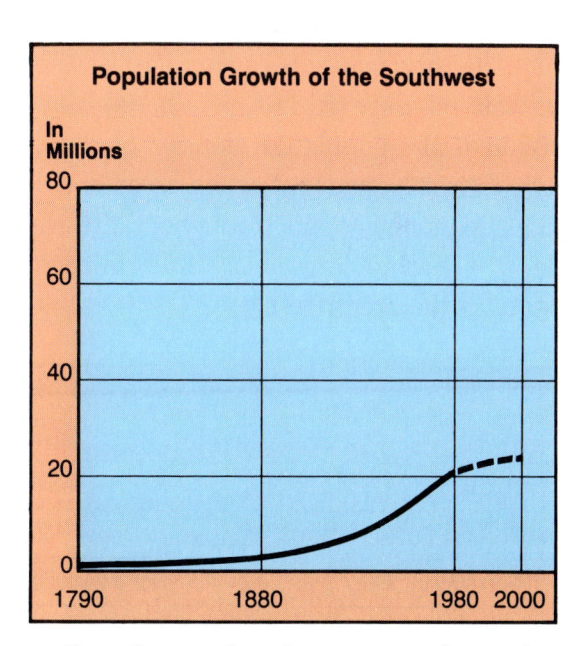

Population Growth of the Southwest

One factor that limits growth in the Southwest is the availability of water. Not only do people need water to drink,

1. All of them. None of them. Houston.
2. 162,933 people. 376,968 people.
3. Urban areas.
4. Between 1880 and 1980. Between 3 and 5 million people.

> **Reading Skill:** Skimming for information. What data are provided in this chapter besides the text to help answer the question, Where are the people?
> **Reading Skill:** Reading for detail. Have students list five facts about where the people live.
> 1. 16,513 people. Houston. 1,594,086 people.

Where Are the People?

In 1945, after World War II, a steady stream of newcomers started moving to the Southwest. At the same time, there was a large increase in population, a population boom, all over the United States. These two facts changed the population patterns in the cities and towns of the Southwest.

Where the People Live

Look at the population density map on this page. Where are the most densely populated parts of the Southwest? the least densely populated parts?

In many regions of the United States, cities are clustered in one or two rather small areas. This is not true in the Southwest. Find the cities of Phoenix, Arizona, and San Antonio, Texas, on your population density map. Use your map of the region on page 378 if you need help. What is the population density of these two cities? Notice that urban areas in the Southwest are found throughout the region. There are large, busy cities in each state in the Southwest.

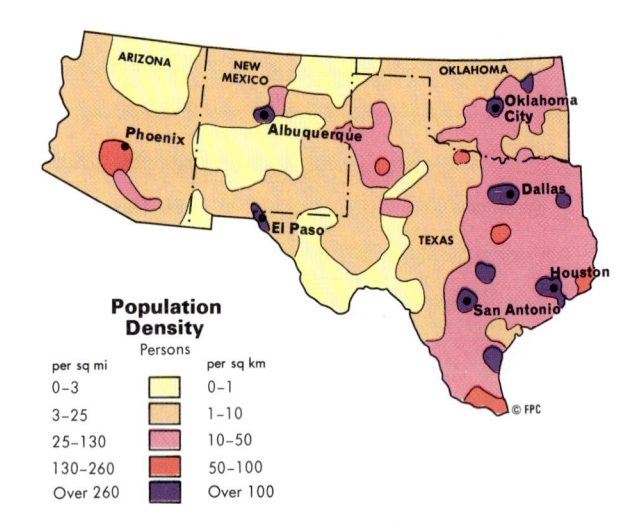

The cities of the Southwest. You have already learned that some of the cities in the Southwest are as old as, or even older than, cities in the Northeast and South. However, their growth in size is more recent. Look at the table on this page. What was the population of Dallas in 1880? in 1980? Which city has had the largest population increase since 1880? What was this city's population in 1980? What was the population increase in Phoenix between 1880 and 1980?

Population Growth of Selected Cities in the Southwest			
City	1790 Population	1880 Population	1980 Population
Dallas, TX	Not Available	16,513	904,078
El Paso, TX	Under 700	736	425,259
Fort Worth, TX	Not Available	6,663	385,141
Houston, TX	Not Available	10,358	1,594,086
Phoenix, AZ	Not Available	Not Available	764,911
San Antonio, TX	Under 700	20,550	785,410

Population Density

per sq mi	per sq km
0–3	0–1
3–25	1–10
25–130	10–50
130–260	50–100
Over 260	Over 100

* **Map Skill:** Symbolization. Review the meaning of the symbols on the growing seasons map.
   Map Skill: Scale. Have students make their own growing seasons map. Show them how to square off the paper to triple the map's size.

Landforms of the Southwest

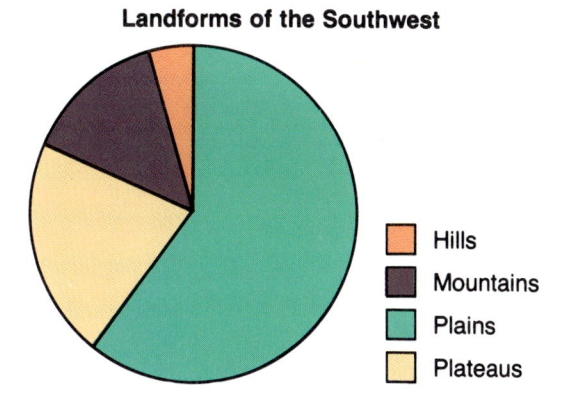

- Hills
- Mountains
- Plains
- Plateaus

Use these graphs to discover which place receives more precipitation in an average year. What is the difference in average temperature between Houston and Flagstaff in January? in July? Which place is warmer during an average year?

Use the map on page 378 to find Houston and Flagstaff. How does the Gulf of Mexico influence the climate of Houston? On what landform is Flagstaff located? How might this landform influence Flagstaff's climate?

Like Houston, much of eastern Texas and parts of eastern Oklahoma benefit from the moist air that blows in from the Gulf of Mexico. However, dry winds from the desert areas of northern Mexico blow across western Texas and Oklahoma, New Mexico, and Arizona.

The growing seasons. Look at the map on this page. How many different growing seasons are there in the Southwest? How long is each one? Where are the areas with the longest growing seasons? Why? Where are the areas with the shortest growing seasons? Why?

Houston, Texas

Average Monthly Temperature
Average Monthly Precipitation

Flagstaff, Arizona

Average Monthly Temperature
Average Monthly Precipitation

Growing Seasons
In Months
- Less than 3
- 3 to 5
- 5 to 7
- 7 to 9
- 9 to 12

© FPC

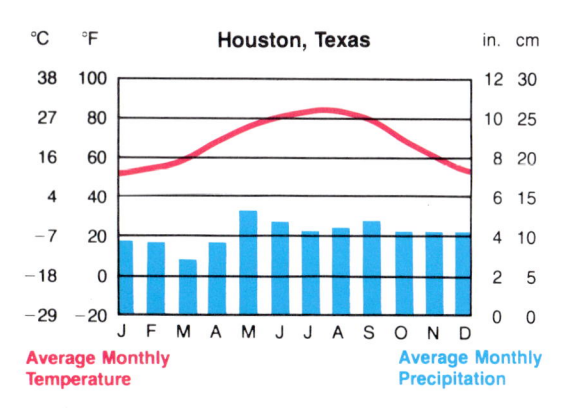

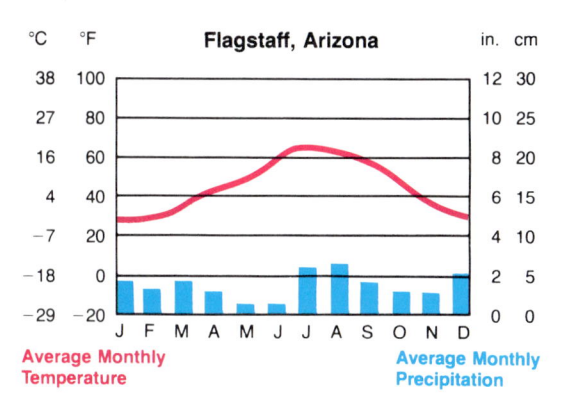

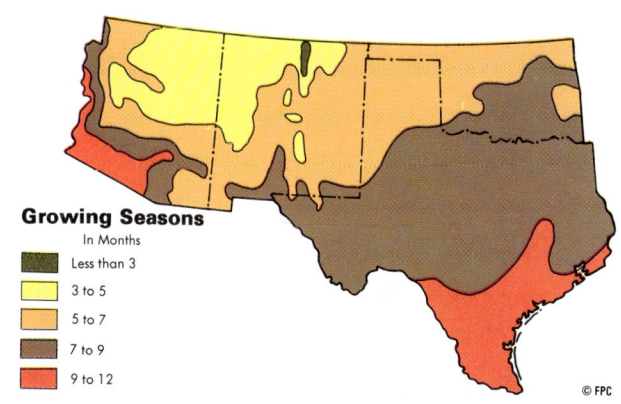

Checking Up

1. What differences in climate are there in the Southwest?
2. What effect does the Gulf of Mexico have on the climate of the Southwest?
3. *Why do growing seasons within the Southwest vary?*

1. About 20 degrees; about 20 degrees. Houston.
2. Houston receives much rainfall as a result of its location near the Gulf of Mexico.

Reading Skill: Using textbook features: As You Read, 3.
1. Ariz. (Phoenix), N.M. (Santa Fe), Tex. (Austin), and Okla. (Oklahoma City).
2. Mexico. 3. Plains.
Background: All four states of the Southwest are in the sunbelt.

Where Is the Southwest?

As You Read This Unit

1. Think about these words.
    water table   irrigation
2. Look for answers to these key questions.
    a. In what ways does the climate of the Southwest vary?
    b. How does population density within the Southwest vary?
    c. What products of the Southwest are important to the rest of the country?
3. Use this reading skill.
    The Index of your book is an important tool. It lists, in alphabetical order, the topics in this book. Turn to the Index on pages 495–510. Find the listings for the Mexican War. Read these pages before you read this unit. How did this war change the future of the Southwest?

A trip to the Southwest would take you through four states: Texas, Oklahoma, New Mexico, and Arizona. You would see giant cacti, cotton fields, oil wells, and large cities.

The Region

Look at the four states of the Southwest on the map on page 378. Find the capital of each state. Use the map scale to find out about how many miles the Southwest measures from east to west, then from the northern border of Oklahoma to the southern tip of Texas. What country borders the Southwest?

The Land

Look at the profile at the bottom of the map on page 378. Compare the elevation of Phoenix, Arizona, with the elevation of Texarkana, Texas. How do the elevations of the land change between these two places?

Although there is not a great difference in elevation between Phoenix and Texarkana, you can see that the Southwest does have a wide variety of landforms. Use your height-of-land key on page 378 and find the location of mountains in the Southwest.

Look at the pie graph on page 380. What is the most common landform in the Southwest?

The Climate

Although the climate of the Southwest is generally warm, there is much variation. The graphs on page 380 show the average monthly temperatures and precipitation for Flagstaff and Houston.

379

*** **Reading Skill:** Doing research. Have students report on the production of petroleum and natural gas.
Map Skill: Location. Have students name cities located near the oil and gas fields.
1. Tex. and Okla.; Tex., Okla., and New Mexico.
2. The Southwest; the Northeast.

What Do the People Do?

Although there are only four states in the Southwest, this region is very important. Other regions depend on the special products of the Southwest.

A Region of Energy

The United States uses a tremendous amount of energy. We need energy to run our cars, buses, trains, and airplanes. We need energy to heat and light our homes and factories. All of us depend on energy.

Two of this country's most important energy resources are petroleum and natural gas. Look at the map on this page. It shows the major deposits of petroleum and natural gas. Which two states in the Southwest are rich in petroleum? in natural gas? Compare the number of petroleum and natural gas deposits in the Southwest with the number of petroleum and natural gas deposits in the Northeast and the Great Lakes regions. Which region has the largest number of deposits? the fewest?

Deposits of petroleum and natural gas are not evenly spread throughout the Southwest. Texas and Oklahoma have more petroleum deposits than Arizona and New Mexico.

Cities have grown near the petroleum and gas fields. People in these cities work to refine and process the fuels. Other people work to make chemicals from the fuels. These chemicals are used to make plastics, paint, and fertilizers.

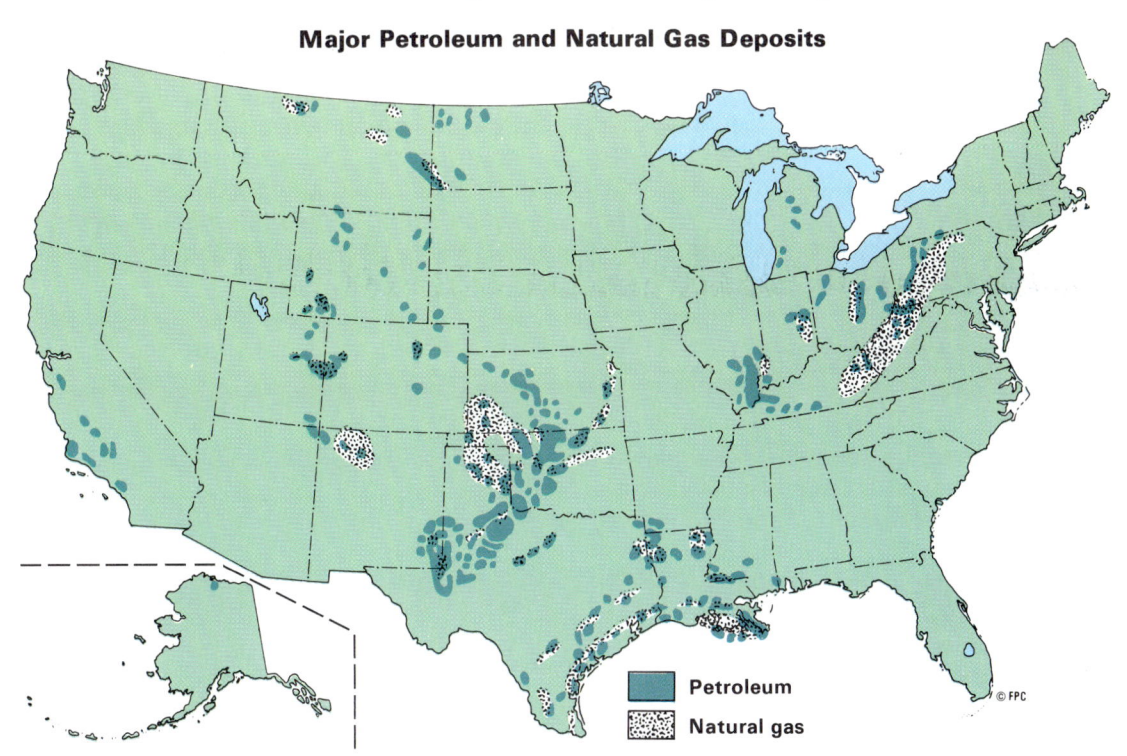

Major Petroleum and Natural Gas Deposits

■ Petroleum
▨ Natural gas

Thinking Skill: Knowing. Have students list uses for natural gas and petroleum.

385

Background: Many members of the Organization of Petroleum Exporting Countries (OPEC) sell oil to the United States. OPEC members are Algeria, Ecuador, Gabon, Indonesia, Iran, Iraq, Kuwait, Libya, Nigeria, Qatar, Saudi Arabia, the United Arab Emirates, and Venezuela.
Map Skill. Location. Have students locate the countries that belong to OPEC.

Since the 1960s, energy needs have grown so much that the United States must buy petroleum and natural gas from other countries. Since factories for refining and processing these fuels already exist in many cities in the Southwest, much foreign petroleum and natural gas is shipped here to be processed and refined. The large shipments of petroleum to this region have made many cities, like Houston, important international trade centers.

Careers

Where Some of the People Work

Scientists working at the Lyndon B. Johnson Space Center in Houston, directed the first landing of men on the moon in 1969. In fact, this space center is the headquarters for all flights carrying astronauts into space. Astronauts receive much of their training here. Scientists design and test spacecraft here. The Lyndon B. Johnson Space Center is one of the most important parts of the National Aeronautics and Space Administration (NASA).

The Los Alamos Scientific Laboratory in Los Alamos, New Mexico, is one of the most important centers in the field of nuclear energy. The scientists in the picture might be adapting nuclear power for public use. Locate Los Alamos near Santa Fe on the map on page 378.

The photo at right shows how important oil is to the economy of the state of Oklahoma and to Oklahoma City. Workers drill for oil right on the grounds of the state capitol building. There is a large oil field under Oklahoma City. Oil is such a valuable fuel that there are many oil wells throughout the city. Oklahoma City is one of the centers of oil production in the United States.

*** **Communication Skill:** Speaking. Have students give their reports on careers.
Communication Skill: Listening. Review rules for being a good listener.

*** **Communication Skill:** Writing. Have several students prepare a visual report on uranium.
** **Thinking Skill:** Comparing. Have students make a chart that compares products made in the Southwest and the Northeast.

Value of Goods Produced in the Southwest

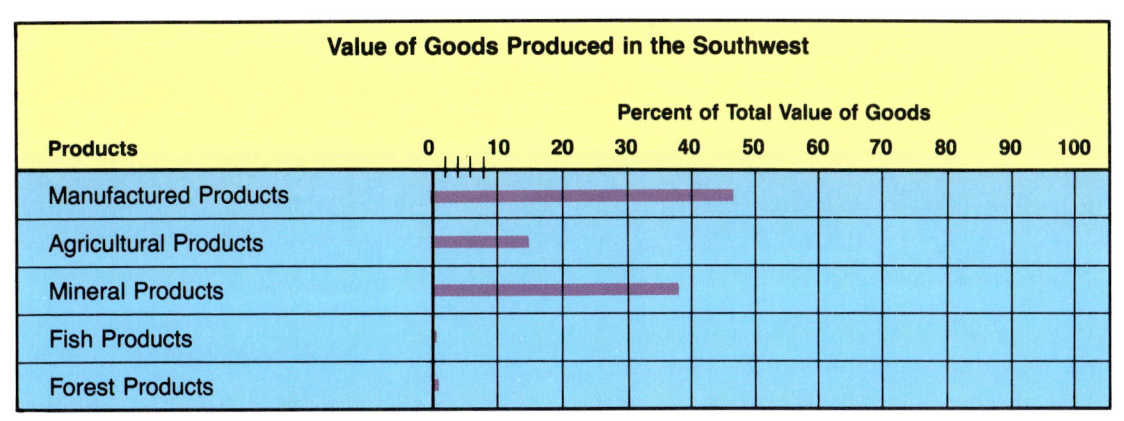

Products	Percent of Total Value of Goods (0–100)
Manufactured Products	~45%
Agricultural Products	~10%
Mineral Products	~40%
Fish Products	~0%
Forest Products	~1%

Other energy resources. The importance of the Southwest to the energy future of this country also involves other resources. You saw on the map on page 385 that New Mexico is rich in natural gas. In addition, New Mexico produces about half the uranium ore mined in the United States. Uranium is used in nuclear power plants. Many cities throughout the country depend on nuclear power plants for electricity to heat and light homes and factories.

The list of energy resources in the Southwest does not end with uranium. There are also rich deposits of coal in each state. The mining of this coal may become more important as energy needs continue to grow.

1 Look at the bar graph of the value of goods on this page. What percent of the total value of goods is mineral products? Compare this with the figure for mineral products in the Northeast on page 319. What does your comparison tell you?

An Agricultural Region

The agriculture of the Southwest is almost as important to the rest of the country as its energy resources are. There is a remarkable variety in the kinds of farming in this region. The types and the sizes of the farms depend on their location in the region.

The farms in the eastern part. You learned earlier that the eastern part of the Southwest gets more precipitation than the western part. The crops farmers grow depend in part on the amount of rainfall. Farmers near the wet Gulf Coast grow rice, sugarcane, and citrus fruits, such as oranges and grapefruits. The farming in the eastern parts of Texas and Oklahoma is much like farming in the South. Crops such as corn, alfalfa, barley, and oats are important

Using irrigation pumps, farmers grow crops in dry areas of the Southwest.

Thinking Skill: Observing. What can be learned about irrigation from the photograph and caption above?
1. About 40%. Mineral products play a major role in the Southwest economy compared with the Northeast's. The Northeast uses many mineral products from the Southwest.

> **Citizenship Skill:** Social participation. Invite an older person who has lived in or visited the Southwest to class.
>
> **Thinking Skill:** Observing. Have students look for products from this region in grocery stores.

here. Beef cattle are raised here, as they are elsewhere in the Southwest.

The farms in the western part. Precipitation falls off the farther west one goes in the Southwest. In western and central Oklahoma, there is still enough rainfall to grow large crops of winter wheat. Central and western Texas have vast rangelands where millions of beef cattle graze. In fact, Texas leads the country in the number of beef cattle raised. Where possible, farmers use **irrigation** to grow feed grains and cotton. Irrigation is a system of supplying land with water by using ditches or sprinklers.

Irrigation from rivers and from deep wells has greatly increased farm production in Arizona, west Texas, and New Mexico. Most of the land in these states is too dry for farming. With the water from irrigation, however, farmers in these states can grow cotton, fruits, vegetables, and feed grains for their beef cattle. Texas grows more cotton than any other state. The melons you see in your supermarket might well have come from one of the irrigated farms in the dry parts of the Southwest.

The Attraction of the Southwest

The Southwest is a growing region. People are moving here for many reasons. Certainly the warm, sunny weather is a major attraction. Thousands of retired people have left their homes in colder parts of the United States to buy or rent homes in Arizona, New Mexico, and the Rio Grande valley of Texas.

The pleasant weather also attracts businesses. Look at the bar graph of employment on this page. What kind of business employs the most people? the [1]

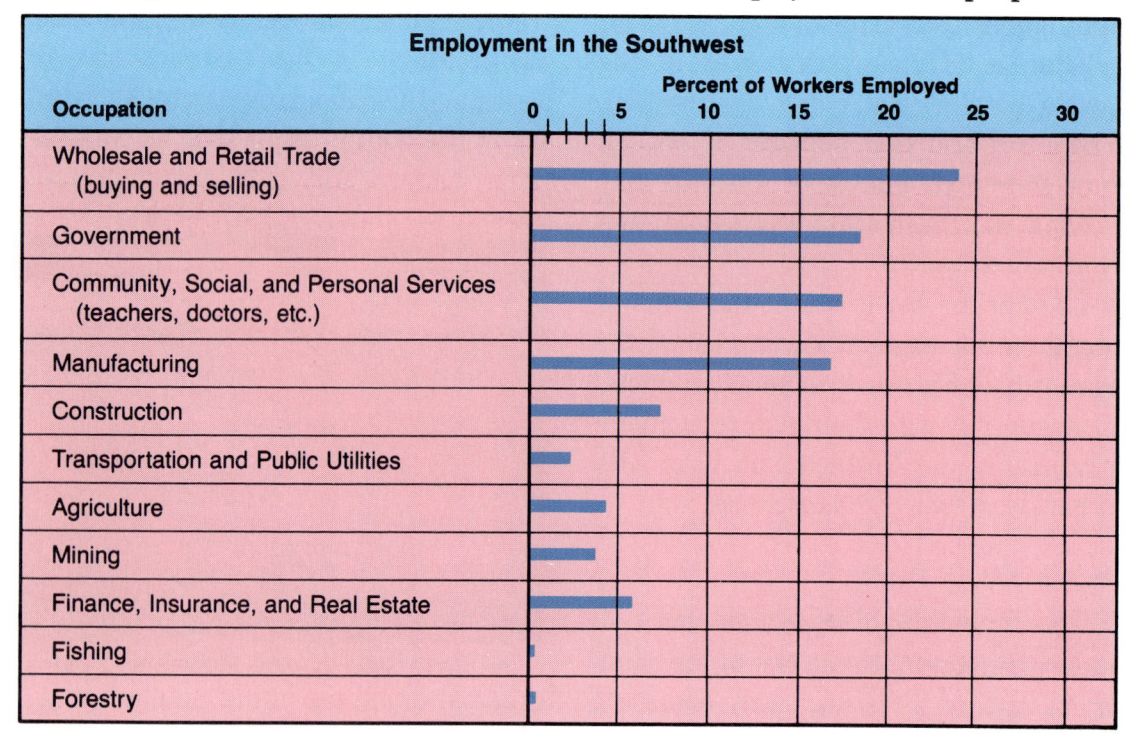

Employment in the Southwest

Occupation	Percent of Workers Employed
Wholesale and Retail Trade (buying and selling)	~23
Government	~18
Community, Social, and Personal Services (teachers, doctors, etc.)	~17
Manufacturing	~16
Construction	~7
Transportation and Public Utilities	~5
Agriculture	~5
Mining	~4
Finance, Insurance, and Real Estate	~6
Fishing	<1
Forestry	<1

> **Reading Skill:** Listing. Have students record reasons for people's moving to this region.
> 1. Wholesale and retail trade.

FACTS ABOUT THE SOUTHWEST

	Nickname	Capital* and Largest Cities	State Bird	Farm Products and Natural Resources	Manufactured Products	Did You Know This?
Arizona	The Grand Canyon State	Phoenix* Tucson Mesa Tempe Scottsdale	Cactus Wren	Cattle, cotton, dairy products, hay, wheat Copper, molybdenum, sand, gravel, silver	Machinery, electrical equipment, metals	London Bridge didn't fall down. It was torn down, sent to Lake Havasu City, Arizona, and rebuilt in 1971.
New Mexico	Land of Enchantment	Santa Fe* Albuquerque Las Cruces Roswell Clovis	Roadrunner	Cattle, hay, dairy products, cotton, corn Petroleum, natural gas, copper, uranium	Processed foods, electronic equipment, chemicals	The oldest road in the United States, el Camino Real, is in New Mexico. The road is now part of Highway 85.
Oklahoma	The Sooner State	Oklahoma City* Tulsa Lawton Norman Midwest City	Scissor-tailed flycatcher	Cattle, hay, dairy products, cotton Petroleum, natural gas, coal	Machinery, processed foods, metals, refined oil	Oklahoma has the largest Indian population of any state in the nation.
Texas	The Lone Star State	Austin* Houston Dallas San Antonio El Paso	Mockingbird	Cattle, cotton, dairy products, corn, hay Petroleum, natural gas, sulfur, seafood	Chemicals, refined oil, machinery, electronic equipment	The headquarters of the National Aeronautics and Space Administration (NASA) is in Houston, Texas.

¹fewest people? About what percent of the people work in manufacturing? The number of people working in manufacturing and wholesale and retail trade will probably grow for many reasons. Many businesses have moved to the Southwest because heating costs are lower here than in most parts of the country. The abundance of energy resources also attracts many businesses. Like any other region in the country, the Southwest faces challenges in its future.

Checking Up
1. What has helped the dry areas of the Southwest become important agricultural areas?
2. What answers would you give to the key questions at the beginning of this unit?
3. *What challenges does the Southwest face in the future?*

Unit 14 Summary
- The population of the Southwest is growing rapidly, particularly in the urban areas.
- Water is scarce throughout much of the Southwest. Irrigation and deep wells are important to the farms and businesses of this region.
- The Southwest is rich in many energy resources, especially petroleum, natural gas, and uranium.

1. Fishing or forestry. About 17%.
Reading Skill: Organizing information. Have students make "Concentration" cards for some facts listed above, putting clues on some cards and the corresponding states on others.

Unit 14 Review Workshop

What Have You Learned?

1. How do precipitation patterns differ within the Southwest? Why?
2. How has the location of the Southwest made it a region of many different cultures?
3. What has happened to the population of the Southwest's cities since 1950?
4. Why is the water table in many parts of the Southwest dropping?
5. Name the energy resources that are found in the Southwest. In which states are they found?
6. How has irrigation affected agriculture in the Southwest?

Use Your Reading Skills

One of the most useful reading skills you can have is the ability to summarize, or put important information in a shorter form. In a chapter of this unit, you read a section about farming in the eastern part of the Southwest and another section about farming in the western part. Try to summarize each section in a paragraph or in a sentence of your own. Compare your two summaries with those of your classmates. What do you think makes a good summary? Writing summaries makes you decide what the important facts in a reading selection are.

Use Your Thinking Skills

You have learned in this unit that parts of the Southwest, like the area around Phoenix, receive very little precipitation. Suppose, though, that suddenly there was a major change in precipitation patterns. Suppose that suddenly Phoenix received as much precipitation as Houston. Turn back to page 380 to see how much precipitation Houston receives in an average year. How would the increase in precipitation affect the Phoenix area in terms of the following: the types of crops grown? the problems of a dropping water table? the movement of retired people to the Phoenix area? the tourist industry?

Use Your Math Skills

Sometimes the easiest way to read information is from a table. Tables often are helpful in presenting information about the number of people or things. The table on page 391 shows the population of the twenty largest American Indian reservations in the United States. Read the table carefully and then answer these questions.

1. Which of the reservations has the most people? Where is this reservation located?
2. Which of the reservations are located in Oklahoma? What is the total population of these reservations?
3. Which state in the Southwest doesn't have a reservation listed in this table?
4. Not counting the Navajo Reservation, how many of the reservations in this table are in Arizona? What is the total population of these reservations?

Reading Skills: Summarizing, interpreting a table.
Thinking Skills: Knowing, comparing, analyzing.

Recent Populations of Largest Indian Reservations					
Navaho (Ariz., N.M., Utah)	154,748	Papago (Ariz.)	10,542	Hopi (Ariz.)	7,177
Creek (Okla.)	26,562	Osage (Okla.)	10,499	Standing Rock (N.D., S.D.)	6,957
Cherokee (Okla.)	23,500	Yakima (Wash.)	9,802	Chickasaw (Okla.)	6,800
Southern Pueblos (N.M.)	20,080	Gila River (Ariz.)	8,777	Wind River (Wyo.)	6,742
Choctaw (Okla.)	17,313	Turtle Mountain (N.D.)	7,850	Blackfeet (Mont.)	6,269
Pine Ridge (S.D.)	12,260	Fort Apache (Ariz.)	7,706	Zuni (N.M.)	6,266
Rosebud (S.D.)	12,186			San Carlos (N.M.)	5,979

5. Not counting the Navajo Reservation, how many reservations in this table are in New Mexico? What is the total population of these reservations?

6. What is the total population of the reservations in the Southwest listed in this table? Be sure to include the population of the Navajo Reservation.

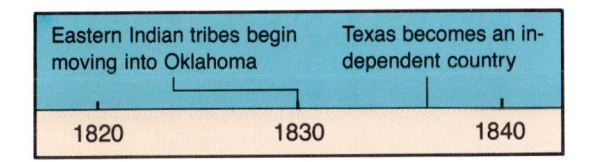

```
| Eastern Indian tribes begin | Texas becomes an in- |
| moving into Oklahoma       | dependent country    |
|          |          |          |
| 1820     | 1830     | 1840     |
```

Learn by Doing

1. Make a time line like the one that appears here. Your time line, however, should cover all the years between 1820 and 1980. The divisions on your time line should be spaced one half inch apart. Each division should stand for ten years. Put a mark in the right space for each of the following events. Write above the mark what event took place that year. Or, draw a picture of the event over the right mark on your time line.

    1820 Eastern Indian tribes begin moving into Oklahoma

    1836 Texas becomes an independent country

    1848 Mexico sells much of what is now the Southwest to the United States.

    1861 Civil War begins

    1901 Opening of Spindletop, Texas's first major oil field

    1912 Arizona becomes 48th state

    1945 First atomic bomb exploded in New Mexico

    1969 American astronauts, directed by NASA headquarters in Houston, land on the moon.

2. The Hopi Indians of Arizona are famous for their Kachina dolls. These dolls are both playthings and ways to learn about Hopi culture. Prepare a report about the Kachina dolls.

Read to Learn More

Find the topics listed below in the card catalog of your library. Read all or part of a book listed under one of the topics. Share what you learn with your classmates.

MEXICAN AMERICANS   PETROLEUM
ATOMIC ENERGY   GRAND CANYON

Reading Skills: Organizing information: *Learn by Doing, 1*; using references, reading widely: *Learn by Doing, 1* and *Read to Learn More.*
Time Skill: *Learn by Doing, 1.*
Communication Skill: Writing: *Learn by Doing, 2.*

Unit Overview: This unit examines the Interior West region, its population density, and the main occupations of the people who live there.

Unit Objectives
To understand:
- the six states in this region
- how population density varies in this region
- the main ways people make a living in this region
- graphics

Skills Emphasized
Map Skills: pp. 392, 406, 407.
Social Studies Reading Skills: pp. 392, 395, 399, 401, 402, 403, 406.
Thinking Skills: pp. 392, 395, 397, 399, 402, 404, 406.
Communication Skills: pp. 392, 400, 403, 404, 406, 407.
Time Skill: p. 399.
Social Studies Math Skill: p. 401.
Citizenship Skills: pp. 401, 407.

Suggested Materials
Workbook
Unit Tests

Suggested Student Activities
1. Work in groups. Each group should make a large wall map on one of the six states in this region.
2. Display newspaper and magazine articles about this region on a bulletin board.
3. Add to the class data-retrieval chart.
4. Write reports on career topics listed on page 403.
* 5. Make product or resource displays on this region.
*** 6. Report on national parks in this region. Include posters.

Skills Emphasized in Suggested Student Activities
Map Skills: Location, symbolization.
Social Studies Reading Skills: Using references, doing research, organizing information.
Thinking Skills: Knowing, classifying, comparing.
Communication Skills: Speaking, writing, listening.

Unit 15

The Interior West

Denver's location in the spectacular Rocky Mountains attracts people and businesses to the city.

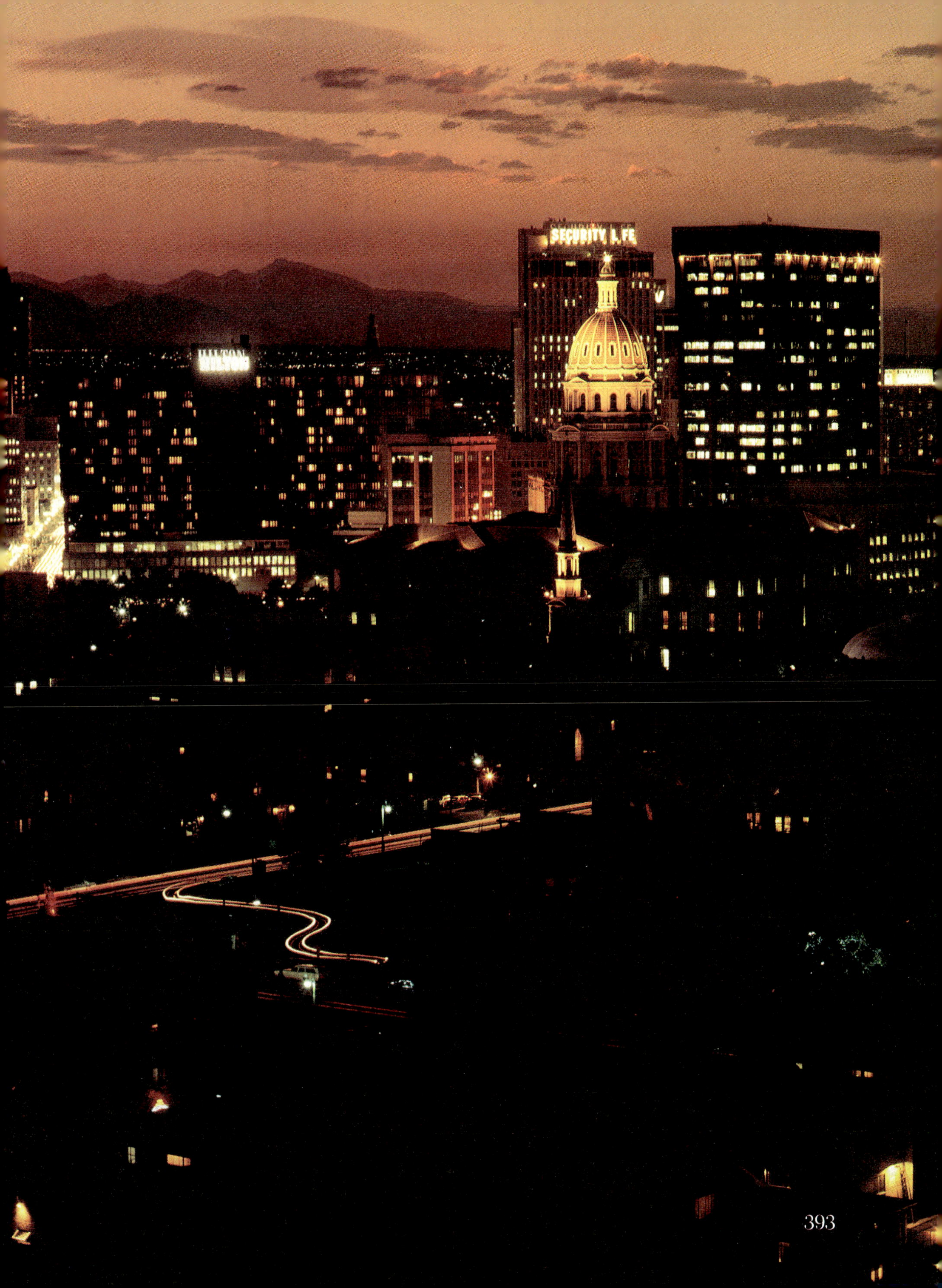
SECURITY LIFE

Region of the Interior West

Physical-Political Map

★ State Capitals   ● Other Cities

SCALE
One inch—about 150 miles

Miles: 0 50 100 150 200 250 300
Kilometers: 0 50 100 200 300 400

HEIGHT OF LAND
- OVER 13,000 FEET
- 6,600 TO 13,000
- 3,300 TO 6,600
- 1,650 TO 3,300
- 650 TO 1,650
- 0 TO 650 FEET

DEPTH OF WATER
- 0 TO 600 FEET
- BELOW 600 FEET

Profile

Reno — Great Basin — Wasatch Range — Green River — Park Range — Front Range — Denver

(Feet: Sea level, 2,000, 4,000, 6,000, 8,000, 10,000, 12,000)

394

Reading Skill: Discovering cause and effect: *As You Read*, 3.
1. Nev. (Carson City), Idaho (Boise), Mont. (Helena), Wyo. (Cheyenne), Utah (Salt Lake City), and Colo. (Denver). Idaho and Mont.

Where Is the Interior West?

As You Read This Unit

1. Think about these words.
   Continental Divide   arid   technology   oil shale
2. Look for answers to these key questions.
   a. Which six states make up the Interior West?
   b. Why is the Interior West so sparsely populated?
   c. What are three major ways in which people make a living in the Interior West?
3. Use this reading skill.
   Discovering the relationship between cause and effect can help you better understand why certain things happen. Causes are the reasons certain things happen. Effects are the results of the causes. As you study this unit, look for the causes of these recent developments, or effects, in the Interior West.
   a. an increasing population
   b. recent mining of new natural resources
   c. growth of manufacturing

The Interior West is a region of wide-open spaces and rugged scenic beauty. It has towering, snow-capped mountains, giant glaciers, thick evergreen forests, and vast deserts and plains. Because of the scenery, the Interior West is also a region of many national forests, parks, and wildlife preserves.

Today the Interior West is undergoing growth and change. Lying beneath the lands of the region are treasures of natural resources such as coal and oil. Many of these natural resources are being developed at a rate that is bringing rapid and drastic changes to the Interior West and its people.

The Region

The Interior West is made up of six states. Look at the map on page 394. What are the names of the six states in the region? What is the capital of each state? Which states share a border with Canada? Use the map scale on page 394 to find out about how many miles the region stretches in a north-south direction. How far does the region stretch in an east-west direction?

The Land

Look at the profile on page 394. Find Reno and Denver. What is the difference in elevation between these two

Thinking Skill: Knowing. Ask whether students have ever visited one of our national parks.

395

1. Because most of the land is either mountains or high plateaus.
2. Mountains; hills.
3. Idaho, Mont., Wyo., Utah, and Colo.

places? Study the profile on page 328. Compare the profile of Rock Island and Cleveland with that of Reno and Denver. Why is the land of the Interior West often described as rugged?

Now look at the pie graph below. Which is the most common landform in the region? the least common?

The mountains. Find the Rocky Mountains on the map on page 394. In which states are the Rocky Mountains located? The Rocky Mountains are the highest and longest mountain range in our country. Find Pikes Peak on the map on page 394. What is its elevation? Use the map on page 360 to compare the elevation of Pikes Peak with the elevation of Mount Mitchell, the highest mountain in the Appalachian Mountains. What is the difference in elevation between the two places?

The Continental Divide. The **Continental Divide** separates our country's waterways. The highest land along the Rocky Mountains is called the Continental Divide. Precipitation that falls along the eastern side of the Continental Divide flows toward the Atlantic Ocean. Precipitation that falls along the western side of the divide flows toward the Pacific Ocean.

The Rocky Mountains are the source of many of our country's major rivers. Use the map on page 394 to find the sources of the Missouri, the Platte, and the Arkansas rivers. Now find the Colorado and Snake rivers. Use the map on page 394 to trace the westward path of these rivers.

Plateaus and basins. West of the Rocky Mountains is a broad basin with many plateaus and small mountain ranges. This region stretches from the Rocky Mountains west to the Sierra Nevada. Find the Sierra Nevada on the map on page 394.

Look at the map on page 394 and find the Great Basin. This basin is surrounded by higher lands. Rivers flow into the Great Basin, but they do not flow out. Some of the rain sinks into the dry soil. Some evaporates, and some drains into salt lakes.

Almost all lakes in the Great Basin are salty. Water dissolves salts from the soil. Streams carry the salts to lakes. Unlike freshwater lakes, saltwater lakes have no outlets. Instead the water evaporates, leaving the salts behind. The largest saltwater lake in North America is the Great Salt Lake. Find this lake on the map on page 394.

The plains. East of the Rocky Mountains is a large area of plains. This area is an extension of the Midwest Plains that you read about in Unit 12. Look at the map on page 394 and find the plains of the Interior West.

Landforms of the Interior West

- Hills
- Mountains
- Plains
- Plateaus

4. 14,110 feet.
5. 7,426 feet.

Background: Almost every large river in this region has been dammed for waterpower, irrigation, or drinking water.

Thinking Skill: Comparing. Have students compare the growing seasons map below with the Southwest's growing seasons map on page 380 and with your own region's growing seasons map.

The Climate

Much of the Interior West has an **arid**, or dry, climate.

Temperature. Study the graphs below. Find the average monthly January and July temperatures for Missoula and Las Vegas. Find both of these places on the map on page 394. How might the landforms and the location of these two places help explain the differences in their temperatures?

Precipitation. Look again at the two graphs on this page. Does Missoula or Las Vegas get more precipitation? Now study the precipitation map above.

The rain and snow that fall on the mountains in the Interior West drain into mountain streams that form the rivers of the region. Because the Interior West gets so little precipitation, however, the people depend on these rivers for most of their water needs.

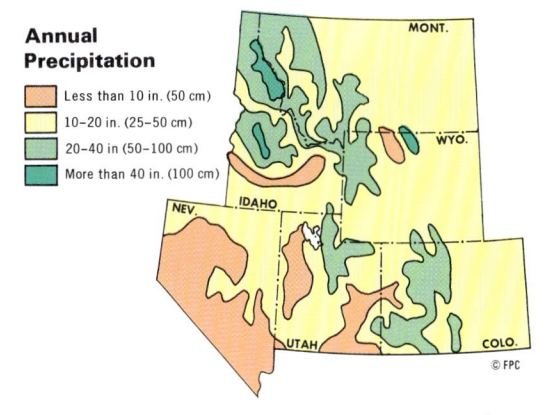

The growing seasons. Look at the growing seasons map on this page. How many months is the growing season in the Rocky Mountains? How long is the growing season in the other parts of the region?

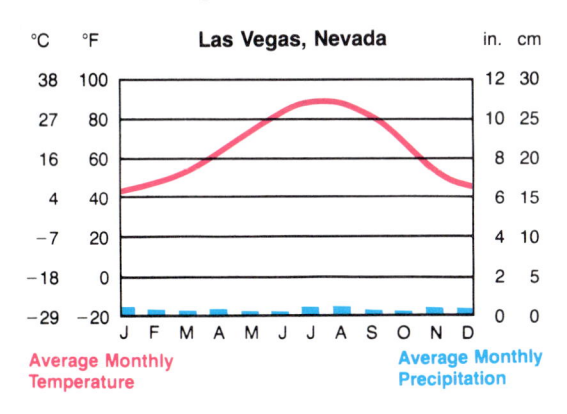

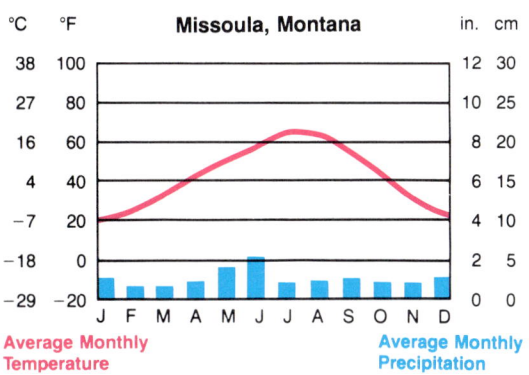

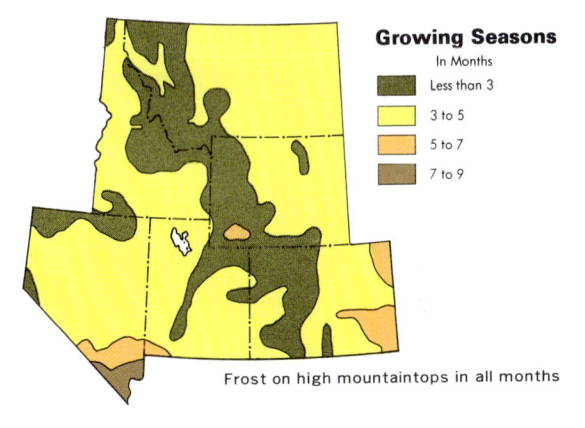

Annual Precipitation
- Less than 10 in. (50 cm)
- 10–20 in. (25–50 cm)
- 20–40 in (50–100 cm)
- More than 40 in. (100 cm)

Growing Seasons In Months
- Less than 3
- 3 to 5
- 5 to 7
- 7 to 9

Frost on high mountaintops in all months

Checking Up
1. What is the Continental Divide?
2. Why are rivers so important to the people of the Interior West?
3. *Why would saltwater lakes be more likely to form in a basin area than in a mountainous area?*

1. Las Vegas's desert location makes temperatures hotter year-round than those in Missoula's mountain valley location.
2. Missoula.

1. These sparsely populated areas are made up of mountains or high plateaus. Both landforms are difficult to settle except in their valleys.
2. Urban areas.
3. Boulder, Fort Collins, or Greeley; Provo, Ogden, or Logan.

Where Are the People?

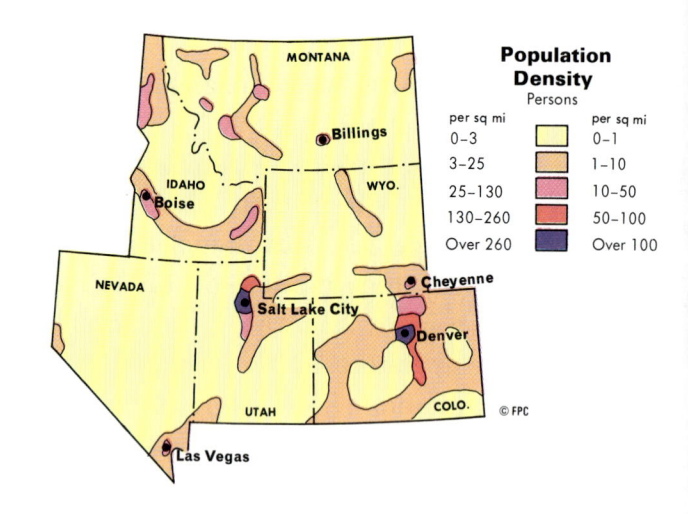

The Interior West is one of the most sparsely populated areas of our country. In more than half of the region, there are fewer than two people per square mile. The rugged land and the arid climate help explain why there are so few people in this region.

Urban and Rural Population of the Interior West

Population Density
Persons
per sq mi
0–3
3–25
25–130
130–260
Over 260

per sq mi
0–1
1–10
10–50
50–100
Over 100

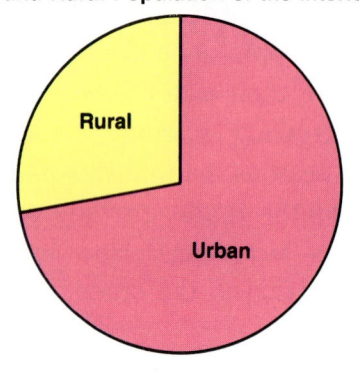

Where the People Live

Look at the population map on page 16. What other parts of the country are as sparsely populated as the Interior West? Find the areas in the Interior West where there are the fewest people. Use the map on page 394 to find the landforms of these sparsely populated areas. How might the landforms explain such a sparse population?

The urban and rural population. Look at the pie graph above. Do most of the people in the Interior West live in urban or rural areas?

Now study the population map on this page. What is the population density for most of the Great Basin? Describe the population density for most of the Rocky Mountain region. Use the population map on page 314 to compare the population density of the Northeastern Seaboard with that of the Rocky Mountains. How much does the population density differ between the two regions in the number of people per square mile?

The urban centers. There are only a few urban centers in the Interior West. In general, these urban areas are small and scattered.

Denver and Salt Lake City are the two major cities of the Interior West. Find Denver and Salt Lake City on the population map on this page. Notice that urban areas extend from these two cities. Now look at the map on page 394. What are two smaller cities that are in the Denver urban area? in the Salt Lake City urban area?

Population Growth in the Interior West

Look at the line graph on page 399. What was the population of the Interior West in 1790? in 1880? How many more

398

4. A few thousand people; about 500,000 people.

Time Skill: Ask students why this region is growing faster than it ever has before.
Reading Skill: Listing. Have students list jobs that might result from the growing tourist industry.

Population Growth of the Interior West

An increasing population. Today the population of the Interior West is growing faster than it ever has. In large part this is because many of the vast natural resources that lie beneath the lands of the Interior West are just beginning to be developed. More and more people are moving to the region to work in the jobs created by the development of these natural resources.

Another reason for the recent population growth is that more and more tourists visit the Interior West each year. As a result, people are moving for the jobs created by the growing tourist industry. In recent years many people have also moved to the Interior West to get away from the crowded urban centers of our country. These people want to enjoy the beautiful scenery and the more rural way of life that the Interior West offers. They often work in the growing industries of the region.

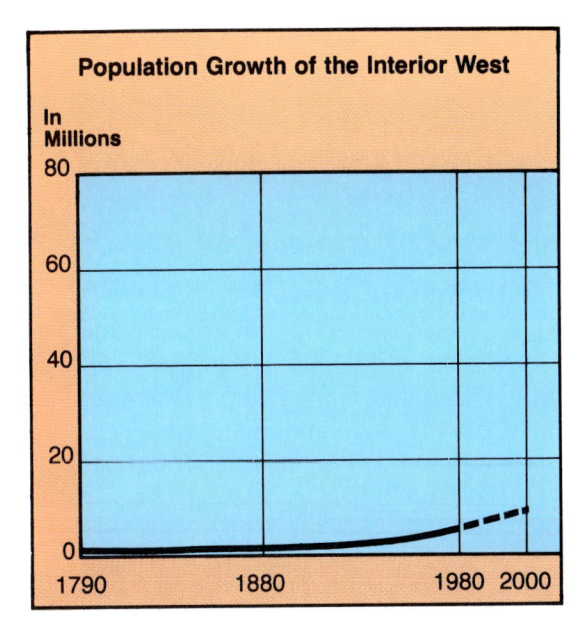

1. people were in the Interior West in 1980 than in 1880? Now look at the table on this page that shows population growth of selected cities. What was the population of Denver in 1880? in 1980? Which city was the second largest in 1980? Which city had the greatest population growth between 1880 and 1980?

Population Growth of Selected Cities in the Interior West			
City	1790 Population	1880 Population	1980 Population
Boise, ID	Not Available	3,214	102,451
Denver, CO	Not Available	35,629	491,396
Las Vegas, NV	Not Available	Not Available	164,674
Salt Lake City, UT	Not Available	20,768	163,033

Recent Populations of Selected Cities in the Interior West				
City	1950 Population	1960 Population	1970 Population	1980 Population
Boise, ID	34,393	34,481	74,990	102,451
Denver, CO	415,786	493,887	514,678	491,396
Las Vegas, NV	24,624	64,405	125,787	164,674
Salt Lake City, UT	182,121	189,454	175,885	163,033

Thinking Skill: Analyzing. Why do some people move from urban areas to this region's rural areas?
1. About 7 million more people.
2. 35,629 people; 491,396 people. Las Vegas. Denver.

399

*** **Communication Skill:** Speaking. Have students give their reports on national parks.
Communication Skill: Listening. Students should listen to the reports and then decide which national park they would most like to visit.

Interesting Places to Visit

The rivers of the Interior West are a popular tourist attraction. Some tourists come to fish in the rivers; others come to ride the rapids. These people are running the rapids on the Middle Fork of the Salmon River in Idaho.

Pictured here is Grinnell Glacier Crevasse in Glacier National Park, Montana. There are more than fifty glaciers on the mountains in this national park.

Salt Lake City, Utah, is the headquarters of the Mormon Church. Pictured here is the world-famous Mormon Tabernacle Choir, which attracts thousands of visitors each year.

Changes in population. The population growth in the Interior West is not all centered in the cities of the region. Like other areas of our country, population growth is often occurring in the suburban and rural areas.

Look at the table of recent populations in selected cities on page 399. What was the largest city in 1950? in 1980? Which cities have shown an increase in population for each of the years listed? Which cities had a population decrease between 1970 and 1980? Now look at the table of recent populations on page 317. Compare the 1980 populations of cities in the Interior West with those of cities in the Northeast. Which region has more cities with populations over 500,000?

Look again at the line graph on page 399. How many people are expected to be living in the Interior West by the year 2000? About how many more people will this be than in 1980?

Checking Up

1. What are the two major cities of the Interior West?
2. What are three reasons for the recent population growth in the Interior West?
3. *Do you think the Interior West will become as densely populated as the Northeast is? Give reasons for your answer.*

1. Denver; Denver. Boise and Las Vegas. Denver and Salt Lake City.
2. The Northeast.
3. About 8,500,000 people; about 1,000,000 more.

Reading Skill: Organizing information. Have students outline this chapter.
*** Citizenship Skill: Social participation. Invite someone who is from or knows about this area to speak to the class.

What Do the People Do?

In the Interior West people have learned to use their land in spite of its rugged landscape and dry climate. Crops are grown. Grasslands provide grazing land for cattle and sheep. Minerals and energy resources are mined and processed. Spectacular scenery is the source of a thriving tourist industry.

Agriculture

As you might expect, farming in the Interior West is done where there is enough water and where the land is generally flat. The largest farming area is on the plains. Here there are large wheat farms. Winter wheat is grown in eastern Colorado, and spring wheat is grown in northeastern Montana.

With the use of irrigation, people are able to farm in other parts of the Interior West as well. For example, there are irrigated farms on the slopes of the Wasatch (wô′sach) Mountains in Utah and along the Snake River in Idaho. Find these two areas on the map on page 394. Crops grown in these areas include wheat, sugar beets, and potatoes. Look at the chart on page 405. What are three other crops grown in the Interior West? 1

Dry grasslands east and west of the Rockies are used for the grazing of cattle and sheep. Cattle and sheep ranches in Wyoming and Montana are some of the largest in our country. They average over 2,000 acres (800 hectares) each. Because the ranches are so large, ranchers often

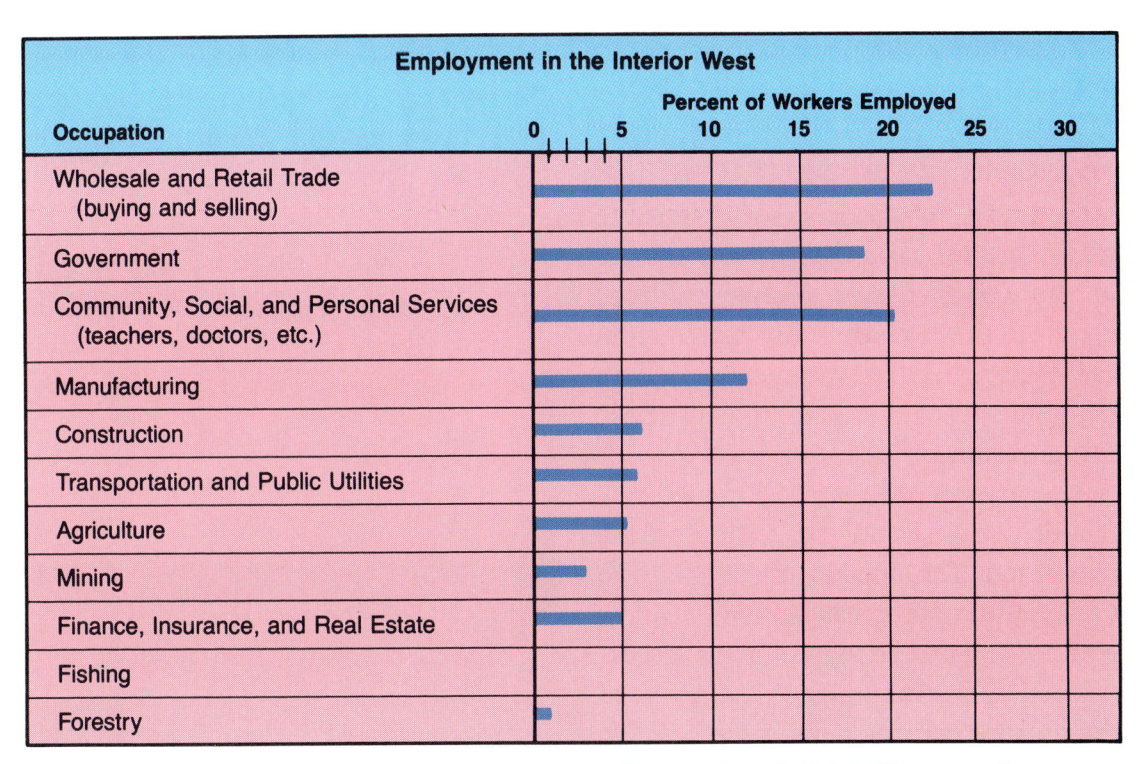

Employment in the Interior West

Occupation	Percent of Workers Employed
Wholesale and Retail Trade (buying and selling)	
Government	
Community, Social, and Personal Services (teachers, doctors, etc.)	
Manufacturing	
Construction	
Transportation and Public Utilities	
Agriculture	
Mining	
Finance, Insurance, and Real Estate	
Fishing	
Forestry	

* **Math Skill:** Talk about how vast an area of 2,000 acres is. The area is equivalent to 3 1/8 square miles. Review the meaning of *average*.
1. Hay, corn, barley, oats, alfalfa seed, cotton, or beans.

* **Reading Skill:** Building vocabulary. Ask students to define *helicopter*. Have them discuss how it would feel to ride in one and how helicopters are used on ranches.
** **Thinking Skill:** Analyzing. Talk about how the federal government is a landowner. Do students think the government should be?

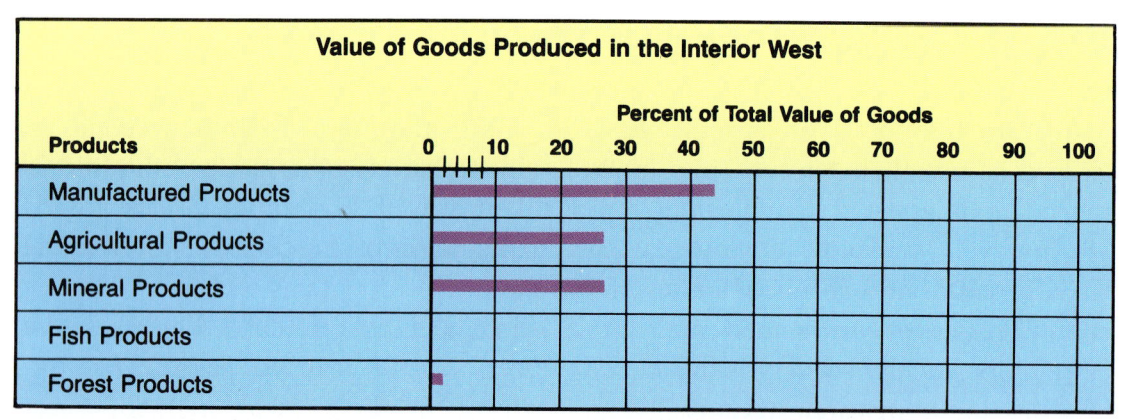

Value of Goods Produced in the Interior West

Products	Percent of Total Value of Goods
Manufactured Products	~45%
Agricultural Products	~30%
Mineral Products	~30%
Fish Products	0
Forest Products	~2%

have to use jeeps and helicopters to round up their herds.

1 Look at the employment graph on page 401. What percent of the workers are employed in agriculture? Now look at the product graph on this page. What is the value of agricultural products? What connections can you make between the number of people who farm and the value of farm products?

The Tourist Industry

Much of the land in the Interior West is owned by the federal government. Look at the map on page 407 and find these areas. As you can see, there are many national parks and recreation areas in the Interior West. People from all parts of the country visit these areas each year. The government employs many people to maintain and supervise this government land.

There are many privately owned recreation areas, such as ski resorts, in the region too. The number of tourists who visit these resorts has grown steadily. New resorts and recreation areas are developed each year to meet the needs of the growing tourist trade.

The Vast Natural Resources

In the late 1800s, large deposits of gold and silver were discovered in the Interior West. With the help of **technology** (tek·näl′ə·jē), or scientific advances in such things as tools and transportation, new deposits of minerals have been found in the Interior West. Look at the map on this page. What are three important minerals in the region? 2

Uranium from the Interior West helps supply nuclear power plants throughout the country. The Interior West also supplies many of our country's factories with mercury and copper.

Natural Resources
- Coal
- Copper
- Forests
- Gold
- Hydroelectric Power
- Iron Ore
- Lead
- Mercury
- Natural Gas
- Oil
- Silver
- Uranium
- Zinc

1. About 5%. About 30%. A small number of people produce a large amount of farm products.
2. Gold, coal, and uranium.

Communication Skill: Speaking. Have students give their reports on these careers.
Reading Skill: Organizing information. Have students make up ads to persuade people to move to this area to work.

Careers

Where Some of the People Work

There are still cowboys and cowgirls in the Interior West! Today these people work on the large ranches of the region. Ranch hands ride horses to trail the cattle herds as they move to new grazing land. When the cattle are ready to be sent to feedlots or to market, the ranch hands round up the cattle and help load them on trucks.

Skiing is a major tourist attraction in the Interior West. There are many jobs connected with skiing. Some people work as ski instructors or ski patrols on the mountain slopes. Others work in the hotels and shops of the ski resorts to serve the needs of the vacationing skiers. Shown here is a ski instructor in Aspen, Colorado.

Many people mine the rich mineral deposits in the Interior West. This picture shows Bingham Canyon Copper Mine near Salt Lake City, Utah. This mine is the largest open-pit copper mine in North America.

Energy Resources. Two of the most valuable natural resources of today's world are oil and natural gas. Recent discoveries have uncovered deposits of these resources in the Interior West. Look at the map on page 402. Which states in the Interior West have deposits of natural gas and oil?

The Interior West also has large deposits of **oil shale,** or rocks from which crude oil can be processed. Many scientists believe that Wyoming and Colorado

*** **Reading Skill:** Doing research. Have students make a diagram showing how oil is processed from oil shale.
1. Natural gas—Wyo. and Colo.; oil—Wyo., Utah, and Colo.

In this mine in Wyoming, coal is dug out of the surface of the land.

might have the largest deposits of oil shale in the world.

Rich deposits of coal are also found in the Interior West. Use the map on page 402 and name the states that have coal deposits.

The coal and oil shale deposits in the Interior West are sometimes thought to be both good and bad. Large areas of land must be disturbed to mine these deposits. Processing these resources is expensive and requires large amounts of water. Some people feel the wilderness areas of the Interior West will be threatened by the continued development of these fuels. Others feel that we must continue to develop the fuels to meet our energy needs in the future.

The Growth of Manufacturing

The Interior West is one of the fastest growing manufacturing regions in our country. Much of this growth is due to the increasing development of the region's natural resources. Each year new factories are built to refine and process these natural resources. Cities such as Denver and Salt Lake City have become important manufacturing centers.

Look at the employment graph on page 401. Find the percent of people in manufacturing. Now find the value of manufactured goods on the graph on page 402. How do these figures show that manufacturing is important?

Checking Up

1. What are three major agricultural products of the Interior West?
2. What answers would you give to the key questions at the beginning of this unit?
3. *How has the recent development of natural resources changed the economy of the Interior West?*

Unit 15 Summary

- The Interior West is a land of rugged mountains, vast plains, and large deserts. Its climate is generally arid. These features help explain the sparse population of the region.
- Today the Interior West is a region of growth and change. The increasing development of its vast natural resources is a major reason for this growth and change.

*** **Thinking Skill:** Analyzing. Should wilderness areas be developed by those searching for fuel?
1. Mont., Wyo., Colo., and Utah.
2. About 12%. About 45%. Manufacturing is the fourth largest employer in this region, yet it produces the highest value of goods.

Communication Skill: Writing. Have students write two-paragraph summaries of this region, using each point in the summary above as the focus of each paragraph.

FACTS ABOUT THE INTERIOR WEST

	Nickname	Capital* and Largest Cities	State Bird	Farm Products and Natural Resources	Manufactured Products	Did You Know This?
Colorado	The Centennial State	Denver* Colorado Springs Aurora Lakewood Pueblo	Lark Bunting	Cattle, sheep, wheat, hay, sugar beets, corn, potatoes Petroleum, gold, silver, lead, tin, zinc	Processed foods and meat, iron and steel, computer equipment, bricks, tile	Colorado has 54 mountain peaks that are at least 14,000 feet (4,200 m) high.
Idaho	The Gem State	Boise* Pocatello Idaho Falls Lewiston Nampa	Mountain Bluebird	Potatoes, cattle, wheat, dairy products, sugar beets Silver, timber, lead, cobalt, phosphate rock, zinc	Lumber and wood products, processed foods, chemicals	The largest silver mine in the United States is located in Idaho.
Montana	The Treasure State	Helena* Billings Great Falls Missoula Butte	Western Meadowlark	Wheat, barley, oats, sugar beets, hay, livestock, potatoes Coal, petroleum, copper, silver, natural gas, timber	Lumber and wood products, processed foods, chemicals	Montana was the home of Charles Russell, world-famous painter and sculptor of life on our western frontier.
Nevada	The Silver State	Carson City* Las Vegas Reno North Las Vegas Sparks	Mountain Bluebird	Livestock, poultry, alfalfa seed, hay, wheat, cotton Copper, gold, sand, mercury, petroleum	Stone, clay, and glass products, chemicals, processed foods, printed materials, electronic equipment	Hoover Dam, on the Colorado River in Nevada, is one of the world's largest dams and supplies electric power to Nevada, Arizona, and California.
Utah	The Beehive State	Salt Lake City* Ogden Provo Orem Bountiful	Sea Gull	Cattle, sheep, dairy products, wheat, hay, sugar beets Petroleum, copper, gold, iron ore, lead, uranium, zinc	Metals and metal products, machinery, processed foods, transportation equipment	Great Salt Lake, the largest natural lake west of the Mississippi River, is about four times saltier than any ocean.
Wyoming	The Equality State	Cheyenne* Casper Laramie Rock Springs Sheridan	Meadowlark	Cattle, hogs, sheep, beans, hay, sugar beets, wheat Petroleum, coal, uranium, timber	Refined oil, processed uranium, lumber products, processed foods	Yellowstone National Park, located in the northwestern part of Wyoming, is our country's largest national park.

Reading Skill: Organizing information. Have students work in pairs to write a ten-point matching exercise based on information in this chart. Have each pair exchange papers with another pair.

Unit 15 Review Workshop

What Have You Learned?

1. What is the most common landform in the Interior West?
2. Why do the people of the Interior West depend so much on the rivers of the region?
3. Why is the population of the Interior West growing?
4. What are two farming areas in the Interior West outside the plains area?
5. In what ways is the tourist industry a major part of the economy of the Interior West?
6. What are three important natural resources of the Interior West?

Use Your Reading Skills

One way to review what you have learned is to organize the information in this unit in an outline. Make the title of each chapter the roman numerals in your outline. The headings within each chapter will be the topics below each chapter title. Depending on their importance, these topics will start with either a capital letter, a number, or a small letter. Below is a start for your outline. Outline the rest of the unit in a similar way. Under each lettered and numbered topic, write a sentence that reviews what you learned in that section of the unit.

I. Where Is the Interior West?
   A. The Region
   B. The Land
      1. The mountains
         a. The Continental Divide

Use Your Map Skills

You learned from reading this unit that the federal government owns much of the land in the Interior West. Study the map on page 407 and then answer the following questions about this government-owned land.

1. Which state in the region has the most Indian reservations?
2. In which state is Yellowstone National Park?
3. Name two wildlife refuges in the Interior West. In which states are these refuges located?
4. Which state has the largest area of national forests?
5. Compare this map with the one on page 394. In which landform region are most of the national parks and forests of the Interior West located?

Use Your Writing Skills

It is often easier to learn the meaning of a word if you put the definition into your own words. Review the four new words for this unit listed on page 395. Look through the unit and find these four new words and their definitions. Put each definition into your own words. Write your own definition on paper. Compare your definitions with the definitions given in the Glossary.

Learn by Doing

1. Many of the animals of the Interior West are not found in other parts of

Reading Skills: Organizing information, building vocabulary.
Thinking Skills: Knowing, comparing.
Map Skill: Location.
Communication Skill: Writing.

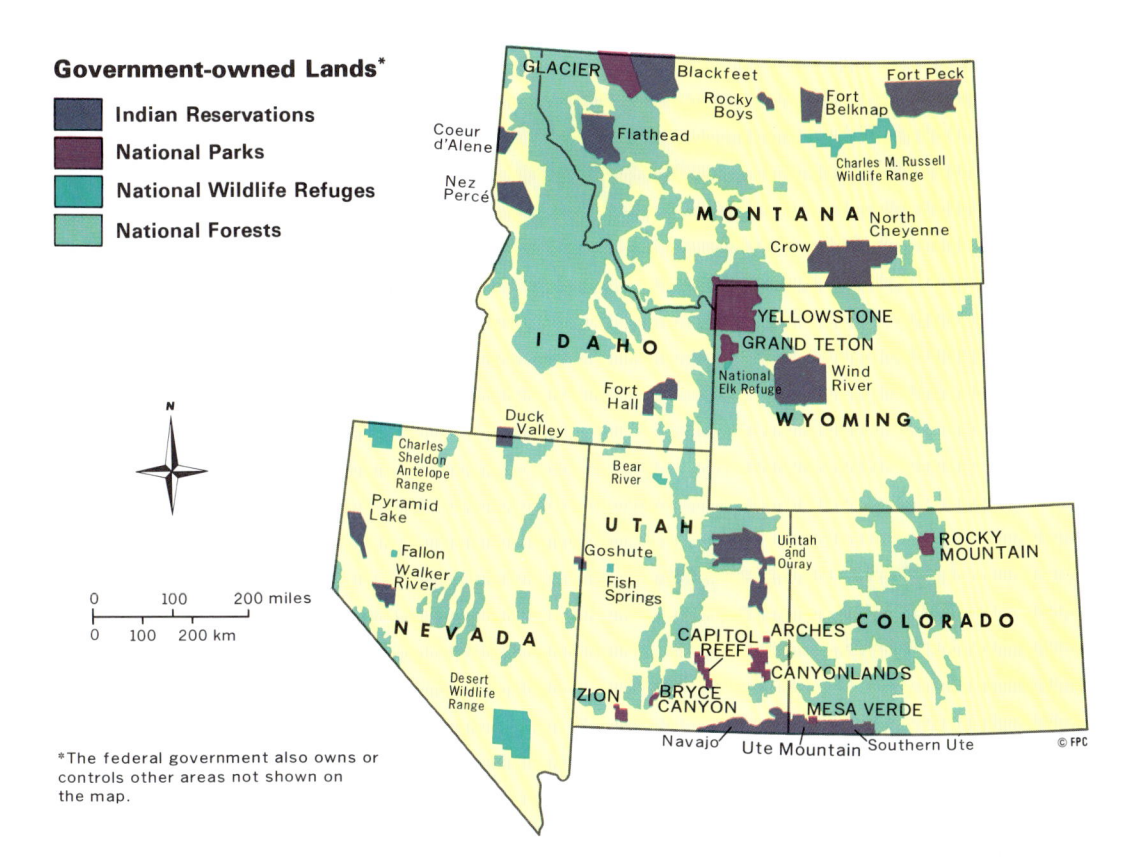

Government-owned Lands*

- ■ Indian Reservations
- ■ National Parks
- ■ National Wildlife Refuges
- ■ National Forests

*The federal government also owns or controls other areas not shown on the map.

our country. Look in books and encyclopedias to find out about golden eagles, jackrabbits, mountain lions, grizzly bears, and bighorn sheep. Draw pictures of each of these animals. Write captions for your pictures describing something interesting about each animal. Post your pictures on the class bulletin board.

2. Pretend you are going to visit a national park in the Interior West. Use the map on page 407 to help you choose a national park. Use a road atlas of the United States to plot a route from your home to the national park you want to visit. On paper, list the distance in miles you would drive.

3. Research the history of one of the American Indian groups, such as the Blackfeet, Crow, Sioux, or Nez Percé, that are living on reservations in the Interior West today. Write a short article about the history of this American Indian group.

Read to Learn More

Find the topics listed below in the card catalog of your library. Read all or part of a book listed under one of the topics. Share what you learn with your classmates.

GREAT SALT LAKE   NATIONAL PARKS
ROCKY MOUNTAINS   HOOVER DAM

Reading Skills: Using references, reading widely: *Learn by Doing, 1, 3* and *Read to Learn More.*
Communication Skill: Writing: *Learn by Doing, 1, 3.*
Citizenship Skill: Decision making: *Learn by Doing, 2.*
Map Skill: Distance: *Learn by Doing, 2.*

Unit Overview: This unit examines the Pacific Coast Region, its population density, and the main occupations of the people who live there.

Unit Objectives
To understand:
- about the three states in this region
- how population density varies in this region
- the main ways people earn a living in this region
- graphics

Suggested Materials
Workbook
Unit Tests

Unit 16

Skills Emphasized
Map and Globe Skills: pp. 408, 422.
Social Studies Reading Skills: pp. 408, 411, 415, 416, 417, 418, 419, 420, 421, 422, 423.
Thinking Skills: pp. 408, 412, 417, 422.
Communication Skills: pp. 408, 416, 419, 423.
Time Skill: p. 415.
Social Studies Math Skills: pp. 412, 417.
Citizenship Skill: p. 420.

Suggested Student Activities
   1. Choose one state. Working in small groups, prepare the pictures and text for a filmstrip.
* 2. Display newspaper and magazine articles about this region on a bulletin board.
   3. Add to the class data-retrieval chart comparing regions.
   4. Report on the topics listed on page 419.
** 5. Make salt relief maps of the region.
*** 6. Report on Mount St. Helens or other volcanoes in the area.

Skills Emphasized in Suggested Student Activities
Social Studies Reading Skills: Using references, doing research, organizing information.
Communication Skills: Writing, speaking, listening.
Map Skills: Location, symbolization, distance.
Thinking Skills: Knowing, classifying, comparing.

The Pacific Coast

Reaching heights of hundreds of feet, sequoia trees grow only in certain parts of the Pacific Coast.

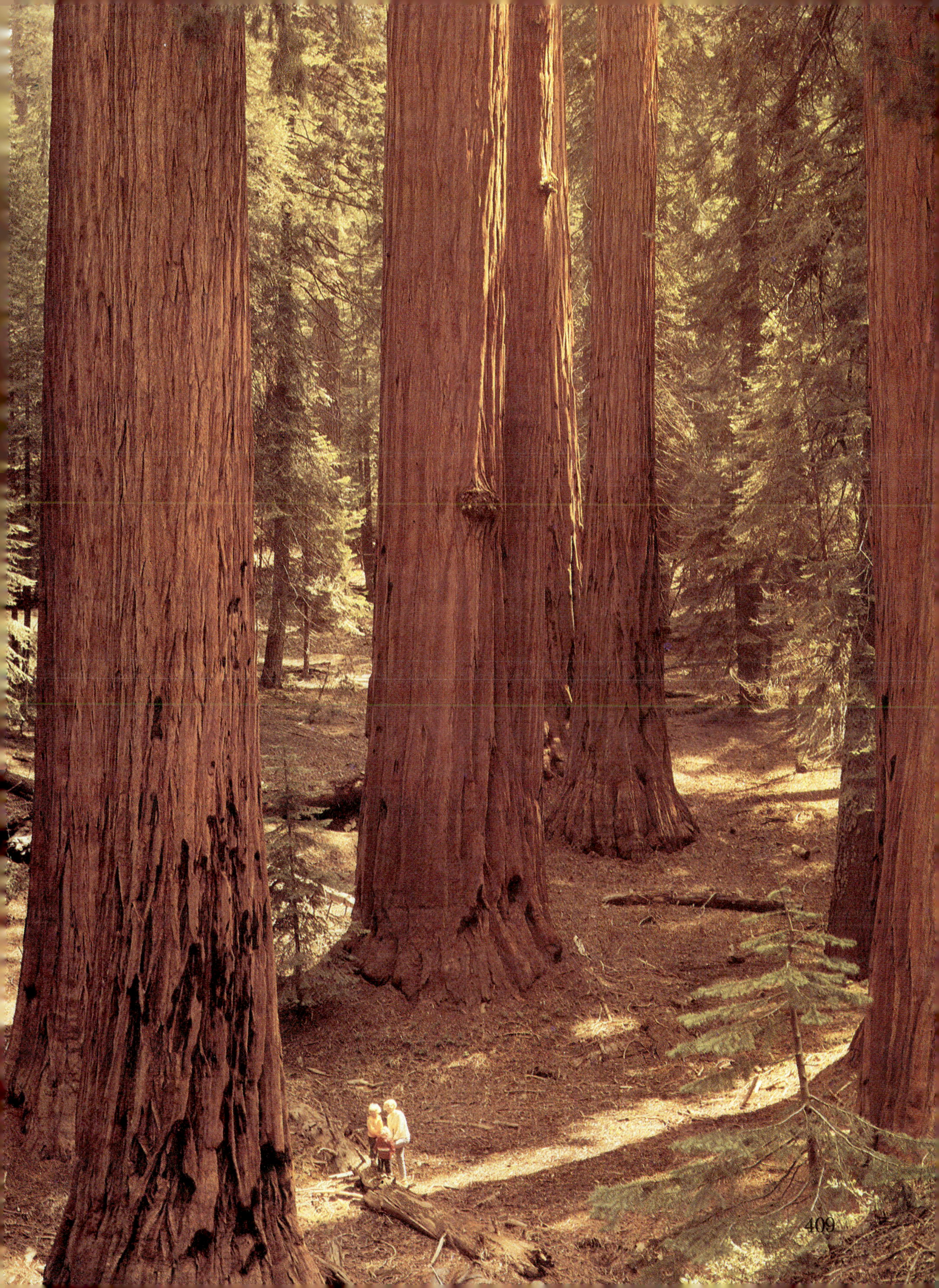

Region of the Pacific Coast

Physical-Political Map

Reading Skill: Recognizing the author's purpose: *As You Read, 3.*

Where Is the Pacific Coast?

As You Read This Unit

1. Think about these words.
   fault   migrant worker   aqueduct   microcomputer
2. Look for answers to these key questions.
   a. In what way does the climate within the region vary?
   b. Where are the areas in the Pacific Coast Region with the greatest population density?
   c. What products does this region ship to other parts of the country?
3. Use this reading skill.
   A good reader must recognize the author's purpose in writing a particular paragraph. Without actually saying "The purpose of this paragraph is . . . ," an author tries to focus on one major point in each paragraph. Sometimes the purpose is to introduce a topic. Sometimes the purpose is to explain a point. What is the purpose of each of the first three paragraphs in this chapter? Try to look for the author's purpose in whatever you read.

Each of the three Pacific Coast states—California, Oregon, and Washington—has high mountains, broad valleys, large plateau areas, and rugged coastlines. Each state has rich natural resources. The beauty of this region and its range of climates are attracting more and more people.

The Region

Look at the map on page 410. What is the capital of each state in this region? [1] Which state borders Canada? Which state borders Mexico? Which river forms the border between California and Arizona? [2] The southern part of California is within the sunbelt.

Use the map scale on page 410 to measure about how many miles this region stretches in a north-south direction. Then find out about how many miles each state in this region measures in an east-west direction.

The Land

Look at the profile on page 410. Find Salinas and Mount Whitney. What is the difference in elevation between these two places? Now find Death Valley. What is the difference in elevation between Death Valley and Mount Whitney? [3] Death Valley has the lowest elevation of any place in the United States.

1. Calif. (Sacramento), Oreg. (Salem), Wash. (Olympia).
2. Washington. California. Colorado River.
3. About 14,800 feet (4,440 m).

Math Skill: Talk about where students would be if they went 750 miles from home.
Thinking Skill: Comparing. Have students compare the heights of Mount Whitney, Mount Hood, and Mount Rainier.

Landforms of the Pacific Coast

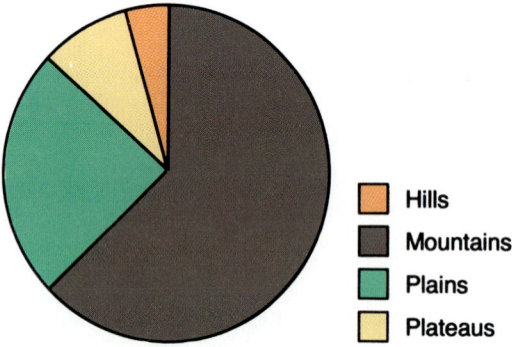

- Hills
- Mountains
- Plains
- Plateaus

The wide difference in elevation between Mount Whitney and Death Valley is only one example of the variety of landscapes in this region. Look at the pie graph on this page. Which is the most common landform? the least common?

Mountains. In each state of the Pacific Coast region, there are high mountains. On page 410, find the Sierra Nevada in California. Then find the Cascade Mountains in Oregon and Washington. Both of these mountain ranges have many tall peaks. You saw on the profile on page 410 that Mount Whitney is over 14,000 feet (4,267 m). Now find Mount Hood in Oregon and Mount Rainier in Washington.

The Cascade Mountains were formed by volcanic activity. In 1980 Mount St. Helens, a peak in the Washington Cascades, erupted. It covered hundreds of square miles with volcanic ash. Some scientists believe other peaks in the Cascades could erupt in the future. Still, the beauty of these mountains draws thousands of tourists every year.

Although people in California may be concerned about volcanoes, they are even more concerned about earthquakes. Most earthquakes in California occur along the San Andreas Fault. A **fault** is a deep crack in the earth's surface. The San Andreas Fault runs more than 750 miles (1,207 km), from northwestern California almost to the Mexican border.

Valleys. Although the mountains of the Pacific Coast are the most common landform, few people live or work in them. The Pacific Coast is a region known for its large valleys. Use the map on page 410 and find the Central Valley of California. Use the map scale to measure the length of this valley from north to south. Between what two mountain ranges is this valley? 1

There are also large valleys in both Oregon and Washington. Use the map

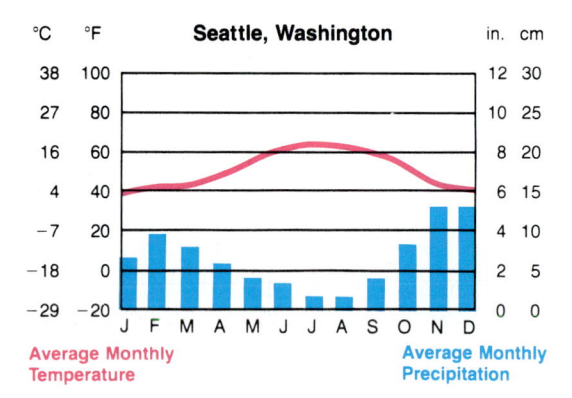

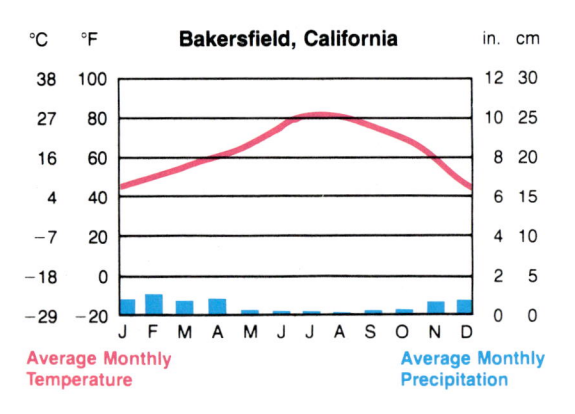

Seattle, Washington

Average Monthly Temperature
Average Monthly Precipitation

Bakersfield, California

Average Monthly Temperature
Average Monthly Precipitation

1. Coast Ranges and Sierra Nevada.
Background: In 1971 an earthquake along the San Andreas fault caused sixty-four deaths and millions of dollars worth of damage in an area north of Los Angeles.

412

1. Seattle—Jan., about 40 °F; July, about 66 °F. Bakersfield—Jan., about 48 °F; July, about 84 °F.
2. Seattle. Winter.

on page 410 and find the Willamette River valley in Oregon. Also find the Columbia River valley in Washington. What other states share part of the Columbia River valley?

The Climate

There is a great variety in the landforms of the Pacific Coast. There is also a variety in the types of climate.

Temperature. Study the graphs on page 412. Find the average monthly temperatures in January and July for both Seattle and Bakersfield. Find both places on the map on page 410. Bakersfield has warmer summer temperatures than Seattle, partly because of its southern location. Because Bakersfield also has an inland location, its temperatures vary more. The location of Seattle on Puget Sound keeps temperatures mild.

Precipitation. Look again at the graphs on page 412. Which place receives more precipitation? During which season do both Seattle and Bakersfield get the most precipitation?

There are some places in this region that are warmer and drier than Bakersfield. Look at the map on page 410. Find the Mojave Desert in California. This is one of the driest parts in the United States.

Some places in the Pacific Coast receive far more precipitation than Seattle. Parts of Olympic National Park in Washington receive over 100 inches (254 cm) of precipitation a year. Moist breezes that blow in from the Pacific Ocean lose their moisture as they travel across land.

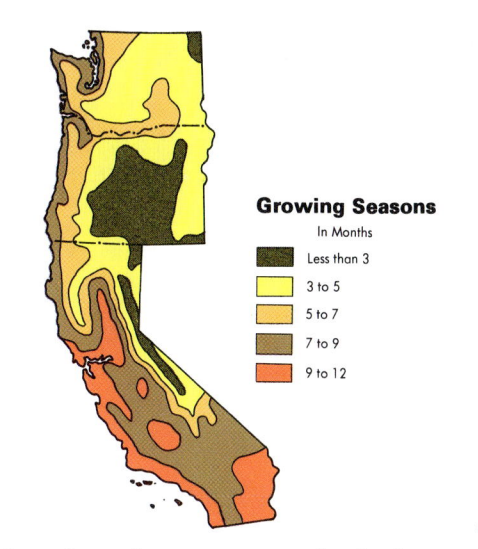

Growing Seasons
In Months
- Less than 3
- 3 to 5
- 5 to 7
- 7 to 9
- 9 to 12

After these breezes cross the high mountains, they have lost most of their moisture. As a result, the eastern part of this region is generally much drier than the western part.

The growing seasons. There is a wide range in growing seasons in the Pacific Coast. Look at the map on this page. What is the longest growing season in this region? Use the map on this page to locate the areas with the longest growing seasons. What reasons can you give for these areas having long growing seasons? Locate the areas with the shortest growing seasons. Why do these places have short growing seasons?

Checking Up
1. What are the two major mountain ranges of the Pacific Coast?
2. Where do most of the earthquakes in California occur?
3. *Why is there such a great range of climates in the Pacific Coast?*

3. Southern location.
4. High elevation and distance from warming ocean.

413

1. Urban areas.
2. San Francisco. Los Angeles grew the most.
3. Los Angeles, San Diego, Seattle, and San Jose. Los Angeles, San Diego, and San Jose, California.

Where Are the People?

You just read about the variety of landforms, climates, and growing seasons within the Pacific Coast region. There are also different population patterns within this region. In terms of population patterns, California is different from Oregon and Washington.

Where the People Live

Compare the population map on this page with the map of the region on page 410. Look carefully at the population density of California. What is the population density in most of California's Central Valley? Notice that the inland areas of both Oregon and Washington are not as densely populated as the Central Valley.

Look at the pie graph on this page. Do most of the people in the Pacific Coast live in urban or rural areas?

The cities of the Pacific Coast. Most of the population increase of the Pacific Coast has occurred in this century. Look at the table on page 415. What was the largest city in 1880? Which city grew the most between 1880 and 1980?

The table on page 415 shows the recent growth of these cities. Which cities had a population increase between 1950 and 1980? Which cities grew by more than 100,000? In what state are they?

In Unit 10, you learned that the area between Boston and Washington, D.C. has grown into almost one completely urbanized area called a megalopolis. The coastal area of California between San Diego and Los Angeles is also becoming a megalopolis. This megalopolis is also growing north of Los Angeles. Which cities on the map on page 410 are part of this megalopolis?

Portland and Seattle are the largest cities in Oregon and Washington. Look at the table on page 415 and find the 1980 populations for these two cities. The eastern parts of Oregon and Washington are not as densely populated as the areas around Portland and Seattle.

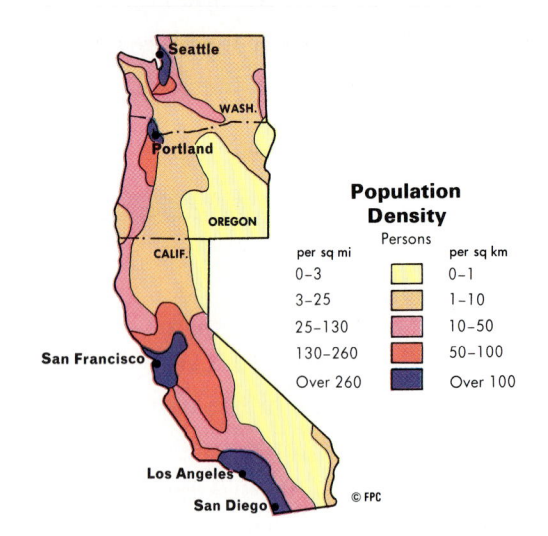

Urban and Rural Population of the Pacific Coast

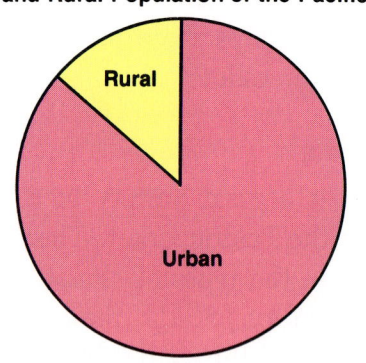

4. Glendale, Pasadena, Long Beach, Santa Ana.

* **Reading Skill:** Building vocabulary. Have students look up the meaning of *migrant*.
Time Skill: Have each student choose one city and write a summary of its population growth from 1780 to 1980.

| Population Growth of Selected Cities on the Pacific Coast ||||
City	1790 Population	1880 Population	1980 Population
Los Angeles, CA	Not Available	11,183	2,966,763
Portland, OR	Not Available	17,577	366,383
San Diego, CA	Not Available	2,637	875,504
San Francisco, CA	Not Available	233,959	678,974
San Jose, CA	Not Available	12,567	636,550
Seattle, WA	Not Available	3,533	493,846

Look at the population density map on page 414. What is the population density of most of eastern Oregon? of most of eastern Washington?

The population of the region. The line graph on page 416 shows the population growth in the Pacific Coast region. When did the greatest population increase occur? What is the prediction for population growth between 1980 and 2000? Not all the population growth will occur in the cities. There will also be growth in rural areas.

Population Patterns in California

California has unique population patterns. These patterns are influenced by location, climate, and history.

You read in Unit 6 about the wave of immigration and migration to California after the discovery of gold. There was another wave of migration to California during the hard times of the 1930s. California still attracts people from other parts of the United States and from other countries. As a result, only about half the people who live in California were born there.

In Unit 6 you learned that California, like much of the Southwest, was part of Mexico until 1848. Mexican Americans have always been a large part of the population. Immigration from Mexico continues today. Some of the present immigrants work as **migrant workers.** Migrant workers move from place to place,

| Recent Populations of Selected Cities on the Pacific Coast |||||
City	1950 Population	1960 Population	1970 Population	1980 Population
Los Angeles, CA	1,970,358	2,479,015	2,816,061	2,966,763
Portland, OR	373,678	372,676	382,619	366,383
San Diego, CA	334,387	573,224	696,769	875,504
San Francisco, CA	775,357	740,316	715,674	678,974
San Jose, CA	95,280	204,196	445,779	636,550
Seattle, WA	467,591	557,087	530,831	493,846

1. Between 1880 and 1980. Population is expected to grow.
Reading Skill: Skimming. Have students look at the population maps in other regions and identify cities the same size as these.

Built in the 1700s, this Spanish mission near Carmel, California, shows a style of architecture that is common in California.

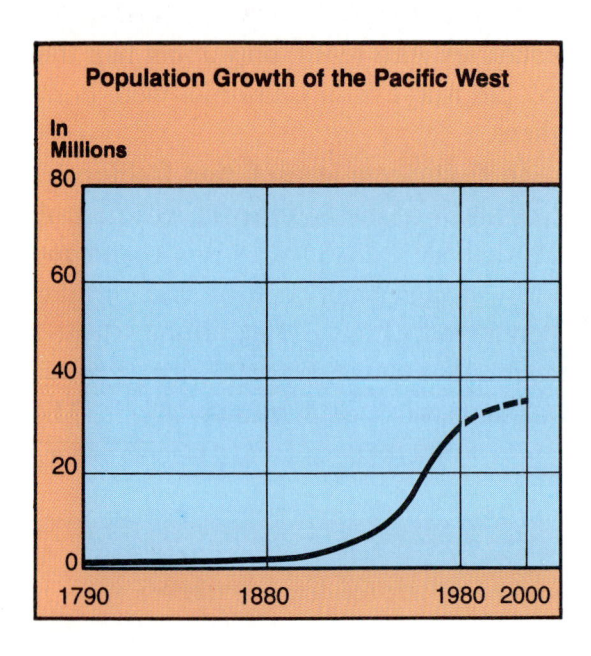

Population Growth of the Pacific West

working on large farms. Like earlier immigrants, these migrant workers come to California hoping for a better life.

The population of California also includes many people of Asian backgrounds. In Unit 8 you read about the Chinese workers who helped build the first railroads. Chinese Americans are still an important part of the population in many cities in California. Many Japanese Americans have also settled in California. Recently, Korean and Vietnamese immigrants have come to California. The influence of so many different cultures is evident in architecture, language, and traditions.

Checking Up
1. Which area in the Pacific Coast region has had the greatest population increase since 1950?
2. Which area in this region is becoming a megalopolis?
3. *Why do you think the population of this region is expected to grow between 1980 and 2000?*

Reading Skill: Doing research. Have students look for information and pictures of Chinatown.
Communication Skill: Writing. Have students prepare reports on the California missions.
Thinking Skill: Comparing. Have students compare this picture of the mission at Carmel with the picture of the same mission on page 118. How has the mission changed?

Math Skill: Review the meanings of ¼ and ⅓ as used here.
Reading Skill: Listening. Have students make an A–Z job list for this region.

What Do the People Do?

The variety within the Pacific Coast region is also reflected in what its people do. Farming is important in all three states. Look at the graph on this page. What percent of the total value of goods are agricultural products? [1] California is a major business center. All three states are trade and transportation centers. Tourism is another important source of jobs for many people in this region.

What the People Do in California

California is a leading state in both farming and business. In fact, it outranks all other states in the value of farm products sold.

Agriculture. California farmers grow nearly every type of crop. Nearly one-third of all vegetables grown in this country come from California. Nearly one-fourth of all the fruit grown in this country is produced in California. Some crops can be grown only in California. For example, dates, figs, olives, and almonds need climatic conditions that are found in California.

The climate and soil in much of California are good for farming. However, the southern parts of California are very dry. Farmers here must irrigate their fields. Some irrigation water comes from nearby rivers. Some water comes from rivers many miles away through **aqueducts.** An aqueduct is a large canal-like structure built above ground to carry water. Aqueducts bring water from rivers in the Sierra Nevada and from northern California to farms in the Imperial Valley and in the southern half of the Central Valley. Without this water, few crops could be grown in the dry valleys of southern California.

The water that aqueducts bring to southern California is also important to industries and to people. One of California's greatest challenges is supplying enough water for the growing populations in southern California.

Manufacturing and trade. The transportation industry employs thousands of people in California. Many people in the transportation industry build airplanes.

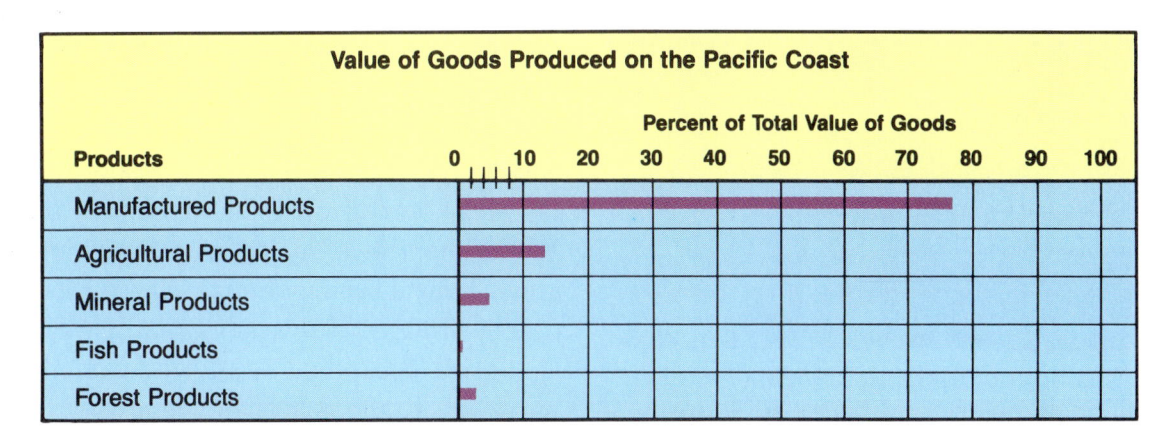

Value of Goods Produced on the Pacific Coast	
Products	**Percent of Total Value of Goods** (0–100)
Manufactured Products	~75
Agricultural Products	~14
Mineral Products	~4
Fish Products	~1
Forest Products	~2

1. About 14%.
Thinking Skill: Observing. Look for products from this region in your grocery.

** **Reading Skill:** Building vocabulary. Have students look for maps of cities with good harbors in this region.
*** **Reading Skill:** Doing research. Have students look for data on the space industry.

Others have jobs related to the space industry. These people design and build satellites, engines, and steering systems. The transportation industry originally came to California because of the good weather for year-round testing. Now many people in and around San Diego, Los Angeles, and San Jose depend on this industry.

Many people in California work in the food-processing industry. The large harvests are processed and shipped to all parts of the country.

Many of the movies and TV shows you see are made in the Los Angeles area. The sunny climate near Los Angeles allowed early moviemakers to film outside all year. Even though much filming is done indoors today, the motion-picture and TV industries employ thousands of workers.

There are good harbors in San Diego, Los Angeles, and San Francisco. The harbors in these cities are busy. Products from California are shipped to all parts of the world.

California has many natural resources. There are petroleum and natural gas. Gold is still mined. People also mine many other minerals. About 10 percent of all the minerals mined in the United States are mined in California.

California is a productive state. People all over the country depend on products from California.

What the People Do in Oregon and Washington

Oregon and Washington have much in common. Their climates and landforms are similar. People in both states have used their good soil, mild climate, and abundant water to create a strong, growing economy.

Agriculture. Much of the farming in Oregon and Washington is done in river valleys. The Willamette River valley in Oregon is famous for its vegetables and strawberries. Central Washington is also a fruit-growing center. Apples and pears grown there are shipped all over the country. Study the map of wheat-growing areas on page 351. In which part of Washington is a major wheat-growing area? Although Oregon and Washington do not produce the variety of crops that California does, their farm products are important to the rest of the country.

Testing models of airplanes in wind tunnels helps build better airplanes.

1. Eastern Washington.

Communication Skill: Speaking. Have students give reports on these careers.
Communication Skill: Listening. Students should listen carefully to reports and then rank the jobs in order of their preferences.

Careers

Where Some of the People Work

The woman at right is hard at work making a **microcomputer.** A microcomputer is a small computer. Smaller and smaller computers have been made. Computers are now small enough to be placed in wristwatches. As recently as the 1960s, most computers were too large for people to lift! The center of the microcomputer industry is between San Francisco and San Jose, California.

Farms in Oregon produce a great variety of crops. The farm above produces bulbs and flower seeds that will be sold to people all over the country. The workers on this farm must do much of their work by hand. The mild climate of western Oregon is perfect for the gardening business.

Look at the photo below. Is that a real bedroom? No, it's part of a movie studio near Los Angeles. Many people build sets like this one to record the sound and to photograph the action.

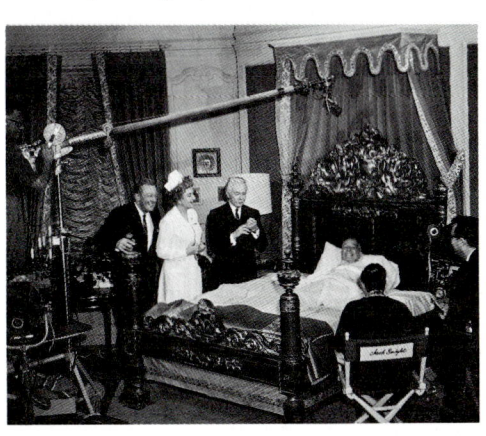

Manufacturing and trade. Earlier you learned that the major cities in Oregon and Washington are Portland and Seattle. Both cities are important manufacturing and trade centers. Seattle, like Los Angeles, is an important aircraft manufacturing center. Portland is a major processing center for Oregon's many farm and wood products.

Both Portland and Seattle are important ports. Look at the map on page 410. On which body of water is Seattle? Al- 1

1. Puget Sound.
* **Reading Skill:** Building vocabulary. Review the meanings of *manufacture* and *trade*.

419

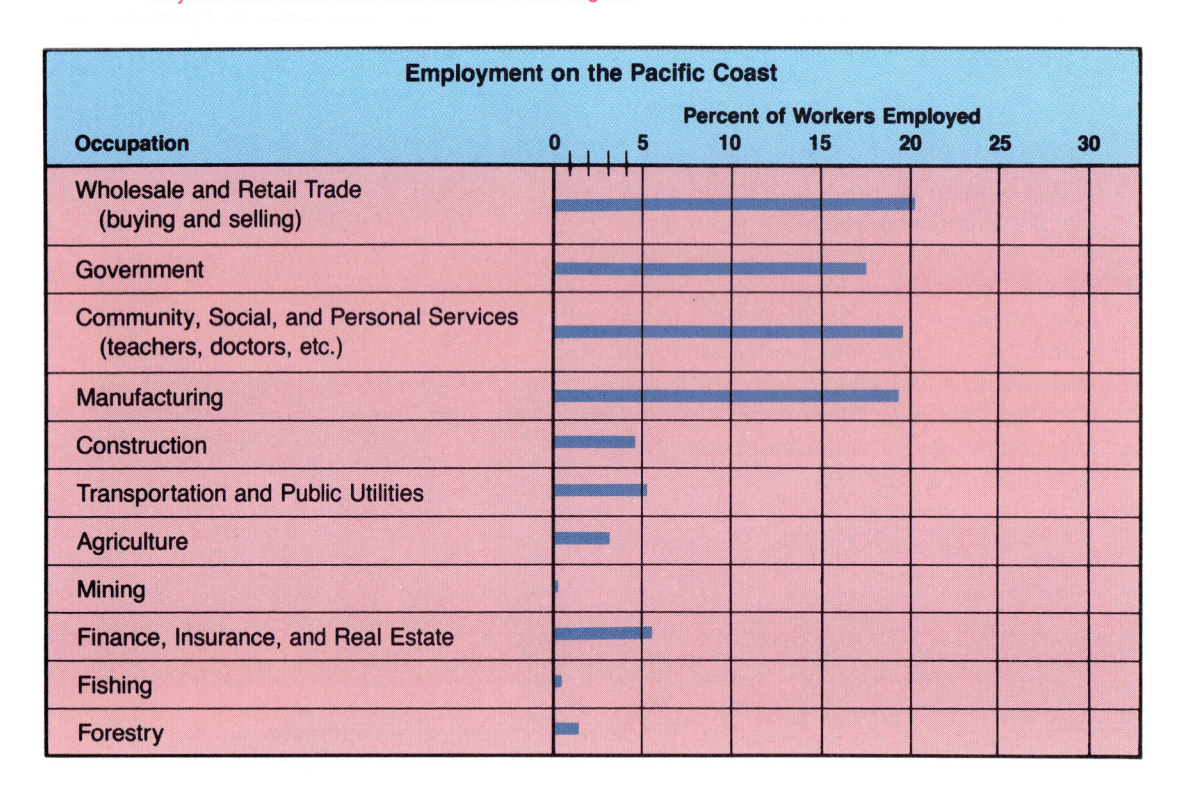

Reading Skill: Doing research. Have several students report on salmon
Citizenship Skill: Social participation. Have a travel agent or other qualified person talk about Disneyland and other tourist attractions in the region.

Employment on the Pacific Coast							
Occupation / Percent of Workers Employed	0	5	10	15	20	25	30
Wholesale and Retail Trade (buying and selling)					~20		
Government				~17			
Community, Social, and Personal Services (teachers, doctors, etc.)					~19		
Manufacturing					~20		
Construction		~5					
Transportation and Public Utilities		~6					
Agriculture		~3					
Mining	<1						
Finance, Insurance, and Real Estate		~6					
Fishing	<1						
Forestry	<1						

though Portland is inland, the Columbia River is deep enough for oceangoing ships to reach Portland. As a result, businesses in Portland can ship their products all over the world.

The Columbia River is more than just a highway for ships. Look at the map on page 410. Trace the route of the Columbia with your finger. Which dams do you see on the Columbia? These dams provide hydroelectric power for homes and businesses. Water, as a source of energy, is one of the great natural resources in Oregon and Washington.

The Region as a Whole

The states within the Pacific Coast region may differ, but they also have much in common. The coastal areas of northern California, Oregon, and Washington are much alike. Forestry and wood products are important in this part of the region. Look at the growing seasons map on page 413. How long is the growing season in this part of the region? The long growing season and the heavy precipitation make trees grow quickly. Much of the lumber used in the United States comes from this area. Look at the bar graph of the value of goods on page 417. What percent of the total value of goods are forest products?

Fishing is important in all three states. Major catches include tuna, halibut, salmon, and shellfish. Look at the bar graph of employment on this page. What percent of the people work in fishing?

Tourism is an important industry in most parts of the Pacific Coast. Visitors come to see the wilderness that has been

1. Grand Coulee and Bonneville dams.
2. About 3%.
3. Less than 1%.

FACTS ABOUT THE PACIFIC COAST

	Nickname	Capital* and Largest Cities	State Bird	Farm Products and Natural Resources	Manufactured Products	Did You Know This?
California	The Golden State	Sacramento* Los Angeles San Diego San Francisco San Jose	Valley Quail	Fruits, nuts, livestock, poultry, dairy products, vegetables, cotton Petroleum, boron, gold, natural gas, seafood	Transportation equipment, processed foods, wines, electronic equipment, refined oil	California has the largest population of any state in the nation.
Oregon	The Beaver State	Salem* Portland Eugene Corvallis Springfield	Western Meadowlark	Cattle, dairy products, wheat, hay, barley, oats, fruits, berries Stone, sand, gravel, timber, seafood	Lumber and wood products, processed foods, paper, chemicals, machinery	Crater Lake, which occupies a volcanic cone, is the deepest lake in the United States.
Washington	The Evergreen State	Olympia* Seattle Spokane Tacoma Bellevue	Willow Goldfinch	Wheat, beans, potatoes, sugar beets, apples, livestock Coal, lead, limestone, sand, gravel, zinc, timber, seafood	Aircraft and missiles, lumber and wood products, processed foods, machinery, chemicals	Washington is the only state named for a president.

preserved in the many national and state parks. Others come to visit the busy cities.

This is a region of dramatic contrasts. Look again at the bar graph of the value of goods on page 417. What is the percent of value of manufactured goods?[1] Now look at the photo that opened this unit. Although the bar graph shows you that this is a region of manufacturing, the photo shows you that it is also a region of great natural beauty.

Checking Up
1. What are three important industries in California?
2. What answers would you give to the key questions at the beginning of this unit?
3. *How does the Pacific Ocean affect the economy of this region?*

Unit 16 Summary
- The Pacific Coast has a wide variety of landforms and climates.
- Southern California has had the greatest population increase of any area in this region.
- California is a leading farm and manufacturing state. Oregon and Washington also produce important crops and manufactured goods.

1. About 77%.
Reading Skill: Organizing information. Have each student divide a sheet of paper into six sections and illustrate six facts about one of the states in this region.

Unit 16 Review Workshop

What Have You Learned?

1. What is the most common landform in the Pacific Coast region?
2. Which areas in the Pacific Coast region receive the most precipitation?
3. Which area in California needs water for people, agriculture, and industry? How is water transported to this area?
4. Which area in this region has had the greatest population increase since 1950?
5. Which cultures have influenced the architecture, language, and traditions of California?
6. Why did the transportation and movie industries develop in southern California?
7. How is the Columbia River important to the economy of Oregon and Washington?

Use Your Reading Skills

You can improve your vocabulary in many ways. One way is to learn meanings of a word or parts of words that are used in other words. For example, you read about microcomputers in this unit. *Micro* means "small." If you remember this, you can make intelligent guesses about the meanings of other words with *micro* in them. Is a microscope a tool for looking at small or large things? Does a micrometer measure small or large objects? What is a microclimate? a microphone? Use a dictionary to check your answers.

Use Your Map Skills

You have learned in this unit that the Columbia River is an important river for people in Oregon and Washington. The map on page 423 shows the system of rivers that flow into the Columbia and the major electric power lines that connect dams with cities. Study the map and answer the following questions.

1. Which countries are part of the Columbia River system? Name the states that are part of the Columbia River system.
2. Which cities on the seacoast of Washington probably receive some power from dams on the Columbia?
3. Which dam do you think probably provides some hydroelectric power for Spokane?
4. Which dam do you think probably provides some hydroelectric power for Portland?
5. Compare this map with the map of the region on page 410. Name some rivers that flow into the Columbia. Near what town does the Columbia flow into the Pacific Ocean?

Use Your Thinking Skills

In this unit, you have learned about some of the well-known landforms and landscapes of the Pacific Coast region. Do you know how to classify these landforms and landscapes? Across the top of your paper, write these four categories: Mountains, Deserts, Valleys, Plateaus.

Reading Skill: Building vocabulary.
Thinking Skills: Knowing, classifying, comparing.
Map Skill: Location.

The Columbia River Basin
- Dams
- Major electric power lines

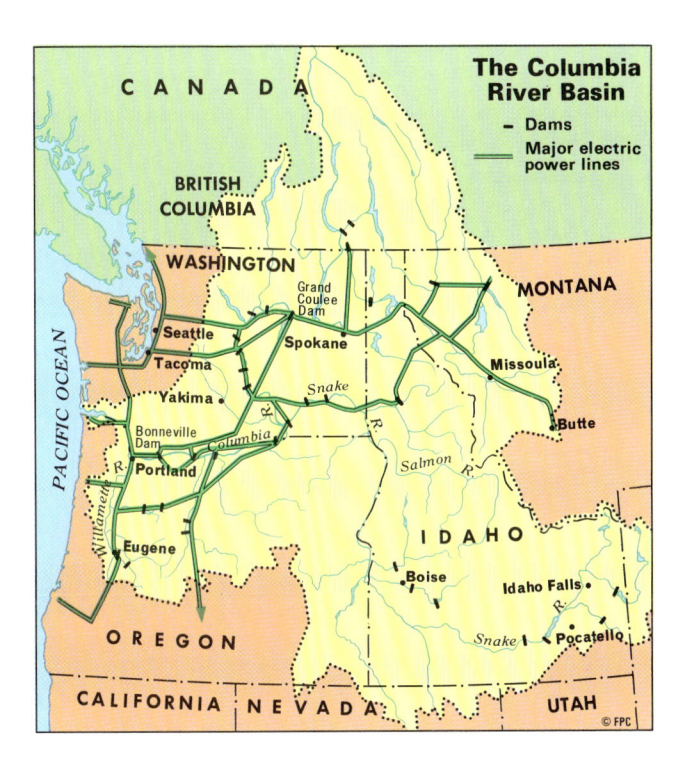

Now turn to the map on page 410. Use the map to help you list examples under each category. For example, under the category Mountains, you could list the Sierra Nevada. List as many landforms and landscapes as you can under the appropriate category.

Learn by Doing

1. You have read that California farmers produce some crops that are rarely grown in any other state. Look in books and encyclopedias to find out about artichokes, pistachios, and pomegranates. Draw pictures of these foods. Write captions for your drawings in which you explain how these foods are used. Post your drawings on the classroom bulletin board.

2. Research the history of aqueducts and their construction. Who were the first people to build aqueducts? Where? Prepare a report on their history and their construction. Include photos and drawings. You may want to study the aqueducts in California that are in use today.

3. Several different flags have flown over California. Spain, Mexico, the United States, and Russia have all claimed this area at certain times in its history. California was even an independent republic for a short time and had its own flag. Use books and encyclopedias to find out what these flags looked like. Then draw your own flag for California. Colors and symbols on flags tell people something important about the state. What will you want to tell people about the state of California when they look at your flag drawing? It may help you to look at other state flags to see what these flags tell you about their states.

Read to Learn More

Find the topics listed below in the card catalog of your library. Read all or part of a book listed under one of the topics. Share what you learn with your classmates.

EARTHQUAKES	TELEVISION
MOTION-PICTURE INDUSTRY	VOLCANOES

Reading Skills: Doing research: *Learn by Doing, 1–3;* using references: *Learn by Doing, 1–3* and *Read to Learn More;* organizing information: *Learn by Doing, 1–3.*
Communication Skills: Writing and Speaking: *Learn by Doing, 1–3.*

Unit Overview: This unit examines Alaska and Hawaii as a region, the region's population density, and the main occupations of the people who live there.

Unit Objectives
To understand:
- about the two states in this region
- how population density varies in this region
- the main ways people earn a living in this region
- graphics

Suggested Materials
Workbook
Unit Tests

Unit 17

Skills Emphasized
Map Skills: pp. 424, 434.
Social Studies Reading Skills: pp. 424, 427, 430, 431, 432, 433, 434, 435.
Thinking Skills: pp. 424, 430, 431, 432, 434.
Communication Skills: pp. 424, 430, 435.
Time Skill: p. 429.
Social Studies Math Skills: pp. 428, 433.
Citizenship Skills: pp. 424, 430.

Suggested Student Activities
    1. Make a map and graph booklet on one state in the region.
    2. Display newspaper and magazine articles about the region on a bulletin board.
    3. Complete the class data-retrieval chart comparing regions of the United States. Review and generalize.
    4. Report on the products and resources of the region.
  * 5. Make relief maps of each state.
*** 6. Invite speakers from each state to class.

Skills Emphasized in Suggested Student Activities
Map Skills: Location, scale, symbolization.
Social Studies Reading Skills: Doing research, using references, organizing information.
Thinking Skills: Knowing, comparing, generalizing.
Communication Skills: Speaking, writing, listening.
Citizenship Skill: Social participation.

Alaska and Hawaii

Denali National Park in Alaska (top) and Kaimu Black Sands Beach in Hawaii (bottom) are open to tourists.

425

Alaska
Physical-Political Map

★ State Capital
• Other Cities

SCALE
One inch—about 280 miles

Hawaii
Physical-Political Map

★ State Capital
• Other Cities

SCALE
One inch—about 70 miles

HEIGHT OF LAND
- OVER 13,000 FEET
- 6,600 TO 13,000
- 3,300 TO 6,600
- 1,650 TO 3,300
- 650 TO 1,650
- 0 TO 650 FEET

DEPTH OF WATER
- 0 TO 600 FEET
- BELOW 600 FEET

Profile
Bering Strait · Nome · Yukon River · Fairbanks · Klondike Region

Dry Leeward Side / Wet Windward Side
Irrigated fields · Pineapple · Northeast Trade Wind · Sugarcane
Honolulu · Kaneohe

426

Reading Skill: Using a textbook feature: *As You Read, 3.*

Where Are Alaska and Hawaii?

As You Read This Unit

1. Think about these words.
   tundra   volcano   ethnic group
2. Look for answers to these key questions.
   a. What is similar about the locations of Alaska and Hawaii?
   b. Why are the populations of Alaska and Hawaii increasing?
   c. What are three major ways that people make a living in Alaska and Hawaii?
3. Use this reading skill.
   The Appendix in the back of your book is an important reference tool. Use the table on page 482 in the Appendix to find out when Alaska and Hawaii became states. What is the capital of Alaska? of Hawaii?

At first you may wonder why Alaska and Hawaii make up a region. They are not located close to each other. Their climates and natural resources differ greatly. In spite of these differences, however, you will learn that Alaska and Hawaii have many things in common.

The Region

Look at the world map on pages 10 and 11. Notice that Alaska and Hawaii are separated from the other forty-eight states of the United States. Find the point at which 40° north latitude touches California. Measure the distance in miles from this point to Kodiak Island in Alaska. How many miles is it from this same point in California to Hawaii?

Now study the two maps on page 426. How many miles separate Alaska from the Soviet Union across the Bering Strait? What ocean lies to the north of Alaska? Hawaii is often called the Island State. How many islands can you find on the map of Hawaii?

The Land

By looking at the pictures in this unit, you can see why Alaska and Hawaii are known for the beauty of their landscapes. Study the pie graph on page 428. Which is the most common landform in the region? the least common? Look at the two maps on page 426. Which landforms do Alaska and Hawaii have in common?

Alaska. The northern part of Alaska is called the Arctic Slope. This region extends from the Brooks Range northward. Find this area on the map on page 426.

1. Alaska (1959), Hawaii (1959). Juneau; Honolulu.
2. The Arctic Ocean is north of Alaska. Nine.
3. Mountains. Hills (notice that plateaus are not shown on the pie graph). Mountains, hills, and plains.

427

Math Skill: Have students compare the height of Mount McKinley with that of other peaks (Pikes Peak and Mount Mitchell) they have read about.
Background: Hawaii has one of the world's most ideal climates. Cool Pacific Ocean breezes help keep the temperature pleasant all year long.

Landforms of Alaska and Hawaii

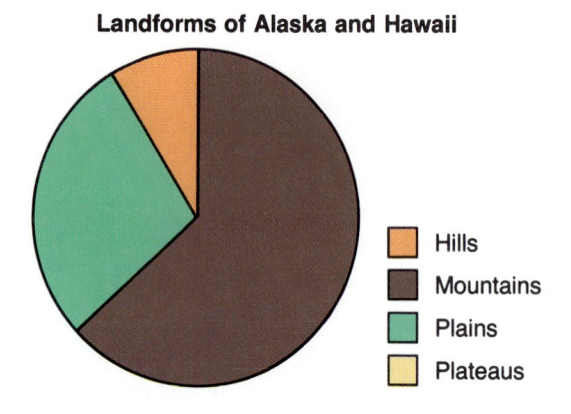

- Hills
- Mountains
- Plains
- Plateaus

The land in this area is **tundra**. The tundra is a cold, treeless plain.

The area between the Brooks and Alaska mountains is central Alaska. Find this area on the map on page 426. What are the major landforms in this area? Find Mount McKinley. This mountain is the highest in North America. What is its elevation? The region south of the Alaska Range is southern Alaska. Describe the landforms in this area.

Hawaii. All the Hawaiian Islands are the tops of **volcanoes**. A volcano is a mountain that is built up, layer by layer, from lava, ash, and rock.

There are two active volcanoes on the island of Hawaii. One of these, Mauna Loa (mou′nə·lō′ə), erupts every few years. Sometimes it only belches smoke and fire. Other times it pours out lava, adding more land to the island.

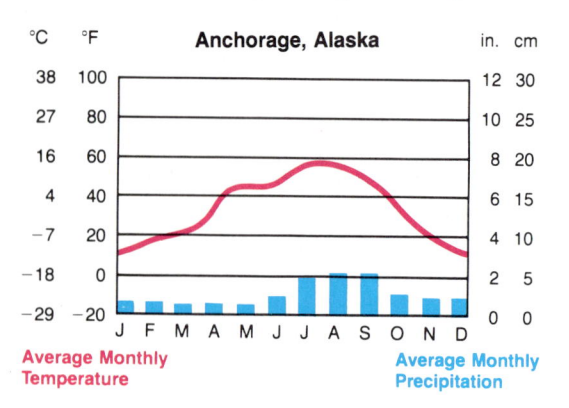

The Climate

The climates of Alaska and Hawaii show the greatest contrast between the two states. As you might expect, their different locations help explain this great contrast.

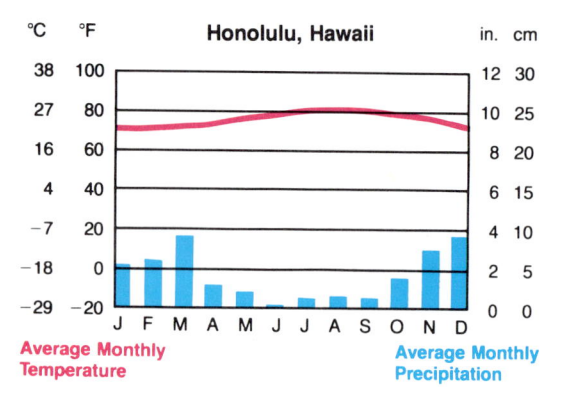

Honolulu, Hawaii

Average Monthly Temperature
Average Monthly Precipitation

Study the climatographs of Anchorage and Honolulu. How many degrees difference is there between Anchorage and Honolulu in January? in July? Which city has the greater range in temperature patterns? Which city gets more precipitation each year?

Anchorage, Alaska

Average Monthly Temperature
Average Monthly Precipitation

Checking Up

1. What is the tundra?
2. How were the Hawaiian Islands formed?
3. *Explain how a description of Alaska as a cold, arctic region is not true for all of Alaska.*

1. Plains and hills. Mount McKinley's elevation is 20,320 feet (32,512 km).
2. About 60 degrees difference in January. About 22 degrees difference in July. Anchorage has the greatest range in temperature patterns. Honolulu gets more precipitation.

1. Anchorage. Honolulu.
2. Oahu.
3. About 218,000. About 1,000,000 more people.
4. Anchorage. About 1,600,000.

Where Are the People?

In both Alaska and Hawaii, many of the people live in each state's largest city. Most of the rest of each state has few people.

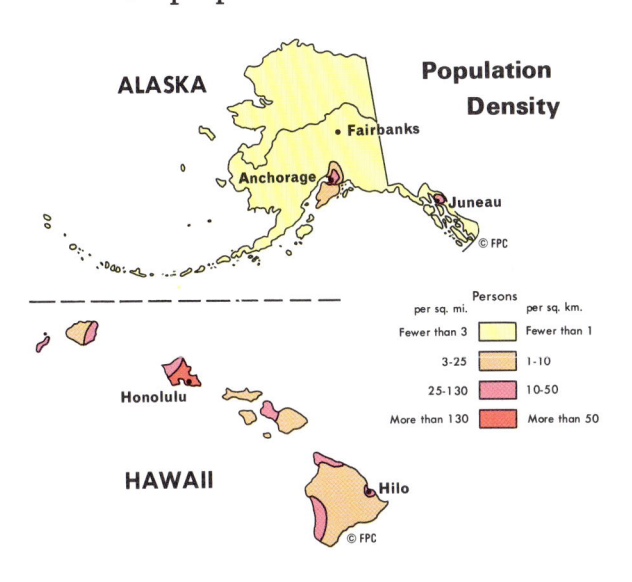

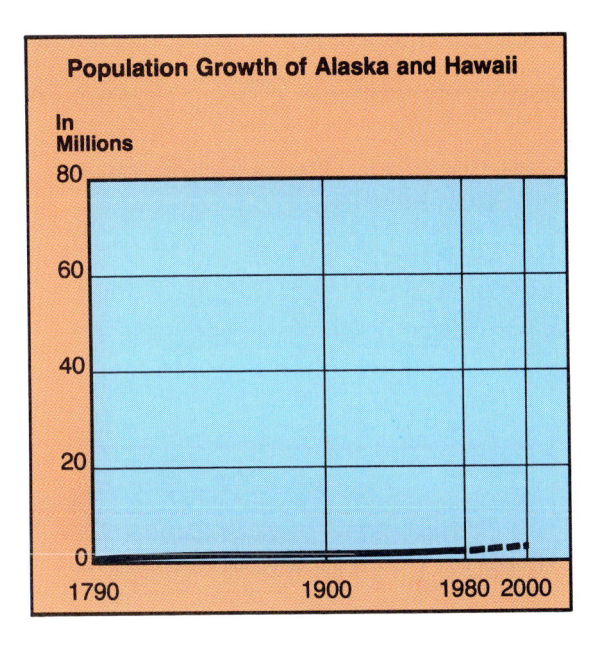

Population Density

Population Growth of Alaska and Hawaii

Where the People Live

Look at the population map on this page. What is the largest city in Alaska? in Hawaii?

Compare the map on page 426 with the population map on this page. Which of the Hawaiian Islands has the most people?

Population Growth

Look at the line graph on this page. What was the population of Alaska and Hawaii in 1900? How many more people were living in Alaska and Hawaii in 1980 than in 1900?

In the past twenty years the populations of Alaska and Hawaii have grown considerably. In Alaska this population growth is due to new discoveries of natural resources. Population increase in Hawaii is due to the rapid growth over the past twenty years of a thriving tourist industry. People have moved to Alaska and Hawaii to fill jobs created by the growth of the economy in each state.

Study the table on page 430. Which city had the greatest population increase between 1970 and 1980? Look again at the line graph on this page. How many people are expected to be living in Alaska and Hawaii in the year 2000?

A Variety of People

Both Alaska and Hawaii have a variety of **ethnic groups.** An ethnic group shares the same ancestry, customs, and language.

The people of Alaska. The earliest settlers in Alaska were Eskimos, American

Time Skill: Why do students think experts have predicted that the population of the region will increase quite a bit by the year 2000?

*** **Reading Skill:** Doing research. Have several students report on the Aleuts and the Polynesians.
Citizenship Skill: Decision making. Have students take turns role-playing a travel agent trying to persuade someone to vacation in Hawaii or Alaska.

Recent Populations of Selected Cities in Alaska and Hawaii				
City	1950 Population	1960 Population	1970 Population	1980 Population
Anchorage, AK	11,254	44,237	48,081	173,017
Fairbanks, AK	5,771	13,311	14,771	22,521
Hilo, HI	27,198	25,966	26,353	37,054
Honolulu, HI	248,034	294,194	324,871	365,048

Indians, and Aleuts (ə·lüts'). Today the descendants of these people make up about one-third of the population of Alaska. Some of these people make a living by hunting and fishing in much the same way their ancestors did. However, in recent years many of these people have been attracted to job opportunities in the cities of Alaska.

The people of Hawaii. Hawaii has a rich blend of cultures. About one half of the population of Hawaii is of European ancestry. The rest of the population is of Asian ancestry. This group includes the descendants of the first people in Hawaii, the Polynesians (päl'ə·nē'zhənz). Today these people are called Hawaiians. These native Hawaiians make up only a small part of Hawaii's population. Other groups of Asians in Hawaii today include people from Japan, China, and the Philippines.

Interesting Places to Visit
Pictured here is Hawaii Volcanoes National Park on the island of Hawaii. This island is the only one that still has active volcanoes. Visitors to this park can walk along trails and view pools of hot, bubbling lava.

The Pribilof Islands, off the southwestern shore of Alaska, attract the world's largest herd of fur seals in the summer.

Checking Up
1. Where do most of the people in Alaska and Hawaii live?
2. What is an ethnic group?
3. Who were the earliest settlers in Alaska? in Hawaii?
4. *How does geography help explain why most of the people in Alaska live in Anchorage?*

*** **Communication Skill:** Writing. Have students write for information on Alaska and Hawaii. Then set up a display for others to view.
Thinking Skill: Evaluation. Which place, Alaska or Hawaii, would students most like to visit? Why?

Reading Skill: Building vocabulary. Talk about the meaning of *cost of living*.
Thinking Skill: Predicting. Where might international flights that stop in Honolulu and Anchorage be going?

What Do the People Do?

The economies of Alaska and Hawaii differ greatly. However, both transportation and the federal government play a major role in the economy of both states.

The Importance of Transportation

As you learned earlier in this unit, Alaska and Hawaii are far from the other forty-eight states. Because of this distance, the people in both states depend on good transportation by sea and by air to get much of the food and other goods they need. Since goods are transported long distances, they often cost more than in other parts of the country. As a result, the cost of living in Alaska and Hawaii is higher than it is in many other areas of the country.

Both Alaska and Hawaii are well located as stopping points for airplanes and ships. The Anchorage airport in Alaska and the Honolulu airport in Hawaii serve as refueling stations for many international flights. Ships crossing the Pacific often stop in Honolulu to take on fuel and supplies.

The Federal Government

Many people work for the military in both Hawaii and Alaska. Hawaii's location explains why the military is important there. The island of Oahu is the center for the American defense of the Pacific area. Look at the map on page 426 and find Pearl Harbor. Our navy's ships get supplies and make repairs

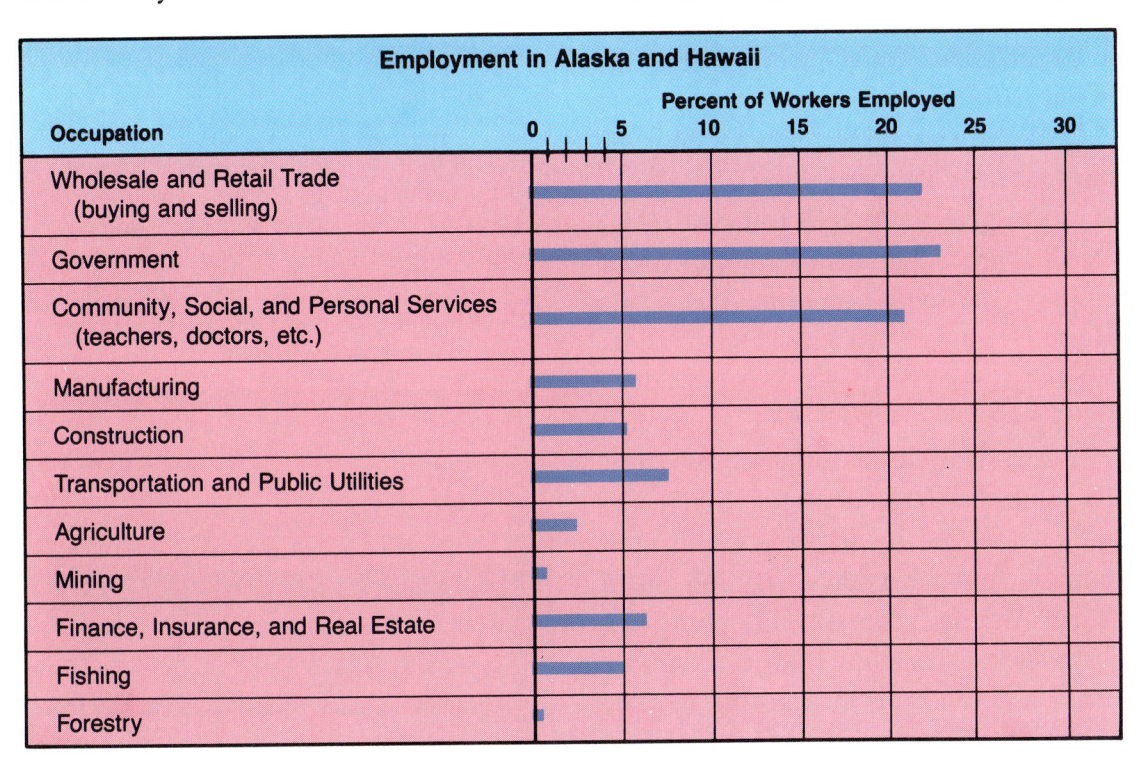

Employment in Alaska and Hawaii

Occupation	Percent of Workers Employed
Wholesale and Retail Trade (buying and selling)	~22
Government	~22
Community, Social, and Personal Services (teachers, doctors, etc.)	~20
Manufacturing	~5
Construction	~5
Transportation and Public Utilities	~7
Agriculture	~3
Mining	~1
Finance, Insurance, and Real Estate	~6
Fishing	~5
Forestry	~1

* **Reading Skill:** Using references. Have students look for pictures of people working in Alaska and Hawaii.

Reading Skill: Building vocabulary. Have students look up the meaning of *radar*. Why is radar important?

Thinking Skill: Comparing. What other region has a lot of government-owned land? How are the two regions alike?

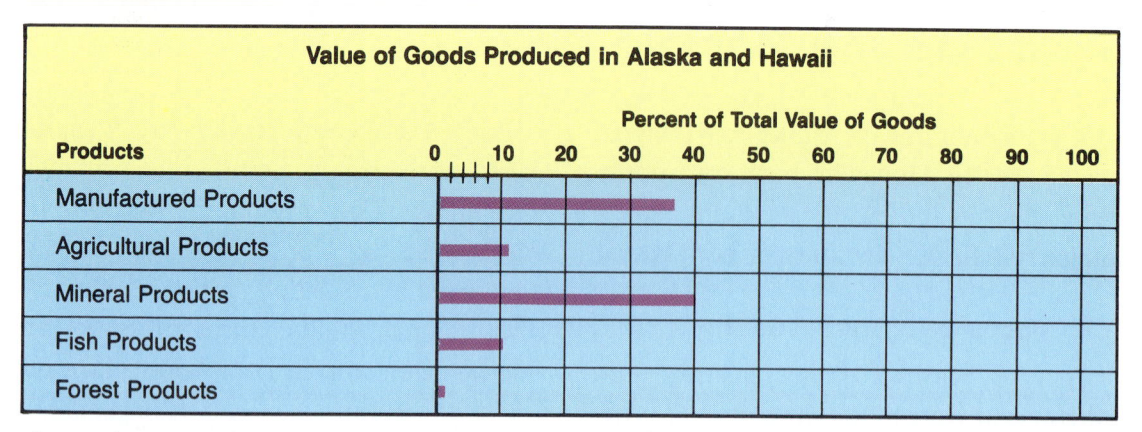

Value of Goods Produced in Alaska and Hawaii

Products	Percent of Total Value of Goods
Manufactured Products	~35%
Agricultural Products	~10%
Mineral Products	~35%
Fish Products	~10%
Forest Products	~1%

there. Army and air force bases are also located on Oahu.

Alaska's location is also important to the defense of our country. Some Alaskans operate radar stations along the northern coast of Alaska. These stations were built to warn our country of possible attack by enemy planes. There are also important military bases in Alaska.

The federal government owns much of the land in Alaska. Most of this land has been set aside by the government as national parks and forests.

Look at the employment graph on page 431. What percent of the people work in government? in transportation? Of all the occupations listed, which one employs the most people in Alaska and Hawaii?

Other Occupations in Alaska

Alaska is rich in mineral resources. The state has large deposits of gold, tin, and coal. However, oil is the state's most valuable mineral product. In 1968 one of North America's largest oil deposits was discovered at Prudhoe Bay on the northern coast. Find this area on the map on page 426.

Careers

Where Some of the People Work

Alaska leads the country in the value of fish caught each year. Salmon and crab are the main catch.

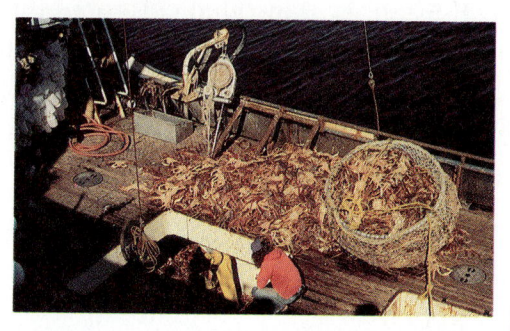

The tourist industry is Hawaii's fastest growing industry. Hotels and resorts, such as those along Waikiki Beach on the island of Oahu, employ many people. In recent years, new resorts have been built on the islands of Hawaii, Kauai, Maui, and Molokai.

1. About 23%; about 8%. Government.

Background: To get the oil near Prudhoe Bay to market, several oil companies worked together to build a pipeline from Prudhoe Bay south to Valdez. From Valdez, oil tankers carry the oil to other parts of the United States.

FACTS ABOUT ALASKA AND HAWAII

	Nickname	Capital* and Largest Cities	State Bird	Farm Products and Natural Resources	Manufactured Products	Did You Know This?
Alaska	The Last Frontier	Juneau* Anchorage Fairbanks Sitka Ketchikan	Willow Ptarmigan	Dairy products, potatoes, hay, cattle, poultry products Petroleum, natural gas, seafood, gold, timber, furs	Processed foods, lumber and wood products, cement and concrete blocks, parkas	Alaska, the largest state in the nation, is more than twice the size of Texas, the second largest state in the nation.
Hawaii	The Aloha State	Honolulu* Kaneohe Hilo Waipahu Pearl City	Nene (Hawaiian goose)	Sugarcane, pineapples, dairy products, cattle, avocados, bananas, papayas Stone, seafood	Processed foods, printed and published materials, glass, stone and clay products	There is a large beach of black sand on the island of Hawaii called Kaimu Black Sand Beach. The black sand is actually small grains of lava.

Thick evergreen forests cover about one-third of Alaska's land. These forests are the basis of an important lumber industry. Fishing and fur trapping are also important ways of making a living in Alaska.

Other Occupations in Hawaii

Unlike Alaska, Hawaii is not rich in mineral deposits. However, Hawaii's ideal climate and beautiful beaches are the source of its major industry, tourism. More than three million tourists visit Hawaii each year.

Like Alaska, Hawaii has to import most of its food. However, specialty crops grown on large plantations are important to Hawaii's economy. Sugarcane and pineapples are the two main crops. Cattle raising is also important. Cattle ranches make up about one-fourth of all the land in Hawaii.

Study the bar graph on page 432 that shows the value of goods produced in Alaska and Hawaii. Of all the goods listed, which has the greatest value? Which state produces this product? [1]

Checking Up
1. What are Hawaii's two major crops?
2. What answers would you give to the key questions at the beginning of this unit?
3. *How are transportation and the government important to the economies of Alaska and Hawaii?*

Unit 17 Summary
- Alaska and Hawaii are similar in that they are far away from the other forty-eight states.
- Both states must import most of their food as well as other goods.
- Both states have a variety of people and have experienced recent population growth.

1. Mineral products. Alaska.
Reading Skill: Interpreting facts. Have students write two facts about each state to support each point in the summary.
Math Skill: Talk about the number of tourists and why they are important.

Unit 17 Review Workshop

What Have You Learned?

1. What are the three regions in Alaska?
2. Describe the temperatures and precipitation in Honolulu.
3. In what way is the population distribution similar in Alaska and Hawaii?
4. What ethnic groups live in Alaska? in Hawaii?
5. How are the economies of Alaska and Hawaii similar?
6. What are three major resources of Alaska?
7. What is the major industry in Hawaii?

Use Your Reading Skills

As you have learned, Alaska and Hawaii are different in many ways. You also learned, however, that they are similar in important ways. Construct a chart of the similarities and the differences between the two states. Use the following topics in your chart: land, climate, population, and economy. Make your chart like the one shown here.

	Similarities	Differences
Land		
Climate		
Population		
Economy		

Use Your Math Skills

The map on page 435 shows the time zones in the United States. Knowing about these different time zones can help you when you travel to or telephone other parts of the country. Study the map. Then answer the questions below.

1. As you move from east to west, does it get earlier or later?
2. How many hours difference is there between New York City and Honolulu, Hawaii?
3. If it is 1 P.M. in Anchorage, Alaska, what time is it in New York? in Montana? in Hawaii?
4. If you lived in Hawaii and you wanted to call someone in Chicago at 3 P.M. Chicago time, what time would you make the call in Hawaii?

Use Your Thinking Skills

A good way to review what you have learned is to see if you can classify, or group, items that belong together. To do this, you must decide which things do not belong in a group.

Read each group below. For each group, tell which item does not belong. Then tell what the remaining items have in common.

1. Mauna Loa, volcano, lava, tundra
2. Anchorage, Barrow, Juneau, Hilo

Learn by Doing

1. Look in books and encyclopedias to find out about one of the following persons: Alexander Baranof, Captain James Cook, Kamehameha the Great, Queen Liliuokalani, or Sanford B. Dole. Write a short report telling why this person is important in history.

Thinking Skills: Knowing, comparing, classifying.
Map Skill: Location.
Reading Skill: Doing research: *Learn by Doing, 1, 2, 4.*

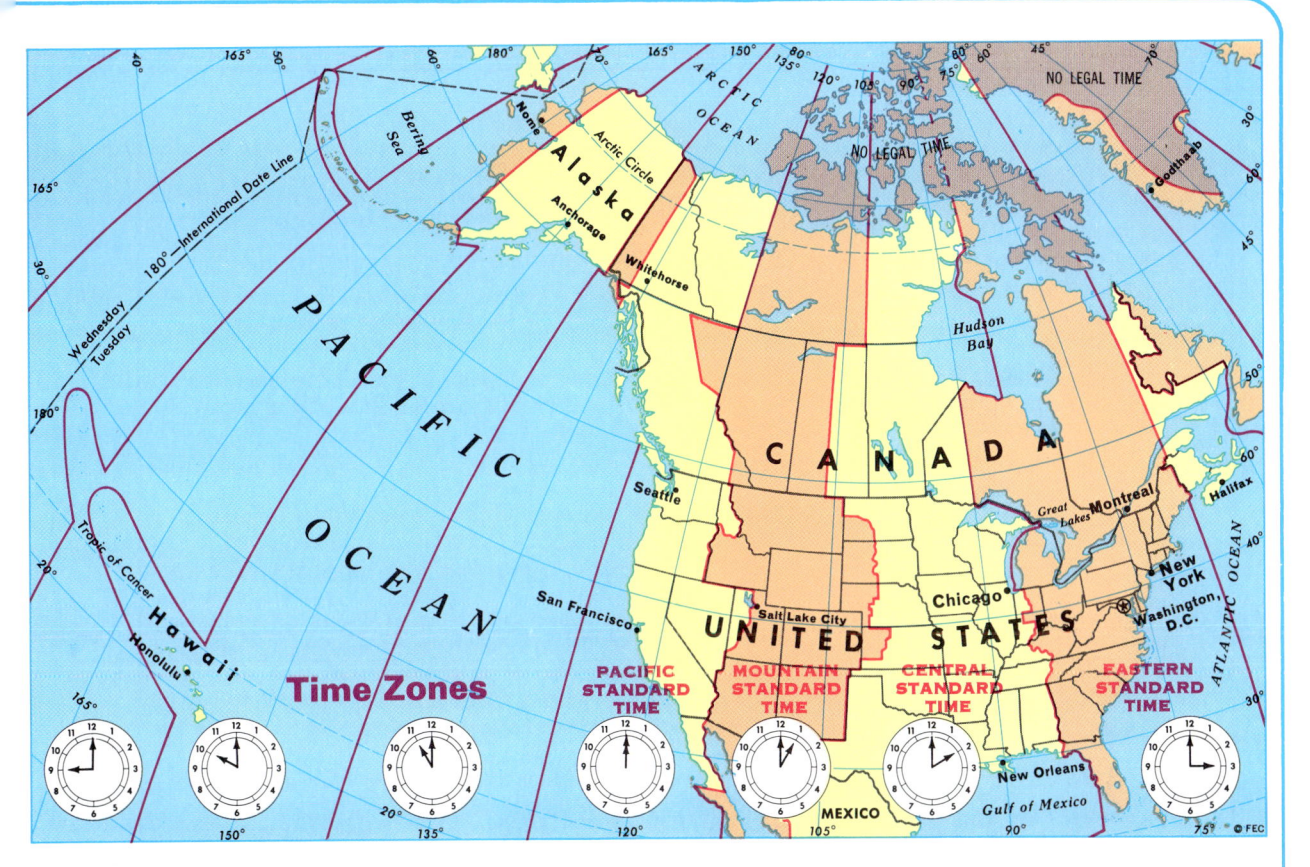

2. Use your school library to find out more about volcanoes. Make a report to your class in which you explain what happens when a volcano erupts. Draw diagrams to use in your report.

3. Draw a picture postcard of the scenery in either Alaska or Hawaii. Look in books and magazines to find photographs of the scenery. Use these photographs to give you ideas for your picture. Write a caption on the back of your postcard that identifies the scene on your postcard. Share this postcard with your class.

4. Find out why Alaska is called the Land of the Midnight Sun. Use a classroom globe to help you explain your findings to your class.

5. Visit your local public library. Use its *Readers' Guide to Periodical Literature* to find articles on the Alaskan pipeline. Read at least two different magazine articles about the construction of the pipeline. Use this information to help you write a description of some of the problems involved in the construction of the pipeline.

Read to Learn More

Find the topics listed below in the card catalog of your library. Read all or part of a book listed under one of the topics. Share what you learn with your classmates.

ALASKA ESKIMOS
HAWAII POLYNESIANS

Reading Skill: Using references: *Learn by Doing, 1–5* and *Read to Learn More.*
Reading Skill: Organizing information: *Learn by Doing, 1–5.*
Communication Skill: Writing: *Learn by Doing, 1, 3, 5.*
Communication Skill: Speaking: *Learn by Doing, 2, 4* and *Read to Learn More.*

Unit Overview: This unit examines Canada, how the geographies of Canada and the United States are alike yet different, how geography influences Canada's population patterns, and the major ways Canadians make a living.

Unit Objectives
To understand:
- how the geographies of Canada and the United States are alike yet different
- how geography influences Canada's population patterns
- the major ways people make a living in Canada
- maps and graphs

Skills Emphasized
Map Skills: pp. 436, 445, 446, 450.
Social Studies Reading Skills: pp. 436, 439, 441, 442, 443, 444, 445, 446, 447, 450, 451.
Thinking Skills: pp. 436, 440, 443, 444, 446, 447, 450.
Communication Skills: pp. 436, 444, 448, 451.
Time Skill: p. 442.
Social Studies Math Skill; p. 442.
Citizenship Skill: p. 436.

Suggested Materials
Workbook
Unit Tests

Unit 18

Suggested Student Activities
1. Find or draw pictures of Canada's seven natural regions to display on a bulletin board.
2. Work in groups. Each group should make a map display of one of Canada's provinces or territories.
3. Make a class data-retrieval chart comparing Canada's provinces and territories.
** 4. Make a salt relief map of Canada.
* 5. Invite someone who has lived in or visited Canada to talk with the class.
*** 6. Write letters requesting information on each province and territory.

Skills Emphasized in Suggested Student Activities
Map Skills: Location, scale.
Reading Skills: Using references, organizing data, interpreting graphics.
Thinking Skills: Knowing, comparing, observing.
Communication Skills: Writing, speaking, listening.
Citizenship Skill: Social participation.

Canada

The Canadian Rockies form the backdrop for mile-high Lake Louise in Banff National Park.

Reading Skill: Building vocabulary. Have students pronounce the name of each province and territory as they use the map on page 438.

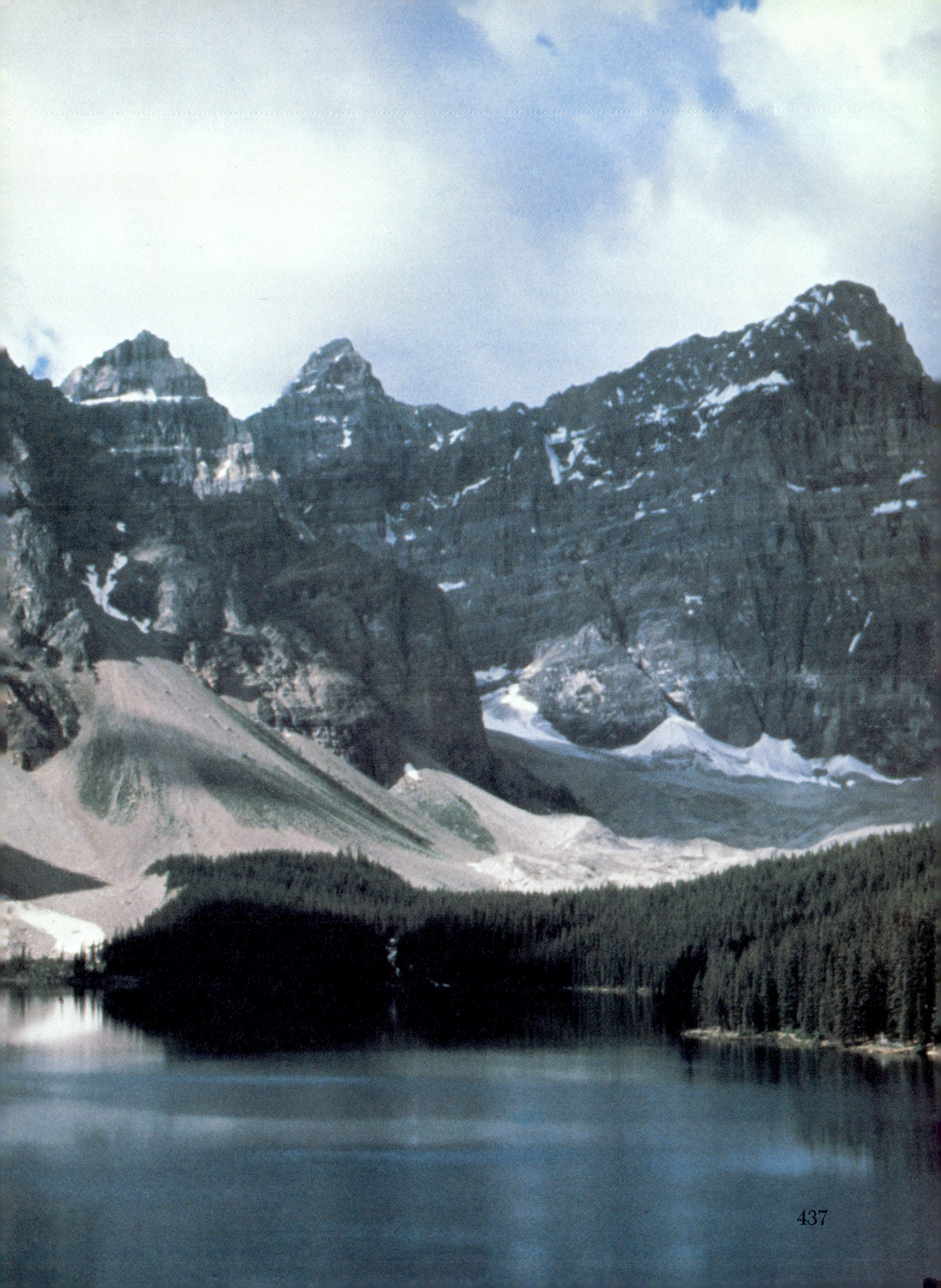

Canada
Physical-Political Map

☆ National Capital ★ Other Capitals
● Other Cities

SCALE
One inch—about 500 miles

Miles: 0 200 400 600 800 1000
Kilometers: 0 200 400 600 800 1000 1200 1400 1600

HEIGHT OF LAND
- OVER 13,000 FEET
- 6,600 TO 13,000
- 3,300 TO 6,600
- 1,650 TO 3,300
- 650 TO 1,650
- 0 TO 650 FEET

DEPTH OF WATER
- 0 TO 600 FEET
- BELOW 600 FEET

Profile

8,000 ft. — Rocky Mountains
6,000 ft.
4,000 ft. — Vancouver Island, Vancouver
2,000 ft. — Winnipeg, Thunder Bay, Lake Superior, Timmins, St. Lawrence River, Gulf of St. Lawrence, St. John's, Newfoundland
Sea level

Natural Regions of Canada

- Pacific Mountain and Valley Region
- Intermountain Region
- Rocky Mountains
- Interior Plains
- Canadian Shield
- St. Lawrence River Valley
- Appalachian Highlands

438

Reading Skill: Interpreting a chart: *As You Read, 3.*
1. Pacific, Arctic, and Atlantic oceans. Asia and Europe. The Great Lakes.

Where Is Canada?

As You Read This Unit

1. Think about these words.
   province   prairie   temperature range
2. Look for answers to these key questions.
   a. In what ways is the geography of Canada similar to that of the United States? How is it different?
   b. How does geography influence population patterns in Canada?
   c. What are three major ways that people make a living in Canada?
3. Use this reading skill.
   Each of the regional units in this book has a chart of interesting facts about the region at the end of the unit. Before you begin reading this unit, read through the chart on pages 448 and 449. When you finish reading the chart, close your book and write a short paragraph listing at least four facts you learned about Canada from reading this chart.

Can you imagine visiting a country so similar to the United States that you might not be sure you were in a different country? This country is Canada, the United States' neighbor to the north. Both countries have rich farmlands, modern cities, and large industrial areas. They also have a wealth of natural resources. Most of the people in both countries speak English.

Yet there are important differences between the two countries. Canada is larger than the United States. In fact, Canada is the second largest country in the world. However, Canada's population is much smaller than that of the United States. The location, land, and climate of Canada help explain why its population is smaller.

Canada's Location

Canada makes up most of the northern part of North America. Study the maps on page 438. What three oceans border Canada? What continents are nearest to Canada across the North Pole? What group of lakes forms part of the boundary between the United States and Canada?

The Provinces and Territories

Canada is divided into ten **provinces,** or smaller political units like states, and two territories. Look at the map on page 438. Find the provinces of Newfoundland, Prince Edward Island, New Brunswick, and Nova Scotia. These provinces are often called the Atlantic, or the Maritime, Provinces because of their location

Reading Skill: Using textbook features. Have students locate this unit in the Table of Contents. Discuss pages 436–437.

Background: Many of the lakes in the Canadian Shield are sources of fast-flowing rivers that provide waterpower for many of Canada's industries.
Thinking Skill: Comparing. Have students make a chart comparing Canada with the United States. Students can later add Latin America to the chart.

along the Atlantic Ocean. Quebec is the largest province in Canada. Find Quebec on the map. Which province borders all but one of the Great Lakes? [1]

Find Manitoba, Saskatchewan (sə·skach′ə·wən), and Alberta. These provinces are called the Prairie Provinces. When settlers first arrived in this area, the land was a vast **prairie**, or large plains area with tall grasses. Now find British Columbia on the map. What ocean borders this province? [2]

Find the Northwest Territories and the Yukon Territory on the map. These territories make up more than one-third of Canada's land.

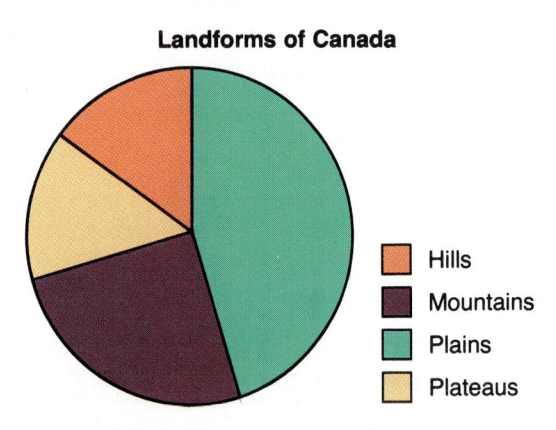

Landforms of Canada

- Hills
- Mountains
- Plains
- Plateaus

The Land

Using the profile and the map on page 438, describe the landforms as you go from west to east in Canada. Look at the pie graph above. Which is the most common landform in Canada? [3]

The natural regions of Canada. Canada has seven major natural land regions. Most of these are part of the same natural land regions that are in the United States. As you read about these regions, find each one on the map on page 438.

The Pacific Mountain and Valley Region. Dense forests cover much of the mountains and valleys in this area. Which province is a part of this region? [4]

The Intermountain Region. This region is a rugged plateau area. Which mountains border this region on the west? on the east? [5]

The Rocky Mountains. This region is an extension of the Rocky Mountains that stretch from New Mexico to Alaska. There are several different mountain ranges here. The largest of these is the Canadian Rockies.

The Interior Plains. This region is an extension of the Midwest Plains and the plains area of the Interior West in the United States. Like the plains in the United States, much of this region is a grassland. Notice that the southern part of the province of Ontario is in this plains region also. The land in this area is similar to the land in northern Ohio and southern Michigan.

The Canadian Shield. Thousands of years ago, glaciers covered this part of Canada. As the glaciers moved south, they carried away most of the topsoil, leaving bare rock, swamps, and lakes. Although the land is not suitable for farming, it has rich mineral deposits.

The St. Lawrence River Valley. This region, the smallest, consists of a series of lowland plains bordering the St. Lawrence River. Some of the best farmland in Canada is in this area.

The Appalachian Highlands. This region is the northern extension of the Appalachian Mountains in the United

1. Ontario. **2.** Pacific Ocean.
3. Plains. **4.** British Columbia.
5. Coast Mountains; Rocky Mountains.

* **Reading Skill**: Building vocabulary. Review the meanings of *sparse* and *dense*.
Reading Skill: Skimming for information. Have students find climatographs of U.S. cities in earlier units that have climates similar to Ottawa and Vancouver.
1. Ottawa. 2. 7–10 inches.

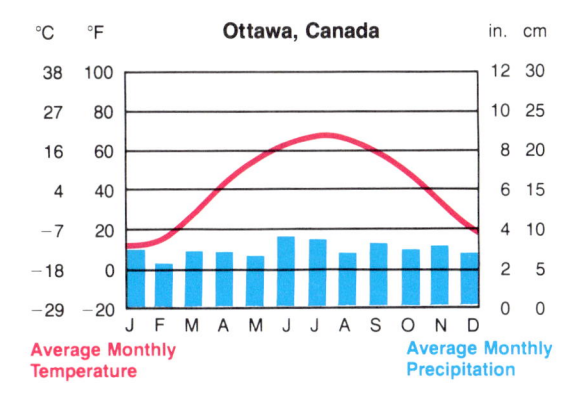

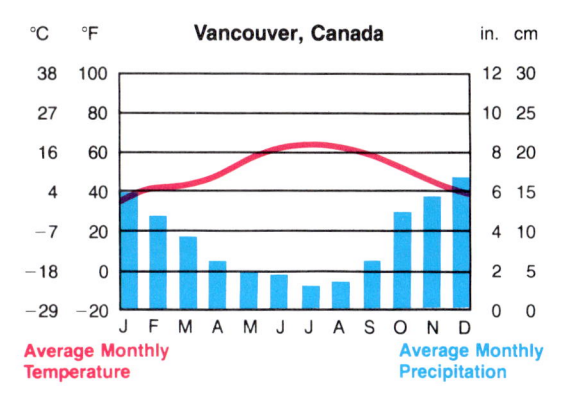

States. Low mountains, valleys, and coastal lowlands make up this region.

The Climate

As you might expect, Canada has a variety of climates. However, because most of Canada is in the high latitudes, much of Canada has a cold climate.

Temperature. Find Vancouver, British Columbia, on the map on page 438. Comparing Vancouver with Ottawa, Canada's capital, illustrates the variety in climates in southern Canada. At any one location, the difference between the highest average monthly temperature and the lowest is called the **temperature range**. Study the two graphs of Ottawa and Vancouver. Which place has a greater range in average monthly temperatures during a year? Warm ocean breezes help keep Vancouver's temperatures mild all year long.

Precipitation. How much more precipitation does Vancouver get than Ottawa? Vancouver's location helps explain its greater rainfall. Moist breezes blowing in from the Pacific Ocean bring rain as they travel inland and up the western side of the mountains.

The growing season. Much of Canada has a growing season too short to grow crops. Study the growing seasons map on this page. Which parts of Canada have the longest growing season? Why?

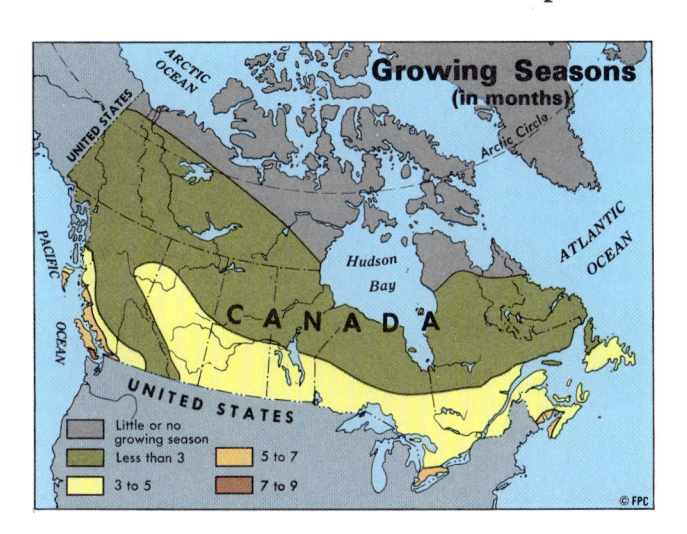

Checking Up

1. How many provinces and territories make up Canada?
2. What are the seven natural regions in Canada?
3. *How might the geography of Canada explain why it is more sparsely populated than the United States?*

441

Math Skill: Have students figure out how many more people live in the United States than in Canada.
Reading Skill: Doing research. Have several students prepare reports on Canada's five largest cities.

Where Are the People?

The size of Canada's population has been influenced by the geography. The harsh climate and rugged land help explain Canada's small population. Canada has only about 25 million people, compared with about 227 million people in the United States.

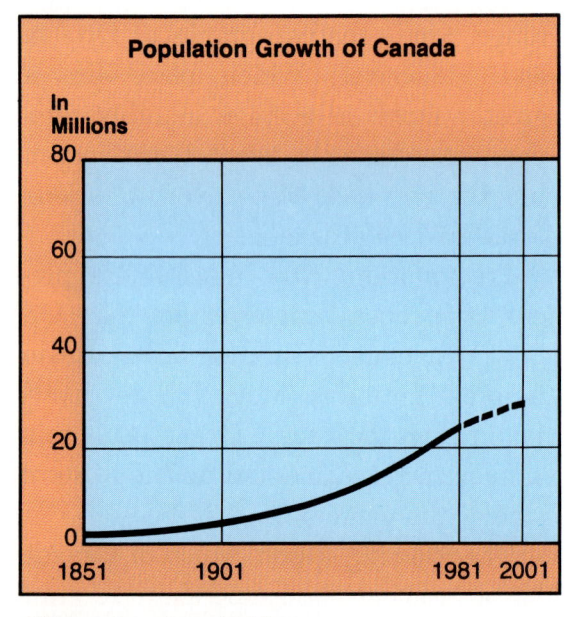

Population Density

Population Growth of Canada

Where the People Live

Most of the people in Canada live within 200 miles (320 km) of the United States border. Montreal, Toronto, Winnipeg, Calgary, and Vancouver are Canada's largest cities. Find these cities on the map on page 438.

Look at the population map on this page. What is the population density along the southern part of Canada's Pacific Coast? along the Great Lakes? How does the population density in these areas compare with the population density in the other parts of Canada?

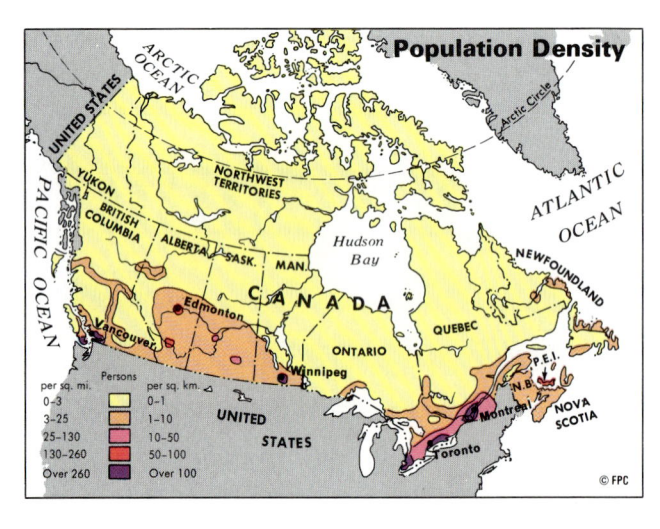

The Growth of Canada

Although Canada and the United States were explored by Europeans at about the same time, large permanent settlements were established in Canada much later than in the United States. In addition, Canada did not become an independent country until 1867. Look at the graph on this page. What was the population of Canada in 1851? in 1901? About how many people are expected to be living in Canada by 2001? How many more people will this be than in 1981? 1

Urban and Rural Population of Canada

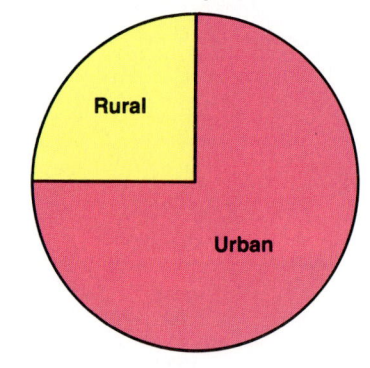

Time Skill: Begin a time line of important events in Canadian history. Each student should add a date and event to the time line.

1. About 2.5 million people; about 5.5 million people. About 34.5 million people. About 9 million more people.

Recent population patterns. As you can see from the pie graph on page 442, most Canadians live in urban areas. However, like cities in the United States, some of Canada's major cities have had a population decrease in recent years. This decrease is due largely to people who have moved from the central cities to newer suburbs surrounding the cities. Study the table on this page. For the years shown, which cities have had a population decrease?

The Two Cultures

Like many other countries in the world, Canada has a variety of ethnic groups. The original settlers in Canada were Eskimos and Indians. The descendants of these people make up only a small part of Canada's population today. Canada also has a number of people who have immigrated from other countries. However, people of British and French heritage make up most of Canada's population.

The French, who were the first Europeans to build permanent settlements in Canada, settled along the St. Lawrence River valley, especially in what is now Quebec. By the time the English defeated the French in North America in 1763, the St. Lawrence valley had many French settlers. These settlers did not leave when the English took over French territory in Canada. Most English settlements in Canada were established farther west in the area of the Ontario peninsula. These early patterns of settlement are still evident and influence the culture in Canada today.

French Canadians live mainly in the province of Quebec. Here French culture is found everywhere. Most of the English Canadians live in the other provinces, particularly west of Quebec. English culture is greatest in these areas.

The official government policy is to recognize both the French and the British cultures as equal. Both French and English are the official languages of Canada. The business of the country can be carried on in either language. All laws must be written in both French and English. Even the capital of Canada is located on the border between the provinces of Quebec and Ontario.

Recent Populations of Selected Cities in Canada				
City	**1951 Population**	**1961 Population**	**1971 Population**	**Latest Estimate**
Calgary, Alta.	129,060	249,641	403,319	470,000
Montreal, Que.	1,021,520	1,191,062	1,214,352	1,080,000
Ottawa, Ont.	202,045	268,206	302,341	304,000
Toronto, Ont.	675,754	672,407	712,786	633,000
Vancouver, B.C.	344,833	384,522	426,256	410,000
Winnipeg, Man.	235,710	265,710	246,246	561,000

> ### Interesting Places to Visit
>
> **Canadian Cities**
>
> Vancouver, at the right, is the busiest seaport in North America. Located between beautiful coastal mountains and the Pacific Ocean, Vancouver's scenic beauty attracts many visitors.  
>
> Toronto, left, is Canada's major industrial city. Unique modern skyscrapers dominate Toronto's business district.
>
> Montreal, pictured at the right, is Canada's largest city. It is the only city in North America built around a mountain. This mountain, called Mount Royal, is shown in the picture here.

In practice, this policy of treating both cultures as equal has not worked very well. The French Canadians, about one-fourth of Canada's population, feel that their culture has not been treated equally in provinces outside Quebec. For example, the French language is rarely spoken outside Quebec. Many French-speaking Canadians, however, speak English as well as French.

Some French Canadians feel that Quebec should become an independent country. The Canadian government is trying to prevent this action. The government is working to bring about better understanding between English and French Canadians. The government, for example, promotes the teaching of both English and French to bring greater feelings of unity to all Canadians.

Checking Up

1. Where do most of the people in Canada live?
2. How does the population of Canada compare with that of the United States?
3. *Do you think all Canadians should be required to learn both French and English? Why or why not?*

Map Skill: Location. Have students locate Canada's agricultural regions on the map on page 451.
* **Reading Skill**: Building vocabulary. Review the meanings of *agricultural* and *industrial*.

What Do the People Do?

Like the United States, Canada began as an agricultural country. Today, however, Canada is one of the world's leading industrial countries. Even so, Canada's farmers produce important crops. Some of these crops are shipped to other countries in the world.

The Agricultural Regions

Canada has two major agricultural regions. The largest of these is the southern part of the Prairie Provinces. This region is a major wheat-growing area similar to the Midwest Plains in the United States.

More wheat is grown in this area than is needed by the Canadian people. As a result, some of the wheat is shipped by rail from Winnipeg and then loaded onto large ships in the Great Lakes for export to Europe. Use the map on page 438 to trace this route. Other cargoes of wheat are shipped west by rail to the port of Vancouver. From there it is exported to countries in Asia. Look at the chart on pages 448 and 449. What are three other crops grown in the Prairie Provinces? **1**

The second important agricultural region in Canada is in southern Ontario and in Quebec along the St. Lawrence River. Dairy farming and livestock raising are important in this area. Also, fruit is grown along the shores of Lake Erie and Lake Ontario.

Look at the graph on page 446 that shows the value of products. What is the value of agricultural products? **2**

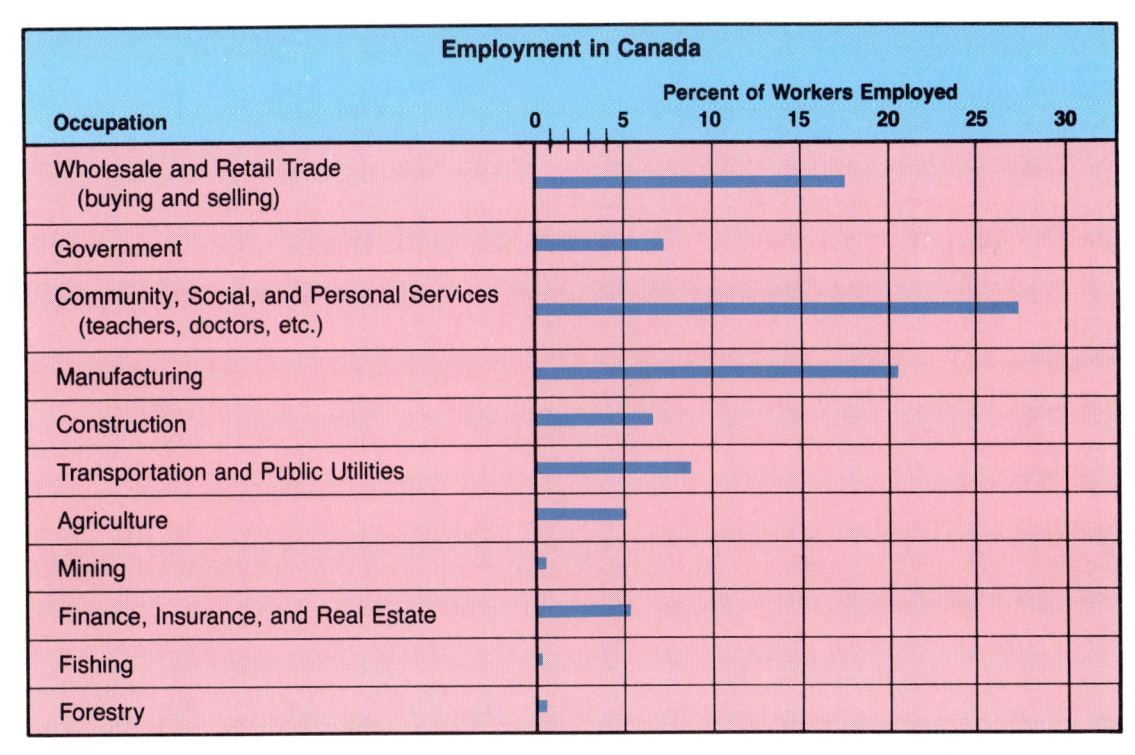

Employment in Canada

Occupation	Percent of Workers Employed
Wholesale and Retail Trade (buying and selling)	~17
Government	~7
Community, Social, and Personal Services (teachers, doctors, etc.)	~26
Manufacturing	~20
Construction	~6
Transportation and Public Utilities	~9
Agriculture	~5
Mining	~1
Finance, Insurance, and Real Estate	~6
Fishing	<1
Forestry	<1

Reading Skill: Interpreting graphs. Ask students how the employment graph helps answer the chapter's title question.
1. Barley, rapeseed, sugar beets, flaxseed, sunflower seeds, rye, oats, or mustard seed.
2. About 14%.

Map Skill: Location. Have students locate Canada's major industrial region on the map on page 438.
Thinking Skill: Comparing. Discuss which U.S. cities compare with Canada's manufacturing centers.
Reading Skill: Interpreting pictures. Have students look for pictures of service jobs performed in Canada.

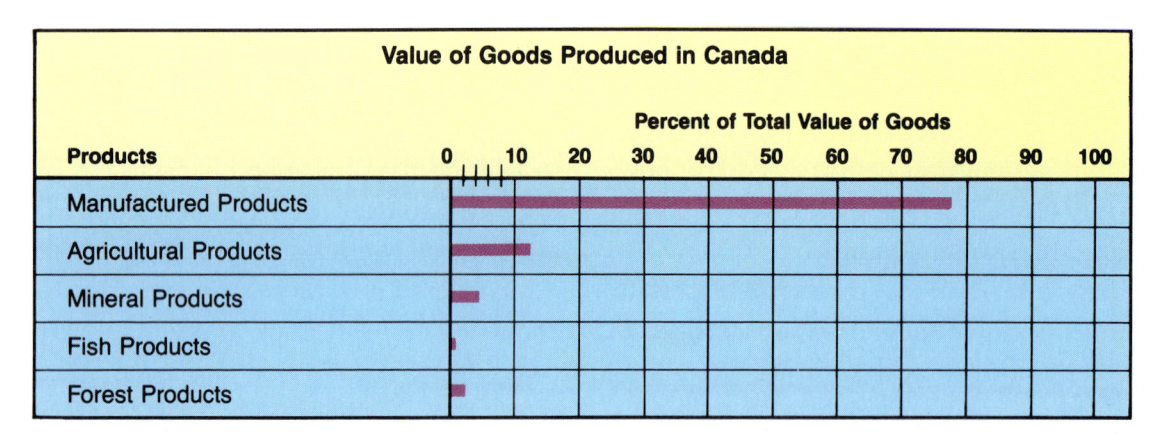

Value of Goods Produced in Canada											
Products / Percent of Total Value of Goods	0	10	20	30	40	50	60	70	80	90	100
Manufactured Products									■		
Agricultural Products		■									
Mineral Products		■									
Fish Products	■										
Forest Products		■									

Major Industries

The major industrial region in Canada includes the southern parts of Ontario and Quebec. This region is located next to one of the largest industrial regions in the United States, the Great Lakes Region. The industrial region in Canada is similar to that of the Great Lakes Region, only smaller. Many of the industries are heavy industries such as steel making and automobile manufacturing. In addition, like the Great Lakes Region, the industrial area in Canada depends on the Great Lakes to transport raw materials from their sources to the factories along the lakes for processing.

Find Windsor, Hamilton, and Toronto on the map on page 438. These cities are major manufacturing centers. Windsor has large automobile plants, and Hamilton has large steel mills. Toronto is a major shipping and processing center. Montreal, the major industrial city in Quebec, has large oil refineries and is an important banking center. There are other smaller industrial areas in Canada, but they are located near the raw materials that their factories process.

Even though Canada is a major manufacturing nation, services employ more people in Canada than any other occupation. Hospitals, advertising agencies, and community services are part of the service business. Look at the graph on page 445. What percent of the people are employed in services? in manufacturing? **1**

Canada's Natural Resources

Canada has a wealth of natural resources. Among these resources are vast deposits of minerals.

Minerals. Canada exports large amounts of minerals to other parts of the world. Look at the map on page 447. Name at least four minerals found in Canada. **2**

Energy resources. In which provinces are oil and natural gas found? Find the **3** Athabasca (ath′ə·bas′kə) River on the map on page 438. There are large deposits of sand soaked with oil in the valley along this river. Many experts believe the oil deposits in this area are among the world's largest known oil reserves.

Forests. Canada's large forests are the source of a major lumber and paper in-

1. About 27%; about 21%.
2. Coal, copper, gold, iron ore, natural gas, nickel, oil, potash, or uranium.
3. Oil—Alberta and Saskatchewan; natural gas—Alberta and British Columbia.

Reading Skill: Listing. Have students name different wood-pulp products. Some students could also organize a products display on a bulletin board.
*** **Reading Skill**: Doing research. Have several students write reports on the Royal Canadian Mounted Police.

Mineral Resources in Canada

Legend: Coal, Copper, Gold, Iron Ore, Natural Gas, Nickel, Oil, Potash, Uranium

Careers

Where Some of the People Work

Paper and wood-pulp industries employ more people in Canada than any other manufacturing business. Shown here are workers in a paper mill in Port Alfred, Quebec. After Quebec, British Columbia leads the provinces in the manufacture of paper and wood-pulp products.

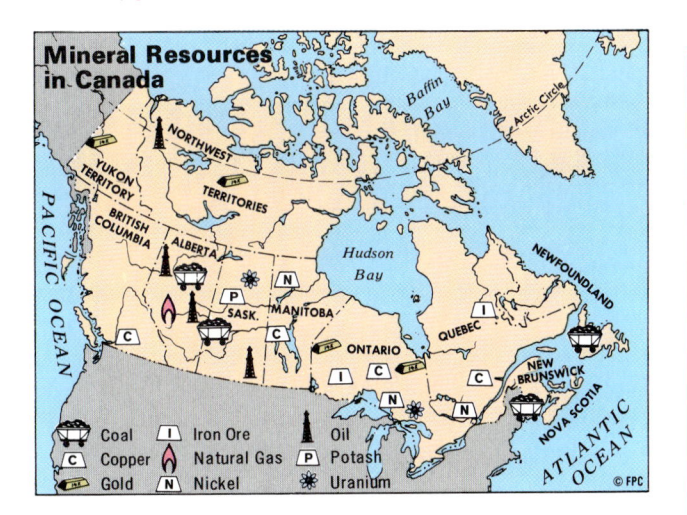

dustry. In fact, Canada is the world's largest manufacturer of newsprint.

Fishing. Canada ranks fourth in the world in the value of its fish exports. Some of the best fishing grounds in the world are off the shores of Nova Scotia and Newfoundland. Fishing is also important in the other Atlantic Provinces and in British Columbia.

Problems and Prospects

Many of Canada's vast natural resources are just being developed. With greater development of these resources, Canada's economy will continue to grow. However, the Atlantic Provinces face several economic problems. Find these provinces on the map on page 438. Notice how they are somewhat isolated from the rest of Canada. These provinces do not have great mineral wealth. The climate in this area is too cool and wet for most crops. Those who do farm in the region find it difficult to compete with farmers in other parts of Canada who are closer to large markets.

The Royal Canadian Mounted Police number over 18,000. This police force is maintained by the federal government of Canada. The major responsibilities of this force include enforcing many federal laws, particularly Canada's criminal code. They are responsible for protecting government property and foreign leaders visiting the country. They are also the only police force in the Yukon and Northwest territories.

Thinking Skill: Analyzing. Discuss why offshore fishing rights are important to many countries.
*** **Reading Skill**: Doing research. Have several students report on Canada's fishing industry off the shores of the Atlantic Provinces.

447

Communication Skill: Writing. Have students use the *Facts* chart to write three facts about one province or territory. Have others guess which province or territory is being described.

The fishing industry in the Atlantic Provinces also faces problems. People come from all over the world to fish off the shores of the Atlantic Provinces. In recent years this has led to decreased supplies of fish in the coastal waters. The Canadian government, however, has taken measures to help its fishing industry. The government has set limits on foreign offshore fishing to protect the supply of fish in the coastal waters off the Atlantic Provinces.

Checking Up
1. Where are Canada's two main agricultural regions?
2. What answers would you give to the key questions at the beginning of this unit?
3. *Why do you think the exports of agricultural and manufactured products as well as natural resources are important to Canada's economy?*

Unit 18 Summary
- Much of Canada has rugged land and a harsh climate. This geography helps explain Canada's sparse population.
- Though similar in many ways to the United States of America, Canada is a country that has both English and French cultures.
- Canada's industrial region is similar in many ways to the Great Lakes industrial region in the United States.

	Province Flag
Alberta Population: 2,153,200	
British Columbia Population: 2,701,900	
Manitoba Population: 1,028,800	
New Brunswick Population: 709,600	
Newfoundland Population: 584,500	
Nova Scotia Population: 856,600	
Ontario Population: 8,614,200	
Prince Edward Island Population: 124,200	
Quebec Population: 6,334,700	
Saskatchewan Population: 977,400	

FACTS ABOUT THE PROVINCES OF CANADA

Capital* and Largest Cities	Farm Products and Natural Resources	Manufactured Products	Did You Know This?
Edmonton* Calgary Lethbridge Red Deer Medicine Hat	Wheat, barley, rapeseed, sugar beets, flaxseed, cattle, hogs, sheep Petroleum, natural gas, sulphur, metals, structural materials	Foods and beverages, wood products, fabricated metal, transportation equipment, refined petroleum	Alberta produces more than 90 percent of Canada's natural gas and petroleum.
Victoria* Vancouver New Westminster Prince George North Vancouver	Fruit, vegetables, cattle, hogs, sheep, poultry, fishing, forestry Metals, fuels, structural materials	Paper, wood products, mineral products, foods and beverages, transportation equipment, chemicals	British Columbia's capital city of Victoria and much of the province's population are located on Vancouver Island, a large island in the Pacific Ocean.
Winnipeg* Brandon Portage la Prairie Flin Flon Selkirk	Grain, sunflower seeds, rapeseed, flaxseed, sugar beets, cattle, hogs, sheep, poultry Metals, fuels	Agricultural implements, processed foods, machinery, transportation equipment, clothing	Half of Manitoba's entire population lives in its capital city of Winnipeg.
Fredericton* Saint John Moncton Bathurst Edmundston Oromocto	Potatoes, apples, blueberries, oats, cattle, hogs, poultry, fishing, lumber Metals, structural materials	Paper, wood products, fish products	New Brunswick has the world's longest covered bridge at Hartland.
Saint John's* Corner Brook Stephenville Gander Grand Falls	Fish, poultry, forestry Iron ore, asbestos, construction materials	Fish products, paper products	More than 95 percent of Newfoundland's electric power is supplied by hydroelectric generators.
Halifax* Dartmouth Sydney Glace Bay Truro	Fish, apples, strawberries, oats, potatoes, hogs, sheep, poultry Coal, structural materials, gypsum	Paper, fish products, dairy products, ships	Nova Scotia's capital of Halifax is a very important port for Canada because it remains open through the winter, when many Canadian ports are closed by ice.
Toronto* Hamilton Ottawa London Windsor	Corn, wheat, oats, barley, rye, tobacco, tree fruits, cattle, hogs, sheep, poultry, forestry Metals, structural materials, fuels	Motor vehicles, iron and steel, foods and beverages, paper and allied products	Ontario's southern boundary touches three U.S. states—New York, Michigan, and Minnesota—and four of the five Great Lakes—Superior, Huron, Erie, and Ontario.
Charlottetown* Summerside Montague Souris East Kensington	Potatoes, oats, barley, cattle, hogs, sheep, poultry, fish Sand and gravel	Paint, farm vehicles, metal products, electronic equipment	Prince Edward Island is Canada's smallest province in both area and population.
Quebec City* Montreal Sherbrooke Sainte Foy Hull	Oats, corn, potatoes, apples, cattle, hogs, sheep, poultry, fish, forestry Metals, asbestos, structural materials	Foods and beverages, clothing, textiles, paper, paper products, furniture	Montreal is second only to Paris as the largest French-speaking city in the world.
Regina* Saskatoon Moose Jaw Prince Albert Swift Current	Wheat, barley, rye, oats, mustard seed, flax, cattle, hogs, sheep, poultry Fuels, potash, metals, structural materials	Foods and beverages, agricultural implements, fabricated metals, nonmetallic mineral products	Saskatchewan produces 60 percent of all Canada's wheat.

Unit 18 Review Workshop

What Have You Learned?

1. What are the names of the provinces and territories of Canada?
2. What are the seven natural regions in Canada?
3. What are the ranges of growing seasons in Canada?
4. How does Canada's geography influence where the people live?
5. What are the two main cultures in Canada?
6. What are three major industries in Canada?

Use Your Reading Skills

Reference tools such as encyclopedias help you gather information about a topic. Choose one of the provinces in Canada to research. Look up this province in your school library encyclopedia. Find out when it became a Canadian province and how many people live in this province. Share this information with your class.

Use Your Map Skills

By comparing two different maps that show the same area, you can learn a great deal about a region. Study the rainfall and agricultural maps on page 451. Then answer the following questions. Answers to these questions will help you see the connections between agricultural regions and geographic features.

1. What part of Canada has the least amount of rainfall?
2. Find the areas where wheat is grown in Canada and in the United States. What is the amount of rainfall in these areas?
3. Which agricultural region requires the least amount of rainfall? the most?
4. What is similar about the pattern of rainfall in both the United States and Canada? Look at the map of North America on page 15. How might landforms and location account for this similar pattern of rainfall?
5. Look again at the maps and pictures in this unit. What geographic features, other than rainfall, might explain why Canada has such a large nonagricultural region?

Use Your Thinking Skills

A helpful way to review what you have learned is to see if you can make a general statement about the major topics you have studied. Below is a list of three of the important topics in this unit. Write one or two general sentences for each of the following topics. Then share what you have written with others in your class.

1. the geography
2. the population patterns
3. the economy

Learn by Doing

1. Work with four or five classmates to put together a current-events magazine about Canada. Group members

Thinking Skills: Knowing, synthesizing.
Reading Skill: Doing research.
Map Skill: Location.

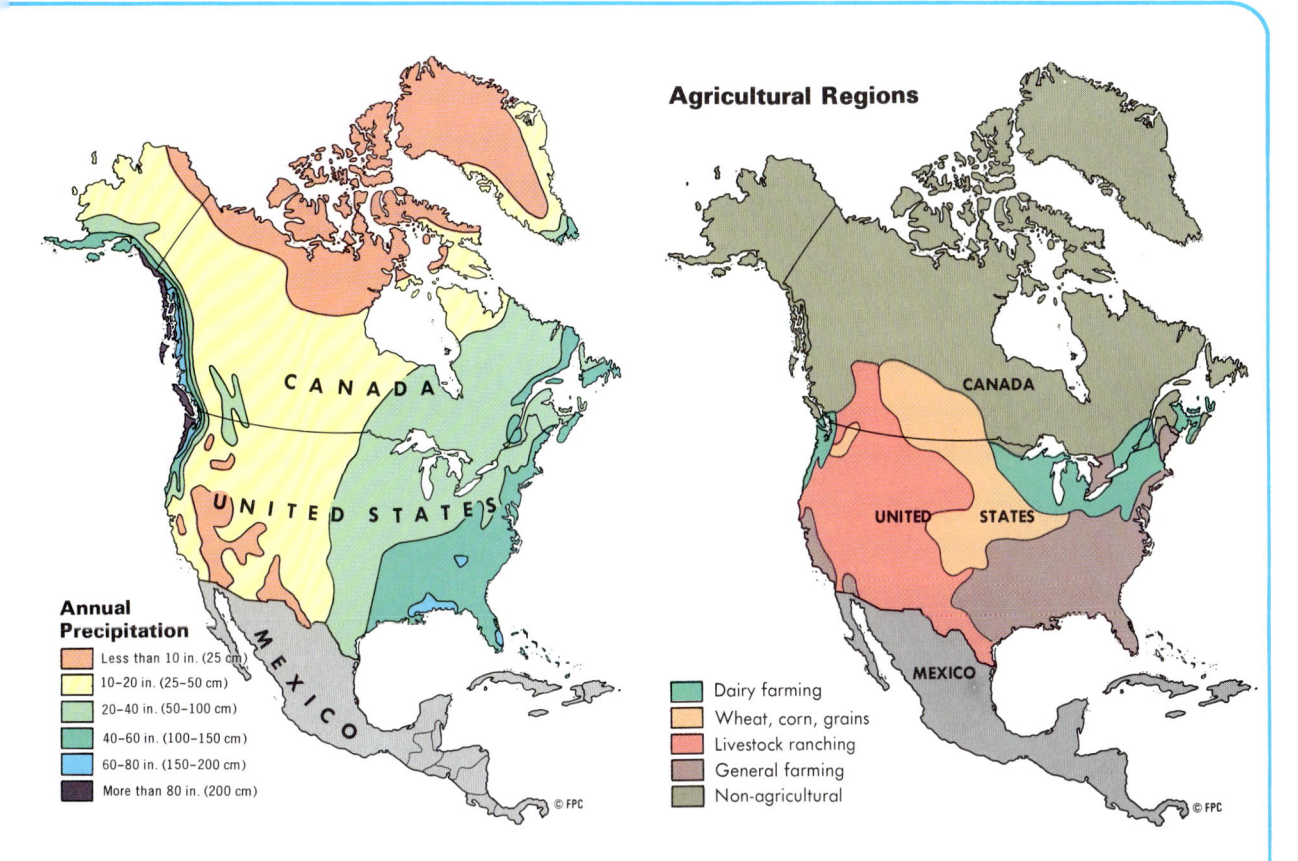

Annual Precipitation
- Less than 10 in. (25 cm)
- 10-20 in. (25-50 cm)
- 20-40 in. (50-100 cm)
- 40-60 in. (100-150 cm)
- 60-80 in. (150-200 cm)
- More than 80 in. (200 cm)

Agricultural Regions
- Dairy farming
- Wheat, corn, grains
- Livestock ranching
- General farming
- Non-agricultural

should look through their home newspapers or newsmagazines for current articles about Canada. Write a short summary for each of the articles. Title the articles and organize them under such topics as Canada's government, its economy, Canadians in the news, and United States–Canadian relations. Paste the articles into a folder under your topic listings.

2. Beginning with the planting of wheat in Saskatchewan, trace all the steps that would go into producing a loaf of bread sold in a store in Toronto. Use books and encyclopedias to help you find out how wheat is made into flour and then into bread. Show these steps on a time line or a picture chart.

3. Farley Mowat is a famous Canadian writer. One of his most famous books is *Never Cry Wolf*. This book is about the living habits of wolves. Research the life of Farley Mowat. Then make a report to your class about the life of this famous Canadian. You may want to read one of his books.

Read to Learn More

Find the topics listed below in the card catalog of your library. Read all or part of a book listed under one of the topics. Share what you learn with your classmates.

CANADA   ONTARIO

QUEBEC   ST. LAWRENCE SEAWAY

Reading Skills: Organizing information: *Learn by Doing, 1, 2*; using references: *Learn by Doing, 2, 3* and *Read to Learn More*; summarizing: *Learn by Doing, 1, 2*.
Communication Skill: Writing: *Learn by Doing, 3*.

Unit Overview: This unit examines Latin America, how the geographies of Latin America and the United States are different and alike, how geography influences Latin America's population patterns, and the major products of Latin America.

Unit Objectives
To understand:
- how the geographies of Latin America and the United States are alike and different
- how geography influences Latin America's population
- the major products grown
- maps and graphs

Suggested Materials
Workbook
Unit Tests

Unit 19

Skills Emphasized
Map and Globe Skills: pp. 452, 456, 457, 468.
Social Studies Reading Skills: pp. 452, 455, 457, 459, 460, 461, 462, 463, 464, 468, 469.
Thinking Skills: pp. 452, 456, 458, 459, 462, 464, 468.
Communication Skills: pp. 452, 460, 465, 469.
Social Studies Math Skill: p. 460.
Citizenship Skills: pp. 452, 469.

Suggested Student Activities
   1. Display drawings and maps of Middle America and South America on a bulletin board.
   2. Use the chart begun in Unit 18 comparing Canada and the United States. Add a column to compare with Latin America.
   3. Work alone or in pairs. Organize a pictorial display of one country in Latin America.
** 4. Make a salt relief map of Latin America.
 * 5. Have someone teach the class some basic Spanish.
*** 6. Invite a speaker from Latin America to speak to the class.

Skills Emphasized in Suggested Student Activities
Social Studies Reading Skills: Using references, organizing data, interpreting graphics.
Communication Skills: Speaking, writing, listening.
Map Skills: Location, scale.
Thinking Skills: Knowing, comparing, observing.

Latin America

Glowing with city lights, age-old Sugarloaf Mountain rises above downtown Rio de Janeiro.

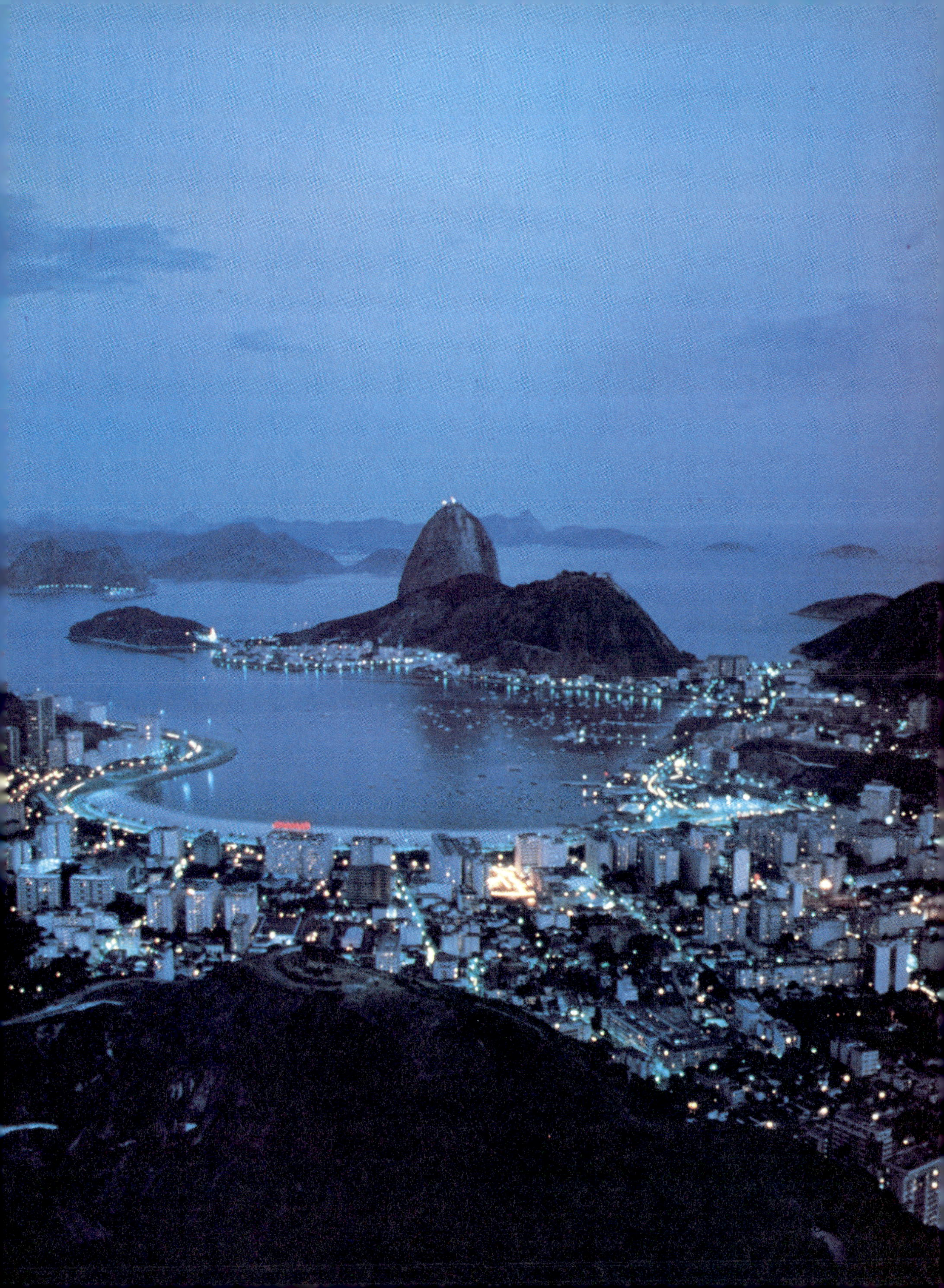

Latin America
Physical-Political Map

- ⊛ National Capitals
- ★ Other Capitals
- • Other Cities

SCALE
One inch—about 825 miles

Miles: 0 200 400 600 800
Kilometers: 0 400 800 1200

454

HEIGHT OF LAND
- OVER 13,000 FEET
- 6,600 TO 13,000
- 3,300 TO 6,600
- 1,650 TO 3,300
- 650 TO 1,650
- 0 TO 650 FEET

DEPTH OF WATER
- 0 TO 600 FEET
- BELOW 600 FEET

Elevation profile (Feet): Quito, Andes Mountains, Río Negro, Amazon River, Belém
15,000 / 12,000 / 9,000 / 6,000 / 3,000 / Sea level

Reading Skill: Using textbook features: *As You Read, 3*.
Reading Skill: Building vocabulary. Have students pronounce the name of each country as they use the map on page 454.

Where Is Latin America?

As You Read This Unit

1. Think about these words.
   low latitudes   mestizo   bauxite
   middle latitudes   developing nation
2. Look for answers to these key questions.
   a. In what ways is the geography of Latin America similar to that of the United States? How is it different?
   b. How does the geography influence population patterns in Latin America?
   c. What are the major products of Latin America?
3. Use this reading skill.
   Using The Atlas Tells a Story section of this book can help you understand more about the geography of an area. Turn to page 32. The drawing at right shows the earth's polar regions, middle latitudes, and tropical region. Compare the map of Latin America on page 454 with this drawing. In which region is most of Latin America? As you read this unit, look for information about the climate of the tropical regions of Latin America.

During the years of European settlement, most of the people who settled in the area known as Latin America came from Spain and Portugal. They brought their customs and languages. Because the Spanish and Portuguese languages developed from Latin, this area is called Latin America. Latin America has a variety of climates, landforms, and cultures.

The Region

Look at the map on page 454. What country in Latin America is the farthest north? Which states in the United States border this country?   1

Which ocean is west of Latin America? Which ocean is east? In which sea are the islands of Cuba and Jamaica?   2

Three important geographical lines run through Latin America. One divides the earth into the Northern and Southern Hemispheres. What is the name of this line? The other two important lines are the Tropic of Cancer and the Tropic of Capricorn. Find these lines. The area between the Tropic of Cancer and the Tropic of Capricorn is called the **low latitudes**, or the tropics. As you can see, most of Latin America lies within the low latitudes.

1. Mexico. Texas, New Mexico, Arizona, and California.
2. Pacific Ocean. Atlantic Ocean. Caribbean Sea.

Reading Skill: Using textbook features. After introducing the unit, have students talk about Latin.

455

Map Skill: Location. Have students compare the longitudes of North and Latin America.
Thinking Skill: Comparing. Have students discuss how the landforms of Middle and South America are alike and different.

Use the map scale to find out about how many miles Latin America stretches from the northern border of Mexico to the southern tip of Argentina. About how many miles does Latin America stretch along the equator from the western coast of Ecuador to the eastern coast of Brazil?

The Land

In this unit Latin America is divided into two parts. Middle America includes Mexico, all the countries south of Mexico to Panama, and all the countries in the Caribbean. South America includes all the countries south of Panama.

Middle American landforms. Look at the pie graph on this page. Which landform is the most common in Middle America? the least common? [1]

Mountains are also a common landform in the Caribbean. In fact, most of these islands are actually the tops of underwater mountains. Erosion, however, has created fairly flat coastal plains.

South American landforms. Look at the pie graph of landforms of South America. Which landform is the most common? the least common? [2]

The Andes and the Amazon River are the two most important geographical features in South America. Find the Andes and the Amazon River on the map on page 454. As you can see, the Andes extend along the entire west coast of South America. Through which country does most of the Amazon River run? [3] The Amazon is one of the earth's longest and largest rivers.

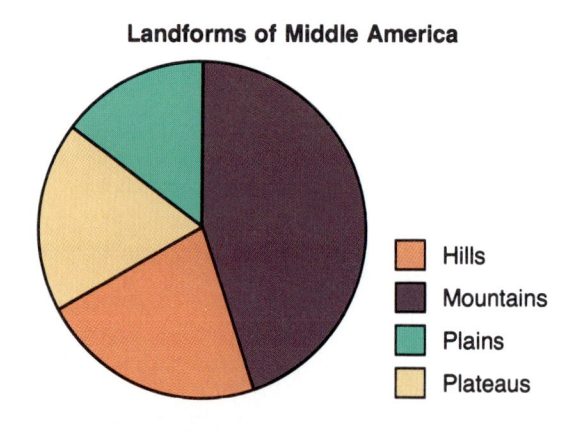

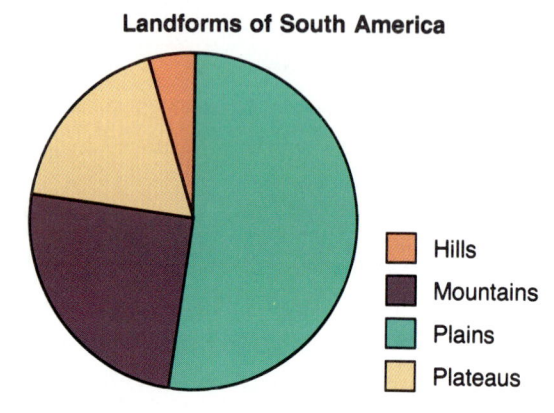

Landforms of Middle America

- Hills
- Mountains
- Plains
- Plateaus

Landforms of South America

- Hills
- Mountains
- Plains
- Plateaus

Look at the profile on page 454. This profile shows a cross section of South America. Find Quito (kē′tō), Ecuador, and Belém (bə·lem′), Brazil, on the profile. Compare their elevations. You can see that elevations in the western part of South America—in the Andes—are much greater than elevations in the eastern part.

The Climate

As you would expect in any large region, the climates of Latin America vary. The climates of this region are influenced by landforms, ocean currents, and tropical location.

The climate in Middle America. Look at the graph on page 457. What are the

1. Mountains; plains.
2. Plains; hills.
3. Brazil.

456

Map Skill: Location. Have students review the influence elevation has on the climate of an area.
*** **Reading Skill**: Doing research. Have several students work together to prepare a report on one of the cities named in these graphs or in the tables on page 460.
Background: Note that the climatograph for Belém has a different precipitation scale.

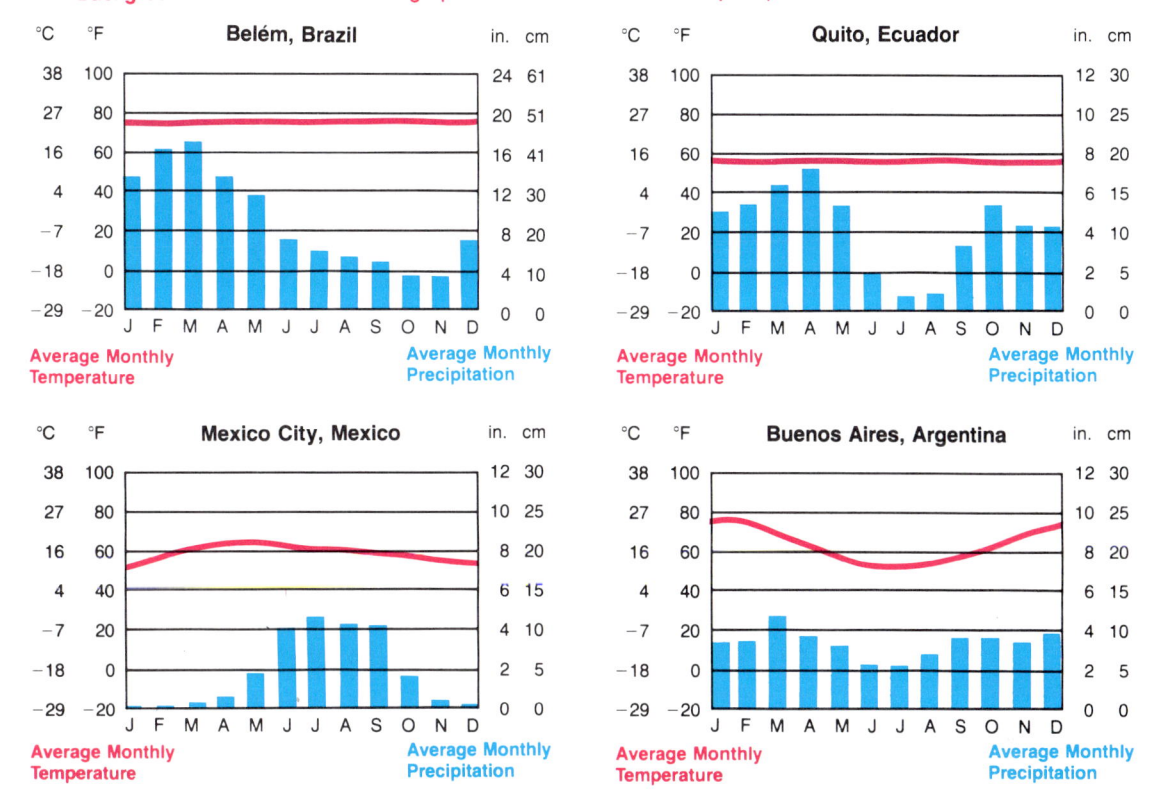

average monthly temperatures for January and July in Mexico City? Although Mexico City is within the low latitudes, temperatures are generally mild. The high elevation of Mexico City—7,575 feet (2,309 km) above sea level—causes temperatures to be lower than those at sea level. On the high plateaus and mountains of Middle America, temperatures are also mild.

About how much monthly precipitation does Mexico City get in January and in July? Although the area around Mexico City can be dry, most of the lower lands in Middle America receive a great deal of precipitation from moist ocean breezes.

The climate in South America. Study the graphs on this page. Find the average monthly temperatures for January and July in Quito and Belém. Which city has warmer temperatures?

The warmer temperatures in Belém result from its location near the equator. Quito is also at the equator. However, Quito is 9,355 feet (2,850 km) above sea level. This high elevation keeps temperatures cool the entire year.

Look again at the graphs on this page. Compare the average monthly precipitation for January and July. Which city receives more precipitation during these months? for the entire year? The large amount of precipitation in Belém is a result of two factors. First, Belém is close to the Atlantic Ocean and its warm, moist breezes. Second, most places in the low latitudes have high temperatures.

1. Jan., about 54 °F; July, about 62 °F.
2. Jan., about .2 inches; July, about 4.5 inches.
3. Belém—Jan., about 77 °F; July, about 78 °F. Quito—Jan., about 56 °F; July, about 56 °F. Belém.

457

Summer in the Southern Hemisphere

Summer in the Northern Hemisphere

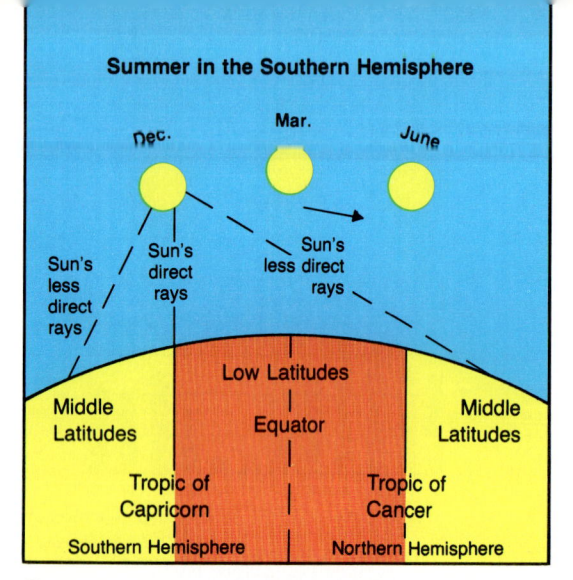

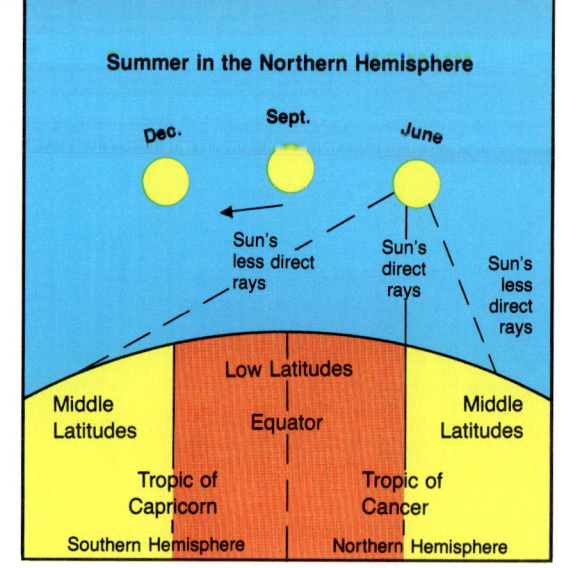

During which month does summer begin in the Southern Hemisphere? in the Northern Hemisphere?

As the land in these places heats up, so does the air. Warm air rises. It also holds much moisture. As the warm, moist air rises, it cools. Cool air cannot hold as much moisture as warm air. The cool air, therefore, releases its moisture as rain.

Not all places in South America near the ocean receive large amounts of precipitation. On the map on page 454, find the Atacama (at′ə·käm′·ə) Desert in Chile and Peru. Although this desert is on the coast of the Pacific Ocean, it is one of the driest places on earth. There is a cold current in the Pacific Ocean off the coast of much of western South America. The winds blowing over the cold current are chilled. The cold, heavy air that comes in from the ocean prevents warm air from rising. For precipitation to begin, air must rise and cool. Cold winds make it almost impossible for precipitation to fall on much of the western coast of South America.

Find Buenos Aires (bwā′nəs ãr′ēz), Argentina, on the map on page 454. Buenos Aires, like much of Argentina and Chile, is in the **middle latitudes.** The middle latitudes are those areas between the tropics and the Arctic and Antarctic.

Places within the middle latitudes have both warm and cold seasons. However, seasons in the middle latitudes of the Northern and Southern Hemispheres are reversed. Look at the graph of Buenos Aires on page 457. What are the average monthly temperatures for January and July? In Buenos Aires the summer months are December, January, and February. Look at the drawing on this page. During the months of June and July the direct rays of the sun are shining more directly on the northern middle latitudes than on the southern middle latitudes. As a result, June and July are winter months in Buenos Aires.

Checking Up
1. Why is this region usually called Latin America?
2. What are the low latitudes?
3. *How do oceans affect the climates of South America?*

1. Jan., about 74 °F; July, about 51 °F.
Thinking Skill: Analyzing. Have students discuss the meaning and possible effects of the reversed seasons in most of South America.

Reading Skill: Using references. Have a student check the latest population figures for Mexico City.
Thinking Skill: Analyzing. Have students talk about the effects of these people's moving to the United States.

Where Are the People?

The population of Latin America is changing in two important ways. First, the population is growing rapidly in almost every country of Latin America. Second, many people in Latin America are moving. Where they move depends on their location within this area.

Where the People Live

Look at the map on this page. Do more people live in the interior or on the seacoasts of Latin America? What is the population density near Rio de Janeiro (rē′ō dā zhə·nãr′ō), Brazil? near Buenos Aires? What is the population density in most of the interior of South America?

Population Density

per sq. mi.	Persons per sq. km
0–3	0–1
3–25	1–10
25–65	10–25
65–130	25–50
Greater than 130	Greater than 50

The population in Middle America. Look at the pie graph on this page. Do more people in Middle America live in urban or in rural areas?

Urban and Rural Population of Middle America

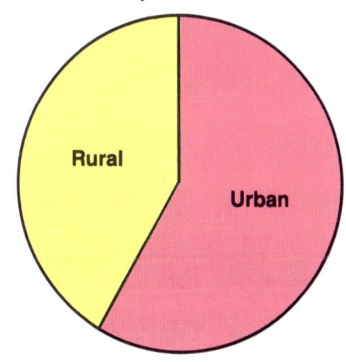

The population in Middle America is both growing and shifting. Many people are moving to the cities. Mexico City, for example, is one of the fastest growing cities in the world. One of the reasons for its growth is the large shift of Mexicans from rural to urban areas. Look at the table on page 460. What was the population of Mexico City in 1960? in 1978?

Many Mexicans have also moved to the United States. This same kind of population shift is also happening in other Middle American countries. Many Puerto Ricans have left their island for cities in the United States. In most of these cases, people have moved to large cities to look for better jobs.

The population in South America. Look at the pie graph on page 460. Do more people live in urban or in rural areas?

1. Seacoasts. 2. Urban areas. 3. 4,825,000; 8,988,230. 4. Urban areas.
Background: Although Puerto Rico is a commonwealth of the United States, its culture and history make it a part of Latin America.

Communication Skill: Speaking. Have students give reports on cities.
Math Skill: Have students discuss the size of Brazil and compare its size with that of the United States.

Population Growth of Selected Latin American Cities					
City	1930	1950	1960	1970	1978
Lima, Peru	265,000	1,000,000	1,212,901	2,415,000	2,833,609
Buenos Aires, Argentina	1,576,597	2,982,580	3,703,000	2,972,453	2,982,000
Mexico City, Mexico	968,443	3,053,588	4,825,000	7,005,855	8,988,230
Santiago, Chile	538,144	952,072	1,627,962	2,447,741	3,448,700
São Paulo, Brazil	879,788	2,218,800	3,850,000	5,901,533	7,198,608
Rio de Janeiro, Brazil	1,468,621	2,418,693	3,288,296	4,296,782	4,857,716

You saw on the population map on page 459 that much of South America's population lives near the seacoasts. There are some important exceptions to this pattern. Find the countries of Peru and Chile on the map on page 454. These countries have dry coastlines. As a result, most of the people in these countries live on high plateaus.

The South American country with the largest population is Brazil. However, most of Brazil's population lives within 300 miles (480 km) of the seacoast. Look again at the table on this page. What were the populations in both Rio de Janeiro and São Paulo (sä'ō poul'ō), Brazil, in 1978? Which city had a larger population increase between 1970 and 1978?

More people are moving into the interior of South America. There are many natural resources in the interior of this continent. However, the tropical climate, the mountains, and the lack of good transportation have been obstacles to the development of this area.

Look at the table below. You can see how the population is changing in some Latin American countries. In which countries did population increase the most between 1880 and 1930? In which country did population increase the most between 1930 and 1979?

Urban and Rural Population of South America

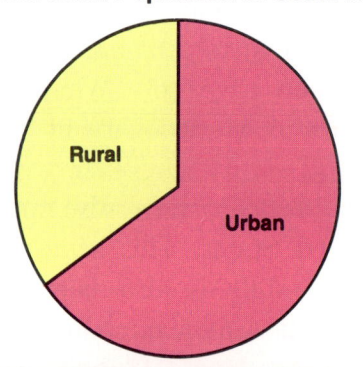

Population Growth of Selected Latin American Countries			
Country	1880 Population	1930 Population	1979 Population
Argentina	2,400,000	12,129,000	27,210,000
Bolivia	Not Available	2,911,000	5,213,000
Costa Rica	190,000	503,856	2,184,000
Mexico	9,343,470	16,404,030	65,770,000

1. Rio—4,857,716; São Paulo—7,198,608. São Paulo had a greater increase in population.
2. Mexico; Mexico.

*** **Reading Skill**: Doing research. Have several students prepare a visual report on Brazil.

Handmade craft items such as pottery attract Mexicans to the market.

A variety of cultural groups can be found in many Brazilian towns.

Who the Latin American People Are

Most of the European colonists, or settlers, in Latin America came from Spain and Portugal. Although these two cultural influences dominate Latin America, they also blend with others.

In Unit 2, you read about the Aztec, Inca, and Mayan Indians in Latin America. The Indian influence is still strong in parts of Latin America. In some countries, such as Bolivia and Guatemala, half the population is Indian. In many Latin American countries, there are large numbers of **mestizos.** A mestizo is a person of both Indian and European ancestry.

The islands of the Caribbean have almost no Indians because the Indians there died from European illnesses. Brazil, Uruguay, Argentina, and Chile also have small Indian populations.

There are many blacks on the islands of the Caribbean, in Brazil, and in northeast South America. These blacks are the descendants of Africans brought to Latin America by Europeans.

Spanish is the most common language in most of Latin America. The Spanish colonists also influenced the architecture, the customs, and the religion of Latin America. In Brazil the most common language is Portuguese, and the customs reflect a Portuguese influence. On many of the islands in the Caribbean, English or French is spoken, and the customs on these islands reflect the influence of these Europeans.

Checking Up

1. What is happening to the population of Latin America?
2. Which language is most common in Latin America?
3. *Why are so many different European languages spoken in Latin America?*

---

* **Reading Skill**: Building vocabulary. Have students use additional references to clarify the meaning of *mestizo.*
Reading Skill: Interpreting pictures. Ask students how these pictures help in understanding the text.

What Do the People Do?

The patterns of employment in Latin America are different from those in most of the United States. Unlike the United States, most countries in Latin America are **developing nations**. A developing nation is a country that is changing from farming to industry and business.

What the People Do in Middle America

Because the jobs people do depend in part on landforms and climates, it is easiest to study the economies of Middle America apart from the economies of South America. Even within Middle America, there are differences from country to country.

Agriculture. Look at the graph on this page. In the countries of Mexico and Costa Rica, what kind of work employs the most people? the fewest? 1

Farmers in northern Mexico grow many of the same kinds of crops that are grown in the United States. They also grow crops such as fruits and vegetables in months when temperatures in the United States are too cool for farming. The United States is a good market for many of these fruits and vegetables.

Middle American farmers also grow crops that cannot be grown in most parts of the United States. Many of the bananas and pineapples and much of the coffee consumed in the United States come from farms in Mexico, Honduras, and other Middle American countries.

Still, there are many problems for farmers in Middle America. Most of them own only small plots of land. They are too poor to buy expensive machinery and fertilizer. Farmers with large fam-

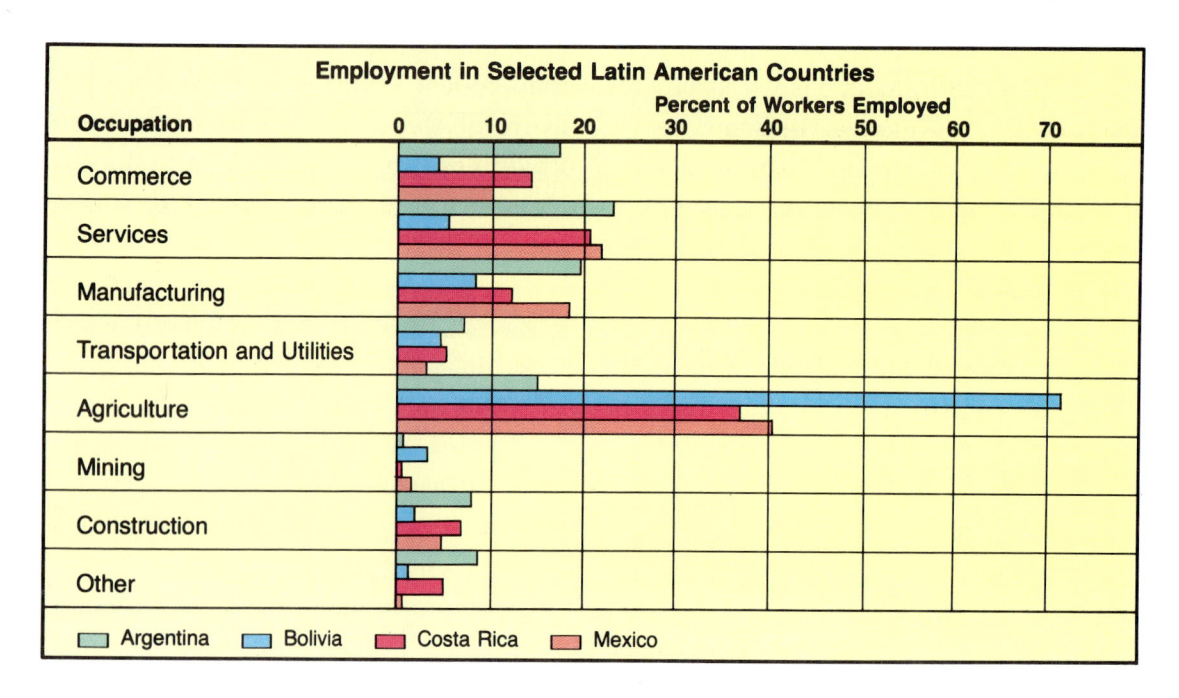

Employment in Selected Latin American Countries

Occupation	Percent of Workers Employed
Commerce	
Services	
Manufacturing	
Transportation and Utilities	
Agriculture	
Mining	
Construction	
Other	

Legend: Argentina, Bolivia, Costa Rica, Mexico

1. Agriculture; mining.

462

* **Reading Skill**: Doing research. Have several students report on the tropical crops mentioned on page 462 and here.
** **Reading Skill**: Using references. Have students look for pictures of farms and ranches in Latin American countries.

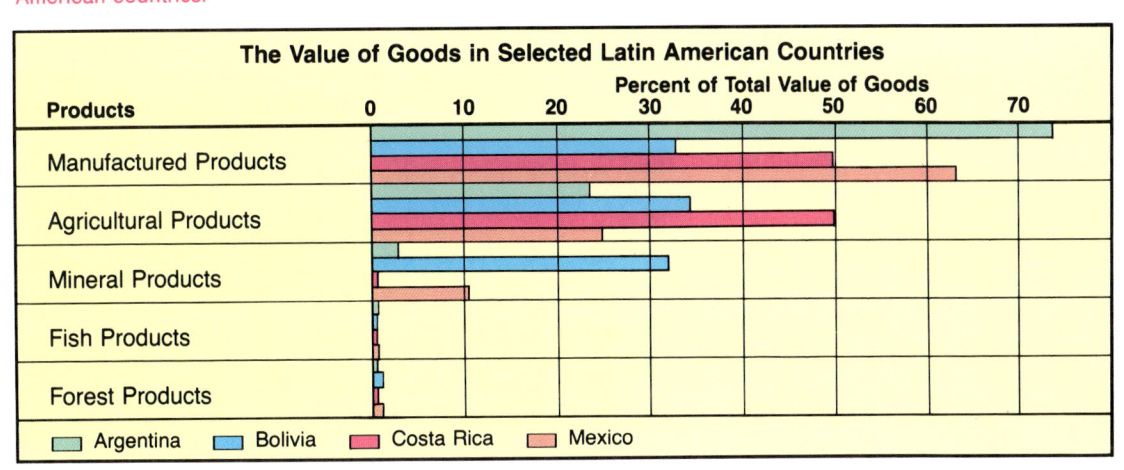

The Value of Goods in Selected Latin American Countries

Products	Percent of Total Value of Goods
Manufactured Products	Argentina ~72, Bolivia ~30, Costa Rica ~62, Mexico (varies)
Agricultural Products	Argentina ~15, Bolivia ~35, Costa Rica ~50, Mexico (varies)
Mineral Products	Bolivia ~32, Costa Rica ~2, Mexico ~18
Fish Products	small amounts
Forest Products	small amounts

Legend: Argentina, Bolivia, Costa Rica, Mexico

ilies to feed are unable to grow enough food. As a result, many people from the rural areas in Middle America must look for some other kind of work besides farming.

Industry and mining. There are important natural resources in Middle America. In addition to its oil, Mexico has large deposits of silver, gold, and iron ore. Jamaica has many large deposits of **bauxite**, the ore from which aluminum is made. Trinidad and Tobago has oil deposits. Many Middle American countries have rivers that could be used for hydroelectric power. In future years these resources and farm products may make Middle America an even more important region of the world.

What the People Do in South America

The economies of South America are changing. Agriculture is still important, but industries and businesses are growing in importance.

Agriculture. South American countries within the low latitudes have climates similar to most countries in Middle America. Many farmers in countries like Brazil, Colombia, and Venezuela grow crops such as coffee, sugarcane, and bananas. Yet these South American countries are not as dependent on tropical crops as are the Middle American countries. Brazil in particular produces large crops of grains, fruits, and cotton in addition to tropical crops.

Farmers in countries like Bolivia and Peru do not grow the same kinds of crops that farmers in Brazil grow. Look at the map on page 454. What landform do you think influences what crops farmers grow? 1

You learned earlier that some countries in South America are located in the middle latitudes. Farmers in these countries—Chile, Argentina, and Uruguay—raise cattle and sheep and grow grain like farmers in the Midwest Plains region of the United States. Meat and grain from these countries are often shipped to Europe and other parts of the world. Look at the graph on this page. What is the percent of total value of agricultural products in Argentina? 2

1. Mountains.
2. About 15%.

463

Careers

Where Some of the People Work

The workers (below right) are helping build a dam on one of the many large rivers in Brazil. This dam, like others elsewhere in Brazil, will generate hydroelectric power for people and businesses. Since Brazil is not rich in oil or coal, the power generated by rivers is important to the growth of industry in this country. There are many dams now under construction in Brazil.

Unlike Brazil, Mexico has a wealth of oil deposits. The workers at right perform the same kind of jobs on this oil rig that oil workers perform in the United States. Mexico is able to export much of the oil it produces. Many of the countries that buy oil from Mexico are also helping build other industries as part of the payment for the oil.

The workers below are loading beef onto a ship in Buenos Aires. Argentina is one of the leading beef cattle producers in the world. Many people across Argentina raise, process, or ship beef cattle. Argentina also sends wheat, cotton, and hides all over the world.

Many Brazilians attend industrial schools to learn trade skills. This factory worker learned how to wire radio transmitters.

Industry and mining. South America has long been famous for its mineral wealth. Gold and silver are still important in Colombia, Peru, and Bolivia. Oil is especially important to Venezuela and Ecuador. Tin and nickel are mined in Peru and Bolivia. Copper mining is important to the economy of Chile.

In countries with a wide variety of resources, the development of industries does not depend on the money from the sale of only one or two products. Brazil, for example, is rich in timber, metals, and farm products. It has several developing industries. Bolivia, on the other hand, depends greatly on the sale of one or two mineral products for money. Look at the graph on page 463. What percent of the total value of goods in Bolivia are mineral products?¹

In the past many South American countries have had to import products such as steel, cars, and machinery. Gradually, more factories are being built to make Latin American countries more independent.

Checking Up
1. Name three tropical crops grown in Middle or South America.
2. What answers would you give to the key questions at the beginning of this unit?
3. *What advantages does a country with a wide variety of natural resources have compared to a country with only one or two major natural resources?*

Unit 19 Summary
- Most of Latin America lies within the low latitudes. As a result, the climate is warm and humid except where elevation and the oceans influence temperature and precipitation.
- The population in Latin America is growing and shifting.
- The economies of Latin America are based on farm products and minerals, but industries are developing.

1. About 28%.
Communication Skill: Writing. Have each student write a paragraph explaining each point in the summary.

FACTS ABOUT LATIN AMERICA

	Flag	Capital* and Largest City	Farm Products and Natural Resources	Manufactured Products
Argentina Population: 27,862,000		Buenos Aires*	Grain, cotton, cattle and sheep, sugarcane, fruit Oil, salt, lead	Processed foods, textiles, metals
The Bahamas Population: 233,000		Nassau*	Bananas, citrus fruits, cucumbers, pineapples Oil	Cement, processed foods
Barbados Population: 275,000		Bridgetown*	Sugarcane, fish Oil	Processed foods
Belize Population: 158,000		Belmopan* Belize City	Sugarcane, citrus fruits Mahogany, other hardwoods, chicle	Almost none
Bolivia Population: 5,286,000		La Paz*	Potatoes, sugarcane, coffee, barley, cacao Tin, tungsten, silver, copper, lead	Hides, processed foods
Brazil Population: 120,386,000		Brasilia* São Paulo	Coffee, cacao, cotton, fruit, sugarcane Iron, manganese, bauxite, rare woods	Textiles, steel, autos, aluminum, appliances
Chile Population: 10,932,000		Santiago de Chile*	Grains, livestock, beans, seafood Copper, iron, nitrates, manganese	Steel, textiles, wood products
Colombia Population: 26,746,000		Bogotá*	Coffee, bananas, cacao, sugarcane Oil and gas, emeralds, gold, silver, platinum	Textiles, steel
Costa Rica Population: 2,193,000		San José*	Coffee, bananas, sugarcane, cacao Timber, gold	Furniture, textiles, leather goods
Cuba Population: 9,883,000		Havana*	Sugarcane, fruit, coffee, rice Clay, nickel, limestone	Processed foods, clothing, machinery
Dominica Population: 78,000		Roseau*	Bananas, coconuts	Processed foods
Dominican Republic Population: 5,621,000		Santo Domingo*	Bananas, cacao, cassava, coffee Bauxite, clay, gold	Processed foods
Ecuador Population: 7,901,000		Quito* Guayaquil	Bananas, rice, other grains, fruits, potatoes Oil, copper, sulphur	Cement, processed foods, textiles
El Salvador Population: 4,714,000		San Salvador*	Coffee, cotton, sugarcane Timber, rubber	Cement, textiles, refined sugar
French Guiana Population: 62,000		Cayenne*	Cacao, bananas, shrimp Timber, gold	Processed foods, hides

	Flag	Capital* and Largest City	Farm Products and Natural Resources	Manufactured Products
Grenada Population: 108,000		Saint George's*	Bananas, cacao, spices Good soil	Processed foods
Guatemala Population: 6,954,000		Guatemala City*	Coffee, sugarcane, bananas, cotton Rare woods, zinc, lead, nickel	Shoes, textiles
Guyana Population: 829,000		Georgetown*	Sugarcane, rice, coffee, fruits, cacao Bauxite, gold, diamonds, timber	Clothing, furniture
Haiti Population: 5,739,000		Port-au-Prince*	Coffee, sisal, sugarcane Copper, bauxite	Processed foods, handicrafts, sporting goods
Honduras Population: 3,702,000		Tegucigalpa*	Bananas, coffee, cotton Timber, silver, gold, zinc	Processed foods, clothing, textiles
Jamaica Population: 2,250,000		Kingston*	Sugarcane, fruits, coffee, coconuts Bauxite, gypsum	Cement, chemicals, processed foods
Mexico Population: 67,296,000		Mexico City*	Cotton, coffee, sugarcane, corn, vegetables, grain Oil and gas, silver, lead, copper, gold	Steel, chemicals, electric goods, textiles, handicrafts
Nicaragua Population: 2,524,000		Managua*	Cotton, coffee, sugarcane, bananas Timber, copper	Processed foods, textiles
Panama Population: 1,830,000		Panama City*	Bananas, cacao, coconuts, sugarcane Timber	Cement
Paraguay Population: 3,206,000		Asunción*	Corn, wheat, cotton, beans, citrus fruits Iron, manganese, limestone, timber	Food and wood products
Peru Population: 17,388,000		Lima*	Cotton, sugarcane, coffee, potatoes, beans Copper, lead, oil, silver, zinc, iron	Fish meal, steel
Saint Lucia Population: 122,000		Castries*	Bananas, coconuts	Clothing, electrical parts
Surinam Population: 402,000		Paramaribo*	Rice, sugarcane, fruit Bauxite, timber	Aluminum
Trinidad and Tobago Population: 1,154,000		Port of Spain*	Sugarcane Oil, asphalt	Oil products, processed foods
Uruguay Population: 2,919,000		Montevideo*	Grain, citrus fruits, livestock, linseed Granite	Processed foods, textiles
Venezuela Population: 14,779,000		Caracas*	Cotton, sugarcane, corn, coffee Oil and gas, iron, nickel, gold	Petroleum products, steel, textiles

Unit 19 Review Workshop

What Have You Learned?

1. What are the two major geographical features in South America?
2. Why are temperatures in Quito, Ecuador, cooler than temperatures in Belém, Brazil?
3. Which city in Latin America has the greatest number of people?
4. What is the most common language in Brazil? in the other countries of South America?
5. Name three countries in Latin America that have important oil industries.

Use Your Reading Skills

It is important to read each paragraph very carefully. Turn to the paragraph on page 458 that begins, "Not all places in South America near the ocean receive large amounts of precipitation." Read this paragraph carefully and answer the following questions.

1. Where is the Atacama Desert?
2. Why are the winds that blow in from the Pacific Ocean cold?
3. What must happen to air for precipitation to begin?
4. Why is it almost impossible for precipitation to occur here?

Use Your Map Skills

Study the maps on the next page. Then answer the following questions. You may also use the map on page 454. The answers to the questions will help you learn more about Latin America.

1. Which parts of Latin America have the longest growing season? the shortest growing season? How does geography explain this short growing season?
2. What is the length of the growing season in most of the area of shifting farming?
3. In which countries is there livestock ranching? What is the length of the growing season in these areas?
4. What is the length of the growing season in most of the area of tropical plantation crops?

Use Your Math Skills

If you were to visit another country, you would probably not be able to use United States money. In many Latin American countries, you would use a unit of money called a peso (pā′sō). Mexico and Colombia are two Latin American countries that use the peso. However, the value of the peso varies from country to country and even from day to day. Assume that there are 20 Mexican pesos to 1 United States dollar and 40 Colombian pesos to 1 dollar. Answer the following questions using those figures.

1. A blanket in a Mexican market is selling for 600 pesos. How much in United States money is the blanket selling for?
2. In Colombia you have a lunch that costs 60 pesos. How much in United

Thinking Skill: Knowing.
Reading Skill: Reading for facts.
Map Skill: Location.

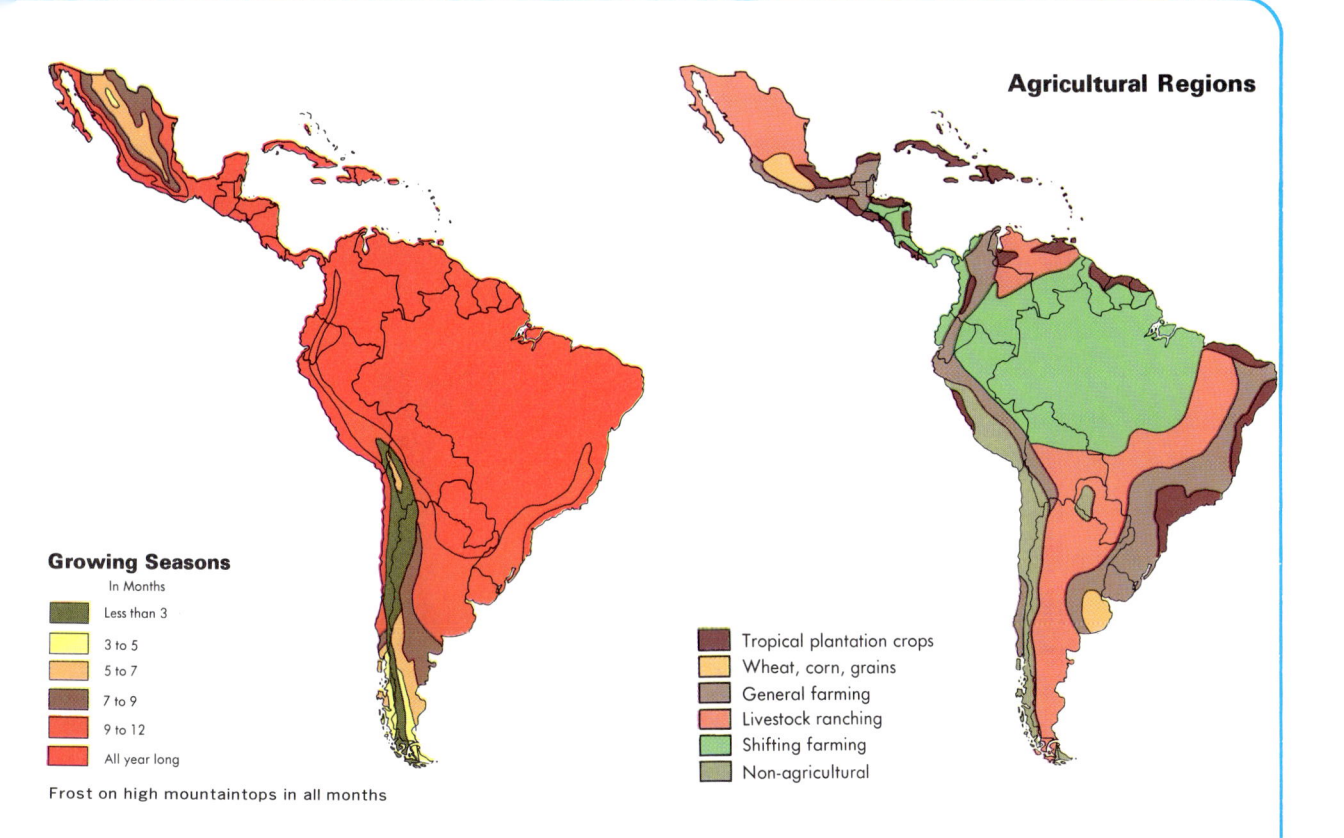

Growing Seasons
In Months
- Less than 3
- 3 to 5
- 5 to 7
- 7 to 9
- 9 to 12
- All year long

Frost on high mountaintops in all months

Agricultural Regions
- Tropical plantation crops
- Wheat, corn, grains
- General farming
- Livestock ranching
- Shifting farming
- Non-agricultural

States money does the lunch cost? in Mexican pesos?

3. In Mexico you take a bus ride that costs 70 pesos. How much in United States money does the bus ride cost?
4. You are traveling from Mexico to Colombia. You have 2,480 Mexican pesos. How many Colombian pesos will you receive for your Mexican pesos? How much in United States money do you have?

Learn by Doing

You learned in this unit that there is a varied European influence on many of the islands of the Caribbean Sea. Jamaica, for example, once belonged to Great Britain. Haiti once belonged to France, and Cuba once belonged to Spain. Prepare a panel discussion with some of your classmates about some of these islands. In your discussion, tell specific ways in which the influence of the European country is still present. You might include language, architecture, and crops in your discussion.

Read to Learn More

Find the topics listed below in the card catalog of your library. Read all or part of a book listed under one of the topics. Share what you learn with your classmates.

MEXICO

INDIANS OF SOUTH AMERICA

CARIBBEAN AREA

Reading Skill: Doing research: *Learn by Doing.*
Communication Skill: Speaking: *Learn by Doing.*
Citizenship Skill: Social participation: *Learn by Doing.*
Reading Skill: Using references: *Read to Learn More.*

Unit Overview: This unit examines the United States at the beginning of the 21st century, how predicted population patterns compare with those of the early 20th century, the importance of energy resources, and technological advances.

Unit Objectives
To understand:
- the population patterns predicted for the beginning of the 21st century compared with those of the 20th century
- the importance of energy resources in the future
- technological advances

Suggested Materials
Workbook
Unit Tests

Unit 20

Skills Emphasized
Map Skills: pp. 476, 480.
Social Studies Reading Skills: pp. 470, 472, 473, 474, 477, 479, 480, 481.
Thinking Skills: pp. 470, 473, 474, 475, 476, 477, 478, 479, 480, 481.
Communication Skills: pp. 470, 478, 481.
Time Skills: pp. 470, 478, 479.
Social Studies Math Skills: pp. 470, 480.
Citizenship Skill: p. 470.

Suggested Student Activities
   1. Organize a bulletin-board display entitled "The Future" that illustrates life in the year 2020.
   2. Work in small groups. Design model buildings of the future.
   3. Collect newspaper and magazine articles on predictions. One topic could be energy.
** 4. Make separate reports on energy resources in the 21st century—one on nonrenewable resources, the other on renewable resources.
* 5. Prepare a report on a career of the future, to be given after covering material on page 478.

Skills Emphasized in Suggested Student Activities
Social Studies Reading Skills: Using references, organizing information, doing research.
Thinking Skills: Knowing, comparing, predicting, hypothesizing.
Math Skill.
Communication Skills: Writing, speaking, listening.
Citizenship Skill: Social participation.
Time Skill.

The United States in the 21st Century

More than a billion miles away, the *Voyager* spacecraft explored and photographed Saturn and its rings.

471

The American People in the 21st Century

As You Read This Unit

1. Think about these words.
   demographer   renewable   telecommunication
   nonrenewable   geothermal   computer
2. Look for answers to these key questions.
   a. How will the population patterns in the United States at the beginning of the 21st century be different from those at the beginning of the 20th century?
   b. Why are energy resources so important to our future?
   c. What are two ways in which technological advances will change the way that people live in the future?
3. Use this reading skill.
   This unit will give you an understanding of some of the future prospects for the United States. You will learn about changes in the population of the future, energy needs in the future, and advances in technology. While you are studying this unit, look through newspapers and newsmagazines for articles about the future. Read these articles. Then make a short report to your class about them. By doing this, you will be helping yourself and your class gain a greater understanding about your future.

The population of the United States is made up of people from many backgrounds. Where these people settled and how they worked together have shaped our history. As in the past, the future of the United States will be determined largely by its people, their ideas, and their choices.

Changes in Population

Who will be living in the United States in the year 2000? Where will people make their homes—in big cities? in small towns? in the North or in the South? in the East or in the West?

People who study such questions are called **demographers** (di·mäg′rə·fərz). Demographers learn all they can about the present population so they can make good predictions about future populations. They predict, for example, where people will live in the next century.

Population growth. Study the line graph on page 473. During which period

Background: Westward migration has slowed in recent years. Except in Alaska, the opportunities offered by the frontier are gone.
Reading Skill: Skimming for information. Have students look back in Units 7 and 8 to find data that explain population migration after the Civil War.

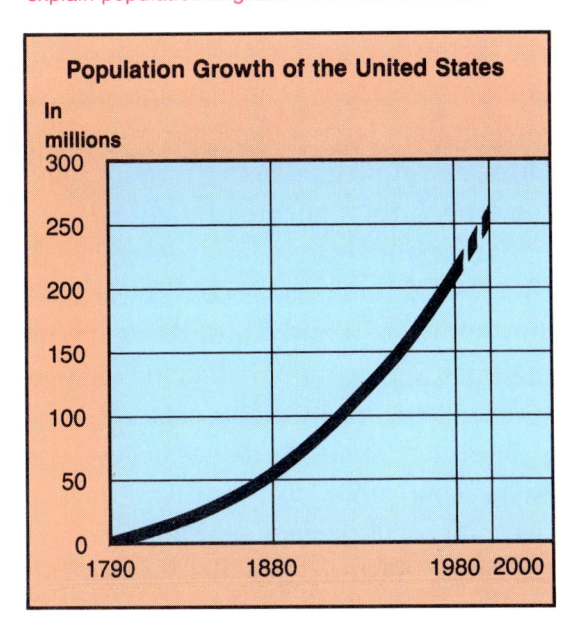

Population Growth of the United States

eral patterns of migration in the United States. Most people first settled in the East, and then later many moved farther west. After the Civil War, another migration pattern developed. Job opportunities in the growing industrial cities of the Northeast and the Great Lakes Region attracted many workers from the South.

By the late 1800s, yet another pattern of migration began to develop. Many farm workers moved from rural farming areas to seek jobs in the urban industrial centers of the Northeast and the Great Lakes Region.

In recent years these patterns of migration have changed. Most demographers agree that the migration from east to west will continue, but at a much slower rate than it has in the past.

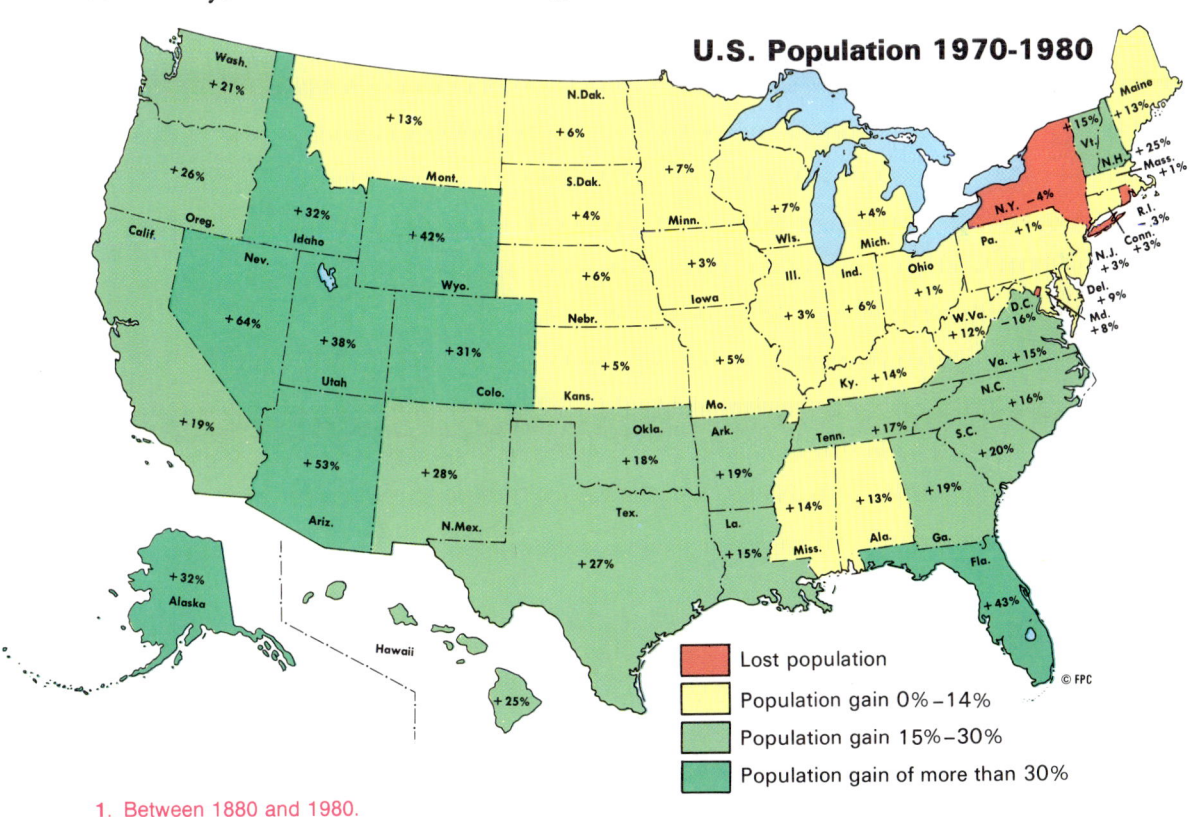

1. of time did the population of the United States grow the most?

Where people will live. For much of our history, there have been three gen-

U.S. Population 1970–1980

- Wash. +21%
- Oreg. +26%
- Calif. +19%
- Nev. +64%
- Idaho +32%
- Mont. +13%
- Wyo. +42%
- Utah +38%
- Ariz. +53%
- N.Mex. +28%
- N.Dak. +6%
- S.Dak. +4%
- Nebr. +6%
- Kans. +5%
- Okla. +18%
- Tex. +27%
- Minn. +7%
- Iowa +3%
- Mo. +5%
- Ark. +19%
- La. +15%
- Wis. +7%
- Ill. +3%
- Miss. +14%
- Mich. +4%
- Ind. +6%
- Ky. +14%
- Tenn. +17%
- Ala. +13%
- Ohio +1%
- W.Va. +12%
- Va. +15%
- N.C. +16%
- S.C. +20%
- Ga. +19%
- Fla. +43%
- Pa. +1%
- N.Y. –4%
- Vt. +15%
- N.H. +25%
- Maine +13%
- Mass. +1%
- R.I. –3%
- Conn. +3%
- N.J. +3%
- Del. +9%
- Md. +8%
- D.C. –16%
- Alaska +32%
- Hawaii +25%

Legend:
- Lost population
- Population gain 0%–14%
- Population gain 15%–30%
- Population gain of more than 30%

1. Between 1880 and 1980.
Thinking Skill: Analyzing. Why do demographers continue to predict westward migration?

473

Reading Skill: Listing. Have students make a list of predictions that demographers are making.
Thinking Skill: Hypothesizing. How will the predictions that demographers are making affect your community?

1. Study the map on page 473. Which parts of the country showed the greatest increase in population between the years 1970 and 1980? Which parts showed the greatest decline in population?

Most demographers predict a continued decline in the population of the Great Lakes Region and the Northeast. They also predict an increase in the population of states in the southern and western parts of the country. However, the areas that will have the greatest population gain will be those like the Pacific Northwest, where there is enough water to support an increasing number of people.

The third change in the pattern of migration recently is that more people are moving from large, older cities to smaller cities and towns. There is even some movement to rural areas. Better transportation and communication will continue to help factories and businesses locate in these areas. Thus, there will be more job opportunities than there used to be outside major urban centers.

Most demographers do not believe this trend from urban to rural living means that cities will become less important in the future. Instead, they believe that the population will become more evenly spread out across the country.

The graphs here show the percent of immigrants to the United States and the regions in the world from which these people came.

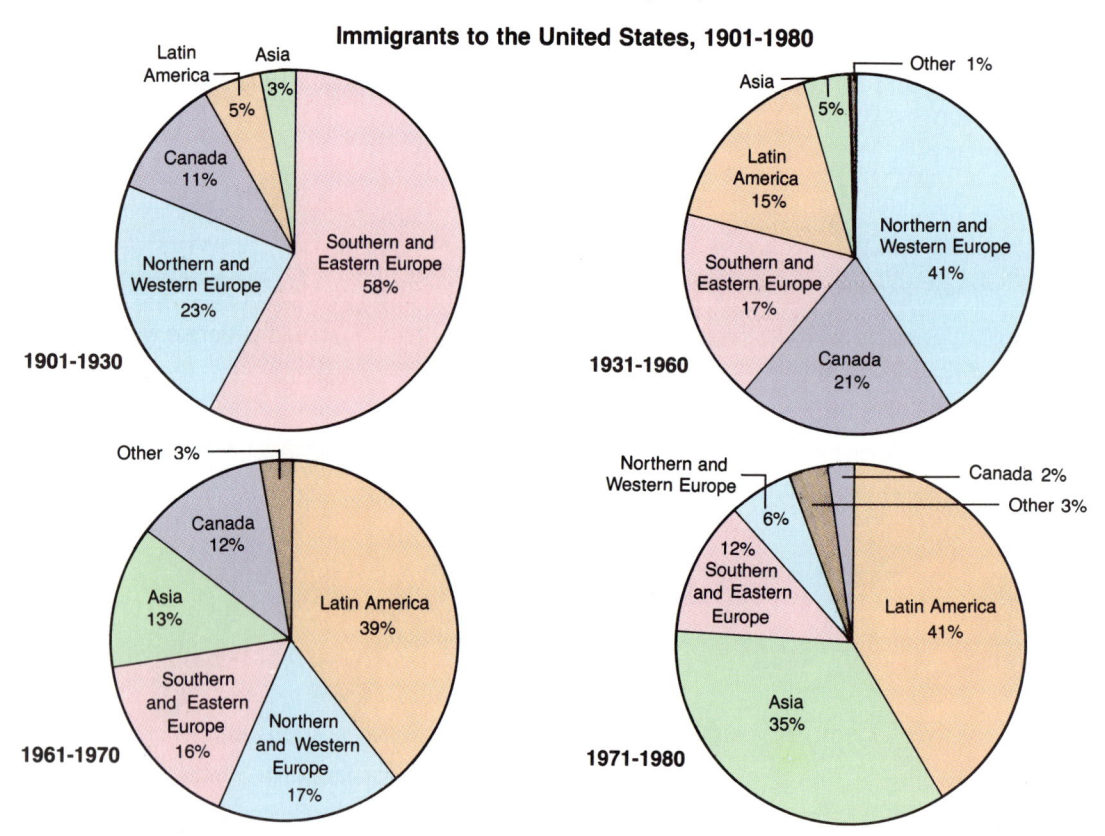

Immigrants to the United States, 1901-1980

1901-1930
- Southern and Eastern Europe 58%
- Northern and Western Europe 23%
- Canada 11%
- Latin America 5%
- Asia 3%

1931-1960
- Northern and Western Europe 41%
- Canada 21%
- Southern and Eastern Europe 17%
- Latin America 15%
- Asia 5%
- Other 1%

1961-1970
- Latin America 39%
- Northern and Western Europe 17%
- Southern and Eastern Europe 16%
- Asia 13%
- Canada 12%
- Other 3%

1971-1980
- Latin America 41%
- Asia 35%
- Southern and Eastern Europe 12%
- Northern and Western Europe 6%
- Other 3%
- Canada 2%

1. The western and southern parts of the country showed the greatest increase in population.
Thinking Skill: Evaluating. Will a more evenly spread-out population be good or bad? Why?

Ethnic and Racial Patterns

One thing will stay the same in the United States in the 21st century. The United States will continue to be a nation of immigrants. Yet the pattern of immigration has been changing. Study the four pie graphs on page 474. From which region did the greatest number of immigrants come to the United States in the years from 1961 to 1970? from 1971 to 1980?

In the years ahead, there will be shifts in the migration patterns of the largest minority group in the United States, the black population. During the first half of the 20th century, far more blacks left the South than moved to the region. Since 1970, however, more blacks have been moving to the South than leaving. This trend is expected to continue.

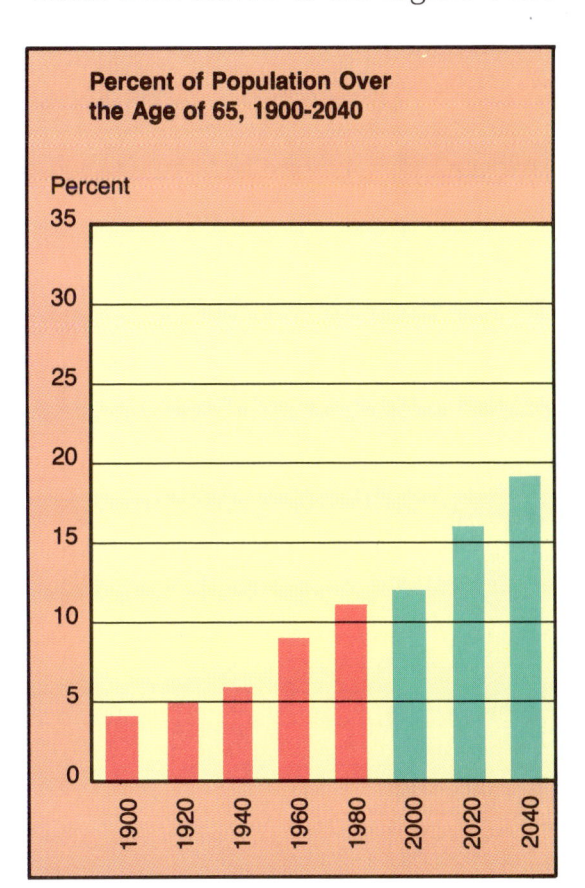

An Older Population

Demographers tell us that older people will make up a larger part of the population of the United States than ever before. Look at the bar graph on this page. What percent of the population is expected to be older than sixty-five in the year 2040?

The number of older people in our population is due in part to the unusually large number of babies who were born in the United States between 1947 and 1964. This time is often called the "baby boom." Smaller numbers of babies were born before and after this time.

Those born during the "baby boom" years will be in their sixties and seventies soon after the beginning of the 21st century. As these people retire, many of them will move to the warmer regions of the South, the Southwest, and the Pacific Coast. They will add to the population growth that is already occurring, and is expected to continue, in these regions.

Checking Up
1. What is a demographer?
2. What are two present-day migration patterns that are expected to continue into the 21st century?
3. *Why do you think the United States will continue to be a nation of immigrants just as in the past?*

Thinking Skill: Predicting. What are some possible new ways of supplying our future energy needs?
* **Map Skill**: Location. Ask students to read the graph on this page. Then have them use the map on pages 10–11 to locate areas that produce more than 10 million barrels of oil per day.

Technology and the Environment

We will face many challenges in the 21st century. One of the most important challenges will be finding new ways of supplying our growing energy needs.

The Importance of Energy

We use more energy per person than the people of any other country in the world. This energy is used for factories, for transportation, and for home use. All the countries in the world get most of their energy from oil, natural gas, and coal. These energy supplies are **nonrenewable**. This means that once they are used they are gone forever.

Decreasing supplies. The earth has only a limited supply of nonrenewable fuels. Someday the supply of these fuels will run out. Some experts believe, for example, that the United States' supply of oil will be seriously low by 2000.

Much of the energy used in the United States today comes from resources that are found in our own country. However, we use more energy resources, especially oil, than we produce. Look at the bar graph on this page. About how much more oil do Canada and the United States consume than they produce? 1

Conserving our energy resources. One of the great challenges facing the people of the United States will be to conserve, or use less of, their energy resources. In the past few years, we have reduced our use of gasoline for cars. Industries have also decreased their use of fuels.

Still, there are other ways we can conserve energy resources. Engineers can design more-efficient power plants and engines. A car engine, for example, uses only about one-fifth of the energy in gasoline. The rest of the energy goes into wasted heat.

More energy-efficient buildings can be built. For example, buildings in the future might make better use of natural lighting to conserve energy. Many experts also believe that better insulation of buildings could save up to half the

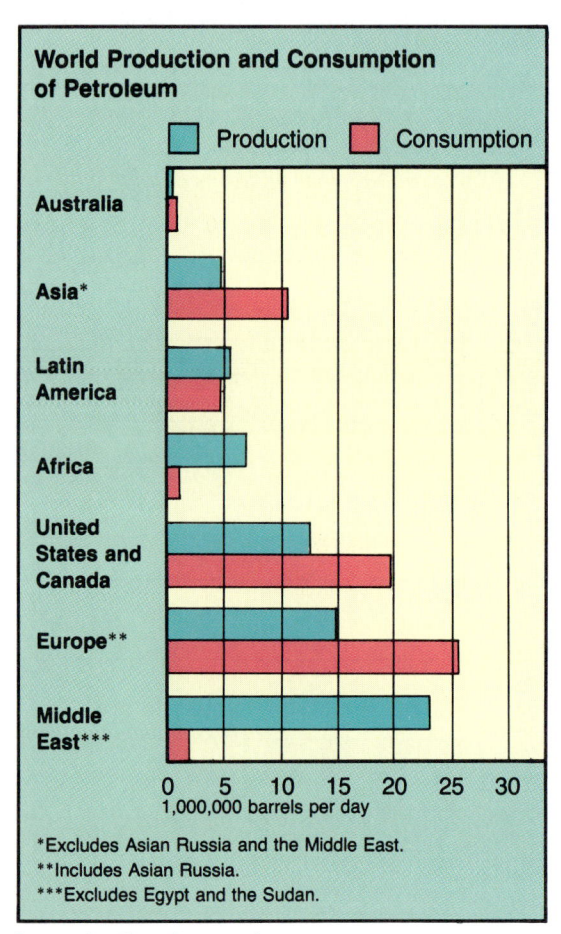

World Production and Consumption of Petroleum

Region	Production	Consumption
Australia		
Asia*		
Latin America		
Africa		
United States and Canada		
Europe**		
Middle East***		

0   5   10   15   20   25   30
1,000,000 barrels per day

*Excludes Asian Russia and the Middle East.
**Includes Asian Russia.
***Excludes Egypt and the Sudan.

1. They consume about 8 million more barrels per day than they produce.
** **Thinking Skill**: Synthesizing. Have students make a poster about energy saving to encourage someone to save or use energy wisely.

Reading Skill: Listing. Have students make two lists—one of renewable resources and one of nonrenewable resources.

** **Reading Skill**: Using references. Have students look for pictures of renewable and nonrenewable resources to share with the class.

Computerized assembly lines speed up much of the work once done by people. Yet people will still design and program these lines.

fuel used for such things as heating and air conditioning.

Other available energy resources. As supplies of oil and natural gas decrease, we will be forced to turn to other energy resources that we do have in large amounts. These include coal, oil shale, and uranium for nuclear power. However, the use of these energy resources presents problems. As yet, there is no way to burn coal without polluting the air. The cost of mining and processing oil shale is higher than the cost of importing oil. Today's nuclear power plants leave dangerous wastes. Safe ways of disposing of these wastes are still being planned.

Renewable energy sources. Many experts believe that the best answer to our future energy needs will be the increased use of **renewable** energy sources. This is energy that can be used over and over. These renewable energy sources include wind power, solar power, waterpower, and **geothermal** power, or power from heat that comes from deep down in the earth.

Much work needs to be done to make these renewable sources of power practical for everyday use. However, experiments using these sources of power are under way. In California, for example, a power plant already uses geothermal power to make electric power.

Experts believe that solar power can be made practical by putting huge solar collectors up in the sky. These satellites can collect solar energy and send it to earth for our use.

The Growth of Telecommunications

Today many kinds of information can be sent and received by **telecommunication** systems. These systems include telephones, televisions, and communication satellites.

In the near future, advances in telecommunications and **computers**, or machines that store and report information, may change the way many people send and receive information. For example, we may soon have electronic mail. Instead of writing letters on paper, we will send the letters from one computer to another electronically.

Jobs will change too. More and more people will have computers that will enable them to work at home. Some people are already doing this. Some newspaper reporters and typists, for example, do their writing and typing at home. They are able to work directly with their office by computer.

Thinking Skill: Knowing. What is being done to conserve energy in your community?

477

Important Careers in the Future

Computer Programmers

Every computer has to be programmed to store information, study information, and report information. Computer programmers are specially trained to write directions, or programs, for computers.

Almost all modern businesses use computers to bill their customers and to pay their workers. Computers are used to keep track of goods on the shelves and to order new goods.

Computers are also used in navigation. Jet planes have computers on board to help pilots plot their courses and to keep track of the fuel they are using. Even the space shuttle uses computers—to relay information back and forth to ground control at the Johnson Space Center in Houston, Texas.

JPL scientists have designed a spacecraft that will take pictures of Venus.

Research Scientists

The Jet Propulsion Laboratory (JPL) in Pasadena, California, is one of the country's major research centers for the study of space exploration. This laboratory employs more than 4,000 people. Scientists at JPL developed America's first space satellite in 1958, Explorer I. Since that time, JPL's scientists have developed technology for United States missions to the moon and the planets.

JPL's major work today involves the exploration of our solar system with unmanned spacecraft. Scientists at JPL also try to find ways of using the technology they have developed to solve problems on earth. Scientists are working on projects in medicine, pollution, transportation, and energy. In the area of medicine, for example, scientists have developed a robotlike wheelchair with a mechanical arm. This mechanical arm can move and pick up objects at the direction of a human voice. Such advances will help many handicapped people.

Many newspaper reporters now type their stories on video display terminals.

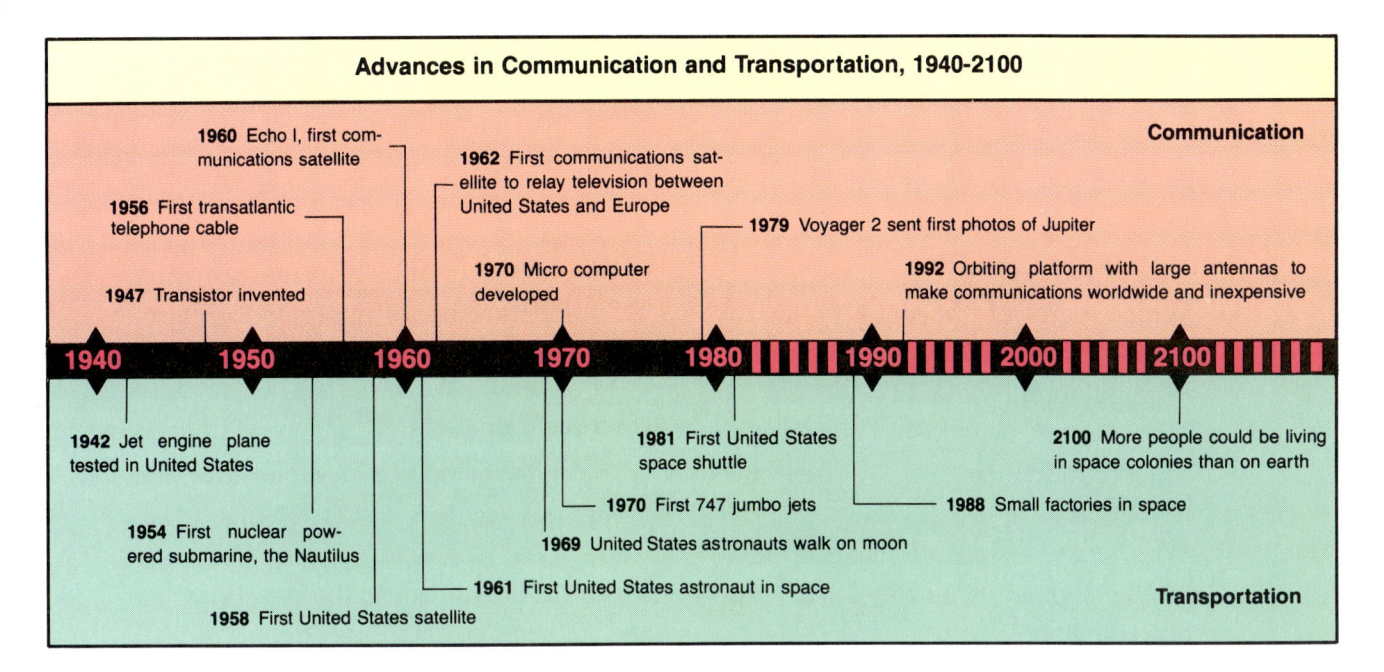

Advances in Communication and Transportation, 1940-2100

Communication
- 1947 Transistor invented
- 1956 First transatlantic telephone cable
- 1960 Echo I, first communications satellite
- 1962 First communications satellite to relay television between United States and Europe
- 1970 Micro computer developed
- 1979 Voyager 2 sent first photos of Jupiter
- 1992 Orbiting platform with large antennas to make communications worldwide and inexpensive

Transportation
- 1942 Jet engine plane tested in United States
- 1954 First nuclear powered submarine, the Nautilus
- 1958 First United States satellite
- 1961 First United States astronaut in space
- 1969 United States astronauts walk on moon
- 1970 First 747 jumbo jets
- 1981 First United States space shuttle
- 1988 Small factories in space
- 2100 More people could be living in space colonies than on earth

The Future of Our Environment

The industries of the United States use huge amounts of energy and natural resources such as oil and coal. Some industrial activity also leaves wastes that pollute the environment. The burning of coal, for example, causes a special kind of pollution called acid rain. As coal is burned, particles of coal dust rise with the heated air. Droplets of moisture collect around the coal dust particles. Coal dust, when mixed with water, creates an acid. These droplets return to earth as acid rain. In recent years acid rain has killed all the fish and plant life in some of the lakes of the Adirondack Mountains in New York State.

We have learned much about pollution and how to deal with it. People, as they approach the 21st century, will continue to try even harder to care for our environment. Americans may have to learn to use fewer goods and to travel less. These, however, are small sacrifices to make if we are to protect the country in which we live.

Checking Up
1. What are three kinds of renewable energy sources?
2. What answers would you give to the key questions at the beginning of this unit?
3. *Why are Americans facing important challenges as the 21st century approaches?*

Unit 20 Summary
- The size, average age, and location of the United States population will be different in the 21st century from what they are today. However, the patterns of these changes can be seen in today's population trends.
- As the 21st century approaches, the people of the United States will be facing the challenges of finding new energy sources and adjusting to technological advances.

Time Skill: How does this time line help explain the future?
*** **Thinking Skill**: Doing research. Have several students report on acid rain.
Reading Skill: Organizing information. Have students organize a visual that includes three facts to support each point in the summary.

Unit 20 Review Workshop

What Have You Learned?

1. Which parts of the country are expected to have the greatest increase in population by 2000?
2. What recent change has occurred in the migration patterns of the black population?
3. Why will older people make up more of the population in 2000 than they do today?
4. What are two ways that Americans can work to meet their energy needs in the future?
5. In what ways will advances in telecommunications change the way in which people live and work?
6. Why do the American people need to find better ways to preserve their environment?

Use Your Reading Skills

The line graph on page 481 shows the major sources of energy used in the United States between 1850 and 1980. This graph also shows the major sources of energy expected to be used through the year 2000. Study the graph and then answer the following questions.

1. What was our major source of energy in 1850? in 1900?
2. In which year did oil become the major energy resource?
3. In which year did oil reach its highest level of use?
4. Which source of energy is expected to be used more than any other in 2000?
5. Why do you think the line showing "other" sources of energy steadily increases from 1980 to 2000?

Use Your Map Skills

The map on page 473 shows how the population of the states changed between 1970 and 1980. Study this map carefully. Then answer the questions below. Answers to these questions will give you a better understanding of current trends in the migration patterns of our population.

1. Name the two states that had a population decrease. In which region of the country are these states located?
2. What happened to the population of Washington, D.C.?
3. Name four states that had a population increase of 30 percent or more. In which regions of the country are these states located?
4. Compare this map with the regional map of the United States on page 307. Which five regions of the country had most of their states increase in population by 15 percent or more? Why might you expect population growth to continue in these areas?

Use Your Thinking Skills

In this unit you learned that one of our major challenges in the future will be to find better ways to conserve our energy resources. Make your own list of ways in which you and your family can help con-

Thinking Skills:: Knowing, analyzing, comparing.
Reading Skill: Interpreting graphics.
Map Skill: Location.

Energy Sources and Use, 1850–2000

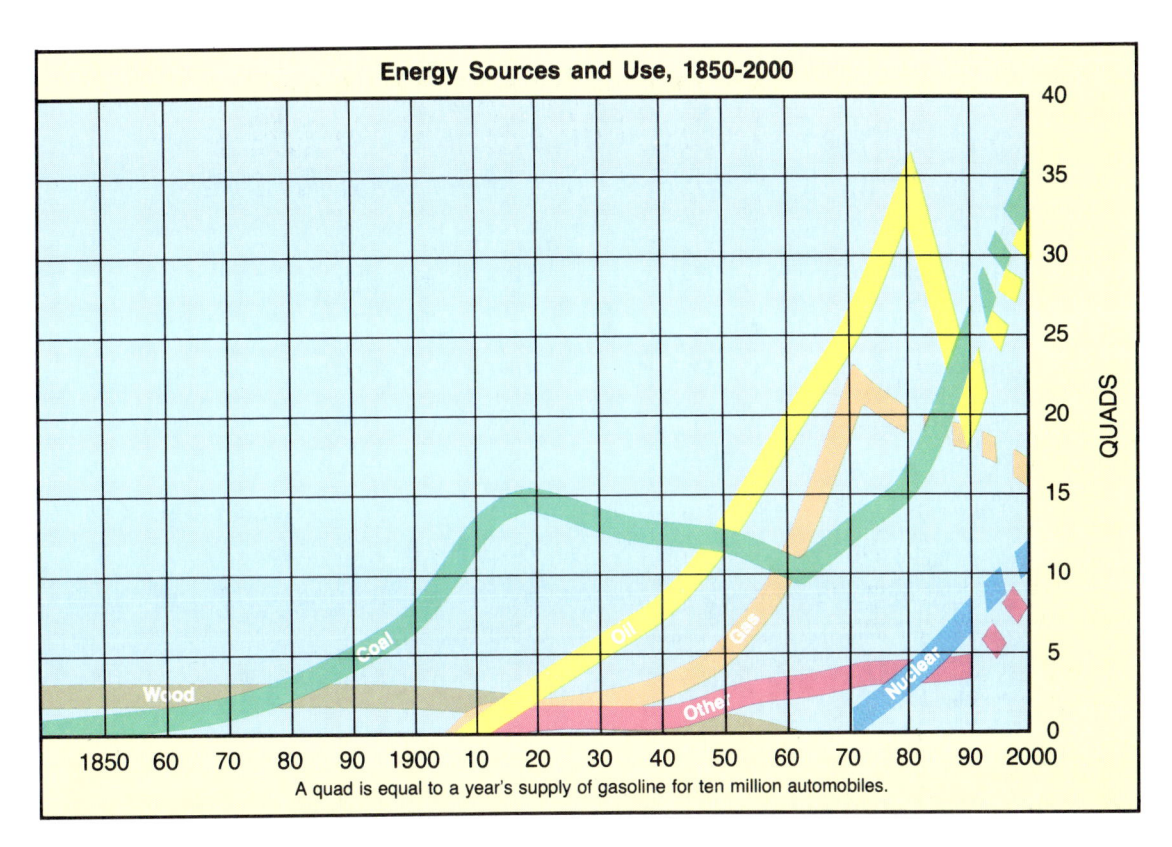

A quad is equal to a year's supply of gasoline for ten million automobiles.

serve energy at home, at school, and at your parents' workplaces. Compare your list with others in your class.

Learn by Doing

1. Research one of the renewable energy sources such as wind power, solar power, waterpower, or geothermal power. Look in books and encyclopedias to learn more about how this kind of power is being developed and what some of the prospects and problems are with its development. Report your findings to the class.
2. Draw pictures of what you think life will be like for most people in the United States in the 21st century. Include pictures of what kinds of work people will do, what kinds of homes people will have, and what sorts of transportation people will use. Write captions for your pictures. Post your pictures on the class bulletin board.
3. Write a short story about life in 2020. This might be a story about life in a space colony. Share your story with others in your class.

Read to Learn More

Find the topics listed below in the card catalog of your library. Read all or part of a book listed under one of the topics. Share what you learn with your classmates.

ENERGY	SATELLITE
POLLUTION	TELECOMMUNICATION

Reading Skills: Using references, doing research: *Learn by Doing, 1* and *Read to Learn More.*
Communication Skill: Speaking: *Learn by Doing, 1* and *Read to Learn More.*
Thinking Skill: Predicting: *Learn by Doing, 2, 3.*
Communication Skill: Writing: *Learn by Doing, 3.*

Appendix

Area and Population of the States of the United States
(Listed alphabetically)

State	Year of Admission	Area in Square Miles	Population (1980 Census)	Capital	Population (1980 Census)
Alabama (AL)	1819	51,705	3,890,061	Montgomery	178,157
Alaska (AK)	1959	591,004	400,481	Juneau	19,528
Arizona (AZ)	1912	114,000	2,717,866	Phoenix	764,911
Arkansas (AR)	1836	53,187	2,285,513	Little Rock	158,461
California (CA)	1850	158,706	23,668,562	Sacramento	275,741
Colorado (CO)	1876	104,091	2,888,834	Denver	491,396
Connecticut (CT)	1788	5,018	3,107,576	Hartford	136,392
Delaware (DE)	1787	2,044	595,225	Dover	23,512
District of Columbia (DC)	N/A	69	637,651	N/A	N/A
Florida (FL)	1845	58,664	9,739,992	Tallahassee	81,548
Georgia (GA)	1788	58,910	5,464,265	Atlanta	425,022
Hawaii (HI)	1959	6,471	965,000	Honolulu	365,048
Idaho (ID)	1890	83,564	943,935	Boise	102,451
Illinois (IL)	1818	56,345	11,418,461	Springfield	99,637
Indiana (IN)	1816	36,185	5,490,179	Indianapolis	700,807
Iowa (IA)	1846	56,275	2,913,387	Des Moines	191,003
Kansas (KS)	1861	82,277	2,363,208	Topeka	115,266
Kentucky (KY)	1792	40,409	3,661,433	Frankfort	25,973
Louisiana (LA)	1812	47,752	4,203,972	Baton Rouge	219,486
Maine (ME)	1820	33,265	1,124,660	Augusta	21,819
Maryland (MD)	1788	10,460	4,216,446	Annapolis	31,740
Massachusetts (MA)	1788	8,284	5,737,037	Boston	562,994
Michigan (MI)	1837	58,527	9,258,344	Lansing	130,414
Minnesota (MN)	1858	84,402	4,077,148	St. Paul	270,230
Mississippi (MS)	1817	47,689	2,520,638	Jackson	202,895
Missouri (MO)	1821	69,697	4,917,444	Jefferson City	33,619
Montana (MT)	1889	147,046	786,690	Helena	23,938
Nebraska (NE)	1867	77,355	1,570,006	Lincoln	171,932
Nevada (NV)	1864	110,561	799,184	Carson City	32,022
New Hampshire (NH)	1788	9,279	920,610	Concord	30,400
New Jersey (NJ)	1787	7,787	7,364,158	Trenton	92,124
New Mexico (NM)	1912	121,592	1,299,968	Santa Fe	48,899
New York (NY)	1788	49,108	17,557,288	Albany	101,727
North Carolina (NC)	1789	52,669	5,874,429	Raleigh	149,771
North Dakota (ND)	1889	70,702	652,695	Bismarck	44,485
Ohio (OH)	1803	41,330	10,797,419	Columbus	564,871
Oklahoma (OK)	1907	69,956	3,025,266	Oklahoma City	403,213
Oregon (OR)	1859	97,073	2,632,663	Salem	89,233
Pennsylvania (PA)	1787	45,308	11,866,728	Harrisburg	53,264
Rhode Island (RI)	1790	1,212	947,154	Providence	156,804
South Carolina (SC)	1788	31,113	3,119,208	Columbia	99,296
South Dakota (SD)	1889	77,116	690,178	Pierre	11,973
Tennessee (TN)	1796	42,144	4,590,750	Nashville	455,651
Texas (TX)	1845	266,807	14,228,383	Austin	345,496
Utah (UT)	1896	84,899	1,461,037	Salt Lake City	163,033
Vermont (VT)	1791	9,614	511,456	Montpelier	8,241
Virginia (VA)	1788	40,767	5,346,279	Richmond	219,214
Washington (WA)	1889	68,138	4,130,163	Olympia	27,447
West Virginia (WV)	1863	24,231	1,949,644	Charleston	63,968
Wisconsin (WI)	1848	56,153	4,705,335	Madison	170,616
Wyoming (WY)	1890	97,809	470,816	Cheyenne	47,283
United States (total)		3,618,772	226,504,825	Washington, D.C.	637,651

Areas Controlled by the United States

	Area in Square Miles	Population	Capital	Population
American Samoa	76	32,395	Pago Pago	3,058
Guam	209	105,821	Agaña	881
Puerto Rico	3,515	3,196,520	San Juan	434,849
Trust Territory of the Pacific Islands	715	116,974	Saipan	7,967
Virgin Islands	133	95,591	Charlotte Amalie	11,756

N/A: Not applicable

Population of United States Cities with More Than 100,000 People
(1980 Census. Listed alphabetically.)

A
Akron, OH	237,177
Albany, NY	101,727
Albuquerque, NM	331,767
Alexandria, VA	103,217
Allentown, PA	103,758
Amarillo, TX	149,230
Anaheim, CA	221,847
Anchorage, AK	173,017
Ann Arbor, MI	107,316
Arlington, TX	160,123
Atlanta, GA	425,022
Aurora, CO	158,588
Austin, TX	345,496

B
Bakersfield, CA	105,611
Baltimore, MD	786,775
Baton Rouge, LA	219,486
Beaumont, TX	118,102
Berkeley, CA	103,328
Birmingham, AL	284,413
Boise, ID	102,451
Boston, MA	562,994
Bridgeport, CT	142,546
Buffalo, NY	357,870

C
Cedar Rapids, IA	110,243
Charlotte, NC	314,447
Chattanooga, TN	169,565
Chesapeake, VA	114,226
Chicago, IL	3,005,072
Cincinnati, OH	385,457
Cleveland, OH	573,822
Colorado Springs, CO	215,150
Columbus, GA	169,441
Columbus, OH	564,871
Concord, CA	103,251
Corpus Christi, TX	231,999

D
Dallas, TX	904,078
Davenport, IA	103,264
Dayton, OH	203,588
Denver, CO	491,396
Des Moines, IA	191,003
Detroit, MI	1,203,339
Durham, NC	100,831

E
Elizabeth, NJ	106,201
El Paso, TX	425,259
Erie, PA	119,123
Eugene, OR	105,624
Evansville, IN	130,496
Ewa, HI	190,037

F
Flint, MI	159,611
Fort Lauderdale, FL	153,256
Fort Wayne, IN	172,196
Fort Worth, TX	385,141
Fremont, CA	131,945
Fresno, CA	218,202
Fullerton, CA	102,034

G
Garden Grove, CA	123,351
Garland, TX	138,857
Gary, IN	151,953
Glendale, CA	139,060
Grand Rapids, MI	181,843
Greensboro, NC	155,642

H
Hampton, VA	122,617
Hartford, CT	136,392
Hialeah, FL	145,254
Hollywood, FL	117,188
Honolulu, HI	365,048
Houston, TX	1,594,086
Huntington Beach, CA	170,505
Huntsville, AL	142,513

I
Independence, MO	111,806
Indianapolis, IN	700,807
Irving, TX	109,943

J
Jackson, MS	202,895
Jacksonville, FL	540,898
Jersey City, NJ	223,532

K
Kansas City, KS	161,087
Kansas City, MO	448,159
Knoxville, TN	183,139
Koolaupoko, HI	109,373

L
Lakewood, CO	112,848
Lansing, MI	130,414
Las Vegas, NV	164,674
Lexington, KY	204,165
Lincoln, NE	171,932
Little Rock, AR	158,461
Livonia, MI	104,814
Long Beach, CA	361,334
Los Angeles, CA	2,966,763
Louisville, KY	298,451
Lubbock, TX	173,979

M
Macon, GA	116,860
Madison, WI	170,616
Memphis, TN	646,356
Mesa City, AZ	152,453
Miami, FL	346,931
Milwaukee, WI	636,212
Minneapolis, MN	370,951
Mobile, AL	200,452
Modesto, CA	106,105
Montgomery, AL	178,157

N
Nashville, TN	455,651
Newark, NJ	329,248
New Haven, CT	126,109
New Orleans, LA	557,482
Newport News, VA	144,903
New York, NY	7,071,030
Norfolk, VA	266,979

O
Oakland, CA	339,288
Oklahoma City, OK	403,213
Omaha, NE	311,681
Orlando, FL	128,394
Oxnard, CA	108,195

P
Pasadena, CA	119,374
Pasadena, TX	112,560
Paterson, NJ	137,970
Peoria, IL	124,160
Philadelphia, PA	1,688,210
Phoenix, AZ	764,911
Pittsburgh, PA	423,938
Portland, OR	366,383
Portsmouth, VA	104,577
Providence, RI	156,804
Pueblo, CO	101,686

R
Raleigh, NC	149,771
Reno, NV	100,756
Richmond, VA	219,214
Riverside, CA	170,876
Roanoke, VA	100,427
Rochester, NY	241,741
Rockford, IL	139,712

S
Sacramento, CA	275,741
St. Louis, MO	453,085
St. Paul, MN	270,230
St. Petersburg, FL	236,893
Salt Lake City, UT	163,033
San Antonio, TX	785,410
San Bernardino, CA	118,057
San Diego, CA	875,504
San Francisco, CA	678,974
San Jose, CA	636,550
Santa Ana, CA	203,713
Savannah, GA	141,634
Seattle, WA	493,846
Shreveport, LA	205,815
South Bend, IN	109,727
Spokane, WA	171,300
Springfield, MA	152,319
Springfield, MO	133,116
Stamford, CT	102,453
Sterling Heights, MI	108,999
Stockton, CA	149,779
Sunnyvale, CA	106,618
Syracuse, NY	170,105

T
Tacoma, WA	158,501
Tampa, FL	271,523
Tempe, AZ	106,743
Toledo, OH	354,635
Topeka, KS	115,266
Torrance, CA	131,497
Tucson, AZ	330,537
Tulsa, OK	360,919

V
Virginia Beach, VA	262,199

W
Waco, TX	101,261
Warren, MI	161,134
Washington, DC	637,651
Waterbury, CT	103,266
Wichita, KS	279,272
Winston-Salem, NC	131,885
Worcester, MA	161,799

Y
Yonkers, NY	195,351
Youngstown, OH	115,436

Population of United States Metropolitan Areas with More Than 1,000,000 People (1980 Census)

15,589,000	New York, NY–Northeastern NJ
9,478,000	Los Angeles–Long Beach, CA
6,711,000	Chicago, IL–Northwestern IN
4,114,000	Philadelphia, PA-NJ
3,809,000	Detroit, MI
3,192,000	San Francisco–Oakland, CA
2,762,000	Washington, DC-MD-VA
2,678,000	Boston, MA
2,452,000	Dallas–Fort Worth, TX
2,413,000	Houston, TX
1,848,000	St. Louis, MO-IL
1,810,000	Pittsburgh, PA
1,787,000	Minneapolis–St. Paul, MN
1,755,000	Baltimore, MD
1,752,000	Cleveland, OH
1,704,000	San Diego, CA
1,613,000	Atlanta, GA
1,608,000	Miami, FL
1,409,000	Phoenix, AZ
1,391,000	Seattle–Everett, WA
1,351,000	Denver, CO
1,244,000	San Jose, CA
1,207,000	Milwaukee, WI
1,123,000	Cincinnati, OH-KY
1,098,000	Kansas City, MO-KS
1,078,000	New Orleans, LA
1,026,000	Portland, OR-WA
1,004,000	Fort Lauderdale–Hollywood, FL
1,002,000	Buffalo, NY

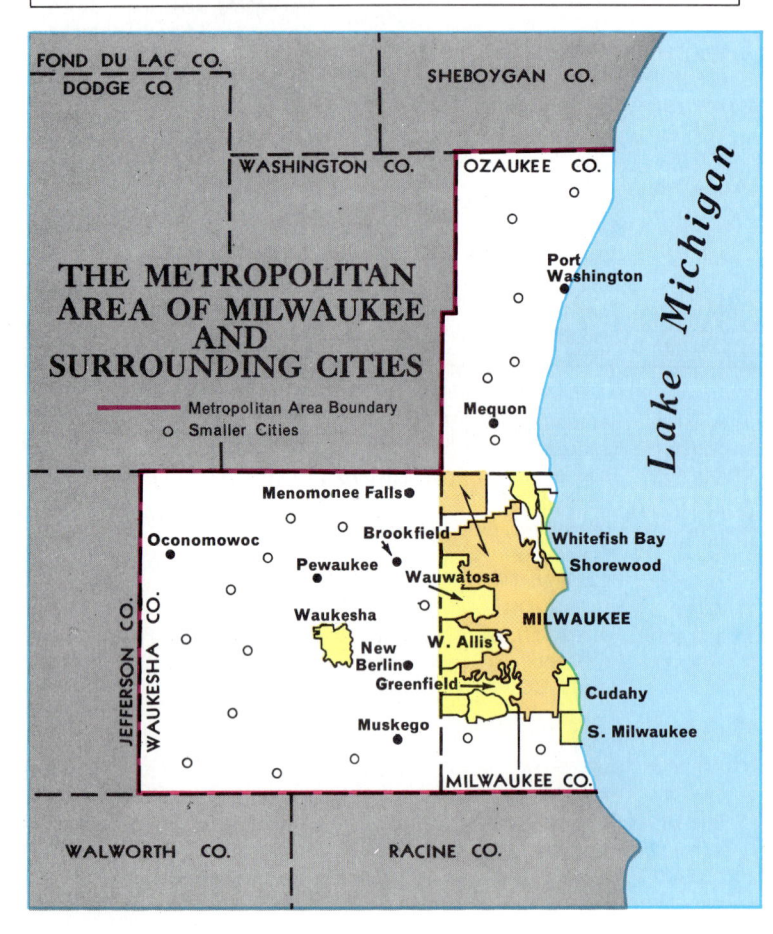

Population of the World's Largest Metropolitan Areas

15,589,000	New York, U.S.A.
13,994,000	Mexico City, Mexico
11,695,000	Tokyo, Japan
10,820,000	Shanghai, China
10,041,000	São Paulo, Brazil
9,863,000	Paris, France
9,749,000	Buenos Aires, Argentina
9,478,000	Los Angeles, U.S.A.
8,569,000	Osaka, Japan
8,329,000	Rio de Janeiro, Brazil
8,011,000	Moscow, USSR
7,570,000	Peking, China
7,500,000	Seoul, South Korea
7,031,000	Calcutta, India
7,028,000	London, England
6,711,000	Chicago, U.S.A.
6,133,000	Cairo, Egypt
5,971,000	Bombay, India
5,490,000	Jakarta, Indonesia
4,904,000	Manila, Philippines
4,835,000	Bangkok, Thailand
4,716,000	Tehran, Iran
4,588,000	Leningrad, USSR
4,280,000	Tientsin, China
4,114,000	Philadelphia, U.S.A.

THE METROPOLITAN AREA OF MILWAUKEE AND SURROUNDING CITIES

A metropolitan area is a group of many cities. The cities of a metropolitan area are much like a series of gears that work together.

The large gear is the central city where most of the people work and where the most banking and trade is carried on. The cities that surround the central city are smaller. They may have business centers and industries of their own, but they depend on the central city as a marketplace, a banking center, a distribution center, and a transfer point. The map shows the metropolitan area around the central city of Milwaukee, Wisconsin.

METRIC CONVERSION TABLE
Converting Standard Measurement to Metric Measurement

	To Convert	Into	Multiply by
Length	inches (in.)	millimeters (mm)	25.4
	inches	centimeters (cm)	2.54
	feet (ft.)	centimeters	30.5
	feet	meters (m)	0.3
	yards (yd.)	meters	0.9
	miles (mi.)	kilometers (km)	1.6
Area	square inches (sq. in.)	square centimeters (sq. cm)	6.5
	square feet (sq. ft.)	square meters (sq. m)	0.09
	square yards (sq. yd.)	square meters	0.8
	square miles (sq. mi.)	square kilometers (sq. km)	2.6
	acre (a.)	hectares (ha)	0.4
Volume	cubic inches (cu. in.)	cubic centimeters (cu. cm)	16.4
	cubic feet (cu. ft.)	cubic meters (cu. m)	0.028
	cubic yards (cu. yd.)	cubic meters	0.765
	cubic miles (cu. mi.)	cubic kilometers (cu. km)	4.1
Weight	ounces (oz.)	grams (gm)	28.35
	pounds (lb.)	kilograms (kg)	0.45
	short tons	metric tons	0.9
Liquid Capacity	fluid ounces (fl. oz.)	milliliters (ml)	29.57
	liquid pints (liq. pt.)	liters (l)	0.47
	liquid quarts (liq. qt.)	liters	0.95
	gallons (gal.)	liters	3.8

Temperature To convert Fahrenheit (F) to Celsius (C), subtract 32, then multiply by 0.556.

To convert Celsius (C) to Fahrenheit (F), multiply by 1.8, then add 32.

485

PRESIDENTS OF THE UNITED STATES

Terms of Office

States Where Born

George Washington
1789–1797
Virginia

James Monroe
1817–1825
Virginia

William Henry Harrison
1841
Virginia

John Adams
1797–1801
Massachusetts

John Quincy Adams
1825–1829
Massachusetts

John Tyler
1841–1845
Virginia

Thomas Jefferson
1801–1809
Virginia

Andrew Jackson
1829–1837
South Carolina

James K. Polk
1845–1849
North Carolina

James Madison
1809–1817
Virginia

Martin Van Buren
1837–1841
New York

Zachary Taylor
1849–1850
Virginia

Millard Fillmore
1850–1853
New York

Ulysses S. Grant
1869–1877
Ohio

Benjamin Harrison
1889–1893
Ohio

Franklin Pierce
1853–1857
New Hampshire

Rutherford B. Hayes
1877–1881
Ohio

Grover Cleveland
1893–1897
New Jersey

James Buchanan
1857–1861
Pennsylvania

James A. Garfield
1881
Ohio

William McKinley
1897–1901
Ohio

Abraham Lincoln
1861–1865
Kentucky

Chester A. Arthur
1881–1885
Vermont

Theodore Roosevelt
1901–1909
New York

Andrew Johnson
1865–1869
North Carolina

Grover Cleveland
1885–1889
New Jersey

William Howard Taft
1909–1913
Ohio

Woodrow Wilson
1913–1921
Virginia

Harry S. Truman
1945–1953
Missouri

Gerald R. Ford
1974–1977
Nebraska

Warren G. Harding
1921–1923
Ohio

Dwight D. Eisenhower
1953–1961
Texas

James E. Carter, Jr.
1977–1981
Georgia

Calvin Coolidge
1923–1929
Vermont

John F. Kennedy
1961–1963
Massachusetts

Ronald W. Reagan
1981–
Illinois

Herbert C. Hoover
1929–1933
Iowa

Lyndon B. Johnson
1963–1969
Texas

Franklin D. Roosevelt
1933–1945
New York

Richard M. Nixon
1969–1974
California

Glossary

In this Glossary you will find many words and phrases used in this book, including all those listed at the beginning of each unit section. You may use the Glossary as you would a dictionary. But only the word meaning that will be most helpful to you in the study of this book is given in the Glossary. You can find more meanings if you look up the words and phrases in a dictionary. Every word has been spelled phonetically, or by sounds, within parentheses following the word, and those sounds are marked to help you pronounce the word correctly. The Pronunciation Key below shows what the marks mean and gives examples of how to pronounce the sounds.

Pronunciation Key

a *a*t	e m*e*t	ī h*i*ke	o͝o g*oo*d
ā f*a*de	ē m*e*	ō *o*pen	o͞o s*oo*n
â *ai*r	ə *a*bout; aft*e*r; *u*p	ô f*o*r; *aw*ful	ou l*ou*d
ä f*a*r; f*a*ther; h*o*t	i *i*t	oi *oi*l	zh gara*g*e

abolish (ə·bäl′ish) To do away with.
acre (ā′kər) A measure of land equal to 4,840 square yards or 4,047 square meters (.4 hectares).
adobe (ə·dō′bē) A mixture of earth and dried grass, sometimes used as a building material.
agency (ā′jən·sē) A group that is formed to achieve a special purpose or goal.
alliance (ə·lī′əns) A friendly agreement between countries to help one another.
ally (al′ ī′) One who agrees to help another.
amendment (ə·mend′mənt) A change that adds to or takes out a part of the U.S. Constitution.
ancestor (an′ses′tər) A person from whom another person is descended.
annex (ə·neks′) To add an area to another.
apprentice (ə·prent′əs) A person who lives and works with a master of a trade in order to learn the trade.
aqueduct (ak′wə·dəkt′) A large canallike structure built above ground to carry water.
archaeologist (är′kē·äl′ə·jəst) A person who studies the way that people lived in the past.
arid (är′əd) Dry.
armed forces (ärmd fôrs′əs) The army, navy, and air force of a country.
artifact (ärt′ə·fakt′) An item from the past.
assembly line (ə·sem′blē līn) An arrangement of machines, equipment, and workers that permits work to pass from one stage to another until a product is put together.
astrolabe (as′trə·lāb′) An instrument for measuring how far north of the equator a ship sails.

astronaut (as′trə·nôt′) A pilot or technician of a spacecraft crew.
astronomy (ə·strän′ə·mē) The study of the stars.
barbed wire (bärbd wīr) A wire with twisted points, or barbs, spaced along it, used for fences.
bauxite (bôk′sīt′) An ore from which aluminum is made.
blockade (blä·kād′) (*n.*) A military action in which ships and troops are used to prevent people and supplies from entering or leaving an area.
boycott (boi′kät′) (*v.*) To refuse to buy certain goods, usually to show disapproval or to force change.
canal (kə·nal′) A channel dug for irrigation or transportation.
capital (kap′ət·əl) The city in a country or state where laws are made.
Capitol (kap′ət·əl) The building in which Congress meets in Washington, D.C.
caravan (kãr′ə·van′) A group of traders with goods carried by animals.
caravel (kãr′ə·vel′) A small, fast sailing ship used in the 1400s and 1500s.
cargo (kär′gō) The goods carried on a ship, plane, train, or truck.
cartographer (kär·täg′rə·fər) A person who draws maps.
cash crop (kash kräp) A crop that is grown mostly for sale rather than for use by a farmer.

489

cause (kôz) (*n.*) A person, thing, or event that brings about an effect or a result.
century (sench′ə·rē) A period of 100 years.
chief (chēf) (*n.*) The leader of an Indian clan or tribe.
civilian (sə·vil′yən) A person who is not in the armed forces.
civil war (siv′əl wôr) A war fought between people of the same country.
clan (klan) A group of people who have a common ancestor.
climate (klī′mət) The kind of weather a region has over a period of years, partly determined by patterns of temperature and precipitation.
climatograph (klī·mat′ə·graf) A graph that gives climate information for a location.
colonist (käl′ə·nəst) A person who settles in a new land.
colony (käl′ə·nē) A permanent settlement made by a group of people who left their own country to start life in a new land.
commonwealth (käm′ən·welth′) A political unit with self-government but joined to another country by its own choice.
compass (kəm′pəs) An instrument that gives directions using a needle that always points north.
compass rose (kəm′pəs rōz) A symbol on a map used to show directions.
compromise (käm′prə·mīz′) (*n.*) An agreement in which both sides are partly satisfied.
computer (kəm·pyōōt′ər) A machine that stores and prints information.
congress (käng′grəs) A formal meeting of delegates to discuss and act on certain matters.
conqueror (käng′kər·ər) A person who takes land by force.
conservation (kän′sər·vā′shən) The protection of forests, land, water, and other resources.
constitution (kän′stə·tōō′shən) A written plan of government that tells what powers and duties the government has and what rights and duties the people have.
consumer goods (kən·sōō′mər gōōdz) Goods used by people for their own needs or wants, such as clothing or food.
continental (känt′ən·ent′əl) A type of climate with hot summers and cold winters.
Continental Divide (känt′ən·ent′əl də·vīd′) The highest land along the Rocky Mountains that separates rivers flowing toward the Atlantic Ocean and rivers flowing toward the Pacific Ocean.

contour line (kän′tōōr′ līn) A line on a map that joins together all the points that have the same elevation.
contour map (kän′tōōr′ map) A map that uses different contour lines instead of colors to show differences in elevation.
convention (kən·ven′chən) A meeting held for a special reason.
corduroy road (kôrd′ə·roi′ rōd) A road built of logs.
corn belt (kôrn belt) A large corn-growing area in the Great Lakes Region and Midwest Plains.
cotton gin (kät′ən jin) A machine invented by Eli Whitney that separates seeds from cotton fibers.
culture (kəl′chər) The arts, customs, and knowledge of a group of people.

decade (dek′ād′) A period of ten years.
degree (di·grē′) A unit of measure for latitude, longitude, or temperature.
democratic republic (dem′ə·krat′ik ri·pəb′lik) A system of government in which the people govern through elected representatives.
demographer (di·mäg′rə·fər) A person who studies population changes such as growth or settlement.
developing nation (di·vel′əp·ing nā′shən) A country that is trying to build a stronger economy by changing from farming to industry and business.
dictator (dik′tāt′ər) A person who has total control over a nation's government.
discriminate (dis·krim′ə·nāt) To show a preference in the treatment of a particular group of people.

earth lodge (ərth läj) A building made of wooden poles and sod and used as a home by the Mandan.
economy (i·kän′ə·mē) The way people make their living or the way people produce and use resources.
effect (i·fekt′) (*n.*) Something that happens as a result of a person, thing, or event.
elevation (el′ə·vā′shən) The height above sea level.
empire (em′pīr′) A group of nations or territories ruled by the same government.
equality (i·kwäl′ət·ē) A condition in which people have the same rights.
erosion (i·rō′zhən) The wearing away of earth and rock by wind and water.

ethnic group (eth′nik gro͞op) A group of people who share the same ancestry, customs, and language.
executive (ig·zek′yət·iv) Related to the branch of our government that carries out the laws.
expedition (ek′spə·dish′ən) A journey made for a special purpose, such as to search or explore new lands.
expressway (ik·spres′wā′) A highway that is built for travel at high speeds and that links the suburbs with the cities.

factory (fak′tə·rē) A place where machines produce goods.
fault (fôlt) (*n.*) A deep crack in the earth's surface where the land on either side has moved up or down along the crack.
federal (fed′ə·rəl) Having to do with the central government of a nation.
fiber (fī′bər) A long, threadlike strand.
food processing (fo͞od präs′es′ing) The method in which farm products are prepared for human or animal use.
fort (fôrt) A settlement protected by high fences or walls.
frontier (frən′tir′) The edge of a settled area.

geography (jē·äg′rə·fē) The study of the physical makeup of the earth, its climate, customs of people, and products.
geothermal (jē′ə·thər′məl) A type of heat that comes from deep down in the earth.
glacier (glā′shər) A large body of slowly moving ice.
globe (glōb) A round model of the earth.
graph (graf) A diagram that gives information, such as a pie, bar, or line graph.

hacienda (häs′ē·en′də) A large farm in many former Spanish colonies that included homes, gardens, and other things needed by the owner and the workers.
headwaters (hed′wôt′ərz) The beginning or source of a river or stream.
heavy industry (hev′ē in′dəs·trē) Factories and mills that produce parts for heavy equipment.
hemisphere (hem′ə·sfir′) Half of the earth.
heritage (her′ət·ij) The ideas, beliefs, and customs passed from generation to generation.
high latitudes (hī lat′ə·to͞odz′) The parts of the world between the North Pole and the Arctic Circle and between the South Pole and the Antarctic Circle, also called the polar regions.

hill (hil) A rounded part of the earth's surface with sloping sides, smaller than a mountain.
historian (his·tôr′ē·ən) A person who studies or writes about important events of the past.
hogan (hō′gän) A building made of wooden poles, mud, and bark.

immigrant (im′i·grənt) A person who comes to a new country to make a home there.
indentured servant (in·den′chərd sər′vənt) A person who works for another person for a certain number of years in exchange for travel, housing, and a job.
independent (in′də·pen′dənt) Free from outside forces.
industrial revolution (in·dəs′trē·əl rev′ə·lo͞o′shən) A time in history when machines began doing the work people had done by hand.
integrated (int′ə·grāt′əd) Made available to all people regardless of race or background.
interstate highway (int′ər·stāt′ hī′wā′) A main road that connects two or more states.
irrigate (ir′ə·gāt′) To bring water to farmland.
irrigation (ir′ə·gā′shən) A system of supplying land with water, especially to grow crops.
isthmus (is′məs) A narrow strip of land that connects two larger land areas.

journal (jərn′əl) A written record of day-to-day events, thoughts, or ideas.
judicial (jo͝o·dish′əl) Related to the branch of our government that interprets the laws.

landform (land′fôrm′) A feature of the earth's surface created by natural forces.
latitude (lat′ə·to͞od′) The distance in degrees north or south of the equator.
legislative (lej′ə·slāt′iv) Related to the branch of our government that makes the laws.
legislature (lej′ə·slā′chər) A governing body that passes laws.
local relief (lō′kəl ri·lēf′) The difference or change in elevation from one place to another in the same area.
lode (lōd) A rich deposit of metal.
log (lôg) A written record of a ship's voyage.
longhouse (lông′hous′) A building made of wooden poles covered with bark.
longitude (län′jə·to͞od′) The distance in degrees east or west of the prime meridian.
low latitudes (lō lat′ə·to͞odz′) Area between the Tropic of Cancer and the Tropic of Capricorn, often called the tropics.

manufactured goods (man′yə·fak′chərd goodz) Goods made from raw materials by machinery in factories.

map scale (map skāl) The measuring device found on a map that compares distances on the map with distances on the earth's surface.

mathematics (math′ə·mat′iks) The study of numbers.

megalopolis (meg′ə·läp′ə·ləs) A large urban area made up of many cities and suburbs.

merchant (mər′chənt) A trader who buys and sells goods.

meridian (mə·rid′ē·ən) A line of longitude.

mestizo (me·stē′zō) A person of both Indian and European ancestry.

microcomputer (mī′krō·kəm·pyoot′ər) A small computer.

middle latitudes (mid′əl lat′ə·toodz′) The two areas between the tropics, or low latitudes, and the Arctic and Antarctic regions.

migrant worker (mī′grənt wər′kər) A person who moves from place to place to find work on large farms.

migration (mī·grā′shən) The movement of people from one place to another.

militia (mə·lish′ə) A group of people who serve as soldiers in times of emergency.

mill (mil) A place where grains are ground into flour.

minuteman (min′ət·man′) A member of a group that prepared for war and were ready "to fight on a minute's notice" before and during the Revolutionary War.

mission (mish′ən) A settlement that centered around a church.

missionary (mish′ə·ner′ē) A person who teaches religion to others.

mountain (mount′ən) High, rocky land, usually with steep sides and a pointed or rounded top, higher than a hill.

nation (nā′shən) A country; a group of American Indian tribes.

natural resource (nach′ə·rəl rē′sôrs′) Something found in nature that people use.

naval stores (nā′vəl stôrz) Liquid products made from pine trees that were once used to build and repair wooden ships.

neutral (noo′trəl) Not taking one side or another.

New World (noo wərld) Term once used by Europeans to refer to the continents of North and South America and the islands near these continents.

nonrenewable (nän′ri·noo′ə·bəl) Referring to something that, once used, can never be used again.

Northwest Passage (nôrth·west′ pas′ij) A northern water route across the Atlantic Ocean and around or through North America to the Pacific Ocean.

ocean current (ō′shən kər′ənt) A flow of water that moves in a definite direction in the ocean at all times.

oil shale (oil shāl) A certain type of rock from which crude oil can be processed.

overland (ō′vər·land′) Across the land.

parallel (pär′ə·lel′) (n.) A line that runs across the surface of the globe and that marks latitude.

pass (pas) (n.) A gap, or low place, in a mountain range.

patent (pat′ənt) (n.) The right to make, use, or sell an invention.

Patriot (pā′trē·ət) A person in the former thirteen American colonies who wanted the colonies to separate from Britain and become a separate country.

percent (pər·sent′) A part in a hundred.

percentage (pər·sent′ij) A part of a whole expressed as a part in a hundred.

petrochemical (pe′trō·kem′i·kəl) Referring to an industry that uses oil and gas as chemical building blocks to make goods such as plastics, paints, and fertilizers.

petroleum (pə·trō′lē·əm) Crude oil.

physical map (fiz′i·kəl map) A map that uses shades of black to show land that is hilly or mountainous.

Piedmont (pēd′mont′) A hilly area at the foot of the Appalachian Mountains.

pioneer (pī′ə·nir′) A person who moves to unsettled lands.

plains (plānz) An area of broad, level land.

plank road (plangk rōd) A road built of heavy, thick boards.

plantation (plan·tā′shən) A very large farm where cotton, rice, tobacco, or other crops are grown.

plateau (pla·tō′) An area of high, flat land.

plaza (plaz′ə) A public square in a village or town.

polar regions (pō′lər rē′jənz) The parts of the world between the North Pole and the Arctic Circle and between the South Pole and the Antarctic Circle, also called the high latitudes.

political map (pə·lit′i·kəl map) A map that shows how the land is divided into countries and states. Political maps also show the location of cities and capitals.

political party (pə·lit′i·kəl pärt′ē) A group of people who share the same ideas about running the government and who try to have party members elected or appointed to office.

population (päp′yə·lā′shən) The number of people in a given area.

population density (päp′yə·lā′shən den′sət·ē) The average number of people living within a given area.

port (pôrt) A harbor, town, or city where ships can load and unload their cargoes.

potlatch (pät′lach′) A feast given by many Northwest Coast Indians during which the host gives away presents to everyone at the feast.

poverty (päv′ərt·ē) The condition of being needy or poor.

prairie (prer′ē) A large plains region with tall grasses, usually found in the United States or Canada.

precipitation (pri·sip′ə·tā′shən) Any form of moisture that falls upon the earth.

prevailing wind (pri·vā′ling wind) A wind that usually blows from the same direction.

prime meridian (prīm mə·rid′ē·ən) An imaginary line on the earth's surface running through Greenwich, England, from the North Pole to the South Pole and used as the starting point from which degrees of longitude are measured.

profile (prō′fīl′) A drawing of a cross section of land from its highest point to its lowest point.

prospector (präs′pek·tər) A person who searches for valuable minerals, such as gold or silver.

province (präv′əns) A political unit like a state, such as that found in Canada.

quadrant (kwäd′rənt) An instrument for measuring how far north of the equator a ship sails.

range (rānj) The difference, or distance, between the highest and lowest of something; a series or row of mountains.

rationing (rash′ə·ning) A government program in which the government decides how much of some goods people may buy or receive.

raw materials (rô mə·tir′ē·əlz) Things in their natural state before they have been processed or manufactured into something else.

reaper (rē′pər) A machine that harvests grain.

rebellion (ri·bel′yən) An uprising or show of force against those in power or control.

Reconstruction (rē′kən·strək′shən) A time in history of rebuilding and reuniting the United States after the Civil War.

refining (ri·fīn′ing) The process by which the impurities of a mineral are removed.

renewable (ri·nōō′ə·bəl) Referring to something that can be used over and over.

repeal (ri·pēl′) To pass a law that makes another law no longer in effect.

representative government (rep′ri·zent′ət·iv gəv′ər·mənt) A government in which the people elect leaders to govern them.

reservation (rez′ər·vā′shən) A certain area of land that the government has set aside for American Indians.

retail trade (rē′tāl′ trād) The selling of goods in a store directly to the users.

revolt (ri·vōlt′) (n.) An uprising or rebellion against a government or leader.

rural (rŏŏr′əl) Having to do with an area that is away from cities.

saga (säg′ə) A long story of adventures of Norse heroes.

satellite (sat′əl·īt′) An electronic object that circles the earth.

sea level (sē lev′əl) The level or place where the ocean meets the land.

secede (si·sēd′) To leave or withdraw from an organization.

segregation (seg′ri·gā′shən) A way of separating black people from white people, especially in schools and other public places.

sharecropping (sher′kräp′ing) A system of renting land and giving the owner part of the crops raised as payment of the rent.

site (sīt) The location on which something is built.

slavery (slāv′rē) The ownership of people by other people.

slum (sləm) A crowded area of a city or town where people live in dirty, run-down buildings.

sod (säd) The tightly packed mixture of soil and grass roots found on the grasslands.

sphere (sfir) A round object such as a globe.

springhouse (spring′hous′) A deep pit dug in a cool area and used to store food.

steamboat (stēm′bōt′) A boat driven by the power of steam.

steam engine (stēm en′jən) An engine powered by the force of boiling water.

stock (stäk) (*n.*) A share of ownership in a company.

strait (strāt) A narrow stretch of water that connects two larger bodies of water.

subsistence farmer (səb·sis′təns fär′mər) A farmer who grows only enough crops to support one family.

suburb (səb′ərb′) A smaller community just outside or near a city.

suffrage (suf′rij) The right to vote.

sunbelt (sən′belt) The southern row of states that stretch from the Atlantic Ocean to the Pacific Ocean.

survey (sər·vā′) (*v.*) To examine and measure land for size, shape, boundaries, and quality.

symbol (sim′bəl) A drawing that represents something else.

tack (tak) (*v.*) To take a zigzag course when sailing.

tariff (tãr′əf) A tax on goods shipped into or out of a country.

tax (taks) The money collected to run a government.

technology (tek·näl′ə·jē) The scientific advances in such things as tools, machines, and transportation.

telecommunication (tel′i·kə·myōō′nə·kā′shən) A system that sends and receives information at a distance.

telegraph (tel′i·graf′) A way of sending messages on electrical wires.

temperature range (tem′pə·choŏr′ rānj) The difference between the highest average monthly temperature and the lowest.

tenement (ten′ə·mənt) An apartment building that is run-down and crowded.

tepee (tē′pē) A large tent in the shape of a cone used as a home by many Indian tribes living on the Great Plains.

terrace (ter′əs) A steplike field on the side of a mountain or hill.

territory (ter′ə·tôr′ē) An area of land organized under a local government before being admitted as a state into the Union.

textile (tek′stīl′) (*n.*) Cloth. (*adj.*) Having to do with cloth making.

toll (tōl) A fee paid to use a road or bridge.

totem pole (tōt′əm pōl) A tall cedar log carved with symbols of ancestors and animals by many Northwest Coast Indians.

tourist (tŏŏr′əst) A person who visits a place to enjoy its scenery or its culture.

trading company (trād′ing kəmp′ə·nē) A group of people that put their money together to make more money from trade.

transcontinental (trans′känt′ən·ent′əl) Across the continent.

transportation (trans′pər·tā′shən) The act of moving things.

treaty (trēt′ē) A formal agreement made especially between two countries or groups of people.

tribe (trīb) A group of Indians who share certain customs.

tropics (träp′iks) The warm region lying on both sides of the equator.

tundra (tən′drə) A cold, treeless plain in polar regions.

underground railroad (ən′dər·ground′ rāl′rōd′) A system by which people who were against slavery secretly helped slaves escape to freedom in the North.

union (yōō′nyən) A group of people, especially a group of workers, who join together to work for things they believe they should have.

Union (yōō′nyən) The United States of America; a term used to refer to the North during the Civil War.

urban (ər′bən) Of or having something to do with a city and its surrounding towns.

volcano (väl·kā′nō) A mountain formed of rock or ash thrown up from inside the earth.

volunteer (väl′ən·tir′) (*n.*) A person who decides to do something without being forced.

wagon train (wag′ən trān) A long line of covered wagons traveling together.

water table (wôt′ər tā′bəl) The top part of the ground in which water has collected.

wheat belt (hwēt belt) A large wheat-growing area in the western Midwest Plains and some bordering states.

wholesale trade (hōl′sāl′ trād) The buying and selling of goods in large quantities to retail stores.

wigwam (wig′wäm′) A building made of wooden poles covered with mats of cattails, tree branches, and bark and used as a home by many Eastern Woodlands tribes.

Index

This Index will help you find the topics, pictures, maps, charts, graphs, and diagrams you need in your work. It is arranged in alphabetical order. It has guide words like those in your dictionary. It will show you what you can find in the book about persons, places, or things.

Italic letters before page references refer to the following: *c.* stands for chart; *d.* stands for diagram; *g.* stands for graph; *m.* stands for map; and *p.* stands for photo or illustration.

A

Abilene, Kansas, 236
abolitionist movement, 208–210, 218
Adams, John, 177; *c.* 486; *p.* 486
Adams, John Quincy, *c.* 486; *p.* 486
Addams, Jane, 265; *p.* 265
airplanes, 252, 276, 277, 295; *p.* 277
Alabama, *c.* 372, 482
  farming in, 205
  mining in, 369
  settlement of, 64, 183
Alamo, 196; *p.* 196
Alaska, 424–435; *c.* 430, 433, 482; *p.* 425
  climate, 428; *g.* 428
  employment in, 431–433
  fishing in, 430, 432
  hunting in, 430
  land, 427–428; *g.* 428
  mineral resources in, 432
  natural resources in, 429
  population of, 429–430; *c.* 430; *g.* 429; *m.* 429
  purchase of, 269
  size comparison map of, 426
  tourism, *p.* 430
Alberta, 440; *c.* 448–449
Albuquerque, New Mexico, 383
Aldrin, Edwin, 96, 297; *p.* 96
Aleuts, 52, 53, 55, 63–64, 430
amendments, to Constitution, 169
  See also the specific amendments
American documents
  Constitution, U.S., 168
  Declaration of Independence, 162–163
  Emancipation Proclamation, 227
  Mayflower Compact, 123
American Indians. *See* **Indians**, **American**
American Revolution. *See* **Revolutionary War**
Anthony, Susan B., 268
anthropology, 80
Antin, Mary, 257
Apollo 11, 96; *p.* 96
Appalachian Mountains, 330, 362
archaeology, 56, 86–87
architecture, 66, 119, 366, 416; *p.* 66, 67, 366, 416
Arctic Circle, 32
Argentina, 461, 463; *c.* 466
Arizona, *c.* 389, 482
  exploration of, 107
  settlement of, 65
Arkansas, *c.* 372, 482
  as Confederate state, 227
  exploration of, 190
Arkansas River, 396
armies
  Civil War, 227
  Continental Army, 162, 163; *p.* 163
  minutemen, 161, 162
Armstrong, Neil, 96, 297; *p.* 96
Aroostook Valley, 319
art
  painting of mammoths, *p.* 58
  Mandan painting, *p.* 70
  Navajo sand painting, *p.* 68
Arthur, Chester A., *c.* 487; *p.* 487
Asian Americans, 261, 262, 287, 299, 416, 430; *p.* 47, 256, 301
assembly line, 251, 336; *p.* 336
  computerization of, *p.* 477
astronauts, 96, 296; *p.* 96, 296
Atlanta, Georgia, 361, 364–365, 367, 371; *p.* 370
Atlantic Provinces, 439–440, 447
Atlas Tells a Story, 28–35
Austin, Stephen, 195
automobiles, 294–295
  assembly line, 336; *p.* 336
  changes brought by, 276
  growth of industry, 274–275; *p.* 274
  invention of, 251–252; *p.* 252
Aztec civilization, 105

B

Badlands, 346, 352; *p.* 346
Bahamas, 96; *c.* 466
Baltimore, Lord, 135
Barbados, *c.* 466
Baton Rouge, Louisiana, 371
Bell, Alexander Graham, 252
Bering Strait, 57, 58, 427; *p.* 57
big business, growth of, 253–254
Bill of Rights, 169
biographies
  Addams, Jane, 265; *p.* 265
  Columbus, Christopher, 89–98; *p.* 91
  Darragh, Lydia, 164
  Douglass, Frederick, 210; *p.* 210
  Edison, Thomas, 250; *p.* 250
  Harvard, John, 139
  Hays, Mary Ludwig, 164; *p.* 164
  Hutchinson, Anne, 133; *p.* 133
  Sampson, Deborah, 164
  Vespucci, Amerigo, 105
Birmingham, Alabama, 369

495

black codes, 231
blacks
  in Civil War, 228
  Douglass, Frederick, 210; *p.* 210
  education for, 266
  free, 223
  in government, 232; *p.* 232
  growth of urban population of, 1870-1930, *g.* 263
  migration of, to cities, 231, 333
  post–Civil War problems, 230-233
  and segregation, 233, 298-299
  Tubman, Harriet, 210; *p.* 210
  See also **slavery**
Blue Ridge Mountains, 362
Bolivia, 463, 465; *c.* 466
Boone, Daniel, 200-201; *p.* 166
Booth, John Wilkes, 230
Boston, Massachusetts, *p.* 312
  growth of, 152-153
  in Revolutionary War, 163
Boston Massacre, 158-159
Boston News-Letter, 160
Boston Tea Party, 159; *p.* 159
Boundary Waters Canoe Area, Minnesota, 349; *p.* 349
Brazil, 461, 463; *c.* 466
  careers in, *p.* 464
Buchanan, James, *c.* 487; *p.* 487
buffalo, 72, 238-239; *p.* 239
  hunting of, by American Indians, 71-72
Buffalo, New York, 321
Bunker Hill, Battle of, 162
Butterfield Overland Mail Company, 243

C
Calgary, Alberta, Canada, 442
California, *c.* 421, 482
  admission as state, 198
  discovery of gold in, 198, 234; *p.* 198
  employment in, 417-418; *p.* 419
  ethnic diversity of, 119; *p.* 47, 118
  population patterns in, 415-416
  settlement of, 197, 198
  Spanish colonization of, 119; *p.* 416
California Trail, 198; *m.* 196
Canada, 436-451; *c.* 448-449
  Appalachian Highlands, 440
  Canadian Shield, 440
  climate of, 441; *g.* 441
  cultural heritage in, 443
  employment in, 445-448
  farming in, 445; *m.* 451
  fishing in, 447, 448
  forests and forest industries, 446-447
  growing seasons, 441; *m.* 441
  industry in, 446
  Interior Plains, 440
  Intermountain Region, 440
  land of, 440-441; *g.* 440
  location of, 439
  mineral resources, *m.* 447
  natural regions of, 440-441; *m.* 438
  natural resources in, 446-447
  Pacific Mountains and Valleys, 440
  population of, 442-444; *c.* 443; *g.* 442; *m.* 442
  precipitation, *m.* 451
  provinces and territories of, 439-440
  Rocky Mountains, 437, 440
  St. Lawrence River valley, 440
canals, 206
  Erie, 183-184; *p.* 181
  Panama, 271-272; *p.* 271
Cancer, Tropic of, 32, 455; *c.* 458
careers
  assembly line worker, 336; *p.* 336
  in Brazil, 464; *p.* 464
  computer programmers, 478; *p.* 478
  cowboys and cowgirls, 403; *p.* 403
  farmer, 353, 419; *p.* 353, 419
  fishing, 432; *p.* 432
  Los Alamos Scientific Laboratory, 386; *p.* 386
  Lyndon B. Johnson Space Center, 386; *p.* 386
  microcomputer industry, 419; *p.* 419
  mining, 336, 353, 403-404; *p.* 336, 353, 403
  movie industry, 419; *p.* 419
  oil fields, 386; *p.* 386
  paper and wood pulp industries, 447; *p.* 447
  Peachtree Center Complex, 370; *p.* 370
  Pentagon, 370; *p.* 370
  physician, 353; *p.* 353
  research scientists, 478; *p.* 478
  retail store buyer, 320; *p.* 320
  Royal Canadian Mounted Police, 447; *p.* 447
  ski instructors, 403; *p.* 403
  stock broker, 320; *p.* 320
  tourism, 432; *p.* 432
  treasury employees, 320; *p.* 320
  Walt Disney World, 370; *p.* 370
  wholesale buyers, 336; *p.* 336
Carmel Mission, 118; *p.* 118, 416
Carnegie, Andrew, 254
Carolinas, colonization of, 135
  See also **North Carolina**; **South Carolina**
Carter, James E., Jr., *c.* 488; *p.* 488
Cartier, Jacques, 109; *m.* 110
cartographer, 35, 125; *p.* 35
Cascade Mountains, 412
case study
  Jamestown, 120-122
  Plymouth, 122-123
Castro, Fidel, 367
Catt, Carrie Chapman, 268
cattle ranching, 235-237, 433; *m.* 236; *p.* 237
Centennial Exposition, 252-253; *p.* 253
Central Overland Company, 243-244
Central Valley, 417
Champlain, Samuel de, 110
Charleston, South Carolina, 159
charts
  area and population of states, 482
  branches of government, 168
  colonial population growth, 1700-1770, 153

European exploration and discoveries, 113
facts about
Alaska, 433
Canada, 448–449
Great Lakes Region, 339
Hawaii, 433
Latin America, 466–467
Midwest Plains, 355
Northeast, 322–323
Pacific Coast, 421
Presidents, 486–488
South, 372–373
Southwest, 389
inventions of late 1800s and early 1900s, 252
metric conversion, 485
population
Alaska, 430
black, 263
Canada, 443
Great Lakes Region, 334
Hawaii, 430
Indian reservations, 391
Interior West, 399
Latin America, 460
Midwest Plains, 348
Northeast, 315, 317
Pacific Coast, 415
selected cities, 1880–1940, 259
South, 366, 367
Southwest, 381, 382
U.S. cities, 483
U.S. metropolitan areas, 484
world metropolitan areas, 484
voters in presidential elections, 300
Chicago, Illinois, 55; *p.* 327, 332
children, working conditions of, 254
Chile, 458, 461, 463, 465; *c.* 466
Chinese, explorations by, 84–85
Chinese Americans, 262, 416; *p.* 47
Chisholm Trail, 236; *m.* 236
Cipangu, 100
cities
American Indians in, 54–55
growth of, 275
migration from, 296
need to improve, 264–265
population of world's largest, *c.* 483
See also **towns and cities**
citizenship
Addams, Jane, 265; *p.* 265
contribution to education, 139
freedoms, 45
for immigrants, 258
Civil Rights Act (1964), 299, 300
Civil War, 225–228; *p.* 215
battles of, 226–228; *m.* 247
blacks in, 227, 228
civilians in, 227
comparison of North and South, 226
destruction of South in, 229–230
end of, 228; *p.* 228
prewar conditions, 216–225
soldiers in, 227
South and border states, *m.* 225
start of, *p.* 226
women in, 227; *p.* 227
See also **Reconstruction**
Clark, William, 187–190; *p.* 187
Clermont, 185
Cleveland, Grover, *c.* 487; *p.* 487
climate
Alaska, *g.* 428
Canada, 441; *g.* 441; *m.* 441
Great Lakes Region, 330–331; *g.* 331
Hawaii, 428; *g.* 428
Latin America, 456–458; *g.* 457
Midwest Plains, 346–347, 352; *g.* 347
Northeast, 312–313; *g.* 313
Pacific Coast, 413; *g.* 412; *m.* 413
South, 362–363; *g.* 363; *m.* 363
Southwest, 379–380; *g.* 380; *m.* 380
climatographs
Anchorage, Alaska, 428
Bakersfield, California, 412
Belém, Brazil, 457
Buenos Aires, Argentina, 457
Chattanooga, Tennessee, 363
Cincinnati, Ohio, 331
Flagstaff, Arizona, 380
Honolulu, Hawaii, 428
Houston, Texas, 380
Las Vegas, Nevada, 397
Mexico City, Mexico, 457
Miami, Florida, 363
Missoula, Montana, 397
Mt. Washington, New Hampshire, 313
Ottawa, Canada, 441
Quito, Ecuador, 457
Sault Saint Marie, Michigan, 331
Seattle, Washington, 412
Springfield, Missouri, 347
Vancouver, Canada, 441
Washington, D.C., 313
Williston, North Dakota, 347
Colombia, 272, 463, 465; *c.* 466
colonial life
education, 139, 140
farming, 134, 135, 136, 138
furniture, 140; *p.* 140
government, 137
housing, 139
towns and cities, 138
transportation, 139
colonies
British, 120–162; *m.* 132
development of cities in, 152–153
development of trade in, 153–155; *m.* 153
formation of new government, 166–169
government in, 156–157
growth of, 152; *g.* 136, 153
Spanish, 116–119; *p.* 117, 118, 119
taxes of, by Great Britain, 157–159
ties to Great Britain, 155
Colorado, *c.* 405, 482
discovery of gold in, 234–235; *m.* 235
exploration of, 190
settlement of, 65
Colorado River, 396
Columbia, p. 283
Columbia River, 43, 189, 413, 420
Columbus, Christopher, 89–98, 100–101; *p.* 91

497

Columbus *(continued)*
  discovery of San Salvador by, 83
  ships of, 94; *p.* 94
  voyages of, 95-98; *m.* 97, 101
  written records of, 93
communication
  development of, 207
  improvements in, 295
compass, 86
compass rose, 33, 125; *p.* 33
computers, 295
Comstock Lode, 235
Conestoga wagons, 198, 200, 242; *p.* 200
Confederate States of America, 225; *m.* 225
Connecticut, *c.* 322, 482
  colonization of, 133
  early factories in, 204
Connecticut River valley, 319
conservation, 267
Constitution, U.S., 167-169; *c.* 168
  acceptance of, 169
  amendments to, 169
  See also the specific amendments
  Bill of Rights, 169
Constitutional Convention, 167
  Washington as president of, 167; *p.* 167
Continental Army, 162, 163; *p.* 163
Continental Congress
  First, 160
  Second, 162
Continental Divide, 396
contour lines, 192-194; *d.* 193
Coolidge, Calvin, *c.* 488; *p.* 488
Corliss steam engine, 253; *p.* 253
corn belt, 337, 351; *m.* 351
Coronado, Francisco, 107; *m.* 106
Cortes, Hernando, 105; *m.* 106
Costa Rica, *c.* 466
cotton, 208, 219-220; *p.* 218, 220
cotton factories, 204-205; *p.* 205
cotton gin, 205-206; *p.* 205
Cuba, 97, 271, 290, 367, 455; *c.* 466
cultural influences, 46
  in Canada, 443
  in New Orleans, 366; *p.* 366
  Spanish, 119
Cumberland Road, 183, 191

D

Dallas, Texas, 381; *c.* 381, 382
Darragh, Lydia, 164
Death Valley, 411-412
Declaration of Independence
  ideas in, 162-163
  signing of, *p.* 162
  Thomas Jefferson as author of, 162
degree, 31, 291
Delaware, *c.* 322, 482
  colonization of, 135
Delaware Bay, 154
democracy, 123, 168
democratic republic, 168
Denver, Colorado, 55, 235, 395, 398-399, 404; *p.* 393
De Soto, Hernando, 107; *m.* 106
developing nations, 289-290
diagrams
  contour lines, 193
  elevation and relief of landforms, 59
  ocean currents of North Atlantic, 102
  ocean currents of North Pacific, 85
Diagrams Tell a Story
  early exploration, 99-102
Dictionary of Geographical Terms, 26-27
direction, finding on maps, 32-33
distance, 33-34
District of Columbia, *c.* 482
Dominican Republic, *c.* 466
Duquesne, Fort, 149-150
Dutch East Indies Company, 131

E

Earhart, Amelia, 276
Earth, *p.* 9
  model of, 28
  roundness of, 28; *d.* 28
earthquakes, 412
Eastern Hemisphere, 29; *p.* 29
ecology
  protection of natural resources, 267
  in United States, 479
economics, 330
Ecuador, 465; *c.* 466
Edison, Thomas, 250-251; *p.* 250
education
  advances in, 265-266; *p.* 266
  for blacks, 232, 266; *p.* 232
  colonial, 139
  growth of, 296
  for women, 211, 266
Eisenhower, Dwight D., 287; *c.* 488; *p.* 488
elevation, 59
El Paso, Texas, 119
El Salvador, *c.* 466
Emancipation Proclamation, 227
energy resources, *g.* 481
  in Canada, 446
  conservation of, 476-477
  consumption and production of, *g.* 476
  in Interior West, 403-404
England. *See* **Great Britain**
English colonies. *See* **colonies, British**
environment. *See* **ecology**
equality, 298-299
  for blacks, 230, 268, 298-299
  for women, 210-211, 268, 299
Ericson, Leif, 86
Erie Canal, 183-184; *p.* 181
erosion, 346
Eskimos, 52-53, 55, 63-64, 429
Estevan, 106-107
ethnic groups, 429
executive branch, 168; *c.* 168
explorations
  Chinese, 84-85
  Dutch, 110
  English, 108-109
  French, 109-110, 128-129; *m.* 110, 129
  Spanish, 89-98, 107; *m.* 97, 101, 104, 106

F

factories
  U.S., in 1850, *p.* 218
  working conditions of, 254

farming
  by American Indians, 60–61, 69, 70, 71, 73; *m.* 71
  in Canada, 445
  in colonies, 134, 136, 138
  during Great Depression, 279; *p.* 279
  in Great Lakes Region, 337–338; *p.* 343
  in Hawaii, 433
  in Interior West, 401–402
  in Latin America, 462–463; *m.* 469
  on Midwest Plains, 351–352; *m.* 351
  on Pacific Coast, 417, 418
  pioneer, 201–203
  on plains, 239–241
  in South, 219–222, 230–231, 368; *p.* 218, 231
  in South America, 463
Federalist Party, development of, 176
Ferdinand, king of Spain, 92–93
Fifteenth Amendment, 230
Fillmore, Millard, *c.* 487; *p.* 487
First Amendment, 169
fishing
  in Alaska, 430, 432, 433; *p.* 432
  by American Indians, 55, 73, 78
  in Canada, 447, 448
  in colonies, 134
  on Pacific Coast, 420
Florida, *c.* 372, 482
  in Peace of Paris, 151
  settlement of, 64
  Spanish colonization of, 119; *p.* 119
  in Treaty of Paris, 165
Ford, Gerald R., *c.* 488; *p.* 488
Ford, Henry, 251–252, 277
forests and forest industries
  in Alaska, 433
  and American Indians, 73–74
  in Canada, 446–447
  in colonies, 134
Fourteenth Amendment, 230
France
  aid to American colonies in Revolutionary War, 164–165

  claim for control of North America, 148–151; *m.* 148
  colonies of, 128–130; *m.* 130
  explorations of, 109–110, 128–129; *m.* 110, 129
free blacks, 223
Freedmen's Bureau, 231
  schools set up by, *p.* 232
freedom
  of religion, 45
  of speech, 45
  to vote, 45
  to work, 47
free enterprise. *See* **New York Stock Exchange**
French and Indian War, 149–151, 157; *m.* 151; *p.* 150, 151
frontier
  settlement of, 166, 176–177, 182–183, 199–203; *m.* 177; *p.* 166, 201, 203
furniture, colonial, 140; *p.* 140

G
Gadsden Purchase, 197
Garfield, James A., *c.* 487; *p.* 487
Garrison, William Lloyd, 209–210
Gary, Indiana, *p.* 335
gasoline engine, 251–252
geography
  human, 314–317, 332–334, 348–350, 364–367, 381–384, 398–400, 414–416, 429–430, 442–444, 459–461
  physical, 28–35, 311–313, 329–331, 345–347, 361–363, 379–380, 395–397, 411–413, 427–428, 439–441, 455–458
George III, king of England, 156, 162, 166; *p.* 156
George Washington Bridge, *p.* 309
Georgia, *c.* 372, 482
  colonization of, 135
  farming in, 205, 219
  settlement of, 64, 183
  textile industry in, 204
Germany
  and World War I, 272–273
  and World War II, 284–285

Gettysburg Address, 44
Gettysburg, Battle of, 226
glaciers, 57; *m.* 57
Glidden, Joseph F., 240
gold
  discovery of, *m.* 235
  in California, 198, 234, 415; *p.* 198
  in Colorado, 234–235
Golden Gate Bridge, *p.* 42
Grand Banks, 109, 110
Grand Canyon, 43, *p.* 39
Grant, Ulysses S., *c.* 487; *p.* 487
  as Union general, 227; *p.* 228
graphs
  climatographs. *See* **climatographs**
  employment
    Alaska, 431
    Canada, 445
    Great Lakes Region, 337
    Hawaii, 431
    Interior West, 401
    Latin America, 462
    Midwest Plains, 352
    Northeast, 318
    Pacific Coast, 420
    South, 368
    Southwest, 388
  energy sources, 481
  goods produced
    Alaska, 432
    Canada, 446
    Great Lakes Region, 337
    Hawaii, 432
    Interior West, 402
    Latin America, 463
    Midwest Plains, 354
    Northeast, 319
    Pacific Coast, 417
    South, 369
    Southwest, 387
  immigration, 260, 261, 474
  landforms
    Alaska, 428
    Canada, 440
    Great Lakes Region, 330
    Hawaii, 428
    Interior West, 396
    Latin America, 456
    Midwest Plains, 346
    Northeast, 313
    Pacific Coast, 412

499

graphs *(continued)*
    South, 362
    Southwest, 380
  miles of railroad track, 244
  older people, 475
  population
    Alaska, 429
    Canada, 442
    changes in urban and rural, 262
    colonial, 136, 153
    Great Lakes Region, 332, 333
    Hawaii, 429
    Interior West, 398, 399
    Latin America, 459, 460
    Midwest Plains, 348, 350
    Northeast, 314, 315
    Pacific Coast, 414, 416
    South, 364, 365
    Southwest, 382
    United States, 260, 473
  women in work force, 1950-1980, 299
  world production-consumption of petroleum, 476
Graphs Tell a Story
  population changes, 260-263
  transportation in the West, 242-245
Great Basin, 234, 396
Great Britain
  claim for control of North America, 148-151; *m.* 148, 151
  colonies of, 111, 120-127, 132-140, 152-160; *m.* 120, 130, 132; *p.* 121, 122, 124
  exploration of North America, 108-109
Great Depression, 278-279
  bread lines, *p.* 278
  dust bowl farm during, *p.* 279
Great Lakes Region, 326-341; *c.* 339
  climate in, 330, 331; *g.* 331
  economy of, 330
  employment in, 335-338; *g.* 337; *p.* 335, 336
  farming in, 330, 337-338; *p.* 341
  goods produced, *g.* 337
  growing seasons in, 331
  land in, 330-331; *g.* 330; *m.* 330
  lumber industry in, 338
  manufacturing in, 335
  mining in, 338
  population of, 332-334; *c.* 334; *g.* 332, 333; *m.* 332; *p.* 332, 333
  precipitation in, 331
  states in, 329, 339
  temperatures in, 331
  tourism in, 330, 338
Great Plains, 43, 234
Great Salt Lake, 234, 396
Great Smoky Mountains, 362
Greenland, Norse exploration of, 85-87
Grenada, *c.* 467
Grinnell Glacier Crevasse, *p.* 400
growing seasons
  Canada, 441; *m.* 441
  Great Lakes Region, 331; *m.* 331
  Interior West, 397; *m.* 397
  Latin America, 468; *m.* 469
  Midwest Plains, 347; *m.* 347
  Northeast, 313; *m.* 313
  Pacific Coast, 413; *m.* 413
  South, 363; *m.* 363
  Southwest, 380; *m.* 380
Guam, 271; *c.* 482
Guatemala, 61; *c.* 467
  Mayan ruins in, *p.* 61

H

haciendas, 118
Haiti, *c.* 467
Hamilton, Alexander, 175-176; *p.* 176
Hamilton, Ontario, Canada, 446
handicapped, equality for, 299; *p.* 46
Harding, Warren G., *c.* 488; *p.* 488
Harrison, Benjamin, *c.* 487; *p.* 487
Harrison, William Henry, *c.* 486; *p.* 486
Harvard, John, 139
Harvard College, 139
Hawaii, 424-435; *c.* 433, 482; *p.* 433
  acquisition of, 270-271
  cattle raising, 433
  climate, 428; *g.* 428
  employment in, 431-433
  farming in, 433
  land, 428
  population, *c.* 430; *g.* 429
  tourism in, 429, 433; *p.* 424, 430, 432
  volcanoes in, 40
Hawaii Volcanoes National Park, *p.* 430
Hayes, Rutherford B., *c.* 487; *p.* 487
Hays, Mary Ludwig (Molly Pitcher), 164; *p.* 164
health care, improvements in, 300
heavy industry, 335
hemispheres, 29; *p.* 29
Henry VIII, king of England, 122
hills, 59
Hiroshima, Japan, 287
Hispanic Americans, 116-119, 299, 315, 333, 367, 383-384, 415-416; *g.* 261, 474; *p.* 117, 118, 119, 299, 383, 416
Hispaniola, 97, 101, 102
history, 50-305
Hitler, Adolf, 284, 285
Homestead Act, 239
Honduras, *c.* 467
Hoover, Herbert C., *c.* 488; *p.* 488
House of Burgesses, 137
housing
  American Indian, 66, 67, 69, 71, 74, 75; *p.* 51, 66, 67, 70, 72, 76
  colonial, 139
  on Great Plains, 240-241; *p.* 241
  pioneer, 201-202; *p.* 201
  tenement, 265; *p.* 264
Houston, Sam, 196; *p.* 197
Houston, Texas, 379, 380, 386; *c.* 381, 382; *p.* 386
Howard University, 232
How Things Work
  Conestoga wagons, 200; *p.* 200

Norse navigation, 86; *p.* 86
How We Know What Happened
  diary of Laura Ingalls Wilder, 240; *p.* 240
  story of young immigrant girl, 257; *p.* 257
  written records of Columbus, 93
Hudson, Henry, 110, 130; *m.* 109
Hudson River, 131, 154, 184
Hull House, 265
humanities. *See* art; architecture; archaeology; music
hunting
  in Alaska, 430
  by American Indians, 55, 58, 67, 70, 72–73
Hutchinson, Anne, 133; *p.* 133

I
Ice Age, 57
Idaho, 400, 401; *c.* 405, 482; *p.* 400
Illinois, 183, 225, 336, 338; *c.* 339, 482; *p.* 327, 332, 336
  farming in, 207
  settlement of, 256
immigration, 255–263, 475; *c.* 256; *p.* 256, 257, 258
  Chinese, 262, 416
  country of origin, 1820–1930, *g.* 261
  to U.S., 1871–1940, *g.* 260, 474
Imperial Valley, 417
Incas, 62
indentured servants, 136
Independence Hall, *p.* 147
Indiana, 183, 338; *c.* 339, 482; *p.* 335
  farming in, 207
Indians, American, 44, 52, 299
  Aleuts, 55, 63–64
  Algonquin Indians, 130, 149–150
  Blackfeet Indians, 69; *p.* 72
  changing ways of life of, 60
  Cherokee Indians, 190
  Cheyenne Indians, 69
  Chickasaw Indians, 166
  Chinook Indians, 79
  Chippewa Indians, 73
  Choctaw Indians, 75, 142, 166
  in cities, 54–55
  and Columbus, 96–97
  Comanche Indians, 69
  Creek Indians, 64, 142, 166
  Croatoans, 111
  Crow Indians, 71–72
  Eastern Woodlands tribes, 73–76, 142; *p.* 74, 76
  Erie Indians, 73
  farming by, 60–61; *p.* 61
  games of, 75; *p.* 75
  Great Plains and Great Basin tribes, 69–72; *p.* 70, 72
  growth of culture of, 61–62
  Hopi Indians, 66
  housing of, 53–55, 64, 66, 67, 69, 71, 74, 75, 78; *p.* 51, 55, 61, 66, 67, 70, 76
  Huron Indians, 109, 130, 149–150
  Iroquois Indians, 73, 75–76, 150, 163; *p.* 76
  Iroquois League, 76
  Kiowa Indians, 69
  Mandan Indians, 69–70, 188; *p.* 70
  Mohawk Indians, 76
  Mound Builders, 63; *p.* 63
  Navajo Indians, 67–68, 384; *p.* 67, 68, 384
  Nootka Indians, 78
  Northwest Coast tribes, 77–79; *p.* 78
  Oneida Indians, 76
  Onondaga Indians, 76
  Pawnee Indians, 69
  Pequot Indians, 142
  Plains Indians, 238–239
  Powhatan Indians, 121
  present-day, 53
  Pueblo Indians, 68, 117, 143, 195; *p.* 143
  relations with British, 121, 123
  relations with colonists, 141–143; *p.* 141
  relations with Dutch, 131
  relations with French, 129–130
  on reservations, 53–54, 190, 239; *c.* 391
  Sacagawea, 188–189
  Seneca Indians, 76
  Shoshone Indians, 72
  Sioux Indians, 69
  in small towns, 54
  southeastern tribes, 64, 142–143
  southwestern tribes, 65–68; *p.* 66, 67, 68
  Wampanoag Indians, 123, 142
  Zuñi Indians, 66, 107
Indies, trade routes to, 88–89; *m.* 89
industrial revolution, 204, 219
industry, growth of, 251–252
Ingstad, Helge, 87
Inouye, Daniel, *p.* 301
interchangeable parts, 206
Interior West, 392–407; *c.* 405
  climate of, 397; *g.* 397; *m.* 397
  Continental Divide, 396
  employment in, 401–404; *g.* 401; *p.* 403, 404
  energy resources in, 403–404; *p.* 404
  farming in, 401–402
  goods produced, *g.* 402
  growing seasons, 397; *m.* 397
  land, 395–396; *g.* 396
  manufacturing in, 404
  mining in, 403–404; *p.* 403, 404
  mountains in, 396
  natural resources in, 402; *m.* 402
  plains in, 396
  plateaus and basins in, 396
  population of, 398–400; *c.* 399; *g.* 398, 399; *m.* 398
  temperature, 397; *g.* 397
  tourism in, 400, 402; *p.* 400
  urban centers of, 398
inventions
  assembly line, 251–252
  farm, 205–206, 207; *p.* 205, 207
  and growth of industry, 251–252
  interchangeable parts, 206
Iowa, *c.* 355, 482
  farming in, 353; *p.* 353
  settlement of, 256
Irish Americans, 255
Iroquois League, 76

501

Isabella, queen of Spain, 92–93, 98; *p.* 93
Italian Americans, 256; *g.* 256
Italy, and World War II, 284–286

J
Jackson, Andrew, *c.* 486; *p.* 486
Jamaica, 455, 463; *c.* 467
James I, king of England, 120
Jamestown colony, 120–127, 136; *p.* 121
Japan, 285, 286, 287
Japanese Americans, 416; *p.* 301
 treatment of, in World War II, 287
Jay, John, 175, 176–177
Jefferson, Thomas, *c.* 486; *p.* 486
 as author of Declaration of Independence, 162; *p.* 162
 as President, 187
 as secretary of state, 175–176; *p.* 176
Jet Propulsion Laboratory (JPL), 478; *p.* 478
Jews, in World War II, 284–285
Johnson, Andrew, *c.* 487; *p.* 487
 as President, 230, 269
Johnson, Lyndon B., *c.* 488; *p.* 488
Joliet, Louis, 128–129; *m.* 129
judicial branch, 169; *c.* 168

K
Kansas, *c.* 355, 482; *p.* 343
 cattle ranching in, 236
Kansas City, Missouri, 354
Kansas Pacific Railroad, 236; *p.* 239
Kennedy, John F., *c.* 488; *p.* 488
 as President, 289
Kentucky, *c.* 372, 482
 farming in, 368
 mining in, 369
 settlement of, 183; *p.* 166
Key, Francis Scott, 185; *p.* 185
King, Martin Luther, Jr., 299; *p.* 299

L
labor unions, 254
Lafayette, General, 165; *p.* 165

Lake Erie, 149, 184
landforms
 depiction of, on contour maps, 191–194
 North American, 42–43, 58–59; *d.* 59; *p.* 41
 in United States. *See* **graphs, landforms**
L'Anse aux Meadows, Newfoundland, Norse remains at, *p.* 87
La Salle, Robert de, 128–129; *m.* 129; *p.* 129
Latin America, 452–469; *c.* 466–467
 climate in, 456–458; *g.* 457
 cultural heritage of, 461; *p.* 461
 employment in, 462–465
 farming in, 462–463; *m.* 469
 goods produced, 462–465
 growing seasons, 456–458
 industry in, 463
 land, 455–456; *g.* 456
 mining in, 463
 population of, 459–461; *c.* 460; *g.* 459, 460; *m.* 459
latitude, 291
 using lines of, 31–32, 291–293
Lee, Robert E., 226, 228; *p.* 228
legislative branch, 169; *c.* 168
legislatures, 137
Lewis, Meriwether, 187–190; *p.* 187
Lewis and Clark expedition, 187–190, 191; *p.* 189
Lexington, Battle of, 161, 162; *p.* 161
Liberator, The, 209, 210; *p.* 209
Lincoln, Abraham, 44, 224–225; *c.* 487; *p.* 224, 487
 assassination of, 230
 and the Emancipation Proclamation, 227
 plan for Reconstruction, 230
Lindbergh, Charles A., 276; *p.* 277
local relief, 59
locations, finding on maps, 33
longitude, 291–293
Los Angeles, California, 54–55, 414, 418; *c.* 415; *p.* 47, 419
Louisiana, *c.* 372, 482

M
McCormick, Cyrus, 207
McHenry, Fort, 185; *p.* 185
McKinley, William, *c.* 487; *p.* 487
Madison, James, *c.* 486; *p.* 486
Magellan, Ferdinand, 103–105
 voyage of, *m.* 104
Magellan, Strait of, 104
mail service, 243–244
Maine, *c.* 322, 482
 admission as state, 218, 271
Manhattan Island, 131
Manitoba, 440; *c.* 448–449
maps
 agricultural regions of Latin America, *m.* 469
 annual precipitation of Interior West, *m.* 397
 annual precipitation of North America, *m.* 451
 Caribbean area, *m.* 292
 color relief, of the Narrows, *m.* 192
 Columbia River basin, *m.* 423
 contour, 192–194
 contour, of the Narrows, *m.* 193
 corn belt, *m.* 351
 direction on, 125
 District of Columbia, *m.* 170, 171, 172
 Eastern and Western Hemispheres, *m.* 29
 Fall line cities, *m.* 362
 finding directions of, 32–33
 finding locations on, 33, 291–293
 globe gores, *m.* 34
 government-owned land in the Interior West, *m.* 407
 interstate highways, *m.* 305
 lines of latitude for, 31–32, 291; *m.* 31
 low, middle, and high latitudes, *m.* 32
 major petroleum and natural gas deposits, *m.* 385
 metropolitan area of Milwaukee, Wisconsin, *m.* 484
 mineral resources of the Midwest Plains, *m.* 357

502

maps–maps, special purpose

Northern and Southern
  Hemispheres, *m.* 29
ocean currents of the North
  Atlantic, *m.* 102
ocean currents of the North
  Pacific, *m.* 85
place-names on, 127
prevailing winds, *m.* 102
reading keys to, 30
regions of the Northeast, *m.*
  312
scale, 170–173
shaded relief, of the Narrows,
  m. 191
symbols for, 30, 34–35,
  125–126
tourist spots in Florida, *m.* 375
use of color, 191–192
wheat belt, *m.* 351

Maps Tell a Story
  early exploration, 99–102
  Jamestown, 124–127
  population changes, 260–263
  settling the Americas, 56–59
  transportation in the West,
    242–245
  United States and world,
    291–293
  the way west, 191–194

maps, historical
  American Indian tribes in
    1600s, 62
  cattle trails, 236
  Civil War battles, 247
  colonial trade in 1760, 153
  Confederacy and border
    states, 225
  early routes of Americans, 56
  Eastern North America after
    1763, 151
  Eastern North America before
    1763, 148
  European claims in North
    America, 1600s, 116
  European land claims and
    colonies, 1700s, 145
  explorations of the Mississippi
    River, 129
  French and English claims in
    North America in 1685, 130
  French explorations in the
    New World, 110
  globe of 1492, 100

growth of industries and
  cities, 1860, 1900, 1920, 251
Indian farm crops, 71
Indian reservations, 54
Indian tribes in New York
  State, 81
Jamestown and Plymouth
  colonies, 120
John Smith's Map of Virginia,
  126
journey of Lewis and Clark,
  188
lower Chesapeake Bay, 124
mining strikes and western
  towns, 235
New Netherland, 131
Norse routes to North
  America, 99
Revolutionary War battles,
  163, 173
search for the Northwest
  Passage, 109
Spanish explorations of New
  World, 106
thirteen English colonies, 132
trade routes to Indies, 1400s,
  89
transcontinental railroads in
  1900, 245
travel routes west, 1850–1870,
  243
United States in 1790, 183
United States in 1803, 186
United States in 1853, 196
United States in 1854, 217
U.S. possessions in 1900, 270
voyage of Magellan,
  1519–1522, 104
voyages of Columbus, 97, 101
western America, 1783–1795,
  177
western routes, 1800–1850,
  184
World War I, 272
World War II, 285

maps, locator
  Alaska, 426
  Canada, 438
  Great Lakes Region, 328
  Hawaii, 426
  Interior West, 394
  Latin America, 454
  Midwest Plains, 344

Northeast, 310
Pacific Coast, 410
South, 360
Southwest, 378

maps, physical, 30, 192
  Narrows, 192
  North America, 15
  Puerto Rico, 293
  South America, 23
  United States, 20–21
  world, 12–13

maps, physical-political
  Alaska, 426
  Canada, 438
  Great Lakes Region, 328
  Hawaii, 426
  Interior West, 394
  Latin America, 454
  Midwest Plains, 344
  Northeast, 310
  Pacific Coast, 410
  South, 360
  Southwest, 378

maps, political, 30
  North America, 14
  Northeast megalopolis, 325
  South America, 22
  United States, 18–19
  world, 10–11

maps, special-purpose
  growing seasons
    Canada, 441
    Great Lakes Region, 331
    Interior West, 397
    Latin America, 469
    Midwest Plains, 347
    Northeast, 313
    Pacific Coast, 413
    South, 363
    Southwest, 380
  landforms, 191–194
    North American glaciers, 57
  land use
    North America, 17
    South America, 25
  population
    Alaska, 429
    Canada, 442
    Great Lakes Region, 332
    Hawaii, 429
    Interior West, 398
    Latin America, 459
    Midwest Plains, 348

503

maps, special purpose
(continued)
North America, 16
Northeast, 314
Pacific Coast, 414
South, 364
South America, 24
Southwest, 381
United States, 473
regions, 312, 330, 438, 451
time zones of U.S., 435
Maritime Provinces, 439–440
Marquette, Jacques, 128
Marshall, George, 288–289
Marshall Plan, 288–289
Maryland, *c.* 322, 482
colonization of, 135
growth of cash crops for trade, 154
Massachusetts, 158–159, 161–162, 164; *c.* 322, 482
colonization of, 132–133
early factories in, 204
Massachusetts Bay Colony, 132
Mauna Loa, 428
Mayflower, 122, 123
Mayflower Compact, 123
Mayflower II, p. 122
Mayo Clinic, 353; *p.* 353
Meat Inspection Act, 268
megalopolis, 316, 414; *m.* 325
Memphis, Tennessee, 362, 371; *g.* 366, 367; *m.* 360
Mesabi Range, 353; *p.* 353
mestizos, 461
Mexican Americans, 116, 383–384, 415–416; *p.* 301, 383
See also **Hispanic Americans**
Mexican Cession, 197; *m.* 196
Mexican War, 196–197; *m.* 196
Mexico, 61, 463, 464; *c.* 467; *p.* 464
Mexico City, 106, 116–119, 195–197; *climatograph* 457
Miami, Florida, 363; *c.* 366, 367; *m.* 375; *climatograph* 363
Michigan, 183, 331, 336; *c.* 339, 482; *p.* 336
Middle colonies, 134–135; *m.* 132
making a living in, 135
and trade, 154

middle latitudes, 32, 458
Midwest Plains, 342–357; *p.* 343
cities of, 353, 354; *g.* 348
climate of, 346–347, 352; *g.* 347; *m.* 347
employment on, 351–354; *g.* 352, 354; *m.* 351; *p.* 353
farming on, 351–352; *m.* 351
growing seasons, 347; *m.* 347
industry on, 354; *g.* 354
land of, 345–346; *g.* 346; *p.* 346
mining on, 352
population of, 348–350; *g.* 348, 350; *m.* 348
precipitation, 347
rivers of, 346
temperatures, 346–347
tourism, 352
transportation on, 354
migrant workers, 415–416
migration, 262–263
of blacks, 263
early American routes of, 56–58; *m.* 56; *p.* 57
rural to urban, 263
Milwaukee, Wisconsin, *m.* 484
mineral resources
in Alaska, 432
in Canada, 446; *m.* 447
in Great Lakes Region, 338
in the Interior West, 402–404; *m.* 402; *p.* 403, 404
on Midwest Plains, 352, 353; *m.* 357; *p.* 353
in South America, 465
in the West, 234–235; *m.* 235
Minneapolis, Minnesota, 55, 349, 354
Minnesota, 349, 352, 353; *c.* 355, 482; *p.* 349, 354
settlement of, 256
Minuit, Peter, 131
minutemen, 161–162; *p.* 161
missionaries
French, 130
Spanish, 117
missions, Spanish, 118; *p.* 118, 416
Mississippi, *c.* 373, 482
as Confederate state, 227
farming in, 205
settlement of, 64, 183

Mississippi River, 43, 226, 227, 346; *p.* 43, 129
exploration of, 128–129
Missouri, *c.* 355, 482
admission as state, 218
exploration of, 190
Missouri River, 43, 187, 346, 396
exploration of, 188
Mitchell, South Dakota, 349; *p.* 349
Mobile, Alabama, 371
Mohawk Indians, 76
Mojave Desert, 413
Monmouth, Battle of, 164; *p.* 164
Monroe, James, *c.* 486; *p.* 486
Montana, *c.* 405, 482; *p.* 49
cattle ranching in, 236
wheat fields in, *p.* 41
Montreal, Quebec, Canada, 109, 130, 150, 442, 446; *p.* 444
Mormons, 234, 400; *p.* 400
Mormon Trail, 198; *m.* 196
Morse, Samuel, 207
motion pictures, 277–278, 418, 419; *p.* 278, 419
Mott, Lucretia, 211
Mound Builders, 63; *p.* 63
mountains, 43, 59; *p.* 41
Mount Hood, 412
Mount McKinley, 428; *p.* 425
Mount Mitchell, 362
Mount Rainier, 412
Mount St. Helens, 412
Mount Whitney, 411, 412
Mount Holyoke College, 211
music, 40, 48, 49, 85
Mussolini, Benito, 284, 285
Mystic, Connecticut, 154

N
Nagasaki, Japan, 287
Nantucket, Massachusetts, 154
Narrows, 191; *p.* 191, 194
Nashville Road, 183
Natchez, Mississippi, *p.* 220
Natchez Trace, 202; *p.* 202
National Park Service, establishment of, 267
National Road, 183
Native Americans. *See* **Indians, American**

natural resources
  in Alaska and Hawaii, 429, 432
  American Indian use of, 78–79
  in Canada, 446–447; *m.* 447
  in Great Lakes Region, 338; *p.* 336
  in Interior West, 402; *m.* 402
  in Latin America, 465; *p.* 464
  on Midwest Plains, 353; *m.* 357; *p.* 353
  in Northeast, 321
  on Pacific Coast, 418
  protection of, 267, 476–477
  in South, 368–369, 371
  in Southwest, 385–387; *m.* 385; *p.* 377, 386
  in United States, 43
navigation
  movements of air and water, 101–103
  by Norse, 86; *p.* 86
  sailing west to reach east, 91
  use of compass, 86–87
  use of stars in, 86; *p.* 86
Nebraska, *c.* 355, 482
  cattle ranching in, 236
Netherlands
  aid to American colonies in Revolutionary War, 165
  colonies of, 130–131; *m.* 131
  explorations by the, 110
Nevada, *c.* 405, 482
  discovery of silver in, 235
New Amsterdam, 131
New Brunswick, 439
New England colonies, 132–134; *m.* 132
  making a living in, 134
  and trade, 154
Newfoundland, 439
  English exploration of, 109
  Norse explorations of, 87
New France, 128–130, 150; *m.* 129, 130, 145; *p.* 129
New Hampshire, *c.* 323, 482
  colonization of, 133–134
New Jersey, *c.* 323, 482
  colonization of, 134
New Mexico, 197, 379, 384, 385; *c.* 389, 482
  exploration of, 107

settlement of, 65, 116–119; *p.* 117, 118
New Netherland, 130–131
  See also **Netherlands**
New Orleans, Louisiana, 151, 166, 187, 371
  cultural influences, 366; *p.* 366
newspapers
  abolitionist, 209–210, *p.* 209
  colonial, 160; *p.* 160
  present-day, 160
New World, 96
New York City, 153, 207, 319, 320; *p.* 135, 320
  purchase of, from Indians, 131
  tenements in, 265; *p.* 264
  urban crowds in, 315; *p.* 309, 315
New York State, *c.* 323, 482
  colonization of, 134
  early factories in, 204
New York Stock Exchange, 320; *p.* 320
Niagara Falls, New York, 321
Nicaragua, *c.* 467
Niña, 93, 94, 97; *p.* 94
Nineteenth Amendment, 268
Nixon, Richard M.; *c.* 488; *p.* 488
Norfolk–Newport News, Virginia, 371
Norse
  exploration of North America by, 85–87
  knarrs, *p.* 85
  navigation methods of, 86; *p.* 86
  routes to North America, 99
  settlement remains, *p.* 87
North America
  Dutch exploration of, 110
  English exploration of, 108–109
  French exploration of, 109–110, *m.* 110
  Spanish exploration of, 103–107; *m.* 106
North Carolina, *c.* 373, 482
  colonization of, 111
  farming in, 154, 219, 368
  settlement of, 64
  See also **Carolinas**

North Dakota, *c.* 355, 482
  settlement of, 69
Northeast, 308–325
  climate, 312–313; *g.* 313
  employment in, 318–321; *g.* 318; *p.* 320
  energy resources in, 321
  farming in, 319, 321
  growing seasons, 313, 319, 321
  land, 311–312; *g.* 313
  less-crowded areas of, 316–317
  lumber industry, 321
  as manufacturing center, 319
  mining in, 321
  natural resources in, 321
  population of, 314–317; *g.* 314, 315; *m.* 314; *p.* 315, 316
  precipitation, 313
  profile of, 310
  quarrying in, 321
  states in, 311; *c.* 322–323
  temperature, 312–313
  trade in, 318–319
  transportation in, 318–319
  urban growth in, 314–315
Northeasterly trade winds, 102
Northeastern Seaboard, 312, 316
Northern Hemisphere, 29; *d.* 29
Northwest Passage, 108; *m.* 109
Northwest Territory, 182–183, 440; *m.* 183
Nova Scotia, 439; *c.* 448–449

O
Oahu, 431, 432
Oberlin College, 211; *p.* 211
ocean currents, 84, 102
  Canary Current, 102
  Labrador Current, 102
  of North Pacific, 84–85; *d.* 85
O'Connor, Sandra, *p.* 301
Oglethorpe, James, 135; *p.* 142
Ohio, 183, 335; *c.* 339, 482; *m.* 328
  farming in, 207
Ohio River, 149
Ohio River valley, employment in, 338
oil industry, growth of, 253–254; *p.* 254
Oklahoma, 385, 386; *c.* 389, 482; *p.* 386

505

Oklahoma *(continued)*
  exploration of, 190
  Indian reservations in, 384
older persons, 366, 475; *g.* 475; *p.* 290
Old Spanish Trail, 198; *m.* 196
Olympic National Park, 413
Omaha, Nebraska, 349, 354
Oñate, Don Juan de, 117
Ontario, 443, 445, 446; *c.* 448–449
Oregon, *c.* 421, 482
  employment in, 418–421
  settlement of, 197–198
Oregon Territory, 197–198
Ozark Plateau, 346, 352

P
Pacific Coast, 408–423; *c.* 421; *p.* 409
  cities of, 414–415
  climate of, 413; *g.* 412; *m.* 413
  employment on, 417–421; *g.* 420; *p.* 419
  farming on, 417, 418
  fishing on, 420
  growing seasons of, 413
  land, 411–413; *g.* 412
  manufacturing and trade on, 417–418, 419–420; *g.* 419, 420
  mountains on, 412
  natural resources of, 418
  population of, 414–416; *c.* 415; *g.* 414, 416; *m.* 414
  precipitation of, 413
  temperature of, 413
  tourism, 420–421
  valleys on, 412–413
Pacific Ocean
  currents in, 84–85; *d.* 85
  discovery of, 104
Panama, 456; *c.* 467
Panama, Isthmus of, 271–272
Panama Canal, 271–272; *p.* 271
Paraguay, *c.* 467
parallels, 31, 291
Paris, Peace of, (1763), 151
Paris, Treaty of, (1783), 165
patriotism, 40, 185
Patriots, 158, 160; *p.* 158
Peace Corps, 289–290; *p.* 290
Pearl Harbor, 286, 431

Penn, William, 134–135; *p.* 134
Pennsylvania, 311–312, 313, 319, 321; *c.* 323, 482; *m.* 310
  colonization of, 134–135
Pennsylvania Journal, 160; *p.* 160
Pennsylvania Road, 183
Pentagon, 370; *p.* 370
People Who Made a Difference
  blacks in government, 232; *p.* 232
  Douglass, Frederick, 210; *p.* 210
  Edison, Thomas, 250; *p.* 250
  Hutchinson, Anne, 133; *p.* 133
  Indian farmers, 71; *m.* 71
  Shepard, Alan, 296; *p.* 296
  Vespucci, Amerigo, 105
  women in Revolutionary War
    Darragh, Lydia, 164
    Hays, Mary Ludwig, 164; *p.* 164
    Sampson, Deborah, 164
Pequot War, 142
Peru, 62, 458, 463, 465; *c.* 467
Philadelphia, Pennsylvania, 152, 160, 162, 164, 167, 207; *g.* 315, 317; *m.* 310; *p.* 147, 199
Philip, King, 142; *p.* 142
Philippines, 104, 271
Phoenix, Arizona, 381, 383; *g.* 381, 382
Pictures Tell a Story
  Jamestown, 124–127
  settling of the Americas, 56–59
  transportation in the West, 242–245
  the way west, 191–194
Piedmont, 362
Pierce, Franklin, *c.* 487; *p.* 487
Pike, Zebulon, 190, 191
Pikes Peak, 40, 396
Pinta, 93, 94, 95, 97; *p.* 94
pioneer life, 199–203; *p.* 200, 201, 203
Pitcher, Molly. *See* **Hays,** Mary Ludwig
Pittsburgh, Pennsylvania, 321; *g.* 315, 317
plains, 43, 59

plank roads, 202; *d.* 202
plantation, 136, 219–220; *p.* 139, 220
plateaus, 43, 59
Platte River, 43, 346, 396
Plymouth Colony, 122–123, 132
  restoration of, *p.* 138
Pocahontas, 121
polar lines, 32
political parties, 176
political science, 167–169; *c.* 168
Polk, James K., *c.* 486; *p.* 486
Polo, Marco, 88
Polynesians, 270, 430
Pony Express, 244
population
  Alaska, 429–430; *c.* 430; *g.* 429; *m.* 429
  Canada, 442–444; *c.* 443; *g.* 442; *m.* 442
  differences in, between North and South, 216–217
  Great Lakes Region, 332–334; *c.* 334; *g.* 332, 333; *m.* 332; *p.* 332, 333
  growth of U.S., 1800–1940, *g.* 260
  Hawaii, *c.* 430; *g.* 429; *m.* 429
  Interior West, 398–400; *c.* 399; *g.* 398, 399; *m.* 398
  Midwest Plains, 348–350; *c.* 348; *g.* 348, 350; *m.* 348
  Northeast, 314–317; *c.* 315, 317; *g.* 314, 315; *m.* 314; *p.* 315, 316
  Pacific Coast, 414–416; *c.* 415; *g.* 414, 416; *m.* 414
  South, 364–367; *c.* 366, 367; *g.* 364, 365; *m.* 364
  Southwest, 381–384; *c.* 381, 382; *g.* 382; *m.* 381
  states, *c.* 482
  U.S. cities over 100,000, *c.* 483
  U.S. metropolitan areas, *c.* 484
  world metropolitan areas, *c.* 484
population density, 314
Portland, Oregon, 414, 419
Portugal, explorations by, 90–91
potlatch, 79
Prairie Provinces, 445

precipitation
  Canada, 441
  Great Lakes Region, 331
  Interior West, 397; *m.* 397
  Midwest Plains, 347
  Northeast, 313
  Pacific Coast, 413
  See also **climatographs**
prevailing winds, 102; *d.* 102
primary sources, 93, 240, 253, 257
prime meridian, 291
profiles
  Alaska, 426
  Canada, 438
  Great Lakes Region, 328
  Hawaii, 426
  Interior West, 394
  Latin America, 454
  Midwest Plains, 344
  Northeast, 310
  Pacific Coast, 410
  South, 360
  Southwest, 378
Prudhoe Bay, 432
Puerto Rico, 271, 292–293, 315, 459; *c.* 482; *m.* 293
Pure Food and Drug Act, 268
Puritans, 122–123, 132, 133

Q
Quaker religion, 134–135
Quebec, 110, 128, 130, 440, 443, 444, 445, 446
  Battle of, 150–151; *p.* 151

R
radio, 276; *p.* 276
railroads
  and cattle transport, 236; *p.* 236
  development of, 206; *p.* 206
  growth of, in West, 244–245; *g.* 244; *m.* 245; *p.* 244
Reagan, Ronald W., *c.* 488; *p.* 488
reaper, 207; *p.* 207
Reconstruction
  congressional plan for, 230
  end of, 233
  life during, 230–233
  Lincoln's plan for, 230
  resentment over, 232–233

religion, freedom of, 45
renewable energy sources, 477
Reno, Nevada, 395
representative government, 134
Republican Party
  Jeffersonian, 176
  pre–Civil War, 224–225
reservations, Indian, 53–54, 190, 239, 384; *c.* 391; *m.* 54; *p.* 55, 384
Revere, Paul, 162
Revolutionary War
  aid from abroad, 164–165
  battles of, 163–165, 173; *m.* 163, 173; *p.* 161, 165
  fighting begins, 161–162
  recruitment in, 163; *p.* 163
  Second Continental Congress, 162–163
  women in, 164; *p.* 164
Rhode Island, *c.* 323, 482
  colonization of, 133
  early factories in, 204
Rio de Janeiro, Brazil, 460; *p.* 453
Rio Grande, 43, 117, 197
roads and highways, 183, 202, 295; *d.* 202; *m.* 305; *p.* 202
Roanoke Island, North Carolina, 111
Rockefeller, John D., 254
Rocky Mountains, 43, 189, 190, 234, 396; *p.* 189
Rolfe, John, 122
Roosevelt, Franklin D., *c.* 488; *p.* 488
  as President, 279, 284
Roosevelt, Theodore, *c.* 487; *p.* 487
  as President, 267, 272
Roosevelt Dam, Arizona, *p.* 268

S
Sacagawea, 188–189
Sag Harbor, New York, 154
St. Augustine, Florida, 361; *p.* 119
St. Lawrence, Gulf of, 109
St. Lawrence River, 130, 443, 445; *m.* 130
St. Lawrence River valley, 443
St. Louis, Missouri, 188, 354; *c.* 348

Saint Lucia, *c.* 467
St. Paul, Minnesota, 349; *c.* 348
Salinas, California, 411; *m.* 410
Salt Lake City, Utah, 234, 398, 400, 404; *p.* 400
Sampson, Deborah, 164
San Andreas Fault, 412
San Antonio, Texas, 119, 381; *c.* 381, 382; *p.* 299
Sand Hills, 352
San Diego, California, 119, 414, 418; *c.* 415
San Francisco, California, 243, 418, 419; *c.* 415; *p.* 42
San Jose, California, 418, 419; *c.* 415
San Salvador, 95; *p.* 83
Santa Anna, 196
Santa Fe, New Mexico, 117, 197
Santa Fe Trail, 195, 198; *m.* 196
Santa Maria, 93, 94, 95, 97; *p.* 94
São Paulo, Brazil, 460
Sarasota, Florida, *p.* 365
Saratoga, Battle of, 164, 173
Saskatchewan, 440; *c.* 448–449
sea level, 30
Seattle, Washington, 55, 413, 414, 419; *c.* 415
Sedalia, Missouri, 236
Sedalia Trail, 236; *m.* 236
segregation, 233, 268, 298–299
Seward, William H., 269
sharecropping, 231; *p.* 231
Sierra Nevada, 396, 412, 417
silver, discovery of, 235; *m.* 235
skills
  graphics-reading, 48, 212
  group, 246
  map and globe, 28–33, 56–59, 80, 99–102, 112–113, 124–127, 144, 170–173, 178, 242–245, 246, 291–293, 304–305, 324–325, 340, 374, 406, 422, 450, 468, 480
  math, 144–145, 304, 374, 390–391, 434, 468–469
  reading, 40, 48, 49, 52, 65, 77, 80, 81, 84, 95, 108, 112, 113, 116, 128, 137, 144, 145, 152, 156, 174, 178, 179, 182, 195, 204, 212, 213, 216, 219, 234, 246,

507

skills *(continued)*
  247, 255, 264, 269, 280, 281, 294, 298, 304, 305, 311, 324, 325, 329, 340, 341, 345, 361, 374, 375, 379, 390, 391, 395, 406, 407, 411, 422, 423, 427, 434, 435, 439, 450, 451, 455, 468, 469, 472, 480, 481
  research, 48, 280, 356
  speaking, 112
  time, 212–213
  thinking, 80, 178–179, 280, 324, 340, 390, 422–423, 434, 450, 480–481
  writing, 340–341, 406
Slater, Samuel, 204
slavery, 155, 208–210; *p.* 155, 209, 210, 218, 223
  disagreement on, between North and South, 218
  free blacks, 223
  fugitives, 222–223; *p.* 222
  life of slave, 221–222; *p.* 221
  in Southern colonies, 136
  uprisings, 223
  See also **abolitionist movement**
Smith, John, 121, 124–127, 191; *p.* 121
Snake River, 43, 396, 401
sociology, 52–55, 60–79, 472–475; *g.* 473, 474, 475; *m.* 473
solar energy, 477; *p.* 294
South, 358–375; *p.* 359
  climate, 362–363; *g.* 363; *m.* 363
  employment in, 368–371; *g.* 368; *p.* 369, 370
  farming in, 368–369
  forestry in, 368–369
  growing seasons, 363; *m.* 363
  industry in, 369, 371; *g.* 369
  land in, 361–362; *g.* 362
  mining in, 369
  population, 364–367; *c.* 366, 367; *g.* 364, 365; *m.* 364
  slavery in, 219–223
  states in, 361; *c.* 372–373
  temperature, 363
  tourism, 366

South America
  climate in, 457–458
  farming in, 463
  industry in, 465
  mining in, 465
  population of, 459–460; *c.* 460; *g.* 460; *m.* 24, 459
South Carolina, *c.* 373, 482
  farming in, 154, 219
  settlement of, 64
  See also **Carolinas**
South Dakota, 349, 351; *c.* 355, 482; *p.* 55, 349
Southern colonies, 135; *m.* 132
  making a living in, 136
  and trade, 154
Southern Hemisphere, 29; *d.* 29
Southwest, 376–391
  attraction of, 388–389
  careers in, 386; *p.* 386
  cities of, 381–383; *c.* 381
  climate of, 379–380; *g.* 380; *m.* 380
  cultural heritage of, 383–384; *p.* 383, 384
  employment in, 385–388; *g.* 388
  energy resources of, 385–386, 387; *m.* 385; *p.* 386
  farming in, 387–388; *p.* 387
  growing seasons, 380; *m.* 380
  land, 379; *g.* 380
  mining in, 387
  population, 381–384; *c.* 381, 382; *g.* 382; *m.* 381
  states in, *c.* 389
Southwestern states, climate of, *p.* 65
Southwest Territory, 182; *m.* 183
Soviet Union
  relations between U.S. and, 290
  and World War II, 285
space exploration, 96, 296–297, 478; *p.* 96, 283, 296, 297, 471, 478
space industry, 418
Spain
  aid to American colonies in Revolutionary War, 165
  claims of, in North America, 151; *m.* 132, 145, 148, 151

explorations by, 103–107; *c.* 113; *m.* 104, 106
  settlements of, in North America, 116–119; *m.* 116; *p.* 117, 118, 119
Spanish-American War, 271
speech, freedom of, 45
sphere, 29
Spice Islands, 88, 104; *m.* 89, 104
springhouse, 203
stagecoaches, 242–244; *p.* 242
Stamp Act, 157; *p.* 157
Stamp Act Congress, 158
Stamps Tell a Story
  United States history, 302–303
Stanton, Elizabeth Cady, 211, 268
stars, use of, for navigation, 86; *p.* 86
"Star-Spangled Banner," 185
Statue of Liberty, 256; *p.* 37
steamboats, 185
steam engine, 206
steel industry, 253, 335; *p.* 249, 335
Stuyvesant, Peter, 131
suburbs, growth of, 276, 296, 316
Sugar Act, 157
Sugarloaf Mountain, *p.* 453
Sumter, Fort, firing on, 225; *p.* 226
sunbelt, 362, 363, 411
Surinam, *c.* 467
Sutter, John, 198
Swedish-Americans, 200

T

tacking, 101; *p.* 101
Taft, William Howard, *c.* 487; *p.* 487
Tampa, Florida, 371
Taos, New Mexico, *p.* 66
tariff issue, 218
Taylor, Zachary, *c.* 486; *p.* 486
technology, 251, 294, 298, 300, 402
telecommunications, advances in, 477
  time line, 479
telegraph, 207
telephone, 252

television, 295
temperature
    Canada, 441
    Great Lakes Region, 331
    Interior West, 397
    Midwest Plains, 346–347
    Northeast, 312–313
    Pacific Coast, 413
    South, 363
    See also climatographs
Tennessee, c. 373, 482
    farming in, 219
    settlement of, 64, 166, 183
tepee, 71
Terre Haute, Indiana, 338
Texas, 385–386; c. 389, 482; m. 196; p. 196, 197, 299, 377, 383, 386
    cattle ranching in, 235–236; m. 236
    as Confederate state, 227
    farming in, 368, 387–388
    settlement of, 65
    Spanish colonization of, 119
    and statehood, 195–197
Thanksgiving, p. 45
    celebration of first, 123
Then and Now
    colonial furniture, 140; p. 140
    Indian games, 75; p. 75
    newspapers, 160, p. 160
    roads, 202; d. 202; p. 202
    stories of Mark Twain, 267
    United States voters, 300
    voyages of Columbus and Apollo 11, 96; p. 96
Thirteenth Amendment, 227, 230
Ticonderoga, Fort, Battle of, 162
time lines, 50–51, 82–83, 114–115, 146–147, 180–181, 214–215, 248–249, 282–283, 479
Tobago, 463; c. 467
Toronto, Ontario, Canada, 442, 446; c. 443; p. 444
tourism
    Canada, 444; p. 444
    Great Lakes Region, 338
    Hawaii, 433; p. 432
    Interior West, 400; p. 400
    Midwest Plains, 349, 352; p. 349
    Pacific Coast, 420–421
    South, 366, 370; m. 375; p. 366, 370
towns and cities, 138
    blacks in, 231
    colonial, 138
    development of, 203
    growth of colonial, 152–153; c. 154
    growth of mining, 235; m. 235; p. 235
    population growth in, 258–259; c. 259
    See also cities
Townshend Acts, 158
trade and trading, colonial, 153–155; m. 153
Trail of Tears, 190
transcontinental railroad, 244–245; m. 245
transportation
    airplanes, 252, 277, 295, 418; p. 277, 418
    in Alaska, 431
    automobiles, 294–295
    canals, 183–184, 206; p. 181
    changes in, 294–295; c. 295; d. 479
    Conestoga wagon, 242
    development of, p. 181
    differences in, between North and South, 217
    in Hawaii, 431
    Pony Express, 244
    railroads, 206, 244–245; m. 245; p. 206
    roads and highways, 183, 202, 295; m. 305; p. 202
    in South, 371
    stagecoaches, 242–244; p. 242
    steamboats, 185
    wagon trains, 197–198, 200; p. 200
transportation industry, 417–418
Treasury Department, development of, 175; p. 320
tribes, 53
    See also Indians, American
Trinidad, 463; c. 467
tropic lines, 32; m. 32
Truman, Harry, c. 488; p. 488
    as President, 289
tundra, 428

Twain, Mark, 267; p. 267
twenties, life during, 276–278
Tyler, John, c. 486; p. 486

U
underground railroad, 222–223; p. 222
United Nations, 289
    UNICEF, p. 289
United States
    branches of government, 167–169; c. 168
    early relations with Great Britain, 166, 176–177, 185
    environment, 479
    ethnic and racial patterns in, 475
    formation of government, 166–169
    form of government, 168
    immigration, 255–263; c. 256; g. 260, 261, 474; p. 256, 257, 258
    importance of energy, 476–477
    landforms of, 42–43
    landscapes of, 40; p. 41, 42
    national anthem, 185
    natural resources of, 43
    See also natural resources
    population growth, g. 136, 473; m. 473
    See also population
    pre-Civil War differences, 216–218
    relations with Communist countries, 290
    relations with developing nations, 289–290
    relations with Mexico, 197
    telecommunications in, 477
    Treasury Department, 320, p. 320
Uruguay, 461, 463; c. 467
Utah, c. 400, 405, 482; p. 400, 403
    settlement of, 65, 198, 244
    Wasatch Range in, p. 41

V
Vaca, Cabeza de, 106
Van Buren, Martin, c. 486; p. 486

509

Vancouver, British Columbia, Canada, 442, 445; *p.* 444
Vargas, Don Diego de, 143
Venezuela, 463, 465; *c.* 467
Vermont, *c.* 323, 482
Vespucci, Amerigo, 105
Vicksburg, Battle of, 227
Vikings. *See* **Norse**
Vinland, 86–87
Virginia, *c.* 373, 482
   colonization of, 135
   farming in, 219, 368
   growth of cash crops for trade, 154
   mining in, 369
Virginia Company, 120, 122, 124, 125
Virgin Islands, *c.* 482
volcanoes, 40, 412, 428, 430; *p.* 430
vote, freedom to, 45
voting
   by blacks, 233; *p.* 233
   by women, 210–211, 268
   in colonies, 137
   right to, 300; *c.* 300
Voyager, p. 471

W

wagon trains, 197–198, 200; *p.* 200
Walt Disney World, 361, 370; *p.* 370
War Between the States. *See* **Civil War**
War of 1812, 185; *p.* 185
Washington, George, *c.* 486; *p.* 150, 486
   as commander of Continental Army, 162, 163, 165; *p.* 165
   in French and Indian War, 149, 150
   as President, 174–175; *p.* 174
   as president of Constitutional Convention, 167; *p.* 167
   return to Mount Vernon, 177
Washington, *c.* 421, 482
   employment in, 418–420
   volcanoes in, 40
Washington, D.C., 319; *p.* 44
   See also **District of Columbia**
Washington Monument, *p.* 44
water table, 383; *d.* 383

West
   opening of, 234–237; *m.* 235, 236; *p.* 235, 237
   settlement of, 238–241
   transportation in, 242–245
Western Hemisphere, 29; *d.* 29
West Indies, 271
West Virginia, 333; *c.* 339, 482
   mining in, 336
wheat belt, 351–352; *m.* 351
White House, *p.* 44
Whitney, Eli, 205–206
Wilder, Laura Ingalls, 240; *p.* 240
Wilderness Road, 183; *m.* 184
Willamette River, 413
Willamette River valley, 418
Williams, Roger, 133
Williamsburg, Virginia, 178–179, 361; *p.* 45, 179
Wilson, Woodrow, *c.* 487; *p.* 487
   as President, 273
Windsor, Ontario, Canada, 446
Winnipeg, Manitoba, Canada, 442, 445
Wisconsin, 183, 337, 338; *c.* 339, 482; *m.* 484; *p.* 61, 266
women
   Addams, Jane, 265; *p.* 265
   Anthony, Susan B., 268
   Antin, Mary, 257
   as astronauts, 297
   changes for, 276
   in Civil War, 227; *p.* 227
   Earhart, Amelia, 276
   education for, 210–211, 266
   equality for, 210–211, 268, 299
   in factories, *p.* 205
   first Supreme Court justice, 301; *p.* 301
   Hutchinson, Anne, 133; *p.* 133
   jobs of, *p.* 46
   Mott, Lucretia, 211
   during the 1920s, 276
   in Revolutionary War, 164
      Darragh, Lydia, 164
      Hays, Mary Ludwig, 164; *p.* 164
      Sampson, Deborah, 164
   rights of, 210–211, 268
   Sacagawea, 188–189
   in South America, *p.* 465

   Stanton, Elizabeth Cady, 211, 268
   Tubman, Harriet, 210; *p.* 210
   Wilder, Laura Ingalls, 240; *p.* 240
   in work force, 1950–1980, *g.* 299
   working conditions of, 254
   in World War II, 286
work, freedom to, 47; *p.* 46
World War I, 272–273; *p.* 273
   airplanes during, 277; *p.* 277
   United States entrance into, 273
World War II, *m.* 285
   beginning of, 285–286
   end of, 287
   postwar conditions, 288–289; *p.* 286, 287, 288
   prewar conditions, 284–285
   and the United States, 286–287
   women in, 286
Wright, Orville, 252; *c.* 252
Wright, Wilbur, 252; *c.* 252
Wyoming, 401, 403; *c.* 405, 482; *p.* 404
   cattle ranching in, 236
   rights of women in, 268

Acknowledgments

Artwork

Burwell, Ted, 138, 139
Caputo, Vince, 28, 31
Killgrew, John, 101
Newman, Deirdre, 202, 252, 322, 323, 339, 355, 372, 373, 383, 389, 405, 421, 433, 458

Photographs

Cover: J. Messerschmidt/Bruce Coleman, Inc.

Page 9: National Aeronautics and Space Administration
28 & 33: Michal Heron
35: United States Department of the Interior
39: Charles Newman
41: top, David Muench/Shostal Associates; bottom left & right, Tom Stack/Tom Stack & Associates
42: Rene Pauli/Shostal Associates
43: Phil Degginger
44: National Park Service
45: top, H. Armstrong Roberts; bottom, Colonial Williamsburg Foundation
46: top left, Michael Philip Manheim/Photo Researchers, Inc.; top right & middle, Michal Heron; bottom left, George Cassidy/Shostal Associates; bottom right, E. R. Degginger
47: Delores McCutcheon Brown/Monkmeyer
49: Tom Stack/Tom Stack & Associates
51: Byron Crader/Tom Stack & Associates
55: left, John Shaw/Bruce Coleman, Inc.; right, Victoria Beller-Smith
57: Alissa Crandall/Alaska Photo
58: Courtesy of the Field Museum of Natural History
61: left, Charles Henneghien/Bruce Coleman, Inc.; right, Courtesy of the Wisconsin Division of Tourism
63: top right, Tony Linck/Shostal Associates; bottom left, Courtesy of the Ohio Historical Society
65: D. Mattusch/Tom Stack & Associates
66: Ray Manley/Shostal Associates
67: Vernon Sigl/Shostal Associates
68: Michal Heron
70: top, Courtesy of the American Museum of Natural History; bottom, Courtesy of the Field Museum of Natural History
72: Courtesy of the Royal Ontario Museum, Toronto, Canada
74: Courtesy of the American Museum of Natural History
75: top, Courtesy of the American Museum of Natural History; bottom, Philbrook Art Center, Tulsa, Oklahoma
76: Courtesy of the American Museum of Natural History
78: Rasmussen Collection of Northwest Coast Indian Art, Portland Art Museum, Portland, Oregon

83: A detail from First Landing of Columbus, William Kemmelmeyer, National Gallery of Art, Washington; Gift of Edgar William and Bernice Chrysler Garbish
85: Courtesy of the Viking Museum, Denmark
87: C. Lindsay/Parks Canada
90, 91, 93: Historical Pictures Service
94: Models Courtesy of the Museum of Science and Industry, Chicago. From The World Book Encyclopedia. © 1981 World Book-Childcraft International, Inc.
96: National Aeronautics and Space Administration
105: Joseph Barnell/Shostal Associates
115: Virginia State Library
117: New Mexico Commerce & Industry Department
118: The Newberry Library
119: Florida Department of Commerce, Division of Tourism
121: left, Virginia State Library; right, Colonial Williamsburg Photograph
122: left, Massachusetts Department of Commerce; bottom, Historical Pictures Service
124: Bradley Smith/Photo Researchers, Inc.
126: Courtesy of the Geography and Map Division, Library of Congress
129: top right, CHIEF OF THE TAENSA INDIANS RECEIVING LA SALLE, MARCH, 1682; George Catlin; National Gallery of Art, Washington; Paul Mellon Collection; bottom right, Historical Pictures Service
133: The Bettmann Inc. Archive
134 & 135: Historical Pictures Service
138: Courtesy of Plimouth Plantation
140: Thorne Room, Gift of Mrs. James Ward Thorne, Collection of The Art Institute of Chicago; bottom left, Bruce Roberts/Photo Researchers, Inc.
141: Rare Books and Manuscripts Division, The New York Public Library/Astor, Lenox and Tilden Foundations
142: left, Courtesy of the American Antiquarian Society; right, Courtesy of The Henry Francis du Pont Winterthur Museum
143: Poster, 1980 © Boyiddle-Bahti, Photo by Michal Heron
147: Helena Kolda
150: left, Washington-Curtis-Lee Collection, Washington and Lee University; right, State Historical Society of Wisconsin
151: Courtesy of the Royal Ontario Museum, Toronto, Canada
155: Library of Congress
156: Colonial Williamsburg Photograph
157: Board of Inland Revenue Library, London
158 & 159: Culver Pictures, Inc.
160: The New York Public Library/Astor, Lenox and Tilden Foundations
161: Courtesy of The Lexington Historical Society

162: Yale University Art Gallery
163: Courtesy of Pennsylvania Historic Society
164: The Granger Collection
165: Library of Congress
166: Courtesy of Washington University Gallery of Art, St. Louis
167: Historical Pictures Service
174: Courtesy of The New-York Historical Society, New York City
175: Gene Ahrens/Bruce Coleman, Inc.
176: left, Roloc; right, Historical Pictures Service
179: Colonial Williamsburg Photograph
181: Courtesy of The New-York Historical Society, New York City
185: The Granger Collection
187: Historical Pictures Service
189: top left, Missouri Historical Society; bottom right, Nicholas de Vore III/Bruce Coleman, Inc.
194: Richard O. Springer
196: D. C. Clark/Bruce Coleman, Inc.
197: Library of Congress
198: California State Library
199: Library of Congress
200: The Granger Collection
201: Courtesy of Hudson's Bay Archives
202: National Park Service
203: Abby Aldrich Rockefeller Folk Art Center, Williamsburg, Virginia
205: top, Courtesy of Yale University Art Gallery/Mabel Brady Garvin Collection; bottom, Historical Pictures Service
206: Albany Institute of History and Art
207: Historical Pictures Service
209: Kennedy Gallery
210: Historical Pictures Service
211: Courtesy of Oberlin College
215: Black Star
218: top, Courtesy of Yale University Art Gallery/Mabel Brady Garvin Collection; bottom, Courtesy of the Museum of the City of New York
220: top left, Library of Congress; bottom, Gene Ahrens/Bruce Coleman, Inc.
221: top, The Granger Collection; bottom, Bettmann Inc. Archive
222: Courtesy of the Cincinnati Art Museum
223: Historical Pictures Service
224: Library of Congress
226: The Granger Collection
227: Historical Pictures Service
228 & 229: The Granger Collection
231: Brown Brothers
232: top right, Courtesy of the Louisiana State Museum; bottom left, Library of Congress
233: Historical Pictures Service
235: Montana Historical Society
237: The Granger Collection
239: top, Library of Congress; bottom, Courtesy of The Taft Museum

511

240: Courtesy of the Laura Ingalls Wilder Home & Museum, Mansfield, Mo.
241: Courtesy of DeGolyer Library
242 & 244: Historical Pictures Service
249: Josef Scaylea/Shostal Associates
250: The Granger Collection
252: Courtesy of Texaco Archives
253: The Granger Collection
254: Drake Well Museum
256: The Granger Collection
257: top right, Historical Pictures Service; bottom left, The Granger Collection
258: Courtesy of the Museum of the City of New York
259: Courtesy of The New-York Historical Society, New York City
264: Museum of the City of New York
265: The Granger Collection
266: Courtesy of the State Historical Society of Wisconsin
267: Historical Pictures Service
268: Ray Manly/Shostal Associates
271: Dr. Anne LeBastile/Bruce Coleman, Inc.
273: United Press International
275: top, The Granger Collection; bottom, Library of Congress
276: Courtesy of Radio Corporation of America
277: top, Courtesy of the National Archives; middle, Brown Brothers; bottom, Courtesy of American Airlines
278: top, Courtesy of San Diego Historical Society; bottom, The Granger Collection
279: The Granger Collection
281: Yale University Art Gallery/The Mabel Brady Garven Collection
283: National Aeronautics and Space Administration
286: Wide World
287: United Press International
288: Scherschel/Life Magazine
289: Courtesy of UNICEF
290: Courtesy of the Peace Corps
294: Michael Gallager/Bruce Coleman, Inc.
296 & 297: National Aeronautics and Space Administration
299: Wide World
301: left, Wide World; right, Michael Evans/The White House
302 & 303: Michal Heron
307: Victoria Beller-Smith
309: Ken Lax
312: Peter Southwick/Stock Boston
315: Ken Lax
316: John Lewis Stage/The Image Bank
320: top, Ken Lax; bottom left, Ken Karp; bottom right, Jim Moore/Liason Agency, Inc.
327: Robert Frerck
332: Jim Anderson/Woodfin Camp
333: Carole Hapke
335: E. R. Degginger/Bruce Coleman, Inc.
336: top, Robert Frerck; bottom, Dick Durrance II/Woodfin Camp; middle, V. Hinz/The Image Bank

341: James A. Sugar/Woodfin Camp
343: Jim Brandenburg/Bruce Coleman, Inc.
346: Breck P. Kent/Earth Scenes
349: top, Ivor A. Parry/Design Photographers, Inc.; bottom, Jim Brandenburg/Woodfin Camp
353: top right, Courtesy of Mayo Clinic; bottom left, Robert Frerck; bottom right, Grant Heilman
359: Zig Leszczynski/Earth Scenes
365: Lynn M. Stone/Earth Scenes
366: Luis Villota/The Image Bank
369: Arthur d'Arazien
370: top, Al Stephenson/Woodfin Camp; bottom left, Gabe Palmer/The Image Bank; bottom right, Courtesy of the Pentagon
377: C. C. Lockwood/Earth Scenes
383 & 384: Michal Heron
386: top & middle, National Aeronautics and Space Administration; bottom, Richard Weiss/Peter Arnold, Inc.
387: Grant Heilman
393: David Muench/Freelance Photographers Guild
400: top, Rickers Film Productions; middle, Bob and Ira Spring; bottom, Courtesy of the Church of the Latter Day Saints
403: top, Timothy Eagan/Woodfin Camp; middle, Rod Hanna/Woodfin Camp; bottom, Horst Schafer/Peter Arnold, Inc.
404: Al Kaplan/Design Photographers, Inc.
409: David Muench/Freelance Photographers Guild
416: E. R. Degginger
418: Courtesy of Lockheed
419: top, M. Beebe/The Image Bank; middle, Ray Atkeson; bottom, Movie Star News
425: top, E. R. Degginger; bottom, Werner Stoy/Camera Hawaii
430: top, Camera Hawaii; bottom, E. R. Degginger
432: top, E. R. Degginger; bottom, Werner Stoy/Camera Hawaii
437: National Film Board of Canada
444: left and top right, National Film Board of Canada; bottom right, Bernard G. Silverstein/Freelance Photographers Guild
447: National Film Board of Canada
453: Loren McIntyre/Woodfin Camp
461: left, Robert Frerck; right, Milt & Joan Mann
464: top right, Robert Frerck; bottom left, Eric Carle/Shostal Associates; bottom right, Michael Folco/Liason Agency, Inc.
465: Milt & Joan Mann
466 & 467: Flags courtesy of Annin & Coe, Verona, New Jersey
471: National Aeronautics and Space Administration
477: Dick Durrance/Woodfin Camp
478: top right, National Aeronautics and Space Administration; bottom left, Milt & Joan Mann
486, 487, 488: Library of Congress

Text

Page 154: Chart information from *Cities in Revolt* by Carl Bridenbaugh. Copyright © 1955 by Carl Bridenbaugh. Reprinted by permission of Alfred A. Knopf, Inc.

240: Text excerpt from *On the Way Home* by Laura Ingalls Wilder. Courtesy of Harper & Row, Publishers, Inc.

257: From *The Promised Land* by Mary Antin. Copyright 1912 by Houghton Mifflin Company. Copyright renewed 1940 by Mary Antin. Reprinted by permission of Houghton Mifflin Company.

123456789/8685848382

512